Sharon Yvonne Rodgers
35 Margaret avenue
San Francisco, Calif. 94112
586-3732 or 585-7093

History Dept, Princeton

CONTEMPORARY ARCHAEOLOGY

A Guide to
Theory and
Contributions

Edited by

Mark P. Leone

SOUTHERN ILLINOIS UNIVERSITY PRESS
Carbondale and Edwardsville

Feffer & Simons, Inc.
London and Amsterdam

Printed in the United States of America
Designed by Gary Gore

International Standard Book Number 0–8093–0513–5
Library of Congress Catalog Card Number 79–156779

Contents

Contents

Contents

5, 23, 24, 25, 28, 29, 30, 31, 32

Preface

THE PURPOSE of this volume is to present in one place the coherent theory and concrete results of recent developments in anthropological archaeology. This volume is meant as much for professional archaeological use as it is for general anthropological judgment. Although the volume is not a complete representation of contemporary advances in archaeology, I have tried to include enough material in it to allow it to stand as a compendium of current issues, discussions, and solutions. These may be used as handbook and source book by the professional archaeologist interested in assessing what is new in archaeology.

I have tried to include in this book those statements of theory that are most important in creating what is now commonly called the new archaeology. Taken as a whole, they represent most of the ideas that make current archaeology somewhat different from the archaeology most anthropologists grew up with. Also when taken in toto, these statements are meant to outline the shared assumptions which differentiate what is usual from what is recent in archaeology. The idea of theoretical coherence is significant because it is necessary to identify to the outside world what it is that is behind the concrete solutions one can find scattered widely throughout the archaeological literature. Recent archaeological innovations have not occurred by chance nor through ideosyncratic strokes of imagination. They form a unified corpus that can be identified.

For the archaeological world, on the other hand, I feel two goals are accomplished by presenting in one place the coherence of recent archaeological theory. Many claim there are no real theoretical differences between new archaeologists and their intellectual fathers. This conclusion comes about because the theoretical statements are often obscure and hidden. It also comes about because it is often impossible to tell when reading a piece of contemporary archaeology that identifies itself as new, what there is about it that distinguishes it from what is not new. Since the data of the discipline have not changed nor has the range of problems been expanded in many instances, a reader has difficulty in picking out elements, theoretical or concrete, that were not present in substantial research prior to the arrival of the new, processual, or evolutionary archaeology. As a result, I hope one of the functions of this volume will be the unmistakable delineation of the theoretical base of much of contemporary archaeology.

Within the house built by new archaeologists there is variability in theory and, as a result, in aims. The house has not always been at peace with itself, and I think one of the reasons for that proceeds from our failure to recognize our theoretical differences. The differences are no doubt real in some cases. But I think, in other cases, they result from our possessing a new and very powerful body of theory which, depending on the archaeologist, is in different stages of assimilation. I think the assumptions are shared but are differentially internalized and used. That would reduce many differences between us to functions of time and problems addressed. This book is then aimed at three different constituencies, my colleagues in anthropology, in archaeology, and those who differentiate themselves into the new or processual archaeology.

There are used above a whole series of terms to label the contributions in this book.

It is commonly agreed that the new archaeology is least happy among these. But it is the most common term and I suspect no amount of posturing is going to make it go away. And it also needs to be said that the phrase is not used without some justification. I have tried to underuse the phrase in this book borrowing, instead, processual archaeology, evolutionary archaeology, and contemporary archaeology. The last phrase is used with a qualifier to signal that not all contemporary archaeology shares the same theoretical base. And indeed much contemporary archaeology is, to use a truly unhappy phrase, traditional as opposed to new archaeology. This is a lexical problem that is not easily solved and it is a function of the fact that some things really are new. The proper label to identify the different, while not irritating unnecessarily, is not in hand, however.

The aims of this book are served in several organizational ways. I have tried to avoid producing a reader that forced the whole job of synthesis on the user. As a result the book has been about evenly divided between theory and its ramifications on the one hand, and substantive accomplishments tied to the theory on the other. The first half of this book provides the key theoretical statements in recent archaeology. These are accompanied by an attempt to discover the historical origins within archaeology for the outburst of the last decade and more. At the beginning of the book there are four essays, mostly of an interpretive sort, that attempt to assess the theory and contributions of the last ten years. They are both critical and complementary and serve to provide background for the core of the book. A section on method completes consideration of the ideas and sources that produced those papers found in the second half.

Inevitably a movement within a discipline that raises a storm such as was done in the 1960s provokes a whole exegetical literature. The four original articles that open this book are such, and they take very varying approaches to the problem of understanding what is really going on. There is no doubt that all are *amici curiae,* and two consider themselves practitioners of the new paradigm. This section can not pretend any more than the section on origins can pretend to represent a comprehensive attempt to address all issues within the specific domain. Other archaeologists would undoubtedly approach these two topics differently, and I must own my own biases as well as the shortcomings resulting from them. As a result of these biases, I may have claimed a man, and possibly an idea, for the new archaeology that others will feel is improper and even unjustified. The factor that makes differing identifications possible is the differing degree to which people are willing to publicly own or practice this approach to archaeology. Since the field has had its share of recriminations as a result of pretty massive theoretical revisions, many have felt labels are better foregone while men simply do research and let that be interpreted as people care to. The wisdom of that approach can not be denied. Therefore, should anyone find himself an unwilling member of a group he is uncomfortable with in these circumstances, I assume the blame for putting him here and extend an early apology.

It also needs to be said that all movements have their predecessors, and this one is not excepted. New archaeologists are berated for ignoring the processes and contributions that created them. I can not say that I have adequately represented the men and ideas that preceded the new archaeology either in the section on origins or in the substantive contributions. Only comprehensive research will outline the processes that created what we now have.

The substantive half of the essays in this book is organized according to a scheme that uses as its chief criterion the complexity of the economic base of a culture. Such schemes are not infrequently used both by ethnologists and archaeologists. Service's *Primitive Social Organization* and Cohen's *Man in Adaptation* employ ordering criteria ranked in terms of complexity and degree of differentiation. Such classificatory schemes are explicitly evolutionary, but beyond that they appropriately complement and accurately represent the assumptions, problems, and areas of substantive work which much recent archaeological research has been directed toward.

There are a number of original articles that appear first with this volume. The most important book in which one finds representatives of recent breakthroughs in archaeology is *New Perspectives in Archaeology,* which Sally and Lewis Binford brought out several years ago. Since then the field has undergone expansion as was inevitable. I have attempted to select some of the more recent contributions made by their colleagues and print them here. Because of my own training and because of the high activity there, many of the original articles and some of those reprinted draw on data from the prehistoric southwestern United States. I think there is minimum risk in narrowing focus by using these since every author who uses that region uses it explicitly as a laboratory where a specific case of a more general problem is investigated. These essays are not historical treatments. These original substantive articles, regardless of where they draw data from, are attempts to present research that builds explicitly on the initial contributions made by some of the earliest of the recent innovators. The original essays are 2, 3, 4, 15, 24, 25, 31, and 32 written respectively by myself, Walter W. Taylor, Raymond H. Thompson, John M. Fritz, Fred T. Plog and Cheryl K. Garrett, Michael A. Glassow, William L. Rathje, and Craig Morris. Essay 19 by Frederick Gorman, though previously published, has been substantially revised for this volume.

To aid in unifying the theory and accomplishments of the work represented here, a single bibliography has been created for the volume. The bibliography is the work of Louis A. Hieb. And with that, references have been unified throughout the book. Although there is naturally a great amount of periphera in the citations, these can stand as a working bibliography for the field. There is in addition a short introduction to each of the major sections within the book. These serve as much to introduce the articles as to identify the issues discussed in the section or underlying that particular domain in archaeology.

Importantly, there are a number of themes running through this book that are not always visible at the surface. Two that are closely allied are the relationship between archaeology and the contributions made by archaeology to its constituencies. Throughout the nineteenth century, archaeology was not tied to anthropology or was tied only in a nacent way. And simultaneous with its autonomy, archaeology made two contributions to general knowledge that had effects more profound than any it has been responsible for since. Archaeology demonstrated the antiquity of man and, in so doing, provided the empirical basis for the radical revision of Western man's concept of time. Certainly we tend not to dwell on these contributions because they have been so completely assimilated into Western culture. But their effects, once called to mind, are readily recorded. However, these contributions and their ramifications occurred at a time when archaeology was autonomous from anthropology and was allied with, although not a subdivision of, the natural, historical sciences. As an era within archaeology, it is not dealt with in this book.

Within the twentieth century, however, these two themes play out differently. In the twentieth, not only had archaeology been differentiated within itself into classical and prehistoric, but the latter became firmly attached to anthropology. In the United States and Western Europe, prehistoric archaeology became one of the historical divisions in a social science whereas classical archaeology, in the course of maintaining its autonomy, became a firmly historical discipline. Classical archaeology is fundamentally at variance in its aims from anthropological archaeology, and most of the data of the two have been mutually exclusive. Prehistory as a part of anthropology lost its autonomy as a purely historical discipline and received in return a set of goals which linked it firmly to anthropology in rationale. It therefore had some obligation to be scientific or comparative as well as to concern itself with society or culture. Yet as this link was forged and as the constituencies of archaeologists changed, there developed a gap between the expectations for and accomplishments of archaeology. In the nineteenth century, archaeology had established the fact of man's domain in the past. But in the twentieth century, archaeology's major accomplishment has been the description and delimitation of that domain. The scope of man's existence in the past, in time and in space—the original goal of archaeology—continued to be the goal after archaeology left the company of the natural historical disciplines and became allied with social science. And it has generally been felt that the description and delimitation of man's past is a foundation for social scientific work but is, in itself, an insufficient end. Hence while autonomy was given up in theory, it was not in practice. As a result of changing constituencies, archaeology continued to satisfy its former but not always its new one. Hence one has to assess quite carefully the contributions made by what is now a subdiscipline in the twentieth century. Some of the underlying themes in the essays in this book provide the basis for such an assessment.

From the point of view of history, there is no doubt that archaeology in the twentieth century has contributed in the most massive and successful ways. Certainly what we know about the prehistory of our own species biologically as well as culturally is so immense that it nearly defies assessment. I think we may justifiably point to archaeology's role in clarifying man's past, especially when one considers the myths, frauds, and misconceptions that have been counterbalanced as a result.

However, as a part of anthropology the contributions of a now dependent subdiscipline are different. One such contribution and theme is precision. Accurate description is so essential to knowledge, yet so often identified as a means, that we sometimes fail to recognize the importance of the methods and techniques that enable precision in the first place. Ethnology has long been famous for the crudeness and imprecision of its descriptive tools. And linguistics, by contrast, as well as genetics have been equally renowned for the precision of their own descriptive concepts. Ethnologists have, of course, borrowed heavily from linguistics for method and descriptive devices in the last two decades.

Part of the environment producing a demand for precision has come from archaeology's occupation with means for obtaining descriptive rigor. That preoccupation has been part of archaeological research efforts for decades and has been one of the field's identifying traits. In addition to the ranges of techniques for dating, palynology, stratigraphy, floatation, and the descriptive classifications for data so precisely recovered, archaeology pioneered in the use of statistics and computer analysis in anthropology. Archaeology also had its debate over the reality of native categories and the relationship between them and analytical categories fifteen years before ethnology had its argument over whose head held more truth, the native's or the anthropologist's. The authors whose work is within this book all take the use of precision in description as a *sine qua non* for research. This represents the continuity of rigorous description within archaeology and as a goal is often unspoken. But as a part of the anthropological world, this has also been one of archaeology's frontier interests.

While archaeology has been conscious of the need for technical accuracy, it has not so often been aware of the need for rigor of the same quality in linking its data to its conclusions. Inductive inference has usually been used as the logical method to provide such links. It is recently argued that the unalloyed use of such a device is debilitating to archaeology. It is within the domain of the methods of logic, methods within the philosophy of science and very closely linked to considerations of accuracy and precision, that archaeology continues to contribute to the environment of anthropology. The occupation in archaeology now with problems of logical procedure parallels the continuing debate among other anthropologists over the validity of types of taxonomies and the proper places of induction and deduction in research. Many of the authors within this book have such a concern and many others act on recently suggested solutions.

A second area in which archaeology has made and continues to make noteworthy contributions to anthropology is in its ability to consider natural factors and their relation to cultural context. Factors like demography, nutrition, and the natural environment, the last often expressed as ecology, have played important roles in archaeological research, and by reflection have had an impact in the anthropological world. There are certainly areas within anthropology where ecological, demographic, geographic, and a host of other biological and environmental factors are considered as critical variables in describing and explaining cultural behavior. Archaeologists have been responsible for providing many of the test cases where the relationship between demographic and ecological variables, on the one hand, and cultural variables, on the other, have been worked out experimentally. And with all of this, archaeology has not been guilty of environmental determinism although it has sometimes emphasized the importance of environmental factors over cultural variables.

Although archaeologists are not especially responsible for founding cultural ecology, they are responsible for providing that approach with massive support in the form of performing critical research, of perfecting methods, and of inventing techniques. When one considers the work of Gordon Childe, Grahame Clark, Robert Braidwood, the long and continuing work of Scandinavian and British archaeologists in the domain of building models incorporating and measuring natural variables, one sees the habitual regard of archaeologists for factors that influence, if not govern, large portions of human behavior.

That is a legacy to anthropology that is neither inconsiderable nor over. There are very few substantive articles in this book that do not consider natural variables, whether these be ecological or demographic or geographic. There is hardly an article either that does not follow the rule that culture is to be explained in terms of culture. What is represented as a result is a complex, often nondeterministic statement about the relation between cultural and noncultural variables.

For this discussion, the third and final area in which archaeology has contributed to anthropology and an area which can be seen moving through the essays in this volume is technology. More than any other discipline archaeology has provided us with an idea of how objects reflect the culture that created and distributed them. Our ideas of how objects function at economic tasks is remarkable. The information derived from chipped stone tools from the paleolithic, for example, covers tasks of food preparation and use, techniques of tool manufacture and use, type of food dealt with, the divisions of the economic base, hunting habits, and several more domains. We have developed the use of settlement patterns to inform on kinship patterns, land use patterns, social stratification, defense and competition, population growth and decline and population proliferation and aggregation, and the subdivision and function of urban centers to give only an incomplete list. Here is the use of patterned sets of material objects to impute the form of several other subsystems in culture. It is a listing of how ranges of objects reflect and function at other levels. We have contributed enormous amounts of clearly specified information about how technology, in its large sense, reflects human behavior. That is still one of our major tasks in archaeology, and it is undergoing an emphasis of unusual strength today. The artifacts of prehistoric archaeology are being applied to demographic, social, and even religious problems as well as to a continuing interest in ecological problems.

Archaeologists have not always been aware of the knowledge about technology or ma terial culture that they have. The information about how items and artifacts reflect and inform on the less permanent aspects of cultural systems has rarely been codified and identified as such. The principles of technology's reflective properties have rarely been specified. They are in hand none the less, and more important is every archaeologist's ability to use objects and patterns of them to talk about the nonmaterial behavior they were a part of. The full range of reflective abilities of objects, or material culture, or technology, will undoubtedly be in hand one day. As a continuing contribution to anthropology, this domain represents a major theme expressed in the volume. But expressed also is a new question about technology. How does technology perform the tasks it does? Not how does it reflect, but how does it reinforce, enforce, and even determine the tasks and functions that it is involved with? Assuming technological determinism for a moment, we are allowed to ask as archaeologists how items from axes to village plans to machines influence behavior. This is different from asking how ecological arrangements or social structure are exhibited in objects; the question here is what role do items play in economics, social organization, and religion. And another question: what are the properties of specific artifacts that allow them to behave as they do?

In outlining some of the areas in which archaeology has been positively allied with anthropology, I have emphasized contributions in the range of larger theoretical and nonhistorical issues. I have not discussed the exemplary achievements our subdiscipline has made in addressing substantive issues like the origins of man, domestication, the rise of cities, and the peopling of the New World. But here are areas where archaeology alone has contributed the only viable hypotheses to address the problems and provided the evidence to verify the hypotheses. These are universally recognized issues on which the only solutions offered have come from archaeologists. Some of these issues are addressed within this book and provide some of the explicit organizing problems around which modern research is organized. These are usually self-evident problems whereas those I mentioned earlier are often implicit motifs that run through most articles here. Such motifs are, however, counted as the firm contributions of archaeology to anthropology.

Just as it has been impossible to deal with all of the contributions made by modern archaeology, it is also impossible to deal adequately with the reasons for those I have chosen to emphasize. As with any book of such scope, there was the necessity of seeking much advice. Many colleagues suggested contributions as well as domains that would be appropriately covered. In many cases I have taken their advice and am grateful for it. In all cases I have made the final choices and accept the errors that may be latent in those. Since I have wanted to collect the most important pieces of recent archaeology, I have had to duplicate articles that have been reprinted elsewhere. Presented here are also a few pieces readily available in major journals. My rationale for what may seem to be redundance is the desire to present the new paradigm as a whole with its theoretical statements and concrete accomplishments juxtaposed in one place.

None of these essays has been cut. The bibliography has been maintained for all articles, and notes appear following individual essays. Where there has been any rewriting, it has been minimal and functioned to adapt an essay to a presentation such as this. Rewriting never interfered with an author's thoughts as originally stated in his article.

This book has been two years in the planning and execution, and during that time I have built up many debts for assistance given by colleagues. To them I am grateful. Two that I wish to mention particularly are Thomas Lewis who suggested the phrase and title, "Contemporary Archaeology," and Jeannette Mirsky who provided continual encouragement.

Mark P. Leone

Princeton, New Jersey
January 1972

Notes on Contributors

ROBERT M. ADAMS is Professor of Anthropology in the Oriental Institute and Department of Anthropology of the University of Chicago.

LEWIS R. BINFORD is Associate Professor of Anthropology at the University of New Mexico.

V. GORDON CHILDE, 1892–1957, was Director of the Institute of Archaeology at the University of London.

GRAHAME CLARK is Disney Professor of Archaeology at Cambridge University.

JAMES F. DEETZ is Professor of Anthropology at Brown University.

EDWIN S. DETHLEFSEN is Associate Professor of Anthropology at Franklin Pierce College.

KENT V. FLANNERY is Associate Professor of Anthropology at the University of Michigan.

JOHN M. FRITZ is Assistant Professor of Anthropology at the University of California at Santa Cruz.

PETER T. FURST is Professor of Anthropology at the State University of New York at Albany.

CHERYL K. GARRETT is a graduate student in the Department of Anthropology at the University of California at Los Angeles.

MICHAEL A. GLASSOW is Assistant Professor of Anthropology at the University of California at Santa Barbara.

FREDERICK GORMAN is a graduate student in the Department of Anthropology at the University of Arizona.

JAMES N. HILL is Associate Professor of Anthropology at the University of California at Los Angeles.

CLYDE KLUCKHOHN, 1905–1960, was Professor of Anthropology at Harvard University.

MARK P. LEONE is Assistant Professor of Anthropology at Princeton University.

WILLIAM A. LONGACRE is Associate Professor of Anthropology at the University of Arizona.

PAUL S. MARTIN is Chief Curator of Anthropology, Emeritus, of the Field Museum of Natural History.

CRAIG MORRIS is Assistant Professor of Anthropology at Brandeis University.

FRED T. PLOG is Assistant Professor of Anthropology at the University of California at Los Angeles.

SONIA RAGIR is Assistant Professor of Anthropology at Richmond College of the City University of New York.

WILLIAM L. RATHJE is Assistant Professor of Anthropology at the University of Arizona.

ROBERT L. SCHUYLER is Assistant Professor of Anthropology at the City College of New York.

ALBERT C. SPAULDING is Professor of Anthropology at the University of California at Santa Barbara.

STUART STRUEVER is Assistant Professor of Anthropology at Northwestern University.

WALTER W. TAYLOR is Professor of Anthropology at Southern Illinois University.

RAYMOND H. THOMPSON is Professor of Anthropology at the University of Arizona.

EDWIN N. WILMSEN is Associate Professor of Anthropology at the University of Michigan.

EZRA B. W. ZUBROW is Assistant Professor of Anthropology at Stanford University.

PART 1

The Scope of the Changes
in Contemporary Archaeology

Introduction

The following four essays represent the agreement of most contemporary archaeologists that the changes occuring now in archaeology are unlike those most remember from the past. Whether the present changes are summed up as a revolution or simply as faster than ordinary change, there is no substantial disagreement that archaeology in the United States and within anthropology is, to one degree or another, being transformed. There is disagreement over the rate, the nature, the origins, and the tone of the transformation, but there is no disagreement that at the moment and for the last ten years, the pace has changed.

There is another common feature in these essays as well. No author regrets the change, and none condemns it. That is not to say that all American archaeologists agree on the beneficial character of the present changes. But the discipline as a whole, while perhaps flinching at the rhetoric and squabbling, has accepted recent innovations with increasing equanimity. Any number of sociologists and allied analysts of American culture have pointed out the receptivity Americans show to change and even to radical innovation. The fact that archaeologists belong to the larger culture is surely in part responsible for the rapid recognition, albeit at differing levels, given to the new archaeology. Within archaeology itself, the reasons for the rapidity of the change and its acceptance are not so clear. Many of the reasons are identified and evaluated by the following essays.

In an attempt to identify the causes for change in archaeology, the principles that have been changed, and the origins for what is now going on, the four authors here have used different models depending on their predispositions. W. W. Taylor has assessed the new archaeology, or really parts of it, against his monumental *A Study of Archeology*. Taylor's 1948 work was one of the most valuable intellectual services American archaeology has had performed for it. A massive collection of evidence clarified the aims and accomplishments of archaeology up to that time and assessed the fit between the two. To remedy the discrepancy he found, Taylor suggested an alternative theoretical approach which has itself rarely been used by archaeologists. Taylor's work brought to a new level of consciousness matters of goals and methods in archaeology and its relation to anthropology, history, and science. Since his study, it has not been possible for archaeology to be unaware of any of the major issues centering on its rationale. The level of critical awareness he created has been part of the backdrop in front of which the new archaeology has grown.

Appropriately, W. W. Taylor examines here the fit between his own study of 24 years ago and several of the crucial theoretical innovations of the new archaeology. This assessment is especially useful because Taylor provides one of the ways for discovering the roots of contemporary change. The problem of the intellectual origins of the new archaeology has not yet been adequately addressed. It may also be impossible to do so for some time. But Taylor points an unambiguous finger at his own seminal study as one of the theoretical factors in the current scene. The claim can not be dismissed.

Paul Martin, who is unquestionably the senior archaeologist in this section, exercises the rights of experience and seniority and calls current events in archaeology revolutionary. From the perspective of 40 years in the field, Martin sees both it and himself revitalized by the new archaeology. There is no contradicting the data of his personal experience. What remains to be seen is how widespread among other archaeologists that experience is. Paul Martin has voiced in the opening of his essay a sentiment that is not a part of the new archaeology but is found among a few of its members. Long before the word relevant became slang, he supported the idea that if archaeology were really linked to anthropology, and if anthropology were directed at problems that were truly pertinent to modern conditions, then archaeology need be neither moribund nor beside the point. Besides enunciating that idea, he argued for its logical corollary: archaeologists should address problems that have real significance for the larger society, that society being archaeology's sponsor in the first place. Martin argues that there should be some explicit fit between the world's problems and archaeology's. That thought is not so unacceptable as it is novel.

As mediator in the assessments offered here, Raymond Thompson plays a significant role. Arguing justifiably that more claims are made by the sponsors of contemporary changes than are empirically verifiable, he further points out the position of many archaeologists on the issue of spontaneous invention versus gradual development for the new archaeology. Using a favorite archaeological device, the continuum of development, he argues that the new archaeology is not so divorced from traditional archaeology as some of its adherents have said. He further argues that fruitful research can most profitably occur when it is understood that there are not two archaeological strategies, but a series of exciting innovations

2

coupled with essential and older practices that will enable the development of archaeology to a new level of accomplishment. Although many new archaeologists would disagree with Thompson's interpretation of the uninterrupted nature of archaeology's growth from the past to the present, none would fail to recognize the reasonableness of what Thompson suggests on the plane of social relations. In fact, over the last two or three years there has been far more cooperation and far less castigation between the various sides than was the case just earlier. The unity that Thompson suggests may be becoming a reality.

My own essay is complimentary to Martin's. The major point is not simply to agree with the other essays here and the opinions they represent, but rather to suggest that the changes everyone willingly admits have happened are not so much over as they are only beginning.

The Revolution in Archaeology

BY A large section of the public, anthropologists are thought of as people who study the quaint customs of "primitive people." Archaeologists, emerge in the public image as adventurers and/or antiquarians who classify pottery types, "find" and dig in "lost" cities for "treasure," for beautiful objects. The question most frequently asked of archaeologists by the public is: "What did you find?" Rarely are we asked if we have other goals and purposes and if these can contribute to the shaping and guiding our world towards humane changes. While these stereotypes are possibly overdrawn, the general public often regards anthropology as an esoteric subject pursued by dilettantes and misfits.

I think we anthropologists are to blame for these misconceptions. Anthropology has been largely unstructured—irresponsibly so— and anthropologists have resisted the idea of formulating a research strategy that would follow the general rules of the logic of science. Archaeologists have preferred to apply themselves to limited problems and have dodged the vexing questions of causality and explanations concerning how and why cultures change. And the idea of advancing probabilistic laws shocks many of my colleagues and is regarded as improper, impossible, and mad. They prefer to remain "neu-

Reproduced by permission of the Society for American Archaeology from *American Antiquity,* vol. 36, no. 1, 1971, pp. 1–8. The bibliographical references have been placed in the general bibliography for this volume and revisions made in the text by permission of the author.

tral," to be students of man who are out of touch with men; to be "value-free."

A few years ago, Professor Barber wrote an article called "Resistance by Scientists to Scientific Discovery" (1961). Barber lists several cultural and social sources that may cause resistance to scientific discoveries by scientists:

1) Substantive concepts and theories at any given time (Mendel's theory of genetic inheritance was originally held to be unacceptable because it ran counter to the predominant conception of joint and total inheritance of biological characteristics).

2) Methodological conceptions (the antitheoretical bias of Bacon or Goethe (and others) who preferred scientific work to be based on intention and direct evidence of the senses; or the tendencies of some to think in terms of established models or to reject propositions that can not be put in the form of some model).

3) Partiality for or hostility toward the usefulness of mathematics (Galton used statistics in application to a biological problem in a paper submitted to the Royal Society, that later requested him in future papers to keep mathematics apart from biological applications).

4) Scientists of higher standing often resist discoveries made by scientists of lower standing or by unknowns, or by amateurs. (Mendel was considered by the distinguished botanists of the time as an unimportant monk with no professional standing.)

5) Specialists or "insiders" in their field

resist new theories or innovations promoted by "outsiders" (Pasteur's ideas were resisted by medical men of his day, because he was not a medical specialist.).

6) Scientific organizations are a social source of resistance to innovations in science. Papers submitted may be read and rejected by a publication committee whose members are not experts or authorities in the matter.

7) "Schools" may be a source of resistance in science (historical-particularism versus cultural-materialism).

8) Older scientists tend to react slowly to new ideas because they are subject to one or several of the sources of resistance outlined above.

Hence, resistance would seem inevitable. I hope, however, that the tradition of receptivity and open-mindedness in science, and the objective tests that will validate new concepts and theories will permit anthropologists to examine with good will the arguments that I shall present. I do not claim that the philosophy, methods, and goals set forth herein are *the only ones* or the "correct" ones. But for myself, I think the goals mentioned constitute a strategy of archaeological research. I make two assumptions and if they are acceptable, then much of the rest will follow.

1) That anthropology, and therefore archaeology, is a social science; and as such it is concerned with the explanation of human behavior and cultural change. As social scientists we must evaluate and suggest guide lines for human society. If we present the inferences from our knowledge as clearly and responsibly as we can, then we are fulfilling our obligations as social scientists.

2) One of the better ways to arrive at causality, explanation, and the development of nomothetic theory is to develop a research strategy that will help anthropologists achieve these goals.

Earlier in this essay, I referred to the public image of anthropology. Perhaps, some will not consider this a prime reason for rethinking and restructuring our research. I think it is important for several reasons. Support for our research comes ultimately from the public and private purses. Federal support for teaching and research is under fire. We are approaching major decisions in Congress as to how it will support science. If Congress and our nation are to reach a wise decision, we must, as scientists and anthropologists, devote more time and thought to the presentation of our research, our goals, our successes as well as our failures, and our conclusions in nontechnical language to the general public. We must show that we do not live in an ivory tower and that we possess knowledge and skills that will help solve many problems. I think we have done too little to increase public understanding of the social need for broad support of research. It is imperative to couple research with broad social issues in order to bring about a popular expression of faith in science as a benefactor and not a malefactor of mankind. We must make clear that the uses to which science may be put require that scientists be permitted to have a strong voice in all decision-making policies. These suggestions mean that we must formulate an adequate public information program that will permit the public to know what we have achieved and what problems face us. I think this fact is clear: unless we as anthropologists and archaeologists take steps to make our research relevant to the problems of our contemporary societies, we may find that the world can get along quite nicely without us. Chronicle and classification are not enough, and such work is sterile and very costly.

The search for the social responsibilities of the intellectual is not confined to anthropology. A cursory survey of articles in scientific journals makes it evident that men in other sciences, too, are engaged in a reexamination of their goals and purposes. We can no longer bury our heads in the sand and pretend that we practice a science that is value-free.

I have stressed the fact that anthropology and therefore archaeology is held in dubious esteem by the general public and by the es-

The Revolution in Archaeology
Paul S. Martin

tablishment who might interpret and manipulate data about which they know little. And I have pointed out that some or many of these misconceptions and misjudgments are the direct result of our resistance to new ideas. They come too, from our failure to envision anthropology, including archaeology, as a social science that has an obligation to structure research so that we can achieve goals compatible with the relevant problems of today and of the future. We must make these goals free of the values of any establishment. By clearly stating our hypotheses, we are at least aware of our biases because they are explicit. Tacit or unconscious goals are dangerous because they are not publicly stated.

I have dwelt on these points, not because they are new, but because they are important in understanding and emphasizing the decline of our paradigm and the revolution that is taking place in anthropology and especially in my own subfield, archaeology. Recently Harris (1968:3) has pointed out that a priority must be given to evolving a general theory of sociocultural change because it is of paramount importance if anthropologists are to assume a fruitful role in planning and carrying out international development programs. Without such a theory, the results could be disastrous. We must reverse the trend towards noncommitment and redirect our research energies towards discovering how we can meet and deal with current and future situations.

Now, what has all of this to do with archaeology and the revolution that is taking place? Needless to state the "new" approach, with different emphases, is a far cry from what I did in the earlier stages of my career. What is this "revolution"? Briefly, it is an attempt to bring about new research strategies that are superior in power to those that Harris (1968:1–7) deprecates and to those that archaeologists have been wedded to for more than a century. It is an attempt to replace the declining paradigm with a more viable one that temporarily, at least, is agreed upon as constituting better research methodol-

ogy and more acceptable results. This whole matter will be dealt with later in this essay.

Before doing so, I should like to examine the "old" paradigm, and its collapse. Recently, for the purposes of a report requested by the National Science Foundation, I had occasion to review my research activities of the past two decades. Prior to 1960, in common with most of my colleagues, I had emphasized culture traits, trait lists, histories of sites and/or areas—all organized in a time-space dimension. I entertained the idea that the facts would speak for themselves once presented. I was carrying on what Kuhn (1962) calls "normal science" or solving jigsaw puzzles.

Since 1960, my goals and interests have been modified by a trend that is now widespread in American science—a trend that involves a shift from emphasis on particularisms to an imaginative era in which anthropologists and archaeologists build a cultural-materialist research strategy that can deal with the questions of causality and origins and laws. The trend towards a reexamination of goals, research methodology and paradigms seems apparent in other fields—sociology, linguistics, geology, biochemistry, and physical anthropology—to mention only a few. As a result, the bearing, emphasis, and procedures of my research have been substantially altered. Thus a conceptual transformation, a revolution, has taken place for me.

In describing this adaptation to my physical, social and intellectual environment, I shall try to explain how this revolution came about. I do this, not because my metamorphosis is important to anyone but myself, but because the changes that I describe are the product of the dissatisfactions shared by many archaeologists. This essay may be of help to younger, creative men who recognize that something is lacking in their research strategies but who do not quite know how to remedy it.

Some years ago, Robert Maynard Hutchins is alleged to have described archaeology as a "tool course" that belonged in the curricula of vocational schools and not in those of a university. This scornful evaluation really racked me, but it had enough truth in it to make it impossible to disregard. Actually, he was not far off target, especially when one recalls the then current definitions of archaeology:

"Archaeology, 'the science of what is old' in the career of humanity, especially as revealed by excavations of the sites of prehistoric occupation," and "Archaeology, of course, is a sort of unwritten history" (Kroeber 1948:4–5, 538). "Archaeology deals with the beginnings of culture and with those phases of culture which are now extinct" (Linton 1945:8). "Archaeology reconstructs human history from earliest times to the present. . . . It is concerned with the beginnings of culture and also with cultures and civilizations that are now extinct" (Martin et al. 1947:3).

In general, then, there was agreement at that time among most American archaeologists that archaeology was concerned with reconstruction of 1) culture history, 2) past lifeways, and 3) the delineation of cultural processes. We had a model for working out culture history, but lacked a model for explaining culture change. We were slowly realizing the importance of understanding cultural processes over vast periods of time.

These goals of archaeology had at one time been satisfactory, but, gradually, the mortar fell out of the joints of our "edifice"! Crucial questions arose which could not be answered with the existing models. For instance, why did the hunting and gathering culture of the Southwest change to a sedentary one; or why did cultures of Mesoamerica become urban? I began to feel that our research was futile; we were, in fact, not increasing our knowledge of the past nor applying it to contemporary problems of our society.

At this time a crisis took place in my professional career. I had been vaguely aware of new trends, of fresh breezes that were

disturbing my mouldering ideas. I finally awakened to the fact that I had to resolve this crisis either by catching up with what was going on, or by resigning myself to becoming a fossil. I must admit that at first the different ideas and approaches outraged me. I was hostile to them, probably because a 35-year professional investment was at stake. I was afraid of things strange and new. This type of hostility has been explained earlier in this essay.

Long before my dissatisfaction and unfulfillment became articulate, a few archaeologists and anthropologists from 1930 on had concluded that our traditional methods were leading them astray, down dead ends, and up against blank walls (Bennett 1943:208; Binford 1962, 1965, and 1968d; Kluckhohn 1939:328; Steward 1936, 1948, and 1949; Steward and Setzler 1938:4; Strong 1936; Taylor 1948). It was borne in on these disaffected students that archaeology is part of anthropology and is, therefore, a social science. As practiced, however, it was at best a stunted history and presentation of facts for their own sake; and, at worst, a kind of stamp-collecting pursuit. The interpretation of interrelationships of events in time and space could go on ad infinitum and never get anywhere. We were in a cul-de-sac because comparing forms and systematizing our data were not leading to an elucidation of the structure of social systems any more than did the ordering and taxonomy of life forms by Linnaeus explain the process of organic evolution (Binford and Binford 1968:8).

Archaeology was, in fact, at a turning point similar to that of astronomy in the late Rennaissance (1500–1700). At that time, some astronomers recognized that the Ptolemaic model had failed to solve many of their traditional problems (for example, the constant length of the seasonal year). Accordingly, slowly, reluctantly, and fearfully, Copernicus, Brahe, and Kepler were led to search for a new model.

We archaeologists, too, were confronted with the bewildering and perplexing fact of a disparity between what we wanted to accomplish—an explanation of why cultures change—and what we were actually doing—histories of sites. For example, we recognized though dimly, the desirability of explaining past cultural processes, but a research strategy for conducting such studies had not been developed in archaeological theory. In fact, we had no theory and we lacked goals. We were in a vexing and painful predicament. We were digging up sites, towns, and cities; classifying pottery and tools with a fatuous obsession; dating places and things; and writing reports and arriving nowhere. Rarely were explanations and predictions attempted; seldom, generalizations or probabilistic laws.

True, archaeology had contributed significantly to general knowledge: probable antiquity and origin of man; delineation of biblical and Grecian history; origin and antiquity of the American Indians; separate developments of cultures in the Old and New World; evolution of cultures; origins of agriculture; elucidation of systems of writing; the destruction of many myths and much folklore concerning giants, races, human origins, etc.

I do not disparage or belittle these achievements. They were not, however, concerned with contemporary problems in behavioral science. Clearly, such an impasse would be resolved as it always has been in science—by the emergence of a new paradigm. This would not be an extension of the older models that had guided us, but would be, rather, a reconstruction of the field from new fundamentals. As I look back with the benefit of hindsight, I think we began to realize that goals (explanations), investigative techniques, and collecting of data are not independent variables. On the contrary, they stand in a dependent relationship, one to the other. After that a preparadigm came slowly into being—a temporary agreement about what constitutes good research strategy and what results were acceptable.

Then, in 1961, by good fortune I was launched into a new stream of events that was to bring me hope of renewed progress and meaning in archaeology. Lewis R. Binford, a student of Leslie A. White, and his students were discovering what others had stumbled on, namely that the traditional ways of archaeology were unpromising and ineffective. Fortunately, they were not deeply committed to the archaeological establishment; they perceived that the old rules no longer "defined a playable game" (Kuhn 1962:90). It is interesting to note that, as was true of other great innovators, they were young!

At this time, four of Binford's students—James A. Brown, Leslie G. Freeman, James N. Hill, and William A. Longacre—were collaborating with me in archaeological analyses. They showed me how we could build on what had been done and how advances could be made. They were kind, patient, stimulating mentors. I perked up. I listened. I attended seminars. I reread Binford (1962:217), Childe (1952), Sahlins and Service (1960), Steward (1936, 1948, 1949), Strong (1936, 1948), White (1949, 1959), Willey (1948), and Wittfogel (1956), in the light of a new theoretical approach. I was greatly influenced by my readings in Braithwaite (1960), Hanson (1958), Hempel (1966), Kuhn (1962), and Nagel (1961). As a result of this reexamination from a new perspective, I found most of the theories and practices of the past obsolete. I slowly became acquainted with new concepts and new principles, began to perceive what is meant by the nature of scientific explanations and devices for systematizing knowledge. Hence, a small group of archaeologists in various parts of the country accepted cultural materialism as a valid strategy. They rejected historical particularism; they stressed the need for devising a research design that would conform to uniform or accepted rationales on which to base acceptance or rejection of hypotheses. This group, and I now consider myself part of it, has reoriented its theoretical and methodological systems. These men are creating a new paradigm.

This change may not seem to some so profound as the shift from geocentrism to heliocentrism or those changes brought about by Kepler, Newton, or Boyle, to name but a few. The point I wish to stress is that a new paradigm permits one to see things differently today than one did yesterday, even if and when looking at the same phenomena.

Let us consider two men looking at the console of a large pipe organ. One man is an organist; the other, unlearned musically. The organist "sees" instantly many things: the various manuals (keyboards) as representing separate organs—the solo, the swell, the great, the choir, and the pedal keyboard, on which the feet play; the stops, each controlling a single rank or multiple ranks of pipes; the couplers, the thumb pistons, toe studs, expression pedals, and more. The nonorganist is looking at the same details, but is not seeing that a certain stop will produce a loud tone or one of a deep pitch or that one's feet can "play" the pedals as nimbly as one's fingers. All he sees is a complex looking "thing" with black and white keys, strange looking knobs, en masse, a bench, and a rack. They are not both visually aware of the same object. The nonorganist must learn music and study the organ before he can see (hear, feel, sense) what the organist sees. Thus, the two men may be said to have vastly different conceptual organizations and, since their visual fields have a different organization, they observe different things.

So it is that the archaeologist armed with a different conceptual organization and a new paradigm can now see in familiar objects what no one else has seen before. He has a new way of thinking about his universe; he knows now how to "see" ancient sites, stratigraphy, stone tools, in a new and meaningful perspective. For example, I used to be a virtuoso of pottery types. Given almost any sherd from the southwestern United States, I could place it spatially and temporally. But I was unable to tell you a thing about the interrelationship of shapes, designs, types, and functions. I had not "seen" that a given pottery type might have been used almost exclusively for ritual or burial purposes. Nor did it ever occur to

me to postulate that pottery was more than a type or that it represented part of an articulated system that had been adapted by man to his environment in order to carry on the business of living. I was unable to see that the patterning of human behaviour might be explained by the variability in the archaeological record.

The force of what I am trying to make clear about the ability to "see" may be made clearer by examples. It is said that prior to the time of Copernicus, Western astronomers, obsessed by the Ptolemaic model, regarded the heavens as immutable; whereas the Chinese astronomers during the same centuries (prior to A.D. 1500) had recorded the appearances of new stars (novae), comets, and sunspots (Kuhn 1962:115). In other words, the Ptolemaic model held by Western astronomers (pre–A.D. 1500) prevented them from actually observing what was there to see. Their model blinded them. By the same token, our models and our hypotheses must be created in such a way as to include multivariate explanations in order that we may not be blind to reality. The paradigm within which we work determines what one is going to "see"—to observe.

Thus, as a result of a new paradigm, I live and work in a different world. The new paradigm that has emerged was a direct response to the crisis that had arisen because the traditional archaeological paradigm was askew (Kuhn 1962:175). This kind of crisis leads to what Kuhn calls a scientific revolution (1962:91). What, then, are some aspects of this revolution-inciting paradigm and how is archaeology redefined?

To claim that some archaeologists have adopted a new paradigm is equivalent to asserting that when they look at their world they see something new and different. If the claim is true, then I should be able to specify some of the principal changes in their conceptual organizations and the different things they observe. I think it is possible to point out some of the major differences in how they view the following:

1) The discipline.—According to the old

view, archaeology was defined as a special kind of history. Data were regarded primarily as the function and result of unique events, and the task of the archaeologist was to collect random facts and from them to create a reconstruction of past events and of by-gone life-ways. A whole was to be formed from random data.

According to the new view, archaeology is a science, for "science" includes not only physical and biological fields but also the social sciences—anthropology, sociology, economics (Braithwaite 1960:7). Even historical inquiry (explanation of past human actions) does not differ radically from the generalizing natural or social sciences, in respect to either the logical patterns of its explanations or the logical structures of its concepts (Nagel 1961:575). Archaeologists now regard data as unique expressions of recurring cultural processes. Understanding data is worthwhile primarily as a means of understanding these recurring processes.

2) The desirable goals.—In the old view, reports or monographs concerned with archaeological survey and/or complete descriptions of all recovered data from a site were considered all-important. Usually, such reports included a history of the region or a reconstruction of the history of a site. In a sense, it was at best highly sophisticated antiquarianism.

In the new view, the function of science—and hence of archaeology—is to establish general laws covering the behavior of the observed events or objects with which the science in question is concerned. This enables us to connect our knowledge of separated events and to make reliable predictions (Braithwaite 1960:1). Statements with a high degree of probability covering a broad range of phenomena are among the important aims of science.

Our ultimate goal in anthropology and archaeology is to formulate laws of cultural dynamics; to seek trends and causes of human behavior; and, as noted above, to make probabilistic predictions.

To apply this to an archaeological situation is neither difficult nor impossible (Plog, 1969, is an example of what I mean). Human behavior is patterned (demonstrable and demonstrated); and if the patterning has not been disturbed by erosion, plough, or pothunters, it can be recovered by proper techniques of limited excavation (sampling). Most of the data relevant to all parts of the extinct sociocultural system are preserved. We have only to devise a proper definition of culture and appropriate techniques for extracting this information from the extant data. Thus, a systems approach to culture permits us to view a site at a single point in time. When one system is compared to another, we perceive process at work—that is, change with or without continuity. By process, I mean the analysis of a system at one point in time and at one place, and how it is transformed into a different system in the same area at a later time. The comparison of systems—not individual "traits"—provides data for understanding trends and for comprehending regularities. Once these are comprehended, one can make probabilistic predictions.

3) The concept of culture.—Under the old view, culture was defined implicitly or explicitly as a set or an association of traits, qualities, properties, or features. Arrowheads, pots, houses, fire pits, orientation of the dead, bone tools, manos, axes, ornaments—all of these and hundreds more are traits. Thus, archaeologists spoke of the Effigy-Mound "culture," the Desert "culture," the Beaker "culture," the Megalithic "culture." Each of these was characterized as possessing certain traits that set it off from all other neighboring or distant "cultures." Archaeologists even spoke of certain tribes as being the "brown-ware (pottery) people." Minute differences in projectile-point shapes were thought of as being important in distinguishing one people from another; and whole migrations of people were postulated on the basis of a single trait or a unique association of traits.

Under the new view, culture is thought of as man's extrasomatic adaptation to his total sociological and ecological environment

(White 1959:15). Prehistoric communities (sites) are studied as whole systems—i.e., technological, sociological, ideological—each subsystem of which is a closely knit, interrelated set of functional parts (Binford 1962: 217). Patterns of significantly covarying clusters of stylistic categories and attributes of data derived from all subsystems are sought.

4) The methods to be employed.—From the old view, insofar as archaeology held any logical structures, it was thought to be inductive. To some, it demonstrated a kind of mysticism in that artifacts recovered from a dig were assumed to speak to the archaeologist who thereby identified (supplemented the real with the ideal) himself with the objects. However, facts cannot be expected to unscramble themselves and produce a theory in the same way as scrambled letters in an animated cartoon unscramble and form a word. Random facts were avidly collected in the belief that this was good procedure and that the end (prehistoric lifeways) justified the means (haphazard collecting of data, with no goals or hypotheses in mind except a reconstruction of past events).

From the new view, the time to retool is here (Kuhn 1962:76). It springs from the concensus that the fruitful approach to a science of the past (as in all sciences) lies in those systems of logic in which deduction and induction interplay. Archaeology can be structured, not haphazard or vague. By this, I mean that tentative hypotheses may be deductively formulated to give direction to scientific investigation. Such hypotheses determine what data should be collected at a given point in an investigation by means of test implications (Hempel 1966:3). It can be shown that the old method of fact collecting is a sterile procedure and produces a morass. Worse, such a procedure will fail to reveal regularities and will lead to no conclusion. (Recently, I heard a colleague describe the data from an impressive series of excavations and then tell his audience that he did not know what to do with these data!)

Actually, most archaeologists have prior or implicit ideas and postulates and even derived theories, but they often fail to make these explicit. They shrink from the ridicule that might beset them if they were to make known these hypotheses. It would take but little intellectual shift to train themselves in the so-called hypothetico-deductive approach. They would then realize that hypotheses are formulated or invented to account for observed facts and not the other way around (Fritz 1968; Hempel 1966:3).

Our knowledge of the past can only be increased by these procedures of interplay and feedback of deduction-induction, formulating hypotheses concerning human behavior and then testing them by relevant archaeological data. The only limits to increasing our knowledge of the past lie in poor intellectual training and in failing to understand that all archeological remains have relevance to propositions bearing upon cultural processes and events of past times (Binford and Binford 1968). The accuracy of our knowledge of the past may be measured by the degree to which our hypotheses about the past are confirmed or rejected.

In the light of the above suggestions, we redefine archaeology as a discipline that deals with the sociocultural systems and cultural processes of the past. Archaeology is a social science because its goal is to explain human behavior. Archaeology is anthropology because it uses the concept of culture. Because these goals are accomplished by using data from the past, the science is *archaeology*. Using data from the past, however, does not make it a type of history. It is not history because archaeology deals with general relationships between variables of human behavior, and not with explaining sequences of unique events.

Up to and including 1960, I pursued four goals: 1) environmental reconstruction using techniques like palynology; 2) the closing of the gaps in the archaeological record by working in relatively unexplored areas; 3) an historical reconstruction of the relationship between the prehistoric "cultures" of eastern Arizona and the historic Hopi and Zuni cultures; and 4) the establishment of a stratigraphy of traits for the area.

In 1961–62, the subject matter of my researches changed slightly—to wit: I developed the desire for information on cultural ecology of eastern Arizona; but I was still concerned with the historical relationships mentioned above. Further, I expanded my interest in the stylistic traits of the "Snowflake Culture" (Arizona) and its ties with both its Anasazi and its Mogollon neighbors.[1]

By 1963–64, substantial changes appeared in my research design. I was still committed to the old stance of writing the "culture history" of our eastern Arizona area. Two new dimensions, however, were added: one was theoretical. It consisted of focusing on culture, not as an aggregation of traits but as an extrasomatic adaptive mechanism that permitted man to cope with the daily problems of living. The facets of culture were subdivided: a) economic, b) sociological, and c) ideological. The other dimension was methodological. It was concerned with sophisticated statistical techniques, sampling, statistical models, and computer aid at all levels of research. It was not, as is naïvely assumed, "computer archaeology," for there is no such thing.

These shifts hastened to displace my old interest in regional cultural history by the analysis of individual sites as sociocultural adaptations—as ongoing social systems (Binford 1962; Hill 1965; Longacre 1963). By studying the patterns of culture represented by the distributions of artifacts at each site, I hoped to make contributions to anthropology. In 1965, many of these emerging trends had become more solid and firm. If a site represented a once flourishing social system, I felt we should analyze it by asking questions about the subsystems of which it was composed. I focused not upon traits but upon the patterned covariation of groups of traits. I studied ecological, sociological, technological, economic, and ideological problems. I set contributions to the understanding of human behavior as the primary goal.

I now feel in a better position to make contributions to anthropology. I now regard the use of logic and of scientific methods as the minimum acceptable standard for good archaeology. By this I mean the procedure of advancing an hypothesis (defined as a statement of relationship between two or more variables (Binford 1967)) to explain observed data or behavior. By the interchange of deduction and induction, the hypothesis can and must be tested with independent but relevant data. Thus, by taking as our hypotheses general propositions concerning causes for culture change, we shall be able to make contributions to anthropology, to formulate probabilistic laws of cultural dynamics, the results of which may be relevant to contemporary world problems.

NOTE

1. "Snowflake Culture"—a name bestowed on archaeological materials that are found near the contemporary Arizona town, Snowflake, originally applied to a black-on-white pottery type. Anasazi, derived from the Navaho language, is the generic term given to the prehistoric peoples of the Colorado Plateau. Mogollon is the name applied to the prehistoric peoples who lived in the vicinity of the Mogollon Mountains, west central New Mexico.

Issues in Anthropological Archaeology

FOR ROUGHLY the last ten years, archaeology has been conceived by many to have been changing both at a faster rate and in a different direction from the previous three or four decades. Is that impression valid, and if it is, what is the explanation for the change? If one were to look at just the arguments, recriminations, pious diatribes, and righteous polemics that have characterized the public rituals of American archaeology, one would say, indeed, something is unusual. The rhetoric of rapid culture change is there to see. What is there behind the rhetoric? (For a thoughtful statement on many of these same questions see Adams 1968.)

The usual schemes used to write the history of American archaeology are stage devices which have the discipline—or subdiscipline, to be narrowly correct—processing diagonally from curiosity satisfaction to history to scientific anthropology. Such schemes have produced a series of categories or historical stages and present no plan for the dynamic transformation of one stage into another (Schuyler 1971:383–409). One cannot expect a discipline which in its substantive work was not able to overcome the problem of static stages to overcome the same problem when writing its own history. These stages cannot be used to cope with what is happening now in American archaeology. Moreover, such schemes have no predictive capacity beyond postulating the further commitment of archaeology to anthropology. They have no predictive power because whatever the dynamic principle is that governs the transformation of stages, it is never

pointed out. And one suspects that as most biologists never saw the flaw in the Linnaean system, most archaeologists do not realize the weakness of the many stage constructions of their own history.

One of the reasons none of the historical stage analyses of the development of archaeology can deal successfully with the decade of the 1960s is that those stage conceptions lack a notion of radical invention, of the existence of the kind of change that is neither gradual nor incremental. They have never heard of a scientific revolution. They are also incapable of coping with that decade because they have explained neither how nor why any of the past changes in archaeology have occurred.

It is because of the possibility that the last ten years' activity in American archaeology represents the beginning of a scientific revolution, a period of radical and swift evolutionary change, that I have borrowed Thomas Kuhn's (1970) model for coping with scientific innovation. *The Structure of Scientific Revolutions* is the most complete model we currently have in hand to describe and explain change in science. It has already been used quite powerfully by George Stocking (1968) to handle the evolution of anthropology as a whole discipline. It strikes me as a vehicle for seeing whether there really is something fundamentally new in American archaeology, or, as many suspect, there are some brilliant new techniques coupled with a lot of "flamboyant symbol mongering" (Geertz 1964:68).

To analyze scientific change, Kuhn has

nominated a series of linked criteria. Central to these is his notion of paradigm. A paradigm is a theory or set of propositions assumed or known to govern the operation of an isolated body of phenomena. A paradigm is as simple as the rule for conjugating a verb or as complex as a theology. In science, a paradigm is the consistent and all but universally agreed-upon way in which, for example, the physical, biological, or economic worlds are supposed to be governed. Such views are those invented by Einstein for physics, the synthetic theory of evolution in biology, and neo-Keynesian economics.

In anthropology, the problem is not what the paradigm is at present but whether there is one or several extant simultaneously. Stocking feels that anthropology, and he would include archaeology, still operates under a paradigm founded by Boas and articulated by his followers. The paradigm is a particular view of what culture is—and is not—as well as all of the propositions, generalizations, and methods deducible from and established as a result of that definition. No one has taken issue with Stocking's analysis but, depending on the level of analysis applied when contrasting paradigms, one somehow intuits that Leslie White and Lévi-Strauss may want to. I personally suspect that the field as a whole, since its founding in the nineteenth century, has moved through a series of protoparadigms which have resulted today in no ultimate agreement about what culture is and is not, as well as, and following therefrom, no unity on what it is that anthropologists should be doing, what problems they should be solving, should consider solved, and which are irrelevant. The protoparadigms which followed the fact-gathering or natural history stage are classic evolution, historicalism, and structural functionalism. What is unclear and is producing a miasma now is that the present paradigm has yet to be fully articulated and identified. The seeming diffuseness of the field now may come because, as Kroeber and White have suggested, we are the catchall for leftover subject matter other disciplines had no use for, or more

plausibly because we are in a state between paradigms. Without a single paradigm to guide, unity of ultimate ends and proximate goals can not be achieved. This exists either because the paradigm for anthropology is as yet incomplete—as it probably is—or because there are several competing paradigms within the field at the moment. This latter is also true, and it is to be observed that none of those used now is complete.

If we suggest that two of the present incomplete paradigms are cultural materialism, or evolutionism, and structuralism as exemplified by Lévi-Strauss and his followers, it is clear that neither is complete as a theory. Evolutionism simply cannot cope as yet with ideological phenomena. Calling religion a reflecting and reinforcing system says nothing when one looks around the corner of the paradigm and sees Parsons, Bellah, and Geertz performing so effectively with religion. Indeed, these latter men participate in another type of evolution which at some theoretical points is in conflict with cultural materialism, and at others is complementary and expanding. Cultural materialism is often contrasted with cultural idealism, a form of which is often seen in Parsonian evolution. It should be pointed out that both types of evolutionary strategy conceive of the systemic nature of culture, but the latter has a more complete and sophisticated notion of culture's subsystems. Neither, however, has completed its own internal evolution. And on the matter of incompleteness, the structuralist paradigm would seem to reveal intrinsic and serious limits in its inability to deal with culture change. The incompletenesses in the paradigms and the competition between their practitioners indicates fairly clearly that whatever it was that Boas has left us, it is not unity.

For ease of analysis, the several levels at which paradigms can exist simultaneously should be pointed out. It is possible to identify a paradigm for science, one for social science, one for anthropology as a discipline as well as paradigms for its recognized subdisciplines, and also for topical areas like economic anthropology. To be sure, all would be overlapping and increase in catholicity of scope in direct ratio to the range of phenomena included under them. Furthermore, the paradigms should be conceived as systemically related, so that paradigm changes are more rapid but have far less long-term impact the narrower the range of phenomena, and slower but far greater overall effect the broader the phenomena and more general the level. A change in the paradigm under which anthropology operates would affect archaeology profoundly, even if only in the long term, whereas an innovation in the paradigm of archaeology is largely lost in the levels above it. Because of this relationship, archaeology will always reflect the paradigm changes in general anthropology since it is a part of what goes on in the larger discipline.

If the problem of the state of the paradigm—single, plural, or incomplete—characterizes anthropology generally, then the problem also characterizes archaeology. Is contemporary archaeology really the product of Boas's genius, or, as the articles in the section of this volume labeled "Origins" attempt to answer, are we the inheritors of parts of plural and diverse protoparadigms: materialistic evolutionism, British functionalism, and cultural ecology? If American archaeologists do march to a different drummer today, has one, evolutionism, suddenly become much more strident? The problem comes down to identifying the nature of the change going on in archaeology. Is it a scientific revolution, or a prelude to one? Or is it best characterized as the completion of a paradigm already present for decades in the field?

When histories of archaeology have been written, stage devices have been used to describe and categorize the events of the field. Not only do these stage taxonomies uniformly lack any dynamic mechanism for transforming stages, most ignore what no archaeologist will deny: archaeology is a part of anthropology. The two have been joined since some time between 1860 and 1880.

I would like to suggest that this relationship has been somewhat more dynamic than has usually been thought. Histories of archaeology usually make the field pass through stages based on its concrete accomplishments (Willey 1968; Wissler 1942). If these stages are lined up and compared with a similar set describing the accomplishments and paradigms of general anthropology for any era, it can readily be noted that while anthropology demonstrates a coincidence between accomplishment and theory, archaeology at any given time has acknowledged the theoretical requirements of the current anthropological paradigm, but in practice has actually addressed its substantive contributions to the preceding paradigm. This is paradigm lag. It can also be readily remembered that archaeologists and other anthropologists have always been aware of that discrepancy. Herein lies a dynamic that has made archaeology go.

The descriptive scheme recently used by Gordon Willey (1968:29–53) to order the history of accomplishment in archaeology aptly illustrates the hypothesis of paradigm lag. Willey divides archaeology into four periods: speculative (1492 to mid-nineteenth century), descriptive (to early twentieth century), descriptive-historic (to 1950), and comparative-historic (since 1950). The periods describe the type of field work accomplished and can also be used to characterize the stages of anthropology's development. Although they are coarse-grained divisions, it is immediately obvious that homotaxially archaeology has been consistently one stage behind anthropology in its concrete accomplishments. General anthropology left its descriptive period in the 1880s, abandoned historicism after World War I, and since then has been firmly comparative.

Willey's stages describe the contributions of the field. They do not accurately reflect the public commitments made by archaeologists to support general anthropological theory. At any one time, archaeologists produced description when stages were called for by the field as a whole, or chronicle was established when functionalism was the common expectation in general anthropology, or functionalist interpretations were offered when anthropologists were concerned with the dynamics of culture change. It is because archaeologists usually acknowledged the theoretical lead of general anthropological theory that they have found themselves committed to an ideal and falling short in practice. At any given time, archaeology actually has been providing answers to problems one paradigm old. Because of the discrepancy between the expected and the achieved, the ideal and the real in anthropological archaeology, ethnologists as well as many archaeologists themselves have regarded archaeology as the poor stepchild of anthropology.

Tallgren (1937), Steward and Setzler (1938), Kluckhohn (1940), and Taylor (1948) have all discussed the discrepancy. The tension created in the field by being one paradigm behind anthropology as a whole, and being conscious of it, has actually been one of the dynamic forces impelling archaeology from stage to stage in its own career. Our evolution as a subdiscipline up to this point has come about precisely because of paradigm lag, not in spite of it.

Why does the lag exist? Probably because all knowledge of the past is ultimately derived from the present, a point we have always been aware of in archaeology. As Spaulding (1968) has pointed out, we are borrowers and consumers. We use the past to test ideas others have had while they were trying to understand the present. We help to articulate the paradigm thereby, but we do not create it. Archaeology is governed by paradigm lag because the ideas we work with are not derived from our own data.

General anthropology has had a variety of scientific revolutions, times when ideas having great promise were introduced and the future was seen to hold great interest. The revolutions have, in fact, usually been less than complete and are represented by protoparadigms like structural-functionalism, modern evolutionism, and French structuralism, rather than by complete theoretical syntheses. However, the lag in archaeological accomplishment has been such in the past that the impact of the revolutions has been felt in a diluted way, when at all. Archaeology has never seen the direct effects of a scientific revolution, at least not until recently.

A Change of Goals

When paradigms change in a scientific revolution, the aims of the field change. When antiquarianism became archaeology, the celebration of unique and precious aspects of antiquity was replaced by reconstruction of the prehistoric past. Can one say that such a change is afoot now? The claims and official rhetoric are enough to lead any susceptible graduate student to the new archaeology. People are now said to be doing science as opposed to writing history, deducing as opposed to inducing, testing hypotheses as opposed to speculating, and so on down the whole litany of procedural requirements for being legitimate as opposed to tainted in the domain of anthropological archaeology. People—young, old, and disguised—are in fact still reconstructing the past and studying extinct lifeways. People are also studying culture change. And that may be new.

As Walter Taylor pointed out, the problems of culture change, the dynamics of cultural transformation, have been part of the conscious concern of archaeologists in Britain and the United States for decades. If anything is new, that goal does not qualify. Are we any closer to realizing that goal now than in 1948? Two decades ago, the specifics of the goal were probably not even understood by most archaeologists. As the essays in this book were meant to demonstrate, that goal is far more frequently realized now. Is that enough to cause a revolution? A lot of gleeful and some pretentious shouting possibly, but a revolution? If the criterion is a change of aims, I think the answer is no, a revolution is not going on. But one may be starting.

If one looks at Deetz's article in this volume, it contains the first hint of a total reorientation of American archaeology. Were archaeology to become the science of material culture or material objects, past and present, the entire field could be revolutionized. At the moment, material culture as a category of phenomena is unaccounted for. It is scattered between interior decorators, advertising firms, and historians of technology. But when one considers how little we know about how material culture articulates with other cultural subsystems, one begins to see the potential. There exists a completely empty niche, and it is neither small nor irrelevant.

Should archaeology become the science of material objects or technology, many of the aims, problems, methods, and data of the field would be completely transformed. A scientific revolution would take place. But as things stand, we are more fully doing the job appointed for us by previous generations of archaeologists. We are doing it better than it has ever been done before. Indeed, it never has been done before successfully. But we are not leading a scientific revolution if the criterion is a change of aims.

New Theory

Nevertheless, a change of aims is not the sole way of measuring a scientific revolution. If it can be demonstrated that fundamental aspects of the old paradigm have been discarded and have been replaced by a new group of assumptions, the change thus characterized is more than gradual evolution. There are three candidates which can be entertained as being essentially new in anthropological archaeology. These are the explicit use of evolutionary theory, an increasingly sophisticated cultural ecology, and the advent of systems theory. With the possible exception of systems theory, which at an ab-

stract level is evolved functionalism and at a more specific level is a way of measuring precise interrelationships between subsystems, both evolutionary theory and cultural ecology have predecessors throughout the history of archaeology. One of the reasons Gordon Childe is the best archaeologist the field has produced is that he possessed and used a powerful paradigm, Marxian materialism. And as Grahame Clark so ably shows, cultural ecology is not new for us. But the combination of these two with systems theory is new. The synthesis is based on the postulates 1) that systems are self-regulating, 2) that evolutionary adaptation is based on the existence of variation, and 3) that cultural systems adjust autonomously by selecting from the variability available to them.

Two events are new concerning the paradigm fragments mentioned above. One is that a partial synthesis of the principles of archaeology based on these fragments is in hand, and the second is that the synthesis is used. The elements, but not the synthesis, come from anthropology or, at any rate, outside of archaeology. But the theoretical synthesis, incomplete though it admittedly is, has been achieved within archaeology. The synthesis is in tune with much of contemporary anthropology. The field has never seen such close coincidence between theory and practice before, and in it may lie the definition of a new relationship between the field and anthropology as a whole.

Glimmerings of that potentially new relationship can be seen in the excitement generated today within archaeology. Many feel that whole new ranges of problems can be tackled by the subdiscipline: social organization, demographic and paleonutritional problems, technological systematics and ideology. Archaeology has suddenly become much more attractive as its ability to address a broader range of issues has been demonstrated. Which of these sets of problems and issues the field settles on for its immediate career is cause for some debate now, and it is as certain that one or some will be selected for as it is that some may be declared irrelevant. After being subjected to this selective pressure archaeology may overcome the subordinate relationship it has had with anthropology and participate in it in a more immediate way.

Problems Addressed

The combination of evolutionism, cultural ecology, and systems theory has resulted in some more convincing answers to inadequately addressed issues. The most important of these is the problem of domestication. Archaeologists consider domestication to be their special province. Childe legitimized the topic, and for decades archaeologists have addressed it. The issue may not now be considered solved, but consider the progress that has been made. Beyond the beginnings established by Childe and so successfully added to by Braidwood who used aspects of cultural ecology, note the essays of Binford and Flannery in this volume, as well as some of the contributions in *The Domestication and Exploitation of Plants and Animals* (Ucko and Dimbleby 1969). Not only do these men variously exhibit an explicit evolutionary attitude and reduce cultural ecology to the subsidiary and useful theory that it is, but for them the interrelationship and interdependence of cultural and natural phenomena are precisely characterized. These are interrelationships that produce stated and measured dependencies.

The most convincing piece of evidence of the productivity of the wedding of evolutionary theory, its specific variant cultural ecology, and systems theory is that we now have a series of testable hypotheses about the origins of the innovation called domestication. And those hypotheses not only have enough generality to predict other loci of domestication but can be used to apply to the nature of ecological innovation generally. When that happens, archaeology will begin to overcome its single most disadvantageous handicap, its inability to contribute general knowledge about how culture, not specific cultures, changes.

My claim here is not that the problem of domestication is solved, although it may well be, but that fundamentally new ideas have been invented to address the problem. That has come about through the use of a different theoretical approach. The difference lies not in using well-measured botanical or climatological data, but in the construction of hypotheses whose variables 1) are both cultural and environmental, 2) are stated in precise interrelationship to one another, and 3) are measurable.

One could take other problems that had not been successfully addressed before and demonstrate the effectiveness of a new body of theory when applied to them. Adams's ideas on the rise of cities, Struever's on the economic base of the Hopewell, the Binfords' on Mousterian adaptability, and Deetz's on prehistoric social organization and on ideological change as shown through technological innovations—all required a new insight of a more than ideosyncratic kind for solutions to be invented. Problems of social organization, ideology, demography, and primitive exchange were simply not issues that had been seen as such before paradigm change. In effect, a new world view has been created for the archaeologist. Paul Martin's essay, "The Revolution in Archaeology," in this volume, does it more than ample justice.

The still-unanswered issue is whether or not this is sufficient reason to claim a scientific revolution or incremental development. The major criterion I have considered here has been the solution of hitherto unsolved problems. A look at the substantive selections in the second half of this volume will show simultaneously two aspects of the criterion. Some recognized but unsolved problems have been successfully addressed. Witness the articles by Wilmsen, Hill, and Rathje as almost random names from the list. And second, the fundamental assumptions all three operate under are so different as to be mutually exclusive with those expressed by the founders of scientific archaeology—Kidder, the great Englishmen, McKern, and others whose work is so faithfully described in several places by Glyn Daniel (1950; 1967) and by Walter Taylor in *A Study of Archaeology* (1948).

New Methods

One of the most strident claims made by many new archaeologists is greater sophistication in the use of scientific method. The claim is also one of the most annoying. People often find it so because it is soon clear that what passes for sophistication in the philosophy of science is really rhetoric. Usually the training in philosophy of science is new, slipshod, and often untried. There are few archaeologists old, new, or indifferent who really use multiple hypothetical explanations or who knowledgeably distinguish between deduction and induction and, appallingly, abduction. This is probably the area in archaeology where more mistakes have been made and less justice done. There has been a series of fraudulent claims which are based on no empirical fieldwork about the way scientists in their guise as archaeologists think.

Kuhn has argued for most philosophers of science that methods are subsidiary to a paradigm and spring from it. They do not create it, although under some circumstances they can help kill it. Methodological innovation ultimately makes no difference in establishing the newness or the oldness of a paradigm. New methods and techniques do not change world views, nor do they ultimately produce better science. That includes radiocarbon techniques and dendrochronology, as well as scientific method itself. We may produce more secure knowledge by using the more rigorous logic of scientific method, but we do not produce new knowledge that way.

If one assumes the priority of a paradigm in any science for that discipline's normal operation, then any methodological innovation, including the use of scientific method, becomes a function of the paradigm and not a device for expanding knowledge. Paradigms are self-fulfilling systems. They identify the pertinent facts—indeed a new paradigm may even bring some of them into sight for the first time. This happened when Deetz identified ceramic variation with aspects of kin units. The paradigm provides the assumption base, the generalizations, and the hypothetical tests. The methods deducible from the paradigm serve to bring the facts into closer harmony with the paradigm. But because one implicitly already knows the range of generalizations that can be established before any experiment begins, no methodological innovation is going to expand them. Scientific method itself is not a way around the paradigm's imperfections, it is rather a logical vehicle to permit greater accuracy in establishing the paradigm's accuracy. No method permits any more knowledge about the "real world" than the paradigm permits.

The one positive function of the precise use of the logic of science is to allow greater validity in the results of experimentation. Since all of the philosophy of science is based on historical knowledge, one should be aware that it has no ability to transcend the contemporary science that it describes. Unlike science, which has a built-in dynamic because of its basic assumptions, the philosophy of science is a far more static system. Often, too, it is used as a tool for legitimation rather than verification.

Paradigm Crisis

Although it requires more than an innovation in methods to mark a scientific revolution, it is sometimes the case that new methods provoke a crisis with the existing paradigm by exposing data so disabling to established views and solutions that scientists begin to question the accepted paradigm. Archaeology is especially rich in methodological innovation and virtuosity. So rich is the subdiscipline that it has seemed justified to some, Taylor for example, to label the whole field a technique. The devices for creating precision in dating, digging, even in creating taxonomies establish in the minds of many outside the field an aura of exactitude and accomplishment that permits us to be called "scientific" by many of our colleagues in other disciplines who simultaneously deny that accolade to our fellow anthropologists.

There is no doubt that radiocarbon dating, palynology, flotation devices, paleonutritional techniques, and dozens of analogous means have allowed archaeologists to recreate the pre- and protohistoric past and to develop satisfying ideas of past lifeways better than ever before. These means are often near the heart of some of the finest of the articles in this volume. But as all this inevitably makes us better archaeologists, it inevitably exposes our true subsidiary role to anthropology (Spaulding 1968:33–39). As we have more fully recreated a picture of life in the past, we become more fully aware that it is not the past we adapt to. What we all aspire to is active participation in anthropology. No one in social science has ever convincingly argued that the past is valuable in itself. The creation of satisfying reconstructions by using the many techniques developed especially since the Second World War has provoked a crisis of accomplishment in American archaeology. Now that one set of expectations is fulfilled (i.e., we have created an outline of world prehistory) it has become more noticeable that we are still ignored by most anthropologists.

Part of the crisis provoked by the myriad techniques available to archaeologists, mostly by loan from other sciences, has come about by realizing that the recreation of the past and the reconstruction of dead lifeways is as impossible for the technologically well equipped archaeologist as it is for the historian and, more especially and pointedly, for the ethnographer. The satisfying history is usually produced by an individual who is as much novelist-artist as social scientist. And the ethnographies that recreate a culture for a reader and revivify a lifeway are only slightly more frequent in ethnology than they are in archaeology. It takes talent, art, and imagination to achieve these aims, not techniques. That J. Eric Thompson's *Rise and Fall of Maya Civilization* has so few peers has nothing to do with the presence of techniques. The absence of equals is explained by the impossibility of achieving archaeology's present goals using the equipment of science, whether that equipment be theoretical or methodological.

If there is a crisis in archaeology, it is because one of our goals, an outline of prehistory, is largely in hand. And another of the goals of archaeology, the reconstruction of past lifeways, simply cannot be achieved by applying scientific techniques, no matter how well or badly science itself may be understood. However, the one goal these techniques, coupled with science, is amenable to is understanding how culture works. Our forebears in archaeology were dedicated, at least verbally, first to the general, then to the prehistoric. And that goal would seem to be one that still is ours to try on for size. It could be that when we discover, as we well might, that it, too, is beyond our reach as archaeologists, the truly anomolous state of archaeology will be exposed.

As a part of the anomolous state already facing us it is observable that archaeologists play almost no role in the major public controversies extant in anthropology today. Cognitive anthropology, structuralism, even the issue of how best to represent nonmodern economic systems are domains quite beside the point for us. Their importance to anthropology cannot be denied; neither can it be denied that we are beside the point to the issues. Our own meetings are almost completely devoted to historical reconstruction. Our major journal has been a tragedy of marginalia.

What is becoming clear is that a double-headed crisis will soon face us as archaeologists. We will have completed the essentials for an outline of world prehistory at the same time that we discover that a reconstruction of a picture of life in the past is theoretically unjustified as well as technically impossible. We have discovered the limits of the paradigm. A concern with time and space and past lifeways is neither trivial nor evil, as some would have it. They simply do not offer any challenge. And there are challenges in abundance in what archaeology may become.

What Is Really Going On

It is very hard to sit back and ask what are the assumptions that hold archaeologists together. But one that seems crucial to the argument I am interested in here is the stage taxonomy. We all know these as lower, middle, and upper something, or early, middle, and late, or pre-, full, and post-, and so on with several combinations. The first important such stage device that all archaeologists are introduced to is the so-called Three Ages system. This is the prototype, although it may not have been the first such, for all similar ideas that form a conceptual umbrella over the entire field. All uses of such schemes are incomplete statements of evolutionary processes, including those produced by ethnologists espousing neo-evolutionism. The implicit question in every one of the stage schemes is how does one stage become another. This latent flaw has been understood by most modern anthropologists studying culture change, but it has required a transformation of that message for archaeologists to be informed. That message is part of the core of the new archaeology. Witness the emphasis Binford and Flannery, for example, put on culture process.

The new archaeology has been labeled by some the process school. Objections can readily be found to either label, but that there is a school, or community of mutually shared understandings, is not hard to establish. And the school's interest in process certainly matches that expressed by all anthropological evolutionists: the so-called neo-

evolutionists as well as the Parsonian and symbolic anthropologists. The theoretical lead is well established with White, Sahlins, Harris, and Service but also with Parsons, Bellah, Turner, and Geertz. Processual archaeology is identified as much by its rhetoricians as by those hurrying to incorporate "sociocultural integration," "sociotechnic," and dozens of other verbal tricks into their official lexicons. There are many who recite the very special and very cumbersome litany. There are many more who identify the school by its ritual language and assume that there is nothing more to it.

In the process of establishing their identity, this explicitly evolutionary school has created a foil called traditional archaeology. The characteristics of the traditional paradigm are identified as much by an examination of its own literature as by the continued evolution of a newer archaeology. It is only with the full definition of the new that a complete understanding of the parts of that which is not new will be in hand. It is easy enough to say that among the attributes of pre-evolutionary archaeology are concerns with temporal and spatial taxonomies and diffusionary explanations. But it is only with the emergence of evolutionary archaeology that the inability of the older paradigm to deal with change, social organization, the real complexity of ecological relationships, demography, the relationship of material culture to technology, and economics becomes apparent. The older paradigm is being identified by contrast as the new one emerges. Schools usually missionize displaying impressive results and ungentlemanly prose. This one is no different. Part of the process of inventing the new paradigm is to make the old one seem as unappetizing as possible. We can only take refuge from the rhetoric under the inevitability of the evolutionary process the rhetoric symbolizes.

The existence of a group of archaeologists who think they are different from other archaeologists is observable. Its theoretical baggage is less easy to identify completely because no major, complete synthesis of that theory exists. One can look into the articles, have conversations with the natives, and reach into one's own head for the essence of the paradigm. I have used three labels to describe fragments of the paradigm—evolutionism, cultural ecology, and systems theory —but that neglects to identify the whole synthesis by name. Furthermore, it may create the idea that there is no whole. And I do not think that is the case.

What creates the whole out of the paradigm fragments mentioned is the relationship of those fragments to science. Here I do not mean scientific method, I mean science as a world view. A world view that creates a level of reality quite distinct from the historical or particular. Science in the particular case of anthropology is after a level of reality that can be removed from time, space, and particular cultures. It creates an analytical reality well described by Kroeber (1952:22–50) and White (1959:3–32), one which supercedes that of particular cultures. That level of reality was firmly established as the proper domain for anthropologists in the 1920s and thirties. And when it was established unequivocally, a number of other changes inevitably followed. The level of generality of the field changed, as did the level of problems addressed. Comparative method was invented and the criteria for acceptability of solutions to problems was revised as well.

Operating under the umbrella of science has a number of other implications. Among others it means that a paradigm focuses on particular problems which in turn bring certain data into view. In other words, the paradigm and problems coming from it dictate reality. That is standard enough, but it also means that the same data can have a different appearance and different interpretations from problem to problem. This is part of what can happen with the change in level of reality under the use of a scientific world view. Reality shifts from a specific and historic set of events centered around one cul-

ture to a generalized, cross-temporal set of observations drawn from plural cultures depending on the issue addressed.

If the earlier hypothesis about paradigm lag in archaeology has any validity, it will describe our subdiscipline's relationship with scientific world view. What the history of archaeology reveals is a public consciousness that general, and hence scientific, knowledge has been the ultimate goal for decades. But it also reveals that the contributions of the field have not demonstrated until very recently that they participate in that generalizing world view. What it is essential to note is that science as a way of looking at the world, along with its various and subsidiary methods, is actually becoming a part of the archaeological life way. And that is new.

The place of science as ideal or practical guide is another example of the process of paradigm lag archaeology is governed by. Science as a world view became a truly acceptable and practicable part of anthropology in the second quarter of the twentieth century. At that time it also filtered inevitably into archaeology. But it has required the passage of an entire generation of archaeologists for scientific world view to become archaeological practice. It is completely inappropriate to take note of these events of archaeology's development, to come to unflattering judgments, and to dismiss the field a populated by blind men. That is the great-man fallacy in reverse and simply does not befit anyone who assumes the superorganic exists. Archaeology is governed by evolutionary processes, one of which is paradigm lag, and the history of the field as well as the contributions of the vast majority of its practitioners should be viewed in that light.

Concurrent with the rise of a scientific world view in archaeology has been the introduction of three parts of the as yet fragmentary paradigm in general anthropology. The origins of evolution and cultural ecology within anthropology are clear enough. Why they should show up at this time in archaeology is another matter. General systems theory, which in its more precise aspects is probably being used more by archaeologists than ethnologists, comes, I think, from the general culture as much as it may from anthropology. Its advent is undoubtedly tied up with the pervasiveness of certain aspects of technology in modern American culture. It should not be considered accidental that evolution, cultural ecology, and systems theory are all generalizing notions and come into actual use in archaeology at the same time the use of science has created a level of analytical reality to which these notions can be applied.

In anthropology as a whole at the moment, several diverse groups are preoccupied with culture process. The cultural materialists or evolutionists have been visible for two decades at least. That group inspired by Weberian and Parsonian sociology, however, also has the means of directional change as its concern. The group includes Geertz, Bellah, and many of the men concerned with modernization. No overall paradigm has been invented yet for studies of culture process; in fact, the area of ethnological theory appears very diffuse at the moment. The field appears to be in a state witnessing the incompleteness but complementarity of functionalism, structuralism, and at least two notions of evolution. The situation seems pregnant for synthesis and the emergence of a normal paradigmatic state.

For various reasons, archaeology has been looking to anthropological theory at a time when that area presents alternative and incomplete paradigms. It is likely that archaeology had never witnessed a similar event when it turned to anthropology for theory in the past. Yet why should archaeology turn to anthropology at this specific time? Furthermore, if we can say, as Willey does, that archaeology has begun a transfer from historical to comparative studies, then it would seem that the paradigm we are in line to borrow from is structural-functionalism, not the paradigm of culture process. Structural-functionalism developed in part as a reaction to particularistic anthropology, and it would seem to be the stage archaeology should logically enter after its own historicalist era.

There are few indices that place any aspect of contemporary archaeology in the functionalist camp. The studies in the early and mid-1960s using stylistic variation in ceramics to reconstruct aspects of social organization may superficially look like functionalism, but as they were perfected, they fell squarely into line with evolutionary theory. Part of the explanation for this involves the use of cultural ecology. Most studies using cultural ecology produce ethnologies. (Sahlins 1958; Rappaport 1968) which have a distinct functional cast to them. The subject occurs more or less at a moment in time, usually concerns the specific adaptation of a specific culture, and usually concentrates on the linked relationships between sets of cultural factors in the single system. The reason, however, cultural ecologists in ethnology and archaeology do not usually produce functional studies, in the Radcliffe-Brown sense, comes from their preoccupation with continual adaptation.

Equilibrium or stasis actually oscillates. Dynamism is consequently present in the most static of cultures. And the more complex the culture the more likely there will be more built-in devices for giving equilibrium a dynamic caste. Given the existence of oscillating equilibrium and the concern of most archaeological studies with lengthy periods of time, it seems unlikely that cultural ecology will become the new functionalism.

I would like to suggest that by and large archaeology has skipped the functionalist stage. Consider Walter Taylor's conjunctive approach. It is a suggested means for establishing functional interrelationships. It is functionalism. Taylor is uniquely valuable as an illustration here. He represents not only the visible signal that announced to the field that a paradigm crisis was at hand, but at the same time suggested what the next paradigm ought to be. He suggested functionalism which at the time was undergoing a period of paradigm questioning and crisis in general anthropology. But because it was the major paradigm in anthropology it seemed to be the inevitable choice for archaeology. Taylor's analysis pointed out paradigm lag and by doing so he illustrates one of the tension-creating vehicles causing archaeology to evolve. As an alternative, however, Taylor suggested the impossible, which is why his device has never been used, not because people got angry at him. The goal of reconstructing past lifeways may be impossible and probably is unrealistic, and that is what the archaeological equivalent of functionalism demands. Moreover, the functionalist paradigm has been selected against in archaeology because the appropriate data are not readily available, because it is either impossible or enormously costly to bring them into exist ence, and most importantly, because functionalism provides no problems calling for the use of a prehistoric laboratory.

Taylor's judgment in 1948 was essentially correct. But no revolution happened then because the anthropological paradigm was not practicable in archaeology. Rapid change is happening now in archaeology because anthropology is experimenting with a new paradigm. The conceptual tools for handling processual change, which were rudimentary twenty-five years ago, have now been perfected enough for adaptation to archaeological use.

To recapitulate briefly before carrying the argument farther, the advent of the conscious use of science in archaeology occurs at the same time that archaeology has begun to employ a notion of the precisely articulated evolution of cultural systems and sub-systems. This presents the conjunction of science, evolution, cultural ecology, and systems theory. It is also clear that when one looks at the goals of archaeology, 1) we have not had much success at reconstructing past lifeways, 2) we have achieved broad knowledge of the culture history of extinct peoples and events, and 3) we are beginning to address an old but untried goal, processes of culture change. We are therefore in an interstitial area in our own evolution and it may be called a time of paradigm crisis. If the normal relationship between archaeology and anthropology were to be counted on, functionalism would be the paradigm we would inherit and begin to employ. But the paradigm we are in line to inherit has no use for data from the past, a fact that has dawned on many archaeologists. Furthermore, the paradigm crisis occurs at a time when there is no well-established paradigm current in anthropology which is an inevitable substitute. As a result, we are feeling the full brunt of the emerging scientific revolution in anthropology, something that has never occurred before to us as archaeologists. The events current in archaeology now come as a result of the process of paradigm lag, but should archaeology choose a course which involves it directly with data from the present, it will have freed itself from that process. It would then participate on a peer basis in anthropology.

The Alternatives Open to Archaeology

While I think various parts of the emerging paradigm in archaeology can be identified without great struggle, I do not think the activities of the school's practitioners can be singled out with anything like clarity. Although there is some coherence among the substantive contributions in this book, it will be obvious at once that two prominent categories of articles produced by new archaeologists and their colleagues are missing. There are no articles on statistical methods, one exception. And there are none on ethnographic archaeology, again one possible exception. They are two sets of activities archaeologists do. They also do historic archaeology, which may or may not be the wave of the future. New archaeologists do all of these things. Can one conclude, therefore, that they do all those activities that all other archaeologists do and that they are merely "living into" the field? There may be another explanation.

Archaeology is evolving toward a scientific

revolution. One certainly may have begun, but one certainly has not been completed. Archaeologists will soon realize that two of their aims are outworn. One, the reconstruction of events in the past, is nearly complete; it offers little in the way of challenge today. And once the outline is in hand, there will remain nothing more than the prehistoric analogues to those studies produced in history under the rubric, "History of the three-tined fork." The other aim, a picture of past lifeways, is a scientific impossibility. And although homage is paid to it in museums, few if any archaeologists strive actively to achieve a "satisfying" reconstruction. That goal has largely been fulfilled by the coffee table picture books. They succeed by using art and photography where archaeologists—famously impoverished wordsmiths—fail.

I do not mean to suggest that either chronologies or reconstructions have suddenly become irrelevant. There are certain basic tools with which the prehistoric laboratory has to be equipped before it can be used for an experiment. One is a basic outline of the events in the past. What I am suggesting, however, is that ever fewer people find that goal sufficient in itself. And some find it simply unchallenging. Nor am I suggesting that our society finds archaeology as it stands beside the point. Clearly class enrollments and book sales to the public suggest that archaeology is remarkably popular with Americans. But the books that are produced to reconstruct the past are picture books. There are lots of them and they do their job well. Degree of accuracy aside, the picture book reconstructions of the past are usually illuminating and sometimes exciting. And archaeologists play a subsidiary role in their production. We produce the artifacts but not the artistic synthesis. What I think can be concluded is that the goal of chronicle and stage construction is becoming truly subsidiary for archaeology and that of reconstruction is being taken out of our hands.

The third aim, the cultural analogues to theories like natural selection, remains both incomplete and potentially fruitful. Because this third aim of archaeology has been so notoriously unrealizable, there is the possibility in theory at least that it is beside the point until a sufficiently powerful paradigm addressing it is invented. We may or may not see it aborning. But what we do see emerging are attempts at answering evolutionary questions using very radical interpretations of what archaeology is all about. Three that are distinctly classifiable are historic archaeology, ethnographic archaeology, and the science of material objects, or material culture. To be sure, at the moment interest in all three is not central to the field, and few conceive of these as holding a fundamental departure for archaeology.

I would like to suggest that these three marginally affiliated types of archaeology represent, among other things, potential tangents allowing archaeologists data amenable to their sole unaddressed aim. Studies of culture change may either be too expensive or yield too prosaic a set of results when using a prehistoric laboratory. In finally focusing concerted attention on this aim, it may be necessary both to extend the horizons of the field for data and to address ourselves to the more pressing needs of our own culture. These calls may be met in some of the developments going on in historic archaeology, ethnographic archaeology, and the study of material objects. Fuller sources of data covering lengthy periods are available using historic materials. Material culture, on the other hand, has so long been neglected by ethnographers that archaeologists have seen themselves forced to build their own analogues. Although this may be the immediate aim, the number of archaeologists involved may be used to argue that there is more here than is at first obvious. In adaptive terms archaeologists are, consciously or unconsciously, proliferating the range of data and problems open to them. Further, considering the range of pressures on archaeologists, the exigencies of our own culture point out quite clearly that we know almost nothing about the effects of technology and material culture on other cultural subsystems and vice versa. That archaeology should expand into such domains would seem implausible, if it had not already begun. The area which we are as yet only dimly aware of is the study of material culture, objects, or technology.

The scholarly and scientific study of technology as a cultural subsystem has very diffuse roots and even more disparate practitioners. Some of the obvious who come to mind are Joseph Needham, Lynn White, Margaret Hogbin, Jacques Ellul, and Marshall McLuhan. None is an anthropologist let alone an archaeologist, yet every one of them has treated technology and its relationship to the rest of culture in remarkably anthropological ways. Yet there is no coherence to these studies when taken as a group, and a list of such names is almost a list of mavericks. These examples provide incomplete models for the study of material culture at the same time that they demonstrate the openness of that niche which archaeologists have been preadapting to for a century.

The explicit reasons archaeologists give to explain interest in what was formerly foreign and unknown territory are quite likely to be aside from the fact that those areas provide a more amenable laboratory for studies of culture change. And that, too, may be quite incidental to the evolutionary direction archaeology itself is subject to. I do not claim to know what that course is, but it is clear that the niche we have adapted to since around the turn of the century is both full and crowded with competitors. Not only do we have a very substantial notion about what went on in the prehistory of this planet, but we are having to reach further and further into the ranges of marginalia for "unsolved issues" as the topics for doctoral theses and kindred exercises.

More to the point, however, is the skill we barely know we possess. The average archaeologist knows an enormous amount about the artifacts of prehistory. He can tell reams about the most arcane item. Or so it would seem. But no one can analyze what plastic has done to American culture and, ludicrous as it may seem, the archaeologist is better fit to do the job than anyone. This is more to the point when one realizes his acknowledged accomplishments using technology to discuss ecology, demography, the evolution of technological forms, and so on.

If the suggestions in this essay about the theoretical and substantive state of archaeology have any validity, there is a unique combination of circumstances facing us. That combination is best seen through the law of evolutionary potential. By having been one step out of phase with anthropology, and by now being unable to become immediately attached to an established paradigm, our field has been left open to select and to be selected for that role most suitable to it within the future of anthropology. However, what that specific role is does not seem immediately apparent, but there is no doubt that it need not revolve solely around the exotic and the long dead.

I think the way this discussion must be left is to acknowledge a very rapid rate of change in anthropological archaeology for the past ten years. We can probably single out the causes for this. But just as no evolutionist can predict the future of the specific case, we can not be sure what is going to happen to archaeology. It may become extinct. But it more surely is going to be radically transformed.

NOTE

This essay was markedly improved through the criticisms of A. Thomas Kirsch, Craig Morris, Martin G. Silverman, and Ezra B. W. Zubrow. I am very grateful for their positive contribution to it and in no way involve them in the burden of any errors this essay may contain.

Old Wine and New Skins: A Contemporary Parable

I HAVE been asked to comment on the new, the not-so-new, and the downright old in contemporary archaeology in the United States. The specific question was put: "what happened between 1948 and 1970?" The task has been rather uncongenial and the writing difficult. I have tried to navigate the waters between a Scylla of adverse criticism and a Charybdis of self-approbation—only to end up with what sadly seems to be a bit of a shipwreck on each side of the straits. This may be the neatest seafaring trick of the week. But that is the way it is, and I offer my results without further apology.

Contemporary archaeology in the United States is certainly in a state of flux. Archaeologists having traditional goals and using traditional theory are still very much with us. There has also developed a sort of "neo-traditionalism," an archaeology having traditional goals but working with an expanded range of data and modern techniques which have evolved in response to a somewhat modified, but still recognizably traditional conceptual scheme. Then there is the so-called new archaeology which, justifiably or not, has set itself apart from traditionalism of any kind and trumpeted its breakthrough to science and the scientific method. Other heterodoxies have been proposed. Rouse, usually rather conservative in his outlook, has suggested the radical possibility that in the not-too-distant future archaeology may separate into two professions, one technological and the other interpretive (1968:12). Chang has argued for a "science of prehistoric so-ciety" or "settlement archaeology," by which he labels what he claims is a more logically consistent and practical archaeology than either the traditional or the "new," one that is "more interested in the larger picture of culture and society" (1968:vii, viii).

I like to think that this turmoil, insofar as it represents an active dissatisfaction with traditionalism and a questing for more productive research design, is, at least in part and however belatedly, a result of the ideas and exhortations of *A Study of Archeology* (Taylor 1948). As I see them now, the basic tenets of the conjunctive approach, as explicitly set forth in that monograph, can be particularized as follows:

1) Since archaeology in the United States has long been considered a subdiscipline of anthropology, the subject of archaeological inquiry is the nature and workings of culture —with the corollary that it is interested in the "nature of culture" in all its particularistic, partitive variability, as well as in its "workings" or processes relative to some more generalized, holistic concept of culture.

2) Like cultural anthropology, archaeology is an historical discipline, but one whose empirical data fall within only four categories: chemico-physical specifications, provenience, quantity, and relationships or "affinities" (Taylor 1948:111 f.) and whose recourse to inference must therefore be proportionately great—with the corollary that its conclusions are not provable but are in the nature of ever closer approximations to some finitely unknowable reality, i.e., work-

ing hypotheses which must be tested and refined by specifically programmed investigations.

3) Culture is integrated, or "systemic" as modern jargon has it, to such an extent that cultural manifestations cannot be truly depicted or understood apart from their contexts—with the corollary that construction of cultural context is an absolute requisite for anthropological archaeology (or archaeological anthropology).

4) Cultural context consists not merely of material objects, singly or in categories, but includes relationships between and among cultural and noncultural phenomena, which relationships or "conjunctives" serve to connect the meaning as well as the construction of archaeological contexts.

5) One of the most efficient and productive ways of utilizing these conjunctives is by multiple categorizations based upon the many inherent characteristics and relationships which each archaeological datum has.

6) The concrete, empirical findings of archaeology can be manipulated and interpreted to provide evidence of cultural behavior, of the nonmaterial results of cultural behavior, and of culture itself—with the corollary that this evidence, specifically and explicitly argued, may be used to enrich the cultural contexts and to support subsequent and consequent studies of culture itself and of cultural process.

If these tenets sound familiar to contemporary archaeologists, especially to those of the "new" or "processual" school, it does not surprise me at all. Much of the "new archaeology" is operating with a conceptual scheme which is virtually identical, in its basic ideas, with that anticipated in *A Study of Archeology*. What does surprise me, however, is that it has taken the many years since 1948 for that conceptual scheme to take hold! Perhaps it is as one colleague predicted: that *A Study of Archeology* would not be widely accepted until a new generation of archaeologists had come along without so much subjective and emotional involvement

in the then status quo. Perhaps the popularly held view that my criticism of Americanist archaeology was a polemic aroused such partisan and defensive animosity that the message of the rest of the volume was lost. Perhaps it is somehow indicative that, only a few months ago on the latest of not a few similar occasions, I heard a colleague pay formal, public tribute to the influence upon him of *A Study of Archeology,* only to discover that his most recent theoretical publication cites the monograph only once, a parenthetical page reference, but does quote at considerable length more recent works by other authors as the sources of some of the most basic and distinctive ideas of *A Study of Archeology.*

Perhaps there have been academic-pedagogic generational reasons for the lag: the older generation taking umbrage but maintaining a dignified silence and largely ignoring my insurgency, at least in public and in print; the next generation (that of my peers) in some cases taking up the cudgels which their mentors and idols had declined to wield, in others tempering their own traditional viewpoint to accept some of my ideas and consequently being more tolerant of their own students' attitudes and actions; and the third, the present generation, once removed from the traditional archaeologists and with more permissive instructors, accepting the insurgency to varying degrees and in varying segments of their archaeological theory.

Perhaps another obstruction has been the object-mindedness of many American archaeologists (Taylor 1952). Gordon Willey is a self-identified example of this and, in discussing Lewis Binford, says:

. . . however, with the outlook of one who grasps the tangible example more readily than the abstract theoretical statement, I await with interest some large-scale demonstrations of [Binford's] principles with the data of New World prehistory. (1968:53)

And Paul Martin was saying practically the same thing a number of years earlier:

I think Taylor's ideas would have been far more favorably received and more widely accepted if he had first put out an archaeological report embodying his ideas. . . . To me a concrete example is more easily grasped than an abstraction or a theory; and we who teach could then point to the applications of his principles. I still await with pleasure Taylor's publications of his archaeological work in Mexico. (1954:571)

It is unfortunate that Martin must still wait for my final report on the Mexican material and that Binford has yet to publish a full-scale archaeological monograph. But it has always seemed to me that both Binford and I have provided our colleagues with enough pertinent material for them to chew on for quite a spell. The fact that they have not chosen to do so and have been waiting so patiently for us to provide them with spelled-out applications using masses of material objects appears to me to be more a commentary on their outlook and standards of value than a justifiable demand upon us.

I for one regret as much as they not having produced a monograph based upon the conjuctive approach, but I cannot see that my default explains or condones the complete lack, in the literature of American archaeology, of any objective, thorough critique of A Study of Archeology. Had there been such, it would have constituted a scholarly response rather than, as actually happened, an emotional reaction in defense of a theoretical cotradition inherited by the critics and their cohorts (e.g., Woodbury 1954). In view of our stated aims, the fact that Binford and I have not seen fit to play their game, but have gone ahead with our own, cannot be justifiably held against us.

And finally perhaps, as some have said, there may be intrinsic and/or practical difficulties which have worked against acceptance and use of the conjunctive approach. With present methods, this may possibly be true, although in the absence of any full-scale test I do not see how the critics can be so sure. My own experience leads me to believe that any such difficulties can be largely overcome through developing and applying new, more efficient methods and techniques, both in the field and in the laboratory. What is needed is a flexible, ever-changing, "lively" approach which will demand, and thus have a better chance of getting, more productive methods. This is precisely what the "new archaeology" has demanded and, in many ways, gotten— although of recent days I have an uneasy feeling that their approach is becoming less flexible and more dogmatic, a situation not unusual among evangelical sects. Let me say once more that what we need is not one approach but a series of approaches which will remain receptive to new ideas and which, thus, can be both broadened and refined as we go along. Only by constantly making more specific and more stringent theoretical demands upon our data can we realize their full potential.

But whatever may or may not have been the influence from A Study of Archeology upon contemporary archaeological theory, many of the latter's methods and techniques are new or are appreciable advances over anything discussed or even envisaged in 1948: the use of computers and backhoes for example. But after all, the conjunctive approach was explicitly stated to be just that, a "theoretical foundation for a viewpoint, a point of attack, or an approach rather than for a particular method" (1948:7). I could and did expect that practical implementation would take turns which, at that time, were unforseeable. Therefore, despite mutterings of denial from some of its practitioners, I allow myself the presumption of looking upon much of the "new archaeology" as practical application of a basic conceptual scheme, the earliest more or less complete expression of which was the conjunctive approach. When progeny will not own their parentage, it becomes the undignified and distressing but incumbent responsibility of parents to claim their posterity as they understand it. False modesty that obscures genealogy can leave a serious blot on the 'scutcheon!

Then what can be said of contemporary

archaeology as it is being practiced? Is it possible to accept it without reservations? The answer, as might be expected, is no, at least in my opinion. As an example, if we take a close look at the "new archaeology," which is the substance of this volume, I believe that several aspects invite comment and a gentle caveat. I feel unhappy about certain matters of theory and would like to elaborate briefly upon two of them here. But before doing so, however, let me emphasize what I have said elsewhere: "Archeology in the United States today is a remarkably different discipline from what it was in 1948 and, from my viewpoint, the outlook for the future is tremendously encouraging and exciting" (1968:i).

Perhaps my principal worry concerns the new archaeology's attitude toward the construction of cultural contexts. It was not to plead for storybook pictures of ancient life that I so strongly advocated cultural context as the minimum performance incumbent upon archaeology as history or as social science, as a part of anthropology. Ford, among others, quite misunderstood my point when he said that I had made a "plea for a more vivid reconstruction of cultural history on the basis of archaeological evidence" (1952:317). I made no such plea, nor was vividness or lack of it any part of my argument! My point was very explicitly stated to be that context is needed because cultural isolates can neither be understood nor properly used without it. This is the old Boasian doctrine and should not have required a lengthy disquisition in order to be comprehended! Furthermore, it should also have been abundantly clear that by the "fullest possible cultural contexts" was meant integrations ranging from the most elaborate narrative descriptions of past lifeways to the immediate matrix of some artifact, event, cultural system, cultural-ecological relationship, or other such isolate: in other words, as much or as little context as required to set the subject of research in its temporal, cultural, and natural perspective.

But it is precisely context of any sort that is skimped or lacking in the published work of the "new archaeologists." They seem to be so impatient to get on with their hypothesis-testing that they do not bother to provide either themselves or their readers with the contexts which alone can set their tests and results in an appropriate and necessary relevance. In fact, some of them have gone so far as to deny the possibility of ever making what they rather anachronistically call "reconstructions of past lifeways." The fallacy of using the word *reconstruction* was dealt with at some length in *A Study of Archeology* (Taylor 1948:35), and to use it today is to set up a straw man, to saddle other archaeologists with an admittedly impossible goal and then deny its possibility. In addition to perpetrating this dubious circularity, they have fallen into the very trap against which they were warned:

Finally, . . . it will be well to comment on the fallacy and mental hazard engendered by the use of the term *historical reconstruction*. The words *reconstruction* and *resynthesis* are fundamentally erroneous and have been responsible for much loss of confidence, particularly among the anthropologists. . . . If it cannot be told for sure whether past actuality has, or has not, been recreated in detail or in essence, it cannot be claimed that these contexts are, or are not, *resyntheses* or *reconstructions*. These terms imply a re-building to exact former specifications which, from the above, are not verifiable and, hence, not knowable. The unknowable cannot be taken as a standard of value. Therefore, arguments both for and against historical reconstruction in anthropology or in any other [historical] discipline are irrelevant, and it becomes apparent that the work of all historical disciplines really leads to construction and synthesis, not reconstruction and resynthesis. From this, it is further apparent that the real task of the students in historical disciplines settles down to seeing how sound, how plausible, and how acceptable their constructions can be made. Neither the anthropologists nor the historians should use the term *reconstruction* and thus make himself feel inadequate because he knows that his research will never permit him actually to reconstruct the life of past times with certainty and completeness. Rather, he should realize that even the contexts written from the best and fullest archives are constructions and that the differences lie in the nature of the respective data, not in the procedures or basic theoretical factors. (Taylor 1948:35–36)

And also in the same vein:

Some archeologists forget that proof of culture and cultural relationships in the past is simply not possible. In archeology we are dealing, and perforce must deal, with probabilities and, we hope, with "ever closer approximations" to some finitely unknowable reality. Our only tribunal is professional acceptability or our personal values. If this is remembered, then much of the steam is taken out of arguments about "knowledge of the past," "verifications," and other such absolutistic value concepts in archeology. (Taylor 1969: 384)

Can it be that their love affair with science has not only led the "new archaeologists" to reject what they know (and everybody else knows!) they cannot prove but has also blinded them to what is the only solution to this predicament: a recognition and an acceptance of the essential nature, the relativism, of their research materials? I hope that as they mature, individually and as a school, they will relinquish their shibboleth of proof and their denial of cultural context to become more relaxed and understanding and tolerant of their lot. If they do this, I believe that they will have a much greater chance of attaining their goals. If they do not, I feel that they will only raise more problems.

For example, it has been stated by Binford and others that the ultimate goal of the "new archaeology" is the formulation of laws of cultural process, which goal is to be attained by the explication and explanation of cultural similarities and differences. But I would ask: how are they going to describe these cultural similarities and differences, much less explain them, without recourse to the very cultural contexts which they claim are impossible of achievement? Or must we believe that they will come upon these explanations a priori or by some decree ex cathedra? Once again I sense an impatience with what other anthro-

pologists consider to be a most necessary procedural step. The "new archaeologists" seem to wish to deal with abstract, universal concepts without dealing with the individual, partitive cultural contexts from which alone such abstractions can be derived or have meaning. In his reply to Leslie White, Robert Lowie made much the same point with regard to the work of Tylor and Morgan, asking how their evolutionary formulae had been derived:

Are they empirical inductions? In that case they must rest on observations of the history of specific tribes. Or are they all *a priori* constructs. . . . the Boasians do claim the right to check evolutionary generalizations by the facts they are meant to explain. . . . (1946:231)

In other words, if the "new archaeologists" claim that it is impossible to make what they call "reconstructions of past lifeways" from the data of archaeology, then on what bases are their processual studies to be made and checked? Adapting a phrase from Lewis Binford, I may say that they appear to have painted themselves into a theoretical corner!

My second point of issue concerns the concept of culture. I do not believe that it is coincidental that the "new archaeologists" should find themselves aligned with the evolutionary anthropologists in this matter. Leslie White, avowed champion of Evolutionism, has obviously been a guiding theoretical spirit behind the "new archaeology." Many of its practitioners use his concept of culture: the extrasomatic means of man's adaptation to his environment. Whether or not this definition is practical in working with living cultures is not a moot question here. But its application to archaeological research most certainly is—and I have serious doubts as to the utility of White's definition in our field. His definition is explanatory and hence dynamic; it tells what culture does. It does not tell what culture is, what culture consists of; it is not a descriptive definition. Now the ethnographer can observe culture in action in the form of cultural behavior and in its adaptive relation with the environment. Therefore, he can use a dynamic, explanatory model from the inception of his studies. This is not possible for the archaeologist. His empirical data are static and, in order to accomplish his first task which is to delimit his empirical data, he must use a static model, i.e., a descriptive concept of culture, not a dynamic one. Only after he has identified his data and then only by use of inference from that data, can he apply a dynamic, explanatory model. By using only a dynamic model, that is by using it first, the "new archaeologists" are once again skipping a necessary procedural step and weakening their results.

I should like to close on a rising pitch. Despite what I have said about certain faults I find with the "new archaeology," I have no inclination to throw the baby out with the bath. I am excited and enthusiastic about what the "new archaeologists" are producing. Given the brief time-span of their work, they have made great strides and notable contributions. I believe their future holds much promise. I hope that they will take these few thoughts of mine as they are meant, as a way of showing my interest and, hopefully, of making a small contribution to their work, to "our" work.

Interpretive Trends and Linear Models in American Archaeology

ARCHAEOLOGISTS have long used various graphic devices as an aid in communicating their ideas to others. Familiar forms are chronological charts, developmental sequences, and diagrams of taxonomic relationships. In recent years it has become popular to identify a scheme that has theoretical validity and explanatory value as a model. These schemes or models are best understood when presented graphically. Both graphic devices and models are similar in many ways. For example, they share a danger pointed out by Phillips (1955:250; Willey and Phillips 1958:7) who comments that they "have the happy facility of proving whatever they are designed to prove." Probably the very best way of avoiding the danger of distortion that seems to be inherent in models and graphs is to strive for devices that possess the elegance of simplicity. A complex and contorted model can serve as a hiding place for all sorts of misrepresentation, distortion, and bias, both intentional and unintentional. A simple model, of course, may also distort, especially if simplicity is an excuse for avoiding the true complexity of a problem. By simplicity, I mean a combination of directness of presentation, clarity of explanation, and honest adherence to reality, rather than a reduction of all factors to a simplistic model or graph whatever the practical and intellectual cost.

One of the great adventures of teaching undergraduate students is that one is forced to try to be clear and convincing without being simplistic and patronizing. As a result

of making such an effort for almost twenty years, I have become intellectually and emotionally attracted to a linear explanatory model, not only because it is a useful teaching device, but also because it provides a theoretically sound basis for understanding and resolving many interpretive and theoretical controversies.

By linear model, I mean a simple straight-line scale characterized by polar extremes that, though often strikingly dissimilar when compared directly, can be shown to be closely related when compared along the gradations of the scale. Such a linear model is often called a continuum. We use continua frequently in everyday life because many situations seem to be most easily analyzed in terms of contrasting and dissimilar alternatives. We often find it convenient to organize a set of facts by emphasizing the kinds of differences that lead to polar extremes, but we ultimately find that these facts only achieve relevance when they are seen in the context of the middle range of the continuum that stretches between the poles. Anthropologists have long made good use of the contrastive values of the concept of continuum. Familiar examples are the Gemeinschaft-Gesellschaft distinctive of Tönnies (1957) and the folk-urban continuum of Redfield (1947).

It is my belief that when two apparently opposing methods or theories reach the state of confrontation that forces the supporters of each to defend and promote their views vigorously, we have clear-cut evidence that we are dealing with a true continuum or linear model. It seems to me that the application of the linear model in such situations is not only a means of clarifying the controversy, but also a way of insuring that the energy generated by the controversy is channeled into constructive rather than destructive directions. One might insist that once the polar extremes have been defined and defended to the point that the polemic leads to the creation of detractors, defenders, messiahs, and cults, it is more economical to turn one's attention to the intervening portion of the continuum.

I do not want to imply by these comments that the lively exploration of either of the polar extremes is without merit. On the contrary, careful examination of either pole of the linear model has great pedagogical and heuristic value. The farther out toward either pole of a continuum one goes the more extreme a position one must take and the more one rejects all other positions. It can be said that such a position is a "purer" one, because the closer one gets to the pole or extreme of the linear model, the more one expresses the position in splendid isolation. The idea is developed in a kind of experimental context in which all other factors are held constant because they are ignored. This approach is truly heuristic because it enables us to examine a single idea without any complicating and entangling relationships with other ideas. However, the clarity with which we thus see the pole of the continuum does not reflect its true relative position in the complex world of reality.

Polar Extreme	The interplay and balance of reality	Polar Extreme

The Linear Model

I offer some examples of the application of the linear model in the explanation of some well-known developments in method and theory in American archaeology in the hope that they will support my suggestion that the linear model is the most productive way of deriving lasting value from any current controversy based on theoretical confrontation.

During the time from World War I to about 1950, American archaeologists invested a great deal of energy in debating the relative value of various field techniques. There was much discussion of the need for careful excavation and much worry about the use of earth-moving machinery as an excavating tool. Two extreme positions were taken. There was the camel-hair school versus the bulldozer school. It ultimately became clear that in fact there were many different ways of moving dirt in archaeology and that the camel hair brush and the bulldozer were only the poles of a linear model. American archaeologists are now well accustomed to using any and all of the techniques of excavating in this model depending on the problem to be solved. A given investigator may use a shovel at one moment, a dental tool at another, as well as a backhoe or bulldozer, in the course of a single day's work on a site. The major result of this recognition of the value of the linear model is that the archaeologist has maximum flexibility without either loss of control or waste of effort and resources.

The excavations of the Nevada State Museum at the Tule Springs Site provides a good example of the value of this flexibility to the archaeologist (Haynes 1967b). This excavation was an attempt to test the claims of very high antiquity for the Tule Springs finds by uncovering very extensive areas with maximum provenience control. Trenches almost one kilometer long, six meters wide, and fifteen meters deep were excavated with bulldozers and other large earth-moving machines. Each machine removed only a few millimeters of earth from the floor of the trench at any one time. A trained archaeologist followed each machine on foot and examined the freshly exposed surface for archaeological evidence. Of course, whenever any hint of archaeological material was found, the machines gave way to hand tools.

An example of the conversion of a major theoretical controversy into a related system

36

of ideas is to be found in the half century or so of discussion about typology. For a long time now, American archaeologists have been worried about whether types or classes of artifacts are the product of arbitrary systems imposed on the evidence for the convenience of the archaeologist or whether these classificatory units mirror the cultural reality that the archaeologist discovers in the evidence (the "Ford-Spaulding" controversy; Willey and Phillips 1958:13). We have finally come to recognize that the emphasis on these two polar views is quite sterile. On the one hand, all classifications are arbitrary in part. At the same time, the very clustering of similarities that makes classification possible demonstrates some patterning of the evidence that reflects, even though imperfectly, the pattern of reality in the past. Again, the application of the linear model results in greatly increased flexibility. The investigator who wishes to gain the most from the study of his data asks many different questions and develops different classifications to help provide the answers. Brew (1946:6) and Rouse (1960) have both emphasized the need for many classifications. One can achieve this goal by moving back and forth along the scale or linear model of classification without compromising theoretical commitment, because the existence of the scale provides the many gradations that demonstrate the ultimate compatibility of the polar views.

Other anthropological examples of the integration of seemingly opposing views include: the question of whether American anthropology is historical or scientific (Kroeber 1935), or humanistic or scientific, (Hammel 1968) and the question of whether the concept of culture is enumerative and descriptive or ideational and value-based (Kroeber and Kluckholm 1952; Osgood 1951; Thompson 1958b:2–3). These examples involve major theoretical and interpretive controversies that first generated polar positions and then moved gradually by trial and error, discussion and compromise, to the theoretical integration of the linear model that we enjoy today.

One of the most common examples of the utility of the linear model involves the kind of controversy that occurs over and over again in the history of science: whether the contributions of the moment are incremental or revolutionary in nature. The authors of new ideas, methods, theories, and interpretations are afflicted with the pride of parenthood. Therefore, they claim that their ideas are not only revolutionary, but in fact more revolutionary than any previous ideas. Those whose ideas are inevitably being modified, perhaps rather drastically, by the new developments are often offended by the brashness and arrogance of their critics. They tend to defend the products of their intellectual efforts as the platform from which the newer ideas have been derived and upon which they are built. Both of these points of view represent polar positions so extreme that they are no longer part of reality. All new ideas add new dimensions, but the degree of "newness" is frequently challenged and the supposed revolutionary character may always be questioned. By the same token no new idea is completely divorced from the past, even when it is only a gross reaction to existing constructs. The problem, therefore, is not the question of whether the discipline changes by incremental or revolutionary growth. It is, rather, the task of identifying the point on the linear model that properly reflects the balance between the new and the old.

At the present time, American archaeology is experiencing such a controversy, one that promises either a new level of theoretical and interpretive achievement or a divisive and bitter setback. American archaeology has re-received major theoretical stimulus as a result of the introduction of a theoretical approach derived from the rigorous application of a scientific method based on the deductive generation of multiple hypotheses from general anthropological theory that are then tested by sophisticated quantitative methods. The approach has been outlined in several position papers, notably those of Lewis Binford (1962, 1964b, 1965, 1967, 1968d), in which there is an emphasis on the intellectual fail-ings of all previous approaches, the revolutionary character of the "new" methodology, the primacy of the processual approach in all archaeological endeavors, and therefore, the promise that it holds for archaeology (Flannery 1967). The discussions have often been accompanied by a rhetoric that contrasts the rich potential and theoretical elegance of the newly proposed method with the inadequate performance and theoretical poverty of the existing methods. The inevitable result of this development has been the polarization of theoretical positions. We now seem to have a "traditional" or "historical" archaeology and a "new" or "processual" archaeology. In this terminological scheme both "traditional" and "new" have either positive or prejorative connotations depending on the theoretical bias of the speaker. Despite the short time since the introduction of this stimulating "new" or processual approach to archaeology, the polemics that surround this controversy have already taken on all of the characteristics of extremism. Discussions abound in aggressive, defensive, arrogant, jargon-laden, even messianic and cult-oriented statements (Binford 1967, 1968*d;* Bayard 1969; Jennings 1968: 329, Fritz and Plog 1970; Martin 1971).

For example, Sabloff and Willey (1967), though insisting on the priority of their "historical" approach, made an important contribution to the literature by turning away from the historical pole of the linear model to work toward the processual pole. Both Erasmus (1968) and Binford (1968*d*), in commenting on the Sabloff-Willey paper, actually demonstrate the importance of the interplay between the historical and processual approaches, despite their efforts to establish the primacy of the processual over the historical. It is as if the polemics of the recent past have pushed each group of defenders so far out on the ends of the linear model that the arguments, isolated by rejection of all other points of view, have become sterile. These extreme positions are the result of what might be called the isolative quality of the comparative method. At the moment, the

more positive integrative qualities of the comparative method are being brought back into play in order to avoid such intellectual sterility. The efforts of each group to look down the linear scale toward each other and seek new comparative definitions of their positions constitute the first steps toward reaching a promising new theoretical plateau. I predict that the history versus process controversy will be a most productive example of the value of the linear model.

Another example of the utility of the linear model is provided by the argument of whether induction or deduction is to be identified as the archaeological Truth-Discovering Machine. Binford (1968*d*:271) has argued strongly for a deductive approach, but in the same paragraph he states (apparently for the first time) that it is necessary to work back and forth between induction and deduction. Moreover, his "Hide Smoking" paper (Binford 1967) is an excellent example of inductive reasoning (especially as amended by Munson 1969), despite the fact that Binford presents it as an example of the deductive approach. The efforts of Fritz and Plog (1970) to contrast the inductive or empirical approach (Thompson 1958*b*) with the deductive or nomothetic approach (Martin 1971) also illustrate the integrative quality of comparison along the scale of the linear model. This kind of contrast has all the earmarks of a chicken-and-egg controversy. Ultimately, it becomes clear to all that the question of which came first (or deserves to be first) is secondary to the question of how the two are related – that is, what kind of a linear model is involved. Some individuals find a closed line, or circle, a more satisfying model for this type of controversy. If the induction-deduction linear model is seen as a circular model (as many epistemologists apparently do), then the question is not which is more important, but rather where does one enter the circle for dealing with a particular kind of problem. Obviously, Binford prefers to enter the circle on the deductive side of the moon, as his "Hide-Smoking" paper shows (Binford 1967). On the other hand, I tend

38

to enter on the inductive side, even though I hope to point the way to subsequent deductive tests (Thompson 1958*b*). At any rate, whether one prefers a linear or a circular model, it is clear that induction and deduction, like history and process, or discovered types and created types, do not exist in isolation from one another. Rather, they interact along the scale of the linear model to provide even more sophisticated and more powerful resources for archaeology.

I seek not to pass judgment on the relative merits of the two polar extremes, even though my training and experience perhaps equip me to be identified more with the "traditional" end of the scale. Rather, I see as inherent in the character of the controversy the inevitability of the definition of a continuum that will demonstrate the coordinate and complementary relationship and interdependence of the two approaches. In fact, American archaeologists have an opportunity to move ahead rapidly to new theoretical levels by turning the energy that is now devoted to the definition and refinement of extreme positions inward toward the continuum that joins them together with a linear model (Sabloff and Willey 1967; Erasmus 1968; Kushner 1970). On the other hand, American archaeologists could delay progress in theory by waiting until present energies are expended in the defense of the poles of the continuum so that we will have to look for a new source of energy to achieve the inevitable linear integration.

Other possible results of continuing the present polarization with increasing religious fervor are a kind of intellectual standoff, or a schism in the discipline. A third, and certainly even more destructive, possibility is that one of these polarized theoretical and philosophical systems may dominate and even largely destroy the other. In fact, there is good evidence that some of the most vigorous proponents of the so-called new approach would welcome just such a development. There is frequent reference in their rhetoric to the idea that archaeological work that is not carried out under the theoretical umbrella of the "new" or processual approach is unworthy, even invalid. The rationale for this view stems from the often stated belief that the great common denominator for the anthropological disciplines is rigorous and unflinching application of "the method of science" as it is defined by one's favorite "distinguished philosopher of science" (Binford 1968*d*:267; Fritz and Plog 1970:405–6). I see this movement toward a monolithic theoretical structure for archaeology as a most unfortunate development.

The most fruitful attempts to achieve a better understanding of the anthropological enterprise have come not from single-purpose approaches, but rather from the pluralism of approaches and theoretical positions that have traditionally given anthropology its strength. What good will it do for archaeologists to develop deductive multiple hypotheses from general anthropological theory if the enterprise is dominated by a ruling theoretical structure? How does this differ, practically speaking, from the domination of a ruling hypothesis? In the long run, how does it really differ from the domination of a ruling ideology?

These dangers are real, but as long as we can see them clearly they are not imminent. We are fortunate as a discipline that we already have successfully gained from other potentially destructive controversies by using the synthesizing capacity inherent in the linear model. Let us hope that American archaeology will soon find the intellectual resources to use the linear model profitably once again.

NOTE

An earlier version of this essay was presented as a paper at the Symposium on Methodology and Theory in Archaeological Interpretation held in Flagstaff, Arizona, September 12–26, 1968, under the aegis of the International Union of Prehistoric and Protohistoric Sciences.

PART 2

**The Origins of
Contemporary Change**

Introduction

Archaeology has been called the science of origins. It seems particularly appropriate in a time of more rapid than usual change to acknowledge our historical predecessors in anthropological archaeology. There are many predecessors to the changes that now characterize archaeology, more, in fact, than can be accurately and intelligently cited. The articles in this section were chosen because each piece represents a special and particular glimpse of what its author wanted archaeology to become. Those glimpses are relevant to the present.

The number of pieces in this section could be doubled or tripled. But there are probably not more than a dozen articles by a handful of authors in the last few decades who accurately reflect a dissatisfaction with the usual challenges of the field and who then took on a task unusual for their time. These pieces reflect some of the changes current in American archaeology because each author had sensed the nearing completion of the historicalist approach and had attempted to experiment with additional problems and approaches. These articles are indices and signposts which occurred in the 1940s and fifties pointing to the present changes in archaeology.

Gordon Childe represents systemic evolution, a notion that implies directional change affecting the parts of a cultural system in precisely interrelated ways. "The Urban Revolution" appears in this volume for two reasons. It is a much-used article in a difficult-to-obtain journal. But also because, taken with *What Happened in History* and *Social Evolution,* it outlines the interrelated criteria present as urbanism arises. The article itself does not explain the systemic connections between the traits. Some are obvious, some less so. But never does the reader get the impression that they are a random collection of bits and pieces which happen to mark a stage in human evolution.

Childe witnesses the advent of evolution in archaeology and the erection of stage typologies that categorize phenomena, from simple to complex and from undifferentiated to differentiated. An important addition to this characteristic, however, is his understanding that directional change operates through affecting all parts of a system. Childe was also, in short, a functionalist.

Paul Martin also represents functionalism as he is reprinted here. It is the explicit nonevolutionary functionalism of Radcliffe-Brown, not the implicit functionalism of Marx. "Conjectures Concerning the Social Organization of the

Mogollon Indians" is an attempt to put flesh on the bones of prehistory. And it is a provocative effort. More than an isolated incident, however, I think it should be viewed as one archaeologist's effort to fulfill his obligations to theory, and to go beyond the real requirements of the field at the time he was writing. Here is one man among several who felt, in the early 1950s, that in the Southwest it was time for more than chronicle.

The adaptation of a culture to its natural and social circumstances and the consequences of that adaptation on the culture's subsystems form the base for studies in cultural ecology. Such studies are a means toward understanding how a culture adjusts. They are a means for studying specific evolution. And insofar as cultural ecology copes with the processes maintaining a culture in a stable state or in dynamic equilibrium, it participates in general evolutionary studies.

Grahame Clark has long been interested in the articulation of the ecological, economic, and technological systems of prehistoric cultures. His studies in the ecological adjustment of the European Mesolithic and Neolithic are paradigmatic cases of the success of the ecological approach. "An Economic Approach to Prehistory" is not just a recitation of ecofacts; it is a statement of relationships between basic cultural subsystems. In addition, it considers the articulation of sociological and ideological factors in such adjustments. Cultural ecology would often seem to be a kind of functionalism produced by using the assumptions of cultural materialism. Its potential for avoiding the static trap of functionalism, however, lies in a consideration of the mechanisms of dynamic adjustment. Archaeological experimentation today with such mechanisms for dynamic adjustment involves use of ideas derived from general systems theory and demography, to name but two sources. This current interest is one of the indices that differentiate between an archaeology concerned with process and one trapped in functionalism. The latter is probably being avoided.

Julian Steward, who is unrepresented in this volume, is among the most important influences on those archaeologists concerned with cultural ecology. In a series of very influential articles written in the postwar period, he combined his interests in cross-cultural research, development of civilization, and ecology. In creating the method as well as rationale for cultural ecology, he made the approach comparative and identified the economic base and ecological adjustment of a culture as critical variables. He is in good part responsible for demonstrating the practical utility of evolutionary theory and cultural materialism. In doing so, he reduced Leslie White to practice for many anthropologists the way Binford has done for many contemporary archaeologists.

Clyde Kluckhohn is only one of many people who have from time to time been vocal about the discrepancy between archaeological theory and accomplishment. My purpose in reprinting his essay is not to celebrate his sharp tongue. It is rather to illustrate one of the specific devices extant in archaeology and anthropology for creating the tension which has been responsible for archaeology evolving from paradigm to paradigm. Kluckhohn's essay is a specific example for the general class of evolutionary instruments that announce a crisis in the paradigm. Crises are usually announced by citing shortcomings and making practitioners aware that a new approach may be necessary and possible.

Periodically one sees dissatisfactions expressed within a discipline and accompanying them are attempts at renovation. As Kluckhohn's article is an example of dissatisfaction, Walter W. Taylor's *A Study of Archaeology* (1948) is an example of an attempt at renovation. As Kluckhohn was Taylor's mentor at Harvard, so Kluckhohn's call for reform is one side of the evolutionary process the complement of which is Taylor's prescription for innovation.

Complimentary to Walter Taylor's concern with method is Albert Spaulding's as voiced in his review reprinted here. The famous debate between Spaulding and Ford livened the middle 1950s in archaeology with a consideration of the nature and function of typology. In the opening sally of the debate that appears here, Spaulding attacks more than methodological flaws standard at the time in archaeology; he castigates an entire archaeological world view. He points out archaeology's unqualifiedly dependent relationship to anthropology and corrects the notion that disciplines using historical data do not have scientific method available to them or have it available only in attenuated form. This review essay should be read in conjunction with Binford's article on research design in Part 4 of this volume. Spaulding cites many of the flaws and correctives that Binford later helped to develop into a systematic research strategy. Spaulding's influence as seen through important reviews and articles was a major catalytic agent leading to renovation in archaeology. Unambiguously pointing out both theoretically unjustified assumptions and methodologically weak procedures, he systematically helped to make many archaeologists aware of the need for reconsidering some of the foundations of their discipline.

The innovative articles and the article that suggests innovation should be tried are prefatory and catalytic to the current changes in anthropological archaeology. They are not an early part of processual archaeology in the sense that they are lone or diluted examples of what faces us now. They are signals of change and attempts to innovate. But they lack a coherence and conceptual concreteness one finds, for example, in Binford's theoretical statements. Without articles like those in this section and others scattered throughout the field, nothing unusual would be happening now in archaeology. These articles are an integral part of the evolutionary process that has been transforming archaeology.

The Urban Revolution

THE CONCEPT of "city" is notoriously hard to define. The aim of the present essay is to present the city historically—or rather prehistorically—as the resultant and symbol of a "revolution" that initiated a new economic stage in the evolution of society. The word *revolution* must not of course be taken as denoting a sudden violent catastrophe; it is here used for the culmination of a progressive change in the economic structure and social organisation of communities that caused, or was accompanied by, a dramatic increase in the population affected—an increase that would appear as an obvious bend in the population graph were vital statistics available. Just such a bend is observable at the time of the Industrial Revolution in England. Though not demonstrable statistically, comparable changes of direction must have occurred at two earlier points in the demographic history of Britain and other regions. Though perhaps less sharp and less durable, these too should indicate equally revolutionary changes in economy. They may then be regarded likewise as marking transitions between stages in economic and social development.

Sociologists and ethnographers last century classified existing pre-industrial societies in a hierarchy of three evolutionary stages, denominated respectively "savagery," "barba-

Reprinted by permission from *Town Planning Review,* vol. 21, 1950, pp. 3–17, and by permission of the Institute of Archaeology of the University of London. Fifteen of seventeen figures have been deleted from the text.

rism" and "civilisation." If they be defined by suitably selected criteria, the logical hierarchy of stages can be transformed into a temporal sequence of ages, proved archaeologically to follow one another in the same order wherever they occur. Savagery and barbarism are conveniently recognized and appropriately defined by the methods adopted for procuring food. Savages live exclusively on wild food obtained by collecting, hunting or fishing. Barbarians on the contrary at least supplement these natural resources by cultivating edible plants and—in the Old World north of the Tropics—also by breeding animals for food.

Throughout the Pleistocene Period—the Palaeolithic Age of archaeologists—all known human societies were savage in the foregoing sense, and a few savage tribes have survived in out of the way parts to the present day. In the archaeological record barbarism began less than ten thousand years ago with the Neolithic Age of archaeologists. It thus represents a later, as well as a higher stage, than savagery. Civilization cannot be defined in quite such simple terms. Etymologically the word is connected with "city," and sure enough life in cities begins with this stage. But "city" is itself ambiguous so archaeologists like to use "writing" as a criterion of civilization; it should be easily recognizable and proves to be a reliable index to more profound characters. Note, however, that, because a people is said to be civilized or literate, it does not follow that all its members can read and write, nor that they all lived in

44

cities. Now there is no recorded instance of a community of savages civilizing themselves, adopting urban life or inventing a script. Wherever cities have been built, villages of preliterate farmers existed previously (save perhaps where an already civilized people have colonized uninhabited tracts). So civilization, wherever and whenever it arose, succeeded barbarism.

We have seen that a revolution as here defined should be reflected in the population statistics. In the case of the Urban Revolution the increase was mainly accounted for by the multiplication of the numbers of persons living together, i.e., in a single built-up area. The first cities represented settlement units of hitherto unprecedented size. Of course it was not just their size that constituted their distinctive character. We shall find that by modern standards they appeared ridiculously small and we might meet agglomerations of population today to which the name city would have to be refused. Yet a certain size of settlement and density of population, is an essential feature of civilization.

Now the density of population is determined by the food supply which in turn is limited by natural resources, the techniques for their exploitation and the means of transport and food-preservation available. The last factors have proved to be variables in the course of human history, and the technique of obtaining food has already been used to distinguish the consecutive stages termed savagery and barbarism. Under the gathering economy of savagery population was always exceedingly sparse. In aboriginal America the carrying capacity of normal unimproved land seems to have been from .05 to .10 per square mile. Only under exceptionally favourable conditions did the fishing tribes of the Northwest Pacific coast attain densities of over one human to the square mile. As far as we can guess from the extant remains, population densities in palaeolithic and pre-neolithic Europe were less than the normal American. Moreover such hunters and collectors usually live in small roving bands. At best several bands may come together for quite brief periods on ceremonial occasions such as the Australian corroborrees. Only in exceptionally favoured regions can fishing tribes establish anything like villages. Some settlements on the Pacific coasts comprised thirty or so substantial and durable houses, accommodating groups of several hundred persons. But even these villages were only occupied during the winter; for the rest of the year their inhabitants dispersed in smaller groups. Nothing comparable has been found in pre-neolithic times in the Old World.

The Neolithic Revolution certainly allowed an expansion of population and enormously increased the carrying capacity of suitable land. On the Pacific Islands neolithic societies today attain a density of 30 or more persons to the square mile. In pre-Columbian North America, however, where the land is not obviously restricted by surrounding seas, the maximum density recorded is just under 2 to the square mile.

Neolithic farmers could of course, and certainly did, live together in permanent villages, though, owing to the extravagant rural economy generally practised, unless the crops were watered by irrigation, the villages had to be shifted at least every twenty years. But on the whole the growth of population was not reflected so much in the enlargement of the settlement unit as in a multiplication of settlements. In ethnography neolithic villages can boast only a few hundred inhabitants (a couple of "pueblos" in New Mexico house over a thousand, but perhaps they cannot be regarded as neolithic). In prehistoric Europe the largest neolithic village yet known, Barkaer in Jutland, comprised 52 small, one-roomed dwellings, but 16 to 30 houses was a more normal figure; so the average local group in neolithic times would average 200 to 400 members.

These low figures are of course the result of technical limitations. In the absence of wheeled vehicles and roads for the transport of bulky crops men had to live within easy walking distance of their cultivations. At the same time the normal rural economy of the Neolithic Age, what is now termed slash-and-burnt or jhumming, condemns much more than half the arable land to lie fallow so that large areas were required. As soon as the population of a settlement rose above the numbers that could be supported from the accessible land, the excess had to hive off and found a new settlement.

The Neolithic Revolution had other consequences beside increasing the population, and their exploitation might in the end help to provide for the surplus increase. The new economy allowed, and indeed required, the farmer to produce every year more food than was needed to keep him and his family alive. In other words it made possible the regular production of a social surplus. Owing to the low efficiency of neolithic technique, the surplus produced was insignificant at first, but it could be increased till it demanded a reorganization of society.

Now in any Stone Age society, palaeolithic or neolithic, savage or barbarian, everybody can at least in theory make at home the few indispensible tools, the modest cloths and the simple ornaments everyone requires. But every member of the local community, not disqualified by age, must contribute actively to the communal food supply by personally collecting, hunting, fishing, gardening or herding. As long as this holds good, there can be no full-time specialists, no persons nor class of persons who depend for their livelihood on food produced by others and secured in exchange for material or immaterial goods or services.

We find indeed to day among Stone Age barbarians and even savages expert craftsmen (for instance flint-knappers among the Ona of Tierra del Fuego), men who claim to be experts in magic, and even chiefs. In palaeolithic Europe too there is some evidence for magicians and indications of chieftainship in pre-neolithic times. But on closer observation we discover that today these experts are not full-time specialists. The Ona flintworker must spend most of his time hunting; he only adds to his diet and his prestige by making arrowheads for clients who reward him with presents. Similarly a pre-Columbian chief, though entitled to customary gifts and services from his followers, must still personally lead hunting and fishing expeditions and indeed could only maintain his authority by his industry and prowess in these pursuits. The same holds good of barbarian societies that are still in the neolithic stage, like the Polynesians where industry in gardening takes the place of prowess in hunting. The reason is that there simply will not be enough food to go round unless every member of the group contributes to the supply. The social surplus is not big enough to feed idle mouths.

Social division of labour, save those rudiments imposed by age and sex, is thus impossible. On the contrary community of employment, the common absorbtion in obtaining food by similar devices guarantees a certain solidarity to the group. For co-operation is essential to secure food and shelter and for defence against foes, human and subhuman. This identity of economic interests and pursuits is echoed and magnified by identity of language, custom and belief; rigid conformity is enforced as effectively as industry in the common quest for food. But conformity and industrious co-operation need no State organization to maintain them. The local group usually consists either of a single clan (persons who believe themselves descended from a common ancestor or who have earned a mystical claim to such descent by ceremonial adoption) or a group of clans related by habitual intermarriage. And the sentiment of kinship is reinforced or supplemented by common rites focussed on some ancestral shrine or sacred place. Archaeology can provide no evidence for kinship organization, but shrines occupied the central place in preliterate villages in Mesopotamia, and the long barrow, a collective tomb that overlooks the presumed site of most neolithic villages in Britain, may well have been also the ancestral shrine on which converged the emotions and ceremonial activities of the villagers below. However, the solidarity thus idealized and concretely symbolized, is really based on the same principles as that of a pack of wolves or a herd of sheep; Durkheim has called it "mechanical."

Now among some advanced barbarians (for instance tattooers or wood-carvers among the Maori) still technologically neo-lithic we find expert craftsmen tending towards the status of full-time professionals, but only at the cost of breaking away from the local community. If no single village can produce a surplus large enough to feed a full-time specialist all the year round, each should produce enough to keep him a week or so. By going round from vilage to village an expert might thus live entirely from his craft. Such itinerants will lose their membership of the sedentary kinship group. They may in the end form an analogous organization of their own—a craft clan, which, if it remain hereditary, may become a caste, or, if it recruit its members mainly by adoption (apprenticeship throughout Antiquity and the Middle Age was just temporary adoption), may turn into a guild. But such specialists, by emancipation from kinship ties, have also forfeited the protection of the kinship organization which alone under barbarism, guaranteed to its members security of person and property. Society must be reorganized to accommodate and protect them.

In pre-history specialization of labour presumably began with similar itinerant experts. Archaeological proof is hardly to be expected, but in ethnography metal-workers are nearly always full time specialists. And in Europe at the beginning of the Bronze Age metal seems to have been worked and purveyed by perambulating smiths who seem to have functioned like tinkers and other itinerants of much more recent times. Though there is no such positive evidence, the same probably happened in Asia at the beginning of metallurgy. There must of course have been in addition other specialist craftsmen whom, as the Polynesian example warns us, archaeologists could not recognize because they worked in

perishable materials. One result of the Urban Revolution will be to rescue such specialists from nomadism and to guarantee them security in a new social organization.

About 5,000 years ago irrigation cultivation (combined with stock-breeding and fishing) in the valleys of the Nile, the Tigris-Euphrates and the Indus had begun to yield a social surplus, large enough to support a number of resident specialists who were themselves released from food-production. Water-transport, supplemented in Mesopotamia and the Indus valley by wheeled vehicles and even in Egypt by pack animals, made it easy to gather food stuffs at a few centres. At the same time dependence on river water for the irrigation of the crops restricted the cultivable areas while the necessity of canalizing the waters and protecting habitations against annual floods encouraged the aggregation of population. Thus arose the first cities—units of settlement ten times as great as any known neolithic village. It can be argued that all cities in the old world are offshoots of those of Egypt, Mesopotamia and the Indus basin. So the latter need not be taken into account if a minimum definition of civilization is to be inferred from a comparison of its independent manifestations.

But some three millennia later cities arose in Central America, and it is impossible to prove that the Mayas owed anything directly to the urban civilizations of the Old World. Their achievements must therefore be taken into account in our comparison, and their inclusion seriously complicates the task of defining the essential preconditions for the Urban Revolution. In the Old World the rural economy which yielded the surplus was based on the cultivation of cereals combined with stock-breeding. But this economy had been made more efficient as a result of the adoption of irrigation (allowing cultivation without prolonged fallow periods) and of important inventions and discoveries—metallurgy, the plough, the sailing boat and the wheel. None of these devices was known to the Mayas; they bred no animals for milk or meat;

The Urban Revolution
V. Gordon Childe

47

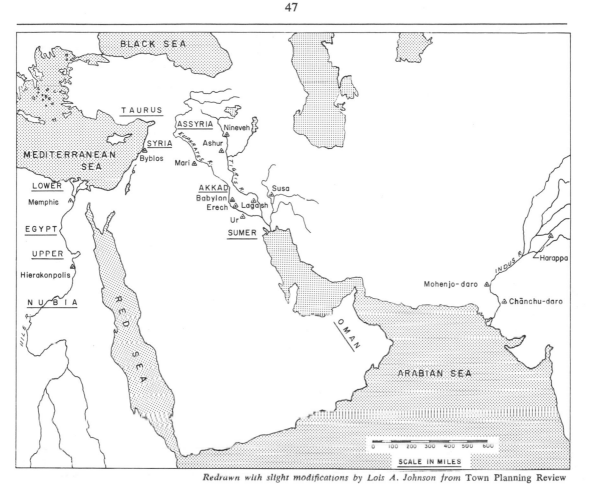

Redrawn with slight modifications by Lois A. Johnson from Town Planning Review

FIG. 1. *First centres of urban civilization in the Old World.*

though they cultivated the cereal maize, they used the same sort of slash-and-burn method as neolithic farmers in prehistoric Europe or in the Pacific Islands today. Hence the minimum definition of a city, the greatest factor common to the Old World and the New will be substantially reduced and impoverished by the inclusion of the Maya. Nevertheless ten rather abstract criteria, all deducible from archaeological data, serve to distinguish even the earliest cities from any older or contemporary village.

1) In point of size the first cities must have been more extensive and more densely populated than any previous settlements, although considerably smaller than many villages today. It is indeed only in Mesopotamia

and India that the first urban populations can be estimated with any confidence or precision. There excavation has been sufficiently extensive and intensive to reveal both the total area and the density of building in sample quarters and in both respects has disclosed significant agreement with the less-industrialized Oriental cities today. The population of Sumerian cities, thus calculated, ranged between 7,000 and 20,000; Harappa and Mohenjo-daro in the Indus valley must have approximated to the higher figure. We can only infer that Egyptian and Maya cities were of comparable magnitude from the scale of public works, presumably executed by urban populations.

2) In composition and function the urban

48

Redrawn with slight modifications by Lois A. Johnson from
Town Planning Review

FIG. 2. *First centres of urban civilization in Central America.*

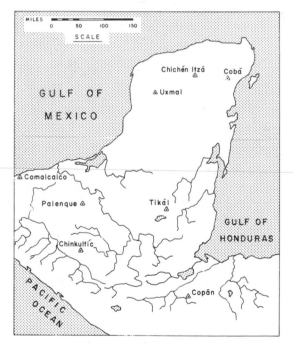

population already differed from that of any village. Very likely indeed most citizens were still also peasants, harvesting the lands and waters adjacent to the city. But all cities must have accommodated in addition classes who did not themselves procure their own food by agriculture, stock-breeding, fishing or collecting—full-time specialist craftsmen, transport workers, merchants, officials and priests. All these were of course supported by the surplus produced by the peasants living in the city and in dependent villages, but they did not secure their share directly by exchanging their products or services for grains or fish with individual peasants.

3) Each primary producer paid over the tiny surplus he could wring from the soil with his still very limited technical equipment as tithe or tax to an imaginary deity or a divine king who thus concentrated the surplus. Without this concentration, owing to the low productivity of the rural economy, no effective capital would have been available.

4) Truly monumental public buildings not only distinguish each known city from any village but also symbolize the concentration of the social surplus. Every Sumerian city was from the first dominated by one or more stately temples, centrally situated on a brick platform raised above the surrounding dwellings and usually connected with an artificial mountain, the staged tower or ziggurat. But attached to the temples, were workshops and magazines, and an important appurtenance of each principal temple was a great granary. Harappa, in the Indus basin, was dominated by an artificial citadel, girt with a massive rampart of kiln-baked bricks, containing presumably a palace and immediately overlooking an enormous granary and the barracks of artizans. No early temples nor palaces have been excavated in Egypt, but the whole Nile valley was dominated by the gigantic tombs of the divine pharaohs while royal granaries are attested from the literary record. Finally the Maya cities are known almost exclusively from the temples and pyramids of sculptured stone round which they grew up.

Hence in Sumer the social surplus was first effectively concentrated in the hands of a god and stored in his granary. That was probably true in Central America while in Egypt the pharaoh (king) was himself a god. But of course the imaginary deities were served by quite real priests who, besides celebrating elaborate and often sanguinary rites in their honour, administered their divine masters' earthly estates. In Sumer indeed the god very soon, if not even before the revolution, shared his wealth and power with a mortal viceregent, the "City-King," who acted as civil ruler and leader in war. The divine pharaoh was naturally assisted by a whole hierarchy of officials.

5) All those not engaged in food-production were of course supported in the first instance by the surplus accumulated in temple or royal granaries and were thus dependent on temple or court. But naturally priests, civil and military leaders and officials absorbed a major share of the concentrated surplus and thus formed a "ruling class." Unlike a palaeolithic magician or a neolithic chief, they were, as an Egyptian scribe actually put it, "exempt from all manual tasks." On the other hand, the lower classes were not only guaranteed peace and security, but were relieved from intellectual tasks which many find more irksome than any physical labour. Besides reassuring the masses that the sun was going to rise next day and the river would flood again next year (people who have not five thousand years of recorded experience of natural uniformities behind them are really worried about such matters!), the ruling classes did confer substantial benefits upon their subjects in the way of planning and organization.

6) They were in fact compelled to invent systems of recording and exact, but practically useful, sciences. The mere administration of the vast revenues of a Sumerian temple or an Egyptian pharaoh by a perpetual corporation of priests or officials obliged its members to devise conventional methods of recording that should be intelligible to all their colleagues and successors, that is, to invent systems of writing and numeral notation. Writing is thus a significant, as well as a convenient, mark of civilization. But while writing is a trait common to Egypt, Mesopotamia, the Indus valley and Central America, the characters themselves were different in each region and so were the normal writing materials—papyrus in Egypt, clay in Mesopotamia. The engraved seals or stelae that pro-

vide the sole extant evidence for early Indus and Maya writing, no more represent the normal vehicles for the scripts than do the comparable documents from Egypt and Sumer.

7) The invention of writing—or shall we say the inventions of scripts—enabled the leisured clerks to proceed to the elaboration of exact and predictive sciences—arithmetic, geometry and astronomy. Obviously beneficial and explicitly attested by the Egyptian and Maya documents was the correct determination of the tropic year and the creation of a calendar. For it enabled the rulers to regulate successfully the cycle of agricultural operations. But once more the Egyptian, Maya and Babylonian calendars were as different as any systems based on a single natural unit could be. Calendrical and mathematical sciences are common features of the earliest civilizations and they too are corollaries of the archaeologists' criterion, writing.

8) Other specialists, supported by the concentrated social surplus, gave a new direction to artistic expression. Savages even in palaeolithic times had tried, sometimes with astonishing success, to depict animals and even men as they saw them—concretely and naturalistically. Neolithic peasants never did that; they hardly ever tried to represent natural objects, but preferred to symbolize them by abstract geometrical patterns which at most may suggest by a few traits a fantastical man or beast or plant. But Egyptian, Sumerian, Indus and Maya artist-craftsmen—full-time sculptors, painters, or seal-engravers—began once more to carve, model or draw likenesses of persons or things, but no longer with the naïve naturalism of the hunter, but according to conceptualized and sophisticated styles which differ in each of the four urban centres.

9) A further part of the concentrated social surplus was used to pay for the importation of raw materials, needed for industry or cult and not available locally. Regular "foreign" trade over quite long distances was a feature of all early civilizations and, though common enough among barbarians later, is

not certainly attested in the Old World before 3,000 B.C. nor in the New before the Maya "empire." Thereafter regular trade extended from Egypt at least as far as Byblos on the Syrian coast while Mesopotamia was related by commerce with the Indus valley. While the objects of international trade were at first mainly 'luxuries," they already included industrial materials, in the Old World notably metal the place of which in the New was perhaps taken by obsidian. To this extent the first cities were dependent for vital materials on long distance trade as no neolithic village ever was.

10) So in the city, specialist craftsmen were both provided with raw materials needed for the employment of their skill and also guaranteed security in a State organization based now on residence rather than kinship. Itinerancy was no longer obligatory. The city was a community to which a craftsman could belong politically as well as economically.

Yet in return for security they became dependent on temple or court and were relegated to the lower classes. The peasant masses gained even less material advantages; in Egypt for instance metal did not replace the old stone and wood tools for agricultural work. Yet, however imperfectly, even the earliest urban communities must have been held together by a sort of solidarity missing from any neolithic village. Peasants, craftsmen, priests and rulers form a community, not only by reason of identity of language and belief, but also because each performs mutually complementary functions, needed for the well-being (as redefined under civilization) of the whole. In fact the earliest cities illustrate a first approximation to an organic solidarity based upon a functional complementarity and interdependence between all its members such as subsist between the constituent cells of an organism. Of course this was only a very distant approximation. However necessary the concentration of the surplus really was with the existing forces of production, there seemed a glaring conflict on economic interests between the tiny ruling

class, who annexed the bulk of the social surplus, and the vast majority who were left with a bare subsistence and effectively excluded from the spiritual benefits of civilization. So solidarity had still to be maintained by the ideological devices appropriate to the mechanical solidarity of barbarism as expressed in the pre-eminence of the temple or the sepulchral shrine, and now supplemented by the force of the new State organization. There could be no room for sceptics or sectaries in the oldest cities.

These ten traits exhaust the factors common to the oldest cities that archaeology, at best helped out with fragmentary and often ambiguous written sources, can detect. No specific elements of town planning for example can be proved characteristic of all such cities; for on the one hand the Egyptian and Maya cities have not yet been excavated; on the other neolithic villages were often walled, an elaborate system of sewers drained the Orcadian hamlet of Skara Brae; two-storeyed houses were built in pre-Columbian *pueblos,* and so on.

The common factors are quite abstract. Concretely Egyptian, Sumerian, Indus and Maya civilizations were as different as the plans of their temples, the signs of their scripts and their artistic conventions. In view of this divergence and because there is so far no evidence for a temporal priority of one Old World centre (for instance, Egypt) over the rest nor yet for contact between Central America and any other urban centre, the four revolutions just considered may be regarded as mutually independent. On the contrary, all later civilizations in the Old World may in a sense be regarded as lineal descendants of those of Egypt, Mesopotamia or the Indus.

But this was not a case of like producing like. The maritime civilizations of Bronze Age Crete or classical Greece for example, to say nothing of our own, differ more from their reputed ancestors than these did among themselves. But the urban revolutions that gave them birth did not start from scratch. They could and probably did draw upon the capi-

51

tal accumulated in the three allegedly primary centres. That is most obvious in the case of cultural capital. Even today we use the Egyptians' calendar and the Sumerians' divisions of the day and the hour. Our European ancestors did not have to invent for themselves these divisions of time nor repeat the observations on which they are based; they took over—and very slightly improved systems elaborated 5,000 years ago! But the same is in a sense true of material capital as well. The Egyptians, the Sumerians and the Indus people had accumulated vast reserves of surplus food. At the same time they had to import from abroad necessary raw materials like metals and building timber as well as "luxuries." Communities controlling these natural resources could in exchange claim a slice of the urban surplus. They could use it as capital to support full-time specialists—craftsmen or rulers—until the latters' achievement in technique and organization had so enriched barbarian economies that they too could produce a substantial surplus in their turn.

priests before specialists?

Chapter **6** PAUL S. MARTIN

Conjectures Concerning the Social Organization of the Mogollon Indians

FOR SOME time we have been interested in making historical reconstructions and in achieving a deeper understanding of a culture by inferring the type of social organization that was present in archaeological horizons for which no written records exist. We recognized that, lacking a quantity of materials with which to work, we had to assess the value of every tool of bone and stone and every potsherd. We were convinced that these poor remains of a culture were important and that each object represented a problem that had been solved by men in terms of their cultural patterns.

But, after all the analyses of tools, pottery, architecture, burials and the like were in, what principles of culture growth and change could be established? Some of these growths and changes have been presented in our previous reports (Martin, Rinaldo, and Antevs 1949; Martin and Rinaldo 1950).

But we wanted to go farther. Could we analyze our data in such a way that we could perceive trends, if any existed, in culture growth? Could we interpret these trends and raw data—such as location of house sites, kind and number of houses per time phase in a given area—to see if they would lead to

Reprinted from *Sites of the Reserve Phase, Pine Lawn Valley, Western New Mexico;* Fieldiana: Anthropology, vol. 38, no. 3, 1950, pp. 556–69. By permission of the author and the Field Museum of Natural History. This essay was written with the help of Donald Collier and George I. Quimby.

probable inferences concerning social organization of the long-dead Mogollon Indians? Would it be possible to utilize the analyses of fully described recent social systems to make guesses concerning the social structures of dead cultures?

We thought we could do all this, and the following paragraphs represent a condensation of our striving, brooding, and conferring of several months. If we knew the linguistic affiliations of the Mogollon people, or what had become of them, our problems would have been simplified and our inferences less shaky.

We shall first present the trends that have been abstracted from graphs, tables, and intense study of the minutiae of the last seven years of digging.

No one should quarrel with these, since they may properly be considered as observable raw data—"facts" in other words, from which abstractions have been carefully made. Mixed with these trends will be some assumptions that seem to flow out of the trends. Before going on to state the trends, it may be well to list the sequence of phases as manifested by our excavations.

The evidence for the earliest occupation of the Valley consists of milling stones, choppers, and scrapers that had been dropped along camp sites located on the banks of a stream. These artifacts, which were uncovered by a recent erosion cycle, are more like those of the Chiricahua stage of the Cochise

53

culture than any other nonpottery horizon in the Southwest. In addition, several hearths and one house-site — all Cochise — have been discovered. Antevs has dated the deposits in which the artifacts were found at about 1500 B.C.

The next archaeological horizon of which we have certain knowledge is called the Pine Lawn Phase — which has been tentatively dated at about A.D. 500. The traits of this phase include pit-houses (twenty-nine of which have been excavated, only twenty-three of which were used for comparative purposes), pottery, stone, and bone artifacts, and some agriculture.

For the purpose of this synthesis and reconstruction, we have lumped together the next three phases — Georgetown, San Francisco, and Three Circle. We did this in order to have a comparable number of houses in this grouping with which to balance the twenty-three houses of the Pine Lawn Phase and the twenty-three of the Reserve Phase. The Georgetown, San Francisco, and Three Circle phases would cover roughly about 400 years (A.D. 500–900). Gradual changes in house structure, pottery and tool types have been noted and described (Martin, Rinaldo, and Antevs 1949; Martin and Rinaldo 1950).

The Reserve Phase, of which we have data on twenty-three rooms (or "houses" as herein defined), is dated at about A.D. 1000. Abrupt changes in architecture and pottery types have been noted along with a continuity of other traits. We feel fairly certain that Anasazi influences or actual migration of Anasazi people were responsible for the introduction of surface, multi-roomed, contiguous masonry rooms (which completely displaced pit-houses) and black-on-white pottery.

These phases from Pine Lawn through Reserve are all part of one continuum, which is demonstrated by our chart of pottery types (Martin, Rinaldo, and Antevs 1949:192–193).

In concluding this brief summary of the sequence of cultures in Pine Lawn Valley, we should point out that our analysis and trends are based only on data that we have actually recovered. We have, however, made similar analyses of Haury's work at Mogollon 1:15 and at the Harris Site (Haury 1936), and Nesbitt's work at the Starkweather Ruin (Nesbitt 1938). We found that their data coincided neatly with ours, and, as a result, strengthened our case and caused us to feel that we were on the right course.

Trends in Pine Lawn Valley
(Figs. 1–4)

Houses. — (Fig. *1;* a house is defined as a pit-house or a single surface room.)

The Cochise house (probably Chiricahua stage) found near Wet Leggett Pueblo and the Cochise house of the San Pedro stage found by Sayles at Pearce 8:4 (Sayles 1945: 3) are both small (about 3 meters in diameter).

Houses of the Pine Lawn Phase were larger than those of any other time period in the Pine Lawn Valley (range in diameter, 3.4–10.4 meters; average diameter, 6.1 meters; median diameter, 5.6 meters).

The houses of the subsequent phases (Georgetown, San Francisco, Three Circle, Reserve) become progressively smaller. The houses of the Georgetown–Three Circle periods range in diameter or greatest dimension from 3.1 to 8.0 meters (average 5.1, median 4.8). During the Reserve Phase the greatest dimension ranges from 1.9 to 9.5 meters; the average length is 3.9 meters; and the median length is 3.4 meters. This average for rooms of the Reserve Phase is slightly larger than the measurements of a second story room at Mishongnovi mentioned by Mindeleff (1891:108). According to him, this second story room measures about 12 feet square and is smaller than the average size room at Mishongnovi. Analysis of sixteen rooms at three Hopi protohistoric pueblos (Awatovi, Burned Corn House, and Kishu; unpublished notes in the Museum files)

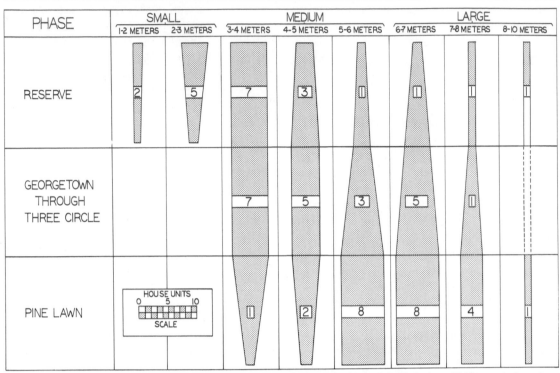

Redrawn by Michael J. Merle from Fieldiana: Anthropology

FIG. 1. *Size frequency of houses from Pine Lawn to Reserve Phase. Figure within block indicates number of houses in that dimension category. A house is defined as a pit-house or a single surface room.*

indicates that the maximum length of these rooms ranges from 2.1 to 5.8 meters and that the average of the greater dimensions is 3.7 meters. This average is almost the same as for the rooms of the Reserve Phase.

A typical dwelling room (Watson 1940: 82) at Cliff Palace, Mesa Verde, measures 1.8 by 2.5 meters. This is considerably smaller than the rooms of the Reserve Phase.

We would assume then that only a nuclear family could be housed in the Cochise dwellings because they are small, that perhaps a larger household population—perhaps an extended family—could have been accommodated in houses of the Pine Lawn Phase (because they are much larger) and that in the later phases (Georgetown to Reserve) only one family could have lived in a room, because the rooms of these last-mentioned phases are small.

Population Increase.—Linked with the

trend in decrease in size of house from early to late is a related trend—namely, an *increase* in the number of houses per phase from early to late (Table 1). Data from excavations and from our surveys show that there are more rooms and more clusters of rooms or villages in the Reserve Phase than there were in the Pine Lawn Phase. This trend may be correlated with an increase in population density from early to late, with a change from band to village organization and perhaps with the development of the clan.

Correlated with increased density of population, in Reserve times as compared with Cochise times, may be a change in the subsistence pattern, and this change in the economic basis might have repercussions on the formation and/or dissolution of certain social units. If, for example, agriculture assumed an increasingly larger importance in

TABLE 1

Frequency of sites and houses * by phases

Number of houses on surveyed sites estimated on basis of size (in square feet) of sherd area as compared with equivalent area and number of houses located therein at the excavated sites.

Pine Lawn Phase		Reserve Phase	
Site	Est. no. of houses	Site	Est. no. of houses
SU ....(25 excav.)	26	South Leggett Pueblo..(4 excav.)	6
Promontory..........(5 excav.)	12	Oak Springs Pueblo....(6 excav.)	7
59.........................	3	Wet Leggett Pueblo....(6 excav.)	6
81.........................	4	Three Pines Pueblo....(4 excav.)	5
84.........................	4	Starkweather Pueblo..(12 excav.)	12
4.........................	12	1...........................	4
6.........................	2	2...........................	5
16.........................	2	5...........................	1
63.........................	2	7...........................	8
25.........................	5	10...........................	4
42.........................	11	12...........................	3
43.........................	1	20...........................	12
50.........................	12	23...........................	5
53.........................	11	28...........................	6
54.........................	1	29...........................	12
96 †.........................	20	35...........................	12
121 †.........................	20	37...........................	7
124 †.........................	2	39...........................	5
Apache Hill †.................	12	40...........................	8
19 sites	**162**	48...........................	8
		49...........................	5
		56...........................	3
		58...........................	6
		65...........................	7
Georgetown through Three Circle		67...........................	3
Site	Est. no. of houses	68...........................	5
Turkey Foot Ridge...(15 excav.)	17	70...........................	5
Twin Bridges..........(4 excav.)	5	71...........................	2
SU (Late occupation)..(4 excav.)	5	72...........................	2
13.........................	14	73...........................	6
14.........................	24	74...........................	7
15.........................	5	75...........................	6
17.........................	14	79...........................	4
19.........................	26	82...........................	4
21.........................	14	85 †...........................	4
22.........................	2	88 †...........................	7
45.........................	6	90 †...........................	2
62.........................	5	91 †...........................	2
83.........................	4	97 †...........................	2
Starkweather.........(18 excav.)	20	100 †...........................	5
49.........................	12	102 †...........................	5
115.........................	16	105 †...........................	5
Wheatley Ridge †.....(10 excav.)	12	107 †...........................	3
Mogollon 1:15 †......(11 excav.)	20	111 †...........................	6
94 †.........................	4	113 †...........................	5
106 †.........................	34	114 †...........................	5
110 †.........................	14	116 †...........................	3
112 †.........................	7	117 †...........................	5
120 †.........................	24	118 †...........................	4
23 sites	**304**	119 †...........................	4
		50	**268**

	Total of valley sites	Total of houses in valley	Total of sites	Total of houses
Reserve..........................34		199	50	268
Georgetown through Three Circle..........................16		189	23	304
Pine Lawn.....................15		108	19	162

* A house is defined as a pit-house or a single surface room.   † Outside valley.

56

PHASE	MEDIAN FREQUENCY OF METATES PER HOUSE UNIT
RESERVE	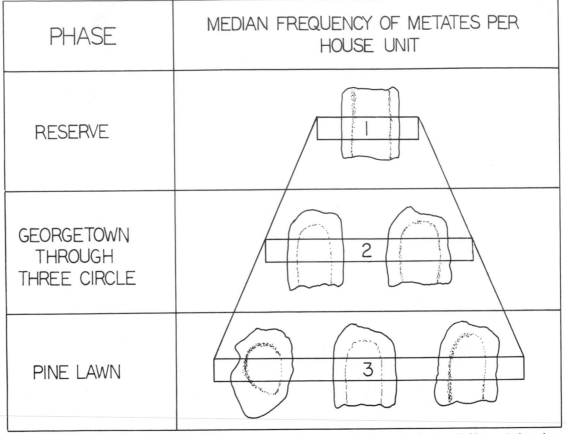
GEORGETOWN THROUGH THREE CIRCLE	
PINE LAWN	

Redrawn by Michael J. Merle from Fieldiana: Anthropology

FIG. 2. *Median frequency of metates per house unit.*

the life of the later Mogollon people, one might find more emphasis on ownership of farm plots and the inheritance of them.

Metates. – The downward trends in number of metates per house and the accompanying decrease in the remainder of the assemblage of artifacts through time (from early to late) might yield some clues that could be fitted in with inferences concerning social organization (Fig. 2).

The number of metates per house decreased through time – that is, from early to late. We find that in modern pueblos three metates per room (that is, per family) is typical (Mindeleff 1891:211; Hough 1915: 62; Owens 1892:163; Winship 1896:522). In many houses of the Pine Lawn Phase we found three or more metates; in pueblos of the Reserve Phase we often found only three metates for the *whole pueblo!* If, as in modern pueblos, three metates per room and per family is typical, might we not have an indication in the Mogollon culture that more than one family lived in some of the houses of the Pine Lawn Phase (because there are three or more metates in several houses and because Pine Lawn houses are on the average bigger than houses of later times)? And, since only three metates are found in an entire pueblo of the Reserve Phase, might we not have inferential evidence for assuming that one, and only one, extended family occupied the entire village?

We should like to correlate basin metates

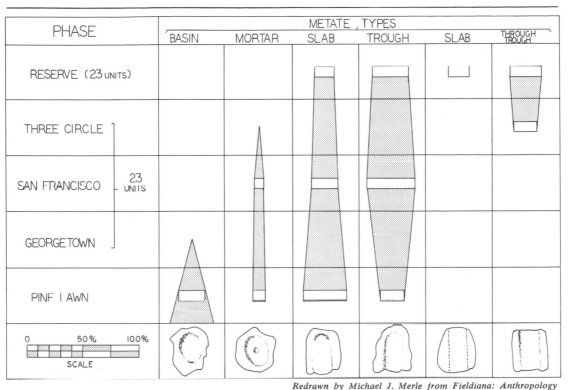

Redrawn by Michael J. Merle from Fieldiana: Anthropology

FIG. 3. Relative frequency of metate types by phases.

with a seed-gathering economy and trough metates with agriculture. We have an intuitive feeling that these assumptions have merit, but proof for this correlation is lacking. True, in the Sulphur Springs stage of the Cochise culture trough metates are absent and, by inference, agriculture is absent, also. In the Chiricahua stage, as exhibited in the Pine Lawn Valley, an oval-basin metate with one end slightly open appears in association with basin and slab types. If the Pine Lawn Valley branch of the Chiricahua stage may be correlated with the lower levels of Bat Cave (excavated by J. Herbert Dick, but not yet described) — and we feel that this correlation is permissible and sound — one would expect the Cochise people in the Pine Lawn Valley to have had some maize agriculture (Mangelsdorf and Smith 1949). Furthermore, an analysis of the trends in metate types (Fig. 3) from say 1500 B.C. to A.D. 1000 shows unmistakably that basin and slab metates *decline*

in frequency during these two thousand years and that trough metates *increase* in frequency during the same span.

On the whole, then, what we are trying to show but cannot prove is that beginning at about 1000 B.C. agriculture was introduced into the Pine Lawn Valley and adjacent areas, but that food gathering was still the main basis for subsistence; but as we come upward in time, we find that seed gathering dwindles in importance and that agriculture becomes the dominant form of food economy.

In other words, trends in number and kinds of metates per house may indicate a decline in household population from the Pine Lawn to the Reserve Phases and also a change in the economy.

Other Artifacts. — Accompanying this downward trend in numbers of metates per room, we have also noted a similar decrease in the number of other artifacts (Fig. 4). To

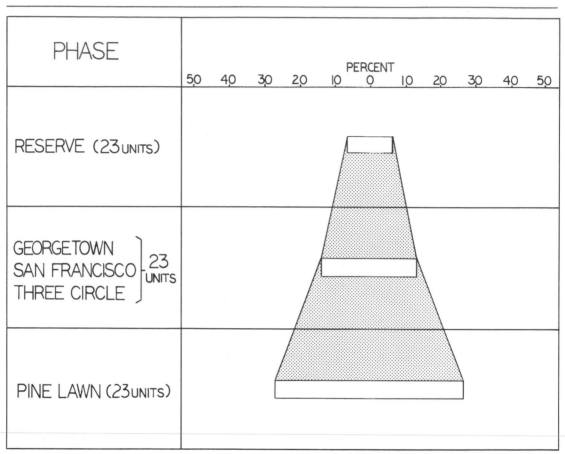

PHASE	PERCENT
	50 40 30 20 10 0 10 20 30 40 50
RESERVE (23 UNITS)	
GEORGETOWN SAN FRANCISCO THREE CIRCLE } 23 UNITS	
PINE LAWN (23 UNITS)	

Redrawn by Michael J. Merle from Fieldiana: Anthropology

FIG. 4. *Comparison of number of artifacts per phase with total number of artifacts found in sixty-nine house units. A house unit is defined as a pit-house or a single surface room.*

put the matter in another way, fewer tools occur per room in the Reserve Phase than occur per room in the Pine Lawn Phase. This trend suggests that fewer tools were used per room and that there were fewer people per room in the Reserve Phase than in the Pine Lawn Phase.

To sum up the trends and a few of the inferences resulting therefrom: we note a decrease from early to late times in actual house size and in the number of metates and other tools per room, and an increase in number of villages or houses per phase. These trends suggest that in the Pine Lawn Phase the number of persons per house was larger (perhaps from 5 to 10) and that the number of villages, that is, the population density,

was restricted; but that in later times—in the Reserve Phase—the number of persons per house was small (perhaps from 3 to 5) and the number of villages—i.e., population density—was greatly expanded.

Now, with these trends and assumptions in mind, what historical reconstruction can be made concerning the social organization of the Mogollon culture of Pine Lawn Valley from the Chiricahua manifestations of the Cochise culture (roughly 1500 B.C.) to the Reserve Phase (about A.D. 1000)? We have several suggestions to offer and these are based on our trends and inferences plus data based on the 250 societies studied by Murdock (1949). Without this brilliant synthesis and suggestive study our reconstructions would have been impossible. We are much indebted to Dr. Murdock and wish to acknowledge our obligation.

The inferences presented below seem highly probable to us, but of course cannot be proven.

The Chiricahua Stage of the Cochise Culture (about 1500 B.C.)

During this stage, it seems probable that food gathering was the principal source of food and that agriculture was in an incipient stage (slab and basin metates plus an oval basin-metate with one end slightly open). Some agriculture is inferred, as stated above, because of the presence of corn in the lowest layer of Bat Cave, New Mexico (Mangelsdorf and Smith 1949). The task of gathering food and tending the corn was probably assigned to the women (Murdock 1949:205, 213).

In the Southwest and adjacent areas, bilateral descent is characteristic of societies with a food-gathering economy, even after they take up agriculture.

Hence the Indians of the Chiricahua stage may have been organized as follows: a nuclear family (i.e. a married man and woman and their offspring) living in a house (because the house is physically small); politically independent endogamous bands (Murdock 19, 85, 214); bilateral descent (Murdock 212); matrilocal residence (Murdock 204, 205, 213); no slavery and no social classes (Murdock 88); monogamy, if both sexes contributed equally to support of household, or polygyny, if the woman's contribution was the larger (Murdock 36).

Pine Lawn Phase (about A.D. 500)

In this period, houses were larger than in any other time-period under consideration. Under the conditions existing in a primitive society, more people could have occupied some of these large houses, many of which yielded three or more metates per house (Fig.

2). More than three metates may indicate more than one family (on the basis of a study of conditions in modern pueblos). More trough metates and fewer basin milling stones occur, which may be interpreted to mean more agriculture and less food gathering. Many stone tools per house may also indicate a population larger than a nuclear family per house.

Since social organization has "drift" similar to that phenomenon in linguistics, we assume that, once started on a certain path, social organization will tend to follow along in the same general direction (Murdock 1949:198–201). A fairly stable equilibrium would have been set up, within which certain changes might take place if they conformed to the general pattern already established, and a balance that would have been relatively immune to external forces, unless changes were in accord with the prevailing rule of residence.

With the increase in importance of agriculture in this phase, matrilocal residence would have been intensified, giving rise to matrilocal extended families. In consequence of matrilocal residence, definite matrilineal descent and matrilineal inheritance would probably have developed by this time. Inheritance of corn plots (a major form of wealth) would have strengthened the economic position of women, and would have helped to bind nuclear families into extended families and would have favored matrilineal descent.

Since we have no evidence of a change in residence rules, we assume that the set-up for the Pine Lawn Phase was similar to that of the Cochise stage: extended families living in the larger houses (7–10 people; Murdock 1949:18); matrilocal residence (Murdock 204, 205, 213); matrilineal descent (Murdock 59, 205); matrilineal inheritance because of increasing importance of corn plots (Murdock 38); politically independent villages (Murdock 85, 214); probably monogamy, because both sexes contribute equally towards subsistence.

The normal formation of extended families

might have been hastened by another factor —that is, one of defense against enemies. Since many villages of the Pine Lawn Phase are located on high and easily defended ridges, and since living space was limited there, it may have been necessary for several families to share one house.

Georgetown Through Three Circle Phases (about A.D. 500–900)

Unfriendly groups had apparently been conquered or dispersed during these periods, for we find houses built in any choice spot, without an eye to defense, and fewer of them bunched together. Furthermore, the size of the houses tended to decrease during these centuries (Fig. *1*). Along with this shrinkage in size of houses, we find that the number of metates and other artifacts tended to decrease per house (Fig. *2*). Basin milling stones markedly decreased during this span and trough metates increased in frequency (Fig. *3*). Agriculture, then, may have supplanted food gathering. Hunting became more important (the ratio of projectile points to metates increases from the Pine Lawn to the Reserve Phase. Presumably, lack of enemies permitted the population to spread out and certainly there are more villages of the Three Circle Phase and a greater population density than in the Pine Lawn Phase. The size of each house, however, was notably smaller than in the Pine Lawn Phase and it would have been physically impossible for more than a nuclear family to occupy any one of the houses of the Georgetown or Three Circle phases. This probably means that an extended family did not occupy one house. Just why this change occurred is not clear. It might have been brought about by disputes between factions or by wrangles concerning witchcraft and sorcery. It is also possible that a desire to be closer to their corn fields and sources of water caused the population to expand. This seems logical, because if more people were practicing more agriculture, more farm lands would have been needed.

For the reasons given under the section on the Pine Lawn Phase, we feel that the continuity of the social organization flowed on without any major ruptures: extended families, perhaps several to a village, and perhaps one such family occupying several houses (houses were too small to accommodate more than 3 to 5 people); matrilocal residence; matrilineal descent and inheritance; exogamous clans, caused perhaps by an increase in population (Steward 1937:91; Murdock 1949:66, 70, 75); one or more clans to a village, politically independent villages; no slavery, no social classes; monogamy.

Reserve Phase (about A.D. 1000)

Profound alterations in the material aspects of the Mogollon culture took place at this time (appearance of surface, contiguous, multi-roomed houses with walls of masonry, and black-on-white pottery, etc.). We have some evidence for believing that these changes were brought about by influences emanating from the Anasazi area or by direct immigration of Anasazi people into Pine Lawn Valley.

One might expect, then, that there were important parallel changes in the social organization of the people. But there is ample reason for thinking that these external forces —that is, changes in material culture—did not necessarily affect the continuum of the social structure (Murdock 1949:197–205). Since we believe that agriculture in the Mogollon area was becoming increasingly important and that it had been borrowed from elsewhere and grafted on a pattern of seed gathering, probably a task carried on by the women; and since the women had at their disposal, as a result of agriculture, most of the wealth, the matrilocal and matrilineal forms would have been strengthened and would have continued. Add to these probabilities the likelihood that the Anasazi, from whom the significant changes in material culture had been received, had also developed the same matrilocal and matrilineal

61

forms, and one might have another argument for conjecturing that the existing social organization, which had been handed down from Pine Lawn times, continued without any important reorganization.

For these reasons, we think it highly probable that the social organization of the people of the Reserve Phase was much the same as that of the preceding phases: matrilocal, extended families, but only one extended family per hamlet (the reason being that only three metates are found on the average in a hamlet and fewer tools are found per room than, say, in the Pine Lawn Phase; Fig. *4*); numerous hamlets (Table 1), indicating a greater density of population (basin metates had disappeared by this time and trough metates were the dominant form; this may mean an increase in dependence on agriculture); matrilineal descent and inheritance; clans occupying several hamlets; monogamy; no slavery and no social classes. Perhaps the absence of kivas with the "hamlets," or clusters of rooms, is explained by the fact that one extended family might not need a kiva. We may find in the area a medium-large kiva or two that would have served several hamlets or one clan unit.

Summary

These are assumptions and nothing more. We do not think of them as provable or proven. We suggest them as probabilities.

We consider this essay as a preliminary attempt to achieve greater understanding of and time depth for one aspect of the Mogollon culture. As our knowledge of this culture grows and we know more of its processes and development, these conjectures may be strengthened or altered.

We felt that this study was worthwhile to see how far we could go with our available data and to call the attention of other anthropologists to this type of study. If others deem it good, then perhaps they will collect data that are susceptible to this kind of analysis—population density, relation of houses one to another, size and location of houses and hamlets, number and kinds of tools per house, functions of various rooms and tools—so that trends may be abstracted and minutiae may be more valuable. If these data are collected and really utilized we should be able to give more significance to the bare material cultural remains available to the archaeologist. Some may say that it is too soon to make such reconstructions, that enough data are not yet collected. If one doesn't start to collect such data, one may overlook material or information which may subsequently assume greater importance and no longer be available for study.

This attempt to reconstruct total culture might best be done on a basis which would include all culture patterns in the Southwest from earliest horizons to the present. This broader approach would permit us to check our guesses and would yield a higher degree of probability to the forthcoming overall picture.

The Economic Approach to Prehistory

FOR MORE than one reason it was appropriate that in opening this biennial series of Reckitt Archaeological Lectures [1] Professor Stuart Piggott should have chosen to speak on William Camden and the *Britannia* (1951). Those who were present on that occasion will agree that the lecturer covered his field with singular felicity and no one is more keenly aware than he who is now called upon to follow of the high standard of wit and learning set by the first Reckitt Lecturer. By thus celebrating the quartercentenary of the birth of William Camden the Academy acknowledged in a manner the place of antiquarianism in the genesis of archaeology: it was surely right to emphasize that the studies, which Camden did so much to further, gave birth to and nurtured the early childhood of those methods of distilling history from material remains that we recognize as specifically archaeological.

Yet, if Camden's role in the prologue to archaeology is acknowledged, it is only right to recall that in Professor Piggott's words the prime object of the *Britannia* was "to establish Britain as a member of the fellowship of nations who drew their strength from roots struck deep in the Roman Empire" (1951:207–8). Camden was concerned with history in the restricted sense of that term and it is only natural that he should have relied first and foremost on literary sources: when he had recourse to archaeological evi-

Reprinted from the *Proceedings of the British Academy,* vol. 39, 1953, pp. 215–38. By permission of the author and the British Academy. The notes have been renumbered.

dence he confined himself almost entirely to coins or to monuments mentioned by ancient authors—such notice as he took of what we should now term prehistoric antiquities was perfunctory even when he was impelled to wonder by their very grandeur. Of Stonehenge he grieved mightily "that the founders of this noble monument cannot be trac'd out" (1695:95) and in his Preface he made no secret of his doubts about the chances of discovering the truth about the first inhabitants of Britain, who "had other cares and thoughts to trouble their heads withal, than that of transmitting their originals to posterity" and who, even had they so desired, could not "have effactually done it" (1695: iii). The fact is that Camden lived at a time before scholars conceived it to be possible to learn anything worth knowing about peoples who had left no written records.

The achievements of prehistoric archaeology during the last century and a half and more particularly during the last fifty years have shown, on the contrary, how much it is possible to recover of the unwritten history of mankind through diligent study of material remains. It would indeed be tedious to expatiate on the merits of archaeological research in the rooms of an Academy which has done so much to advance its cause. The suggestion one would make rather is that archaeological data has exerted if anything too exclusive a fascination over students of prehistoric times. A certain professional myopia is a common penalty of success and this is especially true of a subject like archaeology: it is not merely that the evidence on which it

Economic Approach to Prehistory
Grahame Clark

depends perpetually increases with the progress of exploration and the refinement of technique, but—thanks to the growth of museums and despite the bombs—it survives and accumulates in the form of tangible objects, objects moreover which are often aesthetically and sometimes even financially attractive in themselves. It is small wonder that archaeologists should often have succumbed to their own material and squandered on empty analyses of form energies which might more profitably have been devoted to the understanding of prehistory (1937).[2] It was inevitable that the earlier generations of prehistorians should have been engrossed in the collection and classification of data and it is certain that for a long while to come such activities will continue to absorb a large part of the time of those engaged in prehistoric research. Yet, already for some quarter of a century a sound beginning has been made with the writing of prehistory, at least in those few territories for which the preliminary and essential work of chronological and cultural definition has been brought to the requisite degree of precision (1952a).

It is widely accepted today that prehistory ought to be classified as a historical discipline: in the sense that it is concerned with development and change in the sphere of human affairs this is hardly to be questioned. Yet it seems essential to recognize that prehistory differs radically from the kind of history based even in some measure on written sources, not merely in its methods and procedures, but also in what it is capable of telling us. Since it is anonymous, prehistory can take no cognizance of the moral and psychological problems confronting individuals: it is concerned and can only be concerned with social problems; its subject-matter is culture, whether in the abstract or in relation to a specific community, region, or period. In this lecture I shall be concerned in effect with the study of the economic aspects of prehistoric cultures.

At this point it is well to reflect on what we mean by culture in the present context. If current archaeological usage is vague—

the term is loosely applied to denote congruencies among such traits as happen to be at hand as a result mainly of accident or of haphazard excavation—this is due partly to the inherently vestigial nature of the archaeological record, but partly also to lack of awareness of the achievements of the social sciences and of their implications for archaeology. As an expedient the archaeological usage can be defended, but it can hardly be accepted as more than a temporary necessity: indeed, one might measure the validity of archaeological studies by the degree to which they approximate in their reconstruction of ancient cultures to the functioning entities investigated by modern anthropologists. For their part the anthropologists have defined culture in numerous ways—in their recently published *Culture. A Critical Review of Concepts and Definitions* (1952), Professors Kroeber and Kluckhohn marshal no less than 166 significant definitions in 7 categories, not to mention 100 statements under 6 heads—revealing a diversity of definition which transcends temperamental differences and the varying levels of abstraction sought or attained by individual authors and emphasizes both the many-sidedness of culture and the multiplicity of ways in which it can usefully be approached.

One of the few things on which all authorities agree is the artificiality of culture: culture is not something that sprouts from rocks or trees—it is made by man and is man's distinctive contribution to the totality of nature or being. Further, there is a significant measure of agreement among the authors cited by Kroeber and Kluckhohn (1952:97–98) in recognizing different dimensions of culture, which, though variously labelled, may conveniently be termed material, social, and spiritual. The first of these, categorized by Franz Boas (1938:4) as including

the multitude of relations between man and nature; the procuring and preservation of food; the securing of shelter; the ways in which the objects of nature are used as implements or utensils, and all the various ways in which man utilizes or controls, or is controlled by, his natural environment: animals, plants, the inorganic world, the seasons, and wind and weather,

in effect defines pretty closely the aspect of culture which comes directly within the purview of economic prehistorians and at the same time emphasizes the theme I have particularly in mind, namely, the interplay between culture, habitat, and biome, as illustrated by the food and raw materials consumed by prehistoric communities (1952*b*:7–8 et passim).

The artificiality of culture is in itself a sufficient argument against studying prehistory as though it was a natural science. Yet it is surely an equal error to suppose that culture is something outside nature: man after all is a natural organism and his culture is in essence a traditional medium for harmonizing social needs and aspirations with the realities of the physical world, that is with the soil and climate of the habitat and with all the forms of life, including man himself, that together constitute the biome. One reason for the inadequate treatment of prehistory has been that prehistorians have too often failed to remember that archaeology is only one of a number of disciplines needful for advancing their subject. It is largely because the economic activities of man, in the course of which he utilizes natural resources to support the way of life patterned by his social inheritance, illustrate so vividly the interrelations of culture and physical environment that their study is so rewarding.

Students of modern primitive societies are in the happy position of being able to study in detail, not only the overt activities of economic life, but also, through language, the way in which different preliterate peoples classify and organize their knowledge of their physical environment. Donald Thomson, for instance, was able to observe directly how the Wik Monkan of northern Queensland "classified the types of country as accurately and as scientifically as any ecologist, giving to each a name and associating it with spe-

cific resources, with its animal and vegetable foods and its technological products" (1939: 211), or, again, how they divided the year into "a cycle of four, or more accurately, of five, seasons, each with its distinctive and characteristic climatic and other conditions, and each related to a food-supply, and hence to a definite kind of occupation" (Thompson 1939:216). Alternatively one might quote from a recent report (1952:57) by Paul A. Vestal on the Ramah Navaho, an agricultural and stock-raising group of the American Southwest:

Of the 465 uncultivated plant species collected in the area, there were only three of which no Navaho name was given when shown to two or more informants, and for one of these a use was known . . . the people are observant of their plant-surroundings and can readily distinguish between plants of major, secondary, or minor importance in their lives. . . . Plants enter into all their activities from birth until death. The uses of plants are multiple, and from the Navaho standpoint they fit into that harmony of related parts which is the Navaho view of the universe, and with which the people must make harmonious connections for an abundant life.

This detailed knowledge of ecological conditions was as much a part of the Wik Monkan or Navaho way of life as the tools they made from natural products. The same must have been true of prehistoric man, but in his case we can only infer this from a study of biological traces.

Modes of subsistence confront us with the most vital aspect of economic life or indeed of life itself, since, not merely does survival itself depend on food, but the methods by which food is acquired affect more or less closely all other departments of cultural life. From a theoretical viewpoint subsistence represents no more in essence than the appropriation of animal and plant substances for the nourishment of human beings at standards and in manners conditioned by the societies to which they belong. As such it reflects both the economic level and the individual characteristics of different cultures. Above all, it illustrates how, in the case of man, the preliminaries to even such an overtly biological activity as eating conform to patterns of social behaviour. A knowledge of the methods by which early man maintained life is essential to an—understanding both of individual cultures and of the process of change unfolded in prehistory.

Under the economic and social conditions prevailing in Upper Palaeolithic and Mesolithic times—the earliest for which we yet have adequate documentation—it must be conceded that the field of choice open to individuals or communities was limited by the varieties of animal and plant occupying the habitat. One may emphasize, though, that, if freedom of choice was limited by biological and ultimately by physical factors, this by no means disposes of it. Freedom of choice is after all very relative and no living organism or association of such can exist unless by coming to terms with the extraneous factors which condition to a greater or less degree all forms of life. Other animals, indeed, conform instinctively to these, but it is after all the hall-mark of man that he behaves at least ideally with reference to an artificial pattern evolved and transmitted by society. The evolution of culture, indeed, has been a story of ever-widening range of choice. Already among primitive hunter-fishers there was scope for the exercise of preference—at the most elementary level, for instance, there was the choice from among those available of which animals to hunt and which plants to gather and in what proportions.

It is not difficult to measure accurately the proclivities of prehistoric hunters in regard to meat, since bone commonly survives and the practice of extracting the marrow makes it obvious which animals have served for food. For instance, the fauna from the Magdalenian cave of Petersfels (Fig. *1*) in southeast Baden (Peters 1930; Peters and Toepfer 1932) reflects, in the rarity of forest and the abundance of tundra-steppe species, the ecological conditions prevailing there at a particular phase of Late Glacial times. Yet,

if it would be folly to interpret such a table solely in economic terms, it would be wrong to do so in purely zoological ones. The skeletal material from Petersfels, apart perhaps from a few rodents, is, like that from any other archaeological site, the product of human selection: it represents social choice operating within the limits set by definable biological and physical factors. By and large the Magdalenians of Petersfels relied for their meat (as well as for many of their most important raw materials) on reindeer and to a lesser degree on wild horses, but during the season of snow cover they evidently trapped Ptarmigan, Arctic Fox, and Arctic Hare. On the other hand the Late Glacial stations of Meiendorf and Stellmoor[3] (Fig. *2*) show an unrelieved predominance of reindeer. Analysis of the faunal remains makes it clear that the sites were inhabited only during the summer.[4] During this time of the year the hunters attached themselves to reindeer herds during their migrations to the north, depending on them almost entirely for meat, clothing, and shelter, as well as drawing on their antlers and bones for tools and weapons, so that almost every item in the archaeological inventory of both cultures finds an explanation in terms of the hunting or utilization of this one animal. By contrast, the animals hunted by the inhabitants of east Yorkshire during the initial Pre-boreal phase of the Post-glacial period, as illustrated by the fauna from Star Carr (Fig. *3*), belonged, almost without exception, to forest-dwelling species.[5] Further, in this case we appear to be confronted with the food and industrial debris of the winter months, and it has to be admitted that none of the animals available to the Mesolithic hunters encouraged specialized hunting to the extent that the gregarious and migratory reindeer undoubtedly did. Even so, the Star Carr people showed a marked preference for Red Deer, though they took Aurochs, Elk, and Roe Deer in considerable numbers. Examples could be multiplied, but my point will have been made if I have shown that an element of social choice existed, even if the range

66

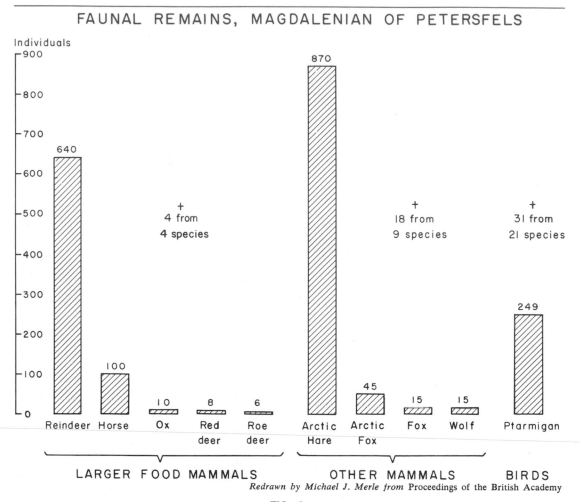

FIG. 1.

within which this could be exercised was limited by the facts of climate and animal and plant ecology. What above all else limited the possibilities of life for the hunters of Petersfels, Meiendorf, or Star Carr was the nature of their economy.

The great turning-point in prehistory, the point at which men first escaped from the closed cycle of savagery and became free to advance towards literate civilization—often termed the Neolithic revolution, though it should be remembered that the great discovery of domestication must in fact have been made by Mesolithic hunters and gatherers (Clark 1952c:325)—may be conceived of as in essence the outcome of a change of atti-

tude on the part of human societies towards the animals and plants with which they were associated. This change was fundamentally from a predatory to a productive régime, away from mere seizure and appropriation to protection, nurture, and selective breeding, so that from among wild species men were able to elicit others endowed with qualities which they regarded as desirable. The species domesticated by human societies over the course of generations were moulded in conformity with the ideas and requirements of these societies and so acquired characteristics determined at least in some measure by the cultural patterns of the societies into which they were in a sense incorporated by

67

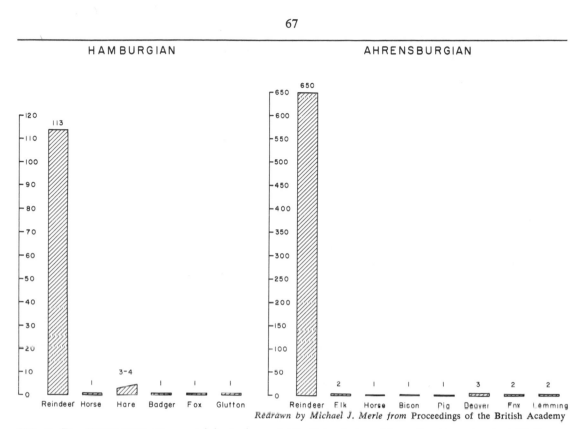

HAMBURGIAN   AHRENSBURGIAN

Redrawn by Michael J. Merle from Proceedings of the British Academy

FIG. 2. *The Hamburgian figures relate to fauna from Meiendorf and from the lower level at Stellmoor combined, the Ahrensburgian ones to the upper level at Stellmoor.*

domestication. Viewed from a slightly different angle the change was one from a relatively passive to an active, dynamic attitude towards nature: men ceased to be satisfied not merely with the character of the animals and plants they found around them but also with their distribution. The need to expand the area within which crops could be grown and herds grazed sprang logically from the control of breeding by domestication. The increased density of population which this made possible, together with the advances in technology which flowed from and at the same time encouraged these, created demands which could most easily be met by expanding the territories over which farming could be carried on. It was, of course, the spread of the new economy from western Asia and north Africa which marked for successive zones of Europe the transition from mesolithic to neolithic culture. The magnitude of this

change, which transcended the purely economic sphere and affected the entire social structure and spiritual outlook of the peoples concerned, can only be fully appreciated in biological terms. The introduction of farming to temperate Europe was nothing less than majestic, not only in its historical consequences, but also as an achievement in creative evolution. It implied not merely the introduction of domesticated animals and plants into an environment quite different from that in which they were originally bred, but also the modification of the incoming economy to suit these different conditions and conversely the initiation of processes by which the physical environment was itself ultimately transformed to accord with developing social needs.

From the point of view of prehistoric research it is these biological and specifically ecological changes which provide the fullest

68

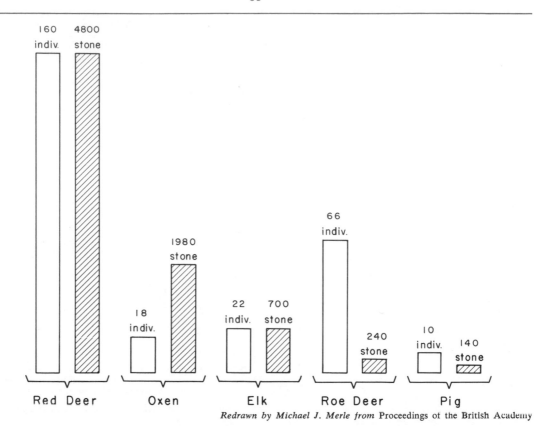

Redrawn by Michael J. Merle from Proceedings of the British Academy

FIG. 3. *The number of individuals represented among the material actually recovered from Starr Carr were half of those shown, but allowance has to be made for areas unexcavated and for the fact that antler bone had decayed on the northern part of the site.*

and most reliable index of the progress and extent of the economic transformation wrought during Neolithic times. Neither of the archaeological traits identified by the earlier prehistorians with the introduction of neolithic culture were in themselves of great significance: the polishing of flint axe and adze blades is still, it is true, of local value as an indicator, even though the technique was taken over from the working of antler, bone, and stone practised by upper Palaeolithic and Mesolithic hunters (Clark 1952*b*:172); and it now appears that farming antedated the appearance of pot-making in the Old as well as in the New World,[6] quite apart from the fact that the manufacture and use of pottery by no means implies the practice of husbandry.[7] As farming techniques developed, the material equipment

needed for tilling the soil, harvesting crops, and the like forms an increasingly valuable source of evidence, but in the earliest stage this was hardly the case: primitive stock-raising could be carried on without leaving any trace in the archaeological record; and crops could be grown without elaborate tillage and harvested by reaping-knives indistinguishable from those employed for gathering wild grains.[8] The most decisive criteria for determining the origin, spread, and progress of farming are biological, notably indications of domestication exhibited by remains of animals and plants, and evidence of ecological disturbance resulting from the practice of farming and from the ever-increasing transformation of the habitat which this entailed.

The practice of agriculture inevitably involves occupation of the soil in a manner more intimate and more intensive than does hunting and gathering: conversely the increasing intensity with which the habitat was settled reflects the dynamism of the new economy with its accompanying growth of population and technological advance. It is hardly too much to claim that we owe our present understanding of the agricultural prehistory of temperate Europe in the first instance to biologists working within the general framework of Quaternary Research (Clark 1945*a*, 1945*b*, 1947*a*). From the very beginning agriculture had to be carried on at the expense of, though also in partnership with, the existing vegetation. The Neolithic settlers were really only the forerunners of deforestation, since, as Iversen and his botanical colleagues over much of northwestern Europe have shown,[9] the first clearances were strictly temporary in character. Iversen's hypothesis (1941) that the Neolithic pioneers practised the slash and burn system, clearing small patches, burning the undergrowth and felled timber (in so doing enriching the soil with potash), taking two or three crops and passing on to fresh tracts of forest, is supported by economic history and comparative ethnology as well as being confirmed experimentally: there is after all plenty of evidence for the practice in medieval Europe (Bloch 1931:27–29) and during the colonization of eastern North America (Schott 1935); it survived until yesterday in the forests of Finland and Carelia (Manninen 1932:274–75); and it still operates among primitive agriculturists in many parts of the world today, notably in Malaya where its progress has been so admirably recorded from the air (Williams-Hunt 1949). The whole process of clearing, burning, and raising cereal crops has recently been reproduced in Jutland by the authorities of the National Museum of Denmark, using only such equipment as was available to Neolithic man; and it is significant that cereals were only able to compete with weeds on soil mixed with ash from the burning.[10]

It is in the light of this hypothesis that we are enabled for the first time to view the earliest agriculturists of temperate Europe as functioning in a convincing setting. The disconnected distribution of the Danubian peasants, the apparent speed with which they spread over their extensive loess-lands (Childe 1929:46–47; Clark 1952*b*:95–96, fig. 45), the frequency with which even their most important setlements were abandoned and reoccupied,[11] all these and many other details fit easily into the context of *Brandwirtschaft*. It is for instance amusing to note the effect of the new concept on our evaluation of so familiar and so solid an archaeological fossil as the shoe-last celt. So long as we thought of the loess as an open corridor it seemed most reasonable to interpret the *Schuhleistenkeil* as an implement of tillage — plain ones as hoe-blades (Childe 1929: 29 et passim.) and perforated ones as ploughshares.[12] Once the forest cover and the régime of slash and burn is accepted, there is no need for hoes, let alone ploughs, since the seed had only to be raked among the ashes (Manninen 1932:30), and there is every occasion for felling trees and for working wood: so it was really no surprise when re-examination [13] of the shoe-last celt revealed a slightly hollow working-edge, a feature meaningless in relation to a hoe-blade, but very much in keeping with the D-shaped section and pointing beyond doubt to use as an adze. Thus, not even the most established types are impervious to ideas, a main function of which in archaeology should be to lead us back to reinterpret the material data. Any regrets for that discarded landmark of prehistory, the shoe-last hoe, will be more than compensated for by the reflection, brought home with increasing force by the continued revelation of traces of massive timber-framed houses, that the Danubian peasants had every need for their adzes as well as every opportunity to use them.

The ecological approach has further provided a convincing clue to the changes in land-utilization which underlie so much of the later prehistory of our region. The initial phase of shifting agriculture could endure only so long as forest regeneration approximated to the rate of clearance. It was inevitable that the growth of population made possible by farming, not to mention the depredations of livestock maintained under a very imperfect system of domestication,[14] should have slowed down and in due course brought to an end the whole cycle. The crisis of subsistence, reflected for instance in the widespread movements of warrior herdsmen at the close of Neolithic times, was to some extent deferred by the annexation of marginal lands and by the intensification of herding and hunting: in the long run, though, it could be resolved only by adopting a more settled and at the same time a more intensive form of agriculture.

Precisely when the new régime, based on permanent as distinct from temporary clearance of forest and involving the cultivation of definite fields by means of the *ard* (Clark 1952*b*:100–103),[15] the light ox-drawn implement of tillage evolved in the dry farming zone of the Near and Middle East, spread into successive parts of temperate Europe is still subject to research. The system seems to have worked well enough on the light, relatively well-drained soils of the area first taken up for tillage in temperate Europe,[16] but inevitably the time came once again when the needs of a growing population outstripped the available sources of food and towards the end of the prehistoric period it became necessary to incorporate intermediate loams and ultimately to make a start on the heavier clay soils. With the colonization of the secondary area of settlement new problems arose (Clark 1952*b*:105–7), which the onset of wetter conditions only served to emphasize, and it was in response to these that the régime familiar from medieval times was originally developed. The topic of land-utilization during prehistoric times is indeed one of inexhaustible interest, but we must not lose sight of the object of all this activity, namely, the supply of animal and plant protein, more

even in flow and more substantial in volume than was possible under a régime of hunting, fishing, and gathering.

The importance of research on the nature of domesticated animals and plants as a source of information about the economy of prehistoric farmers need hardly be emphasized, having in fact been widely recognized ever since the revelation of the Swiss lake-villages a hundred years ago (Heer 1866). On the other hand the purely historical questions which occupied the older prehistorians—the sources of different domesticated species and the routes by which they were diffused—have now been replaced or at least supplemented by others more functional in character. Among such one may note the relative importance of domesticated and wild forms (by which the respective roles of hunting and stock-raising can be measured); the character and degree of domestication; the proportions in which different species were maintained, considered in relation to the total environment;[17] and the precise manner in which different species contributed to the subsistence of the societies which maintained them. Many of these questions—like the more elementary ones already treated when speaking of hunting groups—are capable of scientifically precise answers, in the sense that they are susceptible of exact statistical treatment. Further, when material from successive periods is analysed, any significant trends or developments are likely to be made manifest. This is well seen in the results of Hans Helbaek's work on cereals imprinted on handmade pottery and other clay-fictiles (Jessen and Helbaek 1944; Helbaek 1952). The beauty of his method is that it rests on a random selection—on imprints of whatever material happens to have lain about while potting was actually in progress—and that the cultural and temporal relevance of the data is automatically fixed by the pottery on which imprints occur. Even when restricted to Denmark, the country where it was first worked out,[18] the method disclosed changes in the composition of crops, for instance the swing

71

during the Bronze Age from wheat to barley and the appearance towards the end of prehistoric times of such crops as oats and rye. Now that it is being applied to a much more extensive territory, including the British Isles, and that the imprints are being interpreted in conjunction with other sources of information, it is beginning to throw light on such topics as the origin and spread of domesticated species and in some instances even on the sources of folk-movements indicated by archaeology. Thus, just as the functionalist school of anthropology, though avowedly anti-historical in bias, has in practice made it possible for the first time to appreciate what is involved in social evolution, so in the case of prehistoric crops the ecological approach is making possible a renewed and more profound understanding of genetical-historical problems.

It rarely happens that we can supplement inferences drawn from discarded meat-bones or impressions of plants with more direct evidence about the food of prehistoric man. The autopsy recently carried out in the National Museum of Denmark by the chief pathologist of a Copenhagen hospital, assisted by a specialist in forensic medicine, on the body of an Early Iron Age man recovered from a bog at Tollund, near Silkeborg, Jutland, is one of the rare instances to the contrary (Thorvildsen 1950; Helbaek 1950). When the digestive tract was washed out, it was found to contain the residue of a kind of gruel, recalling that described by Pliny as the common diet of peasants in Greece and Italy. The chief ingredients were barley, linseed, Cameline seed, and the fruits of *Polygonum lapathifolium,* a common weed of cultivation, but remains of fifteen other plants including oats and a number of weeds were also identified. Traces of most of these plants have been found on contemporary settlements in Denmark and there seems no doubt that the peasants of this period were fond of certain oil-bearing seeds and, further, that they took the trouble to gather the seeds of a number of weeds. The investigation of residues in various kinds of container is a not uncommon source of information about food and drink: thus, the evidence from Tollund is reinforced by the discovery of a quantity of linseed and Cameline seed, evidently from a perishable container, in an Iron Age house at Østerbølle, Jutland; [19] and as regards drink one recalls the long-published evidence from Danish burials—cranberry wine mixed with myrtle and honey from the Bronze Age and a brew of barley, cranberry, and bog myrtle from the Roman Iron Age (Shetelig and Falk 1937:149, 313). Although occasional clues to methods of cooking are given by finds of ovens, baking platters, and the like, it has to be admitted that we know far less about the ways in which food was prepared than we do about the selection and provision of the actual raw materials, despite the profound significance of cuisine as an expression of culture.

If prehistoric man lived by eating animals and plants, he depended equally on natural substances, whether organic or otherwise, for the fabric of his material culture, seeking out what he needed and shaping it to meet the requirements of his social life. The artifacts, whether structures, objects of utility, ornaments, or works of art, on which archaeology mainly depends may be thought of as embodiments of ideas, which, however, could only be realized through techniques applied to materials present in or elicited from the natural environment. Thus we are faced in the sphere of technology with the same kind of dynamic relationship between culture and ecosystem that we encountered in the case of subsistence. Whereas in the animal world raw materials were utilized to satisfy merely instinctive needs, among men their very selection has from the beginning been determined by cultural considerations (Fig. *4*). If prehistory is the study of man's growing control over forces external to himself down to the time when through his invention of writing he first emerged on the stage of history, it is significant that this progress has for over a hundred years been epitomized for archae-

Redrawn by Lois A. Johnson from Proceedings of the British Academy

FIG. 4.

ologists by the dominant raw materials used for implements and weapons (Thomsen 1936; Nilsson 1838–43; Daniel 1943, 1950: 42–51). By and large prehistoric man used the materials available to him which most adequately fulfilled his requirements within the limits of his capacity to shape them: his selection of raw materials thus provides important information about the extent of territory from which he obtained supplies, whether by seasonal migration or trade, and about the pattern of his social needs, as well as about the general level of his technology.

One of the most striking characteristics of the technology of modern primitive peoples is the use made of materials derived from wild animals and plants—skins, sinew, bone, antler, wood, bark, resin, stems, leaves, and so on—and no doubt such materials played a much more prominent role among prehistoric peoples subject to the limitations of a stone-age technology than the archaeological record suggests: even so antler and bone often survive in sufficient quantities to provide adequate material for study. When one considers the items selected by any group of stone-age man from among the skeletal remains of the animals taken for food, it soon becomes evident that we are confronted with the results of discrimination; that this discrimination is the outcome of cultural inheritance and of the actual mode of life pursued; and that in consequence this choice is as germane to prehistoric studies as the material equipment fabricated from the raw materials in question.

One may illustrate this by reference to the hunters of Star Carr (Clark 1954: Chapter 5); (Fig. 5). Of their principal food-animals they ignored the roe deer and wild pig; of aurochs they used only the metapodials and femurs and these exclusively for making a particular kind of leather-working tool; of elk they utilized the lower portions of the antlers and the attached frontal bone for mattock-heads, the small lateral metapodials for bodkins and, in rare instances, splinters from the metapodials for barbed points; but, most instructive of all, in the case of their principal quarry, red deer, they entirely neglected the limb bones and ribs, concentrating on the antlers, almost every one of which they turned to account as sources of material for their favourite barbed spearheads. The blanks from which these objects were made were won by cutting parallel grooves up and down the beam and levering out the intervening splinters, a highly characteristic technique and one which had been inherited and transmitted over a long period of time. The groove and splinter technique was apparently first applied to stag, as well as possibly to reindeer antler, by the Aurignacians of south-western France during the first interstadial of the last glaciation.[20] In the territories over which red deer was replaced by reindeer during the ensuing late glacial phase basically the same technique was applied, both by the Mag-

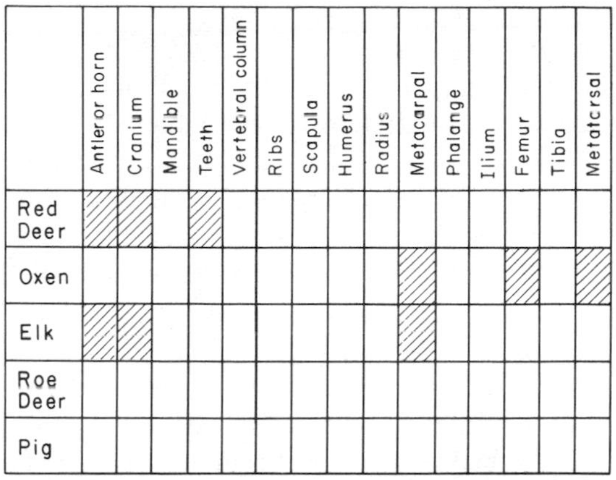

	Antler or horn	Cranium	Mandible	Teeth	Vertebral column	Ribs	Scapula	Humerus	Radius	Metacarpal	Phalange	Ilium	Femur	Tibia	Metatarsal
Red Deer	X		X												
Oxen										X			X		X
Elk	X														
Roe Deer															
Pig															

Redrawn by Michael J. Merle from Proceedings of the British Academy

FIG. 5.

dalenians[21] and also by the Hamburgians;[22] but in each case it was modified in practice to suit the differing character of reindeer antler, the splinters stopping short at the brow tine instead of continuing down to the root of the antler. When, with the onset of Post-glacial conditions the red deer regained and extended their old territories, the technique was once more practised in its original form: the Azilians of north Spain[23] and south-west France, as well as the proto-Maglemosians of the north (as exemplified at Star Carr), removed splinters down to the lower end of the beam in precisely the same fashion as the Aurignacians of France and the early Magdalenians of eastern Spain had done in Late Pleistocene times.

If, however, one turns to the Maglemosians proper, as known from so many sites of Boreal age from eastern England to west Russia (Clark 1936: Chapter 3), one finds on the one hand a more catholic use of the skeletal parts of game animals and on the other a radical change from antler to bone as the material perferred for fabricating barbed points. Red deer was still the commonest game animal, but the antlers were now used almost, though not quite,[24] exclusively for mattock-heads and holders for flint adzes. Uniserial spearheads were an outstanding feature of material equipment, but these were now as a rule cut from the ribs of red deer or the metapodials of roe deer,[25] both materials abundantly available to, though conspicuously neglected by, the hunters of Star Carr. This change in the use of raw materials is all the more striking since the flint component of the Boreal Maglemosian culture, on which the possibility of working antler and bone depended, is so evidently in the same tradition as that represented at Star Carr. How then are we to interpret this? Does it reflect simply an advance in technical dexterity—barbed points being more difficult to work in bone than in antler, though for some purposes more effective—or is it that the finished products were intended for different uses? It is not my present purpose to suggest a solution, but simply to point to the existence of a problem of a kind which ought to abound in prehistoric archaeology. The choice of raw materials is worthy of research precisely because it prompts questions which might otherwise remain unasked, and it is only by questing that we can hope to discover.

The adoption of farming affected the choice of raw materials drawn from organic nature in much the same way as it did the supply of food: it increased their volume and availability and it led to the development of new substances. It was for instance the eliciting of *Linum usitatissimum* and the domestication and selective breeding of fleecy sheep that made possible the rise of textile crafts based on the weaving of linen (Vogt 1937) [26] and wool (Broholm and Hald).[27] Further, it is relevant to recall that sheep-breeding, and consequently a woolen industry, could not be carried on over extensive territories of temperate Europe until permanent deforestation had proceded far enough to provide adequate open pasturage (Clark 1947*b*). This is only another illustration of the need to view the various aspects of economic life in relation to the ecosystems which comprehend human societies.

The adoption of farming was associated with a progressively more extensive and effective use of the inorganic resources of the habitat. The greatly increased use of fired clay among peasant communities, epitomized above all by the craft of potting, though of great value as an archaeological indicator, was not in itself of any marked significance. It was the adoption of the working of copper and its alloys, and later of iron, that brought about major increases in control over physical environment (Childe 1944*a*), not only in working such organic materials as wood and bone, but even more significantly in helping to improve the food-supply through more effective felling and clearance and through the provision of such things as pruning- and lopping-knives, plough-shares, coulters, and the like. The cheaper and the more effective metal tools became, the greater must have been their impact on food-production and so on population. Conversely, every increase in the density of population made possible a finer subdivision of labour, a most essential condition for further technical improvements. The interaction between food-production, population growth, and the ability to use more effective materials for implements and gear was both intimate and continuous, and it is certain that a more adequate understanding of economic prehistory waits on a much fuller and more precise knowledge about the growth of population during prehistoric times than we at present possess.

The importance attached to obtaining the most effective materials from which to make the tools needed to win a better living from the physical environment—and for that matter to forge the weapons for competing with neighbouring groups—is reflected in the care with which they were sought out and if necessary traded over great distances. The size of the territories over which primitive hunters had commonly to range in quest of food meant that in the normal course they were able to gather raw materials from different parts of what might be a variegated habitat. One effect of adopting agriculture was, as we have seen, to tie communities more closely to the soil, even if at first temporarily, so that the area from which raw materials could be gathered was much more restricted. The contraction in living-area, which was only one

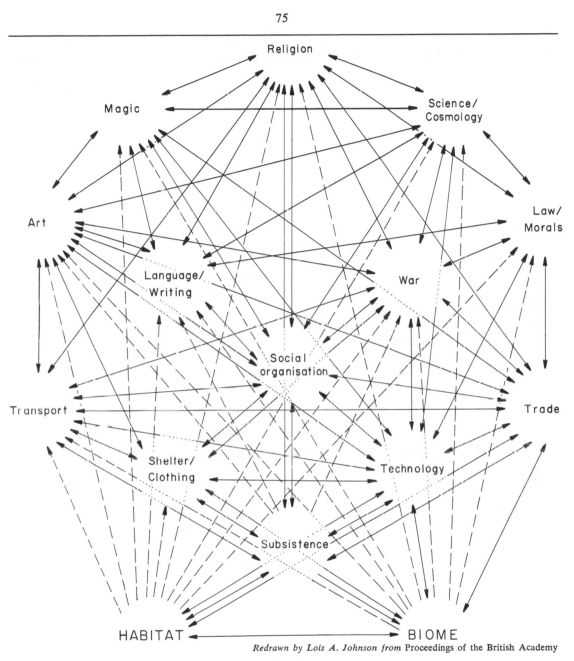

Redrawn by Lois A. Johnson from Proceedings of the British Academy

FIG. 6.

aspect of the increasing density of population made possible by the new economy, came at a time when advances in technology were making great calls on raw materials of uneven and often very restricted occurrence in nature. This was undoubtedly one factor in the development of trade of the kind dramatically exemplified by the rise of bronze metallurgy in regions lacking either tin or copper—but this is a subject altogether too important to embark on at the close of a lecture.

At an early stage I made it clear that I was concerned with prehistoric economy primarily as an approach to prehistory. I ought not to conclude without reminding you that ways of approaching this subject are as numerous as culture and indeed as man himself is many-sided, and further that no aspect of culture, by which I mean everything acquired by individuals as members of societies, can be fully understood in isolation (Fig. 6). Thus, not even the most prosaic activities of daily life can be adequately interpreted solely in terms of economic factors: even the selection of animals for food or of the skeletal remains of these for implements or weapons may depend on traditional beliefs in the field of law, magic, or religion, or on some circumstance of social organization, as much as upon such material factors as the means available for hunting or manufacture. Conversely, it is no less true that the influence of economic factors permeates all levels of social life, so that a knowledge of these is necessary for the understanding even of such apparently remote spheres as art or religion.

My theme has been the interaction between subsistence and technology and between each of these and habitat and biome. The thesis I have sought to sustain is first that even at this basal level, at which economy so to speak interlocks with ecology, the decisive factor has been social choice, and second that every advance in the control of the natural environment has enlarged the scope within which this choice could operate. In other words, economic progress in the sense of a growing capacity to utilize natural resources, such as we can trace in prehistory, marks stages in the liberation of the human spirit by making possible more varied responses and so accelerating the processes of change and diversification over the whole realm of culture. Advances in the means of production have indeed determined history, but only in the sense that they have widened the range of choice open to human societies.

NOTES

1. The Albert Reckitt Archaeological Lecture, British Academy, 1953.

2. Cf. A. M. Tallgren, *Eurasia Septentrionalis Antiqua* 10:16–24.

3. W. Krause in A. Rust (1937:48–61); W. Krause and W. Kollau in A. Rust (1943:49–105).

4. Reconsideration of the evidence raises serious doubts about this interpretation. The sites were occupied seasonally, but the time of the year is in question. Rust's idea that the reindeer abandoned the northern territories during the winter is strongly contradicted by the fact that, of the reindeer antlers from Denmark, a high proportion are shed ones. Since the antlers are cast in October–November, it seems evident that reindeer herds were present even in northern Jutland during the early winter. The probability is that the Hamburgians and Ahrensburgians culled herds as they moved north during the late autumn.

5. F. C. Fraser and J. E. King, *Proceedings of the Prehistoric Society* 15 (1949):67–69 and 16 (1951):124– ; also Chapter 3 in J. G. D. Clark (1954). For further consideration of Star Carr, see J. G. D. Clark (1971).

6. e.g. the pre-ceramic levels at Jarmo (Braidwood and Braidwood 1950) and Jericho (University of London 1953).

7. Pottery was for instance used in a late Mesolithic milieu in the west Baltic areas (see especially T. Mathiassen 1942:62–3), as well as much more extensively in the later hunter-fisher cultures of the circumpolar region northern (see G. Gjessing 1944:40–46).

8. e.g. by the Mesolithic Natufians of Palestine, see D. A. E. Garrod and B. M. A. Bate (1937:pl. xiii). The technique of setting flint flakes in slotted hafts was widely employed for weapon-heads by Mesolithic hunter-fishers from north-western Europe to inner Siberia.

9. Iversen 1941; Faegri 1943; H. Godwin, *Nature* 153:511 and 154:6; Firbas 1949:353–66.

10. Information from Dr. H. Godwin, F. R. S., who observed crops growing in the experimental clearing in the Draved forest, south Jutland.

11. e.g. Köln-Lindenthal (Butler and Haberey 1936) and Brześć Kujawski (K. Jażdżewski, *Wiadomości Archeologiczne* 15(1938):93 and pl. ii).

12. P. V. Glob, *Acta Archaeologica* 1939:131–40.

13. A. Rieth, *Prähistorische Zeitschrift* 34/35 (1949/50):230 ff.

14. Hay-making was developed only at the end of the prehistoric period and roots and other fodder crops came in quite late in the historical period. During prehistoric times livestock depended mainly on what they could secure by grazing on natural vegetation.

15. An important work, not available to me in time for my own book (1952b), is P. V. Glob's (1951).

16. Corresponding to Cyril Fox's primary area of settlement as defined in his *Archaeology of the Cambridge Region* (1923:313–14).

17. e.g. the proportions between cattle and swine on one hand and sheep on the other in relation to the progress of deforestation. See Clark (1947*b*).

18. The basic research was done at the turn of the century by G. L. F. Sarauw. His Danish results are set out in G. Hatt (1937:20–23).

19. G. Hatt, *Aarbøger* 1938:221–25 and fig. 91.

20. A fine example of the base of a stag antler, from which at least four longitudinal splinters have been detached as far down as the burr, is illustrated by P. Girod (1906:pls. xcv–xcvi) from a deposit at Gorge d'Enfer B in association with characteristic split-base bone points. Other evidence for the still sparing use of this technique in Aurignacian times may be cited from Les Cottés, l'abri Blanchard, and Isturitz.

21. Most notably at Meiendorf (Rust 1937:90–98) and Stellmoor (Rust 1943:143–44), but also on stray finds, e.g. from the Havel Lakes (*Mannus Zeitschrift,* 1917, Bd. viii, Taf. iv, 8).

22. The lower parts of reindeer antlers showing traces of the groove and splinter technique have, for instance, been noted at La Madeleine, Laugerie Basse, St. Marcel, Badegoule, and Montgaudier in south-west France; at Petersfels and Schussenquelle in south Germany; and in central Europe at Pekárna in Moravia. It is significant that the barbed harpoon-heads, recognized type fossils of the later Magdalenian, are almost invariably made from reindeer antler, as are also the lance-heads (*sagaies*) of earlier stages of this culture.

23. M. W. Thompson, *Proceedings of the Prehistoric Society* 19 (1954).

24. Only isolated barbed points made from stag antler have been found on Maglemosian sites of Boreal age, e.g. *Danske Oldsager,* i, no. 173.

25. The great majority of the barbed points from Mullerup were made from ribs (*Aarbøger* 1903: 245–46). From Svaerdborg only 40 of the 213 found during the 1917–18 excavations were made from ribs, the remainder from metapodial bones, mainly of roe deer (*Mém. des Antiq. du Nord,* 1918–19:320–24). The proportions from Holmegaard were similar to those from Svaerdborg (*Mém. des Antiq. du Nord,* 1926–31:58).

26. Also *Ciba Review* 54:1938–64.

27. Cf. A. Geijer and H. Ljungh, *Acta Archaeologica* 8(1937):266–75.

8 CLYDE KLUCKHOHN

The Conceptual Structure in Middle American Studies

FOR ONE who has published but a single very trivial contribution in Middle American research (Kluckhohn 1935) to attempt a critical review of the theoretical bases of work in this field may well seem a gratuitous impertinence. Perhaps, however, the significance of the forest as a whole can be envisioned a little more easily if the student is not preoccupied with a particular set of trees. An intensive interest in a given set of facts is often (as Dr. Kidder has suggested) productive of a certain intellectual myopia. We can hope, therefore, that the fact that the writer has only a nonspecialist's familiarity with the data is in part compensated for by the detachment which tends to be associated with lack of a research stake. Full and detailed factual knowledge would, of course, be a prerequisite to any useful commentary on the interpretation of specific assemblages of evidence, the status of concrete problems, or present frontiers of information. But (particularly since Professor Tozzer (1934, 1937b) and Dr. Mason (1938) have recently given us admirable surveys of just this sort) this is exactly what I do not propose to do. I wish, rather, to turn to a general survey of the

conceptual bases to investigations which have been carried out in this field.

Any discussion which could be given in a few pages will necessarily be somewhat schematic and generalized and will inevitably rest more upon impressions than upon exhaustive examination of the evidence and satisfactory, documented induction. First, however, I must be careful to state and discuss briefly two postulates upon which my analysis will rest: 1) archaeologists and ethnologists wish to be "scholarly" at least in the sense of working systematically (with provision for verification by other workers) toward the end of enriching our intellectual grasp of human experience; 2) in scholarly procedure there is a rational or conceptual element as well as a factual or evidential element. The first postulate implies that Maya archaeologists, for example, should not be interested merely in any set of facts as such—no facts are, from this point of view, their own justification simply because they satisfy our intellectual curiosity on a given point. Gathering, analyzing, and synthesizing all the data on, let us say, the calendar system of the Aztecs is justified only if all this industry can be viewed as contributing, however indirectly, toward our understanding of human behavior or human history. Clearly, it cannot be demanded that the precise relevance of each research undertaking to some broad induction should be known and stated in advance. But unless data are gathered and

Reprinted from *The Maya and Their Neighbors,* edited by A. M. Tozzer (New York, London: D. Appleton-Century Co., 1940; Salt Lake City: University of Utah Press, 1962), pp. 41–51. By permission of Mrs. George E. Taylor and the University of Utah Press.

presented in such a way that they can be so conceptualized by other workers they are intellectually useless. Hence the broad outlines of a conceptual scheme should be present in the consciousness of the investigator and clearly stated. It is not sufficient that there should be a sense of problem in so far as clearing up obscurities of fact are concerned. The second postulate is very closely related to the first. As my colleague, Professor Talcott Parsons, has long insisted: "The content of science cannot be wholly fact. For if it were there would be no 'crucial experiments.' . . . The facts do not speak for themselves; they have to be cross-examined." The thesis that the conceptual aspect of anthropological procedure needs at least as careful examination as the verificational aspect (Whitehead's "observational order") I have elaborated elsewhere (1939).

Let us now turn directly to Middle American studies. To begin with, I should like to record an overwhelming impression that many students in this field are but slightly reformed antiquarians. To one who is a layman in these highly specialized realms there seems a great deal of obsessive wallowing in detail of and for itself. No one can feel more urgently than the writer the imperative obligation of anthropologists to set their descriptions in such a rich context of detail that they can properly be used for comparative purposes. Yet proliferation of minutiae is not its own justification. Authors of research monographs ought to make it plain (in few words but lucidly) that they have given such amplitude of detail only toward the end of elucidating such and such larger questions. And from time to time in any field there should appear books or articles on a somewhat higher level of abstraction which suggest the pertinence of various constellations of data to the primary problems of human interaction. It is the candid opinion of this writer that such efforts by Middle American specialists have been pitifully few. Professor Tozzer has pilloried activity of the sheer fact-grubbing type

(1934), but the problems which continue to be attacked in this field appear to be primarily of an informational order. Do researches which require large funds for their support require no social justification other than that of quenching certain thirsts for knowledge on the part of a relatively small number of citizens? If archaeologists and ethnologists have hardly begun to ask themselves the tough-minded query—so what?, evidence is not lacking that this question has occurred to research foundations and other sources of financial support. Personally, I suspect that unless archaeologists treat their work quite firmly as part of a general attempt to understand human behavior they will, before many generations, find themselves classed with Aldous Huxley's figure who devoted his life to writing a history of the three-pronged fork. In Middle American studies up to this time I have been unable to find much evidence of awareness of or interest in the relevance of research and publication to what Linton has asserted to be the prime task of all anthropologists; "to discover the limits within which men can be conditioned, and what patterns of social life seem to impose fewest strains upon the individual."

One almost dares to say quite flatly: the industry of workers in this field is most impressive as is, for the most part, their technical proficiency in the field and the scrupulous documentation in their publications, but one is not carried away by the luxuriance of their ideas. Let me elaborate these considerations. In discussing the various types of intellectual activity carried on by scholars, I have found it convenient to distinguish the following hierarchy of abstractions: methodology, theory, method, technique. Each of these concepts is, of course, progressively more concrete. The category of methodology refers to the logical bases of all intellectual work; the category theory refers to the conceptual framework of a single discipline; the category method refers to the sheer analysis and ordering of data (as opposed to the formulation of abstract concepts in terms of which such ordering is carried on); the category technique refers to a highly concrete systematization of principles for dealing with a particular aspect of a particular subject. Thus methodology deals with the fundamental general problems: what evidence is admissible in the court of learning? in accord with what principles may relations be validly inferred between the various elements of such evidence? Theory, on the other hand, operates within a particular system: how can given sets of data best be conceptualized congruently with accepted principles of general methodology? As for the distinction between theory and method, Goring has expressed this with singular felicity:

. . . we must pass to some extent from the strict and narrow confines of ascertained certainty into the wider latitudes of theory, where the laws which govern the imagination in the construction of ideas are more paramount than those which regulate the intellect in its analysis of facts. The interpreting of fact involves operations different and distinct from those by which facts are established—it involves work of synthesis and exposition, not of analysis and discovery.

Technique is distinguishable from method only in so far as method involves the interrelations and consistency of a number of techniques. For example, archaeological method encompasses a number of techniques such as surveying, photographing, field cataloging and the like. Such techniques emphasize the details of the expert method.

Now if the reader does not like the words with which I have labeled these four somewhat separable types of operations, let him substitute other words or symbols. It is also perfectly true that these categories interdigitate and overlap at various points in our concrete activities. Nevertheless I maintain that such discriminations are useful toward developing greater awareness of what is inevitably involved in the acts of anthropologists as scholars. And I suggest that the greater number of students in the Middle

American field ignore the categories "methodology" and "theory" almost entirely in so far as one can judge from their published writings. If they use the word "theory" at all, they tend to use it as a pejorative synonym for "speculation." No anthropologist, however, can perform intellectual operations without some reference to the logics of scholarship in general and a theoretical system of premises and concepts pertinent to the data of anthropology. The practical question always becomes: is the anthropologist conscious of begging methodological questions and of choosing one theoretical position rather than another? If the methodology and theory are almost wholly beneath the level of consciousness it is axiomatic that they are inadequate. For all aspects of intellectual procedure must be made explicit in order that they may be subject to criticism and empirical testing.

In respect of the operations by which facts are established Middle American studies appear to be relatively sophisticated. The methods and techniques through which analysis and discovery proceeds seem to be subject to rigorous scrutiny and to be advancing constantly. By comparison, the methodological and theoretical development appears stunted indeed. Dr. Vaillant has indicated his awareness of the inevitable dependence of data, technique, and method upon theoretical preconceptions (1935a). In general, however, almost no realization of the dependence of one system of categories upon another is evident. The tradition is accepted; fundamental premises are not questioned, and development occurs only within the limitations imposed by the traditional premises and concepts. Even the Carnegie Institution's well-known and justly praised scheme for a many-sided attack by specialists drawn from varied disciplines is but an extension of the received system, an improvement of method by intensification and intellectual cross-fertilization.

No one, of course, has greater abhorrence of an archaeology which is on the intellectual

The Conceptual Structure
Clyde Kluckhohn

level of stamp collecting than Dr. Kidder. In the Year Book of the Carnegie Institution he has insistently reaffirmed the necessity for "work of synthesis and exposition," for interpreting facts as well as collecting them. Little effort seems, however, to have been given to developing an explicit and consistent logical scheme for attaining these ends. Thus far the published record suggests that his staff are still predominantly preoccupied with answering questions of a factual order. Dr. Kidder might reply that until we have a considerably fuller control of the facts generalization would be premature and misleading. Certainly the history of New World archaeology during this century gives us cause for alarm lest more synthetic interpretations which have an utterly inadequate observational basis become crystallized as sacrosanct dogmas. But unwarranted and stark synthesis is not to be identified in too cavalier a fashion with theory which means, first of all, examination of overt and covert premises (postulates and assumptions) and the general problem of the conceptualization of discrete data. There are, I think, grounds for believing that anthropologists generally have not quite kept on the forward march to the scientific frontiers in this respect. In a scientific world which was dominated by the *simpliste* mechanistic-positivistic philosophy to which Karl Pearson gave a definitive statement in "The Grammar of Science," it is true that the word *theory* wasn't quite respectable. In my observation the greater number of anthropologists still feel that "theorizing" is what you do when you are too lazy, or too impatient, or too much of an arm-chair person to go out and get the facts.

But for the point of view that ratiocination can properly begin only after *all* the facts have been garnered and harvested by observation anthropologists will get little support from their colleagues in science. There are many in the so-called social sciences today who subscribe to the naïve view that their subjects have failed of attainment because of too much "theory," whereas the sciences of matter have achieved honor and glory by eschewing theory and relentlessly observing facts. There is truth, to be sure, in the latter belief and it is undoubtedly true that there has been too little devotion to this task in some branches of "social science." But who has ever *seen* gravitation? One sees bodies fall and the theory of gravitation serves in a very satisfying manner as an explanation of their falling. Since, however, an element of reasoning, an element of inference (of drawing a conclusion which was not observed but in terms of which observations "make sense"!) enters into the matter, gravitation is not fact but conceptual scheme. Similarly, "Boyle's Law," with which every schoolboy is familiar and which has come to stand (in that vulgarization of physics and chemistry which is the common property of educated persons today) as a sort of type instance of scientific law is far from having that character of straightforward *description* of observed uniformities which is ordinarily imputed to it. No, inference is not a mode of thought with which the "natural sciences" have been able to dispense. If anyone affirms that theory has no place in Middle American studies until some fabled day when our factual knowledge approaches completeness, let him be reminded of the words in the "Manifesto on Freedom of Science" which has recently been signed by nearly fifteen hundred American scientists, including most of the members of the National Academy of Sciences:

The charge that theory leads to a "crippling of experimental research" is tantamount to a denial of the whole history of modern physics. From Copernicus and Kepler on, all the great figures in Western science have insisted, in deed or in word, upon the futility of experimental research divorced from theory.

Since no science can progress without inference, it becomes of critical importance that inference should not proceed along lines which are haphazard or capricious or controlled by unconscious prejudice. Since probably no fact has meaning except within the context of a conceptual scheme, archaeologists need to give their attention to these conceptual schemes as well as to the methods and techniques in accord with which data can be most efficiently discovered and analyzed. One lesson which the history of science seems most clearly to teach is that no science has prospered until it has defined its fundamental entities. A system of theory in any science involves a small number of categories and elementary relations between them. In mechanics, for example, these are: mass, location in space, direction of motion, velocity of motion. It is a symptom of the immaturity of anthropology that the logical instruments, the choice between alternative categories has been scandalously neglected. Ask an archaeologist to set forth and justify his conceptual scheme. It is an induction from my experience that the betting odds are enormous against this having even occurred to him as a problem. But if more archaeologists had given systematic thought to the logical implications of one concept which they continually use ("typology"), the problem of pottery classification in various areas in the New World would not be such a welter of confusion. Anthropologists generally have troubled themselves very little with what their conceptual tools actually meant if reduced to concrete human behaviors. The principal explanation for the misunderstandings surrounding the "Q-Complex" is assuredly that the referent for "complex" has been most ambivalent. This may be but the prejudice of a social anthropologist, but I do feel that, of late, the situation in social anthropology is more encouraging. Linton has made what seem to me to be major contributions to the conceptual structure of social anthropology. And, within the field of Middle American studies, Redfield and his coworkers appear to have formulated what they are trying to do much more explicitly and realistically than their archaeological associates.

What has been said of concepts holds very largely for premises also in the Middle American field. Most of the premises are indeed assumptions (covert premises) or axioms (premises taken as self-evident and not requiring proof). Scientific experience suggests that reasoning so premised is more than usually dangerous and treacherous. When one reasons by enthymemes one is proceeding blindly—not by conscious choice between points of departure which (while it may not prove in the light of facts later available to have been the wisest alternative), is at last patent to the investigator and to others as a choice and hence the more open to detection as a possible fallacy in the argument. Implicit in the reasoning of some of the leading workers in this field may be detected many unanalyzed, far-reaching assumptions as to cultural stability; the mechanics of diffusion; relationships of race, language, and culture; poly- and monogenesis; and the like. As for axiomatic reasoning, may it not simply be said that we are as yet hardly in a position to regard any feature of human behavior as altogether self-evident? And yet we find, for example, some of the most undemonstrated beliefs as to instinctive human needs taken as perfectly trustworthy axioms. Mathematics and most sciences have found it more satisfactory to proceed by the method of postulates (stated premises). The method of postulates is the "if . . . , then . . ." method. The scientist says, in effect, "The facts hardly enable us at present to make an absolutely clear-cut choice between the following alternative points of departure: However, since all discourse must proceed from premises we must make a highly provisional selection. I shall choose premises A, B, . . . X as my postulates simply because, on the whole, they seem to me most compendent with the available evidence. But all I assert for my thesis is that *if* future research supports the choice of these postulates, *then* my interpretation of the facts about to be discussed here should still hold true." In terms of what the psychoanalysts and others have taught us about the dangers of emotional identification with unconscious premises, the psychological ad-

83

vantages (and we should never forget in our scholarly work that we and our fellow scholars are always human beings!) of the method of postulates are tremendous.

In the writings of Middle American specialists I have found but little realization of the fact that all discourse proceeds from premises and that there should be some justification for the choice one makes between alternative premises. Even the very central issue seems hardly to have been grappled with. Are Middle American students interested in their data primarily as evidencing (to some extent at least) certain trends toward uniformity in the responses of human beings toward types of stimuli (environmental, contractual, biological, and the like) or are they primarily interested in their data as unique events, to be described and imaginatively recreated (in so far as possible) in all their particularity? Interests of both of these types seem perfectly legitimate—as opposed to the antiquarian interest which makes the collection of specimens an end in itself. It will be convenient and in conformity with contemporary usage to designate these two legitimate types of interest as "scientific" and "historical" respectively. The position of the leaders in this field can only be inferred for the most part. That of Tozzer,[1] Lothrop, Spinden, the Pennsylvania group, and most of the German scholars appears to be resolutely historical. Such a position seems to me quite defensible, but a reasoned justification of the stand would seem to be in the interests of clarification. Perhaps these are not, ideally, two distinct types of interest. The thesis that they are but two sequent phases of a planned research might even be maintained. Actually, however, it is an experiential generalization that material collected and published by the "historically" minded is seldom suitable for "scientific" analysis. A focus of interest upon events in their uniqueness, a concentration of effort upon recapturing the sequence of one specific set of events (rather than upon the elements which a class of events may have in common) is most unlikely to provide that quantitative basis for generalization which is scientifically essential. As a practical matter, then, choice rather than combination of premises, seems to be involved and one's choice of premise here very definitely has consequences for one's whole conceptual structure. It should also have consequences for method and techniques, for a method of discovering and analyzing facts should not be incongruous with fundamental premises and the related concepts which are to be used as instruments in synthesizing the facts.

The interests of Kidder and Vaillant appear to be verging upon the scientific, but a full discussion of this very critical question from them would assuredly be most helpful and welcome. Dr. Kidder has recently written: "Archaeology and history seek to picture man's past; ethnology and the other social sciences to record the conditions under which he lives today. Both groups gather and analyze data necessary for understanding the nature of man and the structure of the modern world" (Kidder und Thompson 1938:493).

But are we to "understand the nature of man" through the reflections which the reading of history stimulates in the thoughtful person? Is the "structure of the modern world" to be revealed by flashes of intuition catalyzed by historical insight or by the inductive generalizations of science? A systematic and rigorous exposition of the conceptual means by which these admirable objectives can be achieved would seem useful. Possibly Dr. Kidder's insistence upon archaeology as history is simply with a view to giving "a time-backbone" to the data which are to be grist to the mill of the generalizing approach. If so, one can only applaud. However, the light in which the members of the Carnegie staff view various specific questions reveals fairly consistent historical rather than scientific interests. Take, for example, the problem of the end of the "Great Period" and possible evacuation of Peten and Usumacinta sites. The many references to this in the writings of this group indicate a desire to explain these phenomena in all their historical uniqueness rather than a wish to extract from the events whatever bears upon the recurring regularities in human behavior. At all events, one wants to know whether the work of the Carnegie Institution aims, to use Kroeber's phrases, at historical integrations in terms of sequences and larger culture wholes or at processual integrations in terms of conceptual constants. Is the cardinal intention to preserve phenomena intact as phenomena or "to decompose phenomena in order to determine processes as such?" The scientific attack would seem to me preferable. While taking account always of the circumstance that the processes which control events are imbedded in time as well as in space and in the structure of social forms, a primary interest in discovering the trends toward uniformity in human behavior under specified conditions will be, I feel sure, the more fruitful. Problems need to be formulated with a view to illuminating the generalities of human action (often inferentially through study of artifacts or other cultural products) by the searchlight of simple induction and the method of agreement and difference.

There are signs, fortunately, that archaeologists are coming to grips with the somewhat more abstract problems which bear upon their studies. Surely a new epoch dawns when the professional journal of American archaeology publishes a leading article entitled "Function and Configuration in Archaeology" (Stewart and Setzler 1938). Even

earlier, Strong gave us his enlightened and enlightening essay "Anthropological Theory and Archaeological Fact" (1936). But while one may agree wholeheartedly with him that anthropology ". . . is a broad, historical science concerned with the relationship of cultural and biological factors through time and space," one must insist in the same breath that the conceptual tools for determining this relationship have very largely yet to be forged. The very sophistication at the levels of method and technique makes the methodological and theoretical naïveté of Middle American studies stand out in shocking contrast. Surely, if the total structure is to be substantially founded and to have balance, methodology and theory must receive the same systematic, persistent, and rigorous treatment which has been accorded to method and technique. Factual richness and conceptual poverty are a poor pair of hosts at an intellectual banquet. A proper hunger for facts and an impatience for an answer to many burning factual questions must not result in a relative sterility and futility of effort. Such, at any rate, is the perhaps mistaken and certainly very humble (but also very honest) opinion of one anthropologist who is a layman in this specialized field.

NOTE

1. See, however, Tozzer 1937a:152, 159; and Tozzer 1937b:338.

Review of James A. Ford's
Measurements of Some Prehistoric Design Developments in the Southeastern States

FORD'S PAPER deals with the relative chronological position of a considerable number of archaeological pottery assemblages. In nearly every case the assemblage is a collection of potsherds found in an arbitrarily defined vertical component of a test excavation in refuse deposits or in a stratum resulting from two or more definable phases of earth mound construction. The chronological positions assigned are said to be inferences derived from 1) the evidence of superposition, 2) an application of the widely accepted proposition that two assemblages which resemble each other closely are not far removed in time, and 3) an evolutionary ranking of certain ceramic attributes and attribute combinations in terms of ancestral and descendant types. A considerable part of the publication is devoted to the closely related problem of determining the point of first appearance (within the area considered) of certain attributes, and the direction and relative speed of their diffusion together with concomitant changes in their physical ex-

Reproduced by permission of the reviewer and the American Anthropological Association from *American Anthropologist,* vol. 55, 1953, pp. 589–91. Originally published as a review entitled: *"Measurements of Some Prehistoric Design Developments in the Southeastern States.* James A. Ford. (35 pp., 23 figs. Anthropological Papers of the American Museum of Natural History, vol. 44, part 3. New York 1952.)"

pression. The term *measurement* presumably refers to use of pottery type percentages; although the word appears a number of times in the text, I was unable to find a coherent statement of what was measured with respect to what scale. It appears, however, to be employed on occasion roughly as an equivalent for counting and ranking, a decidedly misleading practice.

No effort will be made to summarize and discuss specific results, on the ground that the study reveals such serious methodological deficiencies as to make an appraisal of the reliability and implications of the conclusions unprofitable. Under these circumstances, the reviewer's task must be an attempt to validate his judgment by describing and illustrating the putative defects. Since the errors are primarily fundamental misapprehensions of scientific method rather than narrowly technical slips, they are of general interest.

Two characteristic examples can be drawn from the Introduction, which is intended to show the general position of archaeology with relation to cultural anthropology. The first example (pp. 317–18) is the statement:

However, archaeologists have perhaps less excuse than students in any other field to be blind to the fact that not only the methods but the ultimate objectives of their discipline are slowly but inevitably changing. One of the present less-popular concepts of the purposes of archaeological study will become the objective of the majority and then historiography pursued for its own sake will be old-fashioned. Of course, any new objective will in turn be superseded, but we probably cannot now imagine in what way; neither can we be too concerned with this nebulous cultural type that will evolve from a stage of this discipline that is not yet fully developed. It is sufficient to recognize that our study is merely another example of cultural phenomena and to align our activities in the direction of the historical trend. To endeavor to exceed the limits of sound methodology and information is quite as unrealistic as to lag behind. Dissipating effort in some divergent bypath destined to be abandoned is a waste of time. The most productive position is one slightly in advance of the majority.

This statement fails to recognize the fundamental principle that we possess a method of investigation which will disclose real truths (or approximations to real truths) about a real world if it is properly applied. The fact that this method is of cultural origin is inconsequential as a guide for action. Soundness of archaeological methodology and productivity can be gauged only in terms of additions to knowledge. The ultimate objective of archaeology is immutable—it is to achieve a systematic interconnection of facts within the field of archaeological data, and of archaeological data to all other data. This is, of course, an ideal toward which the archaeologist struggles by successive approximations, but it is one which must be kept firmly in mind if archaeology is to be maintained as an intellectually respectable pursuit. The only changes which can occur are those connected with immediate objectives within the framework of this general purpose; they are the result of the continuous process of observation—hypothesis—new observation. Ford's propositions carry the logical implications that truth is to be determined by some sort of polling of archaeologists, that productivity is doing what other archaeologists do, and that the only purpose of archaeology is to make archaeologists happy. This is simply a specialized version of the "life is just a game" constellation of ideas, a philosophical position

which cannot be tolerated in a scientific context.

The second example (p. 318) of defective reasoning is the ascription of logical priority to archaeological studies: "Every living culture is composed of elements inherited from the past and modified. To attempt to describe and analyze any culture without this background resembles the description of a mountain range without reference to historical geology: it is art, not science." One of the implications of this statement is the notion that limited objectives cannot be pursued in a scientific manner, disheartening news to topographers, structural geologists, linguists, ethnographers, and indeed to any working scientist, since the act of working automatically imposes limitations. Descriptions and analyses which are consciously and systematically less than ideal are a fundamental feature of scientific research. A second objectionable implication is the dictum that the present can be understood only in terms of the past. In point of fact, all our knowledge of the past consists of inferences based on observation of current processes and on present material interpreted as relics of the past, a situation which effectively precludes any claim of special priority for historical studies. Historical inferences provide no more than a part of the data required for the understanding of currently existing culture and are indispensable only in the sense that an ideal description demands the marshaling of all relevant evidence.

Similar flaws in reasoning are at least as prevalent at the level of specific problems. An important part of Ford's research consists of ordering components on the basis of their degree of likeness, on the assumption that such an ordering will reflect closely or exactly their chronological rank. The units of likeness are potsherds exhibiting a specified combination of attributes (a "pottery type" in the customary terminology of American archaeology); for ordering, the potsherds of a given type from a component are counted and the total is divided by the total

87

of all potsherds to give a percentage expression of the frequency of the attribute
combination. A component can then be
represented by a histogram, the individual
bars showing on a percentage scale the relative frequencies of each of the pottery types
noted, and the histograms of a group of
successive components drawn from one cultural tradition can ideally be arranged on a
chart so that the bars for each pottery type
form a smooth unimodal curve. There are, of
course, a large number of arrangements
possible if many components are to be
ordered, although in practice most can be
eliminated at once as absurd. A second feature of practical work is the fact that perfect
arrangements are never possible, presumably
owing to such factors as inadequate samples,
multiple occupations, disturbed deposits, errors in typology, geographical variation, and
so on. In Ford's case, arrangements were
made entirely by graphical methods, with the
result that he can only assert that his final
ordering is the best possible under the circumstances and reproduce the graphs to sub-
stantiate the assertion. The absence of any
mathematical expression of degree of fit
leaves the skeptical reader with no recourse
other than reproducing the component histograms and trying new arrangements himself,
a task which is made difficult by the absence
of the original counts on which the percentages were calculated.

A far more serious objection to Ford's attack on the problem can be made, however.
This objection is, briefly, that no effective
consideration is given to negative data. The
numerous discrepancies in the lengths of percentage bars are dismissed on the basis of
sampling error, disturbed deposits, and the
like, but no attempt whatsoever has been
made at an independent classification of components in terms of adequacy of sample or
presence or absence of disturbance. This substitution of ad hoc explanations for systematic classification is not in accord with
basic scientific principles and results in a hypothesis lacking in logical implications and

hence incapable of being tested. The general
impression given by the presentation is that
the true situation is known on the basis of
evidence not available to the reader, and consequently that the cause of any particular
discrepancy is of no great importance and
can be treated in an offhand manner.

An example of this tendency is the treatment of certain data from the western part of
the Florida Gulf Coast (Figure 4). Here, in
accordance with Ford's standard practice,
each set of bars representing a pottery type
is fitted with a "smoothing curve" purporting
to show the unimodal trend of percentage
frequencies. It appeared on inspection that
the smoothing operation was more in the
nature of a bloody amputation. This impression was checked by computing Spearman's
Rank Correlation Coefficient for each type
and then calculating Student's t to test the
significance of the correlation coefficients.
Half of the calculations of t resulted in probabilities between .50 and .10 (and in one
case of more than .50), which indicates that
very often no particular relationship exists
between the smoothing curves and the data
which they are supposed to represent. Although it can be granted freely that these
calculations by no means exhaust the subject,
they are sufficient evidence to establish the
existence of a very serious problem ignored
by Ford, especially when it is realized that
the smoothing curves and not the histograms
are used in drawing chronological inferences.
In this connection, it is interesting to note
that all possible arrangements of a four bar
histogram show a significant trend if one bar
is allowed to be out of place, i.e., they must
show an ascending order, descending order,
or a peak if the bars are of different lengths;
furthermore, either an ascending or a descending order will appear by chance alone
9 out of 24 times and a peak will appear in
16 out of 24 trials.

Other examples of inadequate or erroneous
method could be cited, but it is more important to consider the general problem
raised by Ford's publication: to ask how

these errors could be committed in a field which is scientific in intent. Ford is an energetic and respected archaeologist with a detailed knowledge of southeastern prehistory. Many of his interpretations may prove to be correct, but his methods of analysis and presentation deprive him of the opportunity to prove their correctness. The principles he uses are well-recognized and can be employed to yield valid results. Perhaps there is too much pressure for immediate results. It can only be hoped that careful evaluation of Ford's work will serve as a corrective and demonstrate to all archaeologists the necessity for rigorous methodology.

PART 3

The Theoretical Base
of Contemporary Archaeology

Introduction

The vast bulk of the essays in the second half of this volume are derived implicitly or explicitly from the ideas invented and explained in the articles in this section. Although the assumptions of processual archaeology, as well as the rest of its theoretical framework, are incompletely synthesized yet, enough exists for a very convincing approach to problems.

As the ideas motivating many archaeologists are voiced by Lewis Binford, they represent an archaeology-specific version of materialist-based cultural evolution. Whitean evolution or neoevolution or cultural materialism has been extant since before the 1940s in anthropology. But it has required a readaptation of those concepts before they could be utilized by archaeologists. That readaptation has involved the incorporation of ideas not given explicit emphasis in neoevolution, the most important of which is systems theory. But even that notion proceeds necessarily from primary concern with the processes of cultural change.

Archaeologists of any era are predisposed to cultural materialism, and also, it can be argued, to notions of ordered cultural change, like evolution. The material artifacts, not the ideas, of cultures survive and are the data-base of the subdiscipline. Likewise the data exist over time, and sometimes over enormous spans of time. That the data can be seen to change systematically would seem to predispose archaeologists to ideas of developmental process. Despite the obvious truth of these two statements, archaeologists have only been implicit cultural materialists and have for long periods decried the idea of cultural evolution. Among the contributions made in recent theoretical statements is explicit use of materialistic determinism, of evolution, and, crucially, of the notion that technology in addition to being a critical variable reflects all the cultural sub-systems operating on it.

The idea that an item of material culture, an artifact, as a product of a culture and its various subsystems, is also a statement about those subsystems is new. That painted pottery could be tied to kinship and residence came as a revelation. Archaeologists have always suspected a connection between objects and social organization and religion. Much of the early, provocative speculation of nineteenth-century archaeologists was based on an assumed connection. But their imprecision and speculation differ from the more secure knowledge that exists now. And that security comes not from assuming that some artifacts operate primarily in the economic or social or religious realm, but that any artifact operates in all realms. At least it may to varying degrees, depending on the artifact. And as a result of operating in all realms of culture, an artifact is formed by all and potentially can be made to inform on all the systems which brought it into existence in the first place. This is the logical basis for Binford's claim that all of a cultural system is potentially recoverable. This claim logically proceeds from systems theory which assumes the mutual if unequal interdependence and reflection of the subsystems in a system. The technological subsystem must then necessarily reflect the economic, social, and religious subsystems which are all a part of the same whole.

Allied with the assumption that an artifact can function at all levels of culture is the idea that the variation in any class of artifacts may represent important variation in one of the subsystems in which the artifact operates, or which operated on the artifact. Variations in jar collars or painted designs on pots were connected with variation in family descent and postmarital residence. The stress has been placed on the variability in a type, not on the norm for the type. It was only when Wilmsen, for example (see this volume) dealt with the variation within Paleo-Indian tool kits that he discovered the precision of local ecological adaptations within what had previously been regarded as a far more homogeneous tool tradition. The range of variability within a group of artifacts is connected to the artifacts' function. When it is seen that all purposes tolerate some range of variation, individuals and situations never being identical, then it can be seen how an artifact can be assessed to inform on the system that created it. To state the assumption again, the range of variation within a class of artifacts (size, shape, and a hundred other traits of pots, projectile points, grinding stones and so on) may be a direct reflection of the variability within the cultural subsystems the artifact operated in. The quantity, quality, size and other characteristics of classic Maya funeral pottery are a direct reflection of the scope, divisions, and changes in Classic Maya social stratification (see Rathje in this volume). This follows just as readily as saying that size variation in cooking vessels may be a direct function of the kind of food prepared or served in them. It is not coincidental that the techniques for measurement now so popular in archaeology enter at a time when variation, not the average, is seen to be a key to adaptation and function.

Systems theory's ramifications in archaeology do not end here however. The theory contributes a more sophisticated notion of process. The notion involves groups of related variables, rather than two or three isolated ones, moved through time and whose mutual interaction becomes paramount as opposed to simple statements or assumptions based on a unidirectional notion of cause.

Certainly the concern with evolutionary ideas is a predominating element in the current changes in archaeology. The most convincing citations for that concern revolve around studies in cultural ecology. The adaptive histories of specific cultures and the adaptive efficiency of given subsystems are probably the single major concern for processual archaeologists. Whether it is the reconstruction of the economy, ecological adjustment, settlement pattern, kin organization, or religious postulates, most studies produced by interested archaeologists are concerned with the articulation between one subsystem and some aspect of the economic base. All of this is done with a concern for illustrating how a culture adapts to its environment by processes of differentiation and increasing complexity of organization. The end product of such studies is to show how a culture becomes more autonomous from its environment, natural and cultural, than its less complex predecessors.

The reader will note that much of the background theory used in the articles collected here comes from social science and from general anthropology. That culture should be explained in terms of culture, not in terms of biology or geology or climate, is a completely unmentioned postulate here. Not only is its advent in archaeology fairly recent, but it is one of the crucial ideas gathered from anthropology. The same is true of cultural materialism, scientific world view, the existence of a relative notion of reality, and the very idea of evolution. It is important to note that archaeology is not a private world, but is a part of anthropology and, often without knowing, is subject to the selective pressures of evolution just as all sciences are.

In this section, the careful reader will see two divergences from what is becoming accepted opinion in processual archaeology. James Deetz is suggesting a novel experiment for archaeologists. He is curious about the nature of the relationship between material culture and behavior, a relationship he would remove from the prehistoric straitjacket. Whether this means the advent of a science of technology or something else is unclear. Similar ideas have been suggested by

David Clark in *Analytical Archaeology* (1968:20–24). Not at all unclear, however, is the possible redefinition of archaeology in the light of Deetz's suggestion. At the very least, Deetz's idea is one which archaeology is already heading toward under the guises of ethnographic archaeology and historic archaeology.

It should be kept in mind that as systems theory has allowed us a wider vision of the ranges of culture that can be discussed by using artifacts, it also allows us to see that an artifact must have enormous repercussions on other cultural subsystems. This assumption goes under the name of technological determinism. And it is something about which we know almost nothing. To be sure we understand the direct relationship between tools and productivity and can measure that. But we do not understand the relationship between artifacts and social organization or religion. That there is a relationship we are sure. What is it? Why do good fences make good neighbors, or rather, how? To borrow holy water, White's perennial example to show the arbitrary relation between an object and its meaning, what is it about water that it can be made holy? What are the properties of an artifact (including water, for a moment) that allow it to function in social and religious domains? And even more important, how does an object form and influence social and religious behavior? These are questions asked by a science of technology.

The article by Schuyler on historic archaeology is a dual effort attempting to place that archaeological subfield squarely within anthropology, but also stressing the huge potential for studies of culture change and the science of technology latent in the use of historic materials. If there is any link between the five pieces here, it is concern with processual or directional change, evolution. Underlying that is an enormous excitement at what archaeology is becoming, at what it can be selected for, and of the challenges that make it so especially appealing at this time.

Archaeology as Anthropology

IT HAS been aptly stated that "American archaeology is anthropology or it is nothing" (Willey and Phillips 1958:2). The purpose of this discussion is to evaluate the role which the archaeological discipline is playing in furthering the aims of anthropology and to offer certain suggestions as to how we, as archaeologists, may profitably shoulder more responsibility for furthering the aims of our field.

Initially, it must be asked, "What are the aims of anthropology?" Most will agree that the integrated field is striving to explicate and explain the total range of physical and cultural similarities and differences characteristic of the entire spatial-temporal span of man's existence (for discussion, see Kroeber 1953). Archaeology has certainly made major contributions as far as explication is concerned. Our current knowledge of the diversity which characterizes the range of extinct cultural systems is far superior to the limited knowledge available fifty years ago. Although this contribution is "admirable" and necessary, it has been noted that archaeology has made essentially no contribution in the realm of explanation: "So little work has been done in American archaeology on the explanatory level that it is difficult to find a name for it" (Willey and Phillips 1958:5).

Before carrying this criticism further, some statement about what is meant by explanation must be offered. The meaning which explana-

Reprinted from *American Antiquity,* vol. 28, no. 2, 1962, pp. 217–25. By permission of the author and the Society for American Archaeology.

tion has within a scientific frame of reference is simply the demonstration of a constant articulation of variables within a system and the measurement of the concomitant variability among the variables within the system. Processual change in one variable can then be shown to relate in a predictable and quantifiable way to changes in other variables, the latter changing in turn relative to changes in the structure of the system as a whole. This approach to explanation presupposes concern with process, or the operation and structural modification of systems. It is suggested that archaeologists have not made major explanatory contributions to the field of anthropology because they do not conceive of archaeological data in a systemic frame of reference. Archaeological data are viewed particularistically and "explanation" is offered in terms of specific events rather than in terms of process (see Buettner-Janusch 1957 for discussion of particularism).

Archaeologists tacitly assume that artifacts, regardless of their functional context, can be treated as equal and comparable "traits." Once differences and similarities are "defined" in terms of these equal and comparable "traits," interpretation proceeds within something of a theoretical vacuum that conceives of differences and similarities as the result of "blending," "directional influences," and "stimulation" between and among "historical traditions" defined largely on the basis of postulated local or regional continuity in the human populations.

I suggest that this undifferentiated and unstructured view is inadequate, that artifacts having their primary functional context in different operational subsystems of the total cultural system will exhibit differences and similarities differentially, in terms of the structure of the cultural system of which they were a part. Further, that the temporal and spatial spans within and between broad functional categories will vary with the structure of the systematic relationships between sociocultural systems. Study of these differential distributions can potentially yield valuable information concerning the nature of social organization within, and changing relationships between, sociocultural systems. In short, the explanation of differences and similarities between archaeological complexes must be offered in terms of our current knowledge of the structural and functional characteristics of cultural systems.

Specific "historical" explanations, if they can be demonstrated, simply explicate mechanisms of cultural process. They add nothing to the explanation of the processes of cultural change and evolution. If migrations can be shown to have taken place, then this explication presents an explanatory problem; what adaptive circumstances, evolutionary processes, induced the migration (Thompson 1958a:1)? We must seek explanation in systemic terms for classes of historical events such as migrations, establishment of "contact" between areas previously isolated, etc. Only then will we make major contributions in the area of explanation and provide a basis for the further advancement of anthropological theory.

As an exercise in explication of the methodological questions raised here, I will present a general discussion of a particular systemic approach in the evaluation of archaeological assemblages and utilize these distinctions in an attempted explanation of a particular set of archaeological observations.

Culture is viewed as the extra-somatic means of adaptation for the human organism (White 1959:8). I am concerned with all those subsystems within the broader cultural system which are: (a) extra-somatic, or not dependent upon biological process for modification or structural definition (this is not to say that the form and process cannot be viewed as rooted in biological process, only that diversity and processes of diversification are not explicable in terms of biological process), and which (b) function to adapt the human organism, conceived generically, to its total environment both physical and social.

Within this framework it is consistent to view technology, those tools and social relationships which articulate the organism with the physical environment, as closely related to the nature of the environment. For example, we would not expect to find large quantities of fishhooks among the recent archaeological remains from the Kalahari desert! However, this view must not be thought of as "environmental determinism" for we assume a systematic relationship between the human organism and his environment in which culture is the intervening variable. In short, we are speaking of the ecological system (Steward 1955:36). We can observe certain constant adaptive requirements on the part of the organism and similarly certain adaptive limitations, given specific kinds of environment. However, limitations as well as the potential of the environment must be viewed always in terms of the intervening variable in the human ecological system, that is, culture.

With such an approach we should not be surprised to note similarities in technology among groups of similar levels of social complexity inhabiting the boreal forest (Spaulding 1946) or any other broad environmental zone. The comparative study of cultural systems with variable technologies in a similar environmental range or similar technologies in differing environments is a major methodology of what Steward (1955:36–42) has called "cultural ecology," and certainly is a valuable means of increasing our understanding of cultural processes. Such a methodology is also useful in elucidating the structural relationships between major cultural subsystems. Prior to the initiation of such studies by archaeologists we must be able to distinguish those relevant artifactual elements within the total artifact assemblage which have the primary functional context in the social, technological, and ideological subsystems of the total cultural system. We should not equate "material culture" with technology. Similarly we should not seek explanations for observed differences and similarities in "material culture" within a single interpretative frame of reference. It has often been suggested that we cannot dig up a social system or ideology. Granted we cannot excavate a kinship terminology or a philosophy, but we can and do excavate the material items which functioned together with these more behavioral elements within the appropriate cultural subsystems. The formal structure of artifact assemblages together with the between element contextual relationships should and do present a systematic and understandable picture of *the total extinct* cultural system. It is no more justifiable for archaeologists to attempt explanation of certain formal, temporal, and spatial similarities and differences within a single frame of reference than it would be for an ethnographer to attempt explanation of differences in cousin terminology, levels of sociocultural integration, styles of dress, and modes of transportation all with the same variables or within the same frame of reference. These classes or items are articulated differently within an integrated cultural system, hence the pertinent variables with which each is articulated, and exhibit concomitant variation are different. This fact obviates the single explanatory frame of reference. The processes of change pertinent to each are different because of the different ways in which they function in contributing to the total adaptive system.

Consistent with this line of reasoning is the assertion that we as archaeologists must face the problem of identifying technomic artifacts from other artifactual forms. Technomic signifies those artifacts having their primary functional context in coping directly with the physical environment. Variability in the technomic components of archaeological assemblages is seen as primarily explicable in the ecological frame of reference. Here, we must concern ourselves with such phenomena as extractive efficiency, efficiency in performing bio-compensatory tasks such as heat retention, the nature of available resources, their distribution, density, and loci of availability, etc. In this area of research and explanation, the archaeologist is in a position to make a direct contribution to the field of anthropology. We can directly correlate technomic items with environmental variables since we can know the distribution of fossil flora and fauna from independent data—giving us the nature of extinct environments.

Another major class of artifacts which the archaeologists recover can be termed sociotechnic. These artifacts were the material elements having their primary functional context in the social subsystems of the total cultural system. This subsystem functions as the extrasomatic means of articulating individuals one with another into cohesive groups capable of efficiently maintaining themselves and of manipulating the technology. Artifacts such as a king's crown, a warrior's coup stick, a copper from the Northwest coast, etc., fall into this category. Changes in the relative complexity of the sociotechnic component of an archaeological assemblage can be related to changes in the structure of the social system which they represent. Certainly the evolutionary processes, while correlated and related, are not the same for explaining structural changes in technological and social phenomena. Factors such as demography, presence or absence of between-group competition, etc., as well as the basic factors which affect technological change, must be considered when attempting to explain social change. Not only are the relevant variables different, there is a further difference when speaking of sociotechnic artifacts. The explanation of the basic form and structure of the sociotechnic component of an artifactual assemblage lies in the nature and structure of the social system which it represents. Observable differences and changes in the sociotechnic components of archaeological assemblages must be explained with reference to structural changes in the social system and in terms of processes of social change and evolution.

Thus, archaeologists can initially only indirectly contribute to the investigation of social evolution. I would consider the study and establishment of correlations between types of social structure classified on the basis of behavioral attributes and structural types of material elements as one of the major areas of anthropological research yet to be developed. Once such correlations are established, archaeologists can attack the problems of evolutionary change in social systems. It is my opinion that only when we have the entire temporal span of cultural evolution as our "laboratory" can we make substantial gains in the critical area of social anthropological research.

The third major class of items which archaeologists frequently recover can be termed ideotechnic artifacts. Items of this class have their primary functional context in the ideological component of the social system. These are the items which signify and symbolize the ideological rationalizations for the social system and further provide the symbolic milieu in which individuals are enculturated, a necessity if they are to take their place as functional participants in the social system. Such items as figures of deities, clan symbols, symbols of natural agencies, etc., fall into this general category. Formal diversity in the structural complexity and in functional classes of this category of items must generally be related to changes in the structure of the society, hence explanations must be sought in the local adaptive situation rather than in the area of "historical explanations." As was the case with sociotechnic items, we must seek to establish correlations between generic classes of the ideological system and the structure of the material symbolism. Only·after such correlations have been established can archaeologists study in a systematic way this component of the social subsystem.

Cross-cutting all of these general classes of artifacts are formal characteristics which can be termed stylistic, formal qualities that are not directly explicable in terms of the nature of the raw materials, technology of production, or variability in the structure of the technological and social sub-systems of the total cultural system. These formal qualities are believed to have their primary functional context in providing a symbolically diverse yet pervasive artifactual environment promoting group solidarity and serving as a basis for group awareness and identity. This pan-systemic set of symbols is the milieu of enculturation and a basis for the recognition of social distinctiveness. "One of the main functions of the arts as communication is to reinforce belief, custom, and values" (Beals and Hoijer 1955:548). The distribution of style types and traditions is believed to be largely correlated with areas of commonality in level of cultural complexity and in mode of adaptation. Changes in the temporal-spatial distribution of style types are believed to be related to changes in the structure of sociocultural systems either brought about through processes of in situ evolution, or by changes in the cultural environment to which local sociocultural systems are adapted, thereby initiating evolutionary change. It is believed that stylistic attributes are most fruitfully studied when questions of ethnic origin, migration, and interaction between groups is the subject of explication. However, when explanations are sought, the total adaptive context of the sociocultural system in question must be investigated. In this field of research archaeologists are in an excellent position to make major contributions to the general field of anthropology, for we can work directly in terms of correlations of the structure of artifact assemblages with rates of style change, directions of style-spread, and stability of style-continuity.

Having recognized three general functional

classes of artifacts: technomic, sociotechnic, and ideotechnic, as well as a category of formal stylistic attributes, each characterized by differing functions within the total cultural system and correspondingly different processes of change, it is suggested that our current theoretical orientation is insufficient and inadequate for attempting explanation. It is argued that explanations of differences and similarities between archaeological assemblages as a whole must first consider the nature of differences in each of these major categories and only after such evaluation can adequate explanatory hypotheses be offered.

Given this brief and oversimplified introduction, I will turn to a specific case, the Old Copper complex (Wittry and Ritzenthaler 1956). It has long been observed and frequently cited as a case of technological "devolution" that during the Archaic period fine and superior copper utilitarian tools were manufactured, whereas, during Early and Middle Woodland times copper was used primarily for the production of nonutilitarian items (Griffin 1952*b*:356). I will explore this interesting situation in terms of: 1) the frame of reference presented here, 2) generalizations which have previously been made concerning the nature of culture change, and 3) a set of hypotheses concerning the relationships between certain forms of sociotechnic artifacts and the structure of the social systems that they represent.

The normal assumption when thinking about the copper artifacts typical of the Old Copper complex is that they are primarily technomic (manufactured for use in directly coping with the physical environment). It is generally assumed that these tools were superior to their functional equivalents in both stone and bone because of their durability and presumed superiority in accomplishing cutting and piercing tasks. It is a common generalization that within the realm of technology more efficient forms tend to replace less efficient forms. The Old Copper case seems to be an exception.

Absolute efficiency in performance is only one side of the coin when viewed in an adaptive context. Adaptive efficiency must also be viewed in terms of economy, that is, energy expenditure versus energy conservation (White 1959:54). For one tool to be adaptively more efficient than another there must be either a lowering of energy expenditure per unit of energy of conservation in task performance, or an increase in energy conservation per unit of performance over a constant energy expenditure in tool production. Viewed this way, we may question the position that copper tools were technologically more efficient. The production of copper tools utilizing the techniques employed in the manufacture of Old Copper specimens certainly required tremendous expenditures of both time and labor. The sources of copper are not in the areas of most dense Old Copper implements (Wittry 1951), hence travel to the sources, or at least the establishment of logistics networks based on kin ties extending over large areas, was a prerequisite for the procurement of the raw material. Extraction of the copper, using the primitive mining techniques exemplified by the aboriginal mining pits on Isle Royale and the Keewenaw Peninsula (Holmes 1901), required further expenditure of time and labor. Raw materials for the production of the functional equivalents of the copper tools was normally available locally or at least available at some point within the bounds of the normal exploitative cycle. Extraction was essentially a gathering process requiring no specialized techniques, and could be accomplished incidental to the performance of other tasks. Certainly in terms of expenditures of time and energy, as regards the distribution of sources of raw materials and techniques of extraction, copper required a tremendous expenditure as opposed to raw materials of stone and bone.

The processing phase of tool production appears to present an equally puzzling ratio with regard to expenditure of energy. The processing of copper into a finished artifact normally requires the separation of crystalline impurities from the copper. Following this processing phase, normal procedure seems to have been to pound and partially flatten small bits of copper which were then pounded together to "build" an artifact (Cushing 1894). Once the essential shape had been achieved, further hammering, grinding, and polishing were required. I suggest that this process is more time consuming than shaping and finishing an artifact by chipping flint, or even the pecking and grinding technique employed in the production of ground stone tools. It follows that there was a much greater expenditure of time and energy in the production of copper tools than in the production of their functional equivalents in either bone or stone.

Turning now to the problem of energy conservation in task performance, we may ask what differentials existed. It seems fairly certain that copper was probably more durable and could have been utilized for a longer period of time. As far as what differentials existed between copper and stone, as regards cutting and piercing functions, only experiments can determine. Considering all of the evidence, the quality of durability appears to have been the only possible realm which could compensate for the differentials in expenditure of energy between stone and bone as opposed to copper in the area of procurement and processing of the raw material. What evidence exists that would suggest that durability was in fact the compensatory quality which made copper tools technologically more efficient?

All the available evidence suggests the contrary intrepretation. First, we do not have evidence that the raw material was reused to any great extent once an artifact was broken or "worn out." If this had been the case, we would expect to have a general lack of battered and "worn out" pieces and some examples of reworked pieces, whereas evidence of use is a common characteristic of recovered specimens, and to my knowledge reworked pieces are uncommon if not unknown.

Second, when found in a primary archaeological context, copper tools are almost in-

variably part of burial goods. If durability was the compensatory factor in the efficiency equation, certainly some social mechanism for retaining the copper tools as functioning parts of the technology would have been established. This does not appear to have been the case. Since durability can be ruled out as the compensatory factor, we must conclude that copper tools were not technologically more efficient than their functional equivalents in both stone and bone. Having reached this "conclusion," it remains to explore the problem of the initial appearance of copper tools and to examine the observation that there was a shift from the use of copper for the production of utilitarian tools to nonutilitarian items.

It is proposed that the observed shift and the initial appearance of copper tools can best be explained under the hypothesis that they did not function primarily as technomic items. I suggest that in both the Old Copper and later cultural systems to the south, copper was utilized primarily for the production of sociotechnic items.

Fried (1960) discusses certain pertinent distinctions between societies with regard to systems of status grading. Societies on a low general level of cultural complexity, measured in terms of functional specialization and structural differentiation, normally have an "egalitarian" system of status grading. The term "egalitarian" signifies that status positions are open to all persons within the limits of certain sex and age classes, who through their individual physical and mental characteristics are capable of greater achievement in coping with the environment. Among societies of greater complexity, status grading may be less egalitarian. Where ranking is the primary mechanism of status grading, status positions are closed. There are qualifications for attainment that are not simply a function of one's personal physical and mental capabilities.

A classic example of ranking is found among societies with a ramage form of social organization (Sahlins 1958:139–80). In such

societies status is determined by one's proximity in descent from a common ancestor.
High status is accorded those in the direct
line of descent, calculated in terms of primo-
geniture, while cadet lines of descent occupy
positions of lower status depending on their
proximity to the direct line.

Another form of internally ranked system
is one in which attainment of a particular
status position is closed to all except those
members of a particular kin group who may
occupy a differentiated status position, but
open to all members of that kin group on an
egalitarian basis.

Other forms of status grading are recognized, but for the purposes of this discussion
the major distinction between egalitarian and
ranked systems is sufficient. I propose that
there is a direct relationship between the
nature of the system of status grading within
a society and the quantity, form, and structure of sociotechnic components of its archaeological assemblage.

It is proposed that among egalitarian societies status symbols are symbolic of the
technological activities for which outstanding
performance is rewarded by increased status.
In many cases they will be formally technomic items manufactured of "exotic" material or elaborately decorated and/or pains-
takingly manufactured. I do not imply that
the items could not or were not used tech-
nomically, simply that their presence in the
assemblage is explicable only in reference to
the social system.

Within such a system the structure of the
socio-technic component as regards "contextual" relationships should be simple. Various
status symbols will be possessed by nearly all
individuals within the limits of age and sex
classes, differentiation within such a class being largely quantitative and qualitative rather
than by formal exclusion of particular forms
to particular status grades. The degree to
which sociotechnic symbols of status will be
utilized within an egalitarian group should
largely be a function of group size and the
intensity and constancy of personal acquaint-

ance among all individuals composing the society. Where small group size and general
lack of interaction with nearby groups is the
normal pattern, then the abundance of status
symbols should be low. Where group size is
large and/or where between-group interac-
tions are widespread, lowering the intimacy
and familiarity between interacting individuals, then there should be a greater and more
general use of material means of status communication.

Another characteristic of the manipulation
of status symbols among societies with essentially egalitarian systems of status grading
would be the destruction at death of an individual's symbols of status. Status attainment being egalitarian, status symbols would
be personalities and could not be inherited as
such. Inclusion as grave accompaniments or
outright destruction would be the suggested
mode of disposal for status items among such
groups.

Among societies where status grading tends
to be of a nonegalitarian type, the status
symbols should be more esoteric in form.
Their form would normally be dictated by
the ideological symbolism which rationalizes
and emphasizes the particular internal ranking system or the means of partitioning the
society. The structure of the socio-technic
component of the assemblage should be more
complex, with the complexity increasing directly as the complexity of the internal ranking system. Possession of certain forms may
become exclusively restricted to certain status
positions. As the degree of complexity in
ranking increases there should be a similar
increase in the differentiation of contextual
associations in the form of differential treatment at death, differential access to goods
and services evidenced in the formal and
spatial differentiation in habitations and storage areas, etc. We would also expect to observe differentiation among the class of status
symbols themselves as regards those which
were utilized on a custodial basis as opposed
to those that were personalities. Similarly, we
would expect to see status symbols more fre-

quently inherited at death as inheritance increases as the mechanism of status ascription.

Certainly these are suggestions which must be phrased as hypotheses and tested against ethnographic data. Nevertheless it is hoped that this discussion is sufficient to serve as a background against which an explanatory hypothesis concerning the Old Copper materials can be offered as an example of the potential utility of this type of *systemic* approach to archaeological data.

I suggest that the Old Copper copper tools had their primary functional context as symbols of achieved status in cultural systems with an egalitarian system of status grading. The settlement patterns and general level of cultural development suggested by the archaeological remains is commensurate with a band level of socio-cultural integration (Martin, Quimby, and Collier 1947:299), that level within which egalitarian systems of status grading are dominant (Fried 1960). The technomic form, apparent lack of technomic efficiency, relative scarcity, and frequent occurrence in burials of copper artifacts all suggest that their primary function was as sociotechnic items. Having reached this "conclusion," we are then in a position to ask, in systemic terms, questions concerning their period of appearance, disappearance, and the shift to nonutilitarian forms of copper items among later prehistoric sociocultural systems of eastern North America.

I propose that the initial appearance of formally "utilitarian" copper tools in the Great Lakes region is explicable in terms of a major population expansion in the region following the Nipissing stage of the ancestral Great Lakes. The increase in population density was the result of increases in gross productivity following an exploitative shift to aquatic resources during the Nipissing stage. The increased populations are generally demonstrable in terms of the increased number of archaeological sites ascribable to the post-Nipissing period. The shift to aquatic resources is demonstrable in the initial appearance of quantities of fish remains in the sites

of this period and in the sites of election for occupation, adjacent to prominent loci of availability for exploiting aquatic resources. It is proposed that with the increasing population density, the selective pressures fostering the symbolic communication of status, as opposed to the dependence on personal recognition as the bases for differential role behavior, were sufficient to result in the initial appearance of a new class of sociotechnic items, formally technomic status symbols.

The failure to perpetuate the practice of the manufacture of copper tools on any extensive basis in the Great Lakes region should be explicable in terms of the changing structure of the social systems in that area during Woodland times. The exact type of social structure characteristic of Early Woodland period is at present poorly understood. I would suggest that there was a major structural change between the Late Archaic and Early Woodland periods, probably in the direction of a simple clan and moiety basis for social integration with a corresponding shift in the systems of status grading and the obsolescence of the older material means of status communication.

The presence of copper tools of essentially nonutilitarian form within such complexes as Adena, Hopewell, and Mississippian are most certainly explicable in terms of their sociotechnic functions within much more complex social systems. Within the latter societies status grading was not purely on an egalitarian basis, and the nonutilitarian copper forms of status symbols would be formally commensurate with the ideological rationalizations for the various ascriptive status systems.

This explanatory "theory" has the advantage of "explaining": 1) the period of appearance of copper and probably other "exotic" materials in the Late Archaic period; 2) the form of the copper items; 3) their frequently noted contextual relations, for example, placement in burials; 4) their disappearance, which would be an "enigma" if they functioned primarily as technomic items;

and 5) the use of copper for the almost exclusive production of "nonutilitarian" items in later and certainly more complex cultures of the eastern United States. This explanatory theory is advanced on the basis of currently available information, and regardless of whether or not it can stand as the correct explanation of the "Old Copper Problem" when more data are available, I suggest that only within a systemic frame of reference could such an inclusive explanation be offered. Here lies the advantage of the systemic approach.

Archaeology must accept a greater responsibility in the furtherance of the aims of anthropology. Until the tremendous quantities of data which the archaeologist controls are used in the solution of problems dealing with cultural evolution or systemic change, we are not only failing to contribute to the furtherance of the aims of anthropology but retarding the accomplishment of these aims. We as archaeologists have available a wide range of variability and a large sample of cultural systems. Ethnographers are restricted to the small and formally limited extant cultural systems.

Archaeologists should be among the best qualified to study and directly test hypotheses concerning the process of evolutionary change, particularly slow, or hypotheses that postulate temporal-processual priorities as regards total cultural systems. The lack of theoretical concern and rather naïve attempts at explanation which archaeologists currently advance must be modified.

I have suggested certain ways that could be a beginning in this necessary transition to a systemic view of culture, and have set forth a specific argument which hopefully demonstrates the utility of such an approach. The explanatory potential which even this limited and highly specific interpretative approach holds should be clear when problems such as "the spread of an Early Woodland burial cult in the Northeast" (Ritchie 1955), the appearance of the "Buzzard cult" (Waring and Holder 1945) in the Southeast, or the "Hopewell decline" (Griffin 1960a) are recalled. It is my opinion that until we as archaeologists begin thinking of our data in terms of total cultural systems, many such prehistoric "enigmas" will remain unexplained. As archaeologists, with the entire span of culture history as our "laboratory," we cannot afford to keep our theoretical heads buried in the sand. We must shoulder our full share of responsibility within anthropology. Such a change could go far in advancing the field of archaeology specifically, and would certainly advance the general field of anthropology.

Chapter 11   KENT V. FLANNERY

Culture History v. Cultural Process:
A Debate in American Archaeology

A DOMINANT characteristic of American archaeology has been its long history of reaction to American ethnology. When ethnology was little more than the collecting of spears, baskets and headdresses from the Indians, archaeology was little more than recovery of artifacts. When ethnology increased its attention to community structure, archaeology responded with studies of settlement pattern—an approach in which Gordon Willey was an innovator. Publication of works by Julian H. Steward and others on "cultural ecology" was answered by great archaeological emphasis on "the ecological approach." When the concept of cultural evolution emerged triumphant after years of suppression, archaeology showed great interest in evolutionary sequences and in the classification of "stages" in the human career. The interaction of these two disciplines has been increased by the fact that in the U.S. both are housed in departments of anthropology; as Willey remarked some 10 years ago, "American archaeology is anthropology or it is nothing."

And now, in 1966, Willey—Bowditch Professor of Mexican and Central American

Review of *An Introduction to American Archaeology*, vol. 1: *North and Middle America*, by Gordon R. Willey (Prentice-Hall, Inc.). Reprinted from *Scientific American*, vol. 217, no. 2, August 1967, pp. 119–22. By permission of the author and Scientific American, Inc. Copyright © 1967 by Scientific American, Inc. All rights reserved.

Archaeology and Ethnology at Harvard University—has written a monumental synthesis of New World prehistory (1966a). There is nothing like it. Recently we have had several edited volumes on the New World with contributions by regional specialists, but this book is written cover to cover by one man. Thus the inevitable lack of first-hand familiarity with certain areas is partially offset by the advantage of having one consistent approach and writing style throughout. Although aimed at the student, the book's costly format almost prices it out of the student range. It is a centerpiece for the coffee table of the archaeological fraternity, at least until an inexpensive paperback edition can be produced.

Willey's archaeological career is reflected in monographs and articles on every major land mass of the New World, from the region of the Woodland culture in the U.S. Northeast to the Maya area, the shell mounds of Panama and the coastal border of the Andean civilization. He is a perennial favorite who for a variety of reasons has never come under attack. One reason is his avoidance of any one polarized theoretical position; the other is his adaptability in the face of continual change. While other members of the establishment have clenched their fists and gritted their teeth when their formerly useful theories dropped from favor, Willey has shown no such hostility; younger archaeologists sense he would rather join them than lick them. And he is always free to join them as long as he maintains no vested interest in any comprehensive theory that needs defending.

This book, well organized from the primary literature and from constant conversations with Willey's colleagues, is no exception. It is unlikely to stir up controversy except where Willey commits himself to one of a series of possible theories proposed by others—for example, siding with Emil W. Haury rather than Charles C. Di Peso on the interpretation of the U.S. Southwest, or with Henry B. Collins rather than Richard S. MacNeish on the American Arctic. It is not Willey's aim to intrude his own theories into the synthesis. Indeed, he tells us that he is "not demonstrating or championing any one process, theory or kind of explanation as a key to a comprehensive understanding of what went on in prehistoric America." Clearly Willey feels that it would be misleading to do more than present the student with the facts as most of his colleagues agree on them in 1966. Hence "the intent of this book is history—an introductory culture history of pre-Columbian America."

This statement by Willey makes it appropriate to consider one of the current theoretical debates in American archaeology: the question of whether archaeology should be the study of culture history or the study of cultural process. In view of this debate it is interesting to note that in practically the same paragraph Willey can brand his book "culture history" and yet argue that he is "not championing any one point of view."

Perhaps 60 percent of all currently ambulatory American archaeologists are concerned primarily with culture history; this includes most of the establishment and not a few of the younger generation. Another 10 percent, both young and old, belong to what might be called the "process school." Between these two extremes lies a substantial group of archaeologists who aim their

fire freely at both history and process. And although Willey himself belongs to this group, his *Introduction to American Archaeology* also constitutes a massive restatement of the accomplishments of the culture-history school.

Most culture historians use a theoretical framework that has been described as "normative" (the term was coined by an ethnologist and recently restressed by an archaeologist). That is, they treat culture as a body of shared ideas, values and beliefs—the "norms" of a human group. Members of a given culture are committed to these norms in different degrees—the norm is really at the middle of a bell-shaped curve of opinions on how to behave. Prehistoric artifacts are viewed as products of these shared ideas, and they too have a "range of variation" that takes the form of a bell-shaped curve.

In the normative framework cultures change as the shared ideas, values and beliefs change. Change may be temporal (as the ideas alter with time) or geographic (as one moves away from the center of a particular culture area, commitment to certain norms lessens and commitment to others increases). Hence culture historians have always been concerned with constructing "time-space grids"—great charts whose columns show variation through the centuries. Some have focused an incredible amount of attention on refining and detailing these grids; others have been concerned with discovering "the Indian behind the artifact"—reconstructing the "shared idea" or "mental template" that served as a model for the maker of the tool.

While recognizing the usefulness of this framework for classification, the process school argues that it is unsuitable for explaining culture-change situations. Members of the process school view human behavior as a point of overlap (or "articulation") between a vast number of systems, each of which encompasses both cultural and noncultural phenomena—often much more of the latter. An Indian group, for example, may participate in a system in which maize is grown on a river floodplain that is slowly being eroded, causing the zone of the best farmland to move upstream. Simultaneously it may participate in a system involving a wild rabbit population whose density fluctuates in a 10-year cycle because of predators or disease. It may also participate in a system of exchange with an Indian group occupying a different kind of area, from which it receives subsistence products at certain predetermined times of the year; and so on. All these systems compete for the time and energy of the individual Indian; the maintenance of his way of life depends on an equilibrium among systems. Culture change comes about through minor variations in one or more systems, which grow, displace or reinforce others and reach equilibrium on a different plane.

The strategy of the process school is therefore to isolate each system and study it as a separate variable. The ultimate goal, of course, is reconstruction of the entire pattern of articulation, along with all related systems, but such complex analysis has so far proved beyond the powers of the process theorists. Thus far their efforts have not produced grand syntheses such as Willey's but only small-scale descriptions of the detailed workings of a single system. By these methods, however, they hope to explain, rather than merely describe, variations in prehistoric human behavior.

So far the most influential (and controversial) member of the process school has been Lewis R. Binford of the University of New Mexico at Albuquerque, and it is interesting to note that Binford's name is confined to a single footnote on the last page of Willey's text. It is Binford's contention that culture historians are at times stopped short of "an explanatory level of analysis" by the normative framework in which they construct their classifications. Efforts to reconstruct the "shared ideas" behind artifact populations cannot go beyond what Binford calls "paleopsychology"—they cannot cope with systemic change. And where Willey says that "archaeology frequently treats more effectively of man in his relationships to his natural environment than of other aspects of culture," Binford would protest that most culture historians have dealt poorly with these very relationships; their model of "norms," which are "inside" culture, and environment, which is "outside," makes it impossible to deal with the countless systems in which man participates, none of which actually reflect a dichotomy between culture and nature. The concept of culture as a "superorganic" phenomenon, helpful for some analytical purposes, is of little utility to the process school.

As a convenient example of the difference in the two approaches, let us examine three different ways in which American archaeologists have treated what they call "diffusion"—the geographic spread of cultural elements. It was once common to interpret the spread of such elements by actual migrations of prehistoric peoples (a view, still common in Near Eastern archaeology, that might be called the "Old Testament effect"). The culture historians attacked this position with arguments that it was not necessary for actual people to travel —just "ideas." In other words, the norms of one culture might be transmitted to another culture over long distances, causing a change in artifact styles, house types and so on. A whole terminology was worked out for this situation by the culture historians: they described cultural "traits" that had a "center of origin" from which they spread outward along "diffusion routes." Along the way they passed through "cultural filters" that screened out certain traits and let others pass through; the mechanics of this process were seen as the "acceptance" or "rejection" of new traits on the part of the group through whose filter they were diffusing. At great distances from the center of origin the traits were present only in attenuated form, having been squeezed through so many filters that they were almost limp.

Since process theorists do not treat a given tool (or "trait") as the end product of a given group's "ideas" about what a tool should look like but rather as one component of a system that also includes many noncultural components, they treat diffusion in different ways. The process theorist is not ultimately concerned with "the Indian behind the artifact" but rather with the system behind both the Indian and the artifact: what other components does the system have, what energy source keeps it going, what mechanisms regulate it and so on? Often the first step is an attempt to discover the role of the trait or implement by determining what it is functionally associated with; some process theorists have run extensive linear-regression analyses or multivariant factor analyses in order to pick up clusters of elements that vary with each other in "nonrandom" ways. When such clusterings occur, the analyst postulates a system—tools X, Y, and Z are variables dependent on one another, constituting a functional tool kit that varies nonrandomly with some aspect of the environment, such as fish, wild cereal grains, white-tailed deer and so on. By definition change in one part of a system produces change in other parts; hence the process theorists cannot view artifacts X, Y, and Z as products of cultural norms, to be accepted or rejected freely at way stations along diffusion routes. When such elements spread, it is because the systems of which they are a part have spread—often at the expense of other systems.

Thus the archaeologist James Deetz recently presented evidence that the spread of a series of pottery designs on the Great Plains reflected not the "acceptance" of new designs by neighboring groups but a breakdown of the matrilocal residence pattern of a society where the women were potters. Designs subconsciously selected by the women (and passed on to their daughters) ceased to be restricted to a given village when the matrilocal pattern collapsed and married daughters were no longer bound to

reside in their mothers' villages. In this case, although each potter obviously did have a "mental template" in her mind when she made the pot, this did not "explain" the change. That spread of design could only be understood in terms of a system in which designs, containers and certain female descent groups were nonrandomly related components. The members of the process school maintain that this is a more useful explanatory framework, but even they realize that it is only a temporary approach. They are becoming increasingly aware that today's human geographers have ways of studying diffusion that are far more sophisticated and quantitative than anything used by contemporary archaeologists.

One other example of the difference in approach between the culture historian and the process theorist is the way each treats the use of "ethnographic analogy" in archaeological interpretation. The culture historian proposes to analyze and describe a prehistoric behavior pattern, then search the ethnographic literature for what seems to be analogous behavior in a known ethnic group. If the analogy seems close enough, he may propose that the prehistoric behavior served the same purpose as its analogue and then use ethnographic data to "put flesh on the archaeological skeleton."

The process theorist proposes a different procedure. Using the analogous ethnic group, he constructs a behavioral model to "predict" the pattern of archaeological debris left by such a group. This model is then tested against the actual archaeological traces of the prehistoric culture, with the result that a third body of data emerges, namely the differences between the observed and the expected archaeological pattern. These differences are in some ways analogous to the "residuals" left when the principal factors in a factor analysis have been run, and they may constitute unexpectedly critical data. When the archaeologist sets himself the task of explaining the differences between the observed archaeological pattern and the pattern predicted by the ethnographic model, he may come up with process data not obtained through the use of analogy alone.

Willey is certainly alert to the current debate, and although he summarizes the New World in a predominantly culture-history framework, he concludes Volume I with a discussion of the hopes and promises of the process school. These he leaves for the future: "I shall be less concerned with process or a search for cultural 'laws,'" he says, "than with at times attempting to explain why certain cultural traditions developed, or failed to develop." Certainly the process school would argue that he cannot explain, within a culture-history framework, why such traditions developed or failed to develop; yet, as he explicitly states, explanation is not the purpose of this volume but rather history.

Let us hope, as Willey seems to, that there is a place in American archaeology for both approaches. Certainly we can use both the historical synthesis and the detailed analysis of single processes. By no stretch of the imagination do all process theorists propose to reject history, because it is only in the unfolding of long sequences that some processes become visible.

In fact, what does the difference between the two schools really amount to? In terms of the philosophy of science, I believe the process approach results in moving "decisions" about cultural behavior even farther away from the individual. It is part of a trend toward determinism that the culture historians began.

It was once common to hear human history explained in terms of "turning points," of crucial decisions made by "great men." This view proved unacceptable to the culture historians, with their normative framework of shared ideas, values, and beliefs. They argued convincingly that this body of shared norms determined the course of history—not the individual, who was simply a product of his culture. Possibly the most devastating critique of the individual as decision-maker

was due to Leslie A. White, who in one brilliant polemic concluded that the course of Egyptian history and monotheism would have been the same "even had Ikhnaton been a bag of sand."

Now the process school would like to move crucial decisions still farther from the individual by arguing that systems, once set in motion, are self-regulating to the point where they do not even necessarily allow rejection or acceptance of new traits by a culture. Once a system has moved in a certain direction, it automatically sets up the limited range of possible moves it can make at the next critical turning point. This view is not original with process-school archaeologists —it is borrowed from Ludwig von Bertalanffy's framework for the developing embryo, where systems trigger behavior at critical junctures and, once they have done so, cannot return to their original pattern. The process school argues that there are systems so basic in nature that they can be seen operating in virtually every field—prehistory not excepted. Culture is about as powerless to divert these systems as the individual is to change his culture.

Obviously individuals *do* make decisions, but evidence of these individual decisions cannot be recovered by archaeologists. Accordingly it is more useful for the archaeologist to study and understand the system, whose behavior is detectable over and over again. Obviously this approach is too deterministic for some purposes, but for others it is of great theoretical value.

But then if both historical and processual approaches are useful, why should there be a debate at all? I believe the debate exists because of two basically different attitudes toward science.

The previous generation of archaeologists, who did mostly culture history but also laid the foundations for the process school, were often deathly afraid of being wrong. Many of them felt (and many still feel) that if we will only wait until all the facts are in they will speak for themselves. They spoke in awe of the incompleteness of the archaeological record and of the irresponsibility of speculating on scanty data. Somehow they seemed to feel that if they could get together a few more potsherds, a few more projectile points or a few more architectural details, their conclusions would be unshakable. There has not been, however, any convincing correlation between the quantities of data they amassed and the accuracy of their conclusions.

The process theorists assume that "truth" is just the best current hypothesis, and that whatever they believe now will ultimately be proved wrong, either within their lifetime or afterward. Their "theories" are not like children to them, and they suffer less trauma when the theories prove "wrong." Their concern is with presenting developmental models to be tested in the field, and they have noted no consistent relationship between the usefulness of a given model and the absolute quantity of data on which it is based. To be useful a model need only organize a body of disorganized data in such a way that hypotheses can conveniently be tested, accepted, modified or rejected. Thus the process school will continue to present model after model on the basis of returns from the first few precincts, and at least some of the culture historians will continue to accuse them of being "hasty," "premature" and "irresponsible." And the issue will be settled years from now by another generation that will probably not belong to either school.

Willey's synthesis sums up nearly 100 years of American archaeology, and it comes at the start of one of the most exciting archaeological eras yet begun. My prediction for the next decade is that we shall see general systems theory, game theory and locational analysis all applied successfully to American archaeology in spite of the loudest mutterings of the establishment. I also predict that, in spite of his decision to concentrate his own efforts on producing reliable culture history, we shall hear all these subversive approaches applauded by Gordon Willey.

Archaeology as a Social Science

THAT PART of anthropology known as archaeology is concerned with culture in the past—the extinct lifeways of former peoples, how and why they changed and developed, and the significance of this to developmental process and to our understanding of culture. In short, archaeology adds a vital time dimension to the study of man. As such if it is to achieve the ends which we claim for it, archaeology must remain as closely and intimately bound up with general ethnology as possible and constantly contribute to understandings of social man.

This point needs some stress since much of archaeology in the public mind is involved with radiocarbon dating, pollen studies, glacial geology and other areas of the biological and physical sciences. While modern archaeology could ill afford to forego these contributions of other disciplines, they are still just contributions which make the archaeologist better able to make reasoned and valid statements concerning human culture in the past. To paraphrase Willey and Phillips, then, "archaeology is a social science or it is nothing."

Most archaeologists would agree that they are striving to achieve three related ends: 1) the reconstruction of culture history, often over massive segments of time; 2) the de-

tailing of the daily lifeways of earlier cultures; and 3) the elucidation of cultural process in a broader sense with emphasis on the dynamic aspects of culture. However, these three goals of archaeology are in no sense mutually independent, and it would seem in viewing their interrelationships that two of them are aspects of one larger entity.

If we were able to derive a relatively complete picture of the working of an early culture at one point in time and detail the interrelationships between that culture's various components, then the synthesis of a large number of such cultural statements would at the same time delineate process in a dynamic sense as well as provide a far more detailed historical statement. Thus, sophisticated history and cultural process are but two aspects of the same archaeological goal, differing in emphasis and perhaps in scope.

Until relatively recently, culture history as formulated by archaeologists has been quite coarse-grained, with great stress on the major events of prehistory such as the evolution of lithic technology over tens of thousands of years, the invention and spread of food production, the peopling of the new world or the rise of civilization. This perspective is seen most commonly in overall syntheses, summary statements in effect (I mean here such books as Grahame Clark's *World Prehistory* as an example) of the prehistory of this or that portion of the world, or for that matter the entire world. At a more specific level in space and time, and here I'm really talking about site reports, cultural historical

Reproduced by permission of the American Anthropological Association from Bulletins, vol. 3, no. 3(2), 1970, *Current Directions in Anthropology*, pp. 115–25. The bibliographical references have been placed in the general bibliography for this volume by permission of the author.

statements have concentrated similarly on rather general topics. The generality is much the same and only the time and space dimensions are reduced. Thus, a common and necessary portion of any site report consists of a summary of the prehistory of the region in which the site is located, and matters such as the population of the area by prehistoric culture A, B, or C, the development of subsistence techniques or the increase in community size are the most commonly addressed.

I should make clear that I do not make light of this kind of synthesis. It is basic, important, and represents large quantities of effort expended. It is also probably possessed of a high degree of credibility if only because it is relatively general. It is when archaeology attempts to become more specific and precise, to make inferences concerning more detailed aspects of culture, that the problem of credibility becomes real. And when one moves into the realm of cultural process based on delineation of daily life ways such precision is demanded and one must expect a credibility level comparable to that enjoyed by the more general sort of cultural historical formulation. Ideally, if it were possible to produce precise and totally reliable descriptions of the cultures of prehistoric societies *l* through *n*—and understand their dynamics, then a far more detailed cultural historical statement would naturally follow. But it would seem that the essential first step in achieving such an end would be the development of techniques for generating reliable synchronic cultural descriptions from the past. These in turn permit insights concerning process, and as mentioned above, understanding of process leads to sound and detailed cultural history.

In this sense the three aims of archaeology are but steps in a single process. Perhaps much of archaeology in the past by not following these steps in precisely that order has produced useful but not necessarily general conclusions. If so, then the business before us as archaeologists in the late 1960s is

the development of a body of method and theory which will assure such detail and precision. In fact, such a concern has been characteristic of archaeology since 1960. I should add that that is an approximate date —you could push it back or forward a few years either way you want—and that progress is now being made in a number of directions toward that end. I should like to explore some of these efforts and at the same time make some general observations regarding other possible pursuits, some of these quite tentative and speculative, but hopefully consistent with the stated purpose, and representative in a general way of current trends in modern archaeology.

The actual steps through which an archaeologist proceeds from first to last in working on his data are actually quite simple. He excavates a body of material from his site, using a set of techniques which assures control over its location and the relationship between his various components. Having done this, the next task is the careful description of the material to make it comparable to other lots from other sites. Then the body of data, having been ordered according to any one of a number of classificatory systems, is studied to determine the ways in which it reflects the behavior of the people who were responsible for leaving it behind to be discovered by the archaeologist. Recent developments in archaeology have reflected innovation in all three of these processes.

Before going further, a few words might be in order regarding the nature of archaeological data. Its most salient attributes are that it is fragmentary, and it is buried. For this reason alone much of the archaeologist's time is spent in removing this material from the earth and reassembling it into as complete a condition as possible. As we shall see later, the subterranean aspect of traditional archaeological data may have been an unrecognized impediment to obtaining the maximum understanding from it. The most important thing to realize about archaeological material, however, is that it reflects in its entirety the manner in which human behavior has made an impact upon the environment. This is true from the smallest of artifacts to the largest: a shell bead is shaped through conscious design to a certain form which reflects that design, while a Mayan temple is an aggregate of portions of the environment assembled through the same conscious process. Thus, the most fundamental relationship which the archaeologist must recognize is that between behavior and its productions. And since we agree that behavior is patterned and systematic, it follows that its reflections in its effects on the environment must be similarly patterned and it is the explication of this relationship between behavior and environment which holds the greatest promise for sharpening archaeological studies.

The imperfection and incompleteness of archaeological records has been discussed by numerous writers, all of whom have stressed its effect upon obtaining maximum information concerning its cultural authors. As Lewis Binford (1968a:5–27) has pointed out, however, this concern has at times been overstated. Yet it does pose a real problem in very many cases if one expects all portions of a whole cultural system to be represented in some way or another in the archaeological record. However, this is a totally unrealistic expectation to hold in the first place, and I hope to make some suggestions as to how this problem can be circumvented at least in part.

Looking back over the past decade, there seem to be three major themes which typify current trends in archaeological thinking. Other workers might perceive these somewhat differently, but I would expect at least general agreement. These include 1) an increasing concern over the integrated nature of culture and the necessity for stressing the structure of the varied content of past cultures, 2) a new stress on finer-grain techniques for the description and integration of archaeological materials, aided immensely by

developing technologies in automatic data processing and 3) an increasing concern over the proper role and use of analogy in archaeological inference. These three themes are closely related and when applied with care they have produced some truly impressive and important studies.

The first of these, stressing the interrelationships between various aspects of culture, was of course the dominant theme of Walter Taylor's conjunctive approach, first put forth over 20 years ago (Taylor 1948). Its reawakening in this decade is certainly due in part to Taylor's original thoughts on the subject. An example will show the difference between viewing archaeological cultures in this fashion as opposed to the more traditional perspective. If we look at changes in single categories of artifacts over time and simply describe them, we can certainly make some general statements concerning culture history while at the same time pay little or no heed to the relationship between various classes or between these classes and other nonmaterial aspects of the culture, or to the articulation of the culture as a whole with the environment.

Work in the Santa Barbara Channel region in southern California has produced a sequence of at least three cultures which have been subdivided in a number of ways. (I might interject here for those of you who are specialists in the Santa Barbara Channel sequence that my intention is to boil it down for the purpose of getting through this essay in something less than two hours rather than to do it violence.) In simplest terms, the earliest tradition is one characterized by heavy milling stones used in processing various wild seeds. Projectile points are relatively crude and sufficiently low in number to suggest no emphatic stress on hunting. The economy would seem to be one based on extensive exploitation of vegetable foods with some hunting supplement. Another major food source was shellfish and sites of this tradition are characteristically shell middens, in many instances of considerable depth.

Now this is followed by a second tradition which is markedly different in artifact content. Shellfish seem to have diminished dramatically and a marked increase in projectile points reflects a new heavy emphasis on hunting. These points show affinity with those from the desert areas of eastern California. Milling stones are replaced by basket-hopper mortars, small concave stones on which bottomless baskets are attached, if that's not a contradiction in terms. Someone read this and said, "Well if it doesn't have a bottom it's not a basket." But it's this little basketry cylinder, attached to the stone with asphaltum, used in conjunction with small mortars, to process vegetable materials.

The last major cultural tradition of the region sees a return to maritime orientation and, while hunting seems to be a factor, sites are now again shell middens of impressive size. Standard equipment for seed processing are massive stone bowls weighing in some cases hundreds of pounds and used with large cylindrical stone pestles.

Cultural historical formulations based on these data tend to stress certain general but valid points. There was a change in subsistence technology over time. Milling stones give way to hopper mortars which in turn give way to large stone bowls. Projectile points and their cultural correlate of hunting increase and then show a marked decline relative to other subsistence artifacts.

All of these conclusions are essentially based on considering the formal appearances of certain artifact classes. And, changes in these and the relative frequencies permit the conclusions when viewed against certain settlement data. There is, however, a rather different way to look at these same data and reach somewhat more precise understanding of some basic aspects of cultural process in southern California prehistory and at the same time make a rather more detailed cultural historical statement. This perspective, it should be emphasized, is in hypothesis form and not necessarily to be understood as a statement of fact. What is significant

here is that using a viewpoint which is in accord with a conjunctive approach permits a different final statement. If we consider simply one set of artifacts, those used in processing wild seed materials, and also consider some of the ways in which they relate to other aspects of the culture in question and how those aspects in turn relate to each other, a useful processual statement can be made. Two factors appear to be involved here: portability (of the milling equipment) and the relationship of portability to the area required for seed processing; by that I mean the area on the artifact which gets involved in grinding up all these little seeds. The large early milling stones using a back and forth pattern of grinding with a mano must of necessity be large and heavy since an extensive grinding surface must be supported by a mass of stone. In other words, if you need to rub one rock back and forth on top of another rock in this direction it takes an overall bigger rock on the bottom to get the job done; it can't be just a half-inch thick. It is unlikely that many of these milling stones were moved from site to site frequently if at all. This, in turn, suggests relatively stable settlements with restrictive mobility, with the remote possibility that the stones were cached in some way to be used again and again on periodic return to the site. Due to the rather heavy reliance on shellfish resources and the depth of midden accumulation, the latter alternative seems less likely. I realize I just stepped right into the middle of a relatively large controversy on the early milling stones culture of Santa Barbara County, concerning whether or not they were quite mobile or permanent. But, all I can say is that I know it and I've indicated my own opinion on the subject.

In marked contrast to large heavy milling stones requiring hundreds of square inches of working surface, basket-hopper mortars are light weight and eminently portable devices, requiring working surfaces of less than 100 square inches. The critical factor here is the shift from back-and-forth grinding to up-and-down pulverizing, requiring a minimum of abrading surfaces, with the basketry sides acting as retainers for the processed material. The new emphasis on hunting reflected by the new point types combined with more portable milling equipment may well indicate a marked increase in community mobility. Resemblances with projectile point types to the east could indicate a real movement of influence, and perhaps even people, westward. If, in addition to this, sea level elevations at the same time had an effect upon inter-tidal shellfish resources, more than sufficient factors would have been present to produce a major shift to a nomadic, hunting way of life.

Continuing from the perspective of changes in portability and the seed-processing area on the artifact, the subsequent development shows a return to a more sedentary marine-oriented life. However, seed processing continues an up-and-down pulverizing technique similar to that of the basket-hopper mortars earlier, but with the removal of those pressures which required portability. As a function of mobility, mortars were free to become larger. This would certainly be an advantage in processing large quantities of material at one time and might possibly be attuned to significant population increase and enlargement of community size.

This last tradition was that observed by the early explorers along the Pacific Coast, reaching its climax in the historic Chumash. These people were grouped in very large coastal villages with a high degree of permanence. In this context, massive heavy stone-bowl mortars make perfect sense. The pressures, cultural and environmental, which may have transformed the earlier massive milling stones to light-weight mortars are not present to reverse the trend from milling to pounding back to milling, and subsequent enlargement of seed grinding equipment seems to be in response to population growth and increased permanence of settlement.

In the example just given, it is not neces-

sary at this point, although I suppose maybe it would be sooner or later, to demand that this is the "right" explanation. It is provided to show how change in one class of objects, as a matter of fact change in only one or two attributes of one specific set of objects related to one very specific activity, when considered along with the manner in which this class articulates with a larger set of cultural and ecological imperatives, suggests genuinely processual explanations. The next step in this approach would be further testing of this hypothesis to see if other items in the respective assemblages reflect in yet other ways the suggested changes in community mobility, subsistence and population.

It might legitimately be asked whether these last conclusions are truly so different. They are, to the extent that they result from considering but one small segment of an entire assemblage. In this example, changes in a set of related attributes of milling equipment—working surface and its contingent effect on size and hence portability—can be seen perhaps to reflect a well integrated complex of changes in the culture sequence which produced them. Stress on the essential interrelatedness of cultural systems allows us to reach understandings of many aspects from a relative few. And this certainly is at least a partial answer to the problems posed by the incompleteness of the archaeological record.

This viewpoint, I must stress, is in no way original with me. For a rather similar statement of many of the same things I refer to Lewis Binford's discussion of the limitations of the archaeological record (Binford 1968a).

The second major trend in archaeological thinking in the 1960s is centered around attempts to describe artifacts in a more detailed fashion in the hope that such description might sharpen our abilities to delineate the patterns in the data which hold clues to past behavior. Traditional archaeological description has been based on the *type* concept. Thus artifacts were classified according to their formal similarities and assemblages were compared largely in terms of shared types. The artifact type is, of course, an arbitrary category based on similarities in characteristics selected by the classifier from a much larger range of characteristics. As such, it has been a useful tool to derive relatively coarse-grained groupings which, when compared, permit rather general statements of relationships between archaeological cultures in time and space. With recent emphasis on looking at artifacts in terms of variation in the attributes which, when combined, constitute types, the factors which lead to the creation of these objects can be more clearly understood. For example, a pottery type might be described as having a certain size, type of paste, decoration, a particular rim profile, and tempered with coarse sand. All pots which share in these attributes are placed in this particular type category. Of course, the artifact type is a polythetic category and, in practice, sharing the preponderance of the attributes of the ideal type is sufficient for typological placement of a single artifact. But in making such an assignment the classifier is making a number of other implicit statements. He is saying that the maker of the artifact in question executed operations A, B, and C, and so on—as many operations as there are attributes in the descriptions. And it is equally important that in doing one thing—incising a pot rim, notching an arrowhead or grooving an axe, he did not execute any of the other alternatives known to be available to him from inspection of other type categories or other artifacts in the same assemblage. Thus, the rim might also be cord-impressed, the arrowhead left unnotched, or the axe notched rather than grooved. Two things become obvious with a little thought. The selection is in some way influenced by certain nonmaterial factors in the maker's culture, and the selection of one attribute is not influenced by the same factors as the selection of another. Thus a multi-attribute type construct will be virtually certain to be the end-product of a set of decisions and choices which represent inputs from very different sectors of the maker's culture. As such, it is a useful integrative device, but of little use to an understanding of process.

To resolve this dilemma it becomes necessary to create what is in effect a typology of attributes and consider the data in terms of the manner in which these attributes combine and recombine in response to the culture producing them. It is at the level of the discrete attribute that patterning of the type which represents specific nonmaterial aspects of the culture becomes evident. Certainly behavior shared by a relatively small number of individuals is most likely to be seen in the mode of combination of attributes on artifacts, since it is the individuals who are responsible for combining the attributes creating the artifact in the first place. Elsewhere, in my little paperback *Invitation to Archaeology* (Deetz 1967), I have pointed out that there is an equation between levels of behavior and levels of attribute and artifact grouping. Thus, since individuals are responsible for combining attributes, attribute patterning reflects patterned individual behavior. Likewise the groupings of artifacts into sets which represent certain activities, knives, points and scrapers for example, which relate to hunting and meat processing, reflected patterned behavior on the part of larger social groups within the community. Patterning in entire archaeological assemblages is indicative of behavior representative of whole communities. Thus even if it were possible to agree upon multi-attribute types which possess some cultural reality, they would not permit investigation of the most minimal level of behavior, since individual attribute patterning is the level which is relevant in this case.

There has been a series of studies in recent years which show the validity of attribute analysis in ceramics in assessing past social patterns. I refer to my Arikara study (Deetz 1965), Bill Longacre's study of Carter Ranch Pueblo (1968) and Jim Hill's study of the

Broken K Pueblo (1968) as good examples of this. All indicate in one way or another that the combination of attributes in pottery manufacture is a function of shared behavior which results from the relative solidarity of the social unit. Matrilocal potters who reside together share in certain sets of designs which are more or less distinct from those of other similar residential units. My study showed a progressively more random distribution of attributes of pottery manufacture and design accompanying the breakdown of matrilocal families from historically documented Arikara Indians. The other two studies, Longacre's and Hill's, done in a prehistoric context, tend more to show how distinctive attribute configurations are spatially segregated as were the families which produced them. So, in a way, the latter are synchronic and the former is diachronic.

The study of individual attributes in a large sample of artifacts requires a vast amount of recording and computation, and this in turn would be virtually impossible without the help of data-processing equipment. Thus developments in attribute analysis of archaeological data has in part been a function of the rapidly developing technology in the computer field. Computers were first used in archaeology in 1960 or a little earlier and by now have occupied a prominent position in the field.

The use of analogy in archaeology has been standard from the very beginning. Our view of the meaning of archaeological assemblages must be conditioned by our understandings of cultures of the present. Projectile points are identified as such, not through any inherent quality which they possess, but because similar forms are known from their use in observable contexts. Witness the significant number of unidentified artifacts from any archaeological site. They are unidentifiable in large part because no ethnographic analogue is known. There are, however, certain subtle difficulties in the use of analogy in archaeology. As Lewis Binford has pointed out in the same article I referred to earlier, there is no guarantee that all cultures of the past have analogues in the ethnographically reported present. Thus, total reliance on ethnographic and historic data runs the risk of either restricting our inferential method to an unnecessary degree or even perhaps of making mismatches between archaeological and ethnographic materials.

More fundamental to the entire problem seems to be the manner in which archaeologists implicitly seek analogies between material categories from the past and behavioral categories from the present. Thus, archaeological data, which are tangible material data, are studied to see if they could be made to reflect different aspects of social behavior. Pottery attribute patterns, for example, are said to result from, or to articulate directly with, postnuptial residence. It would seem that implicit in such an approach is the assumption that material culture is more of a cultural byproduct than some nonmaterial categories. It can be argued that an institution such as residence is every bit as much the product of behavior as is a pot or an axe. The only difference is that one can be measured and touched and the other observed and described. This is particularly true in this case because all we are doing is measuring the spatial relationships between individuals inside a hunk of the environment which we call the house. Maybe I should elaborate on this just a little more. I'm struck by the fact that there seems to be some sort of a feeling on the part of archaeologists that the categories used by the ethnographer are possessed of somewhat greater cultural truth than the categories which he imposes on his own data. There is a genuine problem here. It seems that to seek a one-to-one relationship between two different products of similar behavior runs a considerable risk of distortion. It is rather like adding apples and pears. The categories which have been devised by ethnologists to describe the cultural universe they study need not be, and in fact should not be, the categories with which the archaeologists seek correspondence in their data. If there is any logic or validity in this proposition, it follows that a largely ignored task

115

before the archaeologist is the delineation of the nature of the relationships between behavioral and material categories as such without interposed constructs such as residence, descent or exogamy, to name but 3 examples, all examples themselves from a more complex behavioral context. Thus, it might be argued that the most fundamental aspect of analogy in archaeology is the analogue which exists between relationships in archaeological and ethnographic data rather than between artifacts and the ethnographer's categories. I hope I've made that clear. I hate to repeat, but I'll say it one more time because it's the core statement in this whole talk: more important perhaps are those analogues which exist in archaeological and ethnographic data between material and behavior rather than between the artifacts—so many pots let's say, or so many projectile points—and the ethnographer's categories. In other words, perhaps it's time we stopped trying to find postnuptial residence, descent, marriage patterns in our data because these in fact are classificatory rubrics which are about third or fourth order abstractions themselves which the ethnographers are responsible for and this leads us away from the central problem which I think we're involved with here.

One wonders if the development of anthropology over the last century hasn't somehow led the archaeologist into a less than suitable position with regard to the data with which he is normally charged. Material culture of living societies has traditionally been the domain of the ethnographers, and they have not been as concerned with this aspect as with other more exciting subjects. Yet the archaeologist has been restricted to data which is below the sod, and it is a matter of faith that the archaeologist is an anthropologist who digs. Yet this need not be so. And in fact, by taking into account material from above and below the ground, archaeologists are certain to gain much clearer understanding of the materials they do excavate. In other words, perhaps the traditional division of responsi-

bilities within anthropology has unnecessarily restricted the archaeologist in achieving maximum results. A coherent and unified body of subject matter entirely appropriate to the archaeologist is the study of the material aspects of culture in their behavioral context, regardless of provenience.

I realize that in one sense I have just now abolished the field of archaeology as we know it but I sincerely think that as long as we operate in this sense somebody's got to ask these questions and someone has to get at them. We are really not doing ourselves maximum service, and I speak, I think in part at least, from experience, because about five years ago I suddenly discovered a whole new world which wasn't even buried at all. It was all around me. It was called houses and cemeteries, and automobiles, and they're perfectly legal: you can do some pretty groovy things with hub caps and hood ornaments just as much as you can with pre-Columbian ceramics. In this fashion, understandings of the relationship between the material and nonmaterial derived from maximum information well controlled can then be fed back into the traditional archaeological contexts for more precise inferences.

A somewhat lesser theme of archaeology in the 1960s contributes to this perspective in a number of ways. I refer here to historical archaeology—the study of historically documented material through archaeological methods. The kinds of controls available in this sort of archaeology provide a suitable context in which to examine material and nonmaterial relationships in a manner similar to that obtainable from ethnographic data. It has one extra kicker in it which makes it even nicer because it's not ethnographic and it is, to my knowledge, the only archaeological (subterranean) data which you can contend with in which you can pursue certain dimensions of control which allow you to look at it in a somewhat different way. I'll give an example in a minute.

My own work on colonial mortuary art, certainly not buried and certainly supported by historical materials, demonstrates some of the values of this approach. Recent work, as yet unpublished by archaeologists, promises to sharpen our understanding of some of the many factors which affect the frequencies of certain artifact types at different times in the past which go far beyond simple popularity. The method of seriation is based on the assumption that styles appear, increase and decrease and finally vanish as a function of popularity. This is true, but, in aligning archaeological assemblages according to this method, it is implicitly assumed that these changes are uniformly operative on all peoples in a restricted area of time and space. Yet we know now that a simple factor such as socioeconomic status can create a marked difference in just what artifacts are present in a given household and will produce a significant skew in the proposed temporal alignments. I realize this is really operating more at the level of integrative method than it is explanation, but still it's a valid point.

One of the contributions of historical archaeology is an increased awareness that the record of the past is perhaps far more complex than we normally assume. Such a caution is a healthy thing in archaeology today, since, while we are moving toward more detailed and specific inferences about the past, it follows that a greater complexity of relationships will be perceived. And to oversimplify at this point can be quite dangerous, if not in fact disasterous.

An example will make this clear. We've been studying the faunal remains from a series of 7 seventeenth-century house sites in old Plymouth Colony for the past year. From mid-century onwards there is a somewhat surprising pattern in the mammalian food sources. Approximately 98 percent of the meat consumed was from domesticated animals. Hunting was an insignificant factor. Limited documentary research shows that this pattern is probably typical of the earlier portion of the century as well. A domestic-to-feral ratio of this type in the absence of controls would be interpreted as reflecting a level of efficiency of animal husbandry of sufficient height that hunting was no longer necessary. Alternately one might suggest a drastic reduction in the number of game animals. The historical facts, however, provide a very different explanation, one which it is very unlikely could be determined from archaeological analysis, again without the kind of control we've had. Legislation governing hunting rights in their native England was so restricted on the yeomanry that they endured food shortages a number of times without resorting to hunting on any significant scale. Recent research by Patrick Malone of the University of Pennsylvania, as yet unpublished, develops this and the following quite clearly. This reluctance to hunt would appear to result from a retention of attitudes toward hunting engendered prior to colonization, combined with an unfamiliarity with the use of firearms in hunting. Aiming a musket, indispensable to efficient hunting, was so totally foreign a concept that it was not even included in a 40-point manual of arms of the period. This really surprises people—at least it certainly did me. I realize this isn't a session on American history, but the fact is that the whole idea of picking out a target and selecting and shooting the target didn't come until the eighteenth century! Guns of this period were things that you held in rows of 20 or 30 people and fired broadside at the advancing company of soldiers. And if any of them fell, it was an act of God rather than your marksmanship which led to this result. So the idea of pointing it at something and letting it go was totally outside their cognitive view of what one did with a firearm.

Correlated with this was a seemingly disproportionate number of fowling pieces in household inventories of the time and a corresponding high level of waterfowl remains in the sites. (We have up to now transcribed 300 of these inventories and there will be about a thousand of them when we're finished. They are lovely things for archaeological control because they list every single artifact in an individual's house at the time of his death, often by room, and give its value. So you can control this in time over several hundred square miles and over about 70 years. And you can do all sorts of neat things with them. I think this is archaeology even though you don't use a shovel, because it is dealing with the same kind of material.) Shooting ducks requires no aiming. But the difficulty of hunting land mammals when aiming was critical to success and was sufficiently great that it contributed little to subsistence even in the face of shortages.

This essay has been but a general survey and summation of the general directions which archaeology seems to be taking at this time. Central to all of these aspects of current archaeology is its essential and vital relationship to the larger discipline which it serves. As long as this relationship is nourished and developed—I think it is nowadays—archaeology and anthropology are bound to profit in mutual fashion.

Historical and Historic Sites Archaeology as Anthropology: Basic Definitions and Relationships

NORMALLY a discipline either inherits its title from its subject matter, witness for example Egyptology, Classical Archaeology, or more vaguely Prehistoric Archaeology, or it inherits it from its basic approach to its subject matter. In the latter category would fall such neologisms as "new archaeology" and "processual archaeology." Since there is little evidence of anything particularly new about the techniques used in studying materials from historic periods from either an anthropological or historical point of view, it is obvious that such studies in the main must follow the normal pattern and be named after their subject matter.

Considering even the nature and boundaries of the subject matter is apparently no easy task. Among the various titles proffered for the field are found: Historical Archaeology, Historic Archaeology, Historic Site Archaeology, Historic Sites Archaeology, Post-Medieval Archaeology, and a list of more specific terms ranging from Restoration and Colonial to Tin Can Archaeology.

Of course a number of the different terms listed above devolve to sterile points of grammar, euphonics, or at best bare-bones semantics. Nowhere was this clearer than at

Reprinted from *Historical Archaeology,* vol. 4, 1970, pp. 83–89. By permission of the author and the publisher.

the 1967 founding meeting of the Society for Historical Archaeology at Southern Methodist University in Dallas (Pilling 1967:3–4). Debate on the naming of the society, its journal, and its subject matter revolved as much around such semantic questions as around truly substantive points. Noël Hume pointed out at that meeting and elsewhere that the word *site* seemed to exclude artifacts, while *historic* (Hume 1969:5–6) in the minds of many, including politicians, refers to a site on which an event of significant historical impact occurred. Such a stand is incorrect both in reflecting a narrow, archaic view of history (which it is true some government agencies still hold) and even in reference to Webster (or Samuel Johnson). I do not want to argue on this level of meaning, however, and it is readily admitted that the terminological relationship advanced, or more accurately endorsed, in this article is not completely logical or consistent. Periclean Athens is a historic site both in that it dates from a period with historical documentation and in that important events transpired there.

What is proposed is that, putting such minor problems aside, there are presently in the literature two terms which already carry a historical precedent for use. The actual problem is that the terms will be interchanged randomly or one, Historical Archaeology, will crowd the other into extinction and there is already evidence that this is happening. More importantly underlying this terminological tangle is a subject matter, Historic Sites Archaeology, that is vital to both history and anthropology and to which our contribution may be badly curtailed by the imposition of unnecessary limitations.

When and where the two terms in question first appeared in the literature is not clear although as early as 1910 the famous Wisconsin historian, Carl Russell Fish, was discussing the problems involved but without coining any labels. The tradition he represents, however, runs to the present in the writings of such scholars as Carl P. Russell (1967:398–400) who has adopted and proposed the term "historian-archaeologist."

Apparently Historical Archaeology as a name has been in existence for decades and predates Harrington's "Historic Site Archaeology." In the 1930s Woodward (1937:101) was using "Historic Archaeology" and contemporarily or slightly later Frank Setzler (1943:211, 217–18) put in print "Historical-Archaeology" as a hyphenated word. Interestingly Setzler already realized the terminological problems and offered "Colonial Archaeology" as an alternative but with the understanding of its obvious limitations.

Historical Archaeology therefore has been in use for quite some time although its resurgence in popularity is certainly the product of its adoption by the new Society for Historical Archaeology and more publicly by the appearance of Noël Hume's (1969) battle manual for amateurs carrying that title.

Historical Archaeology has never been tightly defined except when it was subsumed the meaning of Historic Sites Archaeology. It is a general and inclusive term and therein lies its usefulness. It is proposed that Historical Archaeology be defined as: *the study of the material remains from any historic period.*

Such a definition does not equate Historical Archaeology with the presence or absence of writing, although there is a vague correlation between level of cultural complexity and the appearance or acceptance of writing. "Historic period" means a period in which the cultures in question have a documentary record and that writing is having a full impact both on the cultures being studied and on the scholarship of the investigation. When records are capable of altering the basic methods and techniques of studying past societies then we are dealing with Historical Archaeology.

For example, all pre-contact New World civilizations would be excluded by this definition. Even if Maya glyphs are deciphered it is extremely unlikely that Maya archaeology will be radically altered by the scanty data they seem to contain.

Historical Archaeology is proposed as a general term, equivalent in many ways to "prehistoric archaeology," because as new areas and time periods began to be studied with a combined archaeological and documentary approach, the same technical problems of how to handle the data will appear that are presently facing historical archaeologists in Europe and America and which certainly were encountered much earlier by Classical Archaeologists. In fact a comparison of the rise of Classical Archaeology on a technical level with our own field might prove very enlightening.

The chronologies, cultural and historical specifics may vary tremendously, but methodologically such fields are (at least in theory) connected. At this moment in its development, however, the field is in truth named for its subject matter, as vague as that may be, more than methodology as that has yet to be spelled out.

More specifically such a covering term includes fields ranging from Colonial to Industrial Archaeology in America and from Classical to Industrial in Europe. The Society for Historical Archaeology and its journal are aptly named in that they are already serving not only scholars dealing with 16th to 18th Century materials, but also as vehicles for the emergence of American Industrial Archaeology. Even the Vikings can be allowed entrance under this definition, with or without the Newport Tower.

Turning to the second term, Historic Sites Archaeology, although it may have its ultimate origin in the Historic Sites Act of 1935 or earlier sources, it was initially defined in 1947 by J. C. Harrington (1952:336; 1955:1128) and redefined from a somewhat different point of view in 1965 by Bernard Fontana.

Harrington emphasized Euro-American remains in his definition of Historic Sites Archaeology although he did not exclude Indian contact sites, while Fontana was certainly working from the reverse perspective as his definition demonstrates (1965:61):

archaeology carried out in sites which contain material evidence of non-Indian culture or concerning which there is contemporary non-Indian documentary record.

Drawing on Harrington and Fontana it is proposed that Historic Sites Archaeology be defined as:

The study of the material manifestation of the expansion of European culture into the non-European world starting in the 15th century and ending with industrialization or the present depending on local conditions.

Historical Archaeology is viewed as covering a subject matter which in no sense is a unified historical entity, although, as already mentioned, there is a developmental relationship. The unity of Historical Archaeology is, or at least should be, primarily technical and involves the methodology of investigation more than the subject matter under investigation. Historic Sites Archaeology in contradistinction deals with a specific historical subject that has temporal, spatial, and cultural boundaries.

Chronologically it would see its inception in the 15th Century perhaps with 1415, the date of the fall of Ceuta signalling initial Portuguese penetration of Africa, as an arbitrary but generally agreed upon point (Parry 1961:7–12). Geographically its boundaries fluctuated from decade to decade but are fairly well documented. Culturally a more

complex problem arises because involved are not only the European cultures in question but also the degree of acculturation on indigenous societies. When is a North American Indian site a historic site? Is the key factor the presence or absence of trade artifacts, the moment of initial contact, or the point of continuous contact?

Many have discussed this problem and Fontana has advanced a typology running from Proto-Contact through Contact, Post-Contact, and Frontier to Non-Aboriginal. As Larrabee (1965:10–11) has pointed out, Fontana's typology is confusing and perhaps too simplistic. Its main shortcoming, however, is its perspective. Fontana seems to be concentrating on the contact situation rather than the ultimate causes and processes involved. For example, he defines (1965:62) Post-Contact sites as:

aboriginal sites which originated after their native populations had been visited by non-Indians and which did not exist prehistorically.

In many cases such a classification has no meaning in that such contact had no influence on basic cultural patterns. Drake's 1579 possible landing and Cermeno's 1595 landing at what today is called Drake's Bay in California may help to date middens there by intrusive artifacts (Heizer 1942), but the sites are still prehistoric both in that the aboriginal cultural patterns seem unaffected, at least the archaeological data does not demonstrate the contrary, and in that the basic research approach is still that of prehistoric archaeology.

Historic Sites Archaeology has temporal, geographical, and cultural boundaries because a complex of fundamental underlying patterns and processes creates the historical studying. These are European in origin and include such factors as the rise of mercantile capitalism, the emergence of national monarchies, and major technological innovations and the impact of these factors outside of Europe. Indigenous sites become historic sites, and thus the subject matter of our discipline, only when their basic cultural and ecological patterns have been altered by contact and when this is displayed in the archaeological data. Such a relationship will frequently correspond to a simultaneous appearance of documentation, as, for example, California Mission records on neophyte villages. Even if such data are lacking for a specific site it is still possible to move from general documentary knowledge to interpret the situation.

Of course direct contact with Europeans is not necessarily a prerequisite for such far reaching changes. Was the rise of the Iroquoian League or the Powhatan Confederacy indigenous or the product of contact, or both? Even if only stimulus diffusion and indirect acculturation are the prime movers, such situations, assuming they can be recognized, are at least in part the subject matter of Historic Sites Archaeology.

Defining Historic Sites Archaeology and its relationship to contact situations as has been done in this article is valid for the New World, all of Oceania, and much of Africa. However, when we turn to Asia a different situation appears. Not only were Europeans observing the natives and recording their observations, but the natives were looking back and also recording. Perhaps such contacts should be called Historic Sites Archaeology to the second power.

More seriously, such a statement is not meant as ethnocentrism, but merely to point out the possible interplay between the various subfields of Historical Archaeology: Historic Sites Archaeology and whatever scholarship has developed around the archaeological and documentary record of the local development of Asian, and for that matter North African, societies. One of the major problems on a global level is our lack of knowledge about what is transpiring in Historical and Historic Sites Archaeology outside of Europe and North America. Are Japanese archaeologists studying those periods of their national emergence that postdate written records including those which reflect

European contact? Are the Indian archaeologists trained under Wheeler excavating Anglo-Indian sites from the 18th and 19th Centuries? The vital importance of such knowledge involves the relationship of these fields to general anthropology.

Turning from this attempt to define Historical and Historic Sites Archaeology and their interrelationship to their relationship to anthropology one finds an even more complex debate. This question has created considerable interest as is seen in Clyde Dollar's recent (1968) essay. Anthropologists tend not to be keenly interested in idiosyncratic behavior and Dollar's use of terminology and concepts was certainly idiosyncratic on occasion. However, what was surprising about the 1968 *Historical Archaeology Forum* was not Dollar's arguments, some of which exposed key problems and questions, but the very poor defense put up by anthropological archaeologists. The papers by Foley (1968) and especially that by Cleland and Fitting (1968) were exceptions.

Harrington in 1955 (:1125) pointed out that although an anthropologically trained archaeologist should bring his theoretical training to bear on the excavation of a historic site there was little evidence for this happening. This is still true and in part is related to the claim of the "new archaeologists" (Binford and Binford 1968) that most American archaeologists, although supposedly trained in anthropology, have not until recently been at all anthropological in their research.

It is not my purpose to go into a detailed discussion of history and anthropology in this article, however, Harrington's sentiments that history is not nor should it attempt to be a social science are fully endorsed. If an archaeologist or anthropologist is trained in the fundamentals of historiography this will not make him a historian any more than a historian with knowledge of surveying and seriation becomes an archaeologist. There is, however, a corollary to this statement which is not true. Anthropologists can use archival data in their research; in fact, such sources can be the basis for their research. Harrington claimed that Historic Sites Archaeology might make contributions to historical data but not to broader history (1955:1124, 1129):

No one supposes that the archaeologist working around Independence Hall will prove that the Declaration of Independence was signed in some year other than 1776.

This example is indisputable but although it is certainly not implied that Harrington, or indeed Fish (cf. 1910:93–94) fifty years earlier, were advocates of a narrow view of history, a few cases, especially the work of Deetz (Dethlefsen and Deetz 1966) and Fontana (Fontana, Greenleaf et al. 1962), have already brought the spirit of such a statement into dispute. Historic Sites Archaeology can correct documentary error, fill in lacunae in the record, certainly, but can it make a major contribution to our understanding of the past? The answer is patently becoming more and more a strong affirmative. How much does a culture record about its basic economic, political, social and ecological structure when frequently the individuals that compose the society in question are only superficially aware of or at least take for granted such patterns and processes?

However the crucial problem is not how much information is excluded or only indirectly reflected in the records, but our habit of thinking of material objects and archival data as separate entities. On a methodological level such a dichotomy is a given, but this unfortunately tends to carry over onto the synthetic and interpretative levels. In the 1920s Arthur Woodward (1932,1937) had already recognized the importance of historic artifacts, now archaeologists are extending his recognition into a full-blown discipline, but usually in the process making reference to historical documents only for chronological or specific, limited data. Even fewer historians are seen either using or advocating

the use (Whitehill 1968:253–63) of such findings to check or supplement their research. The future development of our field, however, does not lie in such attempts to gain specific data, although such data may certainly be useful, nor in an attempt to fuse archaeology and the discipline of American History, but in making Historic Sites Archaeology, including artifacts and documents, an integral part of anthropology.

As previously mentioned, anthropologists, once they have been trained in the use of documentary sources, can use these in their research but from a different point of view than *most* historians. Why can not Historic Sites Archaeologists, as anthropologists, investigate the broadest and most significant questions involved in American history, or any historic record for that matter? Why not redo much of American, or other, history but from an anthropological point of view? Historic Sites Archaeologists conceived their field as an encounter with artifacts and are only now moving into an appreciation of and more than passing interest in primary written sources. The future may well hold a continuing disciplinary evolution that will witness a much more extensive, if not complete, absorption of the documentary record by archaeologists as anthropologists and at the same time a continuing and intensified utilization of material data.

Dollar has discussed the duo-disciplinary nature of our field, but he and Harrington have also hit upon what will terminate this phase. If Historic Sites Archaeology is only a footnote producer for historians, which perhaps it is, it can be much more for anthropologists. A certain amount of research may remain and perhaps should remain in the historian's camp, especially where very specific data are an end goal as with limited excavation in restoration projects, but hopefully problem oriented research free of the impediment of restoration will emerge.

Implied in the above discussion is that anthropology is more holistic than history, and in some ways it may well be. Nevertheless we must not forget that certain schools of historical thought and certain historians also very much take economic, social, political, environmental and ideological processes into account as well as the impact of individuals or specific "key" events. What really distinguishes the two fields, and would distinguish their use of the same documentary or artifactual data, is that anthropology as a social science is ultimately searching for underlying patterns, processes, "laws" (call them what you will) to explain cultural reality.

Specifically how is Historic Sites Archaeology tied into such an approach? The connection is on both a technical and theoretical level, which do, however, merge. Technically Historic Sites Archaeology is a testing ground for methods and approaches used in general archaeology and which on occasion, as in the "new archaeology," arise in part out of anthropological theory. This has been pointed out many times but frequently is viewed as a passing and low level potential. Already specific techniques such as seriation have been checked in historical context (e.g. Barka 1965; Deetz and Dethlefsen 1966), but more importantly major problems of social, economic, and ideological interpretation such as are being debated in the "new archaeology" can be settled in part by Historical and Historic Sites Archaeology as well as Ethnoarchaeology. How is social organization or economic structure reflected in the material inventory of a community? Longacre (1966) or Hill (1966) can only indirectly infer this at a prehistoric site in the Southwest but a ghost town in the same region (Fontana 1968:179–180; Schuyler 1969:2), or better a Classical Greek site where no question of industrialization would intrude, with records on the demographic, social, and ethnic structure would be much more enlightening.

On a theoretical level, besides the holistic perspective, another of the distinguishing traits of anthropology is the comparative approach. Deetz and Larrabee have men-

tioned this in regard to Historic Sites Archaeology, but in a limited sense. Deetz (1968:122–23) in reference to assemblage differences between Jamestown and Plymouth and their significance, and Larrabee (1966:5–6; 14) on a more general level although his example is a narrow comparison of specific historic artifacts of a common source in different geographic and cultural areas.

Prehistoric archaeologists have repeatedly pointed out that the New World on a pre-contact level has because of its isolation importance not in its impact on world history, but as a comparative laboratory for the social sciences. The publication of Robert M. Adams's (1966) *The Evolution of Urban Society* is ample evidence of this potential.

Historic Sites Archaeology has the same potential but for opposite reasons. Just as the lack of diffusion and contact created the situation outlined above so its overpowering and global presence in the Age of Exploration and Colonization creates another laboratory for the anthropologist. There are situations where the same European culture was in contact at the same period, thus giving us a control, with indigenous cultures ranging from the band level to civilization. There were dissimilar European cultures in contact simultaneously with the same native culture. These are built in situations for testing and formulation of hypotheses.

Earlier in this article the complexity of contact situations was discussed and it is natural for anthropologists to immediately notice acculturation potential in Historic Sites Archaeology. However the possibilities on a comparative basis are much broader for anthropology. What of a comparison of European cultures themselves in acculturation situations as in Canada and the Southeastern United States? What of situations where during colonization the same European culture was intruded into radically different environments and the resulting ecological adaptation, or dissimilar cultures into the same ecological zone? What of the selective processes of migration and colonization as Foster (1960) studied in *Culture and Conquest*.

Modern anthropology is rapidly undertaking more research on complex societies and processes and just as Kathleen G. Aberle (1967) has called upon ethnography to study not only conquered non-Western cultures but also the process of imperialism itself, so Historic Sites Archaeology can make a major contribution to modern anthropology by studying the processes of European expansion, exploration, and colonization as well as those of culture contact and imperialism, that underlie one of the most dynamic periods of world history and which are reflected in both artifactual and documentary data.

Methodologically Historic Sites Archaeology, and other branches of Historical Archaeology, should be the most sophisticated archaeology. It is the least sophisticated. Historic Sites Archaeology should be highly productive on a theoretical level but in many ways is inferior theoretically to American prehistoric archaeology. Historic Sites Archaeology should be making major contributions to our understanding of the expansion of Europe and the world wide impact of that expansion, rather than adding marginal footnotes to historical research.

The criticism may be raised that this will all come in good time, that Historic Sites Archaeology is a new field. This attitude, which might be called the "not ready yet hypothesis" has a parallel in the so-called "jigsaw hypothesis" of an earlier generation of American prehistorians: if proper control of the raw data is gained and facts are piled up, they will speak for themselves. Of course the end result was a large number of prehistoric junk piles still housed in American museums. It will indeed be unfortunate if Historic Sites Archaeology, as well as other branches of Historical Archaeology, must blindly repeat the mistakes seen in the rise of prehistoric archaeology.

Specific hypotheses must be applied to the data, artifactual and written, and these hypotheses must be in a broad theoretical structure which will come mainly from anthropology and other social sciences. As Historic Sites Archaeology becomes more and more an integral part of anthropology, and less related to restoration, it will evolve as a valid and relevant field of research and help to maintain general archaeology as a productive part of modern anthropology.

Archaeological Systematics and the Study of Culture Process

WILLEY AND Phillips (1958:50) have expressed doubts that current archaeological concepts such as "phase" have consistent meaning in terms of human social units. It is the purpose of this essay to explore some of the reasons for this lack of congruence and to offer a theoretical framework more consistent with social reality.

In any general theoretical framework there are at least two major components: 1) one that deals with criteria for isolating the phenomenon under study and with the underlying assumptions about the nature of the units or partitive occurrences within the recognized generic class of phenomenon, and 2) assumptions concerning the way in which these partitive units are articulated in the operation of a system or during change.

Most of the analytical means and conceptual tools of archaeological systematics have arisen in the context of a body of culture theory which is referred to here as the "normative school." Under this normative view the phenomenon being studied is variously defined, but there is general agreement that culture with a capital C is the subject. In this the normative theorists are in agreement with others. It is in the definition of partitive concepts and the as-

sumptions concerning the processes of between-unit dynamics that normative theorists differ markedly from the position taken here. A typical normative statement is given by Taylor (1948:110):

> By culture as a partitive concept, I mean a historically derived system of culture traits which is a more or less separable and cohesive segment of the whole-that-is-culture and whose separate traits tend to be shared by all or by specially designated individuals of a group or society.

A similar view is expressed by Willey and Phillips (1958:18) when speaking of spatial divisions of cultural phenomena:

> In strictly archaeological terms, the locality is a geographical space small enough to permit the working assumption of complete cultural homogeneity at any given time.

The emphasis in these two quotations and in the writings of other archaeologists (Ford 1954:47; Rouse 1939:15–18; Gifford 1960:346) is on the shared characteristics of human behavior. Within this frame of thought, culture is defined as an abstraction from human behavior.

According to the concept of culture being developed here, culture is a mental construct consisting of ideas. (Taylor 1948:101).

Or as Ford (1954:47) has argued:

> First, it must be recalled that these buildings are cultural products—not the culture. These arrangements of wood, bamboo, and grass are

Reprinted from *American Antiquity,* vol. 31, no. 2, 1965, pp. 203–10. By permission of the author and the Society for American Archaeology.

of interest to the ethnologists solely because they illustrate the aborigine's ideas as to the proper ways to construct dwellings.

In summary, a normative theorist is one who sees as his field of study the ideational basis for varying ways of human life—culture. Information is obtained by studying cultural products or the objectifications of normative ideas about the proper ways of life executed by now extinct peoples. The archaeologist's task then lies in abstracting from cultural products the normative concepts extant in the minds of men now dead. (For criticism of this general view see White 1954:461–68).

In examining the problem of how we may observe and study cultural phenomena, a crucial question arises: What types of units can be isolated for the meaningful study of culture? For adherents of the normative school, the assumptions about units or the natural "packages" in which culture occurs are dependent upon assumptions about the dynamics of ideational transmission. Learning is the recognized basis of cultural transmission between generations and diffusion the basis of transmission between social units not linked by regular breeding behavior. The corollary of this proposition is that culture is transmitted between generations and across breeding populations in inverse proportion to the degree of social distance maintained between the groups in question. Since culture is viewed as a great "whole" transmitted through time and across space, any attempt to break up this cultural "whole" is considered arbitrary and thought of as a methodological expedient (Ford 1954:51; Brew 1946:49). The partitioning of culture is often termed a heuristic device for measuring the degree of social distance between the groups whose cultural products are being observed. (An excellent criticism of this view is found in Spaulding 1957:85–87). Spatial discontinuities in the distribution of similar formal characteristics are perceived as either the result of 1) natural

barriers to social intercourse, or 2) the presence of a value system which provides a conservative psychological matrix that inhibits the acceptance of foreign traits, or 3) the migration or intrusion into the area of new peoples who disrupt the previous pattern of social intercourse. Formal changes in the temporal distribution of items are viewed as the result of innovations or the operation of a built-in dynamics sometimes designated as "drift" (Ford 1954:51; Herskovits 1948:581–82). (For criticism of this concept, see Binford 1963:89–93.) Both innovation and drift are considered natural to culture and, as Caldwell (1958:1) has said: "other things being equal, changes in material culture through time and space will tend to be regular." Discontinuities in rates of change or in formal continuity through time are viewed as the result of historical events which tend to change the configuration of social units through such mechanisms as extensions of trade, migration, and the diffusions of "core" ideas such as religious cults (Ritchie 1955).

Cultural differences and similarities are expressed by the normative school in terms of "cultural relationships" which, if treated rigorously, resolve into one general interpretative model. This model is based on the assumption of a "culture center" where, for unspecified reasons, rates of innovation exceed those in surrounding areas. The new culture spreads out from the center and blends with surrounding cultures until it is dissipated at the fringes, leaving marginal cultures. Cultural relationships are viewed as the degree of mutual or unilateral "influence" exerted between culture centers or subcenters.

This interpretative framework implies what I choose to call the aquatic view of culture. Interpretative literature abounds in phrases such as "cultural stream" and in references to the "flowing" of new cultural elements into a region. Culture is viewed as a vast flowing stream with minor variations in ideational norms concerning appropriate ways of making pots, getting married, treating one's mother-in-law, building houses, temples (or not building them, as the case may be), and even dying. These ideational variations are periodically "crystallized" at different points in time and space, resulting in distinctive and sometimes striking cultural climaxes which allow us to break up the continuum of culture into cultural phases.

One of the most elegant and complete criticisms of the normative theorists to appear in recent years is that of David Aberle (1960). He has pointed out that adherents of the normative position are forced to explain cultural differences and similarities in terms of two factors, historical and psychic. He summarizes the normative position as follows:

No culture can be understood solely by reference to its current situation. As a result of the accidents of history, it has had contacts with a variety of other cultures. These other cultures provide the pool of potential cultural material on which cultures can draw. Since there is no general basis for predicting what cultures will have contact with what others, the historical factor has an accidental and fortuitous character. With respect to the psychic factor, there are qualities of men's minds—whether general tendencies to imitate or specific attitudes held by a particular group—which determine whether or not any available cultural item will be borrowed. Although the contacts are unpredictable, the laws of psychology may account for acceptance and rejection. Hence the laws of culture are psychological laws. (Aberle 1960:3)

The normative view leaves the archaeologist in the position of considering himself a culture historian and/or a paleo-psychologist (for which most archaeologists are poorly trained). This leaves him competent to pursue the investigation of culture history, a situation which may partially account for failure to develop the explanatory level of archaeological theory noted by Willey and Phillips (1958:5).

It is argued here that a new systematics, one based on a different concept of culture,

is needed to deal adequately with the explanation of cultural process. If we define culture as man's extrasomatic means of adaptation (White 1959:8), in the partitive sense culture is an extrasomatic adaptive system that is employed in the integration of a society with its environment and with other sociocultural systems. Culture in this sense is not necessarily shared; it is participated in by men. In cultural systems, people, things, and places are components in a field that consists of environmental and sociocultural subsystems, and the locus of cultural process is in the dynamic articulations of these subsystems. This complex set of interrelationships is not explicable by reduction to a single component—ideas—any more than the functioning of a motor is explainable in terms of a single component, such as gasoline, a battery, or lubricating oil.

It was stated above that in our definition culture is not necessarily shared; it is participated in. And it is participated in differentially. A basic characteristic of cultural systems is the integration of individuals and social units performing different tasks, frequently at different locations; these individuals and social units are articulated by means of various institutions into broader units that have different levels of corporate inclusiveness. Within any one cultural system, the degree to which the participants share the same ideational basis should vary with the degree of cultural complexity of the system as a whole. In fact, a measure of cultural complexity is generally considered to be the degree of internal structural differentiation and functional specificity of the participating subsystems (White 1959:144–45). Within any given cultural system, the degree to which all the participants share common ideational preferences should vary inversely with the complexity of the system as a whole. The sharing of cultural elements by distinct systems will be a function of the nature of the cultural means of articulating distinct groups with each other.

At present our explicitly stated systematics is based on the degree to which cultural traits are shared. The Midwestern taxonomic system (McKern 1935:70–82; and 1939: 301–13) is a hierarchical arrangement of archaeologically defined culture traits as they appear in spatially or temporally discrete manifestations. Similarly, such units as the phase (Willey and Phillips 1958:50; Rouse 1955:713–14) are groupings of archaeological complexes on the basis of shared traits.

This emphasis on shared traits in our system of classification results in masking differences and in lumping together phenomena which would be discrete under another taxonomic method. Culture is not a univariate phenomenon, nor is its functioning to be understood or measured in terms of a single variable—the spatial-temporal transmission of ideas. On the contrary, culture is multivariate, and its operation is to be understood in terms of many causally relevant variables which may function independently or in varying combinations. It is our task to isolate these causative factors and to seek regular, statable, and predictable relationships between them.

Our taxonomies should be framed with this end in mind. We should partition our observational fields so that we may emphasize the nature of variability in artifact populations and facilitate the isolation of causally relevant factors. Our categories should be justifiable in terms of possessing common structural or functional properties in the normal operation of cultural systems. These categories should then be analyzed in terms of their behavior in various systems and in situations of systematic change.

By such a method we may achieve our aim of expressing the laws of cultural process. Archaeological systematics should be an aid in accomplishing analytical tasks. As an example of the suggested method of partitioning our observational framework, two general problems will be discussed: ceramic classification and the classification of archaeological assemblages.

Formal variation in ceramics occurs because of differences in either the techniques of manufacture or in the general design of the finished product; both kinds of variation may occur independently of each other. (This distinction is analogous to Rouse's [1960:314] distinction between procedural and conceptual modes). One example is the production of an abrupt shoulder as opposed to a gently sloping shoulder while continuing to execute the same basic set of manufacturing techniques. Such variation is termed *morphological variation*. In addition to morphological variation, there is *decorative variation* or modifications that are made as discrete steps in the terminal phases of the manufacturing process. Painted and incised designs are examples of decorative variation. We can therefore speak of two major classes of variation or analytic dimensions, in terms of which ceramic forms can be studied—*technical* and *design dimensions*. Morphological and decorative variation may be observed along either dimension.

With regard to the sociocultural context of formal variability, two broad classes of variation can be recognized which crosscut the categories mentioned above. *Primary functional variation* is that which is directly related to the specific use made of the vessel in question; for example, the difference between a plate and a storage jar. *Secondary functional variation* is a byproduct of the social context of the manufacturers of the vessel or of the social context of the intended use of the item, or both. This variation may arise from a traditional way of doing things within a family or a larger social unit, or it may serve as a conscious expression of between-group solidarity. Certain design characteristics may become standardized as symbols appropriate to vessels used in specific social contexts. At this level of analysis we may recall Linton's (1936:403–21) statement that any given cultural item may vary with regard to form, meaning, use, and function in variable cultural contexts. Such distinctions are particularly important if the social context of manufacture and use are not isomorphic, as in the case of items circulated widely through exchange systems, or are used primarily in the context of institutions functioning for intersocietal articulation.

Formal variation in artifacts need not and, in most cases, probably does not have a single meaning in the context of the functioning cultural system. The study of primary functional variation is essential to the understanding of the sociocultural systems represented by the artifacts, in this case ceramics. The nature and number of occurrences of functionally differentiated container types can yield valuable information about the size of social segments performing different tasks. Even in cases where specific functions cannot be determined for the recognized types, the spatial configuration of their occurrence tells something about the spatial structure of differentiated activities within or between sites.

Variables of primary function may remain stable, change abruptly, or change at rates different from variables of secondary function. The relative rates of change in these two classes of variables can tell us much about the nature of the changes within the systems in question. An example of this can be seen by comparing the Havana tradition of Illinois with the Scioto tradition of Ohio.

Containers of the Havana tradition are predominantly large, open-mouthed cauldrons, but there are occasional flat-bottomed "flowerpot" forms. This suggests that food was prepared in these societies for relatively large groups of people—larger than nuclear families—and that food was stored corporately. This pattern of cooking and storing was common to essentially all the societies participating in the Havana tradition. Secondary functional variation, on the other hand, with respect to both decoration and design exhibits differences through space and time, suggesting that

among the participants in the Havana tradition social contacts and generational continuity were changing.

Container forms of the Scioto tradition in Ohio, which is believed to be contemporaneous with the Havana tradition, were smaller vessels with rounded bottoms; the large cauldron is an infrequent form. Nevertheless, there are common design and technical attributes in the ceramics of both traditions. This suggests that, in the Ohio groups, the social units for which food was prepared were smaller and that modes of food storage were correspondingly different.

In the traditional view, the elements in common between the Havana and Scioto traditions would be interpreted as indicating "cultural relationships," and at present the two are grouped into the "Hopewell phase," with each group sharing different traits of the "Hopewell culture." It is suggested here that the sociocultural systems represented in the two traditions may be and probably are totally different, and that the common ceramic elements reflect patterns of common regional interaction facilitated through different institutions. This view differs markedly from one which pictures the flowing of "Hopewell culture" out of a "culture center."

The comparative study of secondary functional variation within one class of containers makes it possible to determine the degree of work specialization in discrete social segments as well as the degree of craft specialization in the manufacture of specific container classes. Empirical demonstration of the validity of the assumptions underlying sociological interpretation of variability in craft products is accumulating, and a number of recent studies show that this kind of "meaning" is recoverable from ceramic data. For example, Cronin (1962:109) has demonstrated greater similarity in the conventional use of decorative design elements between pottery types at a single site than between types of the same pottery from different sites. Comparable results are suggested by recent discussions of taxonomic problems encountered by others (Sears 1960: 327–28; Smith 1962). I have recently proposed a processual model for this type of phenomenon (Binford 1963). Several recent studies have utilized the measurement and spatial distributions of stylistic minutiae in the construction of sociological models for prehistoric communities (Deetz 1960; Longacre 1963; Freeman and Brown 1964).

If we expand our analytical perspective to include the problem of formal variability in contemporaneous sociocultural systems and sociocultural systems through time, then our analysis must be even more critical. What is ideosyncratic secondary functional variation in one group may symbolize political ties in another. Primary functional variation in one social system may be partially incorporated as secondary functional variation in another.

The complexities facing the archaeologist who attempts this kind of analysis necessitate the use of multiple taxonomies framed to express multivariate attributes. Such taxonomies should replace the conventional ones, which are either classes based on unspecified kinds of likeness or difference, or are hierarchically arranged traits presumed to reflect generic relationships (Willey and Phillips 1958:31; Rouse 1960). We suggest that classification should proceed independently with regard to technical and design attributes and that crosscutting categories should be used to express morphological and decorative variation (Table 1).

TABLE 1

Contingency of formal variation

	Morphological variation	Decorative variation
Technical dimension		
Design dimension		

The result of such an analysis would be the recognition of numbers of classes of variables, referable to one or more of the column-and-row contingency boxes in Table 1. Analysis would then proceed to the question of the cultural context of the observed classes or variables distinguished in the four categories above. This step is schematically diagrammed in Table 2. Each column and row

TABLE 2

Contingency of cultural variation

	Primary functional variation	Secondary functional variation	
		Context of use	Context of Production
Techno-morphological			
Morphological design			
Decorative techniques			
Decorative designs			

contingency box would contain the formal classes of demonstrable variables derived from the initial classification.

The next step would be the definition of populations of artifacts in terms of recognizable and demonstrably different cultural factors. Discussions of differences and similarities would be based on independent and dependent variables and not on an undifferentiated conglomeration of multivariate phenomena.

The current systematics of archaeological assemblages also stresses the quantity of shared traits. Assemblages are referred to a phase or a focus without due allowances for either seasonal or functional variability. Although it is premature to attempt a final presentation of assemblage systematics since such a presentation should be based on more complete knowledge of the range of classes of variability, we feel that at least three major types of broad cultural alignments can be distinguished which may vary independently of one another.

The first such category is the *tradition*, whose meaning we choose to make somewhat narrower than is conventional in archaeological literature. (For a discussion of the concept as generally used, see Willey and Phillips 1958:34–40.) We define tradition as a demonstrable continuity through time in the formal properties of locally manufactured craft items, this continuity being seen in secondary functional variability only. There may or may not be such continuity with respect to primary functional variability. To put it another way, the tradition is seen in continuity in those formal attributes which vary with the social context of manufacture exclusive of the variability related to the use of the item. This is termed stylistic variability (Binford 1962:220), and on a single time horizon such a tradition would be spatially defined as a style zone. Through time we may study the areal extent and stability of style zones and the comparative history of local traditions within the framework of the macrotradition. Historical continuity and social phylogeny are particularly amenable to analysis through the study of stylistic attributes. It should be noted that the concept of tradition as it is used here may refer to either a single class of artifactual materials, such as ceramics, or to several classes of artifacts of a single sociocultural system which exhibit continuity through time. It is assumed that formal variability in secondary function is directly related to the social matrix of production and use. In the case of stability through time in the social matrix of production, we would expect to observe temporal continuity and a regular rate of change. In the case of a changing social matrix of production, we would expect to find discontinuities in rates of change and in the spatial and temporal distribution of formal properties.

A second broad class of sociocultural relationships is reflected in items that are widely exchanged and which occur in a context of social distinctiveness, that is, sociotechnic items (Binford 1962). Such items would be analyzed in terms of their primary functional variability as inferred through correlation with other archaeological remains which define the context of social relations. Through the study of the spatial distributions of such items on a single time horizon we may define *interaction spheres*—the areal matrices of regular and institutionally maintained intersocietal articulation. This term is adopted from Caldwell (1962). It is my impression that I have seen the term used by other archaeologists, but I have not been able to find it in the literature. Caldwell (1962) has pointed to the essential characteristics of the interaction sphere:

An interaction sphere is a kind of phenomenon which can be regarded as having properties different from a culture . . . the various regional traditions were present before there was a Hopewellian situation. The term culture would be better applied to each of these separately than to the overall situation with which they are interacting.

What is essential to the concept of an interaction sphere is that it denotes a situation in which there is a regular cultural means of institutionalizing and maintaining intersocietal interaction. The particular forms of the institutions and the secondary functions which may accrue to them will be found to vary widely in the spectrum of history. Interaction spheres may crosscut both traditions and culture areas. The sharing of symbols and the appearance of similar institutions are less a function of the traditional enculturative milieu of individual societies than of complex articulation of societies of different ethnic backgrounds, levels of cultural complexity, and social types.

The comparative structural and functional analysis of interaction spheres is suggested as an approach which allows us to define, quantify, and explain the observation of Redfield (1941:344) that rates of cultural change may be directly related to rates of social interaction. The distinction between the "shared" culture of a stylistic nature and the "shared" culture of a sociopolitical nature is the basis for distinguishing the tradition from the interaction sphere.

Examples of the interaction sphere come readily to mind. The presence of Mississippian "traits" in local traditions on the Piedmont of the southeastern United States is one. Another is the common "Hopewellian" items in tombs of Illinois (the Havana tradition) and in the charnel houses of Ohio (the Scioto tradition). The nature of the cultural processes responsible for the widespread occurrences of similar cultural items in these two cases cannot be explained by the simplistic reference to sharing of similar ideas concerning the proper ways to manufacture items.

The third category we wish to discuss is that of the adaptive area. An adaptive area is one which exhibits the common occurrence of artifacts used primarily in coping directly with the physical environment. Such spatial distributions would be expected to coincide broadly with culture areas as they are conventionally defined; however, this concept differs from the culture-area concept in that stylistic attributes are excluded from the definition. The adaptive means of coping with changes in physical environment need not coincide with those which are designed to cope with changes in the social environment. Therefore, we need to study traditions (based on styles), interaction spheres (based on intersocietal relations), and adaptive spheres (based on common means of coping with the physical environment), and treat these three isolates as independent variables.

Summary—It has been argued that the normative theory of culture is inadequate for the generation of fruitful explanatory hypotheses of cultural process. An approach is offered in which culture is not reduced to normative ideas about the proper ways of doing things but is viewed as the system of the total extrasomatic means of adaptation. Such a system involves a complex set of relationships among people, places, and things whose matrix may be understood in multivariate terms.

The steps in such an analysis proceed by means of the partitioning of demonstrable variability into a multidimensional framework. Use of such a framework will facilitate isolation of the causes of various kinds of changes and differences and provide the basis for studying comparatively the rates and patterns of change in different classes of cultural phenomena. Such an approach would, it is argued, facilitate and increase our understanding of cultural processes.

NOTE

This essay was originally presented as a paper at the Twenty-ninth Annual Meeting of the Society for American Archaeology, Chapel Hill, North Carolina, 1964.

PART 4

The Methodological Base
of Contemporary Archaeology

Introduction

A distinction should be made between method and technique. In science, method
is generally a series of logical and procedual devices insuring rigor in the match
between data and the variable those data measure. Technique is a much more
particular and narrow set of tools used in obtaining and measuring data. Archaeology
is famous for the techniques it uses: stratigraphy, dendrochronology, radiocarbon
dating, palynology, paleoethnobotany, and a whole litany of others. Archaeology
is not so famous for its methods. Some of these are ethnographic analogy, the
direct historical approach, and a variety of taxonomic principles dichotomized
between native categories thought to represent what the "really real is really like"
on the one hand and arbitrary, problem-designed categories on the other.

The major flaw in archaeological method—a flaw manifestly absent in its
techniques—is imprecision, lack of logical rigor, and a general insecurity of the
knowledge thereby produced. This insecurity in the knowledge we obtain is
manifest in the rhetorical order of archaeology's work. Volumes end with sections
entitled "Speculations" instead of beginning with a section describing the hypothesis
the book will really examine. "Conclusions" occupy totally minimal and dis-
proportionately minor parts of volumes otherwise populated by descriptive data
often unrelated to the ending in any way. It is with this major flaw in archaeological
method that the articles in this section are concerned.

There are two realms of action to improve on the security of the knowledge that
we as archaeologists produce. The first revolves around the logic or arguments of
relevance whereby a variable that is to be measured is linked to the data actually
collected. A classic modern case of this is the logic connecting ceramic style
variation to aspects of social organization: painted design elements measured
residential units of kin groups. It is the strength and imagination of the logic applied
to archaeological data that open an enormously wider range of problems to
contemporary archaeologists than was formerly the case. The arguments which
fashion that logic between data and variable are drawn from the substantive
domain in which a problem resides. If the domain is kinship, the ecology of hunter-
gathers, nutrition, domestication, settlement pattern, economics, or demography,
then the arguments of relevance linking the artifacts to the problem come from the
literature of that substantive domain and from ethnographic cases where similarities
are pertinent. These sources often define new ranges of data and provide the logic
making the data pertinent to the problem. The expansion of archaeology's data

base, one of the real explosions of the last decade, has come about through use of new disciplines to solve older problems. But in addition to expanding the data-base, the initial construction of arguments of relevance borrowed from general anthropology and other disciplines has resulted in fuller and surer use of the data already in hand. Our conclusions are more firm and trustworthy, both through a wider frame of ethnographic and disciplinary reference and through a sub-ordination of archaeological research to the logical rigors of scientific method.

The whole idea of methodological rigor comes with a closer approximation to the methods of science. Although the results of the advent of scientific method in archaeology has been too strongly touted, it is observable that research has greater clarity, and conclusions greater reliability, when the canons of scientific procedure are explicitly used. And it is observable also that these canons are more frequently part of the background of current research designs in archaeology. Since a specific part of such procedure is arguments of relevance or linking logic, their currency in archaeology is easily accounted for.

A distinction should be made between the source of problems and linking arguments on one hand and the explanations for a problem on the other. Much of contemporary archaeology relies on the explanatory framework derived from the disciplines they borrow from, usually adapting those explanations to cultural ecology and process-oriented evolution.

The second realm in which security of knowledge has been improved is quantitative. Descriptive statistics, sampling, and correlational techniques remove the intuitive and haphazard guesswork that cripple an analyst's judgment even before he reaches the conclusion of a project. The introduction of such techniques began several decades ago in archaeology, and their importance has been displayed to the point where other, more crucial innovations in archaeology have been ignored or misunderstood. The emphasis has been so disproportionate that the current innovations have been called computer archaeology. What that epithet accurately implies, however, is the enormous amount of care and precision that may now go into archaeological research planning. A concern with method, and thereby with precision, is exhibited both in the emphasis on logic and the use of quantitative techniques in contemporary archaeology. It is in this domain that some of the most impressive and public advances have been made in the subdiscipline.

Archaeological Systems for Indirect Observation of the Past

THIS ESSAY might better be titled "Toward the Construction of Reliable Indicators in Archaeology." The concerns presented here reflect my conviction that archaeologists seeking to increase the reliability, i.e., credibility, of our knowledge of the past, and seeking also to expend anthropological theory as it relates to the past can borrow profitably from the methodological theory and vocabulary of psychology and sociology. I suggest that just as the answers to psychological questionnaires are considered as indicators of inner psychological factors or states (Boring 1961; Stevens 1951; Thurstone 1959), and just as the answers to census or opinion surveys are considered indicators of social phenomena (Lazarsfeld and Rosenberg 1955:1–18), e.g., class or economic factors, the characteristics of the archaeological record (here termed archaeological data) can be considered as indicators of past phenomena. In this essay, I refer only to past sociocultural phenomena, although past environmental and human biological phenomena could equally well be used.

It is heuristically useful to isolate those archaeological activities that can be termed "natural historiography" from those that are considered subsequently. The philosopher F. S. C. Northrup (1947:35–58) argues that classification and typology are essential characteristics of natural history. Scholars, confronted with masses of empirical data, attempt to reduce their complexities by placing them in smaller, more easily handled categories that may be grouped, in turn, into even fewer classes. The Linnaean system for the classification of animals is archetypical.

Such classification in archaeology can be termed "time-space systematics" (cf. Chang 1967a), or "culture-historical integration" as by Willey and Phillips (1958:4). It consists, first, of the classification of artifacts and features recovered in excavation and survey into types; second, of the grouping of types into assemblages, i.e., classes having similar sets of types; and third, of the grouping of assemblages into "cultures," or "culture-types." Cultures are conceived of as having spatial and temporal boundaries—either natural or arbitrary (cf. Willey and Phillips 1958:14–17)—and are assigned to areas and periods on the basis of the spatial and temporal occurrence of the similar assemblages of which they are composed.

Natural historical archaeology does not, indeed should not, venture beyond the description of the archaeological record. No doubt there are some archaeologists wholly devoted to observation and classification and there are many others whose work entails almost as much devotion. However, almost all archaeologists aspire beyond natural historiography. Almost all archaeologists hope to know the past.

The Need for Observational Systems

Events of the prehistoric past constitute a subclass of those phenomena that are so remote as to be unobservable by any observer now living. Such remote phenomena are numerous and include things too small to be seen, such as subatomic particles; things too distant to be seen, such as the other side of the universe; things too hazardous to be seen, such as the center of atomic explosions; things which may be based in material phenomena but which are not equivalent to them, such as the "id," "collective consciousness," or a morpheme; and events in the past. These phenomena all share the characteristic that they have never and, in many cases, will never, be directly observed by any particular individual.

A second class of remote phenomena consists of sequences of events that extend over considerable lengths of time. These sequences or processes are most notably remote if they extend beyond the lifetime of a given observer. Even if an observer had been present, he could not have seen the evolution of the solar system, or of protoplasm, or the formation of the Rocky Mountains. Similarly, no observer saw, although many observers were present who could have observed short segments of, the evolution of *Homo erectus*, the development of agriculture or of urban centers, or even the industrial revolution.

I must here define "direct observation." We do speak of "observing" atomic particles, of "measuring" their dimensions, of "observing" stars, e.g., pulsars. But "direct observation" here is used in the sense of "experiencing with one's senses." "Senses" here refers to those exterior organs which receive information—the eyes are most important. It is heuristically useful to distinguish that which can be seen with one's own eyes— experience within his own senses—from that which one cannot.

Strictly, by this definition, an individual does not observe phenomena beyond the limits of his senses. Unless he is there, he does not see other nations, other dwellings or other rooms. He does not even see behind his back, although he might sense something in other ways. He certainly does not directly observe events and processes that occurred before his birth. Yet these phenomena *are* observed. We *do* have knowledge of things too small, too distant, too hazardous, or too far in the past to be seen. This is a remarkable situation. Just as we observe the interaction of atoms, we observe the interaction of habitat, human populations, and subsistence techniques which produced the neolithic revolution. Just as we observe the structure of the atmosphere of Jupiter, we observe the structure of society in the past.

All remote phenomena must be observed indirectly. Means must be developed that permit this. They must involve the use of instruments other than our senses, but which articulate with our senses. Occasionally such instruments provide images that are close approximations to many aspects of a remote phenomenon so that we can experience it "as if we were there." Television pictures of the surface of Mars or electron-microscopic photos are examples. But most often instruments provide information about only one or a few characteristics of a remote phenomenon. And most often they do not provide the kind of data we could receive if we were there. Graphs, charts, readings on dials, various numerical values, etc., are not data which men, relying only on their senses, would observe. Rather, instruments translate these phenomena into conventional symbols, e.g., numbers, which must be sensed and interpreted. If technology has extended our senses, it is because it has enabled us to observe many more kinds of phenomena than was possible heretofore.

Past sociocultural phenomena must be observed by instruments developed by archaeologists and other interested scholars. An instrument must be so constructed that when a particular past phenomenon is observed the instrument used gives a distinctive reading or takes on a particular "value." The instrument should not take on that value in the presence of other past phenomena. Otherwise, of course, it would not be possible on the basis of that instrument alone to distinguish which was being observed. Ideally, the absence of a particular value would indicate the absence of the phenomenon. But this is not often possible in archaeology because many other phenomena could intervene to produce distorted values. In short, the presence of a particular value derived from an instrument used for observing the past should be a sufficient condition for establishing the presence of the past phenomenon. Seldom will it also be a necessary condition.

The Structure of Systems for the Observation of Past Phenomena

What are the components of an observational system? If it is conceived of as a process, the observational system consists of an observer (an archaeologist), an instrument, and a product—the observation of a particular past phenomenon. What is the instrument the values of which archaeologists take to be observations of the past? It is obvious that we can observe what we cannot see only by means of what we can see. It is also obvious that only the archaeological record exists in the present to be seen by archaeologists. Clearly the archaeological record is the instrument and its values are its properties, characteristics, and attributes. These we term "archaeological data."

It might be objected that archaeological data are epistemologically distinct from the instrument. Thus data exist whether or not we observe them, while instruments in the sense employed here are created by us. The track of an atomic particle in a bubble chamber would exist even if there were no theory of atomic particles. On the other hand, it can be argued that "to see" is "to see as" (Northrop 1947; Hanson 1958). The physicist does not merely observe some-

thing. Minimally he observes a "line" or "track." He may observe a "track produced by a particular particle" as well. Similarly we assume archaeological data exist independently of our knowledge of them. But as soon as we sense them, we relate our sensations to concepts we have about such things. Something is an "archaeological" datum, not a "geological" one. It is the remains of a "hearth," not a "house." The archaeological datum is both something we sense and conceive. It is this conceptual dimension of archaeological data which enables us to use the archaeological record as an instrument for observing the past.

It might also be objected that the archaeological record is not an instrument in the same sense as an electron microscope or a bubble chamber. An electron microscope is something we have created in the present and by means of which we observe something also existing in the present. The archaeological record is something created in the past by means of which we observe something in the past. The microscope is distinct from that which we hope to observe while the archaeological record is not. But of what does this distinctiveness consist? The archaeological record is not equivalent to the past. Strictly we observe a "shallow, bowl-shaped depression, four meters in diameter," not a "house." When we say that we observe "the remains of a house" we have already lept from the present to the past (see also, Fritz and Plog 1970). Archaeological theory is required precisely because the present archaeological record differs so markedly from the past phenomena archaeologists hope to know. The archaeological record also is not distinct from other instruments in that it was produced in part in the past. This is a matter of degree rather than of kind. There is always some temporal difference between the instance of existence and the instance of observation. Is a telescope less an instrument when it transmits light originating thousands of years ago than seconds ago?

General classes of archaeological data that we employ to observe the prehistoric past includes sites, features, and artifacts; faunal and floral remains; physical and chemical characteristics of soils or of other features of the landscape; and individual and relative distributions of these data in space. Temporal distributions are not data in this sense because they must be observed indirectly using instruments such as stratigraphic position or relative amount of the carbon-14 isotope. An archaeological datum is the only material component of an operational system for indirect observation, per se. An archaeologist acts upon this material by observing it directly, and if he observes an expected datum in the present, he believes that he has indirectly observed the past phenomenon. If he does not directly observe the present datum, he may believe that he has not indirectly observed the past phenomenon.

But why should he believe that the present datum is in any way related to the past phenomenon? To understand this belief, it is necessary to consider the formal structure of his instrument, a system for indirect observation. This refers not to physical hardware or instruments but to the categorical, logical and theoretical systems we must use to know anything at all. Categorical systems can consist of concepts common in ordinary usage, e.g., "large" or of concepts given a technical meaning, e.g., "phase." Logical systems support the reasoning that enables us to confirm our claims that there are relations between present archaeological data and past phenomena. Theoretical systems contain hypotheses about both the nature or content of the present and past phenomena with which we are concerned, and about their interrelationship.

This formal structure has two types of components. One consists of categories or descriptions of a) the properties of phenomena that exist in the present, and of b) the properties of phenomena that are asserted to have existed in the past. The other type consists of arguments which link the described properties of empirical and past phenomena. Another component, viz., the process of justifying the belief that the system works will be considered subsequently.

Descriptions of present and past phenomena require distinct vocabularies. The first consists of primitive terms or concepts that refer to both quantities and qualities of the archaeological record. "Length," "shape," "color," "empirical types" (of objects or features); "texture," "ph," "mineral-type" (of soils); "frequency," "ratio," "correlation" are all examples. "Ph," "mineral-type," and other similar terms are, in fact, rather sophisticated theoretical concepts developed in other disciplines. However, used in archaeology they can be considered primitive with respect to concepts referring to the past in that they are not necessarily defined by any of these concepts.

The same is true of "correlation," "ratio" and similar concepts. However, these concepts depend on the concept of "frequency" which refers not only to number but also to number of *something*. It might be argued that the concept of "something" depends on the concept of a past phenomenon. Thus, the frequency of projectile points might be computed, and clearly the past use of a set of objects is implicitly if not explicitly implied by this concept. However, the referent for this concept need be only an empirical type that describes a set of objects that share attributes that can be observed directly and described by using concepts that do not imply the past. The attributes might include a certain range of size, shape and material properties, e.g., hardness. The posited past use of objects is only indirectly observable, and so is logically distinguished from their directly observable present attributes. Such terms are used in an observational system in which a set of attributes of objects are believed to be indices of the past use of those objects. When frequencies and statistics based on them are computed, however, they refer strictly to numbers of objects and not to their use.

The second vocabulary consists of terms

or concepts whose meaning is given by our conceptualization of the past. In principle, anything we wish to know, can conceive of, and may indirectly observe, can be conceptualized and this concept can be added to this vocabulary. Archaeologists have been concerned with a great variety of past phenomena including the use and function (*sensu* Taylor 1948:115) of objects and features; political, economic, religious, kin, and demographic structures and their changes; the behavior of individuals and groups including the "templates" or psychic structures which are said to produce this behavior (cf. Chang 1967*b*; Deetz 1960); and adaptive systems (Binford 1962).

Vocabularies consist of terms that must be defined if their meaning is to be understood and their use is to be systematic. Terms of the first or primitive vocabulary are said to be antecendently understood, i.e., defined in vocabularies external to and prior to their use in an observational system. (Hempel 1966:88. For a discussion of different views see Shapere 1965:1–29.) Because they are not defined or influenced by terms of the second vocabulary, the system of definitions avoids circularity. They are, in a sense, empirical axioms upon which the second vocabulary rests. In many cases terms of the first vocabulary are given in conceptual systems of common sense or everyday use, and are essentially undefined. Examples include "round," "yellow," "glossy," "hollow," "stone," "twenty-two," and "large." As indicated above, other terms of the first vocabulary are theoretical terms defined in other disciplines, e.g., "carbon-14," "calcarious soil horizon," and "statistical factor."

More complex terms of the first vocabulary, for example, types such as "projectile point," are defined by sets of less complex terms. The purpose of these definitions is "to assign, by stipulation, a special meaning to a given term, which may be a newly coined verbal expression . . . or an 'old' term that is to be used in a specific technical sense." (Hempel 1966:85–86). Such

stipulative definitions have the general form, "By ———, let us understand the same thing as by ———" (Hempel 1966:85–86). Thus the concept of a type of feature, "C," may be defined as "the set of those phenomena that appear as straight lines on aerial photographs, that are longer than one meter but shorter than 100 kilometers, are U-shaped in profile, contain soil that is rich in organic matter and/or mineral salts at their bottoms, and have material similar to that underlying their bottoms located on one or two sides adjacent to their tops."

Indefinitely more complex concepts can be defined using sets of terms referring to less complex concepts. For example, the concept of a feature, "I.S.," may be defined as "the set of those phenomena which consist of 1) feature T, or lines of stones which are located on hillsides and which are at right angles to the direction of slope; 2) features of type C, the higher ends of which terminate below and adjacent to features of type T, and the lower ends of which terminate above and adjacent to features of type P that are rectangular or square depressed areas larger than 10 square meters but smaller than 10,000 meters, deeper than 10 centimeters, but less deep than 3 meters, and are subrectangular in profile."

In the process of defining ever more complex concepts, more and more terms referring to properties of the archaeological record are used. It is often the case that the majority of these properties are used. The empirical referents of certain categories of the McKern system, for instance, are sets of all empirical types that are found in a region (McKern 1939). The empirical data of "settlement patterns" as defined by Binford (personal communication) include spatial distributions and environmental associations of (empirical) site types.

The terms of the second or theoretical vocabulary are defined by sets of primitive terms, by sets of other (antecedent) theoretical terms, or by both. Particular definitions may be given purely by imagination, by reference to the context of a term, i.e., its usage in relation to other terms, or by observation of present day phenomena. The meaning of theoretical terms such as "atom" in physics, or "interaction sphere," "component," or "phase" in archaeology are derived chiefly from the imagination. They cannot be directly observed even in the present. The term "primary functional variability" (Binford 1965:206) may be thought of as defined in part by its relation to other such terms, e.g., "secondary functional variability." However, most terms used by archaeologists are taken from vocabularies referring to sociocultural phenomena defined and observable in the present, e.g., "hunting," "patrilocal," "hearth."

The term "argument of relevance" has been introduced into the archaeological literature by L. R. Binford (1968a:22, 23; Binford and Binford (1968:2). It refers to the components of archaeological reasoning that enable us to relate phenomena to one another. If one were to ask how archaeologists make links between phenomena, the relationships of which are not immediately or intuitively obvious, or, more precisely, how archaeologists justify their assertions of these linkages, the answer is via arguments of relevance.

Two levels of such arguments can be defined. These levels do not distinguish arguments that are logically different or the contents of which are different necessarily or in principle. Rather, these levels distinguish what tend to be different stages in archaeological research as well as those theories or paradigms (*sensu* Kuhn 1962) and those academic disciplines with which archaeologists are involved when they do research at each stage. Hence they are different in practice. At the first level arguments link attributes of the archaeological record to attributes of past events which are believed to have produced them. For example, part of the variation in design elements on ceramics has been related to variation in the residential system of ceramic producers (cf. Deetz 1960; Hill 1965; Longacre 1963). The logi-

cal relation between the first phenomenon and the second as well as our belief that this relationship obtained or does obtain depend on the presence of arguments of relevance. These arguments have included assertions about the nature of ceramic producers, of the transmittal of information within and between generations, and of the relationship between loci of production, use and disposal of ceramics.

At the second level, arguments link attributes of past phenomena to attributes of antecedent past phenomena that are believed to have produced them. For example, it has been argued that the abandonment of the Southwestern United States beginning circa A.D. 1100 was produced by the onset of arid conditions (Antevs 1962), or by changes in the distribution of rainfall (Martin et al. 1961), or by the abandonment of less productive areas for more productive areas (Plog 1969). Each set of arguments includes a (different) set of assumptions about the nature of past conditions, and of groups' responses to those conditions.

Arguments at this level derive from the body of theory an archaeologist believes to be appropriate to the definition and explanation of such phenomena in general. Theory can be defined as the set of concepts and statements or hypotheses referring to some directly or indirectly observed phenomena. Theory defines the characteristics of phenomena, and the relationships, including causal relationship, between and among phenomena. Assuming the general principle of uniformitarianism, as all archaeologists must, past phenomena cannot be considered different in nature or in their interrelationships from present phenomena simply because they occurred in the past. The concepts appropriate for explaining events in the present are used to explain similar events in the past.

One kind of theory may explain variation in the forms of man-made objects by variation in the mental constructs (cf. Deetz 1960; Rouse 1960) of individuals or groups.

Such explanations are most closely related to psychological theory (Binford 1965:204) of a nonbehavioralist type (Harris 1969:66 *et passim*). Another kind of theory might explain the former variation by variation in the adaptive tasks that such objects perform. If they were used as tools for doing subsistence tasks, their variation might be explained in part by technological theory, including mechanics, and, in part, by economic theory.

Arguments of relevance at this level have several roles in relation to theory. First, as previously indicated, they are derived from theory and explain the relationship between phenomena according to the concepts of the theory. They are the explicit and implicit theorems and assumptions of a theory applied to a specific case. Second, to the degree that such arguments produce satisfying explanations for phenomena, they increase our confidence in the *theory* in general, i.e., they help to confirm it. Since theories consist of statements that are or are thought to be explicitly or implicitly logically interrelatable, the demonstration that some of these statements account for empirically observed phenomena can be considered to be a demonstration that related statements tend to have the same power.

Archaeologists making arguments at this second level are archaeologists acting as psychologists, social or cultural anthropologists, economists, etc. They are using the same concepts and statements of relationship as do specialists practicing these disciplines. In this sense Taylor's view (1968:41) that archaeologists are highly skilled technicians appears correct. When archaeologists ascend to the "explanatory level" of Willey and Phillips (1958:5), they are actually *doing* psychology, social anthropology, economics, etc. That the phenomena explained happen to have existed in the past is irrelevant to the selection of the body of theory by which they are explained. Willey and Phillips suggest that "American archaeology is anthropology or it is nothing" (1962:2). This is

less a definition of the theoretical base that archaeologists must employ than of the base or bases that American archaeologists have employed historically.

It is essential to understand arguments at this level when one is concerned with the theoretical systems archaeologists use indirectly to observe and to explain the relationship between past phenomena. This is also essential when one wishes to evaluate the contribution that archaeology can make to social scientific disciplines. However, this level is not as directly relevant to the concern of this essay, i.e., how we can know past phenomena in the first place even before we attempt to explain them via prior past phenomena. Accordingly, I concern myself subsequently with the characteristics of arguments of relevance at the first level.

In the most highly developed sciences, the logical form of such arguments approach the systematization of explicit hypothetico-deductive systems. As in the proofs of geometry, statements express or represent chains of deductive reasoning. Each nonaxiomatic statement is at least a sufficient (if not a necessary) condition for at least one succeeding or consequent statement. It is also at least a necessary consequence of at least one preceding or antecedent statement. The conclusions of such arguments are the product of the logical interrelations of all previous statements and must be logically true if all previous statements are true.

This is particularly the case when phenomena and their interrelationship are expressed by mathematical models. Mathematics can be considered to be a branch of logic (Whitehead and Russell 1925 and 1927), thus the manipulation of mathematical statements by physical scientists, e.g., is a form of logical argumentation. These sciences are not subdisciplines of logic, however. They are concerned with empirical phenomena, not with the syntactical interrelationship between sentences such that some are logically true and others false. Empirical phenomena exist or do not exist. The scien-

142

tific problem is to ascertain the existence of their interrelations and the existence of previously unsuspected phenomena.

In archaeology neither concepts nor their interrelation are usually expressed by mathematical models. Binford (1965:203–4) has presented an excellent critique of the tendencies of archaeologists to partition the archaeological record and past phenomena into qualitative categories, i.e., into "types" and "norms," using unidimensional nominal scales (see also Fritz 1968). Possible exceptions are the use of techniques for analyzing the variance and covariance of measurable phenomena. Correlational, partial correlational, cluster, and factor analytic methods have been used to interrelate the attributes of the archaeological record. As often as not, these attributes have been qualitative or discrete, e.g., types, designs, and shapes, the frequency of which have been quantified. Thus, while archaeologists are beginning to be concerned with variations in amount of material from location to location, and in particular with associated relative variation, they are less concerned with expressing the traditional units of the archaeological record by quantitative mathematical models. Exceptions include Sackett's (1966) attempt to analyze variation and covariation of attributes within types or to "create" types by analyzing covariation among attributes of artifacts (see also Cowgill 1968 for a similar attempt using cluster analytic techniques), and Binford's explanation of variation within a type of artifact by a cultural drift model (1963).

Even less common have been attempts to express past phenomena in quantitative terms. Even the results of factor and other analyses have usually been qualities, e.g., tool kits, clusters of associated types, and types. Measures of strength of association of a type, for example, with a tool kit, have been ignored once it has been determined that a type "belongs" or does not "belong" in a kit. Similarly, the association between tool kits has been ignored except to determine whether they belonged together. It is conceivable that quantitative expressions of association could be related to mathematically expressed models for past behavior. Some examples exist. Leone (1968) attempts to define and measure "dependence on agriculture" and "social distance." Benfer (1967) attempts to measure "culturability." Plog (1969) is concerned, inter alia, with quantitative measures of "population," "economic specialization," and "integration."

In short, archaeologists have tended not to use mathematical models to define either the archaeological record or past phenomena or the relationship between the two. Even where exceptions occur, one can question the degree to which detailed mathematical concepts and relationships have been directly and explicitly related to those employed in archaeology specifically, or in anthropology. Thus, argumentation in archaeology seldom, if ever, achieves the explicit deductive systematization of mathematical reasoning.

Nor does it attain deductive symbolization in reasoning expressed in other than mathematical systematization. One of Binford's intents in raising the problem of arguments of relevance has been to encourage the elaboration of such reasoning in archaeology (Binford 1968a). I suggest elsewhere (Fritz 1968; Fritz and Plog 1970) that arguments of relevance in archaeology tend to be implicit, underdeveloped, unsystematized and sketchy, at best. In archaeological typology, for example, a "type" not only implies a cluster of associated attributes held in common by the members of a set of artifacts or features (cf. Jennings 1968:17), but also implies the past function or use of these members. The type "hearth" refers not only to "hearth form," but also to "hearthness" or hearth-like uses. The fact that hearths can be used for many things—heating, cooking, lighting, producing smoke—and thus that the functional referent is rather broad does not invalidate the suggestion that the term partitions the field of possible past behaviors to some degree. The same implication of form to function can be found in the names of many other types, e.g., "arrowhead," "pit house," "mano," and "metate."

What is noteworthy here is the absence of explicit arguments attempting to demonstrate that a particular cluster of attributes is a relevant indicator of a particular past use or that the past use is a relevant explanation for the occurrence of the set of attributes. Archaeologists certainly do arrive at plausible interrelations of past and present phenomena, for example, from knowledge of analagous artifacts or features in other societies—their own or some other. (cf. Thompson 1958*b*). But having arrived at a plausible interrelation, and having reported the source of our inspiration and a few of the more compelling reasons for accepting it we tend to abandon argumentation. When conflicting interrelations are made of a given datum, the archaeologists holding each position may elaborate on these reasons. But even then, it would be extremely difficult to find a case in which this reasoning has been expanded into anything approaching a deductively valid argument.

In short, the formal aspect of a system for indirect observation consists of theoretical and logical dimensions. These are expressed in terms and arguments employing these terms. Some terms are primitive, and are undefined within the theoretical system, while others are theoretical and are defined within the system. The content of primitive terms is given by observation of the archaeological record and by reference to the theory of ancillary discipline. The content of theoretical terms refers to past phenomena archaeologists hope to know or indirectly observe and is given by contemporary paradigms about human behavior. Arguments of relevance relate the archaeological record to past phenomena through sets of (ideally) deductively interrelated statements. These statements contain both primitive and theoretical terms; they refer both to universal and particular phenomena. That such systems for indirect observations are now absent or underdeveloped in archaeology is exemplified by the present nature of arguments of relevance.

The Construction of Observational Systems

I now turn to how systems for indirect observation are or might be put together. Three steps should be taken. First, the construction of a plausible instrument. Second, the construction and performance of tests for the instrument, and third, the evaluation of the results. I suggest that to the degree that these steps are not taken, such systems lack logical and empirical validity.

These steps are diagrammed in greater detail in Figs. *1–13*. The figures provide a flow chart of the component processes and products of successive stages of the construction of an observational system. I do not claim that these stages are *necessarily* temporally distinct, although they can be. They are at least distinguishable stages in arguments supporting or modifying a particular instrument.

How do we come to the realization that a given datum might indicate that a past sociocultural phenomenon existed or occurred in the past? This is surely one of the most difficult questions in philosophy or psychology. To understand such processes we would have to understand the nature and workings of the human imagination, of our creative process. While long the subject of speculation, and of research (cf. Barron 1969), no one would suggest that we can account for every act of creation or that we can produce conditions in which individuals will create. I do not propose a recipe for discovery. Rather, I discuss situations to which discovery might be germane, and in which it might occur. I discuss post-discovery activities in which an archaeologist would engage in order to construct a formally and operationally plausible system.

There is considerable discussion as to whether science is inductive (cf. Nielsen 1967), deductive (cf. Hempel 1966), or both (cf. Rudner 1966). I consider this mat-

144

ter elsewhere (Fritz 1968) as it relates to archaeology. It is relevant here insofar as it defines different paths along which discovery of subsequent activities takes place (Figs. *1–3*).

FIG. 1. *Construction of a plausible instrument.*

It has often been suggested (B. K. Schwartz 1967; Thompson 1958*b*) that discovery occurs when an archaeologist is confronted with a set of archaeological data. During the process of his analysis, the data "suggest" or "indicate" to the observer a possible relation to past phenomena (Thompson 1958*b*:3). In different terms, during analysis the analyst discovers a possible relation. In either case data are, at least in part, necessary conditions for discoveries. This can

phenomenon and its relation to a (previously observed) datum.

An alternative path of discovery exists when an archaeologist is confronted not with data but with knowledge that leads him to posit the existence of a particular past sociocultural phenomenon. This can be termed the deductive path (Fig. *3*). This knowledge might derive from history, ethnography or some explicit, applicable theory. Historical records might describe the occurrence of particular events in the past. An archaeologist might attempt to find material evidence for them. Schliemann's search for Troy, the attempts to find evidence for events recorded in the Old or New Testament, or,

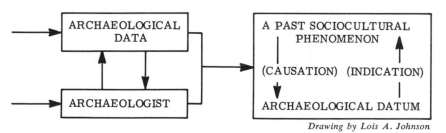

Drawing by Lois A. Johnson

FIG. 2. *Discovery of a plausible instrument: inductive path.*

be termed the inductive path to discovery and construction of systems for indirect observation. In Fig. *2* the context of discovery is one in which the archaeologist deals with archaeological data. Out of this interaction comes a hypothetical instrument consisting of the concept of a past sociocultural phenomena that might have caused a present archaeological datum that indicates the presence of the phenomenon. What has been discovered or created is the concept of a past

in the southwestern United States, the search for Father Kino's grave (Jimenez Moreno 1966*a*) are examples. Similarly, an early ethnography may record the past existence of a particular behavioral pattern, e.g., a house type and associated activities, and an archaeologist might attempt to find evidence for it. In other cases, ethnography might be used in relation to implicit theory to suggest the possible existence of a past phenomenon. Thus Longacre (1963) and Hill

(1965) use information about present western Pueblo residence patterns to posit patterns existing in another area of the Southwest 800 years earlier.

Theory is concerned explicitly and primarily with generals and can be distinguished from history, including ethnography, which deals with particulars (cf. Hempel 1966). Theory deals with particulars only to the extent that generals are thought to have actual or potential particular instances. In other words, theory allows one to predict that

the same historical or ethnographic record that suggested the event, or it may be derived from characteristics of the event or of related events (see following discussion of direct and indirect tests). For example, several archaeologists assume that residential patterning is reflected in the patterning of what Binford (1965) terms the "secondary functional variability" of the archaeological record (cf. Deetz 1960; Hill 1965; Longacre 1963). This assumption permits them to define indicators in data as diverse as

CONTEXT OF DISCOVERY

HYPOTHETICAL
OBSERVATIONAL
INSTRUMENT

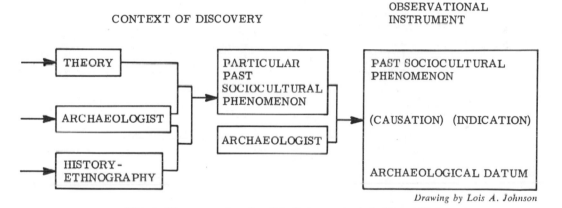

Drawing by Lois A. Johnson

FIG. 3. *Discovery of a plausible instrument: deductive path.*

a particular instance of a general phenomenon will or did occur under specified conditions. When an archaeologist works with theories of sociocultural phenomena he may attempt either to test or to use them. In either case he will deduce a particular past phenomenon from a theoretical general, but in testing them his motivation will be to increase or to decrease the credibility of a theory, while in using them his motivation is the desire to ascertain the existence of a past event.

Whatever his motivation and its source, once an archaeologist posits a particular past sociocultural phenomenon, he must then posit a particular archaeological datum that would indicate its presence. Otherwise the existence of the event would remain purely speculative. A datum may be suggested by

ceramic designs and hearth profiles. What is created or discovered by archaeologists following the deductive path is a hypothetical datum and its relationship to a past phenomenon. In many cases a hypothetical past phenomenon may be created as well.

Once a hypothetical instrument is created it becomes necessary to justify it (Fig. 4). This consists of two heuristically separable stages. In the first, the relevant characteristics of the past sociocultural phenomenon and of the archaeological datum are explicitly defined. This step may only consist of stating characteristics that were implicit or explicit when a hypothetical instrument was created. However, in the process of definition, new or more precisely defined characteristics may be discovered. Is a stone mortar thought to be an indicator for past acorn preparation? We can initiate justification of this hypothesis by defining those characteristics of acorns that might be relevant to given techniques of preparation, for example, of their tough shell or hull and of their interior that must be reduced to a pulp in order that leaching might be effective. Next, we can define those formal attributes of mortars that might be relevant to their use as part of these techniques, for example, the vertical profile of their hole that shows a relatively small horizontal surface at the bottom with respect to depth.

of 1) an initial statement of the characteristics of the past phenomenon, 2) a final statement of those of the datum, and 3) statements necessary for deriving the latter from the former statements. Here the goal is simply to present publicly the statements thought necessary to derive the datum from the phenomenon. In most cases, it is argued that for numerous reasons the phenomenon directly or indirectly caused the datum to occur. A second goal is to permit assessment of the empirical and theoretical validity of those reasons and of the logical validity of

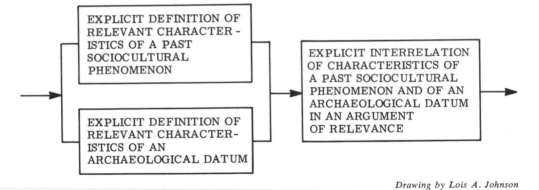

Drawing by Lois A. Johnson

FIG. 4. *Preliminary justification of instrument.*

The first goal of this step is simply definition of terms so that other archaeologists can know what characteristics are being considered and are thought relevant. The second goal is to state those characteristics precisely enough so that other archaeologists can understand and replicate their observation precisely when necessary. The definition of terms by use of primitive terms creates this understanding. Thus to describe the bottom of a set of mortar holes as "relatively narrow" is less precise, primitive, intelligible, and replicable than to say that their mean is 10.0 centimeters, or that the mean of the ratio of their width to depth is 2.0 (cf. Spaulding 1960*b*).

In the second step of justification the explicitly defined characteristics of the past phenomenon and of the datum are explicitly interrelated or linked in an argument of relevance. Minimally, the argument consists

their interrelation. Either the archaeologist making the argument or other archaeologists judging it or both may make these assessments. The criteria for empirical and theoretical validity of these statements that an archaeologist and/or any other scientist uses are many and diverse. Suffice it to say here that they do not necessarily include the presence of known empirical support (cf. Braithwaite 1960; Hempel 1966; Kuhn 1962), although such support should be obtainable in principle (Hempel 1966:30–32).

As suggested above, in the social sciences such arguments are almost never so elaborated as to permit one actually to *deduce* a statement of the characteristics of an archaeological datum from statements about the past phenomenon. It might be questioned seriously whether rigorously and explicitly systematized deductive logic can provide an adequate model for our reasoning in such arguments. Again, this is in part a problem for philosophers and psychologists, but archaeologists can determine whether such models account for or help us to understand this reasoning. At present there seems to be no better candidate than the deductive model, and it should be noted that it is quite adequate for dealing with mathematical reasoning in archaeology and other social sciences (Shapere 1965). It follows that it is almost never possible to analyze completely and to confirm or disconfirm the logical validity of arguments of relevance. However, on the basis of statements given it is possible to make at least an impressionistic assessment of the reasoning and to determine when an intermediate statement or the final statement follows or does not follow. Part of the dynamic development of archaeology consists of the dialectic in which such arguments are stated, questioned, are elaborated and defended or revised, or are abandoned.

In the previous example, it is suggested that mortars might be an indicator of acorn preparation. Potentially relevant characteristics of mortars might include the morphology of mortar holes and of the pestle, while those of acorns might include their size and the structure of their outer covering or hull and of their starchy interior. The arguments necessary to derive the former from the latter might include statements referring to the necessity to break and remove the outer covering in order to recover the interior, to the pliable nature of the hull, to the tendency of such material to split into a few large pieces when struck with considerable force with a blunt object, to the ease of removal of such pieces from the matrix of starchy material, to the inertial force generated by an object with the mass and weight of a pestle, to the tendency of objects with the morphology of acorns to cluster in a cylindrical or conical space defined by the interior walls of objects like mortars, to the morphology of mortars and pestles such that the latter can be thrust into the former with considerable force, etc. Through statements such as these, although more elaborated and bet-

ter defined, it should be possible to justify the assertion that mortars (and pestles) are indicators of acorn preparation.

The particular content of arguments of relevance varies with the nature of a past phenomenon and of a datum. The statements used to justify a given datum as an indicator of a past technological pattern obviously is quite different from one that justifies an indicator for a past kinship relation or a ritual behavior. Arguments dealing with technological patterns might be concerned with the properties of materials and forms, with the laws of mechanics, physics, and chemistry, for example, as they are reflected in the operation of energy sources, for example, manpower, in articulation with instruments and facilities, with principles of technological efficiency, etc. Arguments dealing with subsistence economy might be concerned with technological processes of procuring and processing raw materials including food sources, with human nutritional requirements, with the nutritional properties and spatial and temporal variation of single species and of communities of plants and animals, etc. Arguments dealing with ritual behavior might be concerned with regularities of association of ritualistic acts and of acts with material objects, with biopsychological principles of symbolic expression in colors, morphologies, textures, etc., and their combination, with the spatial and temporal variation of acts, etc.

Whatever their specific contents, the statements of such arguments have several general characteristics. First, they must indicate how and why human actions and behavior generally are correlated with or manifested in the data of the archaeological record. As has long been recognized, behavior not indicated by the archaeological data would be unobservable in all senses. As has been more recently recognized, the number and kinds of behavior that are so indicated are much greater than hitherto suspected.

Second, they should use implicitly or explicitly empirical generalizations and laws that relate such phenomena in general. The

148

former refer to characteristics of and to interrelationships among phenomena that reoccur many times and may be thought to be universal. Thus the general assumption that small, bifacial, lanceolate chipped stone implements are universally associated with hunting is based on repeated observations of their association in history and in the ethnographic present. An empirical generalization may become a law when it is linked to a confirmed theory that explains why such phenomena exist and why they are related. A law—like an empirical generalization—is concerned with no particular phenomenon at a given point in space and time but with all such phenomena irrespective of their loci. Similarly, a law has universal application, i.e., the relationship it defines is true at all times and places. Finally, a law is related to theory such that it is (ideally) deducible from other laws, and other laws may be deduced from it. That is, laws are linked to other laws which explain them, and they may, in turn, alone or in conjunction with other laws, explain still other laws (see also Fritz and Plog 1970).

Third, because laws and empirical generalizations refer to phenomena in general, arguments should include statements asserting and confirming the claim that the characteristics of the particular datum-indicator conform to those of the phenomenon referred to by a generalization or law. Such statements make a general relevant to a particular case. Thus, if "projectile points," in general, indicate "hunting" in general, and if these "projectile points" are defined, inter alia, as being between three and ten centimeters in length, a particular object or set of objects thought to be a particular manifestation of such a "projectile point" should be shown to have a length falling within this range. If a set of objects have all other characteristics of "projectile points" but range between twenty and thirty centimeters in length, they would not be a particular instance of "projectile points" and would not indicate hunting. Such statements and defi-

nitions are quite significant in the development of archaeological theory in that they require one to define the characteristics of both the data and of the general phenomena of which they are particular instances. Thus, they increase the precision not only of the theoretical vocabulary but also of the observations and the descriptions of observations.

Fourth, arguments of relevance should demonstrate and account not only for a past association of a behavioral and a material phenomenon, but also for the deposition and subsequent alteration of the latter into the form observable in the archaeological record. All archaeologists realize that they are dealing with the garbage, debris, and lost and abandoned objects and features of past cultures, and all know that these materials have often been changed considerably between deposition and recovery by subsequent actions of geomorphological forces and of man. Archaeologists have given considerable attention to the forces that alter the forms and/or interrelationships of objects and features, but less to those which produce the initial deposition of these objects and features. The importance of both of these components of arguments of relevance is obvious when one realizes that previous components establish the relationship of nonmaterial and material sociocultural phenomena in the past only at the time the latter were produced and/or used. They do not necessarily account for the form and relationship of material phenomena observed in the archaeological record in the present. We might reasonably expect that a given material phenomenon should have existed in the past, e.g., animal bone resulting from butchering. But we might not observe it in the present, either because it was not deposited at the location we observe at present, or because it was deposited there but through mechanical and/or chemical weathering was reduced to its constituent elements. Thus the absence of a particular datum need not mean that the past phenomenon we hoped to observe indirectly was not present. It might mean that we should revise this component of the argument and either look elsewhere for this data or develop methods by which we can observe their presence in their modified form.

Fifth, ideally arguments of relevance should meet the requirement of deducibility, that is, they should permit us explicitly to deduce the characteristics of the data from those of the past sociocultural phenomena we hope to observe. I suggest that this goal has not been attained in archaeology. Some philosophers state that acceptable scientific knowledge does not always meet this requirement (Hanson 1958). They suggest that such complete derivations are more characteristic of the maturity of a science than of its youth. In Kuhn's terminology (1962) it is an activity of normal science —probably late normal science—rather than of scientific revolution.

Does this mean archaeologists should not be concerned with deducibility? I don't think

(1958:5–6) reaching the "explanatory level." To approach deducibility we must continually improve our observations and descriptions of the archaeological record. We must continue to explicate and to improve our definitions of past sociocultural phenomena. We must continue to discover and to explicate our knowledge of the associations and causal interrelationships of such phenomena—especially among behavioral and material phenomena. And we must continue to expand our knowledge of the forces that alter the forms and interrelationships of past material phenomena into those observable in the archaeological record. Thus, if we determine why the context of a given argument of relevance fails to meet the requirement of deducibility, we also determine inadequacies in archaeological knowledge. If we reduce these inadequacies we also approach more closely to deducibility.

When we have justified a hypothetical in-

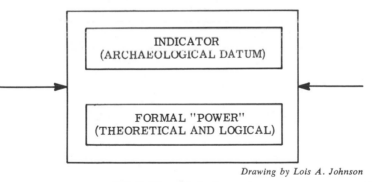

Drawing by Lois A. Johnson

FIG. 5. *Plausible instrument.*

so. It should not be thought of as the irrelevant dictate of some scientific systematist or aesthetician (seeking abstract elegance) that may be attained by some future archaeological generation when there is nothing else to do. In fact, as archaeological theory develops we meet this requirement more and more closely. In seeking to approach this ideal we achieve the eminently practical result of increasing archaeological knowledge, or, in the terms of Willey and Phillips

strument for observing the past, we have both a plausible indicator (datum) and a source of "power," i.e., external theoretical confirmation plus internal logical validity (Fig. 5). If we have taken the deductive path to discovery we can observe the archaeological record to determine if the expected datum exists. If it does, our instrument is plausible; if it does not, we may do any one of a number of things that are discussed subsequently in relation to unfavor-

150

able outcomes of tests. If we have taken the inductive path, we have already observed the datum and after justification automatically have a plausible instrument.

The next step in the creation of the instrument is to test it. This may consist merely of repeated observations of the archaeological record to determine if the datum obtains in several more instances when it is expected. In the case of unique historical events it would not be possible to observe its indicator more than once. However, testing may also consist of discovering additional data which, if they were observed, would increase the plausibility of the instrument (Fig. 6). It should be noted that we seldom if ever achieve a completely confirmed instrument, i.e., one that is true of the world in some absolute sense. A model for this assertion, based on the characteris-

and bases of such credibility can be found in Hempel (1966) and Fritz (1968). It must suffice here to say that credibility increases with the quantity, variety, and precision of related test data.

Tests in which additional data is sought increase the quantity of supporting data by definition. The more such tests we perform with favorable outcomes, the more data support the credibility of our instrument. Thus, we might consider a block of small, contiguous rooms to be an indicator of a past redistributive economy. If we test this and demonstrate that they contain data (pollen, seeds, containers, absence of indicators of use for other activities, etc.) that indicate that they were used for storage and that they are proximate to data indicating association with politico-religious activities (pyramids, cemeteries, great kivas, central plazas, etc.),

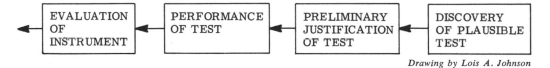

Drawing by Lois A. Johnson

FIG. 6. *Test of plausible instrument.*

tics of deductive logic, is presented by Hempel (1966), and is applied to archaeological reasoning elsewhere (Fritz 1968). This is intuitively comprehensible, however, if we are willing to admit the possibility that a future archaeologist might be able to show that the datum of our instrument is more likely the indicator of another past phenomenon. This could be done by different and more complete arguments of relevance and/or by different and more extensive testing. (See also Flannery 1967.)

While we can never achieve an absolutely confirmed instrument, we can increase its credibility, i.e., our belief that it is more likely to be true than some other instrument. This belief is the basis of our willingness to use the instrument, i.e., to take the pragmatic view that it is probably true enough for our immediate practical requirements. Extended discussions of the nature

then the quantity of supporting data would be considerably increased.

Such tests can also increase the variety of supporting data. Data considerably different from the original datum would be desirable. Thus, an archaeologist might assume and/or demonstrate that redistributive economies are associated with social systems having ranked lineages. He might suggest a datum that would indicate such lineages, e.g., a type of variation in mortuary practices within a site. If observed, such data would be quite different from the original (form of rooms and room blocks), and would add considerable support to the original instrument. Finally, more precisely defined data also add to credibility. If "redistributive economy" is defined in terms of the relative proportion of goods received or dispersed by a redistributive authority, if techniques are developed to observe indirectly these quantities, and if they are observed, the likelihood that previously observed data are indicators is greater. Similarly, we have more confidence that an indicator of an obsidian blade craft-producing area is correct if testing shows that the lithic assemblage contains "85% broken blades" rather than "some stone chippage."

non that we have not considered. This is less likely when a past phenomenon accounts for several kinds of data—especially when they are quite different. Similarly, the more precisely a datum is defined, the fewer the phenomena that can account for its unique form.

How are tests discovered? The context

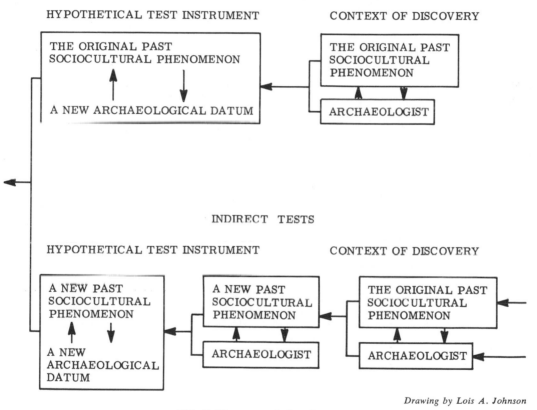

Drawing by Lois A. Johnson

FIG. 7. *Discovery of plausible test.*

Why should tests which increase the quantity, variety, and precision of data related to an instrument increase its credibility more than the repeated observation of the original indicator? This seems intuitively to be related to our belief that one occurrence of an expected datum could happen by chance, and that several repeated occurrences of the same datum might equally well or better be accounted for by some other past phenome-

of discovery is similar to that of the deductive path in the discovery of a plausible instrument. That is, the archaeologist starts with the concept of a past phenomenon and discovers some new present datum that might indicate it. The relation of this datum to the past phenomenon varies with the nature of the test. There are two possible kinds of tests—direct and indirect (Fig. 7). In the first, an archaeologist discovers some datum that would also have been produced by the original phenomenon. Population growth might be indicated by increase in the number of habitation rooms in an area, for example. The same growth might also be indicated by increase in the volume of trash or midden. The latter datum would provide a direct test for the original instrument.

In an indirect test, an archaeologist first discovers the concept of a new past phenomenon that would be expected to exist if the original phenomenon existed. He then discovers a new datum which would be produced directly by the new past phenomenon. Population growth, for example, might be

characteristics of the latter differ only slightly from those cited in the original justification. The linking arguments might differ more in content because a quiet different present datum must be derived from them. When the present datum is linked to a new past phenomenon, the content of the arguments is quite different from that of the previous argument, reflecting their different relevant characteristics.

When indirect tests are justified another level of argument must also be developed, i.e., one explicitly justifying the asserted plausible linkage between the original and the new past phenomena. Here, an archae-

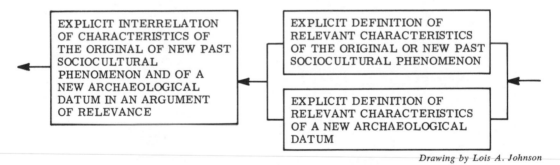

Drawing by Lois A. Johnson

FIG. 8. *Preliminary justification of plausible test.*

accompanied by increased social complexity as new social forms develop to organize and integrate the increased population. Increased complexity might be indicated by increased variability in burial patterns or by changes in the form and distribution of ceramic decorations. Here the new present datum (burials, ceramics) indicates the original past phenomenon indirectly through a new but related past phenomenon (complexity).

Justification of a plausible test is similar to justification of a plausible instrument (Fig. 8). It consists, first, of the definition of the relevant characteristics of the new present datum, and of the original or newly suggested past phenomenon. Second, these characteristics are interrelated in an argument of relevance. When the present datum is linked to the original past phenomenon, the relevant

ologist employs arguments of relevance at the second level, that is, he must use anthropological or other theory to explain why such phenomena would be associated. The theory might assert that one caused the other, that both were caused by a third phenomenon, or that they are generally associated. Thus, one might suggest that "dependence on hunting" produces "patrilocal residence" or that both are produced by "innate male dominance" or simply that in all societies heretofore observed, if the former was present, the latter was also present. In general, these arguments need not refer to associated material phenomena and thus need not account for subsequent modifications of them. The credibility of the association between the past phenomena is dependent both on the logical validity of the argument linking them, and on the theoretical and/or empirical support for or confirmation of the statements and assumptions of the argument.

This empirical support normally is derived from the analysis of present or historically documented societies. However, it is here that archaeology can make a significant con-

in hand. In this case, it may be necessary only to observe it or to analyze it further. No doubt we would save both time and money if we could devise tests which employ old "new" data rather than entirely new data.

TEST OUTCOME   TESTING

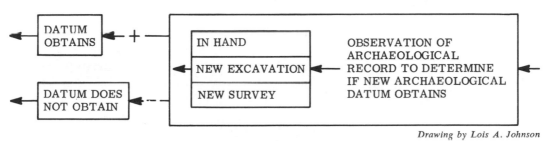

Drawing by Lois A. Johnson

FIG. 9. *Performance of test.*

tribution to anthropological or other theory. An association may be thought to be only somewhat plausible on the basis of historical and present evidence. If archaeological indicators can be discovered for such phenomena, and if they are observed in the archaeological record, greater support for their general association is given. If one or both are not observed, support is decreased. Thus, the outcome of an indirect test of an instrument for observing a past phenomenon necessarily adds to or subtracts from the credibility of, for example, anthropological theory.

When a test has been justified, the next step is actually to perform it (Fig. 9). Tests always require the observation of new data.

A test can have one of two outcomes— either the test datum is observed or it is not. On the basis of the outcomes we evaluate the credibility of our observational instrument. This is the process of confirmation or disconfirmation. In the first or favorable case (Fig. 10), the presence of the datum increases the credibility of the plausible instrument. Depending on our evaluation of the test—the degree to which it increases this credibility—we may decide provisionally to accept the instrument or we may decide to perform additional tests before accepting it. On the one hand, provisional acceptance reflects our belief that an instrument might eventually be shown to be mistaken. That

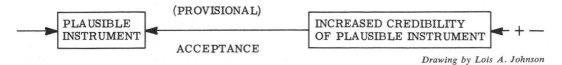

Drawing by Lois A. Johnson

FIG. 10. *Evaluation of instrument: favorable outcome.*

This data may be "new" in the sense that it has not previously been obtained, and thus the performance of the test requires that new or additional data collections be made by excavations, by survey, or by some other technique. "New" data may also be data already

is, a given datum may be shown to be a more credible indicator of another past phenomenon. On the other hand, it reflects our practical need to observe the past.

Provisional acceptance reflects a delicate balance between these two concerns. We do

154

not want to accept an instrument too soon, i.e., when it is hypothetical or plausible, lest we quickly be found mistaken. We also do not want to accept it too late, i.e., after a great many tests, lest we not accomplish our primary goal—to know of the past. There are no strict and universally applicable rules for how, and at what point, we should set the balance. Recently, workers (Binford 1968a; Flannery 1967; Plog 1969) have suggested that we have too quickly accepted the existence of or knowledge about past phenomena without sufficient preliminary justification or testing. As the question of the acceptability of our indirect observations of the past becomes more important, i.e., to the development of anthropological and other theory,

wish to reformulate the test at any stage of its construction (Fig. 12). We could reformulate the performance of the test and then assert that the test conditions were not correct or that the wrong datum was observed. For example, a test of population growth in an area might require the measurement of the volume of midden from a sample of sites occurring in the area. If the sampling program is not systematic or random, it might introduce a bias that leads the recorder to discover and measure a higher relative frequency of earlier than of later sites. If this bias is discovered and eliminated, the test can be performed again with, perhaps, a favorable outcome. Similarly, a test of an indicator for hunting in an area might be

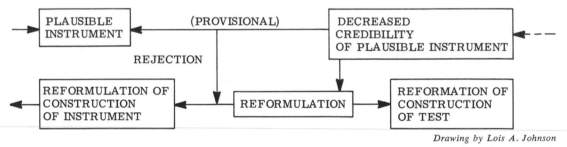

Drawing by Lois A. Johnson

FIG. 11. *Evaluation of instrument: unfavorable outcome.*

the truth of these suggestions will become quite apparent.

If the test datum is not observed, the credibility of the instrument is decreased (Fig. 11). If the plausibility of the test is greater than that of the instrument, we might decide provisionally to reject the instrument. However, if the plausibility of the instrument is greater than that of the test, we might reject the test to seek another test for the still plausible instrument. To follow the latter course does not violate the canons of logic, of theory, nor of correct or customary scientific practice—so long as the instrument has not been discredited by several previous tests. Again, a delicate balance must be struck between giving up a potentially useful instrument too soon, and holding on to it in the face of considerable contrary evidence.

If we provisionally reject the test we might

the presence of projectile points. If observation of data disclosed no small, lanceolate, bifacially chipped implements, we might conclude that while hunting is not here associated with this type of item, it might be indicated by another type. With further observation we might find small, straight, prismatic, pointed flakes that could plausibly have been mounted as projectile points.

We could reformulate the justification for the test. Here we would suggest that one or more of the statements of the argument were theoretically or empirically false, and/or that the logic was incorrect. If so, the characteristics of the test datum could not be derived from those of the past phenomenon. Thus, the depositional context might have been such as to destroy rather than to preserve the test datum, or the past phenomenon might have been associated with a material

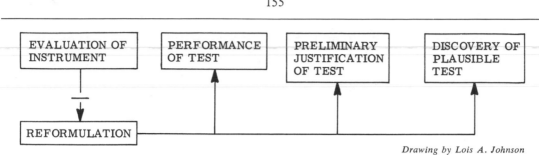

Drawing by Lois A. Johnson

FIG. 12. *Unfavorable outcome: reformulation of test.*

phenomenon of a slightly or radically different form. In both cases a new test datum might be discovered and its relevant characteristics defined and related to the original or new past phenomenon in new arguments of relevance. We might also determine that the arguments justifying an indirect test, i.e., demonstrating the relationship of the new and the original past phenomena, were incorrect. The new past phenomenon might be abandoned and another sought.

Finally, we could reformulate the discovery of the test. We might discover a new test datum that indicates the original past phenomenon or, in the case of indirect tests, the new phenomenon. We might decide that we cannot create another direct test, so attempt to formulate an indirect one. Conversely, we might abandon an indirect test to search for another indirect or a new direct test. Whatever our action, we would then reformulate the necessary definitions and arguments, perform the new test under reformulated test conditions, and would again evaluate the instrument on the basis of the test's outcome. If the outcome is favorable, we might provisionally accept the instrument. If not, we might again reformulate the test. As previously suggested, however, the more unfavorable test's results, the less likely this would be.

If the original test results were unfavorable, we might decide to reformulate the instrument (Fig. *13*). As with the test, we would provisionally reject the datum as an indicator of the past phenomenon. It would be profitable to reexamine our justification for the instrument. As with the test justifica-

tion, we would search for errors in definition, in logic, and most importantly for anthropological and archaeological theory, for errors in the statements relating past behavioral to material phenomena, and relating past material phenomena to the data of the archaeological record. Discovery of these errors might enable us to reformulate the justification with different and better definitions, statements, and logic.

The reformulation of the instrument differs from that of the test because in the first case we have observed a datum. Depending on our original or present goal, we might attempt to discover either a new indicator or a new past phenomenon. We are more likely to seek a new datum if the original context of discovery is deductive. If the past phenomenon is documented historically, we would almost always continue our belief in it, unless perhaps the history is quasi or completely mythological. If the past phenomenon is suggested by ethnography or by some body of explicit theory, and if we believe strongly in their applicability to the past society, we would again seek a new datum. If we believe less strongly in their applicability, the unfavorable test outcome(s) might cause us provisionally to reject their applicability. In the case of past phenomena predicted by theory, if enough expected archaeological data are not observed, we might completely abandon part or all of a theoretical paradigm and attempt to find a better one (cf. Kuhn 1962).

On the other hand, we are more likely to seek a new past phenomenon if the original context of discovery is inductive. How-

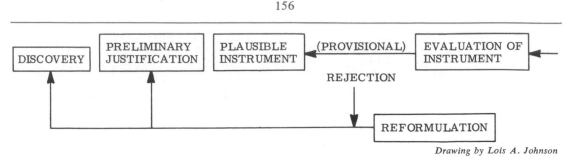

Drawing by Lois A. Johnson

FIG. 13. *Unfavorable outcome: reformulation of instrument.*

ever, if we arrive at a new hypothetical instrument we would repeat the process of justification, test construction, testing, and evaluation. When an instrument has at last been constructed and favorably tested, it, together with its supporting data, their definitions, and justificatory arguments, can be described as a *system* for indirect observation of the past.

Whatever our evaluation of the test results, whether we decide to keep, revise, or abandon our instrument or its test, we have contributed to the development of archaeological and anthropological knowledge. Thus, we might show either that a particular phenomenon existed or that it did not exist in the past, and thus contribute to the knowledge of prehistory. To the degree that we have related or may potentially relate the presence or absence of the phenomenon to the theory, we contribute to the empirical verification of the theory. To the degree that we have more carefully and precisely defined the characteristics of past and present phenomena, and have interrelated them in logically valid arguments, we contribute to the precision and intelligibility of our field. Finally, to the degree that we explicate our arguments of relevance, to that degree we attain the "explanatory level."

Limitations to Observational Systems

There has been considerable discussion about the knowledge that archaeologists can or cannot discover about the past. This discussion is relevant here in that its resolution might determine either phenomena that it

would be wasteful to attempt to observe or sources of limitations to knowledge, many or all of which might then be removed. On the one hand, Hawkes (1954) suggests a scale of credibility on which we can rank knowledge of different kinds of past phenomena. On this scale knowledge of past technological or economic phenomena is most credible and that of past religious or ideological phenomena is least credible. Knowledge of past social phenomena falls somewhere in between. This suggestion has been echoed by Daniel (1962), Thompson (1958*b*), Chang (1967*a*), and Deetz (1967), and can also be found in Childe (1951*b*).

On the other hand, Binford (1968:18–23) suggests that there are no known limitations to the knowledge we may gain of the past.

Data relevant to most, if not all, components of the past sociocultural systems are preserved in the archaeological record . . . (Binford 1968:22).

The position being taken here is that different kinds of phenomena are never remote; they are either accessible or they are not. . . . The practical limitations on our knowledge of the past are not inherent in the nature of the archaeological record; the limitations lie in our methodological naïveté, in our lack of development for [sic] principles determining the relevance of archaeological remains to propositions regarding processes and events of the past (Ibid:22–23).

In an earlier (1968) comparison of the metaphysical and epistemological foundations of these views, I conclude that the first view is based on the belief that knowledge inhers in and derives from data. Because some past phenomena are thought to be more "remotely" related to or less inherently "in" archaeological data than others, inferences derived from the former are necessarily more speculative and less credible than those from the latter.

The second view is based on the belief that phenomena have no inherent properties in the above sense. Only when they are conceived, or interlinked with a set of concepts, do they become data. Data are the perceived characteristics of phenomena defined by the concepts held at the moment by their perceivers. The conceived nature of data can thus vary from one person to the next and from one time to another. It follows that the source of limitation to knowledge is not in the phenomena of the archaeological record but in the conceptual systems of those who spend their lives perceiving this record, i.e., archaeologists.

I advance the second view here. Not only does the first view seem contrary to the nature of the world as anthropologists are trained to see it, i.e., via cultural relativity, but also it severely limits and underestimates the creative role of the archaeologist and the potential dynamic growth of our field. As Binford points out (1968:22) it is highly speculative in that no specific potential knowledge has been empirically demonstrated to be more or less "remote" than some other. Moreover, some phenomena previously thought to be "remote" have recently been shown to be quite observable, e.g., networks of social interaction or residence systems (Deetz 1960; Leone 1968; Longacre 1963; Whallon 1966).

The view that present limits to knowledge are to be found in our present concepts about the past and about the archaeological record frees us and directs us to the difficult but exciting task of refining or abandoning these concepts and inventing new ones. The limitations on what can be indirectly observed of the past are to be found in lack of creativity and unwillingness to change concepts. To the degree that we remove these limits, we can indirectly observe the past. I suggest that the analysis of systems for indirect observation of the past presented here is a useful model for a method that we can follow profitably to add to the systematization, credibility, and content of our knowledge of the past.

A Consideration of Archaeological Research Design

IT SEEMS fair to generalize that archaeologists are becoming more interested in the explanatory potential which studies of paleoecology, paleodemography, and evolution offer for increasing our understanding of formal and structural change in cultural systems. Several anthropologists have recognized a growing interest in questions dealing with the isolation of conditions and mechanisms by which cultural changes are brought about (Adams 1960a; Braidwood 1959; Haag 1959; Steward 1960). In short, we seek answers to some "how and why" questions in addition to the "what, where, and when" questions so characteristically asked by archaeologists. This essay is concerned with presenting certain methodological suggestions, some of which must be adopted if we are to make progress in the study of processes and move archaeology into the "explanatory level" of development (Willey and Phillips 1958:4–5).

In any general discussion of method and theory there is inevitably an argumentative bias on the part of the writer. It should be pointed out that I believe the isolation and study of cultural systems, rather than aggregates of culture traits, is the only meaningful approach to understanding cultural processes (Steward 1960:173–74). A cultural system

Reprinted from *American Antiquity,* vol. 29, no. 4, 1964, pp. 425–41. By permission of the author and the Society for American Archaeology.

is a set of constant or cyclically repetitive articulations between the social, technological, and ideological extrasomatic, adaptive means available to a human population (White 1959:8). The intimate systemic articulation of localities, facilities, and tools with specific tasks performed by social segments results in a structured set of spatial-formal relationships in the archaeological record. People do not cooperate in exactly the same way when performing different tasks. Similarly, different tasks are not uniformly carried on at the same locations. As tasks and cooperating groups vary, so do the implements and facilities (Wagner 1960:88–117) of task performance. The loss, breakage, and abandonment of implements and facilities at different locations, where groups of variable structure performed different tasks, leaves a "fossil" record of the actual operation of an extinct society. This fossil record may be read in the quantitatively variable spatial clusterings of formal classes of artifacts. We may not always be able to state or determine what specific activities resulted in observed differential distributions, but we can recognize that activities were differentiated and determine the formal nature of the observable variability. I have argued elsewhere (Binford 1962:219) that we can recover, both from the nature of the populations of artifacts and from their spatial associations, the fossilized structure of the total cultural system. The archaeological structure of a culture should, and in my opinion does, reflect all other structures, for example, kinship, economic, and political. All are abstracted from the events which occur as part of the normal functioning of a cultural system. The archaeological structure results from these same events. The definition of this structure and the isolation of the archaeological remains of a cultural system are viewed as research objectives. Such an isolation can be made by the demonstration of consistent between-class correlations and mutual covariations among classes of artifacts and other phenomena. The isolation and definition of extinct cultural systems, both in terms of content and demonstrable patterns of mutual formal-spatial covariation, can be accomplished. Once accomplished, such an archaeological structure is amenable to analysis in terms of form and complexity; in short, we can speak of culture types. Methods for correlating archaeologically defined culture types with structural forms defined in terms of behavioral attributes can be developed. When this is accomplished, archaeologists and "social anthropologists" will be in the position to make joint contributions to the solution of common anthropological problems, a condition that hardly obtains today.

In addition to maintaining the position that we should strive to isolate the archaeological structure of extinct cultural systems, it is argued that changes in cultural systems must be investigated with regard to the adaptive or coping situations which are presented to human populations. If we are profitably to study process, we must be able to isolate cultural systems and study them in their adaptive milieu conceived in terms of physical, biological, and social dimensions. The physical and biological dimensions need little explanation because anthropologists are familiar with the problems of the nature and stability of natural environment and in the physical and demographic human basis of cultural systems. However, the social dimension is frequently excluded from considerations of adaptation. There is little need to belabor the point that as the density and complexity of separate sociocultural systems increase within a major geographic zone, the cultural means for articulating and "adjusting" one society with another become more complex. Certainly the coping situations and hence the adaptive stresses associated with a changing pattern of sociopolitical distribution within a major zone must be considered when attempting to understand changes in any given system (Gearing 1962). As long as "cultures" are defined in terms of stylistic similarity, and the question of possible differences in the material inventory of functional classes and in the internal structure of the assemblage is unanswered, there is little possibility of dealing realistically with questions of process. It is a system that is the seat of process.

Because of these convictions I will frequently mention the "regional approach" or the detailed and systematic study of regions that can be expected to have supported cultural systems. The extent of such regions will vary because it is recognized that cultural systems differ greatly in the limits of their adaptive range and milieu. As cultural systems become more complex, they generally span greater ecological ranges and enter into more complex, widespread, extrasocietal interaction. The isolation and definition of the content, the structure, and the range of a cultural system, together with its ecological relationships, may be viewed as a research objective. Admittedly it is an objective which may or may not be successfully accomplished under any given research design. The research design should be aimed at the accomplishment of this isolation which, I believe, is most profitably prosecuted within a regional unit of investigation. Under current programs of salvage archaeology and increased foundation support for archaeological research, we are being given the opportunity to study major regions intensively. In spite of the opportunities currently available, it is my impression that very little thought has been given to research design. Methods and approaches utilized in such investigations seem to be little more than expanded or greatly enlarged field sessions of the type that has traditionally characterized American archaeological data collection. To be sure, the work may be neater, more attention may be given to stratigraphy, more classes of phenomena may be observed and collected than in the field work of years past; yet the general methods of data collection and observation remain unchanged. I wish to argue that current lack of concern with the development of planned research designs generally obviates the recovery of data pertinent to questions which derive from current theoretical interests. Investigatory tools must fit the job; current field procedures were developed to provide data relevant to a limited number of problems. Concern has been with problems of stylistic chronological placement and historical continuity between and among archaeologically defined units. The methodological tools developed for the investigation of such problems are inappropriate for supplying information relevant to our broadening research interests in cultural processes.

Methodological Problem Areas

Laymen frequently ask: "What are you digging for?" I think most of us will agree that we are digging to recover facts for the elucidation of past cultures. In the absence of explicit statements concerning the kinds of facts which archaeologists hope to obtain, we can only assume that we know how to recover the "pertinent" ones. Most of us will agree that this is not true. I not only have been unable to use other investigators' data, but I have also frequently found my own data lacking in many important "facts"—facts which could have been collected had I been aware of the questions to which the given observation was relevant. For instance, I recently wanted to demonstrate that most of the sites in a particular area were located adjacent to streams. This was impossible because I had no data as to where the archaeologist reporting on the area had concentrated his survey efforts. Was the failure to report sites in areas not adjacent to streams the result of sites being absent, or was it simply a lack of investigation in those areas not adjacent to streams? In another instance, I wanted to compare the relative density of Middle Woodland sites in two major river basins in order to make statements about the relative occupational intensity in the two areas. This was impossible because I was unable to determine whether or not the reported differential densities were the result of differences in the intensity of survey, presence or absence of forest cover affecting the likelihood of sites being recognized, or differential aboriginal use of the valleys under consideration. Such uncertainties make it obvious that we are concerned with answering questions for which our research designs, field methods, and reporting procedures are not adequate to supply the "pertinent facts." Such a situation cannot be prevented entirely, but we can strive to devise techniques for gathering the facts which are pertinent to questions currently being asked of our data. As the general theoretical development within archaeology goes forward, more and more facts previously ignored will be recognized as important and pertinent. We can look forward to continued concern with keeping our investigatory tools sufficient to the task; in short, we will be increasingly involved in the development of new and improved research designs and methodologies by means of which they may be operationalized.

One clue to a "methodological problem area" in our current practices can be found in another question which laymen are apt to ask: "How do you know where to dig?" My answer to such a question is that we dig where there are surface indications of past occupations or cultural activity—a seemingly accurate answer, yet we do not excavate every location which yields surface indications. What are the means whereby we select

161

certain sites for excavation and not others? A quick review of 37 regional reports spanning the period from 1954 to 1963 failed to reveal a single exposition by the authors as to the criteria they utilized in selecting sites for excavation. A typical statement may read as follows: "During this time a total of 51 sites was located in survey work and 13 of the more important sites were excavated to some extent."

It is my impression that there is no single set of criteria for selecting "important" sites. Some archaeologists select sites because they represent a time period. Others are selected because they are large and productive. Certainly some have been excavated because they were accessible to modern roads. Despite the lack of systematic statement, it is repeatedly mentioned that sites are representative or that they are large and yield much material. Less frequently, economy is cited as a reason for selecting a particular site. Although it is not commonly expressed, we may generalize that archaeologists want representative and reliable data within the bounds of their restricted time and monetary resources. This is practically the definition of the aims of modern sampling procedures. Sampling, as used here, does not mean the mere substitution of a partial coverage for a total coverage. It is the science of controlling and measuring the reliability of information through the theory of probability (Deming 1950:2). Certainly we are all aware that we must substitute partial coverage for complete coverage in our investigation. Given this situation, there is only one currently known means for accomplishing coverage so that the results can be evaluated as to their reliability in representation of the population investigated. This is through the application of sampling theory in the development and execution of data-collecting programs.

Sampling

In the following discussion of sampling we shall introduce certain terms that are used by writers on sampling and attendant statistical problems. A *universe* is the isolated field of study. In most cases archaeological field work is conducted within a universe of territory, a universe spatially defined. A *population* consists of an aggregate of analytical units within the universe so that, at least in principle, each unit may be assigned a definite location for a given unit of time. The population has a distribution in space consisting of the aggregate of individual locations (Duncan et al. 1961:21). In addition to a distribution, we can speak of the *spatial structure* of a population. Structure suggests a pattern of interrelationships among distinguishable parts of an organized whole (Duncan et al. 1961:2), and for our purposes the spatial structure of archaeological populations derives from the complex interrelationships between people, activities, and material items within a cultural system. In addition, we may speak of the *form of a population,* which is the nature and quantitatively variable constitution of subclasses and the relative frequency of analytical units.

The application of the method of probability sampling presupposes that a universe can be subdivided into distinct and identifiable units called *sample units*. These units may be natural units, such as sites or individual projectile points, or they may be arbitrary units, such as 6-inch levels in an excavation, or surface areas defined by a grid system. Regardless of the basis for definition, the application of the method of probability sampling presupposes the availability of a list of all the potential sample units within the universe. This list is called the *frame* and provides the basis for the actual selection of the sample units to be investigated. The frame varies with the nature of the archaeological population under investigation. When a population of sites is sampled, the frame is normally a list of sites within a stated universe, such as the alluvial bottoms of the Rock River between two specified points. When partial coverage of a population within a stated universe is attempted, the sample units are selected from the frame so that all units of the frame have an equal chance of being chosen for investigation; the selection is governed by the "laws of chance" alone, maximizing the reliability of the sample.

Before we approach the subject of different methods of probability sampling and their range of application in archaeological research, certain principles which underlie and guide the research design aimed at the proper and efficient execution of sampling techniques will be mentioned. This presentation is adapted from a section entitled "Types of Sampling" by Parten (1950).

1) The population to be sampled and the units composing it must be clearly defined so that there will be no question as to what the sample represents.

2) A universe partitioned by a frame composed of many small units is preferable to one composed of fewer but larger units. This is a safeguard against accidental inclusion of an unrepresentative amount of "heterogeneity" in any given sample.

3) The units of the frame should be approximately equal in size. This eliminates bias which could result from a systematic relationship between the structure and the size of the population.

4) All units should be independent of each other so that if one is drawn for sampling, it will in no way affect the choice of another.

5) The same units should be used in sampling, tabulation, and analysis. A sample of mounds is of no use if generalizations about general site distributions are being attempted.

6) The universe must be present or cataloged so that every unit in it is listed or can be given an identifying symbol to be used during the drawing of a sample. For instance, a grid system is established with 12 ten-foot squares on a side, and 20 of the 144 squares are chosen for excavation by a random method. Later, it is decided to extend the grid system six more squares in one direction. The enlarged system does not have the random character of the sample drawn under the frame defined by the original grid system.

7) The method of drawing the sample should be completely independent of the characteristics to be examined.

8) In order for the sample to remain random, every unit drawn must be accessible. For instance, in the case where a site has been selected for sampling and the property owner refuses permission to dig, inaccessibility biases the sample. This is particularly true because refusal of permission may be related to ideas of the "value" of materials on his property relative to those on others' property.

With these principles serving as a background, we can turn to a discussion of types of sampling and their ranges of applicability to archaeological investigation. Although there are many types of sampling, only two will be discussed: simple random sampling and stratified sampling.

Simple Random Sampling

This is by far the simplest of the methods of probability sampling. It implies that an equal probability of selection is assigned to each unit of the frame at the time of sample selection. The term *random* refers to the method of selecting the sample units to be investigated rather than to the method of investigating any given unit. A practical procedure for selecting a random sample is by utilizing a table of random numbers (Arkin and Colton 1957:142). The procedure is to 1) determine the number of units in the frame, identifying them serially from one to (n); 2) determine the desired size of the sample, that is, actual number of units to be investigated; 3) select the required series of numbers from the table of random numbers (the required series is the number determined sufficient to constitute a representative sample of the population); and 4) investigate those units in the frame that correspond to the numbers drawn from the table of random numbers. It cannot be overemphasized that this is a technique for selecting the units to be investigated and does not refer to the procedures used in gathering the data.

Stratified Sampling

It can be shown that the precision of a sample depends upon two factors: 1) the size of the sample and 2) the variability or heterogeneity of the population being sampled. If we desire to increase the precision, aside from increasing the sample size, we may devise means which will effectively reduce the heterogeneity of the population. One such procedure is known as the method of stratified sampling. The procedure is to partition the universe or divide it into classes, each of which is treated as an independent sampling universe from which simple random samples are drawn, following the methods outlined above. This procedure has a number of advantages. Classes may be established with regard to different variables that one wishes to control, which makes possible the reliable evaluation of variability in other phenomena with respect to the class-defining variables.

As has been suggested, the size of the sample is an important factor for consideration in striving for reliability in the sample as representative of the population. An optimum sample is one which is efficient, representative, reliable, and flexible. The sample size should be small enough to avoid unnecessary expense and large enough to avoid excessive error. To arrive at a sample size which is considered optimum in terms of the above criteria, there are a number of factors which must be considered, each largely integrated with the other rather than independent. Each will vary, in different sampling situations, as to their relative importance in influencing decisions about the appropriate sample size. Of particular importance to archaeologists is the realization

that the size of the sample necessary to meet normal requirements of reliability and economy is greatly affected by the number of subclasses into which the recovered data will be divided. For instance, in the case of a sample of ceramics composed of 100 sherds, it is likely that if only two "types" are represented, the sample may be sufficient to give a fairly reliable estimate of the relative proportions of the two types in the population. On the other hand, if within the sample there are 15 "types," then the reliability of the sample as an estimate of the relative proportions of the recognized types in the parent population is very low. A further caution applies to samples drawn from multicomponent sites where there are clearly several recognizable populations of separate historical origin. In the latter case, some of the subclasses are independent of one another, and any given subclass may be representative of only one of the multiple historical populations. Also, in the latter case, sample size must be determined by the relative frequencies of the smallest independent subclass. In other words, sample size should be large enough to give reliable measures of the smallest important breakdowns made within the sample. If the population is relatively homogeneous, then sample size may be relatively small and still reliable. On the other hand, if the population is heterogeneous, more observations are needed to yield reliable data.

This discussion of sampling is very elementary, but enough has been presented to serve as a basis for evaluation of the types of observational populations which archaeologists investigate and their investigatory peculiarities as a basis for further discussion of research design.

Basic Units of Archaeological Observation

Albert Spaulding has provided us with a classic statement of what we as archaeologists are doing, thereby setting forth an operational definition of the field of archaeology

Spaulding's introductory statement is reproduced here as a point of departure for
further discussion of archaeological data
collection.

A science deals with some class of objects or
events in terms of some specified dimensions
of the objects or events. The simplest (and
most elegant) of the sciences, mechanics, has
all physical objects as its center of attention,
and the demensions of these objects as studied
are length, mass, and time; i.e., roughly speaking
mechanics has three kinds of measuring instruments: a yardstick, a set of scales, and a
clock. The interrelationships and transformations of measurements with these scales is the
business of mechanics. It is clear that prehistoric
archaeology also has a class of objects, artifacts,
as its center of attention. The concept "artifact"
presupposes the idea of culture, which I will
treat as a given. Thus we can define an
artifact as any material result of cultural
behavior. Since cultural behavior is our ultimate
referent, it follows that we are interested in
only those properties, characteristics, aspects,
and attributes of artifacts which are the result
of or have a significant relation to cultural
behavior. What arc the dimensions of artifacts
whose interrelationships are the special business
of archaeology? Plainly there are two in the
strict sense of dimension: time and space. We
want to know where and when artifacts were
made, used, and deposited. Plainly there is
another class of dimensions fundamental to
archaeological study; the many dimensions
which are sets of physio-chemical properties of
the artifacts. We can group them for convenient
reference under the label, formal properties,
and collectively as the formal dimension. We
are now in a position to define archaeology as
the study of the interrelationships and transformations of artifacts with respect to the
formal, temporal, and spatial dimensions. As
a footnote, formal and spatial attributes can be
observed directly, but temporal attributes are
always inferred from formal and spatial
attributes. Indeed strictly speaking artifacts are
objects and do not have temporal attributes—
they merely exist. But artifacts do imply events,
and events do have the property of occurring
at a definite time, so when we speak of the
temporal attributes of an artifact, we really
refer to an inference about some event or
process implied by the formal and/or spatial
attributes of the artifact. This leaves us with
describing and ordering formal and spatial
attributes as the primary task. These are the
empirical data of archaeology and this describing and ordering are prerequisite to the chronological inferences (Spaulding, mimeographed
version, revised 1960a:437–9).

Artifacts as a class of phenomena represent a number of different types of populations which are definable in terms of their
spatial, formal, or spatial and formal attributes taken in combination. Because of the
different nature of artifactual populations,
investigation of the several recognizable
populations must differ as regards the appropriate means to provide the necessary
information for their formal, spatial, and
temporal analysis. The several classes of
artifactual populations recognized here will
be termed *types of observational populations,* since it is argued that different sampling techniques, and hence research strategy,
are necessary for the investigation of each.

Populations of Cultural Items

Cultural items are discrete entities, the
formal characteristics of which are at least
partially the result of cultural activity or
events. A further qualification is that the
formal characteristics of the item are not
altered through removal from their matrix;
they are transportable and may be formally
analyzed without recourse to information
about their provenience. This is not to say
that such information is not crucial to interpretation of the formal properties, only that
the formal properties themselves are independent of the matrix and provenience
associations.

The form of the cultural item may vary in
terms of the function of the item as an element in the cultural system, for example,
technologically (manufacturing techniques
and raw materials) or stylistically.

The sampling universe for the investigation of populations of cultural items is
necessarily the site. The sampling and field-
observation procedures utilized do not affect
our ability to analyze items formally, but
they greatly affect our ability to study the

distribution, form, and structure of *a population of cultural items*. It will be remembered that a population necessarily has spatial attributes both in its distribution and its structure. Sampling control is therefore necessary to provide data for the description of populations of cultural items. We as anthropologists hope to be able to assess the range of formal variability in classes of cultural items and to study their distribution and population structure in terms of spatial clusters of quantitatively variant class associations. It is necessary to define accurately the range of formal variation within classes of cultural items as well as relative frequencies among recognized classes within the population. While excavating, we have no precise knowledge of the boundaries of the population of cultural items being investigated, and we generally sample in terms of areal units designed to cover the territory defined by the presence of artifacts. We are sampling "artifact space" as a means to both definition and segregation of populations of cultural items. We can only accomplish this through exercising tight spatial controls for gaining information necessary to the analytic determination of what cultural items are, spatially and temporally clustered one with another and with other artifactual materials. Such insights are a clue to the "role played" by various items in the operation of extinct cultural systems. Similarly, the same control is necessary to the definition of the spatial structure and form of the population. We want to utilize techniques which will insure reliable and representative data regarding the range of formal variability within a given subclass of cultural items, the content of the population of cultural items defined by the relative frequencies of the recognized classes, and the structure of the population defined by the spatial structure of between-class associations of items and other classes of artifacts.

Error arising in the sampling of populations of cultural items normally results from 1) incomplete and nonrepresentative coverage of the universe; 2) failure to partition the universe so that a single undifferentiated collection is made, thereby excluding the possibility of investigating the homogeneity or heterogeneity of the population; or 3) samples are far too small to allow the adequate evaluation of the variability represented in a given class of cultural items or to yield a reliable estimate of the between-class relative frequencies.

Populations of Cultural Features

Cultural features are bounded and qualitatively isolated units that exhibit a structural association between two or more cultural items and types of nonrecoverable or composite matrices. The cultural feature cannot be formally analyzed or at least formally observed after its dissection in the field. Many of the formal observations must be made while the feature is being excavated. Features include such classes of remains as burials, mounds, structures, pits, and hearths. Formal variations among cultural features are dependent upon 1) their functions within the represented cultural system, 2) technology in terms of the raw materials utilized in their production, 3) alterations occurring as a result of their participation in other natural systems, for example, organic decay, 4) their cultural history (how often they were parts of successive cultural events, resulting in their repair, secondary modification, and destruction), and 5) stylistic variation. Unlike cultural items, the cultural feature cannot be formally defined without precise and detailed observation and "analysis" in the field. The field investigator must at least make decisions as to what attributes are culturally relevant and meaningful prior to beginning field observation and recording. This adds an additional field burden to the normal exercise of sampling control characteristic of the investigation of cultural items.

As in the case of cultural items, the sampling universe for populations of cultural features is the site. Similarly, our sampling procedures should insure reliable and representative data regarding 1) the variability within any class of features, 2) the formal content of the population of features, and 3) the structure of the population of cultural features.

Sources of error which frequently arise in sampling such populations are 1) incomplete and nonrepresentative coverage of the "artifact space" so that, while the number of recovered features may be large, there is no way of demonstrating or determining whether the between-class frequencies are representative of the population present; 2) samples are far too small to allow adequate evaluation of the variability represented in a given class of features or to yield reliable estimates of the between-class relative frequencies.

Populations of Cultural Activity Loci: Sites

The site is a spatial cluster of cultural features or items, or both. The formal characteristics of a site are defined by its formal content and the spatial and associational structure of the populations of cultural items and features present.

1) *Sites vary in their depositional context*. Sites exhibiting primary depositional context have not been altered in their formal properties except through the natural processes of the decay of organic material, or the physicochemical alteration of features and items since the period of occupancy. Sites exhibiting secondary depositional context are those whose formal characteristics, defined in terms of soils, features, and items, have been spatially altered through physical movement or deletion from the loci. Some or possibly all of the original associations between the various classes of artifacts have been changed. This disruption in the structure of the site may have occurred through the agency of erosion, geophysical changes, or through destruction as a result of later cultural activity. Sites with primary deposi-

tional context yield the most complete archaeological record. However, sites with secondary depositional context must frequently be studied in order to understand the regional distribution of activity loci.

2) *Sites vary in their depositional history*. The culturally dependent characteristics of a site may have been the result of a single short-term occupation, a single long-term occupation, multiple occupation over a rather limited temporal span, multiple occupations over an extended period of time, or combinations of all of these.

3) *Sites vary in their culture history*. Sites exhibiting a complex depositional history may or may not exhibit a complex cultural history. A site could be repeatedly occupied by representatives of the same stable sociocultural system for the same purposes, in which case there may be a complex depositional history with a simple cultural history. Similarly, a site with a simple depositional history may exhibit a complex cultural history, for example, an extended long-term occupation spanning a period of major structural changes in the cultural system. A single locus may be sequentially occupied by social units of different sociocultural or sociopolitical units, adding to the complexity of the cultural history of the site.

4) *Sites and areas within sites vary functionally*. Since sites are the result of cultural activities performed by social units within restricted spatial bounds, we would expect them to vary formally as a function of the activities of the social units represented. It is a known and demonstrable fact that sociocultural systems vary in the degree to which social segments perform specialized tasks, as well as in the cyclical pattern of task performance at any given location. These differences have spatial correlates with regard to the loci of task performance; hence we expect sites to vary formally and spatially with regard to the nature of the tasks performed at each, and the social composition of the units performing the tasks.

All possible combinations of the above-mentioned basic forms of variation may occur at sites which archaeologists investigate. Archaeologists must be prepared to make the pertinent observations needed to define the form and structure of the populations of artifacts and culturally relevant nonartifactual material present, and to isolate the form and structure of historically different archaeological assemblages represented. Unlike populations of cultural items or features where the normal universe is the site, the sampling universe for populations of sites is of necessity a region. Once the archaeologist has determined the relative homogeneity of the sampled site population as regards the historical and functional nature of the archaeological assemblage present, he is in a position to consider the nature of the site as a whole and to classify it within a typology of sites (based on the attributes of both the form of the artifactual elements present and the structure of their spatial and formal associations). Such an approach is the methodological aim of sampling a universe of sites regionally defined.

Two major sources of error arise in the investigation of site populations. The first source of error is incomplete and nonrepresentative coverage of the range of variation represented among sites within the universe. This arises inevitably as a result of the "selection" of sites for investigation on the basis of criteria other than those of the method of probability sampling. For instance, sites are frequently selected because of a high density of cultural items almost to the exclusion of sites with low density. The density of cultural items at a site is a formal attribute of the specific activity loci and is only relevant to the selection of sites for excavation as an attribute in a provisional site typology. A given universe may have very few sites with dense concentrations of cultural items, while the number of sites exhibiting less-dense concentrations may be quite high. In this case, the sample of sites for investigation must be composed of a proportionally higher number of sites ex-

hibiting low densities of cultural items. The second source of error is failure to sample with sufficient intensity to yield a reliable measure of the variability present in the population. Inadequate sample size measured by the number of investigated sites is one of the major sources of error. Ideally, a sample of sites should be adequate to represent the formal range of variability in site form, the relative frequencies of recognized site types, and their spatial structuring within the universe.

Populations of Ecofacts

In addition to the investigation of cultural items, features, and activity loci, we must sample populations of ecofacts. Ecofact is the term applied to all culturally relevant nonartifactual data. Cultural systems are adaptive systems, and in order to understand their operation and the processes of their modification, we must be in a position to define their adaptive milieu. All those elements which represent or inform about the points of articulation between the cultural system and other natural systems must be sampled. This is an extremely important phase of archaeological data collection and is accompanied by many field complications in terms of methods of observation and sampling. The general class of ecofacts can be broken down into many subclasses representing different populations, such as pollen, soil, and animal bone, each with specific attendant sampling problems. However, for the purpose of this presentation, we will consider ecofacts as a single population which, in general, requires certain methodological considerations distinct from the problems associated with sampling artifact populations.

Basic Sampling Universes

Although we have recognized four major types of observational populations, each differing in the way it must be observed and sampled, there are only two basic sampling universes in excavation or field work, the region and the site. Populations of sites must be investigated within a universe defined in spatial terms, the region. Populations of cultural items and features must be investigated within a universe defined by the bounds of artifactual distribution at a given location, the site. Ecofactual populations may be sampled within both universes, depending on the types of information desired. If culture types are to be defined, it is essential that we isolate a reliable and representative sample of the population of sites characteristic of a given culture. For adequate definition of types of activity loci we need a reliable sample of populations of cultural items and features assignable to any given occupation. In order to obtain such information, we must have well-planned research designs rooted in the application of probability sampling procedures.

Limitations of Current Procedures

It is my impression that archaeologists have not consciously aimed at sampling populations of sites. They have concentrated on collecting "samples" of cultural items within regionally defined universes. The sites have been treated largely as "mines" for such items. In exceptional cases, where sites have been intensively investigated and populations of cultural features studied, there is little attempt to analyze the population of cultural items with regard to its spatial structure or form, while inordinate attention is frequently given to describing the "norms" of recognized formal subclasses within the population. When cultural features are investigated, they are usually reported cartographically, with little attempt to conduct a detailed formal analysis aimed at the description of types of features. One rarely finds a report in which correlations between the spatial structure of populations of cultural features and items have been attempted as a matter of "standard" procedure. For the

most part, archaeologists have concerned themselves with vertical spatial analysis, and the search has been for stratified sites in which a limited "test pit" will yield a stylistic sequence that may be used to develop a regional chronology. This results in "cultures" being isolated on a regional basis and defined largely in terms of the stylistic characteristics of cultural items. The resulting information is insufficient for the structural definition of artifact assemblages and site typologies in precise terms. Cultural "taxonomy" remains almost exclusively in stylistic terms.

On the other hand, there has been inordinate interest in certain classes of cultural features, such as burial mounds and platform mounds. It was early recognized that such mounds were excellent "mines" for exotic and artistically pleasing objects and were therefore attractive to untrained investigators and relic hunters. Work in mounds, whether prompted through humanistic interests or through the "salvage motive," has contributed inordinately to our "sample" of artifactual data which serves as the taxonomic basis of many archaeologically defined cultures. This lack of representative data plus inadequate information on the form of the features is a real and limiting bias in the data currently available for study. Data have been gathered in terms of problems which concentrate investigations on populations of cultural items at the expense of and to the exclusion of cultural features. Investigation has also been concentrated on particular types of obvious features, such as mounds, and there has been very little awareness that the aim of archaeological investigation is the definition of the structure of an archaeological assemblage in addition to its content. These factors have contributed greatly to our current inability to deal systematically with archaeological data.

Current interests demand that we do not perpetuate these limitations in our methodology. We must approach our work with the methodological ideal of sampling a spatial universe, regardless of whether it is conducted under large-scale regional research programs or over an extended period of time through a series of small-scale investigations. Such sampling is aimed at obtaining a reliable and representative sample of the range of variation in formal-structural terms of sites within a given region. Selection of sites for excavation should be made on the basis of some method of probability sampling as the best means of insuring that the expenditure of time and money in excavation will yield the desired information. Sites selected for excavation must be investigated so that they can be formally defined from the standpoint of the nature of the populations of cultural items present, but equal attention must also be given to the population of cultural features. This is the only way to approach the necessary task of developing a site typology in functional and structural terms, an absolute necessity for the definition and isolation of the archaeological structure of extinct cultural systems. The latter is judged a necessary step toward the scientific investigation of cultural processes.

A Hypothetical Research Design

In an initial attempt to think through some of the practical problems associated with the design and execution of a research program which attempts to operationalize some of the suggestions advanced thus far, I will present a "hypothetical" research program. Hypothetical is placed in quotes because many of the ideas and problems discussed are the result of work currently being undertaken in the southern part of Illinois, specifically in the Carlyle Reservoir. Regardless of the projected implementation of many of the ideas set forth, the program remains hypothetical because the suggestions are untried and undemonstrated. It is hoped that by presenting these ideas in the form of a research "model," others may gain a clearer understanding of what is intended by the application of probability sampling approaches in field work. It is further hoped that this model can serve as a "whipping boy" for the improvement and further development of field methods and the execution of well-planned research designs.

Let us assume that we are given the task of investigating the prehistoric remains within a region. Our aim is to determine with the greatest degree of precision and reliability the nature of the extinct cultural systems represented for the entire range of human occupation. We must face the problem of isolating the variable cultural items, cultural features, and sites of activity for the cultural systems represented. In addition, we must gather ecofactual data as a basis for understanding the way in which the extinct cultural systems participated in the regional ecosystems of the past. We want to know the internal structure of the systems, the degree of structural differentiation and functional specialization of the social segments, as well as how these segments were articulated into a functional cultural system. We want to know the demographic basis and how it varies with respect to isolated structural changes in the cultural systems. In short, we want to know all we can about the structure and functioning of the extinct cultural systems and how they relate one to another as regards processes of change and evolution.

The initial problem is the location of the various loci of past cultural activity within the region. This phase of the work should be directed toward determining the density and distribution of activity loci with respect to classes of ecofactual phenomena, such as plant communities, physiographic features, and soil types. In order to accomplish this task, there is only one appropriate procedure short of complete coverage, a procedure rooted in some form of probability sampling. One suggested approach is to stratify the regional universe on the basis of ecofactual criteria judged desirable to control, such as soil types. If we assume for purposes of presentation that soil types have been decided upon for the areal stratification, in most cases the bounds of the various soils will be defined fairly accurately on a soil map, and we can simply determine the extent of each in square miles, acres, or other appropriate units. Having accomplished this, we can impose a frame within each sampling stratum (areas of common soil type). It will be remembered that a universe partitioned by many small sample units is preferable to one with fewer but larger units, and that the units of the frame should be approximately equal in size. Using these guides, we can impose a grid system over the areas of the various soil types. The actual size of a given unit in the frame would be determined by considerations of survey logistics and the need to have multiple but also practicable units for investigation. For purposes of presentation, it is assumed that the grid is composed of squares equaling one-half square mile. We would then count and enumerate each unit in the separate frames for each sampling stratum (soil type). The next methodological consideration is arriving at a "sample size." This can be quite complicated. For purposes of argument, it will be dismissed and we will assume that a 20% areal coverage within each sampling stratum has been judged sufficient. The next step is to draw the sample for each sampling stratum, and this may be accomplished by use of a table of random numbers. The sampling units within each frame will then be completely surveyed for purposes of locating sites.

What are the advantages of such a procedure? If executed under ideal conditions, it will permit the objective evaluation of site density in terms of ecofactual controls and also provide data relevant to summary statements about the intensity of past activities in the region as a whole within definable limits of error. The procedure will also permit the concentration of efforts on intensive study areas, making the logistical expenditure less than if the entire region were surveyed in a haphazard fashion. In addition to these advantages, it eliminates "hidden bias" in the form of differential attention paid to ecological situations which the investigator "feels" were preferred by prehistoric inhabitants. By following such a plan it is possible to demonstrate the ecological preferences of past occupants of the region.

On the other hand, there are certain problems which arise with any attempt to sample in this manner. Of primary importance are the conditions of the area itself in terms of the type of cover, presence or absence of modern communities, and distribution of agricultural land. Such factors could variously affect one's access to the land for site locational survey as well as the relative efficiency of observation. These complications are not new nor are they stumbling blocks to the suggested procedures. They are present no matter what type of research design we attempt to execute. The advantage of this particular approach is that it provides a methodological frame of reference for documenting and evaluating such bias. There are many ways to correct complicated sampling conditions. When approaching the problem of locating sites as outlined, it becomes imperative that the investigator concern himself with the control of bias resulting from differential survey conditions, something not generally considered under normal haphazard survey procedures.

Assuming that we have executed a research plan as outlined, the next step is to define spatially and sample initially the populations of cultural items present at each of the identified loci of cultural activity. This is prerequisite to the evaluation of the formal characteristics of the sites themselves; the ultimate aim is a classification of activity loci as to their degrees of similarity and difference. A working taxonomy of sites is a necessary prerequisite to the selection of sites for excavation and investigation of the populations of cultural items and features present. Limited data are obtainable through sampling populations of cultural items present on the surface of a site as well as through exercising spatial control over the "context" of the artifactual populations as regards ecofactual data. This information provides the classes of attributes utilized in classifying sites. There are three main attribute classes which can be normally controlled through the use of surface-sample data: the size and density of the cluster of cultural items, the formal constitution of the population of cultural items, and the degree of stylistic and functional homogeneity of the population.

The methods utilized to control the attributes of size and density will also allow us to partition the population of cultural items and speak of the relative densities and of its formal classes, that is, the spatial structure of the population. A further class of data, largely ecofactual, can and must be controlled. This is the topographic and physiographic nature of the location. Such information can be obtained at the same time that the spatial controls are established for sampling the population of cultural items.

In order to control the relevant variables and obtain the necessary data, we must have a number of sample units distributed over the area of the site and its immediate environs. These sample units must be rather evenly distributed within and beyond the suspected bounds of the site. In addition to establishing areal limits of the frame, we must determine the appropriate size of each sampling unit to insure the recovery of an adequate sample. A normal topographic survey of the site will provide a basis for the notation of ecofactual data as well as for the spatial control of the sampling frame and the location of sampling units.

Some method of "systematic sampling" is suggested as being the most appropriate to surface sampling. Only the first unit is selected at random and then others are selected in terms of a pre-established interval (Vescelius 1960:463). Systematic sampling ensures an equal dispersion of sample units, a desirable condition when densities and aggregational analysis are attempted. There is a further advantage in that spatial control on the placement of sampling units is easier to maintain with an equal spatial unit between

them; thus, it is easier to lay out and identify the selected sampling units in the field.

A typical example of the execution of such a program is given here. 1) Impose a frame over the area of the site in the form of a grid system composed of sampling units of appropriate size. 2) Enumerate the sampling units in the frame from one to n. Determine the necessary sample size and then determine the appropriate sampling interval. 3) Consult a table of random numbers and draw the initial sample unit. Then draw each sample unit separate from the initial one by the designated sampling interval. 4) Locate on the site the selected sampling units and collect all cultural items within the bounds of that unit.

This procedure can be speeded considerably in open or cultivated areas by use of a "dog-leash" technique. Each person who collects items has attached to his belt a cord of predetermined length to which is attached a stake. The stake is placed in the ground at the appropriate location, and the person collects all the cultural items within the radius of the circle defined by the "dog leash." The location of sampling units can be determined quickly by means of a tape and compass or with a transit. Such a method is considerably faster than setting up a grid and collecting items from a square unit, all four corners of which must be defined.

Regardless of the particular procedure followed, application of the principles of probability sampling to the collection of cultural items from the surface makes possible the objective definition of the site in terms of density clines. This permits objective comparison of sites in terms of site size and item density, in addition to the form, homogeneity, and structure of the population of cultural items present. On the basis of such comparisons, we can arrive at a provisional typology of the range of variability in the population of sites within the regional universe. Working hypotheses can be generated to account for the observable differences and similarities in form, density, and spatial structure, and these hypotheses can be tested by excavation.

A comparative study of information collected through the application of sampling techniques provides a basic set of data for the construction of a stratified sampling frame of provisional site types within which selection of sites for excavation can be made. This brings us to one of the major questions considered: how do we know where to dig? I think that the answer to this question logically rests with a methodology which attempts to test working hypotheses concerning the nature of variation that is observable in populations of surface-collected cultural items and with techniques of probability sampling. Are sites that exhibit similar size, density, and composition of cultural item populations similar with respect to populations of cultural features, depositional and cultural history, and general function within the cultural systems represented? If such a hypothesis were to be confirmed, we would be in a position to generalize far beyond the data derived from direct excavation and could make statements about settlement systems based largely on surface-collected data. This is not possible when sites are not treated within a sampling universe or when surface data are not used in the generation of structural hypotheses.

How do we actually go about the selection of sites for excavation? The following procedure is suggested. 1) Develop a taxonomy of sites based on formal attributes investigated during the surface survey. 2) Determine the relative frequencies and distributions of site types according to the original sampling strata, for example, soil types. 3) Stratify the population of sites into sampling strata based on the typology further stratified in terms of the original areal strata, that is, soil types. 4) Determine in terms of the time and funds available what proportion of the total number of each site type can be excavated to yield reliable information on their internal composition. 5) Enumerate each site in each sampling stra-

tum from one to *n*. 6) Consult a table of random numbers and draw the appropriate sampling units designated by the random numbers. 7) Proceed to excavate all those sites whose unit-designator number was drawn from the table of random numbers.

The use of such a procedure can be justified in a number of ways. First, it will be remembered that the initial taxonomy based on surface-collected materials grouped sites judged to be similar or different. Within each taxonomic class, sites are excavated to test the reliability of this judgment and to further explicate the nature of the variability through more detailed investigation of populations of cultural items and features. Only by the use of such a procedure can we explicate the meaning of observed differences in the surface-collected material and thereby provide the necessary information for confirming the validity of generalizations based on such data. Secondly, the procedure insures an adequate and representative sample of the population of cultural activity loci within the defined universe. It is a complete and unbiased across-the-board investigation of the full range of formal variability within the population.

The next phase of research planning is to many the most important, and it is the phase that has received most attention under the rubric of "field methods." Initially, it must be recognized that in excavation we are not sampling activity loci; we are sampling populations of cultural items, cultural features, and ecofacts at an activity locus that may or may not have a complex cultural and depositional history. We want data which will allow us to understand the historical aspects of the various occupations, as well as the functions of the occupations in the total cultural system represented.

If we view excavation as having a particular role in the scheme of data collection, it is reasonable to think in terms of an excavational strategy. First, it must be kept in mind that all excavation is exploratory in addition to being a method for securing samples. Some phases of excavation may be parametric in the sense of it being possible to enumerate a sampling frame prior to data collection, while other phases are exploratory and sampling must be only provisionally parametric. Spatial control on a horizontal axis makes possible the parametric definition of a sampling frame in terms of spatial units. This type of frame is ideal for investigation of the homogeneity or heterogeneity of the population of cultural items, and it is appropriate for exploratory work that seeks the solution of problems of depositional and cultural history. However, it is with excavation that we hope to accomplish the maximum correlational control and thereby obtain the data that will allow reliable interpretation of the internal variation in the spatial structure of functional and stylistic classes of cultural items. Excavation will further provide well-documented and correlated samples of ecofacts, the basic data relevant to the nature of the local environment, and the way in which the represented social units were adapted to it. It is by correlating the distributions of cultural items with different functional classes of cultural features that insight into the "causes" of differential distributions is obtained, and hence understanding of the range, location, and nature of the various activities conducted at the site. Sampling frames designed solely to obtain cultural items and provide information concerning depositional and cultural history are generally inadequate as a sampling frame for cultural features. Ideally, we should have an X-ray machine which would allow us to locate and formally evaluate the range of variation manifest in cultural features. Given such information, we could construct a frame and excavate features within each recognized formal class in proportion to their relative frequency. Such a procedure would be analogous to excavating sites selected on the basis of a previously defined frame of site types. Unfortunately, no such X-ray machine exists, and we must attempt to obtain the desired sample by opening up areas of the site in

such a way as to 1) allow the recognition of the presence of cultural features, 2) provide a representative spatial coverage of the universe in order to define the spatial distribution and structure of the features, and 3) provide the necessary contextual data for the formal analysis of the recognized features.

This discourse is not intended as a discussion of excavational techniques. However, a limited discussion of some widely utilized approaches as they relate to the general problems of research strategy seem to be in order.

Ideally, once a site is selected as a unit in a sampling frame of sites, it should be completely excavated. In such a case, there will be no question about one's ability to give parametric definition to a sampling frame for cultural items commensurate with the efficient investigation of cultural features. Complete excavation will insure complete recovery of the entire record of past activities at the given location.

In most cases it is impossible to undertake complete excavation of a site; only rarely are funds and personnel available for such an undertaking, particularly when sites are large. One method frequently resorted to when faced with a large site, or when the investigator is interested in obtaining information concerning the constitution of the population of cultural features, is to open up large "block" areas such as was done at Kincaid (Cole 1951). A relatively large number of contiguous excavation units were opened, and this resulted in the complete excavation of a large "block" of the site area. This method insures recovery of the formal range of cultural features present in any given block but, as normally implemented, does not insure that the excavated block is representative of the range of features and activity loci present at the site. As normally practiced, the block or blocks selected for excavation are in the "core" area of the site and therefore bias the sample toward features and activity areas that were centrally located. As previously noted, our

174

aim should be for adequate, reliable, and representative data. Block excavations as normally utilized do not supply this type of information.

Test pits and test trenches are appropriate units of excavation when one is investigating certain limited, formal properties of the site, but they are inappropriate to investigation of the site as a whole. Test pits are by definition small, noncontiguous units. Such units are useful in preliminary investigations of depositional problems and as a means of solving site cultural history problems. They can also be profitably employed in the collection of a dispersed number of samples of cultural items, but they do not normally expose areas large enough to define and sample populations of cultural features.

Test trenches are excellent means of investigating and defining problems of cultural and depositional history, but they have most of the limitations of test pits when sampling cultural features. However, they frequently provide more information on the differential distribution of feature types if they happen to be opened in sufficient density to "cross cut" major areas of the site. Data gathered from test trenches also have the advantage of being particularly useful for analysis of item densities on a linear axis. The limitations of test trenches are those of any technique which does not open up a large contiguous area, and does not cover, in a representative manner, the entire site.

As test pits and trenches are normally utilized, they do not provide adequate data regarding the population of cultural items because they are not normally distributed at random in sufficient numbers over the site. A greater limitation is the failure to expose large contiguous areas, a necessary condition for adequate sampling of cultural features.

Phase excavations seems to be the most appropriate term to apply to the procedures which will be suggested as a means of overcoming some of the difficulties inherent in sampling the different types of observational populations at a site. The term implies that the excavation of a site may involve several different excavational steps, each largely dependent upon the results of the earlier "phase" for the details necessary to the proper planning and execution of the succeeding phase. Each phase is designed to answer certain specific questions with the most economical and expedient means.

As an example, initial discussion will center around a relatively small, single-component site that lacks primary archaeological context below the plow zone (except, of course, cultural features). Initially, we want to know whether or not there are clusters of differential density in cultural items, a clue to the possible location of cultural features. In addition, we want a complete and unbiased sample of the population of cultural items in order to make judgments as to the "meaning" of demonstrable differential distributions of recognized stylistic and functional classes. Such a sample could be obtained by the excavation of a series of "test pits," the size and density of which would be determined by the estimated density of cultural items present. The distribution of the pits would be determined by some technique of probability sampling normally executed within a grid frame. The plow zone would be excavated and sifted for each of the selected excavation or sample units. This methodology could be further implemented by combining controlled surface collection from selected sample units. The data collected in this way should yield the desired information concerning population form, structure, and content. Once this is accomplished the next phase of excavation should be planned to yield the sufficient controlled data on the population of cultural features present. In this particular case, where there is no primary archaeological context below the plow zone, we can most efficiently accomplish our task by complete removal of the plow zone with the aid of power equipment. The result would be the exposure of cultural features which could be mapped and excavated, utilizing techniques designed to yield maximum correlational control.

The suggested excavation program would

amount to a two-phase sequence. The first phase is designed to yield information about the population of cultural items present, whereas the second phase would yield the desired information concerning the population of cultural features.

In many field situations the sites are more complex, having multiple occupations with primary archaeological deposits below the disturbed plow zone. In such a case, a three-phase excavation program may be more appropriate. The initial phase would consist of opening up a series of test pits selected for excavation on the basis of a random or systematic sampling pattern within a grid frame. This procedure, as in the earlier case, should provide the data necessary for the reliable definition and isolation of different stylistic and functional areas within the total site area. Next is the problem of sampling populations of cultural features. Since the site has several components, tight correlational control must be exercised to ensure the possibility of correlating feature forms with forms of cultural items representative of discrete occupational episodes. An appropriate procedure is to employ block excavations as the second phase. Since the multicomponent nature of the site presumably would have been recognized during the early stages of the test-pitting phase, such a procedure also ensures that the initial exploratory exposures will yield information obtained under conditions of maximum correlational control. This hopefully makes possible the correlation of feature types with old soil surfaces, which in turn can be isolated and investigated in terms of cultural-item content. With this type of information we should, assuming that the block exposures have been successful, be able to develop a formal taxonomy of features which can be correlated with the variable populations of cultural items representative of the separate occupations. Once such correlations are established, the third phase of excavation can begin, the "stripping phase." This is removal, by means of power equipment or by hand, without attempting to recover cultural items, of the complete cultural deposit down to the level where cultural features can be observed intruding into the natural. Once this is accomplished, these features can be mapped and excavated, using techniques that will ensure maximum correlational control. The distributional data thus obtained will supplement that already collected and make possible the definition of activity areas and the general internal community structure representative of the separate occupations.

If we have been careful in planning and successful in the execution of the three phases of excavation, we should have the data necessary for the demonstration of differences and similarities between occupations in terms of the formal, spatial, and structural composition of the separate populations defined by both cultural items and features.

Enough has been said to suggest what is intended by phase excavations. As the complexity of a site is compounded in depositional and culture historical aspects, more and more attention must be given to maintaining maximum correlational control. The intensity of sampling or the sample size needed to ensure adequate data increases with the heterogeneity of the universe under investigation. This means that data necessary for justifying the step from one phase to another become expanded, and in general the nature of the appropriate phases changes with the complexity and form of the universe. The more complex the site, the more complex the excavational procedures, and the larger must be the recovered samples for any given phase of excavation.

This recognition provides the justification for what I call the planning of an excavational sequence. In areas where a number of sites have been selected for excavation, the temporal sequence of excavation can be very important in promoting the efficient use of resources in both labor and funds. The initial sites excavated should be the least complex, so that the chances of making false correlations are diminished and the maximum conditions obtain for observing the formal spatial structure of features and cultural items.

Once an understanding is gained of the formal and structural characteristics which may be encountered, one is in a much better position to investigate a complex site where the nature of the variability may not be so clearly depicted. Informed excavation of a complex site can often greatly expedite its efficient investigation.

It is hoped that by following this "hypothetical" research program, the reader has gained a clearer understanding of what is intended by the argument that methods of probability sampling are applicable on all levels of field investigation. By pointing out some of the complications, I trust an appreciation can be gained as to the potential which the application of probability sampling methods holds for improving our data-collection methods. Such methods further provide a basis for a greatly expanded analysis of archaeological data directed toward the definition of archaeological assemblages in structural terms, ultimately with a view toward the isolation and definition of extinct cultural systems.

Of equal importance is the recognition that field work must not be conducted separately from analysis. Running anlysis is a necessary part of feature description, and of even greater importance is the recognition that the results of running analysis largely serve as the basis for the planning and decision-making regarding successive methodological steps taken in the execution of a field program. Much ink has been spilt on the argument that the archaeologist as such is a technician (Taylor 1948:43). Only in a very restricted sense can such a position be defended because the field archaeologist is forever making decisions as to what are pertinent and relevant "facts." Such decisions can only be made with knowledge and understanding of the questions being asked of the data. The field archaeologist must also be an anthropologist to make such decisions efficiently and effectively. As Brew (1946:65) has argued that there is no single or even adequate taxonomy sufficient for "bringing out all the evidence," so I also argue that there is no sufficient set of field techniques. Field work must be conducted in terms of a running analysis and against a backdrop of the widest possible set of questions to which the data are potentially relevant. This is no technician's job. This is the job of an anthropologist specialized in the collection and analysis of data concerning extinct cultural systems. Only after the myth of simplicity which surrounds the training of field archaeologists is dispelled, and after more attention is given to recovering information concerning the operation of extinct cultural systems as opposed to the recovery of things, will archaeologists make significant advances in studies of cultural process.

Summary and Conclusions

It has been argued that as archaeologists we are faced with the methodological task of isolating extinct socio-cultural systems as the most appropriate unit for the study of the evolutionary processes which result in cultural similarities and differences. If we view culture as man's extrasomatic means of adaptation, we must isolate and define the ecological setting of any given socio-cultural system, not only with respect to the points of articulation with the physical and biological environment, but also with points of articulation with the sociocultural environment. It is suggested that changes in the ecological setting of any given system are the prime causative situations activating processes of cultural change.

It is argued that the methodology most appropriate to the study of cultural process is a regional approach in which we attempt to gain reliable and representative information concerning the internal structure and ecological setting of successive cultural systems. It is observed that under current programs of salvage archaeology and greater foundation support for archaeological research, archaeologists are actually being given the opportunity to study such regions.

It is argued that, in spite of such opportunities, our current practices largely obviate the recovery of data necessary to the study of cultural process. The development of techniques for the recovery of data in structural terms is believed to be crucial, for it is the structure of archaeological remains that informs about the cultural system, and it is the cultural system which is the seat of process.

Probability sampling is suggested as a major methodological improvement which, if executed on all levels of data collection in full recognition of the inherent differences in the nature of observational populations which archaeologists investigate, can result in the production of adequate and representative data useful in the study of cultural process.

Observational populations of cultural items, features, and activity loci are recognized as having certain chaarcteristics which demand different treatment in both field observation and sampling methodology. On the other hand, only two major sampling universes, regions and sites, are recognized as appropriate to field investigations. Many of the limitations of currently available data are believed to derive from the failure to sample populations of activity loci within a regional universe. Emphasis has been on sampling populations of cultural items within a regional rather than a site universe. This procedure has made impossible the structural definition of populations of cultural items or the study of activity loci from a structural point of view. Consequently, our current understanding of the prehistoric past is largely in terms of style distributions and cultures defined in terms of discrete traits and stylistic characteristics; this is certainly not a situation conducive to studies of cultural process.

The argument for planned and well-paced execution of research design has been presented in the form of a "hypothetical" research program, along with a limited discussion of the techniques and levels of applicability of probability sampling procedures. Problems attendant upon the recovery of structural information within both the regional and site universe have been made explicit in a number of examples of types of sampling problem and excavational situation. It is concluded that the design and execution of a research program is the job of an anthropologist, and only in a limited way can the field archaeologist be considered a "technician." Field work is an on-going process demanding methodological decisions based on a running analysis of the data recovered from prior field work. It is concluded that if we are to be successful in the collection of data relevant to studies of cultural process, field work must be conducted within the framework of a well-planned research design which provides for the application of probability sampling techniques, at all levels of investigation. The field strategy executed within the framework of the research design must be directed by a well-trained anthropologist capable of making interpretations and decisions in terms of the widest possible factual and theoretical knowledge of general anthropology, and the types of questions must be drawn up which his data may be useful in solving. It is believed that modification of current practices along these lines is a necessary prerequisite for moving archaeology on to the level of development which Willey and Phillips (1958:4–5) have called the "explanatory level."

NOTE

This essay was originally presented as a paper at the Annual Meeting of the Society for American Archaeology at the University of Colorado, Boulder, May 1963.

A Review of Techniques for Archaeological Sampling

I have given you, Adam [says God], neither a predetermined place, nor a particular aspect nor special prerogatives so that you may take and keep that place, that aspect, those prerogatives that you desire all by your own choice and advice. The limitations to the nature of other beings are contained within my prescribed laws. You shall determine your own nature, without being constrained by any barrier, by means of

your own freedom to whose power I have entrusted you. I have placed you in the midst of the world so that from there you might better see what is in the world. I have made you neither heavenly nor earthly, neither mortal nor immortal in order that, like a free and sovereign artifice, you may mould and sculpt yourself into that form you will have chosen for yourself.

—PICO DELLA MIRANDOLA

AN ARCHAEOLOGICAL site is an accumulation of materials which are the residues of cultural activity. These accumulations can provide both qualitative and quantitative information about the activities, ecology, and cultural and chronological relationships of the human occupants of the site. Qualitative analysis consists of the identification of the constituents of a material (or archaeological site) irrespective of their amount. Quantitative analysis is the determination of the amounts in which the various constituents of a material (or site) are present (Chamber's Technical Dictionary, 1962:692). Both types of analysis are basic to archaeology: the qualitative aspect is typological and takes the form of the setting up of categories of countable units without which there can be no quantitative analysis. Quantitative analysis is prerequisite to any comparison between: 1) components of a site (either vertical strata or horizontal facies); 2) individual sites; or 3) constellations of sites or regions. In other words, such an analysis is necessary for any kind of cultural interpretation based on the comparison of the pro-

portion and distribution of cultural and natural elements.

The introduction of quantitative techniques, because they demand greater precision in the definition of categories, usually modifies the existing descriptive framework to a greater or lesser extent. In archaeology these techniques have been important in greatly expanding and modifying the field of study. The discussion of quantitative methods of the last ten years was stimulated by the expansion of goals to include reconstruction of group activity (behavior) from archaeological evidence (Taylor 1948; Spaulding 1960b; Binford 1963; Hole and Heizer 1965:187–249). Moreover, the increasing cooperation between archaeologists and other natural scientists (physiologists, geologists, botanists, paleontologists, etc.) has made archaeologists aware of a long neglect or misuse of quantitative techniques borrowed from the natural sciences in the collection of samples and in subsequent laboratory analysis (Brothwell and Higgs 1963; Stanton 1965). This chapter will briefly review the literature of field sampling techniques and discuss collecting techniques and sampling designs.

Early attempts at systematic sampling in order to obtain "representative samples" of surface archaeological materials were carried out by American archaeologists in response to questions raised by the development of seriation analysis of pottery (Kroeber 1916). The interpretation of surface materials was

Reprinted from Robert F. Heizer and John A. Graham, editors, *A Guide to Field Methods in Archaeology: Approaches to the Anthropology of the Dead* (Palo Alto: National Press Books, 1967), pp. 181–97. By permission of the editors, author, and National Press Books. The "Plan of an Ainu village" (figure) has been deleted.

and is still limited in scope. Three traditional problems have been attacked: 1) cultural identification; 2) ceramic chronology or seriation (temporal sequence of ceramic style changes); and 3) the use of associated ceramic and other material for dating or assigning to cultural context various site features (Cowgill 1964).

Spier's early work on seriation in the Southwest largely ignores the sampling problem, although some test excavation was done to check similarity between surface ceramic collections and those below ground (Spier 1917). The "representative sampling" technique, a method which was intended to eliminate "bias," was first described by Gladwin (Gladwin and Gladwin 1928:1) (the italics have been added).

> When a ruin is found, a collection of sherds is made *at random,* care being taken that all pottery types in evidence are gathered. . . . Occasionally, at large sites; two collections are made, one in which every sherd within a given area is taken, in order to obtain the percentages of types; the other covering the whole area in which only those sherds are picked up which are regarded as significant.

As with Spier, the word "random" simply meant an effort not to collect predominantly painted or pretty sherds (cf. Kroeber 1916: 384, 387). The concept of unconscious selective bias for particular sizes, shapes, colors, materials, densities and known function is not explicitly discussed. However, Gladwin was aware that the sherds collected, utilizing the method quoted above, would not yield significant percentages; a fact not recognized or admitted by many later archaeologists.

In the Viru Valley survey (Ford and Willey 1949) and in the survey of the Lower Mississippi River Valley (Phillips, Ford, and Griffin 1951) the misunderstanding of random sampling procedures reaches absurdity. Ford (Ford and Willey 1949:34–35) writes:

> Two workmen who accompanied Willey and me gathered most of the collections. These usually were made from a small section of each site, not more than 10 meters in diameter. The workmen were instructed not to select sherds when collecting and were watched to see that they did not. Their goal at each place was to fill the required number of bags so that they might rest until Willey had finished writing notes. The men were also repeatedly cautioned and watched to see that they did not gather all material from one spot for at some sites they might have made a collection of the required size without moving.

And as late as 1951 Ford (1951:43) wrote: "Generally speaking, our only concern was to get as large a sample as possible and a reasonably honest one. . . . The only sure way to eliminate this difficulty is to hire local people to pick sherds up at so much per sack." The above methods were succinctly characterized and evaluated by Alcock (1951:75): "The American technique of surface collecting makes use of random samples—so random that they are best collected by untrained and uncomprehending laborers." This, he argues, is not science. Furthermore, it is not "random." Alcock's criticism and reappraisal of surface surveying techniques includes discussion of the kinds of inferences one might make from surface collections other than the traditional typological ones. He specifically mentions their utility in planning excavation (Alcock, 1951:76):

> What is required is not a random sample, but one selected on rational principles, so that each sherd may be significant. Decorated sherds we must have, but we must balance them with plain wares, endeavoring to preserve the proportion between them as they appear on the surface. But is it enough to collect indiscriminately from the entire site and lump all our finds together in one bag? Different parts of a large complex may have been occupied at different times, and there may even be a contouring of cultures, an archaeological treeline above which sherds of the earlier occupations are not found. This evidence could, and should, be obtained when making a surface collection, the more so since sherds are not autogenous, and there is a real danger of completely denuding popular sites.

Alcock's thoughtful article is marred, however, by the continued misunderstanding of what random samples really are. The techniques proposed by him will not necessarily provide a systematically collected sample approaching a representative selection of all the materials from the surface of the site.

With the refinement of ceramic chronologies investigators began to doubt that surface sherds could be relied on to represent an isolated temporal unit. Controlled excavations such as those carried out by Spier (1917) were made to test the assumption of temporal reliability of surface collections (see also Ford and Willey 1949; Ford 1951; Tolstoy 1958). It was concluded from these that "a representative collection of surface sherds does not represent a cultural unit in time" (Bennyhoff 1952:232). This conclusion, right or wrong, is unfounded when reached without the examination of a single truly random (much less representative) sample. In a stratified site there is little doubt that the surface contains some degree of mixture of later and earlier materials. A representative sample will reflect this mixture and indicate the duration of occupation. Short-term, single-period occupation sites result in temporally homogeneous deposits above and below ground, and any kind of sample will contain sherds only from the single temporal unit of the occupation.

One field solution reached by some investigators interested mainly in ceramic chronology was that of "spot sampling," in which "most of the visible sherds of reasonable size in and around the point selected for sampling were gathered until a bagful, generally between 200–800 sherds—about 300 in most cases—was obtained" (Tolstoy 1958: 9). Specifically aimed at obtaining pottery samples for seriation, the refinement of "spot sampling" over other haphazard collecting methods lay in the increased homogeneity of the sample. Its major weakness is that one can have no idea of how representative the collection is of the rest of the site.

Surface surveys and descriptions of collecting techniques in the literature exemplify the confusion existing in the discipline on the definition of "an adequate sample." Even more evident is the positive misunderstanding of the phrase "random sample," often incorrectly considered synonymous with "representative sample." Many archaeologists assume that selected or haphazard collections are truly representative of an artifact population. Such an assumption is unjustified. Grab samples can yield only small amounts of qualitative information (e.g., that the elements collected exist on the site); they cannot be made to yield "demonstrably sound quantitative information" (Vescelius 1960: 461).

All statistical treatment of archaeological material is based on the assumption of a random sample (i.e., any one item or element of the population is as likely to be drawn as any other element and so the collection is free from conscious or unconscious bias). Certainly this is an ideal condition more to be striven for than achieved. In surface collecting and excavation some device must be utilized to minimize selective bias, personal preference, and convenience in collecting as exhibited in the tendency to pick up painted sherds, worked flints, whole items, and conveniently sized pieces, to name only a few. One such device is the use of a randomly chosen sampling unit. The size and shape of the unit can be arbitrarily defined according to the archaeological problem, the physical condition of the surface to be collected (i.e., density of artifact scatter, topography), and obvious cultural differences.

The essential problem in comparing artifact populations is that of evaluating the chances that differences in frequencies of artifact categories in two or more sampling units reflect accidents of sampling rather than real differences in the artifact populations. Sampling, as used here, does not mean the mere substitution of a partial collection of a population for the total population. It is a technique by which one can control and measure the reliability of information through statistical tools based on the theory of probability (Binford 1964b:427). Basically the archaeologist's task is to insure

181

that: 1) the sample is selected from the population in such a way that statistical theory is applicable, and 2) the absolute size of the sample is large enough to permit satisfactory conclusions concerning the problems being studied (Cowgill 1964:467). The first problem, that of sample selection, is treated by Vescelius (1960), Binford (1964*b*), Cowgill (1964), and Rootenberg (1964). Their definitions and techniques are in substantial agreement.

A truly representative sample is a selection of individual elements from a population in the exact proportion that they exist in the original population. In order to obtain a representative sample the original population must be known. Simple random sampling is a method of selection in which every member of the population has exactly the same chance of being included in the sample as does every other member. A random sample is used to estimate a representative sample of a population of unknown constitution. The larger the random sample is, the greater is the probability that it resembles a truly representative sample.

A population is defined (Binford 1964*b*: 427) as an aggregate of analytical units within an isolated field of study. It is imperative that both the analytical units and the field within which they are chosen are clearly defined in a sampling design. Sample units are the subdivision of the universe (the field of study—a geographical region, or an archaeological site) into distinct and identifiable units (natural or arbitrary) approximately equal in size. The sample unit may or may not be identical to the descriptive categories which make up the population. When partial coverage of a population within a universe is attempted, the sample units are selected from a frame (list of all units in the universe) so that all units of the frame have an equal chance of being chosen for investigation. A frame composed of many small units is preferable to one composed of only a few large units because small sampling units are a safeguard against the inclusion of

an unrepresentative amount of heterogeneity in any given sample (Binford 1964*b*:428).

There are a number of basic works such as those of Cochran (1963) and Slonim (1960) containing chapters on each of the sampling techniques mentioned in this section. The sampling of mineral deposits, and indeed of all materials in field sciences, poses problems similar to those encountered in archaeology (cf. Jackson and Knaebel, 1934).

Krumbein's chapter in the *Handbook of Paleontological Techniques* (Kummel and Raup 1965:137–50), called "Sampling in Paleontology," is an extremely clear and complete description of the various kinds of statistical sampling. I have revised some of it in the following pages to fit an archaeological rather than a geologic or paleontological context. Archaeological situations and problems are substituted for paleontological ones; brackets indicate revisions. Similarly, my paraphrasing of Krumbein employs an archaeological rather than a palaeontological context (1965:139):

A principal attribute of statistical sampling is its element of randomization, which assures each individual in the population some chance of being included in the sample. . . . Complexities in obtaining statistical samples from [an archaeological] population are mentioned later; nevertheless, on any one [site] it is possible to collect various kinds of statistical samples.*

Sampling techniques are discussed here in terms of a single site. For this purpose the site may be considered as a subpopulation within some larger population representing, let us say, the distribution of the refuse from an extinct people's activity in a particular geographical region.

The first step in choosing a sampling plan is to define the subpopulation being sampled, in terms of its physical limits and of the individuals that make it up. (Krumbein 1965:139)

* From "Sampling in Paleontology" by W. C. Krumbein, *Handbook of Paleontological Techniques,* edited by Bernhard Kummel and David Raup. W. H. Freeman and Company. Copyright © 1965. Hereafter cited as Krumbein.

In the example mentioned the objects of direct interest are cultural debris of all sorts, and the population to be sampled may be defined in any of several ways. One way is to define the population of artifacts or features directly, and the other is to define a population of unit volumes of earth or equal areas of surface of a site.

Setting up a population, defining its units, devising a problem of archaeological interest with relation to the material at hand, and deciding on a sampling plan all involve a number of purely archaeological decisions.

Once these have been made . . . the statistical model that is to be used in analyzing the data is in turn evident, and this model controls to some extent the kind of samples that are to be collected. There is no assurance that an arbitrarily selected sampling plan will be equally appropriate for different kinds of arbitrarily chosen statistical models. (Krumbein 1965:139)

Since the kind of samples to be collected depends on what is to be done with them, and this in turn depends on the purpose of the archaeological study, four main sampling variants are described: 1) simple random sampling; 2) systematic sampling; 3) stratified sampling; and 4) cluster sampling.

Exactly the same plans are applicable to sampling both in the horizontal and vertical section.

[Areal sampling] requires mainly a modification of the randomization procedure to permit location of points on a map or on an outcrop face. Thus, for simple random sampling, two random numbers are taken, one representing the horizontal distance from some origin, and the other representing the vertical distance from that origin. (Krumbein 1965:145–46)

1. Simple random sampling.—Suppose a large site has 100 roughly circular depressions exposed on its surface. The problem is to obtain a random sample of these features in order that their varied functions and the differences in their use and chronology can be determined. Simple random sampling requires numbering all sampling units (in this case the depressions) and randomizing a

sample from these numbered individuals. Define the features as the sampling unit. Calling the first feature 00, the depressions are numbered serially to 99. Let us take a sample of 10, although in the case of feature units a larger sample is probably necessary to be confident that all variation is included in the sample and that a representative sample is approached. A sample as large as 60 out of 100 units could be called for if the variance of the variable in question was very large. In archaeological sampling of artifact and multiple variable populations (especially in cluster and feature sampling) this is often the case. A table of random numbers is used to select the 10 or more two-digit numbers lying between 00 and 99, omitting duplicates. The corresponding depressions are carefully excavated. In this plan each feature is an individual in a subpopulation of 100, but within each feature is a cluster sample (see below) of the subpopulations of the archaeological refuse characteristic of the site and of the particular feature which is being excavated. The population sampled satisfies the condition that each feature has an equal chance of being included in the sample, but there is no randomization of items within the feature.

The laboratory analysis of this sample may involve: 1) segregating the artifacts into types or classes in order to facilitate counting and measurement; 2) analyzing the soil samples as to physical-chemical composition (animal and fish bone, shell, seeds, pollen and other vegetal remains; organic carbon, charcoal, calcium carbonate, phosphates, acidity, and soil color have all been used to enhance the archaeologist's idea of the activities which took place in any one part of an archaeological site); 3) identifying animal and vegetable food debris as to genera and species (if possible); and 4) comparing vertical and horizontal floor plans in order to finally group the features into functionally differentiated classes. The depressions mentioned above might be classed as house depressions possibly belonging to persons of different status or occupation, storage pits, hearths or fire pits, religious or community structures, or sweat houses, on the basis of the analysis of the materials sampled.

In the process of analysis new types of populations have been generated: the depression is an individual in a population of features, but the artifacts and food debris are individuals in populations of pottery sherds, worked stone, animal and fish bone fragments, shells, seeds, and pollen, and each may in turn be sampled by a randomization procedure if the number of specimens referred to any category is very large in each feature. Soil samples, for example, should be randomly selected from the three-dimensional plan of the feature (either systematic or stratified cluster sampling is a possible procedure; see below).

In archaeology this procedure of simple random sampling is applicable to large features exposed on the surface of a site such as hearths, buildings, pit depressions, and rooms of a large structure, or to arbitrarily defined sampling units. The method involves numbering all occurrences and randomizing a sample from these numbered individuals.

In simple random sampling some samples are taken in clusters and others are widely spaced. As long as the population is homogeneous, showing no trends or gradients, and as long as all individuals in the subpopulation are equally accessible, simple random sampling is a standard procedure for estimating the population mean and variance of measured attributes. (Krumbein 1965:141)

2. Systematic sampling. — Systematic sampling provides a plan in which the sampling units are spread fairly evenly over the area to be sampled. Let us assume the site to cover an area of 2,500 square feet. This area is divided into ten 250-square-foot nonoverlapping segments, each of which contains ten 25-square-foot nonoverlapping grid units. Number the grid squares of each segment from zero to nine. One number in the range zero to nine is chosen at random to locate the individual sample unit in the first seg-

ment. Then, from each segment, the grid square bearing this number is collected to obtain a systematic sample of each segment.

Systematic samples satisfy the condition of equal spacing, but statistical models related to systematic sampling may differ from those based on simple random samples. Regression models for detecting trends are conveniently used with systematic samples, whereas estimates of population means and variances and of statistical correlation among variates are commonly based on simple random samples. . . . systematic samples may give better estimates of mean values (because the whole [site] is involved) than simple random samples will; but estimates of population variances may be larger for systematic than for simple random samples. This arises because . . . random samples allow some clustering, and thus include in the variance estimate the balancing influence of greater resemblance between neighbors, and less between individuals farther away. (Krumbein 1965:142)

Homogeneity of debris is assumed in the systematic samples. They furnish, however, an opportunity for testing this point, in that if the subpopulation does have a gradient or trend, regression analysis can commonly detect it.

This method might be particularly applicable to the detection of dietary or ecological shifts through the successive deposits of a shell midden or habitation mound. The segments in a midden mound would be vertically stratified through the depth of the deposit and the sample could be a column subdivided according to the arbitrarily or naturally defined levels of the segments. In general, systematic sampling is not recommended for archaeological problems. The usual statistical procedures for calculating estimated sampling error are not applicable to this type of sampling procedure.

3. Stratified sampling. — Again quoting Krumbein, "In this method of statistical sampling, some control can be exerted on the spacing of the samples by setting up two or more *sampling strata*" (1965:142). These may be selected arbitrarily, or they may be selected on the basis of depositional or cultural criteria. A common cultural criterion is the division of a deposit into living floors (the material on and above one geologically and culturally defined floor is considered one unit).

The appropriate sampling procedure may be to collect simple random [cluster] samples from each stratum, to obtain a set of *stratified samples.*

The word *stratum* as used in statistical sampling is similar to its use in geology. . . . the population is "sliced" into categories or subpopulations much as geological strata "slice" a stratigraphic section into parts. Stratified sampling permits the variability in each sampling stratum to be evaluated separately, in contrast to evaluation of the overall variability in the whole population. (Krumbein 1965:143)

The archaeologist may decide to use arbitrary sampling strata even on a single surface. Thus, as in the surface collecting example of systematic sampling, the site can be divided into ten 250-square-foot nonoverlapping segments, each of which contains ten 25-square-foot units. Ten separately randomized samples are drawn from the segments. As Krumbein states, ". . . this tends to spread the samples over the outcrop [or site] more regularly than in simple random sampling, but less so than in systematic sampling" (1965:143). Stratified sampling, especially when more than a single sample is collected per archaeologically relevant surface area or depositional stratum, "yields a better estimate of the overall population mean than simple random samples collected over the [horizontal surface or vertical profile] without regard to strata, because the variability in each sampling stratum is taken into account in setting confidence limits on the population mean" (Krumbein 1965:143).

4. Cluster sampling.—In Krumbein's definition, "Cluster sampling is a procedure by which more than one individual in the population being sampled is taken at each randomized position" (1965:143). In terms of a gridded archaeological site a number of randomized grid units are chosen and every item within that unit is collected. This pro-

cedure yields clusters of various kinds of cultural debris, in which the spacing between major positions is random but the spacing within the cluster (of pottery, stone, bone, etc.) is not random. This type of sampling is often used initially in collecting and excavating material which is subjected to other sampling techniques in the field and in the laboratory.

Cluster sampling can be extended to more than two levels, and can be designed as *nested sampling,* in which each sampling level is nested within a higher level. (Krumbein 1965:144)

This system can be illustrated in areal sampling where, for example, the study area may include several townships as the top level, a random sample of square-mile sections within the townships as the second level, a sample of archaeological sites located within the sections as the third level, and cluster samples of grid units on the sites as the fourth level. This kind of sampling is very useful when questions of regional scales of variability are part of the archaeological study.

It is necessary to consider what restraint is imposed upon statistical sampling by the absence of sites in positions that happen to be selected by randomization.

These restraints give rise to the concept of a *target population* that is the object of interest, as against a *sampled population* that represents the accessible portion of the target population. (Krumbein 1965:146)

Limitations on statistical sampling imposed by inaccessible parts of the target population add up to this: the [archaeologist] may derive valid statistical inferences about the sampled population from his samples, but any extension of these generalizations to the target population is substantive. (Krumbein 1965:148)

The archaeologist must draw from his knowledge of variation among archaeological sites from other regions in evaluating the possibilities of differences between the sample and target populations.

There is no direct statistical method by which this comparison can be made, unless the entire target population ultimately becomes available for study. (Krumbein 1965:148)

Thus, "statistical analysis provides a safeguard at various stages of a study," by assuring the archaeologist that his sample is "free of unintentional bias; and that his substantive assumptions, judgments, and decisions are supported by the objectively derived statistical inferences that arise from his sample data" (Krumbein 1965:149).

The most important point emerging from the above discussion is that although there is a close relationship between archaeological objectives and the statistical model with its sampling plan, it is the archaeologist who decides what he wants to study. His decisions involve the evaluation of sources of variability that may enter his data and the choice of sources to be taken into account in reaching generalizations. The archaeologist can be greatly aided in his problems of sampling and statistical design by a professional statistician.

Vescelius (1960) was the first archaeologist to recommend and adapt cluster sampling to the archaeological problem of surface sampling. The method is complex and time-consuming compared to nonrandom sampling; nevertheless, the quality of the returns in information and precision far outweigh the cost in extra effort and time required. The technique of cluster sampling in an archaeological context as described by Vescelius, Binford, Cowgill, and Rootenberg is practically identical to that described by Krumbein. The technique is used for surface collecting as described in the Aschers' article on "Recognizing the Emergence of Man" (Ascher and Ascher 1965).

The concept of 'adequate sample size' is often mentioned but rarely explored in detail. The consensus in the earlier archaeological literature is that a sample of somewhat over 100 sherds is an adequate sample of surface materials. Ford, in the Viru Valley Report (Ford and Willey 1949:36), states:

It seems to be indicated that when a type appears in a strength of over 5 percent the chances are excellent that it will be represented in a collection of over 100 sherds. . . . Further, fairly substantial variation from the theoretical actual percentage conditions on the site is to be expected in types that approach 50 percent popularity, even in collections of 300 to 500 sherds. Variation between the substantial (over 10 percent) type pairs . . . ranges from 3 to 20 percent. . . .

As a result of experience in analyzing classification result, rather than from any basis demonstrated here, I have come to regard a random collection of over 100 sherds as fairly dependable, and anything over 50 sherds as usable for rough dating.

Tolstoy (1958:10) also considers a sample size of less than 100 "definitely suspect." These estimates are for samples to be used only for seriation which is a descriptive, not a quantitative, method of analysis as used in the reports published before 1960.

Vescelius (1960:462) briefly discusses the sample size with reference to the functional analysis of a surface collection.

The problems of sample size are discussed in many elementary textbooks . . . . Suffice it to say that while there is no single optimum, a sample consisting of 5 to 10 percent of all the clusters (grid squares) in the population should yield results of adequate reliability for most archaeological purposes.

An adequate sample is a fraction of the surface elements of the entire site. The size of the fraction depends largely on the size of the site, the density of the surface material, the type of archaeological problem (functional or chronological) to be solved, and, finally and most important, the degree of statistical reliability desired by the investigator. The more powerful statistical tools require a larger, more rigorously controlled sample. In any kind of matrix analysis (i.e., grid sampling and analysis), each grid unit must contain a minimum number of units to be reliable.

Sample size can be calculated for any given degree of accuracy. The estimated size may be different for each variable sampled in the site, depending on the variability within the item or estimated variance. When sampling for more than one variable (more than one kind of information) as is usually the case in archaeological work, the archaeologist may take the maximum sample size if he has unlimited resources, or he may calculate an adequate sample size for most of the variables and sacrifice accuracy in certain areas for convenience. The statistical procedure followed in calculating sample size can be found in either of the statistical texts mentioned previously (Cochran 1963; Slonim 1960) and many others. Cowgill (1964:470) discusses optimum sample size:

Adequacy of the sample is far more a matter of its absolute size than of the proportion it constitutes of the total population; the frequencies of very common attributes and common combinations can be estimated satisfactorily by a properly drawn sample that includes only a small proportion of all examples in the total collection. On the other hand very rare attributes or combinations using every example found in the collections will probably provide none too good a basis for making inferences about this occurrence in target populations.

In the analysis of ceramics a much smaller proportion of the material in common categories is required to reduce the risk of sampling error to any specific level than in rare categories. Cowgill (1964:471) suggests a subdivision of categories into first- and second-rank classes, that is, into one class of numerous and another class of rare elements.

One can then determine roughly what proportion of the lots from these units will be needed to give a large enough sample of the most common categories to permit inferences of the desired precision about their proportions in the target population, on the basis of formulas appropriate for cluster sampling. Enough lots or stratigraphic columns are then drawn at random to provide a sample of this size, and all material from these provenience units is described in detail and saved in some single institution.

This procedure is one of "first-order" sampling. "Second-rank" categories are included in first-order sample lots, but there are not

enough to permit satisfactory conclusions to be drawn.

We can increase our sample of these second-rank categories by drawing a number of additional lots at random (from the list of provenience units relevant to whatever population we are interested in) and thus forming a second-order sample. The size of the second-order sample should be such that when we take both first- and second-order sample data, we have enough information on second-rank categories to permit us to draw satisfactory conclusions. However, all the very common specimens of first-rank categories in this second-order sample do not provide us with any worthwhile additional information. After being cleaned, broadly identified and counted, they may be discarded or distributed.

If there is a third-rank in scarcity one goes through the same procedures as for the second-rank sample. Both first- and second-rank categories in the third-order sample may be discarded or distributed. A major advantage of this procedure is that the whole range of material is preserved for future reference. It can then be restudied or reclassified according to any new dimension or attribute.

Horizontal distribution of artifacts and other cultural debris may be affected by natural and human activity both during and after the original occupation of a site. However, statistically valid associations are possible despite the disturbance of original artifact scatter. Areas of intensive prehistoric activity, where a specialized tool kit was employed, will retain a character distinct from the remainder of the site if the factors acting to disturb the area are relatively uniform over the entire site (e.g., plowing) and/ or are not so intense as to destroy part or all of the site. In dealing with surface collecting, the surveyor may be able to obtain some control information about disrupting agents. He is at leisure to observe the topography of the site and delineate areas of differential erosion or postoccupational deposition. Local inhabitants or recorded information may be able to provide the archaeologist with information on previous surface collecting or excavation. Unplanned and systematic or selective disruptions which have been differentially destructive may be determinable. If these disruptive factors are taken into consideration, artifact clustering may be tentatively interpreted in terms of specialized cultural activity and temporal change. The surveyor or excavator can then proceed to salvage, through proper collecting techniques, significant cultural information.

Random samples taken from archaeological sites can yield information on numerous important questions such as density of debris per unit area; the range of artifact types; the proportion of specific artifact types in the population; and distribution or patterned spacing of amount and kinds of cultural debris within the site. Knowledge of the relative density of artifacts or food debris per unit area may enable one to make a rough estimate of intensity of occupation (i.e., number of people living on the site during the period in question), length of occupation, seasonal inhabitation, or type and intensity of ecological exploitation. An idea of distribution (or dispersion) of elements within the site may supply information which will enable one to distinguish among: 1) a large number of persons occupying the site for a short time; 2) a small group living on the site for a long time; or 3) a large population occupying the site for a long time. The interpretation of length and/or intensity of occupation, however, depends on *a priori* assumptions or documented correlations between cultural activity and the material remains of that activity (Heizer 1960:112–15; Cook and Heizer 1965; Meighan 1958:2–3). Distribution of aggregates of particular tools or artifact configurations can lead to delineation of sections of the site where special activities were performed. The range of tool types and their proportions to one another may give information as to specific activities conducted within the site as well as to the relative importance of these activities.

With the proper sampling design it is possible to isolate not only activity foci within a site but differences in activity between sites in a single area. Regional studies have made it possible to combine what were considered separate cultures into a single multi-facies culture, the variations being a function of different activities which may or may not have been seasonally determined.

Three factors contribute to differences between archaeological samples taken from undisturbed archaeological strata: 1) sampling error; 2) functional differences; and 3) temporal differences between the parent populations from which the samples were drawn. Many archaeologists have explained such differences as due only to temporal variations between parent populations, thereby ignoring sampling error and relegating functional specificity to a minor role (Brown and Freeman 1964:162). In a UNIVAC analysis of the pottery from Carter Ranch Pueblo, Brown and Freeman (1964:166) were able to delineate four functional differences from the pottery distribution of the pueblo: 1) there were four constellations of pottery types that may have been used for functionally diverse purposes, among them a possible mortuary complex; 2) four room types established on the basis of floor features were distinguishable through frequencies of pottery found on their floors, and this suggested that different cultural activities were taking place in each type of room; 3) functional differences were discovered in the deposition of midden materials in five discrete areas, though there were no consistent demonstrable temporal differences between painted and unpainted pottery in the five trenches through the midden; and 4) the largest frequencies of painted pottery were found in the kiva and the four rooms closest to it, leading the investigators to suspect involvement with a mortuary complex. Further, they were able to explain differences between floor and fill debris which would have otherwise gone unnoticed.

Statistical techniques describe associations which exist among elements of a site and/or constellations of sites. It is clear from the UNIVAC analysis done by Brown and Freeman (1964) that such an analysis accomplished merely the description of a body of material. The relationships discovered were associations of the same validity but of a different nature from the more common "visible associations," such as the association of grave goods, skeletal material, and burial pits. The explanation in cultural terms of such association is not the job of the machine nor of the statistical techniques, but of the prehistorian himself. However, description of the data in as nearly complete a fashion as possible using statistical tools will not only help the prehistorian to see pertinent factors involved in that explanation, but may also give insights into aspects of other problems and ease their solution (Brown and Freeman 1964:163). The discussion given by Hill (1966:9–30) of prehistoric communities in eastern Arizona summarizes some of the recent contributions to archaeology by the use of statistical techniques in excavation and data processing. It presents "an example of some of the kinds of inferences which may be made concerning the internal structure and social organization of a prehistoric Pueblo site. It has also examined some of the evidence related to an ultimate explanation of changes in site structure through time" (Hill 1966:27).

Binford (1964b:432–35) outlines procedures for a regional site survey which might serve to exemplify the kind of research design proper to statistical analysis. This design allows for the description of the environment as well as the archaeological sites. Culture is considered an adaptive system. In such a system, the operations and the processes of modification which culture undergoes can only be understood within the context of "the adaptive milieu." "All those elements which represent or inform about the ways and means by which groups have exploited or adjusted to the natural and cultural environment form this milieu" (Binford 1964). Thus, both ecological and cul-

tural aspects of a region must be investigated, and ecological as well as archaeological components are broken down into subclasses representing different populations (pollen, soil, and animal bone) which may be sampled for information about the natural environment.

In Binford's research design, two sampling universes are defined: 1) the region; and 2) the site. The region is divided into "strata" —natural areas (river frontage, forest, plateau, etc.) and/or arbitrary ones (e.g., square-mile grids)—and a combination of stratified and cluster sampling techniques can be utilized to obtain a random sample of sites from all segments of the area. Thus the surveyor is able to cover a randomly chosen proportion of the area and, perhaps, to recognize functional differences between sites associated with specific natural strata. The surface of the sites located in the course of the survey are mapped in detail and sampled. The populations of cultural items (artifacts and debris) present at each of the sites are evaluated in terms of a formal characterization of the sites. The ultimate aim is the classification of activity loci as to their degree of similarity and difference—in other words, a taxonomy of sites. From this frame of sites as many from each of the several categories may be excavated as interest, time, and money will allow.

The major emphasis thus far in this discussion has been on surface sampling rather than sampling techniques used during excavation. Random sampling of midden areas for subsistence and ecological information has been worked out with some precision (cf. Cook and Heizer 1951, 1962; Cook and Treganza 1947, 1950; Gifford 1916; Greengo 1951; Treganza and Cook 1948). This sampling utilizes basically the same assumptions and techniques as those previously described. There are, however, three important differences: 1) the grid or matrix is extended vertically as well as horizontally with arbitrary or natural stratification serving to demarcate vertical boundaries; 2) in shell

189

refuse middens horizontal homogeneity is assumed (Treganza and Cook 1948; Cook and Heizer 1951); and 3) the elements of the samples (bone, shell, and organic material) are often minute if not microscopic. These differences demand some change in technique. The systematically sampled grid units are excavated as free standing columns, as vertical walls of the deposit, or with augers, and the samples are bagged separately by levels. This process yields control over vertical as well as horizontal trends within the deposit. Furthermore, an adequate sample may consist of fewer units of a much smaller size. There is not space to review here the large volume of literature on midden analysis and sampling, but since the principles are basically those of systematic cluster sampling, a reference is made to some of the details of sample collection which differ due to the nature of the deposit being sampled.

Column sampling was originally inspired by A. L. Kroeber (Gifford 1916:1), pioneered by Gifford (*ibid.*), subsequently extensively applied by Cook, Heizer, Treganza, and Greengo, and discussed as a method by Meighan, *et al.* (1958) and Cook and Heizer (1965). It has been used principally in Northern and Central California, although any shell or habitation midden is amenable to such analysis. Much of the original work in California on both habitation and shell mounds in the late 1940s and early 1950s is still methodologically sound. Changes have been primarily in the direction of refinement and speed of data recovery, for example, in adopting standard screen and sample size (Ascher 1959; Greenwood 1961; Cook and Heizer 1962:3–4).

The work is based on the one major assumption: ". . . in order to reconstruct the life of extinct peoples all material residues must be studied, and concomitantly, no tangible material is too crude or insignificant to tell us something about the conditions in which aboriginal populations lived" (Cook and Heizer 1951:281).

Treganza and Cook (1948) established the methodological principles by the complete excavation of a single small habitation mound. From this site all the earth was weighed and screened, and every artifact, bone, and shell was counted. This enabled the investigators to devise a general formula for sampling other sites and comparing sampling results. The method assured adequate statistical treatment of the content and at the same time enabled the investigators to reduce excavation to a minimum. In the work of Cook and Heizer (1951:281) a series of sites were sampled:

It was then possible to point out how these areas differed, both qualitatively and quantitatively, in certain aspects of material culture and to correlate these differences with variations in the physiography and ecology of the corresponding regions. In this particular instance many of our conclusions could have been reached equally well by the use of ethnographic data. However, our results demonstrated that physical analysis leads to essentially correct deductions even in the total absence of any ethnographic knowledge.

The standard procedure for physical analysis entailed the taking of a series of column samples. Each sample was then transported to the laboratory and passed through an $\frac{1}{8}$-inch or 2-mm screen. Comparisons were based upon the material retained by the screen. Screening the column sample in the field can be accomplished most efficiently with a $\frac{1}{4}$-inch screen. A few samples sent to the lab and screened thorough a $\frac{1}{8}$- or $\frac{1}{16}$-inch screen establish the ratio of components in the field sample to those in the more accurate laboratory sample (Cook and Heizer 1962; Ascher 1959). Field identification of mound components has also been proved possible and helpful in guiding the progress of the excavation. "Any mound component occurring in pieces smaller than $\frac{1}{2}$-inch in diameter should be sampled by the column method or its equivalent, with the single exception of artifacts" (Cook and Heizer 1951:291). In the sampling of artifacts many large refuse samples are necessary because of the rarity of artifacts and the unevenness of their distribution. When properly handled, this method of screening large samples is capable of yielding information on the occurrence and distribution of artifacts in one site as well as the differences between sites.

Greenwood (1961:416–17) designed a shell refuse study to test and perfect methods of quantitative analysis.

Experiments were performed to determine the optimum size of sample, dimension of screen, number of samples, and the practicability of rapid analysis in the field to guide the progress of excavation. . . . The methodological experiments demonstrated that a 500gm. sample produces as accurate a measure of the shell in a level as the total sample from the level, that a ¼th inch screen is adequate when brittle types such as *Mytilus* and abalone which break into very small fragments are absent or present in only very small quantities, that rough field sorting produces results which correlate well with those based on closely controlled laboratory analysis. . . . Field identification, weighing, tabulating and interpreting of shell remains could be used to advise the digging crew about horizontal and columnar distributions in time to modify the excavation schedule if that seemed advisable.

The principles for sampling in an archaeological site remain the same, whether the sampling is done on the surface, during excavation (treating each level of excavation as a surface), in the deposit, or when soil, carbon, or pollen samples are taken. As representative a sample as possible is sought by a random sampling technique. Some of the techniques outlined above require time and a number of workers not always available to the weekend student crew or to a lone archaeologist looking over a new site. Any number of modifications are possible in the systems described to adjust for lack of time, labor, and/or money. If a random sample is not possible, then an intelligently selected sample in which biases are relatively explicit is preferable to a haphazard one. Having a map of the site and marking the areas collected are prerequisites. Preferably every item in the small area collected should be bagged together. If two small segments of the site are sampled, each should go into a separate bag or container; large areas can be broken up into smaller units in which everything is collected and each segment is bagged separately.

In the method described by Alcock (1951: 25–26) the entire site is paced off into "zones" which are collected separately. Particular materials are explicitly selected, such as all pottery or all flint, leaving out animal remains, fire-cracked rock, or flint waste (in the case of a largely ceramic site). This type of collection will, of course, tell one only about the distribution within the site of the material collected and nothing about the numerical relations of one component to another or to the total surface population. A sketch map with bags designated according to area, a notebook description of the selective bias (i.e., what was collected entirely, partially, or not at all), and the rationale behind the bias are, as always, imperative.

In the final analysis, cluster or stratified cluster sampling is the most reliable, giving more information on more aspects of the population than any other. Vescelius's article (1960:463–64) contains a description of the statistical methods involved in analyzing cluster samples. Other methods are rougher and useful only when previous work (i.e. excavation) at similar sites has given the archaeologist an added basis for interpretation. In cases where it is unlikely that actual excavation of a site will follow (this is true with the majority of sites), a random cluster sample from the surface can provide valuable information toward the cultural evaluation of an entire region. Prehistory is best understood, however, through the excavation of a carefully planned sampling of a total range of sites in a region. The sampling of an entire region is an invaluable aid in making an intelligent selection of key sites to be excavated. Surface collections of the sites yield clues for excavation strategy. And the random testing of the areas of the site which the archaeologist has chosen not to excavate can give the investigator some assurance that he has not missed an important feature of the site.

This essay has not developed new statistical strategies for the preliminary survey or excavation of an archaeological deposit; it has merely summarized statistical techniques already adapted to archaeological problems. Perhaps a more useful and exciting approach to the discussion of statistical techniques would be to create new statistical designs specifically for the analysis of archaeological field and laboratory problems. This task is beyond this chapter's scope, but must eventually be done in order that particular field problems can be approached more rationally than is now customary. Work by Brown, Freemen, Longacre, and Hill in the Southwest does explore various research designs and techniques "that can be used in recovering and analysing data . . . useful in making more complete description of prehistoric sociocultural systems and more complete explanations of their change in time and space" (Hill 1966:28).

Full development of these techniques will require some time, considering present ignorance about statistical methods as applied to archaeology. More preliminary field analysis directed to an archaeological approach is required because each archaeological deposit may be approached with numerous problems in mind and the research design applicable to their solution is modified by the unique constitution of the individual site. A more detailed discussion of basic statistical methods and their possible uses in archaeology is imperative. Students of prehistory cannot understand published material, much less hope to contribute creatively to the theoretical growth of the subject, without a working knowledge of statistical techniques.

PART 5

Archaeological Strategy for the Study of Hunter-Gatherers

Introduction

For most of man's history, his economy has been based on hunting and collecting. And although few societies have such an economic base today, the archaeological record consists in great part of remains that characterize that longest of human economic eras. It is often suggested that because hunter-gatherers are both simple and nearly extinct, anthropological concern with them is myopic and irrelevant. Their study can be defended, however, since knowledge of them expands our comprehension of the total range of cultural variation in time and space. But a more solid argument resides in our use of that part of the prehistoric laboratory to understand the long-term effects of ecological adjustment, population dynamics, economic exchange, and technological growth. The behavior of organisms entering an empty niche is a particularly useful subject to us now, especially since we as a species are concerned with overpopulation and the potential use of hitherto empty areas. The whole of the prehistoric New World provides a laboratory for testing ideas about population dynamics and cultural change in an empty zone. Likewise, the principles of ecological management and adjustment used by Paleolithic and Mesolithic hunters and gatherers can be used to augment the precision of our present knowledge of ecological change. The laboratory of prehistoric hunter-gatherers is a particularly unexploited one, and one having great promise.

As a whole, hunter-gatherers have a less differentiated and more homogeneous culture than agriculturalists and industrialized peoples. That is not to say their culture is either rudimentary or in some sense simplistic. The sophistication and complexity in the domains of kinship and ecological orchestration are adequate citations of the systemic precision hunter-gatherers use in adjusting to their circumstances. One of the best archaeological illustrations of our improved knowledge of hunting-gathering cultures comes from the work of Lewis and Sally Binford on the Mousterian cultures of the Middle Paleolithic. Mousterian is the designation for assemblages of tools found with the Neanderthal populations throughout the Old World. The Mousterian coincides with the climax and amelioration of the last major glaciation. The Binfords demonstrated (Binford and Binford 1966:2:2:238–95) that specific tool kits very likely corresponded to specific kinds of activities, e.g., killing-butchering, shredding-cutting, manufacture of tools from nonflint materials: wood, antler, etc. They demonstrated further that Mousterian sites presented a variety of distinguishable activities carried on at them.

The popularity of artifact assemblages varied between sites depending on the predominance of the activities carried on at a site. On that basis the Binfords differentiated between two basic types of Mousterian sites, those used principally for maintenance activities like secondary butchering and the manufacture of nonstone tools, and those for extractive activities like killing, primary butchering, and plant food cutting and shredding. Base camps used for maintenance activities are occupied more permanently and witness a larger number of tasks; work camps used for extractive activities are occupied for a short period for a smaller range of activities. It was apparent that all sites were used for the same activities over a long period of time, since the composition of assemblages maintained consistency. In addition, some evidence was found for the replacement of a specialized hunting tool kit by more generalized hunting equipment at some Mousterian localities.

During the Mousterian, such a shift in tool kits occurred with the climatic change accompanying the moderation of the last major glaciation. The shift in tool kits serves to illustrate the generalization that in times of ecosystem change, such as occurred at the end of the Mousterian, general adaptive techniques will predominate over more specific ones. With return of stable circumstances, specialized adaptation to specific resources has distinct adaptive value insofar as it permits members of a species to avoid competition with one another. This latter adaptation of groups of people tied to narrower ranges of resources is one that characterizes much of the Upper Paleolithic.

The Binfords' work has been described here since it is not included in the volume and because it represents a major recent contribution in archaeology. Their extensive study is one of the exemplary citations of the procedures employed and the goals sought by new archaeologists. Their concern with hunter-gatherers mirrors a growing interest by archaeologists and many other cultural anthropologists. Both extinct and extant, hunter-gatherers offer laboratories which are presumed to be better controlled since the groups are uniformly smaller, usually more isolated in space, and generally present cultures with subsystems that can be more easily examined and systemic interconnections that can be more easily described.

Lithic Analysis in Paleoanthropology

ARCHAEOLOGISTS as anthropologists are concerned with the problem of discovering fundamental, underlying properties of cultural processes common to extinct as well as to living cultural systems. This interest weds archaeology to other segments of anthropology in which cultural explanation is sought. Archaeologists must assume that, other things being equal, these processes which structure the ethnographic record have also structured the archaeological record. When ecological conditions, level of social integration, or primary subsistence patterns similar to those known ethnographically can be demonstrated or inferred archaeologically, the archaeologist must orient his investigation toward the elucidation of processual factors which may underlie both cases and he must seek structural explanations for the similarities and differences that are recognized.

Recently a number of archaeologists have come to realize that, in order to achieve their anthropological goals, new procedures for the collection, description, and interpretation of archaeological data must be formulated within a general theoretical framework in which explanatory inferences may be tested against the whole range of anthropological data.

Reprinted from *Science,* vol. 161, 6 September 1968, pp. 982–87. By permission of the author and the American Association for the Advancement of Science. Copyright 1968 by the American Association for the Advancement of Science. The notes have been renumbered.

Archaeological energies have often focused on the recognition of superficial resemblances in form among individually selected specimens. These specimens were labeled "diagnostic traits," and the presence of one or more of these traits in each of several site collections was taken to indicate some sort of relation between the collections. Interpretations were limited to speculations on the significance of the spatial and temporal distributions of these traits. This orientation has served the limited aims of archaeological historiography, but it is inadequate for the formulation of explantory inferences. Flannery has contrasted the goals and strategies of those archaeologists who hope to construct culture histories with those who seek explanations in terms of cultural processes (1967).

Willey and Phillips note the failure of American archaeology to develop in any satisfactory way its theoretical structure at an explanatory level (1958); Binford has suggested that an interpretive framework focused upon selected variations in ideational norms — diagnostic traits — may partially account for this failure. He presents an excellent case for a holistic approach to archaeological systematics and argues for the establishment of multivariate taxonomies as a means for isolating causative factors in the operation of cultural systems and as a basis for identifying regular and predictable relationships among these factors. Binford's discussion is founded on the general cultural theory, formulated by White, in which cul-

196

ture is viewed as a system of adaptive mechanisms with which the member units of human society integrate with their environments (Binford 1965; White 1959).

Within a social system, certain structural poses [1] may be isolated which relate a society's economic, political, and ideological activities to ecological conditions of resource availability and competitor activity. These units function to maintain a sociocultural system within an ecological framework by combining social groups with implements, ideas, habits, and the like. Archaeology can supplement ethnographic attempts to elucidate processes of cultural-ecological articulation by expanding the range of cultural knowledge both in time and in variety. The ethnographic record is limited, and almost daily its scope is diminished by modern industrial expansion. It is, therefore, desirable to establish means for identifying and interpreting structural variation in extinct cultural systems.

Neither Binford nor White was primarily concerned with developing detailed procedures for constructing a systematic descriptive and classificatory methodology aimed at the establishment of formal taxonomies and the identification of articulations between variables within a social system. But Spaulding (1967) has noted that in order to establish "archaeo-sociological" correlations as alternatives to arbitrarily defined taxonomies it is essential that the problem of the classification of archaeological data be satisfactorily treated beforehand.

In the past, attribute-identification procedures have been formulated to meet the particular requirements of a specific data set and have been characterized by *ad hoc* adjustments in the decision-making process when specimen inclusion within a given category was in doubt. Such procedures are subjective and, therefore, cannot be verified by independent investigators. The position taken here is that all conclusions about the meaning of archaeological data, whether inherently correct or not, based upon intuition-bound notions of culture and loose formulations of interpretive procedure, are indefensible because they cannot be independently verified and because they can generate no evaluative mechanisms by means of which preference for one conclusion over another may be demonstrated. This is not to deny a productive role to intuition. The point is that intuitive formulations cannot of themselves lead to internally satisfying results. Intuition provides a creative element to theory formulation and model building, but that creativity must be evaluable. These considerations provide strong motivation for a systematization of archaeological methodology.

In this essay some steps in the formulation of procedures applicable to one category of lithic material are presented. Specifically, the expansion of the scope of lithic analysis through the presentation of certain descriptive and classificatory devices is attempted. These methods are applied to lithic assemblages from a number of late Pleistocene and early Recent North American sites. The results obtained suggest that a more complete understanding of early American hunting life may be gained by application, to the whole range of data pertaining to it, of more rigorous procedures than those used in the past.

The data for this study were derived from eight sites: Blackwater, Horner, Levi, Lindenmeier, Quad, Shoop, Vernon, and Williamson. A total of 2139 artifacts was selected from the collections for intensive examination.

A number of considerations guided the selection of sites. Primary among these was a desire to incorporate into the analysis as representative a geographical range as practicable. A determined effort was made, therefore, to use collections from sites in all parts of the known Paleo-Indian range (Fig. *1*). A second important consideration was that the sites chosen should represent a wide range within the known Paleo-Indian time span. Three sites have been dated by the radiocarbon method. Blackwater—11,170 ± 360 years; Lindenmeier—10,780 ± 375

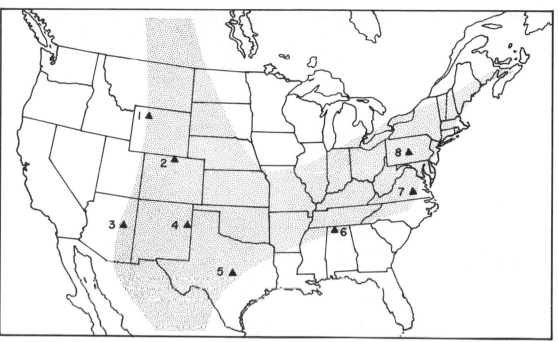

Drawing by Edwin N. Wilmsen

FIG. 1. *Locations of sites discussed in text. 1, Horner; 2, Lindenmeier; 3, Vernon; 4, Blackwater; 5, Levi; 6, Quad; 7, Williamson; 8, Shoop. Shaded area delimits the extent of the known Paleo-Indian range; beyond these limits, only isolated surface finds are presently known.*

years; Horner—6876 ± 250 years. Levi has yielded internally inconsistent ages ranging from 9300 ± 160 years to 6750 ± 150 years. Vernon, Shoop, Williamson, and Quad are not datable by independent methods but on typological grounds they are usually placed between Lindenmeier and Levi in time. The third consideration guiding site selection was collection size. Only large collections and those comprehensive in their representation of the artifact variation in the sites from which they are drawn are useful to a study of the kind presented here (Table 1). Most site assemblages were not collected in ways that are consistent with the requirements of probability sampling.

The first step in working with each collection was the selection of a representative sample from the body of available artifacts. In each of four collections (Blackwater, Horner, Shoop, Levi), the total assemblage size was small enough that the entire collection

TABLE 1

Collection and sample sizes

Site	Collection	Sample
Lindenmeier	7000±	747
Blackwater	175	118
Horner	210	120
Levi	442	139
Shoop	800±	181
Williamson	1500±	191
Quad	1000±	444
Vernon	2334	199

could be used. Apparent discrepancies between assemblage and sample sizes in Table 1 reflect the presence of unchipped and bifacially chipped specimens in the inventories. The four remaining collections were so large, however, that a representative sample was drawn from each.

Although individual site conditions dictated minor modifications, sample-selection procedures for each of these four collections were structured in a generally similar way. The specimens in each collection were divided into sets according to the following criteria: (i) raw material type, (ii) degree of retouch modification, (iii) implement type, (iv) gross size differences, (v) completeness of the specimen. A total sample size was decided upon for each collection, and a proportional number of specimens was drawn from each artifact set resulting from the above steps. Unmodified, unused flakes without striking platforms and chips less than 15 mm in gross length were, in general, not selected.

The geometry of specimens is described in formal terms and presented as grouped data (Table 2). The variables are described be-

TABLE 2

Characteristics of stone inventories from included sites. Symbols for the geometrical variables are defined in the text; debi, ratio of stone waste to tools; M, raw material source ($+$, local; $-$, imported; 0, both); N, number of cases; $\bar{X}$, sample mean; d, standard deviation; t, platform thickness. The data presented are for the total samples drawn from each site except that values for length (L), width (W), and thickness (T) for Quad and Vernon are for finished tools only. β, Flake angle; α, medial axis; δ_D, distal edge; δ_L, lateral edge.

	Dimensions (mm)				Angles (°)				Debi	M
	t	L	W	T	β	α	δ_L	δ_D		
					Blackwater					
$N =$		118	118	118	64	62	39	10		
$\bar{X} =$		44.6	29.2	5.9	67	6.5	48		1:1	$-$
$d =$		19.4	12.4	3.9	12	4.4	12			
					Horner					
$N =$	66	91	91	91	66	66	82	46		
$\bar{X} =$	3.5	33.8	26.4	6.8	67	5.8	45	55	3:1	$-$
$d =$	2.3	14.1	8.4	2.6	10	2.5	12	13		
					Levi					
$N =$	108	70	70	70	108	108	68	31		
$\bar{X} =$	6.9	55.1	42.6	12.8	69	6.9	55	67	25:1	$+$
$d =$	3.0	17.3	13.3	6.3	10	4.5	14	12		
					Lindenmeier					
$N =$	597	578	578	578	597	592	267	122		
$\bar{X} =$	3.1	43.6	31.5	8.0	69	6.6	48	65	6:1	0
$d =$	2.1	16.4	11.1	3.4	10	3.9	13	11		
					Quad					
$N =$	336	210	210	210	336	335	244	57		
$\bar{X} =$	4.3	52.5	31.1	9.2	73	8.4	47	66	2:1	?
$d =$	2.4	13.5	9.2	3.3	12	6.7	11	10		
					Shoop					
$N =$		132	132	132	160	95	139	132		
$\bar{X} =$		28.4	21.5	6.8	73	6.3	54	65	2:1	$-$
$d =$		9.0	6.1	2.5	10	4.1	27	10		
					Vernon					
$N =$	157	12	12	12	157	156	81	36		
$\bar{X} =$	3.5	50.8	36.9	15.0	73	6.5	51	60	20:1	$+$
$d =$	2.3	18.8	15.0	9.0	11	4.2	12	13		
					Williamson					
$N =$	153	181	181	181	153	153	58	38		
$\bar{X} =$	4.5	41.2	30.2	10.2	72	7.2	58	68	19:1	$+$
$d =$	2.5	15.3	11.0	4.4	11	4.3	10	8		

199

low and graphically illustrated in Fig. *2*. Data were recorded on punch cards and processed in the Numerical Analysis Laboratory, University of Arizona.

The flake angle (β) is the angle formed between the plane of the striking platform and the plane of the ventral surface of a flake (Fig. *3*). This angle was measured with a polar coordinate grid and lens stand. In a few cases, a jeweler's comparator was used. The Lindenmeier, Blackwater, Horner, and Levi samples are statistically alike, and each is significantly different ($p = .05$) from the Shoop, Williamson, Quad, and Vernon samples which do not differ among themselves.

The medial axis (α) is measured by the angle formed between the axis of percussion (a line drawn perpendicularly to the striking platform at the point of percussion) and the centroidal axis of the flake (Fig. *4*). A radial grid was used for this measurement. Readings are to the nearest $2°$. The Quad sample displays significantly larger values for this variable ($p = .05$) than do the others.

Length (L) is measured along the medial axis; width (W) is the greatest dimension perpendicular to length; thickness (T) is measured at the base of the bulb of percussion (Fig. *2*). There is a great deal of variation, at $p = .05$, among sample dimensions. Levi, Quad, and Vernon tools are larger than are other tools. Williamson tools, although not especially long, are very thick. Shoop specimens tend to be thick in proportion to other dimensions. Blackwater and Horner specimens are comparatively thin.

Platform thickness (t), the dorsoventral distance at the point of percussion (Fig. *2*), tends to be small in the Horner, Lindenmeier, and Vernon samples but very thick at Levi. This variable was not measured in the Blackwater and Shoop samples.

Edge angles were measured on distal edges (δD) and lateral edges (δL) when these displayed either retouch or use scarring (Fig. *5*). Measurements are to the nearest $5°$. Distal edges as a group are consistently much steeper than are lateral edges. Both edges on

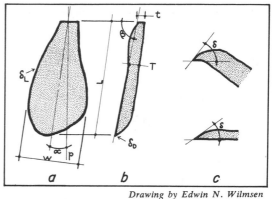

Drawing by Edwin N. Wilmsen

FIG. 2. *Geometry of specimens. a, dorsal view; b, lateral view; c, edge-angle measurement on different edge configurations; L, length; W, width; T, thickness; β, flake angle; α, medial angle; δl, lateral edge angle; δd, distal edge angle; p, axis of percussion. No scale.*

Levi, Shoop, and Williamson specimens, those on Vernon tools but not on unused flakes, and Quad distal edges are significantly steeper ($p = .05$) than are their counterparts in other samples. All Horner edges tend to be more acute than others.

Product-moment correlations were run between pairs of variables. There are strong positive correlations ($p = .001$) between platform thickness, flake angle, and specimen thickness. There is a somewhat less pronounced relation (significance levels remain the same but are not reached in all samples) between flake angle and specimen width and between specimen thickness and lateral edge steepness. Edge angles appear to be independent of other variables except each other and, to a very minor extent, flake width. The medial axis varies independently of all variables except specimen length.

Technological processes in stone tool manufacture are activated in the conversion of raw stone materials into culturally useful forms. It is apparent from the data that in a social group occupying any site from which samples were drawn, a knapper exercised controls over flaking techniques that were widely shared by other knappers in the group. Whether these controls are inherent

200

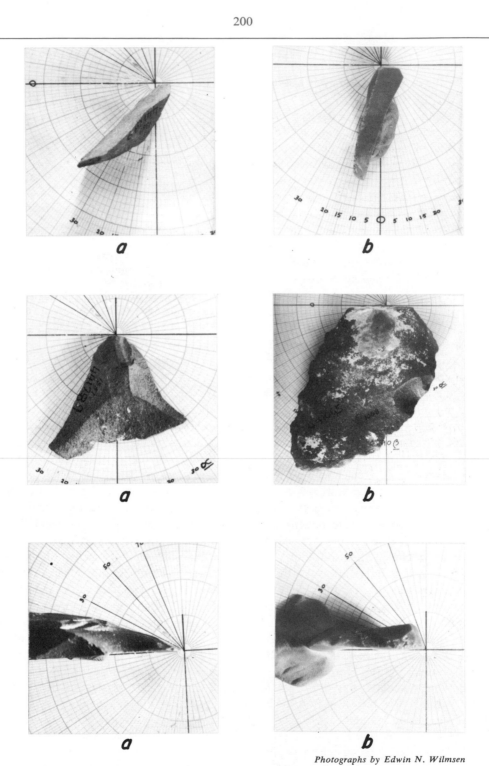

Photographs by Edwin N. Wilmsen

FIG. 3. (top) *Measurement of flake angle.* (a) $\beta = 48°$; (b) $\beta = 74°$.

FIG. 4. (middle) *Measurement of medial axis.* (a) $\alpha = 3°$; (b) $\alpha = 15°$.

FIG. 5. (bottom) *Measurement of edge angles.* (a) $\delta l = 30°$; (b) $\delta d = 70°$.

201

in the processes employed, or whether adjustments must be made when these processes are applied to different stone types, can only be determined by experiment and by testing complete stone inventories from a number of sites where specific activities are known to have taken place. Crabtree suggests that some rocks must be heat treated before being flaked (Crabtree and Butler 1964). Other technical adjustments may be necessary as well.

It seems evident, however, that flaking techniques were directed toward the production of blanks that could be converted into tools with a minimum of further modification. In almost every sample, the mean values of flake angles, medial axes, and length-width-thickness dimensions are essentially the same for tools as for that sample as a whole. Unmodified, unused flakes tend to vary more widely from sample means. Obviously, specific flake forms were being produced and selected for use as tools. It seems reasonable to suggest that technological processes of stone flaking were directed toward the preparation of these preferred flake forms and that these forms were prescribed by functional criteria. This interpretation is supported by the fact that postdetachment modification is minimal on most tools in this series. In many cases, modification appears to have been accomplished by the simple expedient of dragging a flaking baton along one lateral edge of a flake. And in only rare cases were tools (other than points and bifaces) modified beyond the immediate area of use. Significantly, a relatively large proportion of flakes was such that functionally desirable flake forms could be predetermined on and struck directly from cores.

The data suggest that striking platform architecture is of fundamental importance in predetermining at least some flake-form characteristics. Platform thickness is apparently a strong determinate of specimen thickness and width and, to a lesser extent, length. Platform width, because not measured in several samples, was not tested against other variables, but this dimension displays a tendency to vary within those samples for which data are available in a manner similar to that displayed by platform thickness. The flake angle (β) appears to be another factor upon which specimen morphology depends. Although the pattern is not consistent among all samples, the large samples and the pooled data indicate that increases in specimen thickness are strongly related to increases in the steepness of the flake angle. Specimen width is less strongly related to this angle, and length appears to be only weakly correlated if at all. These correlations suggest that a decision to produce thicker, heavier flakes or thinner, sharper flakes could be implemented by controlling the striking direction and the point of striking force application.

We may conclude, therefore, that flake morphology depends upon a number of factors. Among the more important technical factors that can be measured, platform size and striking direction appear to be critical. The amount of force applied in detachment is probably also important, but I know of no way to measure this factor after the flake has been removed. While it is probably not true that a Paleo-Indian knapper could direct every single flake to a specific size and shape, it appears certain that he could regulate any series of flakes to meet intended dimensional and formal tolerances. He apparently did this by varying the distance from the edge of a core at which he applied detaching force as well as the direction and strength of that force.

There is some internal evidence to suggest that other characteristics of platform preparation visible on flakes are indicative of more specific core-flake relations. Transverse preparation and platform abrasion co-occur in greatest frequency in the same samples. These samples—from Lindenmeier, Blackwater, Horner—also contain high proportions of thin flakes with small platforms and relatively acute flake angles. This combination of characteristics should be indicative of a high proportion of thinning, trimming, and resharpening flakes at these sites. Transverse preparation and abrasion would be applied to relatively narrow striking areas in order to provide purchase for a detaching force to "peel" off a thin flake. The core, in this case, might be a flake undergoing modification into a tool. In many cases, abrasion may have been the product of tool use. Such an inference fits well with the previous suggestion that specimen thickness is directly related to platform thickness. A "peeling" force would necessarily be applied near the core platform edge and would, therefore, carry with it only a small remnant from the platform at the same time that it was producing a thin flake. Such a force is also likely to produce relatively high proportions of acute values of β.

The distribution of edge angle values found in the samples in this series displays a distribution with peaks in the 26° to 35°, the 46° to 55°, and the 66° to 75° range. We may reasonably suspect that differential functional capacities are reflected in this distribution. It would certainly be an oversimplification to equate each mode with some specific functional operation; however, general categories of functional effectiveness may be suggested for each mode. We may infer that cutting operations are associated with the most acute mode (26° to 35°). Essentially all angles of this value occur on lateral edges. Semenov (1964) suggests that the optimum angle for whittling knives is 35° to 40°. Knives for cutting meat and skin may be expected to have even more acute working edges. Edge angles in this size range are often not the result of retouch but are simply the natural edges of flakes which have been used in an unaltered state.

The most frequent incidence of edge-angle values falls within the interval 46° to 55°. The prevalence of angles of this size suggests that this was a broadly useful attribute appropriate to a number of functional applications. Angles of this size occur both on lateral and on distal edges. Inferred uses for this range of edge angle values are (i) skinning and hide-scraping; (ii) heavy cutting—

of wood, bone, or horn; (iii) tool-back blunting. Large, unhafted tools retouched on the distal edge and on one or both lateral edges as well as socketed endscrapers are suggested implements for the first set of tasks. The same unhafted tools and tools retouched on both lateral edges would be appropriate to the second group. Tools with natural edge angles of about 50° might have been preferred for bone cutting but edges carefully retouched to this size could also be used for this purpose. Edge blunting is common in all of the Paleo-Indian Collections studied. Retouch of about 50° or more was used to create dulled edges on the backs of many cutting or scraping tools so that greater pressure could be applied to the working edges of the tools. These tools are the analogs of European Upper Paleolithic backed blades. They obviously were not hafted. Burin-like blows were also employed to blunt tool backs.

Edge angles of 66° to 75° are found on about 12 percent of all laterally retouched tools and about 48 percent of all distally retouched tools. Suggested functions for tools with edges in this steepness range are (i) woodworking and (ii) bone working. It is significant that 65 percent of all accessory tool tips and notches are associated with tools having edge angles of this steepness. Socketed endscrapers and heavy, unhafted side tools are included in this group. A large proportion of those tools with edge angles of 56° to 65° (present in significant quantity only in the Levi and Williamson samples) are probably functionally allied with these more steeply edged tools.[2]

With this outline of the data in mind, the artifact contents of the various sites may be briefly summarized.[3] The Blackwater and Horner inventories are characterized by predominantly thin tools with low values for edge angles, relatively few artifacts (but, among these, relatively many projectile points), relatively low proportions of *débitage*, and a great deal of bone waste. Single-edged cutting tools are in the majority in both samples. The associatiated fauna is mammoth (*Mammuthus columbi*) at Black-water and an unidentified bison species at Horner. This assemblage is consistent with kill and butchering operations. In the Williamson and Levi inventories, steep edges predominate. These sites have yielded high proportions of *débitage* and much evidence of stone working. A single raw material type accounts for 95 percent of each assemblage. The sources of raw material are located in the immediate vicinities of these two sites. Heavy, double-edged scraping and cutting tools are common at both; steep-bitted distal end scrapers are abundant at Williamson. These are primarily quarry sites but wood working appears to have been a strong secondary activity. Hunting was apparently only a maintenance activity. Small, extant species predominate at Levi; there are no faunal associations at Williamson. Shellfish remains and hackberry seeds are important components at Levi.

The Lindenmeier inventory is heterogeneous in all respects other than technology. There is a wide range of raw material types, steep and acute edge angles, thick and thin flakes, and a great variety of tool types. Associated fauna include extinct bison as well as deer, antelope, jackrabbit, rodents, and carnivores of species not yet fully identified. Tools, debitage, and bone scraps are mutually localized in a number of discrete clusters within the site. It is possible that several band units simultaneously occupied the site and that this was a relatively long-term camp.

The Quad, Shoop, and Vernon sites may be considered to be band segment camp locations which were occupied briefly during the seasonal round. These sites are characterized by small occupation units. They tend to have rather heavy, steep-edged tools along with relatively large numbers of projectile points and moderate proportions of cutting tools. Activities at these sites appear to have been oriented toward the exploitation of small animals and plant products. There are no associated organic materials of any kind.

Processes involving subsistence activities and specific task performance sequences are intimately related to technological and functional variables. Primary among these processes are those which are directly related to the choice of a particular site. A second set of processes is centered around tool manufacture and maintenance required to perform the primary tasks as well as other activities ancillary to those tasks. A third group of processes includes those employed in sustaining the group regardless of its specific location. These include food preparation and consumption, procurement of water, manufacture and repair of clothing, and a host of everyday tasks.

Paleo-Indian bands probably behaved not unlike later hunter-gatherer groups in adjusting their behavior to their environments.[4] Band movements were likely within a more or less well-defined territory. Even during the initial spread of peoples over the continent, groups moved in relation to other groups. An adequate balance between social relations and resources was maintianed through established interband communications networks. Bands appear to have broken up periodically either under the stress of seasonal fluctuations in resources or to take more efficient advantage of ecological opportunities. Surface quarrying and plant collecting do not require large numbers of workers to be carried out effectively. It may be that one segment of a band exploited one set of resources while other segments directed their attention to different parts of the environment. Band segments regathered periodically and, in fact, bands themselves may have joined with other bands (as at Lindenmeier) in order to exploit the larger environment and to maintain socioeconomic integration. Hunting parties as well as raw material and plant collection parties may have voluntarily moved out from these larger units and returned to distribute the products of their activities to the group as a whole. It may be that hunts for mammoth and bison were carried out principally and perhaps only by groups such as these at times when large band units were assembled.

Multiband units also functioned to maintain technocultural processes among groups and to disseminate change which arose in these processes. When individual groups moved into new environments they began to exploit the new opportunities offered by these environments and adapted their technologies to new exploitative tasks. It is probable that these adaptations involved no more than a realignment of emphasis in a pre-existing technocultural system. Those elements in a familiar technology which were most useful in the new environment were emphasized. Prolonged emphasis in one direction gradually produced a technology which was distinctive from the parent, other-directed, technology. The dynamics of this process may be seen in the eastern sites included in this survey. Technologically, Shoop, Williamson, and Quad tend to be alike. To a lesser extent, they share technological features with Levi but they deviate sharply from Lindenmeier, Blackwater, and Horner. Functionally, Shoop, Williamson, Quad, and Levi are alike. These sites exemplify the tendency of a basic stoneworking tradition to be modified to meet new conditions. The implication is that woodland or scrub forest conditions were being increasingly met. This need not imply any real climatic change. It is more likely that these environmental areas were entered for the first time. Structurally related changes in other sectors of the cultural system no doubt took place along with these technological changes but these changes are not discernible in the existing data. Mac-Neish (1964a) and Flannery (1966) suggest that postglacial adaptations were complex and not necessarily centered about the extinction of megafauna. It is probable that hunting activities at Shoop and Williamson, as at Levi, were directed toward small mammals and deer. These hunting patterns, once established, were maintained well into historic times.

Stability in basic patterns of technological and functional variation is also exemplified in the Blackwater and Horner sites. Blackwater is the oldest and Horner among the youngest sites in our sample; some 4000

years separate them in time. At both, large mammals were killed and butchered and this functional regularity is reflected in both artifact assemblages. Stylistic variation is present in projectile points and as yet unrecognized structural changes may differentiate the two sites. But those technological and functional processes associated with hunting appear to have remained essentially stable.

It is clear that technological, functional, social, and ecological processes were structurally interrelated in the Paleo-Indian cultural system. Technological procedures were directed toward an economy of tool production in which functionally useful artifacts were produced with a minimum of effort. Changes in resource patterns elicited changes in functional responses, and patterns of sociocultural interaction were adapted to ecological opportunities and task performance requirements.

Although Paleo-Indian sites are usually thought of as locations where large animals were killed and butchered, only two of the eight sites examined in this survey may be exclusively characterized as such. The relative chronological status of the Paleo-Indian stage has been fixed (Griffin 1960b; Haury 1962; Haynes 1964), and we now have an opportunity to enquire more deeply into the nature of this Paleolithic way of life. It is because of its early date that this stage takes on special significance for Americanist studies. For Paleo-Indians were the first widely successful, if not the initial, human inhabitants of the North American continent; we may assume that a significant portion of later American cultural development stemmed from this early culture.

NOTES

1. A structural pose is a recurring social unit composed of individual members of a society appropriately organized at a particular time for a particular purpose; see F. Gearing (1958).

2. For a more detailed discussion of functional variation, see E. N. Wilmsen (1968).

3. For more complete site inventories, see the

following: Blackwater—J. M. Warnica (1966); Horner—H. M. Wormington (1957); Levi—H. L. J. Witthoft (1952); Williamson—B. C. McCary Alexander (1963); Lindenmeier—F. H. H. Roberts (1935; 1936); Quad—F. J. Soday (1954); Shoop— (1951). There is no available publication for the Vernon site. I thank P. S. Martin, Field Museum of Natural History, and W. A. Longacre, University of Arizona, for permission to use their material.

4. For the definition of the term *band* as used in this paper and for a discussion of the characteristics of this social form, see E. R. Service (1962).

The Clovis Hunters: An Alternate View of Their Environment and Ecology

THE PURPOSE of this essay is to investigate the extent to which the structure of task groups among ethnographic hunter-gatherers accounts for the extinct system used by Clovis hunters for exploiting and processing post-Pleisticene megafauna. This is attempted through the isolation and definition of formal similarities and differences among cultural items and features which characterize ethnographic data on the one hand, and Clovis archaeological debris on the other. The earliest documented material remains of human hunting activity in North America analyzed in this paper are thirteen assemblages of projectile points and associated fossil remains of megafauna reported from eight sites distributed in an area which includes Arizona, Texas, Colorado, and northern Mexico. Thirteen reliable radiocarbon dates published for five Clovis sites (Haynes 1967a) approach a normal distribution which has a mean value of 11,150 years B.P., and a range of 540 years.

In view of the fact that Clovis culture has been the subject of extensive archaeological study, it is remarkable that so little has been inferred about the modes of life available to hunters during the terminal Pleistocene in the Greater Southwest. While the majority of these reports are descriptive, those which are primarily interpretive may be loosely catego-

rized by two kinds of perspective. Essays written by Sayles and Antevs (1941), Jennings and Norbeck (1955), Moone (1958), Haury, Sayles, and Wasley (1959), and Mason (1962) have attempted to assign a specific subsistence pattern to Clovis culture by reference to types of artifacts and environment diagnostic of either hunting or gathering ecologies. Alternatively, the monographs written by Wendorf (1961) and Bryan (1965) are concerned with relationships between Clovis artifacts and environments as expressions of a special hunting ecology. The monograph of Wendorf and Hester (1962) is a partial exception, for it advances a reconstruction of hunting and butchering techniques, tool manufacture, the delineation of hunting areas, social organization and the regional variation of Paleo-Indian cultural systems. The purpose of the present essay is to provide insight into these aspects of Clovis culture.

The method by which this is attempted requires the construction of an explanation and component hypotheses which can be tested in terms of archaeological and ethnographic data (Binford 1968e:269) in order to diminish the possibility of projecting ethnographic knowledge of living hunters into the past.

The explanation of variability in past and present hunter-gatherer subsistence systems is constructed from a simple axiom: seasonal fluctuations in the ecology of biotic species inhabiting an environment regulate change in the size and composition of human popula-

This article is a completely revised version of one that appeared in the *Kiva*, vol. 35, no. 2, 1969, pp. 91–102. By permission of the author and the Arizona Archaeological and Historical Society.

tions which hunt and gather those species. The dimensions of task-group organization vary with the size and composition of the social units from which they are formed. Variation in the size, composition and spatial structure of artifact assemblages used in the performance of tasks (Binford 1968*e*:272) will reflect variation in the organization of task-specific groups. Two classes of ethnographic data account for methods used by contemporary hunters to secure large game. In one instance large herbivores and edible plants may be separate from each other in a given environment. Simultaneous exploitation of both resources requires fragmentation of the group into smaller social units (Watanabe 1968: 77). Task groups formed for the purpose of hunting megafauna are recruited from social units of a larger size. Hunting parties are recruited through use of the same mechanisms of kinship and residence, which permit larger population aggregations other times in the year. The fragmentation of territorial or regional bands into task-specific hunting groups composed of related nuclear or extended families and individuals linked to them by friendship constitutes a pattern which appears to characterize seasonal shifts in the composition of the following groups: the Ainu, Kuchin, and Iglulimiut (Watanabe 1968:72–76); Netsilik Copper and Iglik Eskimo (Damas 1968:115); Dogrib (tentative) (Helm 1968:121); and Mandan (Spencer and Jennings 1965:345). The formation of Dobe Kung hunting groups appears to be similarly affected by the process of fission (Lee 1968:33) as an adaptation to differing species distribution. In their arid environment, spatial distributions of edible plants and animals coincide, but these zones are small in size and are associated with dispersed seasonal rain pools. It is significant that partnership and kinship among all these groups are the mechanisms which insure uniform distributions of meat obtained in the hunt. Individual hunters need not actually dispatch animals in order to claim a portion of the kill. Of equal significance is the apparent

lack of communal participation in ritual involving the kill directly. If ritual does occur, it seems to be restricted to social segments of the hunting party, rather than to all members of the task group.

A second set of relations exists between large game hunters and their environments, one which is polar in structure to that described above. When zones of edible plants and animals converge in an environment during specific seasons, maximal aggregations of individuals from previously isolated social segments of regional bands will form task-specific groups for simultaneous exploitation of both resources. Most or all adult male hunters from a region will form one hunting party. Fluctuation in the composition of certain bands of Shoshoni, Paiute, and Teton Sioux (Spencer and Jennings 1965:277,378) are part of this adaptation, as is the case with the Ik spear hunters and Mbuti archers (Turnbull 1968:135). Kinship is not a criterion for membership in the hunting party, nor does it have much significance in structuring the distribution of meat. General practice allows each individual the game he himself has taken, portions of which are given to unsuccessful hunters. Recipients are usually members of the donor's age-grade set. Participation of the entire task group in ritual which directly involves portions of the kill appears to characterize most or all populations which practice this type of hunting.

The hypothesis that measurable relationships exist between the composition of task groups and their hunting and butchering activities rests upon two basic assumptions. The first of these is that the organization of task groups for efficient exploitation of large herbivores requires precise coordination of individual hunters, particularly when dangerous species are confronted. Ethnographic data are imprecise on the subject, but the observations of Laughlin (1968:314) and Turnbull (1968:135) confirm the validity of the assumption.

The second assumption basic to this hypothesis is that patterns of coordination in hunting among the ethnographic groups mentioned above are extensions of kinship or residence rules used in the formation of other task groups. When the formation of hunting parties is the product of fission among social units, efficient task performance is accomplished by coordinating individuals who interact with each other as kinsmen or partners in the stalking, immobilizing, and distributing of large game. When fusion of previously isolated social units is necessary for the formation of hunting parties, uniform hunting behavior is required of all individuals for efficient task performance. Each hunter participates in one and the same method of stalking, immobilizing and distributing of game. The validity of the second assumption is not explicitly demonstrated by ethnographic data; however, it is implicit in the observations of Spencer and Jennings (1965: 360) and Laughlin (1968:314).

Both assumptions have specific implications for the hypothesis. Individual hunters share in sets of behavioral patterns which vary with participation in task groups formed either by the process of fission or fusion. Artifact clusters and the attributes of these artifacts used in the performance of hunting tasks vary with task group composition. The patterning of material remains of the hunting activities of each type of group exhibit contrast not only in the attribute relationships of projectile points but also in the spatial configurations of points and skeletal debris of megafauna hunted. One of these two patterns is expected to characterize the activities of the Clovis hunters. Linked behavioral attributes of each pattern are predicted for both kinds of task performance where they are reflected in the archaeological record—the immobilization and processing of megafauna and the manufacture of hunting tools. Each of these is listed separately below.

1) Efficient stalking and immobilization of large game by task groups which are the result of fission requires the coordination of teams of hunters. When these subgroups are composed of individuals who are kinsmen or hunting partners, the distribution of categories of projectile points are expected to vary with target areas on single animals. In situations where a number of individuals of a gregarious species is slain, the animal itself will be the unit of variation. The same activities undertaken by task groups which are the product of fusion require uniformity in communal hunting behavior, and nonrandom associations of projectile points with a specific anatomical region of slain and butchered animals of a species are expected. All hunters dispatch prey in the same manner. Differential association of projectile points would be expected to characterize the remains of animals of the same species which were attacked by hunters but escaped. The spatial distribution of projectile points in the remains of animals which have been hunted but not butchered will differ significantly from the distribution of points in the bodies of animals which have been successfully hunted.

2) The butchering activities of a task group which is composed of fragmented social segments will vary with each segment since they are the participatory units rather than the hunting party itself. The remains of a number of gregarious herbivores killed at one geographic locus would not show evidence of having been processed in a uniform manner by hunters, nor would one pattern of human activity be expected to characterize such manifestations in a series of hunting and butchering loci. Task groups which are the product of fusion will butcher species of game animals in a uniform manner at one or more kill sites. Patterns of game processing will vary with the species killed, and not by subpopulations of those species at a site as is the case with the first type of task group.

3) The differential composition of hunting groups results in the contrasting patterns of behavior which articulate hunters with each other and with large game animals. It follows that contrasting patterns of attributes seen in the manufacture and use of hunting implements might reflect variance in group composition. For example, projectile points, manu-

factured by members of minimal social segments that aggregate to form task groups may exhibit nonrandom associations of color or kind of stone used. There may also be proportional differences between basal and lateral widths of these same points. The assumption is made that proportions in point widths constitute a visually recognizable shape which, when correlated with the distinctive color or material of the point, identified the individual who manufactured them. The presence of identifiable points in the carcasses of slain megafauna may have entitled their owners to substantial portions of meat while reducing the possibility of conflict over the distribution rights to these portions. In cases where the fragmentation of previously articulated social units is prerequisite for task group recruitment, patterns of attribute association characterizing the manufacture of hunting tools would not be expected to exhibit a significant amount of simple covariation.

Complementarity should be seen in the association between proportional widths and materials of projectile points. This is based in part on the assumption that lithic resources available to hunters are limited to the specific region in which the task group is formed. Differences in proportional widths of projectile points produced from one kind of material which are greater than two mm. are assumed to reflect manufacture of those points by different and unrelated individuals. Laughlin (1968) notes that learned behavior relating to the manufacture and use of hunting tools is programmed by kinsmen, and that the parameters of such behavior tend to be constant. If portions of game secured by this type of hunting party are shared between hunters as kinsmen or partners, we would expect the mutual use of one type of lithic material by all individuals involved. The use of finer levels of attribute discrimination to avoid interpersonal conflict in establishing claims upon game would be unnecessary.

The method by which data from the archaeological record were ordered to test the hypotheses is essentially similar to that out-lined by Binford (1964b:425), who points out the need for archaeological investigation which isolates populations of variable cultural items and features within types of activity loci in an ecologically defined geographic region.

Gathering data prior to the analysis of Clovis artifact assemblages was complicated by the fact that many of these archaeological sites are simple in culture history, but complex in deposition. Four locations contain the remains of a number of mammoths. Because it was difficult to determine whether these multiple kills were the handiwork of one or more hunting groups, it was decided to shift analytical perspective from the traditional considerations of sites as discrete entities to individual examinations of each mammoth kill. Each sample unit consists, then, of the remains of one mammoth whose skeleton is in an articulate or disarticulate state, and which is associated with Clovis artifacts. While most of the relationships between artifacts and skeletons were spatially discrete, those from the Lehner, El Llano, and Blackwater Draw sites were not. Fairly accurate artifact associations with three mammoths at the Lehner site were derived by correlating topographical positions with metric depth and soil strata. In contrast, the population of artifacts associated with the remains of four mammoths at the El Llano site was grouped as one sample unit due to inadequate information. Statistical skewing was minimized by excluding this locale from as many analyses as possible. The meager amount of archaeological data reported from Blackwater Draw permitted cautious but arbitrary correlations of artifacts with three mammoths. If reference to individual sample units is to be consistent with the aims of this essay, let each mammoth at any site yielding more than one be designated numerically. To give an example, the multiple remains from the Lehner site are termed Lehner 1, 2, and 3 in Table 2.

A second theoretical assumption is made: chronological data are excluded from analyses because their inclusion hinders the search for the widest spectrum of possible relationships which may have existed between Clovis hunters, their material culture, and the mammoths they hunted.

All quantifiable information used in testing the hypothesis is ordered in two-by-two matrices which are presented in Table 3. Although the data analyzed are derived from investigation of a major portion of the literature, the size of the population obtained is fairly small. Therefore, the construction of adequate tests required the use of categorical data where each and every observation categorized is dependent on each other observation. Fisher's exact test (Edgington 1969) was used to compute the exact probability for a sample's showing as much or more evidence for association than that obtained, given only the operation of chance. A probability level of .05 was chosen to reject the null hypothesis that chance determined the association in each test matrix.

Measures of predictive association for categorical data form a valuable adjunct to randomization of contingency tests. When the value of association defined by application of Fisher's exact test is significant, it can be said with confidence that the dichotomous variables involved are not associated in a random manner. Nevertheless, the significance level alone tells us nothing about the strength of association. The index of predictive association (Goodman and Kruskal 1954) is an important corrective to the investigator's tendency to confuse statistical significance with the importance of the results for actual prediction. This measure takes account of sample size and indicates just how much the discovered relationship implies about real predictions and how much one attribute tells us about another. It would seem desirable in analyses of archaeological data to use a symmetric measure (Goodman and Kruskal 1954:743) of the power to predict where neither contingent categories in a row, nor columns of a matrix, is specifically designated as the entity predicted from or known first. In this circumstance, the index λAB (Hays 1965:610) can be computed from:

$$\lambda_{AB} = \frac{\sum_i \max_k f_{ik} + \sum_k \max_i f_{ik} - \max_k f_{.k} - \max_i f_{i.}}{2N - \max_k f_{.k} - \max_i f_{i.}}.$$

where

f_{ik} is the frequency observed in cell (A_i, B_k)

$\max_k f_{ik}$ is the *largest* frequency in column A_i

$\max_k f_{ik}$ is the largest *marginal* frequency among the rows B_k.

$\max_i f_{ik}$ is the largest frequency in row B_k

$\max_i f_i$ is the largest marginal frequency among the columns A_i

The λAB measures show how one is led to predict differentially in the light of the relationship. This says that knowing either the A or B classification considerably improves our ability to predict the other category, in that the probability of error is reduced by a certain percent. If information about either category does not reduce the probability of error at all, the index is zero and no predictive association exists. On the other hand, if the index is 1.00, no error is made and there is complete predictive association. It is quite possible for some statistical association to exist even though the value of λAB is zero. In this situation A and B are not independent, but the relationship is such that prediction will not vary with information. A value of .40 is arbitrarily considered here to be a significant proportional reduction in the probability of error in prediction, since it should allow correct placement of two thirds of the population in a four-fold table.

In order to justify the examination of Clovis assemblages within the Greater Southwest, it is necessary to construct a regional post-Pleistocene environment characterized by a constant ecosystem. Acceptance or rejection of hypothesized relationships between the carrying capacity of Late Quaternary environ ments and the formation of Clovis task groups to hunt migratory megafauna requires that our knowledge about the ecology of mammoths be tested against the archaeological contexts of fossil mammoth remains and their distributions within post-Pleistocene and Holocene vegetation belts of the Greater Southwest.

Reconstructions of the habits and migration patterns of Pleistocene mammoths appear to be derived from observations made of contemporary North American megafauna (principally bison) which recently inhabited the same environment. Current theory (Haury, Sayles, and Wasley 1959) suggests rather restricted wandering ranges for mammoths, which were thought to have been radially restricted to movement between central waterholes and peripheral feeding grounds. While this postulate may characterize the behavior of American bison (Garretson 1938:57), it is probable that interpretive analogy about mammoth behavior can be more profitably derived from the behavior of African elephants. These creatures inhabit an environment similar to that which mammoths favored. Also, all mammals and their habits are thought to have experienced fewer changes in Africa from the late Pleistocene to the Holocene than have mammals on other continents (Russell 1962:52). Comparative anatomy validates this analogue to a certain extent, for mammoth and the African elephant are characterized by high-crowned teeth adapted to both grazing and browsing (Lundelius 1964:27). Neither of these species would be restricted to foraging exclusively either in gallery forests or savannahs (Findley 1964:25). Rather it is probable that the diurnal wanderings of mammoths resembled those of African elephants which are restricted to regions which offered water in addition to possibilities for browsing and grazing. If effect, the migration of the mammoth along peripheral post-Pleistocene gallery forests is hypothesized.

By extending the analogy between the behavior of mammoths and African elephants into other areas, we may perceive some of the problems which Clovis hunters overcame in killing their prey. Herds of elephants travel daily through a series of favored feeding locations interspaced by distances of 15 to 25 miles, and it is extremely difficult for men to pace them on foot (Stracey 1963:83,191).

The diurnal subsistence requirements for active mature elephants (100 pounds of foliage and 35 gallons of water) necessitate their rapid pace of migration, for a small herd can easily exhaust the resources of any one location through intensive feeding (Carrington 1958:43). Herds are able to maintain this pace by sleeping during very limited periods of time each day. This fact largely negates the possibility of predation by surprise on the part of man or beast (Carrington 1958:47).

Current theories concerning Clovis hunting techniques need revision. Haury, Sayles, and Wasley *et al.* (1959:28) and Wendorf and Hester (1962:167) view this activity as one which involved stalking and somehow containing mammoths in channels, streams or ponds while efficiently killing them. African elephants react to similar situations by habitually charging offenders who surprise or wound them. This initial confrontation is followed by their flight many miles from the area (Carrington 1958:153). Only a bullet of high velocity fired into the brain has been known to kill an elephant instantly (Stracey 1963:191). If 5 to 35 such bullets fired into the body are the usual number required to dispatch an elephant, then traditional assumptions about the efficiency of Clovis projectiles and hunting techniques must be drastically reassessed. African elephants have also been observed to run one to five miles to a source of water when seriously wounded (Stracey 1963:191). If this behavior also characterized mammoths, Clovis bands would practice efficient hunting by attacking these animals some deliberate distance from a nearby source of water known to both. Then the exhausted prey could be killed later with comparative ease.

Wedel (1963:5) noted the absence of documented migratory patterns among pedestrian hunters inhabiting the southern high plains and concluded that their comparatively restricted mobility may have led these groups to intercept herds of animals which had predictable migration patterns. If his premise equates adaptive hunting technique with the efficient expenditure of human energy as it seems to, there is reason to suppose that the statement can serve to generate a testable hypothesis. The adaptation of mammoths to an environmental niche in the Southwest during the early part of the San Jon Pluvial enabled Clovis hunters to intercept migrating herds of these animals. The emergence of this delicate equilibrium between post-Pleistocene hunters and their environment corresponds favorably with the period of 11,500–11,000 B.P. advanced by Haynes (1964:1411) to date the sudden appearance of the Clovis culture in the American Southwest. The relationship between Southwestern paleoclimatic fluctuation and vegetational episodes during the last glaciation is subject to different interpretations. In one instance it has been defined in terms of biological indications of alternation between relatively cool/moist and warm/dry conditions (Oldfield and Schoenwetter 1964; Bryan 1965). An equally valid case has been made in terms of geological and hydrological indications of cool/dry paleoclimate affecting periglacial vegetation belts (Galloway 1970).

A four-thousand foot depression of the full-glacial timber line hypothesized to have resulted from climatic oscillation during the Tahoka Pluvial (22,000–14,000 B.P.) is pivotal to both interpretations however. Post-Pleistocene environmental fluctuation occurring at the end of this period during the initial stages of the San Jon Pluvial (13,000 B.P.) in eastern New Mexico involved replacement of pine forests below the elevation of 4,500 feet by prairie grasslands having pollen rain which is quite similar to that of the present (Oldfield and Schoenwetter, 1964:228). Wedel (1963:14) suggested that the presence of isolated pine groves along stream channels and ravines in this region of the Southwest today attests to the formerly extensive nature of this environment. Pollen evidence also suggests that vegetation zones in one region of southeast Arizona were not characterized by major changes in their composition between 12,000 and 7,000 B.P. (Mehringer and Haynes 1965:23 and Mehringer 1967:271). Analysis of

fossil pollen by Martin (1963) and Mehringer (1967) led them to conclude that full glacial vegetational zones in southern Arizona were about 1,000–300 meters lower than at present. If minor fluctuations characterized the compositions of various post-Pleistocene environments in the Greater Southwest, proportionally small magnitudes of fluctuation in the spatial boundaries of these life zones can be hypothesized. Contemporary borders of contiguous vegetation zones are postulated to have remained relatively unchanged since the Clovis hunters stalked mammoths along them. The assumption is made that recent documented plant invasions (Davis 1966) have not significantly altered or obscured the border zones between different plant assemblages. The ecotones of particular concern in this analysis are those which are located between 4,500 and 6,500 feet in the Colorado Plateau and southern mountain regions of Arizona and eastern New Mexico. Included also are ecotones on the southern Great Plains of western Texas between the elevations of 1,000 and 3,000 feet. Mammoth kill sites are found in each region at these levels (see Table 1).

The montane border zones are characterized today by the association of pinon-juniper woodlands and adjacent grama grasslands. Remnants of tension zones also characterize the distribution of different types of vegetation between elevations of 1,000 and 3,000 feet in the extreme northern region of the southern Great Plains where prairie grasses border deciduous-evergreen woodlands situated on drainage systems (Pound and Clements 1900:349). Forage consumption by populations of humans and large herbivores which have inhabited both ecotones is insufficiently documented to permit rigorous investigation of the carrying capacities of these environments in quantitative terms. Information concerning seasonal variation in the natural production of contemporary forage can be used to postulate cyclical variation in the composition of human task groups exploiting the faunal and floral resources of both zones, however.

TABLE 1

Holocene and late Pleistocene environments of mammoth kill sites

Holocene life zones

	Eleva-tion	Major vege-tation zone	Local vegetation	Local drainage	Distance from ecotone	Reference
Miami	2,900	prairie grassland	unknown, ridges 1 mi.	Bluff Creek 1–2 mi.*	plains grass 5 mi.*	U.S.G.S. maps
Naco	4,515	desert grassland	unknown	San Pedro River 9 mi.	pinon/juniper woodland 3.5 mi.	Haury 1952
Lehner	4,190	desert grassland	willow, ash, oak, cottonwood .04 mi.	San Pedro River .04 mi.	juniper/oak woodland 4 mi.	Haury, Sayles, and Wasley 1959
McLean	2,264	desert grassland	unknown, ridges 1 mi.	Valley Creek 4 mi. Colorado River 10 mi. seasonal creek 1 mi.	oak/hickory woodland 25 mi.	U.S.G.S. maps
Angus	1,650	prairie grassland	hickory/oak woodland 5 mi.	Blue River 1 mi.*	plains grass 30 mi.*	U.S.G.S. maps Pound and Clements 1900
Dent	4,750	plains grassland	pinon/rock pine woodland 2 mi.* marsh .7 mi.	South Platte River .5 mi. St. Vrain River 3.5 mi.	subalpine forest 30 mi.*	U.S.G.S. maps
Blackwater	4,280 *	plains grassland	pinon/juniper/ oak woodland 5 mi.*	Blackwater Draw situ	desert grass-land 5 mi.*	Wendorf 1961 Shantz 1924
El Llano	4,280 *	plains grassland	pinon/juniper/ oak woodland 5 mi.*	Blackwater Draw situ	desert grassland 5 mi.*	Wendorf 1961 Shantz 1924

Post-Pleistocene life zones

	Major vege-tation zone	Local vegetation	Local drainage	Comments	Reference
Miami	unknown	unknown	water hole situ		Sellards 1952
Naco	desert/plains grassland *	unknown	Greenbush Creek situ	parkland, sagebrush, grassland	Mehringer 1967
Lehner	desert/plains grassland *	(fossil pollen) Pinus 12–24% Juniperus 5% Quercus 8% Artemisia 4–16% Graminae 15–40%	Mammoth Kill Creek situ	parkland, sagebrush, grassland	Mehringer and Haynes 1965
McLean	unknown	unknown	stream situ		Sellards 1952
Angus	unknown	unknown	stream situ		Figgins 1931
Dent	unknown	unknown	stream situ		Figgins 1933
Blackwater	prairie grassland *	Arch Lake (fossil pollen) Pinus 20–50% Juniperus 4% Artemisia 4% Quercus 4% Graminae 10–20%	pond situ springs situ	water table unchanged?	Hafsten 1961 Haynes and Agogino 1965
El Llano	prairie grassland *	San Jon (fossil pollen) Pinus 25–35% Juniperus 5% Artemisia 10–16% Graminae 20–25%	pond situ springs situ	water table unchanged?	Hafsten 1961 Haynes and Agogino 1965

Key: * = tentative classification; mi. = miles.

214

Grasses which are extensively grazed by large herbivores in each zone are characterized by dense populations of diverse species. Buffalo and grama grasses associated with montane woodlands (Emerson 1932:348) provide forage for these animals during a major portion of the year. Species of grama, big bluestem (Andropogon furcatus) and little bluestem (A. scoporious) appear to function similarly in the ecology of herbivores inhabiting the tension zone between prairie and plains grasslands (Steiger 1930:182). Other types of vegetation peculiar to each ecotone are available as browse forage for a more limited portion of the year, usually from spring to late autumn. Pinon, juniper, cocklebur (Xanthium) and various types of cactus (Emerson 1932:356) are browsed by herbivores in the montane districts during this season, and a profuse growth of nongrassy subdominants situated in ravines and wet meadows of the prairie-plains association (Steiger 1930:191) provide browse during the same season.

Human forage activities in these tension zones are restricted to specific seasons of relatively short duration. Maturation cycles of edible herbaceous and fruit producing plants coincide with population expansions of burrowing rodent faunas during early and late summer in the prairie-plains tension zone (Steiger 1930:185), while the same forage climax occurs in the juniper-pinon grassland association during the autumnal months (Emerson 1932:357). Seasonal abundance of these food resources would permit simultaneous exploitation of edible flora and fauna by task groups formed through the fusion of previously isolated social units.

The three assumptions defined in detail above are summarized below to clarify the hypothesis that task groups formed by fusion characterized Clovis mammoth hunting in the montane and prairie-plains grass border zones.

1) The ecotones between post-Pleistocene vegetation zones remain relatively unchanged from 12,000 B.P. to the present. The further assumption is made that the population of fossil mammoth remains and the associated artifacts analyzed in this study are a representative sample. It is assumed that biased reconnaissance and differential processes of soil erosion has not characterized the archaeological identification and retrieval of prehistoric cultural items and features in certain land forms and not others.

2) Arguments hold which favor post-Pleistocene adaptations of mammoths to subhumid and semiarid environments in general (Martin 1963c:71), and particularly similar environments of the Greater Southwest discussed in this essay.

3) The feeding habits of mammoths and their behavioral responses to human predation were essentially similar to the behavioral patterns of the African elephant.

Given the assumptions and hypotheses above, we would predict that the geographic distribution of archaeological sites having disarticulated fossil remains of mammoths accompanied with hunting and butchering artifacts coincides at distances of two to five miles with the contemporary ecotones of the type defined earlier. Conversely, the locations of archaeological sites characterized by articulate fossil mammoth remains that exhibit artifactual evidence of prehistoric hunting activity alone are expected to be at least ten to fifteen miles distant from contemporary ecotones. Differential distance of both mammoth remains and African elephant carcasses from ecotones is held to be a function of differential response made by both species to critical wounding by successful human attack, or superficial (and eventually fatal) wounding by unsuccessful attack. If the behavior of mammoths under stress of human predation is to be explained by analogy to African elephant behavior we would expect the average distance from ecotones of butchered remains of mammoths to be one-third to one-half the distance of remains of mammoths which escaped.

Holocene and post-Pleistocene environments of mammoth kill sites are listed in

TABLE 2

Cultural items and features correlated by mammoth kill

Cultural Items	Miami	Naco	Lehner 1	Lehner 2	Lehner 3	McLean	Angus
Number of Mammoths	1	1	1	1	1	1	1
Condition of Skeleton	D *	D	D	D	D	A	A
Mammoth Age at Death	young	adult	young	adult	unknown	unknown	adult
Mammoth Orientation	south	south	south	south	south	unknown	unknown
Position of Humeri	Left of V	Left of V	Left of V	Left of V	Left of V	unknown	unknown
Points per Mammoth	3	8	6	5	2	1	1
Position of Points	V,R†	V,R,S,Sk	H,R,M,P	V,R,M,P	V,R	M	unknown
Damaged Points	1	2	1	1	1	unknown	unknown
Damaged, Reusable Points	unknown	2	1	1?	1	unknown	unknown
Points With Lengths Below 70 mm.	1	4	5	2	none	none	none

Cultural Items	Dent 1	Dent 2	Dent 3	Black-water 1	Black-water 2	Black-water 3	El Llano
Number of Mammoths	1	1	1	1	1	1	3
Condition of Skeleton	A	A	A	D	unknown	D	D
Mammoth Age at Death	young	young	young	unknown	unknown	unknown	2 young 1 adult
Mammoth Orientation	unknown	unknown	unknown	unknown	unknown	unknown	south
Position of Humeri	unknown	unknown	unknown	unknown	unknown	unknown	Left of V
Points per Mammoth	1	1	1	4	unknown	2	8
Position of Points	unknown	M	P	V,H,S	unknown	R,S	unknown(s)
Damaged Points	unknown	1	unknown	unknown	unknown	unknown	4
Damaged, Reusable Points	unknown	unknown	unknown	unknown	unknown	unknown	2
Points With Lengths Below 70 mm.	unknown	none	none	1	unknown	2	3

* Key: A = Articulate; D = Disarticulate; H = Humeri; M = Mandible; P = Pelvis; R = Ribs; S = Scapulae; Sk = Skull; and V = Vertebrae.

† The Number of points in each position is not specified (see site reports).

Table 1. Prehistoric cultural items and features which characterize each fossil mammoth context are presented in Table 2. Data from all sites listed in both tables are correlated to test the proposition that variability in the location and spatial configuration of fossil remains of mammoths associated with Clovis cultural items can be explained by reference to the stress behavior of African elephants. Application of Fisher's exact test to the relevant variables ordered in the first four-celled matrix in Table 3 demonstrates that the association is not significant at the .05 level of confidence, for P = .10. The association between hunting success and differential response made by mammoths to human preda-

tion may be due to chance alone. The index of predictive association is significant ($\lambda AB = .60$), and makes the classification of environmental data from some sites suspect in this matrix (Table 3, No. 1). For example, the association of archaeological and environmental variables at the Dent Site (Table 1) forms the single deviation (Table 3, No. 1) from the pattern expected above. The ecotone at this site is formed by the intersection of a number of vegetation belts, and it is poorly documented in the literature. Further investigation is necessary for an adequate classification of this environment in the test matrix.

The previous discussion has outlined the problems of post-Pleistocene environment

TABLE 3

Tests of association

Test number	Contingency matrix			Contingent categories	Significance of association
1.	B_1 B_2	A_1 A_2 5 1 0 2 5 3	6 2 8	A_1 = Site situated 5 mi.* or less from ecotone. A_2 = Site situated 10 mi. or more from ecotone. B_1 = No. of disarticulate mammoth remains. B_2 = No. of articulate mammoth remains.	P = .10 λAB = .60
2.	B_1 B_2	A_1 A_2 22 0 4 3 26 3	22 7 29	A_1 = Disarticulate mammoth remains. A_2 = Articulate mammoth remains. B_1 = No. of points associated with ribs, vertebrae, humeri, scapulae. B_2 = No. of points associated with cranium, mandible, pelvis.	P = .01 λAB = .30
3.	B_1 B_2	A_1 A_2 8 0 3 3 11 3	8 6 14	A_1 = Point association with ribs, vertebrae, humeri, scapulae. A_2 = Point association with cranium, mandible, pelvis. B_1 = No. of disarticulate mammoth remains. B_2 = No. of articulate mammoth remains.	P = .05 λAB = .43
4.	B_1 B_2	A_1 A_2 3 17 1 17 4 34	20 18 38	A_1 = Sites characterized by remains of mammoths alone. A_2 = Sites characterized by remains of mammoths and other fauna. B_1 = No. of points having lengths longer than 70 mm.† B_2 = No. of points having lengths shorter than 70 mm.	P = .27 λAB = .09
5.	B_1 B_2	A_1 A_2 9 0 1 4 10 4	9 5 14	A_1 = Direct association of points with faunal remains. A_2 = No association of points with faunal remains. B_1 = No. of cases in which mammoths were butchered. B_2 = No. of cases in which mammoths and other fauna were butchered.	P = .05 λAB = .77
6.	B_1 B_2	A_1 A_2 20 10 6 3 26 13	30 9 39	A_1 = No. of points in functional state after previous use. A_2 = No. of points in dysfunctional state after previous use. B_1 = Point repair impossible or unnecessary for reuse. B_2 = Point repair possible or necessary for reuse.	P = .31 λAB = .0
7.	B_1 B_2	A_1 A_2 8 2 2 2 10 4	10 4 14	A_1 = Proportional differences in widths/same material are 1mm./less. A_2 = Proportional differences in widths/same material are 2mm./more. B_1 = No. of occurrances in all mammoth/specific assemblages. B_2 = No. of occurrances between all mammoth/specific assemblages.	P = .27 λAB = .0

Key: mi.* = miles; mm.† = millimeters.

confronted by Clovis hunters. If inference is to be made about the coordination of hunting tasks, then the manufacture and use of hunting tools and butchering activities must be examined in detail. Hypothesized variation in the use of hunting tools is tested in terms of the strategies by which Clovis hunters effectively immobilized mammoths. Clovis projectile points constitute the type of hunting tool selected for analysis because they occur in the archaeological record of every site considered in this essay. Variation in the size, shape, and

condition of projectile points was evaluated in terms of 1) adaptation to game species which were smaller than mammoths, 2) differential breakage and repair, and 3) variation in the composition of hunting task groups.

The effectiveness of the strategy used by Clovis hunters to wound and dispatch mammoths must be demonstrated if it is to be eliminated as an explanation for the variation in projectile point attributes. Verification requires that the regions of projectile penetration and killing efficiency demonstrate systematic and nonrandom patterning. Wendorf and Hester (1962:167) noted that the spatial distributions of projectile points among mammoth skeletons were fairly restricted. The predominent association of points with strategic areas of the postcranial anatomy of mammoths indicate that Clovis hunters attempted to retard and direct their prey's reactive mobility. Distinct spatial clusters of points exist among 10 disarticulate mammoth skeletons associated with butchering tools (Table 2). Within this population 10 points were located among ribs, 5 among vertebrae, 4 with scapulae, 2 with the pelvis, 3 with humeri and 2 in mandibles. Projectile points found within skeletons of 5 articulate mammoths show different spatial clusterings. In each case the presence of only one point was associated with an absence of butchering tools. Points were found in the mandibles in 2 cases, and within the pelvis in 1 other.

The distribution of these variables in the matrix (Table 3, No. 2) permits the inference that penetration of the vertebrae, scapulae, ribs and humeri were essential components of the hunting strategy. The association is significant (P = .01) but its predictive strength is not ($\lambda AB = .30$). While uniformity in the manipulation of projectiles can be inferred, it must also be stated that projectile penetrations of the cranial, mandibular and pelvic regions were not extraneous to the procedure as long as they were accompanied by penetrations of the critical regions of mammoths. Evaluation of the efficiency of this hunting strategy was made by application of both statistical tests to the frequency distributions of mammoth remains where butchering was associated with projectile penetrations of the critical target areas distinguished above (Table 2). Their association in the contingency table (Table 3, No. 3) is significant (P = .05) and has predictive value ($\lambda AB = .43$). The null hypothesis is rejected and the inference is made that the killing procedure used by Clovis hunters was very efficient.

An evaluation was made of the possibility that variation in the size of projectile points is associated to a significant degree with the fossil remains of various game species. Eighteen points of a population totaling 38 from all sites are less than 70 millimeters in length. It is conceivable that 48% (18 points) of the entire population of projectile points may have been manufactured for the hunting of animals smaller than mammoths. An additional observation is made. The fossil remains of mammoths are associated with those of smaller game species at 5 of the 8 sites analyzed. Bryan (1965:41) noted this pattern and suggested that Clovis bands were hunting small game due to a gradual extinction of megafauna. If his postulate is tenable, we would expect those sites (Dent, Angus, McLean) which have only mammoth remains associated with long projectile points alone to be chronologically older than the remaining sites. The postulate is partially confirmed on the basis of radiocarbon dates (Haynes 1967a:269) currently available.

A test was made of the possibility that projectile points of different lengths were manufactured for use on different sizes or species of game killed at these sites. The association between 1) numbers of points from all sites that are no longer or shorter than 70 millimeters and 2) sites having only the remains of mammoths and sites having the remains of mammoths and other fauna in the contingency matrix (Table 3, No. 4) is not significant (P = .27) and has no predictive value. ($\lambda AB = .09$). Therefore the inference must be made that projectile points having lengths shorter than 70 millimeters were not manufactured for exclusive use on game species smaller than mammoth.

If smaller point lengths reflect behavioral adaptation by the hunters we would also expect direct association of projectile points with the fossil remains of animals other than mammoth. With one recent exception, Murray Springs (Hemmings 1970), the expectation is not met. The fossil remains of smaller fauna from four other sites show evidence of their having been butchered and eaten, yet no projectile points were found in direct association with them.

A test (Table 3, No. 5) was made of the possibility that chance can account for the direct association of projectile points with mammoths alone at sites where the fossil remains of other game species are also present. The association is significant (P = .05), and has considerable predictive power (λAB = .77); therefore the null hypothesis can be rejected.

Inferences derived from Bryan's postulate and the two previous tests (Table 3, No. 4 and No. 5) present an apparent contradiction between components of the cultural ecology of Clovis hunters. On one hand it is possible that only long projectile points were used to hunt mammoths alone during the earliest phase of Clovis culture. On the other hand, the converse of Bryan's argument does not hold, for it is not probable that short points were used to hunt smaller game species alone. Nor is it likely that points of either length are associated with the remains of game species other than mammoth.

The limited focus of both tests above (Table 3, No. 4 and No. 5) excludes the possibility that smaller species of game were hunted with tools which did not involve the use of nonperishable projectile points. An alternate interpretation however, may resolve the contradiction. Different lengths of projectile points manufactured by Clovis hunters may reflect prehistoric aspects of a mixed strategy used in hunting. Species of smaller fauna may have been hunted with smaller projectile points at or near the locus of an anticipated mammoth kill. Meat obtained from these animals may have sustained the group during the period while it waited to intercept herds of mammoths. Subsequent immobilization of mammoths involved the reuse of short projectile points in addition to the initial use of long ones. Objection to this postulate may be made on the basis of its direct linkage to the environmental hypothesis which is characterized by an insignificant statistical value of association (Table 3, No. 1) despite its high predictive index. Since predictable stress behavior of mammoths in or near ecotones cannot be demonstrated with confidence, it is difficult to justify the postulate that Clovis hunters intercepted herds of mammoths along these border zones in a systematic manner.

An evaluation was made of the possibility that prehistoric breakage and repair of projectile points accounts for variation in the length and shape of a significant number of Clovis points. The related assumption that these factors reflect retrieval of points from carcasses of mammoths for reuse (Haury, Sayles, and Wasley 1959:15) was simultaneously examined. Nineteen projectile points of the total number of 39 might have been discarded by the hunters because of damage of any kind, yet 9 of these 19 could have been reused effectively without repair. Three points actually showed evidence of secondary repairs made prior to their deposition. It was assumed that if a projectile point could be repaired it would be, particularly since the materials from which they were made appear to have been selected for their fracturing qualities. This factor argues for the retrieval of projectiles from the bodies of completely butchered mammoths. The abandonment due to major breakage of one fourth (10) of all projectile points does not explain why intact points representing three-fourths of the population were left in the carcasses of butchered mammoths. Results of the test (Table 3, No. 6) that undamaged and unrepaired projectile points were abandoned by chance at kill sites does not permit rejection of this null hypothesis. The directionality of association (P = .31) is not great enough to argue against the retrieval and modification of projectile points by Clovis hunters. The very low strength of association (λAB = .04) however, argues against any predictable variation in the attribute behavior of projectile points which could be expected to result from differential deposition. If Clovis hunters systematically retrieved, modified, and reused projectile points at kill sites we would expect the depositional contexts of points damaged beyond repair to be highly predictable. On the basis of this test, we can suspect but not demonstrate that the deposition of Clovis points among mammoth remains may have been deliberate. If future analysis demonstrates ential length, can be explained in terms of functional variation in task performance rather than in terms of repeated performance of the same task.

Variability in the widths of points can not be explicated by the same inferences because width does not behave consistently with re-

TABLE 4

Attribute patterns among projectile points

Mammoth kill	Length *	Maximum lateral width	Basal width	Proportional difference	Material
Naco	116 †	34	27	7	red-brown chert
Naco	72	26	19	7	red-brown chert
Naco	97	30	27	3	gray chert
Naco	68	31	27	4	gray chert
Naco	68	30	27	3	gray felsite
Naco	81	27	27	0	gray felsite
Naco	58	23	22	1	red chert
Naco	96	25	23	2	red chert
Miami	113	30	22	8	mottled chert
Miami	116	30	23	7	mottled chert
Miami	76	25	20	5	mottled chert
Lehner 1	74	28	23	5	dark gray chert
Lehner 1	62	31	25	6	dark gray chert
Lehner 1	83	29	27	2	gray chalcedony
Lehner 1	56	25	23	2	gray chalcedony
Lehner 1	36	17	15	2	clear quartz
Lehner 1	31	17	16	1	clear quartz
Lehner 2	81	29	25	4	gray chert
Lehner 2	97	30	26	4	gray chert
Lehner 2	78	30	22	8	gray chalcedony
Lehner 2	52	28	26	2	jasper
Lehner 2	47	21	21	0	clear quartz
Lehner 3	87	31	27	4	dark gray chalcedony
Lehner 3	79	22	19	3	gray-brown chert

* Length was the only consistently recorded attribute for all sites. Where no other attributes were reported the entire listing was deleted from this table.

† All measurements are in millimeters.

nonrandom patterning in the deposition of undamaged, unrepaired points, the inference may be made that these artifacts were task specific components of hunting paraphernalia used by hunters primarily through their membership in the task group. The utility of these artifacts would be coterminous with the function and composition of the task group. The two preceding tests have argued that one aspect of morphological variability within the population of projectile points, that of differ- spect to variable lengths of projectile points. This observation is based on metric measurements of the lengths and widths of projectile points presented in Table 4, and they are taken from all mammoth sites where such information was available. Proportional differences of 1 millimeter or less and 2 millimeters or greater between basal and greatest lateral widths of projectile points were observed in Table 4 to vary with the lithic material from which points were manufactured. Construc-

220

tion of an adequate randomization of contingency test (Table 3, No. 7) required that single points manufactured from lithic materials which are unique in the population be excluded from analysis. One point associated with the Lehner 2 mammoth and both points associated with Lehner 3 were excluded for this reason. The test of association between lateral measurements and materials of projectile points within and between all mammoth-specific populations of points (Table 3, No. 7) does not permit rejection of the possibility that covariation of these attributes could occur by chance (P = .27). The absence of any predictive value in the association ($\lambda AB = 0$) is important because it permits the inference that projectile point shapes and materials were probably not an important component of a strategy used by Clovis hunters to eliminate conflicting claims made upon slain mammoths.

The spatial distributions of certain fossil bones within the disarticulate skeletons of mammoths exhibit a high degree of uniformity. The topography of eight disarticulate mammoth skeletons excavated at four sites show the mandibles of seven and the teeth of one to lie south of clustered postcranial bones (Table 2). Within each of these same skeletons, most of the related limb bones lay to the left of the spinal column. Warnica (1966: 247) noticed this southward orientation of four mammoth skeletons at the Clovis Site, and attributed it to alignment caused by alluvial flow. On the basis of available information, it can be stated that this orientation characterizes every mammoth skeleton which shows prehistoric evidence of having been killed and butchered. The statistical significance of this association cannot be determined, due to an absence of information concerning articulate skeletal matrices of mammoths (Dent, Angus, McLean) which are associated with Clovis artifacts. We can specify that at least three of the five articulate fossil remains of mammoths represented at these three sites would have to be characterized by alignment of their skeletons in any direction

but southward if the association of the variables in this hypothesis is to have significance and predictive value. The probability of obtaining this is .96, which lends considerable strength to the observation. The tentative inference is made that this aspect of Clovis butchering activity exhibits the homogeneous patterning which has been hypothesized to reflect the behavior of task groups formed by fusion of social units.

It is apparent that the results of certain observations made of the archaeological data are not in accord with the predictions of relevant hypotheses. Abandonment or modification of these hypotheses depends on their potential productivity in addition to their correctness. The hypotheses are evaluated by conclusions which are enumerated to correspond with each contingency test in Table 3.

1) A nonrandom association between the ecology of mammoths and the carrying capacity of their post-Pleistocene environments cannot be demonstrated at the .05 level of confidence. The degree of association which does exist (Table 3, No. 1), however, has considerable predictive value. Simultaneous exploitation of floral and faunal resources under the conditions of this hypothesis requires task group formation by fusion. Direction of association and predictive power make the hypothesis useful as a base from which new lines of investigation should evolve.

2) The nonrandom association of projectile points with one target area of mammoths is demonstrated (Table 3, No. 2). The association has minor predictive value. We conclude that the strategy reflects uniform behavior in attacking mammoths. This strategy of uniformity has been hypothesized to reflect hunting behavior of task groups which form by fusion. The hypothesis can be retained in modified form.

3) The immobilization strategy used by Clovis hunters is demonstrated (Table 3, No. 3) to have been effective. It can be used to predict behavior of variables in the archaeological record and should be retained in unmodified form.

4) Nonrandom association of different projectile point lengths with the presence of game species remains other than mammoths is demonstrated (Table 3, No. 4). The association has no predictive value. It is likely that Clovis hunters manufactured shorter points for use on game smaller in size than mammoths. The hypothesis should be abandoned.

5) Nonrandom association between projectile points and the fossil remains of mammoths alone is demonstrated (Table 3, No. 5). The association also has considerable predictive power. One possible explanation which accounts for this phenomenon is that Clovis hunters subsisted on small game killed with short projectile points. These short points were retrieved and reused on mammoths shortly thereafter.

6) Nonrandom variation in the length and shape of projectile points due to differential breakage and repair can not be demonstrated. The association of these variables (Table 3, No. 6) argues for the deliberate abandonment of projectile points regardless of condition in the carcasses of mammoth. This is not proved, however.

7) Variation between task group composition and differential patterning of attributes exhibited in hunting tools is not demonstrated. Simple covariation between shapes and materials of projectile points does not approach significance (Table 3, No. 7), and there is no support for the hypothesis that this type of attribute patterning reflects the behavior of task groups which form by fusion. The postulate that differential patterning of projectile point attributes reflects intentional behavior by hunters generally and Clovis hunters in particular should be discarded because the association lacks predictive value. This does not imply that systems of material ownership or identification are, or were, not used to resolve conflict over the distribution of game. Rather it indicates that attributes of projectile points have no intentional function in the Clovis culture.

8) Variation in patterns of mammoth butchering cannot be demonstrated because certain data necessary for the kind of analyses undertaken here have not been made available. All information on the subject which does exist points to the uniform use of one butchering method. Uniformity in butchering activities has been hypothesized to reflect the behavior of task groups which form by fusion.

In summary, the conclusion is drawn that many, but not all, facets of the archaeological record investigated can be explained in terms of behavioral adaptations made by certain ethnographically observed populations of hunter-gatherers, populations in which task group formation results from seasonal aggregations of individuals from previously isolated social units. These hypotheses however need to be tested against future evidence.

Archaeological Systems Theory
and Early Mesoamerica

AS WORK on the early periods of Mesoamerican prehistory progresses, and we learn more about the food-collectors and early food-producers of that region, our mental image of these ancient peoples has been greatly modified. We no longer think of the preceramic plant-collectors as a ragged and scruffy band of nomads; instead, they appear as a practiced and ingenious team of lay botanists who know how to wring the most out of a superficially bleak environment. Nor do we still picture the Formative peoples as a happy group of little brown farmers dancing around their cornfields and thatched huts; we see them, rather, as a very complex series of competitive ethnic groups with internal social ranking and great preoccupation with status, iconography, water control, and the accumulation of luxury goods. Hopefully, as careful studies bring these people into sharper focus, they will begin to make more sense in terms of comparable Indian groups surviving in the ethnographic present.

Among other things, the new data from Mesoamerica strain some of the theoretical models we used in the past to view culture and culture change. One of these was the model of

a culture adapted to a particular environmental zone: "oak woodland," "mesquite-grassland," "semitropical thorn scrub," "tropical forest," and so on. New data suggest, first, that primitive peoples rarely adapt to whole "environmental zones" (Coe and Flannery 1964:650). Next, as argued in this article, it appears that sometimes a group's basic "adaptation" may not even be to the "micro-environments" within a zone, but rather to a small series of plant and animal genera whose ranges crosscut several environments.

Another model badly strained by our new data is that of culture change during the transition from food-collecting to sedentary agriculture. Past workers often attributed this to the "discovery" that planted seeds would sprout (MacNeish 1964a:533), or to the results of a long series of "experiments" with plant cultivation. Neither of these explanations is wholly satisfying. We know of no human group on earth so primitive that they are ignorant of the connection between plants and the seeds from which they grow, and this is particularly true of groups dependent (as were the highland Mesoamerican food-collectors) on intensive utilization of seasonal plant resources. Furthermore, I find it hard to believe that "experiments with cultivation" were carried on only with those plants that eventually became cultivars, since during the food-collecting era those plants do not even seem to have been the principal foods used. In fact, they seem to have been less impor-

Reproduced by permission of the author and the Anthropological Society of Washington from Betty J. Meggers, editor, *Anthropological Archeology in the Americas* (Washington, D.C.: Anthropological Society of Washington, 1968), pp. 67–87. The bibliographical references have been placed in the general bibliography for this volume.

tant than many wild plants which never became domesticated. Obviously, something besides "discoveries" and "experiments" is involved.

I believe that this period of transition from food-collecting to sedentary agriculture, which began by 5000 B.C. and ended prior to 1500 B.C., can best be characterized as one of gradual change in a series of procurement systems, regulated by two mechanisms called seasonality and scheduling. I would argue that none of the changes which took place during this period arose *de novo,* but were the result of expansion or contraction of previously existing systems. I would argue further that the use of an ecosystem model enables us to see aspects of this prehistoric culture change which are not superficially apparent.

In the course of this essay I will attempt to apply, on a prehistoric time level, the kind of ecosystem analysis advocated most recently by Vayda (1964) and Rappaport (1967), with modifications imposed by the nature of the archaeological data. Man and the Southern Highlands of Mexico will be viewed as a single complex system, composed of many subsystems which mutually influenced each other over a period of over seven millenia, between 8000 B.C. and 200 B.C. This systems approach will include the use of both the "first" and "second" cybernetics (Maruyama 1963) as a model for explaining prehistoric culture change.

The first cybernetics involves the study of regulatory mechanisms and "negative feedback" processes which promote equilibrium, and counteract deviation from stable situations over long periods of time. The second cybernetics is the study of "positive feedback" processes which amplify deviations, causing systems to expand and eventually reach stability at higher levels. Because I am as distressed as anyone but the esoteric terminology of systems theory, I have tried to substitute basic English synonyms wherever possible.

Let us begin by considering the subsistence pattern of the food-collectors and "incipient cultivators" who occupied the Southern High-

lands of Mexico between 8000 and 2000 B.C.

The sources of our data are plant and animal remains preserved in dry caves in the Valley of Oaxaca (Flannery, Kirkby, Kirkby, and Williams, 1967) and the Valley of Tehucán (MacNeish 1961, 1962, 1964a). Relevant sites are Guilá Naquitz Cave, Cueva Blanca, and the Martínez Rock Shelter (near Mitla, in the Valley of Oaxaca), and Mac-Neish's now-famous Coxcatlán, Purrón, Abejas, El Riego, and San Marcos Caves, whose food remains have been partially reported (Callen 1965; Smith 1965a). Tens of thousands of plants and animal bones were recovered from these caves, which vary between 900 and 1900 meters in elevation and occur in environments as diverse as cool-temperate oak woodland, cactus desert, and semi-tropical thorn forest. Because most of the material has not been published in detail as yet, my conclusions must be considered tentative.

Preliminary studies of the food debris from these caves indicate that certain plant and animal genera were always more important than others, regardless of local environment. These plants and animals were the focal points of a series of procurement systems, each of which may be considered one component of the total ecosystem of the food collecting era. They were heavily utilized—"exploited" is the term usually employed—but such utilization was not a one-way system. Man was not simply extracting energy from his environment, but participating in it; and his use of each genus was part of a system which allowed the latter to survive, even flourish, in spite of heavy utilization. Many of these patterns have survived to the present day, among Indian groups like the Paiute and Shoshone (Steward 1955: 101–21) or the Tarahumara of northern Mexico (Pennington 1963), thus allowing us to postulate some of the mechanisms built into the system, which allowed the wild *genera* to survive.

Each procurement system required a technology involving both implements (projectiles, fiber shredders, collecting tongs, etc.) and facilities (baskets, net carrying bags, stor-

224

age pits, roasting pits, etc.). In many cases, these implements and facilities were so similar to those used in the ethnographic present by Utoaztecan speakers of western North America that relatively little difficulty is encountered in reconstructing the outlines of the ancient procurement system.

Literally hundreds of plant species were used by the food-collectors of the Southern Mexican Highlands. There were annual grasses like wild maize (*Zea*) and fox-tail (*Setaria*), fruits like the avocado (*Persea*) and black zapote (*Diospyros*), wild onions (*Allium*), acorns and pinyon nuts, several varieties of pigweed (*Amaranthus*), and many other plants, varying considerably from region to region because of rainfall and altitude differences (Callen 1965; Smith 1965*b*, and personal communication). However, three categories of plants seem to have been especially important wherever we have data, regardless of altitude. They are:

1) The maguey (*Agave* spp.), a member of the Amaryllis family, which is available year-round; 2) a series of succulent cacti, including organ cactus (*Lemaireocereus* spp.) and prickly pear (*Opuntia* spp.), whose fruits are seasonal, but whose young leaves are available year-round; and 3) a number of related genera of tree legumes, known locally as mesquites (*Prosopis* spp.) and guajes (*Lucaena, Mimosa,* and *Acacia*), which bear edible pods in the rainy season only.

System 1: Maguey Procurement. – Maguey, the "century plant," is most famous today as the genus from which pulque is fermented and tequila and mezcal are distilled. In prehistoric times, when distillation was unknown, the maguey appears to have been used more as a source of food. Perhaps no single plant element is more common in the dry caves of southern Mexico than the masticated cud or "quid" of maguey (Smith 1965*a*:77). It is not always realized, however, that these quids presuppose a kind of technological breakthrough: at some point, far back in preceramic times, the Indians learned how to make the maguey edible.

The maguey, a tough and phylogenetically primitive monocotyledon which thrives on marginal land even on the slopes of high, cold, arid valleys, is unbearably bitter when raw. It cannot be eaten until it has been roasted between 24 and 72 hours, depending on the youth and tenderness of the plant involved.

The method of maguey roasting described by Pennington (1963:129–30) is not unlike that of the present-day Zapotec of the Valley of Oaxaca. A circular pit, 3 to 4 feet in diameter and of equal depth, is lined with stones and fueled with some slow-burning wood, like oak. When the stones are red-hot, the pit is lined with maguey leaves which have been trimmed off the "heart" of the plant. The maguey hearts are placed in the pit, covered with grass and maguey leaves and finally a layer of earth, which seals the roasting pit and holds in the heat. After one to five days, depending on the age and quantity of maguey, the baking is terminated and the hearts are edible: all, that is, except the indigestible fiber, which is expectorated in the form of a "quid" after the nourishment is gone. Evidence of the roasting process can be detected in maguey fragments surviving in dessicated human feces from Coxcatlán Cave (Callen 1965:342).

The Zapotecs of the Valley of Oaxaca, like most Indians of southern Mexico, recognize that the best time to cut and roast the maguey is after it has sent up its inflorescence, or *quiote*. The plant begins to die after this event, which occurs sometime around the sixth or eighth year of growth, and a natural fermentation takes place in the moribund plant which softens it and increases its sugar content. The sending up of this inflorescence is a slow process, which can culminate at any time of the year. The large numbers of *quiote* fragments in our Oaxaca cave sites indicate that the Indians of the preceramic food-collecting era already knew that this was the best point in the plant's life cycle for roasting.

The discovery that maguey (if properly processed) can be rendered edible was of major importance, for in some regions there is little else available in the way of plant food during the heart of the dry season. And the discovery that maguey was best for roasting *after* sending up its inflorescence and starting its natural fermentation meant that the plants harvested were mostly those that were dying already, and had long since sent out their pollen. Thus the maguey continued to thrive on the hillsides of the southern highlands in spite of the substantial harvests of the preceramic food-collectors: all they did was to weed out the dying plants.

System 2: Cactus Fruit Procurement.— Organ cacti of at least four species were eaten at Tehuacán and Oaxaca, and their fruits— which appear late in the dry season—are still very common in Mexican markets. Most are sold under the generic terms *pitahaya* and *tuna,* but the best known "tuna" is really the fruit of the prickly pear (*Opuntia* spp.), the ubiquitous cactus of Mexican plains and rocky slopes. Most cactus fruit appears some time toward the end of the dry season, depending on altitude, but the tender young leaves may be peeled and cooked during any season of the year.

The collecting of cactus fruit had to take place before the summer rains turned the fruit to mush, and had to be carried on in competition with fruit bats, birds, and small rodents, who also find the fruit appetizing. The fruits are spiny, and some of the Tehuacán caves contained wooden sticks which may have been "tongs" for use in picking them off the stem (MacNeish, personal communication). The spines can be singed off and the fruits transported by net bag or basket, but they cannot be stored for long. By sun-drying, the fruit can be saved for several weeks (Pennington 1963:117–18), but eventually it begins to rot. It is worth noting, however, that harvest of most of these wild fruits must be done quickly and intensively because of competition from wild animals, rather than spoilage.

The harvesting and eating of cactus fruits, no matter how intensive it may be, does not appear to diminish the available stands of cactus nor reduce subsequent generations of tuna and pitahaya—for the seeds from which the plant is propagated almost inevitably survive the human digestive tract and escape in the feces, to sprout that very year. It is even possible that such harvests are beneficial for the prickly pear and columnar cacti, in affording them maximum seed dispersal. This is only one example of the self-perpetuating nature of some of the procurement systems operating in preceramic Mexico.

System 3: Tree Legume Procurement.— Mesquite is a woody legume which prefers the deep alluvial soil of valley floors and river flood plains in the highlands. During the June to August rainy season it bears hundreds of pods which, while still green and tender, can be chewed, or boiled into a kind of syrup (called "miel" in the Oaxaca and Tehuacán Valleys).

Such use of mesquite extended from at least the Southern Mexico Highlands (where we found it in caves near Mitla) north to the Great American Southwest, where it was evident at Gypsum Cave and related sites (Harrington 1933). *Guajes,* whose edible pods mature in roughly the same season, characterize hill slopes and canyons, and were abundant in both the Mitla and Tehuacán caves (C. Earle Smith, personal communication).

The amount of food available when mesquite and guajes are at the peak of their pod-bearing season is truly impressive. Botanist James Schoenwetter, standing outside one of our Mitla caves in 1966 during the optimum mesquite-guaje season, personally communicated to us his suspicion that a family of four Indians could have collected a week's supply of legume pods there "practically without moving their feet."

The pod-bearing pattern of mesquite and guaje demands a seasonal, localized, and fairly intensive period of collecting. The pods can be hand-picked, and probably were transported in the many types of baskets and net carrying bags recovered in the Oaxaca and Tehuacán caves (MacNeish 1964a:533;

Flannery, unpublished data). Both pods and seeds can be dried and stored for long periods, but they must be picked at the appropriate time or they will be eaten by animals, like deer, rabbit, and ring-tailed cat.

Mammals were an important year-round resource in ancient Mesoamerica, where winters are so mild that many animals never hibernate, as they do at more northern latitudes. Deer, peccary, rabbits, raccoons, opossums, skunks, ground squirrels, and large pocket gophers were common in the prehistoric refuse (Flannery n.d.). However, wherever we have adequate samples of archaeological animal bones from the Southern Highlands of Mexico, it appears that the following generalization is valid: white-tailed deer and cottontail rabbits were far and away the most important game mammals in all periods, and most hunting technology in the preceramic (and Formative) eras was designed to recover these two genera. Our discussion of wild animal exploitation will therefore center on these animals.

System 4: White-Tailed Deer Procurement.—The white-tailed deer, a major food resource in ancient times, continues to be Mesoamerica's most important single game species. Part of its success is due to the wide range of plant foods it finds acceptable, and its persistence even in the immediate vicinity of human settlement and under extreme hunting pressure. White-tailed deer occur in every habitat in Mesoamerica, but their highest populations are in the pine-oak woodlands of the Sierra Madre. The tropical rain forests, such as those of the lowland Maya area, are the least suitable habitats for this deer. Within Mesoamerica proper, highest prehistoric populations would have been in areas like the mountain woodlands of the Valley of Mexico, Puebla, Toluca, Oaxaca, and Guerrero.

These deer have relatively small home ranges, and although they often spend part of the daylight hours hiding in thickets, they can be hunted in the morning and evening when they come out to forage. Deer have known trails along which they travel within their home ranges, and where ambush hunters can wait for them. In other words, they are susceptible to daylight hunts, on foot, by men armed with nothing more sophisticated than an atlatl or even a fire-hardened spear, such as used by the Chiapanecs of the Grijalva Depression (Lowe 1959:7). On top of this, they can stand an annual harvest of 30 to 40 percent of the deer population without diminishing in numbers (Leopold 1959:513). Archaeological data (Flannery n.d.) suggest that the hunters of the Tehuacán and Oaxaca Valleys did not practice any kind of conservation, but killed males, females, fawns and even pregnant does (as indicated by skeletal remains of late-term foetuses). This does not seem to have depleted local deer populations in any way. In fact, by thinning the herds during times of optimum plant resource availability, it may even have prevented the starvation of deer during the heart of the dry season.

System 5: Cottontail Procurement.—I have already discussed the ecology of Mexican cottontails in a previous paper (Flannery 1966) and will only recapitulate briefly here: cottontails are available year round (though most abundant in the rainy season) and can best be taken by means of traps or snares. Throwing sticks are also effective, and the Indians of northern Mexico use a figure-four rock trap or "deadfall" (Pennington 1963:90 and Plate 12). In the Tehuacán caves there were fragments of whittled sticks and fiber loops or slip knots which may be trap fragments (MacNeish 1964a:533 and personal communication); similar fragments showed up in one of our Oaxaca caves in 1966. The best feature of cottontail trapping is that the only investment of labor is in the manufacture and setting of the trap; it works for you while you go about other tasks. And cottontails are such prolific breeders that no amount of trapping is likely to wipe them out.

The ecosystem in which the hunters and collectors of ancient Mexico participated included many regulatory mechanisms, which kept the system successful, yet counteracted deviation from the established pattern. I will discuss only two of these—"seasonality" and "scheduling." "Seasonality" was imposed on man by the nature of the wild resources themselves; "scheduling" was a cultural activity which resolved conflict between procurement systems.

The most important divisions of the Mesoamerican year are a winter season (October to May), which is dry, and a summer season (June to September), when most of the annual rain falls. Many edible plants and animals of the area are available only during one season, or part of a season. For example, in the semiarid highlands of Mexico some plants like the *pochote* or kapok tree (*Ceiba parvifolia*), as well as many species of columnar cacti, bear fruit in the late winter just before the rains begin, so that their seeds will sprout that same year. Other trees, like the oak (*Quercus* spp.) and the *chupandilla* (*Cyrtocarpa* sp.) bear fruit after the summer season, so their seeds will lie dormant through the winter and sprout during the following year. These differences, which are of adaptive value to the plant (allowing each species to flower and seed itself during the time of year when it is most advantageous), somewhat predetermined the collecting schedule of the preagricultural bands in Mesoamerica: often these Indians had to be able to predict to within a week or two when the maturation of the plant would take place, and then they would have to harvest furiously before the plants were eaten by birds, rodents, or other small mammals.

MacNeish (1964*a*, 1964*b*) has shown some of the ways in which human groups reacted to seasonality. During the rainy season, in areas where many wild plant resources were available, they often came together in large groups which MacNeish calls "macrobands," probably consisting of a series of related families (cf. Steward 1955:101–21). During the heart of the dry season, when few edible plants are available, the group fragmented into "micro-bands," which may have been individual family units. These small units scattered out widely over the landscape, utilizing resources too meager to support a macroband.

The seasonally restricted nature of resources made it impossible for groups to remain large all year, and effectively counteracted any trends toward population increase which might have been fostered by the intensive harvests of the rainy-season macrobands. Thus populations never grew to the point where they could effectively over-reach their wild food resources. MacNeish (1964*a*: Fig. *4*) postulates that as late as 3000 B.C. the population of the Tehuacán Valley was no higher than 120–240 persons, in an area of 1400 square miles.

So many possibilities for exploitive activity were open to these ancient Mesoamericans that it would have been impossible to engage in all of them, even seasonally. It happens that there are times of the year when a number of resources are available simultaneously, producing a situation in which there is some conflict for the time and labor of the group. Division of labor along the lines of sex, with men hunting and women collecting, is one common solution to these conflicts, but not all conflicts are so easily resolved.

The solution for more complex situations may be called "scheduling," and it involves a decision as to the relative merits of two or more courses of action. Such "scheduling decisions" are made constantly by all human groups on all levels of complexity, often without any awareness that a decision is being made.

It is not necessarily true that the lower the level of social complexity, the fewer the conflict decisions, for hunting and gathering groups of arid America had many scheduling problems to resolve. Food gathering bands of the Great Basin, for example, often depended on "scouting reports" from relatives who had passed through certain areas several weeks in advance. If they noticed an unusually high concentration of antelope or rabbit in a particular valley, or if they saw that a particular stand of wild fruit would come ripe within the next two weeks, they would advise other scattered bands of foragers about this resource (Steward 1955:105–6). Often, while they descended on the area to harvest that particular species, new reports would come in from other areas concerning still another resource. This was not the kind of "hit and miss" pattern of exploitation one might think, for the Great Basin Indians had a rough idea that acorns and pinyon nuts would be available in the autumn, wild legumes and grasses in the rainy season, and so on. The outlines of a schedule, albeit with conflicts, were present; the "scouting reports" helped resolve conflicts and gave precision to the dates of each kind of resource exploitation, depending on individual variations in growing season from year to year.

These individual variations, which are a common feature of arid environments, combined with the scheduling pattern to make it unlikely that specialization in any one resource would develop. This prevented over-utilization of key plants or animals, and maintained a more even balance between varied resources. Because scheduling is an opportunistic mechanism, it promoted survival in spite of annual variation, but at the same time it supported the status quo: unspecialized utilization of a whole range of plants and animals whose availability is erratic over the long run. In this sense, scheduling acted to counteract deviations which might have resulted in either 1) starvation, or 2) a more effective adaptation.

Thanks to the plants and animal bones preserved in the dry caves of Oaxaca and Tehuacán, we can often tell which season a given occupation floor was laid down in. Because of the work of botanists like Earle Smith, Lawrence Kaplan, and James Schoenwetter, we know the season during which each plant is available, and hence when its harvest must have taken place. Even the use of animal resources can often be dated seasonally; for example, in the Tehuacán Valley, we studied the seasonality of deer hunting by the condition of the antlers, which indicates the time of year when the animal was killed.

Assuming that each occupation floor in a given cave represents the debris of a single encampment, usually dating to a single season (an assumption that seems to be borne out by the quantity and nature of the refuse), the combinations of plant and animal remains observed in a given level tell us something about prehistoric scheduling decisions. Analyses of our Oaxaca caves and MacNeish's Tehuacán Caves, by roughly the same group of specialists (MacNeish 1962, 1964a; Flannery n.d.), suggest the following tentative generalizations:

1) *Dry season camps* (October–March), depending on their elevation above sea level, may have great caches of fall and winter plants—for example, acorns in the Mitla area, or Ceiba pods in the Coxcatlán area—but in general they lack the variety seen in rainy season levels. And perhaps most significantly, they have a high percentage of those plants which, although not particularly tasty, are available year-round: maguey, prickly pear leaf, *Ceiba* root, and so on. These are the so-called starvation plants, which can be eaten in the heart of the dry season when little else is available. These same levels also tend to have high percentages of deer bone. Some, in fact, have little refuse beyond maguey quids and white-tailed deer.

2) *Rainy season camps* (May–September), as might be expected, show great quantities of the plants available at that time of the year: mesquite, guajes, amaranth, wild avocado, zapotes, and so on. They also tend to be rich in small fauna like cottontail, opposum, skunk, raccoon, gopher, and black iguana. Although deer are often present in these camps, they frequently represent only a small percentage of the minimum individual animals in the debris. Nor are the starvation plants particularly plentiful in these rainy-season levels.

3) What these generalizations suggest, for the most part, is that scheduling gave preference to the seasonality of the *plant* species collected; and when conflict situations arose, it was the *animal* exploitation that was cur-

tailed. I would reconstruct the pattern as follows:

A. In the late dry season and early rainy season, there is a period of peak abundance of wild plant foods. These localized resources were intensively harvested, and eaten or cached as they came to maturity; this appears to have been a "macroband" activity. Because "all hands" participated in these harvests, little deer hunting was done; instead the Indians set traps in the vicinity of the plant-collecting camp, an activity which does not conflict with intensive plant harvests the way deer hunting would.

B. In the late fall and winter, most plants have ceased to bear fruit, but deer hunting is at its best. Since this is the mating season, male deer (who normally forage by themselves) fall in with the does and fawns, making the average herd larger; and since this is also the season when the deciduous vegetation of the highlands sheds its leaves, the deer can be more easily followed by hunters. As the dry season wears on, however, the deer grow warier and range farther and farther back into the mountains. This is the leanest time of the year in terms of plant resources, and it was evidently in this season that man turned most heavily to plants available year round, like the root of the *Ceiba* (which can be baked like sweet manioc) or the heart of the maguey plant (which can be roasted). These appear to have been "microband" activities.

C. By chewing roots and maguey hearts, the preceramic forager managed to last until the late spring growing seasons, at which point he could wallow in cactus fruit again. Essentially, his "schedule" was keyed to the seasonal availability of certain wild plants, which climaxed at those times of the year which were best suited for small game trapping. He scheduled his most intensive deer hunting for the seasons when big plant harvests were not a conflicting factor.

D. Climatic fluctuations, delays in the rainy season, or periodic increases in the deer herds at given localities probably kept the picture more complex than we have painted

it, but this cannot be detected in the archaeological record. The constant evolution of new bags, nets, baskets, projectile points, scrapers, carrying loops, and other artifacts from the caves of the Southern Highlands suggests slow but continual innovation. To what extent these innovations increased the productivity of the system is not clear.

Because the major adaptation was to a series of wild genera which crosscut several environmental boundaries, the geographic extent of the ecosystem described above was very great. This adaptation is clearly reflected in the technological sphere. Implements and facilities of striking similarity can be found in regions which differ significantly in altitude and rainfall, so long as the five basic categories of plants and animals are present. This can be illustrated by an examination of the Coxcatlán Phase (5000–3000 B.C.) as it is represented at Coxcatlán Cave, Puebla (Mac-Neish 1962) and at Cueva Blanca, Oaxaca (Flannery, Kirkby, Kirkby, and Williams 1967).

Coxcatlán Cave, type site for the phase, occurs at 975 meters in an arid tropical forest characterized by dense stands of columnar cacti; kapok trees (*Ceiba parvifolia*); chupandilla (*Cyrtocarpa* sp.); cozahuico (*Sideroxylon* sp.); and abundant Leguminosae, Burscraceae, and Anacardiaceae (Smith 1965b: Fig. *31*). Cueva Blanca occurs at 1900 meters in a temperate woodland zone with scattered oaks; *Dodonaea;* ocotillo (*Fouquieria*); wild zapote (*Diospyros*); and other trees which (judging by archeological remains) may originally have included hackberry (*Celtis*) and pinyon pine.

In spite of environmental differences, implements at the two sites are nearly identical; even the seasonal deer hunting pattern and the size of the encamped group are the same. In the past, such identity would have inspired the traditional explanation: "a similar adaptation to a similar arid environment." But as seen above, the two environments are not that similar. The important point is that the basic adaptation was not to a zone or even a biotope within a zone, but to five critical categories—white-tail deer, cottontail, maguey, tree legumes, prickly pear and organ cactus. These genera range through many zones, as did the Indians who hunted them, ate them, propagated their seeds, and weeded out their dying members. This is not to say that biotopes were unimportant; they played a role, but they were also crosscut by a very important system.

Seasonality and scheduling, as examined here, were part of a "deviation-counteracting" feedback system. They prevented intensification of any one procurement system to the point where the wild genus was threatened; at the same time, they maintained a sufficiently high level of procurement efficiency so there was little pressure for change. Under the ecosystem operating in the Southern Mexican Highlands during the later part of the food-collecting era, there was little likelihood that man would exhaust his own food resources or that his population would grow beyond what the wild vegetation and fauna would support. Maintaining such near-equilibrium conditions is the purpose of deviation-counteracting processes.

Under conditions of fully achieved and permanently maintained equilibrium, prehistoric cultures might never have changed. That they did change was due at least in part to the existence of positive feedback or "deviation-amplifying" processes. These Maruyama (1963:164) describes as "all processes of mutual causal relationships that amplify an insignificant or accidental initial kick, build up deviation and diverge from the initial condition."

Such "insignificant or accidental initial kicks" were a series of genetic changes which took place in one or two species of Mesoamerican plants which were of use to man. The exploitation of these plants had been a relatively minor procurement system compared with that of maguey, cactus fruits, deer, or tree legumes, but positive feedback following these initial genetic changes caused one minor system to grow all out of proportion to

the others, and eventually to change the whole ecosystem of the Southern Mexican Highlands. Let us now examine that system.

System 6: Wild Grass Procurement.—One common activity of the food-collecting era in the Southern Highlands was the harvesting of annual grasses. Perhaps the most useful in preagricultural times was foxtail grass (*Setaria*) (Callen 1965:343), followed by minor grasses like wild maize (*Zea mays*), which may have been adapted to moist barrancas within the arid highland zone (Smith 1965a:95).

We know very little about the nature of the early "experiments" with plant cultivation, but they probably began simply as an effort to increase the area over which useful plants would grow. For example, Smith (1965a:77–78) has suggested that the preceramic food-collectors may have attempted to increase the density of prickly pear and organ cactus stands by planting cuttings of these plants. For the most part, judging by the archaeological record, these efforts led to little increase in food supply and no change in emphasis on one genus or another, until— sometime between 5000 and 2000 B.C.—a series of genetic changes took place in a few key genera. It was these genetic changes, acting as a "kick," which allowed a deviation-amplifying system to begin.

As implied by Maruyama, many of these initial deviations may have been accidental and relatively minor. For example, beans 1) became more permeable in water, making it easier to render them edible; and 2) developed limp pods which do not shatter when ripe, thus enabling the Indians to harvest them more successfully (Kaplan 1965). Equally helpful were the changes in maize, whose genetic plasticity has fascinated botanists for years. While *Setaria* and the other grasses remained unchanged, maize underwent a series of alterations which made it increasingly more profitable to harvest (and plant over wider areas) than any other plant. Its cob increased in size; and, carried around the highlands by Indians intent on increasing its

231

range, it met and crossed with its nearest relative, *Zea tripsacum,* to produce a hybrid named *teocentli.* From here on its back-crosses and subsequent evolution, loss of glumes, increase in cob number and kernel row number, have been well documented by MacNeish, Mangelsdorf, and Galinat (1964).

Another important process, though somewhat less publicized, was the interaction between corn and beans recently emphasized by Kaplan (1965). Maize alone, although a reasonably good starch source, does not in itself constitute a major protein because it lacks an important amino acid—lysine—which must therefore be made up from another source. Beans happen to be rich in lysine. Thus the mere combining of maize and beans in the diet of the Southern Highlands, apart from any favorable genetic changes in either plant, was a significant nutritional breakthrough.

Starting with what may have been (initially) accidental deviations in the system, a positive feedback network was established which eventually made maize cultivation the most profitable single subsistence activity in Mesoamerica. The more widespread maize cultivation, the more opportunities for favorable crosses and back-crosses; the more favorable genetic changes, the greater the yield; the greater the yield, the higher the population, and hence the more intensive cultivation. There can be little doubt that pressures for more intensive cultivation were instrumental in perfecting early water control systems, like well irrigation and canal irrigation (Neely 1967; Flannery, Kirkby, Kirkby, and Williams 1967). This positive feedback system, therefore, was still increasing at the time of the Spanish Conquest.

What this meant initially was that System 6, Wild Grass Procurement, grew steadily at the expense of, and in competition with, all other procurement systems in the arid highlands. Moreover, the system increased in complexity by necessitating a planting period (in the spring) as well as the usual harvesting season (early fall). It therefore competed with both the spring-ripening wild plants (prickly pear, organ cactus) and the fall-ripening crops (acorns, fruits, some guajes). It competed with rainy-season hunting of deer and peccary. And it was a nicely self-perpetuating system, for the evolution of cultivated maize indicates that no matter how much the Indians harvested, they saved the best seed for next year's planting; and they saved it under storage conditions which furthered the survival of every seed. Moreover, they greatly increased the area in which maize would grow by removing competing plants.

As mentioned earlier, 1) procurement of "starvation" plants like *Ceiba* and maguey seems to have been undertaken by small, scattered "microbands," while 2) harvests of seasonally-limited plants, abundant only for a short time—like cactus fruits, mesquite and guajes, and so on—seem to have been undertaken by large "macrobands," formed by the coalescence of several related microbands. Because of this functional association between band size and resource, human demography was changed by the positive feedback of early maize-bean cultivation: an amplification of the rainy-season planting and harvesting also meant an amplification of the time of macroband coalescence. MacNeish (1964*b*:425) anticipated this when he asked:

> Is it not possible as the number of new agricultural plants increased that the length of time that the microbands stayed in a single planting area also increased? In time could not perhaps one or more microbands have been able to stay at such a spot the year around? Then with further agricultural production is it not possible that the total macroband became sedentary? Such would, of course, be a village.

Actually, it may not be strictly accurate to say that sedentary village life was "allowed" or "made possible" by agricultural production; in fact, increased permanence of the macroband may have been *required* by the amplified planting and harvesting pattern.

An aspect of early village agriculture in Mexico not usually dealt with in the literature is the extent to which increased concentration on maize production made it necessary to re-schedule other procurement systems. It is not possible in an essay of this length to discuss all the subtleties of Formative agricultural systems. The basic distinction I would like to make is this: given the technology of the Early Formative as we understand it at present, there were regions where maize could be grown only during the rainy season, and regions where maize could be grown year-round. All differences in scheduling to be considered in this paper ultimately rest on this dichotomy.

Regions where we postulate that agriculture was practiced only during the rainy season include areas with an extremely arid climate like the Tehuacán Valley, or higher valleys where frosts occur in October and continue until April, as is the case in the Valley of Mexico (Sanders 1965:23). Regions where we postulate that agriculture was practiced year-round include very humid areas in the frost-free coastal lowlands (such as the southern Gulf Coast or the Pacific coasts of Chiapas and Guatemala), and areas in the frost-free parts of the interior where one of two techniques was possible: 1) intensive cropping of permanently humid river bottomlands, such as in the Central Depression of Chiapas (Sanders 1961:2) or 2) very primitive water control techniques like "pot-irrigation," such as in the western Valley of Oaxaca (Flannery, Kirkby, Kirkby, and Williams 1967).

What did this mean, region by region, in terms of "scheduling"? It meant that, in regions of year-round agriculture, certain seasonal activities were curtailed or even abandoned, and emphasis was placed on those year-round resources that did not conflict with farming schedules. In regions where farming was conducted only in the rainy season, the dry season was left open for intensive seasonal collecting activities. Even exploitation of permanent wild resources might be deferred to that time of year. Let me give a few examples:

The Rescheduling of Deer Hunting.—Deer hunting in the Formative differed greatly from region to region, depending on whether agriculture could be practiced year-round, or only seasonally. In the Valleys of Mexico and Tehuacán, remains of white-tailed deer are abundant in Formative sites (Vaillant 1930, 1935b; Flannery n.d.), but wherever we have accurate counts on these fragments it is clear that by far the most intensive deer hunting was done in the late fall and winter. Projectile points and obsidian scrapers of many types are plentiful in these sites (MacNeish 1962, Vaillant 1930). On the Guatemalan coast, at Pánuco, or in the western Valley of Oaxaca, deer remains are absent or rare, and projectile points nonexistent (Coe and Flannery 1967; MacNeish 1954). It has occasionally been suggested that the lowland areas had such intensive agriculture that hunting was "unnecessary," whereas the highland areas needed deer "as a supplement to their diet." I do not believe this is the case; it is more likely a matter of scheduling. It so happens that the best season for deer hunting in the oak woodlands of highland Mesoamerica is late fall, after the maize crop has been harvested and the frosts are beginning. This made intensive fall and winter deer hunts a logical activity. By contrast, lowland peoples concentrated on those wild resources that were available year-round in the vicinity of the village. Exploitation of these resources could be scheduled so as not to siphon off manpower from agricultural activities. On the Guatemalan Coast, for example, the very rich perennial fish resources of the lagoon and estuary system were relied upon. Some villages, located near mangrove forests, collected land crabs; others, located at some distance from the mangroves, ignored them (Coe 1961b; Coe and Flannery 1967). None of these resources conflicted with the farming pattern.

Similar rescheduling of wild plant collecting took place in the highlands. The plants that dwindled in importance were the ones that ripened during the seasons when corn would have to be planted or harvested. Plants like maguey, whose exploitation could be deferred until the winter, were still exploited intensively, and in fact eventually came to be

233

cultivated widely in areas where a winter maize crop is impossible. In the arid Mitla region of the Valley of Oaxaca today, maguey is as important a crop as maize, and some years it is the only crop that does not fail (Aubrey W. Williams, Jr., personal communication).

System 7: Procurement of Wild Water Fowl.—Until now, we have not mentioned Mesoamerica's great water fowl resources, since we still have no good archaeological evidence from the food-collecting and "incipient cultivation" periods in any of the lake and marsh areas where those fowl congregate. But beginning with the Formative period, we do have data on wild fowl exploitation from the lakes of highland Mexico and the swamps and lagoons of the coast.

Water fowl in Mesoamerica are as restricted in availability as the seasonal plant resources mentioned above. Only four species breed in Mexico. All the others (perhaps some two dozen species or more of ducks and geese) spend the summer in the prairie marshes of western Canada, principally in Alberta, Saskatchewan and Manitoba. Before the formation of winter ice in November, these ducks and geese head south down a series of four well defined routes, of which only two will be considered here: the Pacific and Central Flyways. Ducks coming down the Central Flyway, terminating at the lakes of the Central Mexican Plateau (Texcoco, Patzcuaro, Cuitzeo, Chapala), include the pintail (*Anas acuta*), the shoveler (*Spatula clypeata*), and the green-winged teal (*Anas carolinensis*). The coot (*Fulica americana*) is resident year round in Lake Texcoco, but constitutes only 3 percent of the water fowl. Ducks coming down the Pacific Flyway reach the extensive lagoon-estuary system of the Chiapas and Guatemala coasts. Among the most numerous ducks taking this route are the pintail (*Anas acuta*), blue-winged teal (*Anas cyanoptera*), and baldpate (*Mareca americana*). There are also a few resident species like the black-bellied tree duck (*Dendrocygna autumnalis*), but they constitute less than 1 percent of the waterfowl. In other words, between 97 and 99 percent of the duck population of Mesoamerica is available only between November and March; by March or April most of these species are either back in Canada or on their way. This necessitated an intense seasonal exploitation pattern similar to that required by perishable seasonal fruits.

It is difficult to compare the relative abundance of waterfowl on the Pacific coast lagoons with Lake Texcoco, because the lake system of the Valley of Mexico was drained by the Spanish, and is now a pale shadow of what it was in the Formative. In 1952, an estimated 33,540 migratory ducks spent the winter in Lake Texcoco (Leopold 1959: Table 4), while the totals for the Chiapas Coast during the same period were over 300,000; some 27,000 of these were in the area between Pijijiapan and the Guatemalan Coast alone, a stretch of only 100 miles of coastline.

The Early Formative villagers responded quite differently to these populations of winter waterfowl. Every Formative site report from the Lake Texcoco area stresses the abundance of duck bones in the refuse. Vaillant (1930:38) claimed that the animal bones from Zacatenco indicated "considerable consumption of the flesh of birds and deer," and his illustrations of bone tools suggest that bones of waterfowl were well represented. Worked bird bone also appears at El Arbolillo (Vaillant 1935*b*:246–47). Piña Chán (1958: 17) likewise lists "bones of deer and aquatic birds" from Tlatilco. At Ticomán, bird bones were also common, and the larger ones apparently were ducks (Vaillant 1931). Recently, I have had a chance to examine faunal remains from Tolstoy's new excavations at El Arbolillo, Tlatilco, and Tlapacoya, as well as the Late Formative site of Temesco near Lake Texcoco (Dixon 1966), and ducks of the genera *Anas* and *Spatula* are abundant, confirming Vaillant's impressions.

On the Guatemalan Pacific Coast, as suggested by Coe and Flannery (1967) the extensive duck populations were virtually ignored. Although rich in fish and mollusks, the Formative middens have yielded not a

234

single bone of the ducks that flew over our heads as we traveled upriver to the site each day. Since other birds, like the brown pelican, were sometimes killed and eaten, we assume that ducks must occasionally have been consumed. But the paucity of their remains is in striking contrast to the Lake Texcoco sites.

I suggest that in areas where agriculture was practiced year-round, heavy exploitation of winter duck resources would have conflicted with farming, and hence was not practiced. In areas like the Valley of Mexico, where winter frosts prevent agriculture, ducks arrive during the very time of the year when farming activity was at its lowest ebb, and hence they could be heavily exploited. This may be one further example of the kind of "scheduling" that characterized the Formative.

The use of a cybernetics model to explain prehistoric cultural change, while terminologically cumbersome, has certain advantages. For one thing, it does not attribute cultural evolution to "discoveries," "inventions," "ex-periments," or "genius," but instead enables us to treat prehistoric cultures as systems. It stimulates inquiry into the mechanisms that counteract change or amplify it, which ultimately tells us something about the nature of adaptation. Most importantly, it allows us to view change not as something arising *de novo,* but in terms of quite minor deviations in one small part of a previously existing system, which, once set in motion, can expand greatly because of positive feedback.

The implications of this approach for the prehistorian are clear: it is vain to hope for the discovery of the first domestic corn cob, the first pottery vessel, the first hieroglyphic, or the first site where some other major break-through occurred. Such deviations from the preexisting pattern almost certainly took place in such a minor and accidental way that their traces are not recoverable. More worthwhile would be an investigation of the mutual causal processes that amplify these tiny deviations into major changes in prehistoric culture.

PART 6

Archaeological Strategy for
the Study of Horticulturists

Introduction

The invention of agriculture and its effects on culture are the special domain of archaeology. The circumstances surrounding domestication as well as the simultaneous and long-term results of it have been appropriate topics in anthropology since the 1870s. In archaeology detailed investigations concerning domestication must go back to the second decade of the twentieth century. But it was probably Gordon Childe who gave the fillip to such studies. He not only outlined the so-called oasis theory, but provided the detailed logic making the rise of urbanism dependent on the use of domesticates. Childe suggested that as the Near East dried up at the end of the Pleistocene, men, plants, and animals were forced into greater proximity and interdependence on one another. And at the remaining places where water was available, propinquity and interdependence resulted in men harnessing the energy of hitherto wild plants and animals. Braidwood demonstrated the hypothesis to be wrong by showing that the post-Pleistocene had little effect on the climate of southern Mesopotamia, the postulated theatre for domestication. But the inaccuracy of the hypothesis is not so important here as is Childe's legitimation of the topic, outlining a research design for studies of domestication, as well as connecting that ecological innovation to the origin of cities. Many of the following pieces speak directly to the problem Childe first outlined.

It is in the study of domestication and of agriculturalists that archaeology has demonstrated its greatest inventiveness with techniques. The precise measurement and description of data, using devices from the natural sciences, has obtained for us an unbelievable range of data through which the origins and effects of the use of domesticated plants and animals have been addressed. Borrowing descriptive techniques from disciplines ranging from physics to geography has been one of our strengths and has permitted an infinitely more fine-grained examination of some aspects of extinct agricultural developments.

In addition to containing two articles devoted to hypotheses concerning the advent of domestication itself, this section attempts to show that archaeologists have become concerned in a more precise way with the interrelationships between agriculture as an economic base, on the one hand, and demography, technology, social organization, and religious conceptions on the other. Domesticated plants and animals provide a completely new source of energy and, in so doing, foster a series of changes in cultural systems that both reflect and reinforce that fundamental innovation. Demographic dynamics are undoubtedly involved in the factors that enter the process of domestication, as are certain factors in the natural environment like rainfall and the native plant population.

Within this section Zubrow has tried to assess some of the demographic consequences involved in primitive agriculture, and Glassow depends heavily on population dynamics in his explanation for the evolution of an agricultural lifeway in the American Southwest. Struever, as well as Plog and Garrett, are concerned with the technological ramifications, as seen through ecological adjustment, that changing reliance on agriculture brings with it.

However, as a system, agriculture brings into existence and is maintained by new forms of social organization and different views of the world. Some of the most notable experiments initiated by contemporary archaeologists center on efforts to reconstruct parts of agricultural kinship systems. These began a decade ago and are discussed by Deetz, Hill, and Longacre in this volume. In some ways, this specific aspect of the new archaeology has been the most controversial. It has probably been the single most important index for cultural anthropologists that something unusual is going on in archaeology. Within the framework of archaeology itself, the status of such studies directed at prehistoric social organization is uncertain. The experiments have been limited. They made a substantial initial impact, but are not much repeated. But taken as a whole, experiments in prehistoric social organization witness one of the most exciting and even catalytic developments in archaeology.

Almost any theory of culture change would allow one to assume that the demographic, ecological, and social changes that accompany the invention of agriculture will be accompanied by a change in religious conceptualization as well. As might be expected from our usual conception of archaeological data, no work has been done on this problem. In fact, for religions connected with agriculturalists per se, one has to go to studies in the history of religion rather than stay within anthropology. In any case, Peter Furst's use of ethnographic analogy to cope with Olmec world view and religion stands as one of the very few efforts to speak to this issue. His article is also one of the best examples of the careful use of ethnographic analogy we have.

Chapter **21** LEWIS R. BINFORD

Post-Pleistocene Adaptations

THIS ESSAY will examine some of the major assumptions underlying the current systematics of the archaeological remains of the post-Pleistocene period. The essay falls into three parts: 1) a brief survey of the history of research on the immediately post-Pleistocene period, with particular attention to the conditions affecting research orientation and, consequently, systematics; 2) an assessment of the utility of current concepts, schemes, and arguments which are advanced to explain cultural events of the post-Pleistocene period; and 3) the outlining of a different approach for understanding the nature and extent of cultural changes occurring during the period.

The archaeological remains of the immediately post-Pleistocene period are generally termed Mesolithic. They are characterized over wide areas by the appearance of small, highly specialized flint implements; these occur frequently on later sites in the coastal and riverine regions in the context of the systematic exploitation of aquatic resources.

Until 1892 there was widespread agreement among European scholars that there was a break, or "hiatus," in the archaeological record between the Paleolithic and Neolithic epochs (Brown 1892; G. de Mortillet 1885: 479–84; Breuil 1946:25).

It has generally been assumed that a break occurred between the periods during which this country, and in fact the continent of Europe, was inhabited by Palaeolithic Man and his Neolithic successors, and that the race or races of Palaeolithic folk who hunted the elephant, rhinoceros, cave bear, hippopotamus, reindeer, *ursus*, bison, etc., were completely separated as by a chasm from the agricultural people, the herdsmen with their oxen and sheep, and the tillers of the soil of the so-called Neolithic epoch, implying that man in Britain had changed suddenly from the low savage hunter to a half-civilized farmer and drover. (Brown 1892:66)

A. C. Carlyle who conducted archaeological investigations in the Vindhya Hills of Central India between 1868 and 1888 was the first to use the term *mezolithic*. Carlyle was also one of the early questioners of the validity of the hiatus between the Paleolithic and Neolithic. Carlyle's excavations yielded typical crescents, trapezoids, and other geometric microliths; it was asserted that these implements were found both with late Paleolithic tools and pottery. This led him to propose that there was no hiatus in India and that the microliths constituted an intermediate industry to which he applied the term "mezolithic." These materials were exhibited in England in 1888 at the Royal Albert Hall.

Carlyle's findings served to stimulate John Allen Brown who published an article summarizing Carlyle's work (Brown 1889). In this article, Brown asked if there had been similar microlithic forms found in the British Isles, pointing out that they were already reported from Tunis, Egypt, Italy, Palestine,

France, Portugal, and the Crimea. Brown's main concern was with documenting the widespread occurrences of microliths, and he offered no chronological interpretation. Wilson (1894) reported that in 1892, the U.S. National Museum acquired much of Carlyle's material, and he proposed the acceptance of the Mesolithic as a transitional period between the Paleolithic and Neolithic.

The following year Brown published an extensive paper (Brown 1892) in which he discussed the problem of the hiatus. He went on to argue in favor of an unbroken continuity between the Paleolithic and Neolithic, setting forth four stages: Eolithic, Paleolithic, Mesolithic, and Neolithic. He based this four-fold division on the transformational sequence of axes, from the crude forms of the "Drift" to the well-made polished types of the Neolithic. He documented finds of "intermediate" forms and used a scale of crude to fine as evidence for historical continuity, citing Pitt-Rivers's argument that such a transformational sequence indicated historical continuity (see Pitt-Rivers 1906:20–44). Occupation of the same caves by Paleolithic and Neolithic populations is cited as further support for the claim of continuity.

The following year, Boyd Dawkins challenged Brown's views:

> I shall first of all address myself to the point as to continuity in this country. Is there any evidence that the Palaeolithic shaded off into the Neolithic age in this country without any such break as I have mentioned above? Next, I shall examine the facts bearing on the point outside of the British Isles, premising that the evolution of the Neolithic from the Palaeolithic stage of culture in some part of the world may be accepted as a high probability, although we may be unable to fix with precision the land where this transition took place. (1894:243)

Dawkins went on to question the validity of the reasoning behind the claims for continuity and concluded: "The exploration of caverns has not, I submit, yet resulted in establishing a 'continuity' but simply a sequence" (1894:274).

The English literature of the early 1890s is full of arguments on these issues, and similar questions were also occupying continental scholars. The formal changes in the archaeological record were the subject of controversy, both with regard to the meaning of the observed changes and the reality of a hiatus. Lartet and G. deMortillet claimed as early as 1872 that the apparent break in the archaeological record was in reality simply a gap in knowledge and did not represent a period during which Europe was not occupied (Piette 1895b:235–36). Cartailhac, on the other hand, stated that the hiatus constituted a major break in the occupancy of the continent. In 1875 the Congress of Prehistory held a meeting at Nantes, and an argument was presented which attempted to disprove Cartailhac's position by pointing to formal similarities between the flints from Solutré and those of the Neolithic period (Piette 1895b: 238).

Shortly after this, artifacts were found which were dated to the period between the remains of the Magdalenian, or "reindeer," period and that of the Lake Dwellers, the Robenhausian. In 1879 Vielle discovered microliths at Fère-en-Tardenois (1890:961). Almost ten years later Piette made his discoveries at Mas d'Azil where microliths were found in association with modern fauna. The deposits in question overlay the Magdalenian and lacked the features then considered diagnostic of the Neolithic (Piette 1895a). These finds were followed by surveys of locations with microliths (A. deMortillet 1896), and there was a proliferation of names for these industries which were said to fill the hiatus (see Coutil 1912). New excavations were also carried out (deLoe 1908; Herve 1899).

In the years following World War I, there was a marked increase of interest in the post-Pleistocene period, and a number of regional syntheses were made (Kozlowski 1926; Clark 1932, 1936; Childe 1931, 1937). Further, there was an extension of European terms to non-European materials which were considered intermediate between the Paleolithic and Neolithic (Garrod 1932; Garrod and

Bate 1937). Some general works also appeared in which data from various regions were summarized and compared (Obermaier 1925; Osborn 1919; de Morgan 1924; MacCurdy 1924; Menghin 1925). Specific syntheses of the Mesolithic period proper have appeared (Burkitt 1925; Gimbutas 1956, 1963). In these various summary and interpretive writings, there are several distinct lines of reasoning, leading to a diversity of opinion as to the historical significance of the archaeological record.

One line of argument sought to demonstrate that the Mesolithic represented a way of life, and a subsistence base, intermediate in a developmental sequence between the reindeer hunters of the terminal Pleistocene and the food-producing villagers of the Neolithic. For example, Piette claimed that there was evidence for the domestication of the horse by the Solutreans, reindeer by the Magdalenians, and cattle by the occupants of Mas d'Azil who also, according to Piette, domesticated plants (Piette 1895b). Less extravagant claims have recently been made for the transitional nature of the Baltic materials (Troels-Smith 1953) and those from Central Europe (Pittioni 1962). Few workers, however, have seriously considered the European Mesolithic as a stage transitional to the later food-producing societies.

Other workers were more concerned with the problem of the continuity (or lack of it) between the human groups responsible for the Paleolithic and Mesolithic. Osborn (1919: 457) saw in each change in form of archaeological assemblages evidence for the invasion of new "races." Others argued that the presence or absence of discrete traits was diagnostic of population stability or change. For example, Grahame Clark (1932:2) and Menghin (1927) based their claims for historical continuity between the Paleolithic and Mesolithic on the continued use of core tools. Obermaier (1925:324), on the other hand, viewed the shift to the exploitation of aquatic resources in Ertebølle and the Auterian as justifying the postulation of movement of new people into Western Europe. DeMorgan (1924:74) saw the adoption of microliths and the loss of graphic arts as "revolutionary" and as proof of a major break in historical continuity. Childe (1925:2), Clark (1932: 1), Gimbutas (1956) and Braidwood (1963) are in general agreement that the Mesolithic of Europe is a continuation of the Paleolithic way of life and that the observed archaeological changes can be related directly to the major climatic changes of the post-Pleistocene period. These authors do differ, however, on the degree to which changes in the form of archaeological assemblages can be explained by reference to new populations or to "influences" from other cultures.

We have attempted to show in this brief historical survey that Mesolithic research has been characterized by a series of changing questions and that the answers to any one question have tended to generate new questions. The initial problem was to determine whether or not Europe was occupied between the end of the Paleolithic and the beginning of the Neolithic. The affirmative answer to this problem led to the question of historical continuity. Consideration of this problem necessitated consideration of the criteria for evaluation of formal archaeological variations in terms of their meaning for population change or lack of change. There was considerable diversity of opinion on this question.

Although problems of interpretive theory and method were never solved, they began to occupy scholars less and less as more detailed knowledge of the archaeological record accumulated. Local sequences were worked out, and a more limited geographical perspective led to greater conservatism in interpretive viewpoints. Most recent workers have used a diffusionist model for interpreting geographic variations in archaeological data, with the postulation of actual movement of peoples playing a minor role (see, for example, Waterbolk 1962). The problem of historical continuity *vs.* population movement has not been so much solved as circumvented; this circumvention has involved two means:

first, application of one's own criteria to an extremely detailed sequence in a very limited area making it almost impossible for other workers to judge interpretations offered; and second, stressing certain widespread "traits" in macroregional syntheses, traits which are usually so generalized that one might question their relevance to the measurement of detailed changes in culture history.

The work of the past 100 years has resulted in the accumulation of sufficient data to justify some generalizations made by workers in the field of European Mesolithic studies. Some of the generalizations made in distinguishing the Paleolithic from the Mesolithic are:

1) *There was a major shift in the centers of population growth in Western Europe.* "During the Upper Magdalenian, the density of population was relatively high in France, as evidenced by the great number of sites occupied for the first time, and by the richness of the sites. . . . The end of the glacial times was fatal to this striking human expansion. The disappearance of the cold fauna and the replacement of the steppe, rich in game, by forests was followed by the demographic recession and breakup of the Upper Paleolithic cultures resulting in the traditions which are grouped together under the general name of Mesolithic" (deSonneville-Bordes 1963a: 354; see also deSonneville-Bordes 1960, 1963b; and Sackett 1968).

2) *There was a major change in the form of stone tools.* "Small, geometric flints became very common, and the bow and arrow became widespread during the immediately post-Pleistocene period. The changes have occasionally been taken as defining features of the Mesolithic" (Childe 1956:96; see also Gabel 1958a:658).

3) *There is greater geographic variety in cultural remains suggesting more specific responses to local environmental conditions.* See de Morgan 1924:74; Garrod and Bate 1937: 121; Braidwood and Willey 1962:333; Schwabedissen 1962:260; Pittioni 1962:218; de Sonneville-Bordes 1960:497–500, 1963 for specific statements of this generalization.

4) *There was a marked increase in the exploitation of aquatic resources and wild fowl.* This statement scarcely requires documentation since it is practically a definition of the Mesolithic (cf. Gabel 1958a:661).

5) *There was a "trend" toward small game hunting.* Braidwood (Braidwood and Willey 1962:332) notes that this phenomenon has traditionally been explained as a response to the extinction of large mammals at the close of the Pleistocene. He points out, however, that this trend occurs before the end of the Pleistocene and characterizes Africa and India as well as Europe (see also Gimbutas 1956:14).

6) *The Mesolithic represents cultural degeneration when compared with the Upper Paleolithic.* This is generally cited in the context of discussions of the Western European materials and the loss of graphic arts (see Osborn 1919:456; de Morgan 1924:73; Clark 1932:1; Sollas 1924:595; deSonneville-Bordes 1960:498). Reference is also made to the less prestigious activity of fishing and shellfish collecting, as opposed to reindeer hunting (Osborn 1919:457).

These generalizations which summarize archaeological observations have been conceived by most European scholars in the following manner (see Clark 1962:100):

1) There are major changes in cultural remains which serve to differentiate the cultural systems of the terminal Pleistocene from those of the immediately post-Pleistocene period.

2) This immediately post-Pleistocene period is further characterized by major changes in pollen profiles, fossil beach lines, and the geomorphology of major drainage systems.

3) The demonstrable correlation between the dramatic cultural and environmental changes at this time is evidence for the systematic articulation of cultural and environmental systems.

Therefore: a) archaeological differences observed between the terminal Paleolithic and the Mesolithic can be explained by reference to environmental changes and b) differences not explained by reference to environmental changes are the result of new social contacts; such social contacts were a result of movement of populations in response to local climatic deterioration (for example, the "desiccation" of North Africa cited by Clark 1936: xiv).

This argument is a relatively straightforward mechanistic approach and is completely compatible with a materialistic, systemic approach to the understanding of cultural change. The extent to which this approach might be questioned and the particulars of its application tested depends upon the degree to which: 1) equally radical changes in culture can be demonstrated in the absence of analogous environmental changes, and/or 2) major environmental changes can be demonstrated to vary independently of analogous changes in cultural systems.

Such test situations can be found either at a contemporary time period outside the area directly affected by the retreat of glacial ice or in the same regions under similar environmental conditions at a different time period. Researchers concerned with the initial appearance of food production, as well as those workers operating in a variety of non-Western European regions, are the ones to whom we now turn for an evaluation of the explanatory approach commonly used on Western European materials.

The shift from food procurement to food production has been examined by many scholars; Childe termed this change the Neolithic Revolution. In *The Dawn of European Civilization* (1925) Childe suggested that the investigation of the origins of the Neolithic and its spread into Europe would be a major step in the understanding of the post-Mesolithic history of Western Europe. In his *New Light on the Most Ancient East* (1952) Childe offered a model to explain the beginnings of the Neolithic Revolution. Until this point, several other workers had considered the problems of understanding the conditions surrounding the origins of agriculture, and some offered idealistic progressions of conditions under which man would have gained sufficient

knowledge of plant and animal biology to permit cultivation (Darwin 1875:326–27; Roth 1887). Others offered mechanistic generalizations about the conditions under which man would have been most likely to have implemented his knowledge (Tylor 1881:214; deCandolle 1959). Childe's consideration of the problem was the most influential, since he presented a series of propositions specific enough to be tested through the collection of paleoenvironmental and paleoanthropological data:

Food production—the deliberate cultivation of food plants, especially cereals, and the taming, breeding and selection of animals . . . was an economic revolution . . . the greatest in human history after the mastery of fire. . . . The conditions of incipient desiccation . . . would provide the stimulus towards the adoption of a food-producing economy. Enforced concentration by the banks of streams and shrinking springs would entail an intensive search for means of nourishment. Animals and men would be herded together in oases that were becoming increasingly isolated by desert tracts. Such enforced juxtaposition might promote that sort of symbiosis between man and beast implied by the word domestication. (Childe 1951:23–25)

If it was Childe who first provided a set of testable propositions as to the conditions under which food production was achieved, it was Braidwood who actively sought the field data to test Childe's propositions. For a short history of the Iraqi-Jarmo project, the reader is referred to Braidwood and Howe (1960:1–8); we shall simply summarize the findings of Braidwood and his coworkers with specific reference to the validity of the oasis theory and to the materialistic approach to the understanding of culture change. In discussing the oasis theory Braidwood states:

So far this theory is pretty much all guess-work, and there are certainly some questions it leaves unanswered. I will tell you quite frankly that there are times when I feel it is plain balderdash. (1951:85)

Braidwood also questioned the relevance of the postulated environmental changes to the origins of food production:

242

There had also been three earlier periods of great glaciers, and long periods of warm weather in between. . . . Thus the forced neighborliness of men, plants and animals in river valleys and oases must also have happened earlier. Why didn't domestication happen earlier too, then? (1951*a*:86)

Braidwood has made the above point on numerous occasions, but it is in more recent publications (Braidwood and Willey 1962: 342) that the comment is less directly aimed at the oasis theory and more toward questioning the role of environmental change in bringing about food production.

Braidwood's work in the "hilly flanks" zone of the Fertile Crescent was carried out over a number of years and involved the collaboration of a number of scientists from the fields of zoology, paleontology, geology, palynology, paleobotany, etc. Their investigations had been directed toward the identification of the physical effects of domestication on plants and animals and the documentation of the environmental events of the period between 10,-000 B.C. and the appearance of "settled village life." The climatological-environmental results have allowed Braidwood to generalize:

It seems most unlikely that there was any really significant difference between then and now in the general land forms and rainfall patterns. (1952*b*:11)

In southwestern Asia . . . our colleagues in the natural sciences see no evidence for radical change in climate or fauna between the levels of the Zarzian and those of the Jarmo or Hassunah phases. (Braidwood and Howe 1960:181)

Discussing specifically the relationship between environmental change and the beginnings of food production, Braidwood states:

We do not believe that the answers will lie within the realm of environmental determinism and in any direct or strict sense . . . we and our natural-science colleagues reviewed the evidence for possible pertinent fluctuations of climate and of plant and animal distributions . . . and convinced ourselves that there is no such evidence available . . . no evidence exists for such changes in the natural environment . . . might be of sufficient impact to have

predetermined the shift to food production. (Braidwood and Howe 1960:142)

Thus Braidwood argues that: 1) environmental conditions analogous to those at the close of the Pleistocene had occurred previously without having brought about food production, and 2) there is no evidence to support major climatic changes in the Near East of sufficient magnitude to have "predetermined the shift to food production." These observations are not only directed against the oasis theory but also against the argument that food production constituted an alternative adaptation to changed environmental conditions at the close of the Pleistocene. Braidwood also argues against the causative role of environmental change in his consideration of the applicability of the term Mesolithic to non-European areas (Braidwood and Willey 1962:332). Garrod (1932) called the Natufian of Israel a Mesolithic industry, and the appropriateness of this terminology has been questioned by Braidwood:

. . . the usual conception of the Mesolithic is as a cultural readaptation to post-Pleistocene environments but the conception has become an awkward one, on a world wide scale, since as we have just seen, there is evidence that the same trends toward readaptation and intensification of collection activities had begun to manifest themselves in certain areas before the conventional date for the end of the Pleistocene. One of us is of the opinion that there was no Mesolithic sensu stricto, in southwestern Asia, at least. (Braidwood and Willey 1962:332)

There is also increasing evidence that there were cultural changes parallel to those occurring in Western Europe in regions where there were no correlated major climatic changes (see, for example, Perrot 1962:147, 151–53).

Braidwood presents a strong case that there was major cultural change in areas where environmental change was minor or absent, as well as in areas such as Western Europe where environmental change was marked. This, together with the fact that earlier interglacial warm periods were not accompanied by drastic cultural changes of analogous form, is sufficient to invalidate the argument that the magnitude of environmental and cultural change can be expected to vary directly in a simple stimulus-response pattern. These data also raise questions about the positive correlations claimed for the form of environmental and cultural changes.

Braidwood, however, is not completely consistent in his application of these findings. He argues *against* the causative role of environmental change in the Near East, yet *for* such an explanation for the cultural changes observed in Western Europe (Braidwood and Willey 1962:341). We do not propose here that there is no relationship between environmental and cultural change in Western Europe but rather argue against the direct and simple causative role of environmental change in view of Braidwood's own findings. What we must seek is a set of explanatory variables which will be valid on a world-wide scale at the terminal- and post-Pleistocene periods.

If Braidwood rejects environmental change as the principal explanation in the Near East, what does he propose instead? After apologizing for Childe's "materialistic philosophy of history" (Braidwood and Howe 1960:7), Braidwood offers his "nuclear zone" theory:

In my opinion there is no need to complicate the story with extraneous "causes." The food producing revolution seems to have occurred as the culmination of the ever increasing cultural differentiation and specialization of human communities. Around 8,000 B.C. the inhabitants of the hills around the fertile crescent had come to know their habitat so well that they were beginning to domesticate the plants and animals they had been collecting and hunting. . . . From these "nuclear" zones cultural diffusion spread the new way of life to the rest of the world. (1960a:134)

A nuclear zone is defined as follows: "A region with a natural environment which included a variety of wild plants and animals, both possible and ready for domestication . . ." (Braidwood 1963:106).

In his statements Braidwood proposes that cultivation is the expected, natural outcome of a long, directional evolutionary trend, limited only by the presence in the environment of domesticable plants and animals. This is clearly an orthogenetic argument (see Simpson 1949:130–59 for a critical discussion of orthogenesis). The vital element responsible for the directional series of events appears to be inherent in human nature; it is expressed by Braidwood in such phrases as "increased experimentation" (1963:106) and "increased receptiveness" (1963:97–98, 137–38). These behavioral traits made it possible for man to "settle into" his environment (Braidwood and Reed 1957:20), and they serve as the basis for Braidwood's taxonomy of subsistence-settlement types (1960b:143–51) in which three long-run trends can be seen: 1) increased localization of activity within the territory of a group, 2) more specific exploitation of the habitat, and 3) increased group size. (For a playful treatment of Braidwood's frame of reference see Binford and Binford 1966a.) It is when we have these trends, based on inherent human nature, operating in the context of a "nuclear zone" that things begin to happen:

Now my hunch goes that when this experimentation and settling down took place within a potential nuclear area . . . where a whole constellation of plants and animals possible of domestication were available . . . the change was easily made. . . . (Braidwood 1963:110)

The explanation for absence of food production during earlier interglacial periods is that: "culture was not ready to achieve it" (Braidwood and Willey 1962:342).

It is argued here that vitalism, whether expressed in terms of inherent forces orienting the direction of organic evolution or in its more anthropocentric form of emergent human properties which direct cultural evolution, is unacceptable as an explanation. Trends which are observed in cultural evolution require explanation; they are certainly not explained by postulating emergent human traits which are said to account for the trends.

In summary, post-Pleistocene research began with the question of whether or not Western Europe was populated between the close of the Pleistocene and the first appearance of the later Neolithic settlements. When this question was answered affirmatively, emphasis shifted to the question of continuity —were the "intermediate" populations indigenous or were they intruders? In seeking to solve this problem scholars were involved in the methodological question of what archaeological data could be cited as proof or disproof of continuity. As local sequences became better documented, this question was dropped, and there was an increasing tendency to view variability as a direct response to local environments which had radically changed with the retreat of the ice. This stimulus-response reasoning was generalized not only for the European foraging adaptation but was also used to explain the origins of food production (the propinquity or oasis theory). Field investigation in the relevant parts of the Near East showed that dramatic environmental change did not characterize the crucial periods of time. The oasis theory has fallen into disfavor, and Braidwood's nuclear zone theory has tended to replace it. We have sought to demonstrate in our analysis that this theory is based on a kind of vitalism and a postulation of causal factors which are incapable of being tested. We also propose that current explanations for the form and distribution of post-Pleistocene cultures in Europe are implicitly, and often explicitly, based on simple and direct environmental determinism which the data from non-European parts of the world tend to refute. What follows is an examination of post-Pleistocene data within a different theoretical framework and the formulation of explanatory hypotheses which, it is hoped, are both more generally applicable and also testable.

If our aim is the explanation of cultural differences and similarities in different places and at different times, we must first isolate the phenomena we designate "cultural." Culture is all those means whose forms are not under direct genetic control (that is, extrasomatic [White 1959:8]) which serve to adjust individuals and groups within their ecological communities. If we seek understanding of the origins of agriculture or of "the spread of the village-farming community," we must analyze these cultural means as adaptive adjustments in the variety of ecosystems within which human groups were participants.

Adaptation is always a local problem, and selective pressures favoring new cultural forms result from non-equilibrium conditions in the local ecosystem. Our task, then, becomes the isolation of the variables initiating directional change in the internal structuring of ecological systems. Of particular importance is understanding the conditions which favor the rearrangement of energy-matter components and their linked dependencies in a manner which alters the effective environment of the unit under study.

The term "effective environment" (Allee et al. 1949:1) designates those parts of the total environment which are in regular or cyclical articulation with the unit under study. Changes in the effective environment will produce changes not only in the boundaries of the ecological community but also in the internal organization of the community. Both of these changes in turn set up conditions favoring adaptive adjustments among the components of the community. In dealing with sociocultural systems and in trying to understand the conditions under which such systems undergo adaptive change, we are necessarily concerned with the effective environment of a given system.

Cultural systems relate man to habitat, and an equilibrium can be established in this relationship as in others. When an equilibrium has been established culturally between man and habitat, it may be continued indefinitely until it is upset by the intrusion of a new factor. (White 1959:284)

If we hope to understand culture change in general, and the changes of the post-Pleistocene period in particular, we must seek the conditions which have brought new factors into play in the effective environments of the cultural systems at the close of the Pleistocene.

Before undertaking our analysis, one further distinction needs to be made—the distinction between functional and structural differences in ecological niches. *Functional differences* are those which result from differences in the form of the elements of a system and which do not necessarily imply differences in the kind of articulation which exists between a cultural system and the ecological community of which it is a part. *Structural differences* refer to communities made up of nonanalogous components which are integrated in different ways. In citing functional variability between niches, we are referring to differences in the form of the gross environment in which ecological communities occur; in such cases there would be no necessary structural differences in the organization of the ecological communities of the system, but only in the form of their environments. A case in point might be two cultural systems, both of which are solely dependent upon terrestrial resources within their home ranges and neither of which possess the technological means for food storage or circulation beyond the locus of procurement. If one such system were located in a tropical rain forest and the other in a temperate deciduous forest, we would observe numerous formal differences between the cultural elements in the two systems, yet both can be said to occupy similar ecological niches within their habitats. Despite obvious differences in raw materials, the form of implements, differences in phasing of activities, and even in social organization, all such differences are explicable directly by reference to differences in gross environment. Therefore, we would term these differences functional, not structural.

Structural differences in ecological niches, on the other hand, refer to differences in the modes of integration between cultural and other components within ecological communities. Such differences imply a different set of relationships between the cultural unit and the variables in the gross environment

with which the cultural unit is articulated. Cultural systems which occupy different ecological niches would therefore have different effective environments. An example of two cultural systems in the same gross environment but occupying different ecological niches would be the commonly occurring case where horticulturalists and hunters and gatherers live side by side. Each cultural group is in articulation with quite different elements of the gross environment and is integrated with the environment differently. Such cultural systems would be subject to qualitatively different types of selective pressure.

We would argue that understanding the selective pressures favoring the adoption of adaptive means as radical and as new as animal husbandry and cultivation in the post-Pleistocene requires the application of the ecological principles outlined above. A first step would be to determine whether food production constitutes a functional variant of analogous ecological niches in different environments, or whether it is a structurally new adaptive means in an ecological niche not previously occupied by cultural systems.

Braidwood's nuclear zone theory is an argument for the former interpretation; the differences between the post-Pleistocene cultures in the hilly flanks and elsewhere are explicable by reference to formally unique elements in the plant and animal populations of the piedmont regions of the Near East. Childe's position is a statement of the latter interpretation, and he cites changes in the physical environment as the cause for bringing about new structural relationships between plants, animals, and men. Our argument also favors the second interpretation but with demographic, rather than gross environmental, variables responsible for the generation of pressures favoring new ecological niches.

At certain times and places in the course of culture history, the threat of a diminished food supply, coming from an increase of population through immigration, or from a decline in local flora due to climatic or physiographic change, was met by various measures of cultural control over plant life, which collectively, we call agriculture. (White 1959:285)

White's citation of population increase through immigration as a relevant variable in explaining the appearance of agriculture is a radical departure from traditional interpretations.

In the traditional approach, changes and variation in the available food supply have been cited as the major factors which regulate population equilibrium systems (Childe 1956:98; Dumond 1965:310).

Man must eat to live at all; food is perhaps the one absolute and overriding need for man. In early and primitive societies the quest for food was and is the most absorbing preoccupation for all members of the group. The enlargement of the food-supply was therefore presumably the indispensable condition for human progress. (Childe 1944:12)

The community of food-gatherers had been restricted in size by the food supplies available. (Childe 1951:61)

Similar statements have been made by Braidwood (1963:121–22), among others.

The inference about population dynamics to be made from these statements is that populations will grow until the food requirements of the group begin to exceed the standing crop in the local habitat. No population could ever achieve a stable adaptation, since its members would always be under strong selective pressure to develop new means of getting food. This assumption of the available food supply as the critical variable in population dynamics has prevented consideration of population variables themselves as possible sources of disequilibrium.

Recent studies in demography have argued strongly against the direct control of population density by the availability of food.

We have the strongest reasons for concluding . . . that population density must at all costs be prevented from rising to the level where food shortage begins to take a toll of the numbers— an effect that could not be felt until long after the optimum density had been exceeded. It

would be bound to result in chronic overexploitation and a spiral of diminishing returns. (Wynne-Edwards 1962:11)

Long term population equilibrium . . . implies some kind of restraint. . . . "Food supply" offers a quick answer, but not, I think, the correct one. At any rate, a forest is full of game for an expert mouse-hunter, and a Paleolithic man who stuck to business should have found enough food on two square kilometers instead of 20 or 200. Social forces were probably more powerful than mere starvation in causing men to huddle in small bands. (Deevey 1960:6)

Most demographers agree that functional relationships between the normal birth rate and other requirements (for example, the mobility of the female) favor the *cultural* regulation of fertility through such practices as infanticide, abortion, lactation taboos, etc. These practices have the effect of homeostatically keeping population size below the point at which diminishing returns from the local habitat would come into play. (See Carr-Saunders 1922; Wynne-Edwards 1962, 1964; Birdsell 1958, 1968; Deevey 1960; Hainline 1965; Dumond 1965; and Halbwachs 1960.)

The arguments of demographers are supported by a number of recent ethnographic studies which document the abundance of food available to even marginal hunters. Some cases of importance are J. D. Clark (1951) on the Barotse, Lee (1965) on the !Kung Bushmen, Woodburn (1968) on the Hadza, and Huntingford (1955) on the Dorobo. Similar conditions of relative abundance have been reported for Australia. For example, life on the Daly River in the Northern Territory led McCarthy (1957:90) to generalize: "For the uncontaminated bush native the food problem hardly exists." Ease in food procurement is also reported for Arnhemland (McCarthy 1957:90; McCarthy and McArthur 1960:145–93). Quimby has described the truly impressive quantities of food obtained in the course of a single year by a Chippewa family in the Lower Peninsula of Michigan in 1763 (Quimby 1962:217– 39). In a quantitative study of food intake by the Onge hunters of Little Andaman, Bose (1964:306) states: "The region surrounding Tokebuea can supply more food than the requirement of the local people."

These data suggest that while hunting-gathering populations may vary in density between different habitats in direct proportion to the relative size of the standing food crop, nevertheless within any given habitat the population is homeostatically regulated *below* the level of depletion of the local food supply.

There are two corollaries of the assumption that population size is regulated almost exclusively by food supply which we also need to examine. The first corollary is: *Man would be continually seeking means for increasing his food supply.* In other words, there would be ubiquitous and constant selective pressure favoring the development of technological innovations, such as agriculture, which serve to make larger amounts of food available to a group. There is a large body of ethnographic data which suggests that this is not the case.

Carneiro (1957) in his study of the Kuikuru, who are horticulturalists, demonstrated that these people were capable of producing several times the amount of food they did. A small increment in the amount of time devoted to planting and harvesting would have brought about substantial increases in the available food, yet the Kuikuru chose not to do this. Enough food was produced to meet local demands, and it was at that point that production stopped. Equilibrium had been reached, and neither population nor production increased.

In writing about the Southeastern United States, Caldwell concerned himself with the question of why no effective early prehistoric agriculture was developed in the region. He concluded:

We have suggested that so many natural foods were available that to place any reliance on cultivation . . . might have seemed risky or irrelevant. The hunting-gathering pattern was developed to a peak of efficiency and jelled,

so to speak, in the very heart of eastern cultures. (1958:72)

If we recognize that an equilibrium system can be established so that populations are homeostatically regulated below the carrying capacity of the local food supply, it follows that there is no necessary adaptive pressure continually favoring means of increasing the food supply. The question to be asked then is not why agricultural and food storage techniques were not developed everywhere, but why they were developed at all. Under what set of conditions does increasing the supply of available food have adaptive advantage?

The second corollary to be examined concerns leisure time: *It is only when man is freed from preoccupation with the food quest that he has time to elaborate culture.* A fairly representative statement of this corollary has been made by Childe (1951:61) and is cited above. Also, Braidwood writes:

Proper village life now came into being, and with it a completely new kind of technology. This latter depends on the fact that time now became available for pursuits other than that of simply collecting food. (Braidwood and Braidwood 1950:189)

Braidwood reiterates the same argument in more detail in another place (1963:121–22). The view of the hunter constantly involved in scrounging a bare subsistence and existing on the brink of starvation has recently received some rather pointed comments by Sahlins:

Almost totally committed to the argument that life was hard in the Paleolithic, our text books compete to convey a sense of impending doom, leaving the student to wonder not only how hunters managed to make a living but whether, after all, this is living. The spectre of starvation stalks the stalker in these pages. His technical incompetence is said to enjoin continuous work just to survive, leaving him without respite from the food quest and without the "leisure time to build culture." (1968)

There is abundant data which suggests not only that hunter-gatherers have adequate

248

supplies of food but also that they enjoy quantities of leisure time, much more in fact than do modern industrial or farm workers, or even professors of archaeology. Lee (1965), Bose (1964), McCarthy and Mc-Arthur (1960), and Woodburn (1968) have shown that hunters on a simple level of technology spend a very small percentage of their time obtaining food. On these grounds we can reasonably question the proposition that cultural elaboration is caused by leisure time which is available for the first time to agriculturalists.

In rejecting the assumption that hunter-gatherer populations are primarily regulated by the available supply of food, we put the problem of the development of new types of subsistence in a different light. As long as one could assume that man was continually trying to increase his food supply, under-standing the "origins of agriculture" simply involved pinpointing those geographic areas where the potential resources were and postu-lating that man would inevitably take ad-vantage of them. With the recognition that equilibrium systems regulate population density below the carrying capacity of an environment, we are forced to look for those conditions which might bring about disequi-librium and bring about selective advantage for increased productivity. According to the arguments developed here, there could be only two such sets of conditions:

1) A change in the physical environment of a population which brings about a reduc-tion in the biotic mass of the region would decrease the amounts of available food. The previous balance between population and standing crop is upset, and more efficient extractive means would be favored. This is essentially the basis for Childe's propinquity theory.

2) Change in the demographic structure of a region which brings about the impinge-ment of one group on the territory of another would also upset an established equilibrium system, and might serve to increase the popu-lation density of a region beyond the carrying capacity of the natural environment. Under these conditions manipulation of the natural environment in order to increase its produc-tivity would be highly advantageous.

The remainder of this paper is devoted to the exploration of this second set of condi-tions. The first step of our analysis is to build models of different types of population sys-tems under different conditions. One such type of system is termed a *closed population system* (Hyrenius 1959:476) in which a steady state is maintained by internal mecha-nisms limiting numbers of offspring at the generational replacement level. Techniques such as abortion, contraception, abstinence, and infanticide serve to lower the birth rate and increase the mortality rate so that a given population would be homeostatically regulated at a given size or density.

The second type of system, the *open popu-lation system,* is one in which size and/or density is maintained by either the budding off of new groups or by the emigration of individuals. This would be an *open system of the donor type*. If the size or density of the system is altered through the introduction of immigrants from other population groups, we have an *open system of the recipient type*.

Given these two types of population sys-tems—closed and open, the latter including two subtypes, recipient and donor—we can begin to analyze differences in the ways in which the two system types can be articulated in a given region.

Closed Systems

We can identify the population of a region as a whole as a closed system, yet find that within the region there would be some vari-ability in optimum group size as a response to geographical differences in the regional distribution of resources. Further, each local group within the region may operate peri-odically as an open system, since we would expect some variability in the degree to which local groups have achieved equilib-rium. There would therefore be some redistribution of population between groups which would promote a more uniform and steady density equilibrium system over the region as a whole.

We would expect selection favoring cultural means of regulating population to occur in situations where the density equilibrium system for the region as a whole was in fact a closed system, and where there were significant imbalances in the losses and recruits for the local subsegments of the regional population. There would be differential selective advantage for cultural regulation of population growth between two closed population systems in different environmental settings if there were discrepancies between the actual birth and death rates on the one hand and the optimal rates for maintaining population size on the other.

Open Systems, Donor Type

We would expect to find this type of population system in areas which are not filled to the point at which density dependent factors are brought into play. The peopling of a new land mass, such as the New World or Australia, would be an example of such a situation in which there would be positive advantage for this type of system.

The rate of expansion of open donor systems into uninhabited territory has been discussed in the literature, and models for this type of expansion have been built (Bartholomew and Birdsell 1953; Birdsell 1957, 1958, 1968; Yengoyan 1960). Birdsell has made two observations which are particularly relevant here. First, the budding off of new groups occurs *before* optimum local population size has been reached (Birdsell 1957: 54). This observation demonstrates the role of emigration in bringing about and maintaining equilibrium and also shows that the unit on which selection for emigration operates is a subunit of the local population, since conditions favoring segmentation appear before the regional population is under pressure from density dependent factors.

Second, the adaptation of any given sociocultural system will determine in part the locus of selection within the social system and the particular selective advantages for different fertility rates. Birdsell writes:

In a population stabilized at the carrying capacity of its given environment, some limitation on procreative activities naturally filter down to the level of the biological family. These may be examined most profitably in terms of the requirements which affect the spacing of the natal survivors. Generalized hunters with their requirements of high mobility present the most exacting model. Australian data indicate that the inability of a mother to carry more than one child at a time together with her female baggage impose the first insurmountable barrier to a large number of children. Strongly reinforced by an equally limiting incapacity to nurse more than one child simultaneously imposes a minimum of a three-year spacing upon children designed for survival. Since human female reproductive physiology does not reliably prevent conception while still nursing, children are frequently conceived and born which cannot be reared. The result is systematic infanticide. (1968)

We have seen that two frequent means of maintaining homeostasis are emigration and cultural regulation of births and deaths. The relative importance to any group of one of these means *vs.* the other will be conditioned by such factors as mobility requirements of the group. Another conditioning factor would be the type of articulation between segments of the population which can directly affect the ease with which budding-off can occur. A third factor would be the degree to which the region as a whole is occupied which would affect the expectations of success in the establishment of daughter communities.

Open Systems, Recipient Type

This type of system could occur under only two sets of conditions; the first would be where there is the expansion of a donor system into an uninhabited region. The frontier of the region would contain a number of population units which could, for a short time, serve as recipient systems. Their change from recipient to donor systems would depend upon the extent to which optimal densities were achieved locally and the frontier continued to advance.

The second set of conditions promoting systems of the recipient type is more relevant to the consideration of early agricultural developments. This is the situation in which two or more different kinds of sociocultural systems occupy adjacent environmental zones. If the adaptation of one sociocultural unit is translatable into the adjacent environmental zone, it may expand into that zone at the expense of resident systems. Cases of this type have been cited by Kaplan (1960) as examples of the Law of Cultural Dominance, and a specific instance referred to by Sahlins are the Tiv and the Nuer (1961). We would expect expansion of the dominant system until the zone to which the system was adapted was occupied; at this juncture there would be selection for increased efficiency of production and/or for increased regulation of the birth rate.

A different kind of situation would obtain in the case of sociocultural systems occupying adjacent zones if the adaptation of the more rapidly growing group is not translatable into the adjacent zone. Population growth within the area occupied by the parent group might well be so great that daughter communities would frequently be forced to reside in an environment which is incompatible with their particular cultural adaptation. There could be a number of effects under these circumstances.

From the standpoint of the populations already in the recipient zone, the intrusion of immigrant groups would disturb the existing density equilibrium system and might raise the population density to the level at which we would expect diminishing food resources. This situation would serve to increase markedly for the recipient groups the pressures favoring means for increasing productivity. The intrusive group, on the other hand, would be forced to make adaptive adjustments to their new environment (for an example of this situation see L. R. Binford 1968b). There would be strong selective pressures favoring the development of more efficient subsistence techniques by both groups.

It should be pointed out, however, that such advantage does not insure that these developments will inevitably occur. In many cases these problems are met by changes which might be called regressive in that the changes in adaptation which occur may be in the direction of less complex cultural forms. Examples of this sort of change can be seen among the hunter-gatherers of the nonriverine tropical forest zones in South America. Steward and Faron write of the Siriono and Guayaki:

These Indians retreated . . . to inaccessible regions where they largely abandoned horticulture to rely on a predominantly hunting and gathering subsistence. Other enclaves of nomads isolated in the tropical forests and interfluvial regions may also have experienced similar deculturation. (1959:378)

Lathrap has offered the possibility that perhaps all of the less sedentary South American groups are "the degraded descendants of peoples who at one time maintained an advanced form of Tropical Forest Culture" (1968).

While in these examples the adaptations along population frontiers were in the direction of less complexity, it is in the context of such situations of stress in environments with plant and animal forms amenable to manipulation that we would expect to find conditions favoring the development of plant and animal domestication. Such situations would be characterized by disequilibrium between population and resources which, in turn, would offer selective advantage to increases in the efficacy of subsistence technology. Rather than seeking the locus for the origins of agriculture in the heart of a "natural habitat zone," we would argue that we must look to those places where a population frontier or adaptive tension zone intersects a "natural habitat zone." This means that archaeological investigations might well concentrate on those areas within the natural habitant zone where there is an archaeologically demonstrated major shift in population density. The presence of such a shift might well indicate a population frontier where rapid evolutionary changes were taking place.

Another archaeological clue to be exploited is the degree to which settlements are characterized by sedentism. The frontier zones would be expected between regions which differed widely in the degree of sedentism practiced by resident groups. In those areas with highly sedentary population, problems of transport of young and belongings would be reduced. Reduced mobility of social units in general and in the daily routines of females in particular would in turn reduce the selective advantages accruing to cultural means of controlling population growth. Therefore, under conditions of increased sedentism we would expect population growth. A consequence of such growth would be the increased relative importance of emigration as a mechanism for maintaining the local group within optimal size and density limits.

Therefore where there is a marked contrast in degree of sedentism between two sociocultural units within a relatively restricted geographical region, there would be a tension zone where emigrant colonies from the more sedentary group would periodically disrupt the density equilibrium balances of the less sedentary group. Under these conditions there would be strong selective pressure favoring the development of more effective means of food production for both groups within this zone of tension. There would also be increasing pressures against immigration, given the failure to develop more effective extractive technologies.

It is proposed here that it was in the selective context outlined above that initial practices of cultivation occurred. Such selective situations would have been the consequence of the increased dependence on aquatic resources during the terminal and immediately post-Pleistocene period. Not all portions of rivers and shorelines favor the harvesting of fish, molluscs, and migratory fowl; it is with the systematic dependence on just these resources that we find archaeological remains indicating a higher degree of sedentism in both the Archaic of the New World and the terminal Paleolithic and Mesolithic of the Old World. This hypothesis is lent strong support by the fact that it is also in the terminal Paleolithic-Mesolithic and Archaic that we find, associated with increased sedentism, evidence for marked population growth and for the development of food storage techniques, the latter being functionally linked to the highly seasonal nature of migratory fowl and anadromous fish exploited as food crops (for an example of the importance of anadromous fish see L. R. Binford 1964a).

Since the systematic exploitation of these food sources (and of markedly seasonally available terrestrial forms as well—for example, reindeer) characterized adaptations of this time range in a wide variety of environments, we would expect that tension zones, with their concomitant selective pressures favoring increased subsistence efficiency, would be widely distributed also. This expectation is in accord with the empirical generalizations that: 1) there were a number of independent loci of the development of cultivation techniques—the Near East, Asia, and the New World—and all the developments of these techniques occur within the time range in question; and 2) these loci were distributed across widely different environmental types—root crops in the tropics and cereals in semiarid lands, for example.

The widespread nature of conditions favoring increased subsistence efficiency also accounts for the rapid transmission and integration of contributing innovations from one cultural system to another. Many authors have cited the rapid "diffusion" of cultural elements as characterizing the immediately post-Pleistocene period.

Finally, in the traditional view the "Neolithic Revolution" is characterized by the appearance of a number of traits which are thought to be linked to the shift to food production. The manufacture of ceramics and textiles, relatively permanent houses, and craft specialization are only a few of those frequently cited (cf. Braidwood 1963:122–23). These traits constitute part of the definition of the "village farming way of life," and the assumption is that they originated in the "nuclear area" from which they spread as a complex, the spread being achieved by diffusion, stimulus diffusion, and/or migration. As more data have been accumulated, it becomes increasingly clear that these traits are not mutually dependent; indeed, it seems to be quite clear that ceramics, for example, were first used in the Old World in coastal Japan (Griffin 1961:92), with a cluster of radiocarbon dates averaging *ca.* 7000 B.C. This is about the same time that effective grain agriculture was initially practiced in the Near East (Mellaart 1961, 1963; Hole 1966; Young and Smith 1966), and the occupations in question have yielded no ceramics. Given our model, such traits insofar as they are functionally linked to sedentism and/or food production would be expected to appear in a variety of regions as the result of numerous independent but parallel inventions.

Further utility for the model presented here can be shown by the degree to which it provides explanatory answers for a series of questions posed by Braidwood and Willey—questions which cannot be satisfactorily answered within the traditional framework.

Why did incipient food production not come earlier? Our only answer at the moment is that culture was not yet ready to achieve it. (Braidwood and Willey 1962:342)

We believe that a more complete answer is possible. The shift to the exploitation of highly seasonal resources such as anadromous fish and migratory fowl did not occur until the close of the Pleistocene. This shift, probably linked to worldwide changes in sea level, with attendant increase in sedentism, established for the first time conditions leading to marked heterogeneity in rates of population growth and structure of the ecological niche of immediately adjacent sociocultural systems. This new set of conditions brought about, in turn, conditions favoring improved subsistence technology. It was not that culture was unready, but rather that the selective conditions favoring such changes had not previously existed.

What were the . . . cultural conditions favoring incipient cultivation or domestication? Certainly there is nothing in the archeological record to indicate that those few instances of cultural build-up and elaboration, as manifested by the varying art styles of the upper paleolithic from western Europe into Siberia . . . provided a favorable ground for incipient food production. On the contrary, those instances of incipient cultivation or domestication of greatest potential are found in contexts of a much less spectacular character. (Braidwood and Willey 1962:343; see also Willey 1966b:141–42)

According to our model, we would *expect* to find the selective situation favoring "incipient cultivation" in "contexts of a much less spectacular character"—in those tension zones where less sedentary populations are being moved in on by daughter groups from more sedentary populations. These are the areas where the development of greater productive means is most advantageous.

The perplexing question of what kinds of natural environmental settings were most propitious for the early development of incipient food production is by no means solved. Nevertheless, the data on hand suggest that generally semiarid regions . . . with adequate but not overabundant collectible food resources were the hearths of the most important beginnings of cultivation and domestication. (Braidwood and Willey 1962:342)

If we look at the semiarid areas where the crops referred to (wheat and barley in the Old World; maize in the New World) were developed, it turns out that they are adjacent to areas which already supported settled (that is, sedentary) villages whose populations depended in large part upon aquatic resources. The Natufian of the Near East (Kenyon 1959; Perrot 1960, 1962) and the coastal settlements of Mexico and Peru (Willey 1966:144; see also Flannery and Coe) are cases in point.

The explanation of the distribution noted above of the hearths of domestication of most economically significant crops within semiarid regions lies in the nature of the seeds produced by the plants in such regions. Seeds of xerophytic plants normally have low moisture requirements and can therefore remain viable without being subject to rots which attack many other kinds of seeds. Their economic value also lies in the fact that semiarid regions are areas with low diversity indices (Odum and Odum 1959: 281), which means that there will typically be many individuals of a given species within a very limited space.

We would like to note in passing that the post hoc evaluation of some "beginnings of cultivation" as "most important" (because of the ultimate economic significance of the crops produced) and the limitation of question-asking to these instances has served to prevent the recognition of the general conditions under which cultivation may have been initiated.

How did the new elements spread into Europe; how shall we conceptualize the nature of the cultural mechanisms of diffusion" and the spread of new "influences" through a vast area of already functioning cultural and environmental adaptations? (Braidwood and Willey 1962:347)

While wheat and barley might have constituted "new influences" in Europe, it has been suggested above that cultivation arose as a response to similar pressures many times and in many places. Given the existence of the selective situation favoring food production and the response to this adaptive situation occurring in a number of places, including Europe, the adoption of easily storable high-yield crops such as wheat and barley becomes readily understandable. However, it is important not to confound the adoption of specific crops with the "spread of the village-farming way of life."

If the model presented here has value above and beyond that of a logical exercise, it must be tested by the formulation of hypotheses and the collection of data. While the outlining of a program of research is beyond the scope of and irrelevant to the aims of this paper, a few predictions follow which, if borne out by field research, would empirically validate some of our assertions.

1) Evidence for the initial domestication of plants and animals in the Near East will come from areas adjacent to those occupied by relatively sedentary forager-fishers. One such area is that adjacent to the Natufian settlements in the Jordan Valley. These settlements have yielded evidence of heavy dependence upon fish and migratory fowl (Perrot 1960:20) and the architecture suggests a sedentary way of life. The areas just beyond these villages would have received "excess" population and would therefore have been areas of disequilibrium in which adaptive change would have been favored. Intermontane valleys and foothills which supported migratory hunters far removed from the kind of villages described above will not yield information on the earliest transition to dependence on food production, regardless of the density of wild ancestors of domesticates.

2) Evidence for independent experimentation leading to the development of agriculture as well as animal domestication will be found in European Russia and south-central Europe. We would expect the relevant areas to be adjacent to those where there was effective exploitation of anadromous fish and migratory fowl. Such areas appear to be the rivers flowing into the Black Sea (Clark 1948b:50).

3) As further research is carried out in Europe, Asia, and the New World, there will be evidence for numerous independent innovations paralleling forms appearing in other areas. Post-Pleistocene adaptations are viewed as the result of the operation of local

254

selective pressures, and the development of food production is one instance of such adaptations. Parallel innovations can be expected where structurally similar ecological niches were occupied, regardless of differences in the general form of the environment.

In conclusion, it is hoped that the theoretical perspective offered here will serve to generate a new series of questions, the answers to which may increase our understanding of the major cultural changes which occurred at the close of the Pleistocene.

Chapter **22** KENT V. FLANNERY

The Ecology of Early Food Production
in Mesopotamia

GREATER MESOPOTAMIA — broadly defined here as the whole area drained by the tributaries of the Shatt al-Arab — has long been the scene of popular interest and scholarly research. In recent years attention has been drawn to the fact that this was one of the few areas in the world where agriculture and animal husbandry seem to have arisen autonomously. A number of excellent cultural-historical reconstructions of the way food production began in the Near East are already available (Braidwood and Howe 1962; Perrot 1962:147), but most of these reconstructions do not deal directly with some of the ecological questions most commonly asked by the interested nonspecialist. This article examines some of those questions.

From the standpoint of agriculture and grazing potential, the area under consideration includes four main environmental zones: the alluvial plain of Mesopotamia proper, the steppeland of Assyria, the woodland belt of the Zagros Mountains, and the edge of the high central plateau of Iran (see Figs. *1* and *2*). The first three of these zones have already been described by Hatt (1959); I have added the high plateau, although it is not

Reprinted from *Science,* vol. 147, 12 March 1965, pp. 1247–55. By permission of the author and the American Association for the Advancement of Science. Copyright 1965 by the American Association for the Advancement of Science. The notes have been renumbered.

actually drained by the Shatt al-Arab system, because its mineral resources figured prominently in the early village period.

1) *The central plateau of Iran.* — Central Iran is an interior drainage basin at altitudes of 900 to 1500 meters, with annual rainfall as low as 100 to 230 millimeters. The basin is filled with sierozem and desert soils, overlain in places by shallow brackish lakes surrounded by salt-crusted flatland. Rugged mountains jut unexpectedly from the plain, some of them ore-bearing; there are veins of copper just east of the prehistoric site of Tepe Sialk, and one of the world's major turquoise sources lies in the northeast corner of the plateau near Meshed. Both turquoise and copper were traded as far away as the Assyrian steppe zone by 6500 B.C. (Hole, Flannery, and Neely 1965).

Herds of gazelle (*Gazella subgutturosa*) and wild ass (*Equus hemionus*) would have been available to hunters in the area, but without irrigation the high plateau is very marginal agricultural land; the only source of hope for the early farmer would have been the alluvial aprons of mountain soil produced where streams break through the Zagros to enter the salt lake basins. Despite the uncertain rainfall, some of these "oasis" locations appear to have been permanently settled by 5500 B.C., especially those near copper sources.

2) *The oak-pistachio woodland belt.* The Zagros Mountains break away from the east-

256

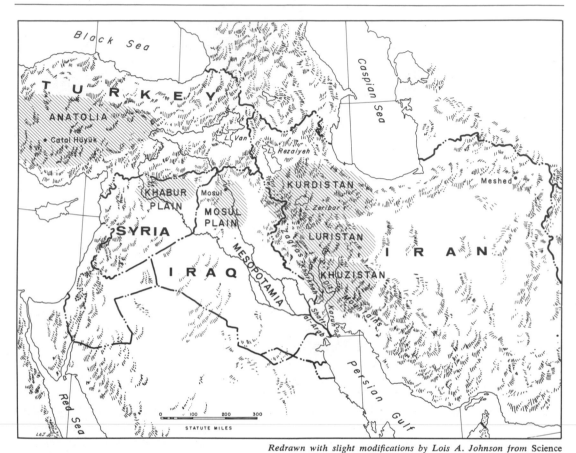

Redrawn with slight modifications by Lois A. Johnson from Science

FIG. 1. *Map of Greater Mesopotamia and adjacent areas today.*

ern edge of the high plateau and descend in tiers toward the Tigris-Euphrates basin. In places the mountains form parallel ridges which are separated by long, narrow, synclinal or anticlinal valleys, frequently poor in surface water; in other areas there are irregular mountain masses bordering wide flat valleys. Acting as aquifers, these porous mountain masses may trap tremendous quantities of winter snow or rain and release it through springs, which in turn feed permanent poplar-bordered streams. At elevations of 600 to 1350 meters there are alluvial valleys of chernozem, chestnut, brown, or reddish-brown soils, with alpine meadows scattered through the surrounding peaks. Summers are warm and dry, winters cool and wet; depending on altitude and topog-

raphy, the annual rainfall varies from 250 to 1000 millimeters, and hillsides have varying densities of oak, maple, juniper, hawthorn, pistachio, and wild pear. On well-watered slopes grow hard-grained annual grasses like wild emmer wheat (*Triticum dicoccoides*), barley (*Hordeum spontaneum*), and oats (*Avena fatua*).

Much of the area is too rugged for large-scale agriculture, but even the narrower and drier valleys have been used for sheep or goat grazing since at least 8500 B.C.; broad valleys with annual rainfall in excess of 300 millimeters have been farmed for at least the same length of time.

3) *The Assyrian steppe.* The Zagros Mountains fall away through a series of foothills and eventually level off onto a steppe

257

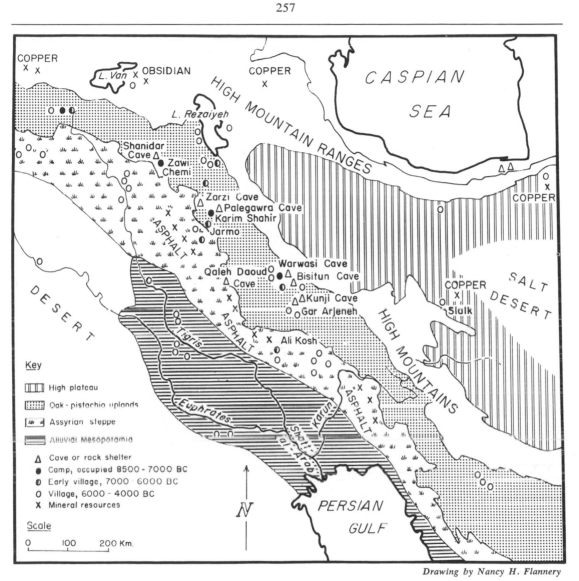

Drawing by Nancy H. Flannery

FIG. 2. *Map of Greater Mesopotamia, showing environmental zones, mineral resources, and archaeological sites. Only sites mentioned in the text are labeled.*

region of great natural winter grassland at elevations of 150 to 300 meters; these plains have reddish-brown or brown prairie soils of high fertility. Here the mountain streams have collected into larger rivers like the Tigris, Karkheh, Diz, and Karun, which flow into the area through erosional valleys and have wide, farmable floodplains. Hot and dry in the summer, the Assyrian steppe is transformed by 250 to 380 millimeters of winter rain into meadows of Bermuda grass, canary grass, and wild narcissus. Herds of gazelle, wild ass, and wild cattle once roamed the plain, and the rivers had carp and catfish. The Assyrian steppe is oil country, and one of its most widely traded commodities in prehistoric time was bitumen or natural asphalt, used for cementing flint tools into their handles.

Some parts of the steppe, too salty for effective agriculture, are used for winter grazing. Other areas are real breadbaskets for

258

winter wheat (like the upper Khabur plain; the area near Mosul, Iraq; or the Khuzistan plain of southwest Iran), and the density of prehistoric villages in these regions is staggering. Adams's comments on northern Khuzistan (1962) – that the adequate rainfall, underlying gravels, and consequent good drainage in this zone facilitated the crucial transition from dry farming to irrigation – may apply to other favored parts of the steppes.

4) *Southern Mesopotamia.* Below 150 meters the Assyrian steppe gives way to the lower drainage of the Tigris, Euphrates, and Karun, as they flow together and empty into the Persian Gulf. Here the annual rainfall is under 250 millimeters (an amount usually inadequate for dry farming) and the grassland is replaced by two kinds of biotopes: alluvial desert and blowing sand dunes on higher ground, and reed-bordered swamps in the low-lying areas. The delta area is a subsiding geosyncline, slowly settling and filling with river alluvium, across which the big rivers run between their own natural levees, flooding and changing courses periodically (Lees and Falcon 1952). Contrary to what was once believed, the area has never been under the waters of the Persian Gulf (at least not since the Pliocene), and in prehistoric times it must have looked much as it does today. It was in this environmental zone that urban life, civilization, and writing began, about 3000 B.C. When permanent settlement began here is undetermined, but villages dating back to 5500 B.C. are known even in the bleak area west of the Euphrates. Surely these villages must have followed the old swamps and watercourses, beyond which agriculture would have been impossible and grazing difficult.

The Local Climatic Sequence

The possibility that the environment in the Near East might have been different during the beginnings of agriculture has intrigued archaeologists for generations. The few prehistoric pollen sequences we have suggest that, although some climatic fluctuations did occur, they were not on a scale capable of creating or destroying the complex of plants and animals that were eventually domesticated. The facts we have are too few to permit us to say dogmatically that climatic change played no role, but it appears that the problem is cultural rather than climatic; the inescapable conclusion is that agriculture began in an area where, then as now, only about 10 percent of the land surface is suitable for dry farming (Cressey 1960:158–60).

One pollen sequence comes from Lake Zeribar in the wooded mountains of western Iran, at an altitude of about 1200 meters. Studies by van Zeist and Wright (1963) show that during the late Pleistocene the area was steppe, characterized by the sagebrush-like *Artemisia,* which implies a cool dry climate. About 11,000 B.C., at the end of the Pleistocene, the area became warmer and the vegetation made the transition to savanna, with scattered oaks and pistachios. The savanna thickened to oak forest about 3500 B.C., either through increased precipitation or through lowered temperature. Cereal-type pollen (possibly wild wheat and barley?) is present throughout the entire sequence, so climatic fluctuation would seem not to have been a determining factor in the beginning of agriculture there.

Six hundred meters lower, in the Zagros Mountains of Iraq, a slightly conflicting pollen story is available from human occupational debris in Shanidar Cave. More striking climatic fluctuations are implied, one of which Solecki interprets as the "shock stimulus" which triggered the beginnings of food production (1963). Actually, however, the late-Pleistocene to early-Recent pollen sequence from Shanidar is not in much conflict with that from Lake Zeribar: at about 10,000 B.C. a "relatively cool climate" changed to "a warmer one similar to the present climate." Cereal pollen is known at least as early as 14,000 B.C., and potential animal domesticates (sheep and goat) are present in the cave debris even at 40,000 B.C.

Neither of these pollen sequences supports the age-old myth that the Near East was once lush and well watered, then suffered from desiccation. Nor do any of the inferred climatic fluctuations imply the sudden, overnight appearance of wheat, barley, sheep, or goats. I do not feel qualified to evaluate the "shock stimulus" theory, but I suspect that, although drastic climatic change explains why certain plants and animals become extinct, it does not explain how or why cultures change.

Preagricultural Subsistence Pattern

Scattered caves, rock shelters, and open-air sites have given us only hints of how man lived in this part of the world before domestication of plants and animals. All appearances are that his way of life conformed to a flexible, "broad-spectrum" collecting pattern, keyed to the seasonal aspects of the wild resources of each environmental zone, with perhaps a certain amount of seasonal migration from zone to zone. The less mobile members of society appear to have collected such resources as snails, turtles, freshwater clams and crabs, and the seeds of wild annuals and perennials, while more mobile members pursued wild ungulates by special techniques, according to the species involved. Although cave remains include fish, birds, and small mammals, the bulk of the meat diet—often more than 90 percent (see, for example, Perkins 1964) came from ungulates, like the wild sheep, goat, ox, pig, wild ass, gazelle, and deer. Note that the first four were early domesticates.

Hunting patterns were influenced by the topography of the region. In the steep, rugged rockslide area around Shanidar Cave, wild goat (*Capra hircus*) was the animal most frequently taken. The goat, a resident of the limestone crags, is difficult to hunt by means of drives; it is best pursued by small groups of agile men who know their country well and are equipped with light projectiles. Rock shelters or caves overlooking broad, flat valleys are usually rich in the bones of the wild ass, a plains-dwelling animal which could best have been hunted by drives or surrounds, then dispatched with a larger weapon, like a thrusting spear. Gazelles and hares are also creatures of the flat valley, while the wild sheep of the Near East (*Ovis orientalis*) frequent rolling, round-top hills and are hunted today by ambush in the brushy stream canyons where they hide during the noon hours. Some of the smaller rock shelters excavated in the Zagros Mountains seem to have been stations or overlooks used mainly for hunting or butchering a single species of ungulate, or two species at most.[1]

In recent years the oak-pistachio uplands, in the 400- to 1000-millimeter rainfall belt at altitudes of 450 to 900 meters, have been singled out as an "optimum" zone which includes all the potential domesticates (Braidwood and Howe 1960). Actually, topography is a much more important ecological factor for wild sheep and goats than either altitude or rainfall; sheep range down to sea level along the Caspian Sea, and up to 2700 meters in the Zagros Mountains, if rolling mountain meadows are available. Goats reach sea level on the foothills flanking the Persian Gulf, and are as much at home on the last rugged sandstone hills separating southwest Iran from southern Mesopotamia (180 meters above sea level) as they are on the 3000-meter crags of the northern Zagros. Pigs range over a wide area, from sea level to timberline, and if we knew more about the ecological requirements of wild cattle we might find their range equally broad.[2] The crucial factor for hunters of wild ungulates, or early herders of semiwild ungulates, would have been the ability to move from upland to lowland as seasonal pasture was available, a pattern known as "transhumance."

Let me give one example. Khuzistan, the Iranian arm of the Assyrian steppe, is lush winter grassland from December to April while many of the mountains to the east are covered with snow. Through late spring and summer the steppe becomes blisteringly hot and dry, while the melting snow on the mountains gives rise to good spring and summer grassland. The Persian herder classifies the steppe as *quishlaq* (winter pasture) and the mountains as *yehlaq* (summer pasture), and he moves his herd from one to the other as the season demands. Prehistoric hunters may have followed game over the same route; and as for prehistoric herders, Adams reminds us (1962): "It is, in fact, erroneous to consider the upper plains as a zone of occupance distinct from the surrounding uplands. Both together constitute a single natural ecosystem, whose seasonal alternation of resources provides as strong an inducement to migratory stock-breeding as to intensive, settled agriculture."

The wild plants of southwestern Asia have much the same seasonal aspect. MacNeish's work (1964) in the New World has shown that a long period of intensive plant collecting preceded agriculture there; archaeologists have long assumed that this was the case in the Near East, but preserved plant remains were not available to tell us which specific plants were used in the preagricultural era. New light was thrown on the problem in 1963 by a collection of some 10,000 carbonized seeds from basal levels at the site of Ali Kosh in lowland southwestern Iran.[3] The area, a part of the Assyrian steppe, lies outside the range of wild wheat and barley, but locally available plants were intensively collected; the most common were wild alfalfa (*Medicago*) and the tiny-seeded wild legumes *Astragalus* and *Trigonella*, as well as fruits like the wild caper (*Capparis*), used today mainly as a condiment. These data indicate that intensive plant collecting may have been the pattern everywhere in southwest Asia, not merely at the altitude where wild wheat grows best. Moreover, the fact that *Astragalus* and *Trigonella* occur in the mountains as well as the lowlands suggests that prehistoric collectors could have harvested one crop on the Assyrian steppe in March, moved up to 600 meters for a harvest in April or May, and arrived at 1500 meters for another harvest in June or July. Somewhere between 600 and 1200 meters these migrant collectors could have harvested

the seeds of the annual grasses ancestral to domestic wheat, barley, and oats. These cereals, which are dependent on annual rainfall of 400 to 750 millimeters, do not range down to the Assyrian steppe today, although they are available over a surprisingly wide area; according to Helbaek (1960*a*), wild barley "grows in the mountain forest, on the coastal plain, in the shade of rock outcrops in semidesert areas, and as a weed in the fields of every conceivable cultivated crop" from Morocco to Turkestan.

Other plants useful to the collector—and eventually, in some cases, to the primitive cultivator—were ryegrass (*Lolium*), *Aegilops* grass, wild flax (*Linum bienne*), and large-seeded wild legumes like lentil, vetch, vetchling, chick pea, and *Prosopis* (a relative of mesquite). The lowlands had dates; the foothills had acorns, almonds, and pistachios; and the northern mountains had grapes, apples, and pears.

Most of the important species occurred in more than one zone, and their months of availability were slightly different at different altitudes—key factors from the standpoint of human ecology. An incredibly varied fare was available to the hunter-collector who knew which plants and animals were available in each season in each environmental zone; which niche or "microenvironment" the species was concentrated in, such as hillside, cliff, or stream plain; which species could be stored best, and which it was most practical to hunt or collect. From 40,000 to 10,000 B.C., man worked out a pattern for exploiting the natural resources of this part of the world, and I suspect that this preagricultural pattern had more to do with the beginnings of food production than any climatic "shock stimulus."

Beginnings of Food Production

Leslie White (1959:283–84) reminds us that "we are not to think of the origin of agriculture as due to the chance discovery that seeds thrown away from a meal subsequently sprouted. Mankind knew all this and more for tens of thousands of years before cultivation of plants began." The cultivation of plants required no new facts or knowledge, but was simply a new kind of relationship between man and the plants with which he was most familiar.

One striking aspect of the late preagricultural pattern in the Greater Mesopotamian area was the trading of obsidian from its source in central and eastern Turkey to cave sites in the central Zagros, such as Zarzi and Shanidar (Braidwood and Howe 1960; Solecki 1963). Natural asphalt was traded in the opposite direction, up from the tar pits of the Assyrian steppe to campsites in the mountains, wherever flints had to be hafted. By 7000 B.C., handfuls of emmer wheat from the oak-pistachio belt had reached the lowland steppe of Khuzistan (Hole, Flannery, and Neely 1965). Typical of the prehistoric Near Easterner was this penchant for moving commodities from niche to niche within environmental zones, and even from zone to zone.

It has been argued that the last millennia of the preagricultural era were a time of "settling in" to one's area, of increasing intensification and regionalization of the exploitation of natural resources (Braidwood and Howe 1960:180). This is indeed reflected in the flint tools, but such "regional specialization" may not be the essential trend which led to food production. From the standpoint of human ecology, the single most important factor may have been the establishment of the above-mentioned pattern of interchange of resources between groups exploiting contrasting environmental situations —a kind of primitive redistribution system. It was this pattern that set the stage for the removal of certain key species of edible grasses from the niches in which they were indigenous, and their transferral to niches to which they were foreign.

With the wisdom of hindsight we can see that, when the first seeds had been planted, the trend from "food collecting" to "food producing" was under way. But from an ecological standpoint the important point is not

that man planted wheat but that he i) moved it to niches to which it was not adapted, ii) removed certain pressures of natural selection, which allowed more deviants from the normal phenotype to survive, and iii) eventually selected for characters not beneficial under conditions of natural selection.

All that the "settling in" process did for the prehistoric collector was to teach him that wild wheat grew from seeds that fell to the ground in July, sprouted on the mountain talus in February, and would be available to him in usable form if he arrived for a harvest in May. His access to those mature seeds put him in a good position to bargain with the goat-hunters in the mountain meadow above him. He may have viewed the first planting of seeds merely as the transfer of a useful wild grass from a niche that was hard to reach—like the talus below a limestone cliff—to an accessible niche, like the disturbed soil around his camp on a nearby stream terrace. Happily for man, wild wheat and barley both grow well on disturbed soils; they will sprout on the back-dirt pile of an archeological excavation, and they probably did equally well on the midden outside a prehistoric camp (Helback 1960a). It is obvious from the rapid spread of agriculture in the Mesopotamian area that they grew as readily on the midden outside the forager's winter camp at 180 meters as they did in his summer camp at 900 meters, in the "optimum" zone.

Viewed in these terms the advent of cultivation may have been a rather undramatic event, and the concept of "incipient cultivation" (Braidwood and Howe 1960) becomes rather hard to define. Was it a fumbling attempt at cultivation, or only the intensification of an already existent system of interregional exchange?

Biological Obstacles to Early Food Production

The transfer of species from habitat to habitat made the products of all zones available to all people; but it was a process not

262

without difficulty, since some of the plant and animal species involved had not yet developed the most tractable or productive phenotypes, from man's point of view.

Some of the biological obstacles faced by early agriculturalists were as follows.

1) The difficulty of harvesting wild, brittle-rachis grains. One adaptive mechanism for seed dispersal in wild wheat and barley is a brittle rachis or axis which holds the seeds together in the mature head of grain. When a dry, ripe head of wild barley is struck by a twig or a gust of wind, the rachis disintegrates and the seeds are spread far and wide.[4] The disadvantages of this mechanism for the prehistoric collector are obvious: the slightest tug on the stem of the plant or the slightest blow with a flint sickle might send the seeds scattering in every direction.

2) The difficulty of removing the grain from its husk. Even after a successful harvest, the prehistoric collector's troubles were not over. Primitive grains like emmer or einkorn wheat have a tough husk, or glume, which holds each kernel in a stubborn grip long after the brittle rachis has disintegrated. Even vigorous threshing will usually not release these primitive grains from the glume so that they can be eaten.

3) The difficulty of farming in the niche to which the grain was adapted. Both wild wheat and barley are grasses of hillsides and slopes, and they usually do not occur on the flat stream floodplains, where it would have been most convenient for prehistoric man to farm. The deep alluvial soils in the valley centers, prime areas from an agricultural standpoint, were already occupied by competing grasses and wild legumes.

Research on archaeological grain remains by Danish botanist Hans Helbaek has shown us some of the ways in which early farmers either consciously or unconsciously overcame these three obstacles.

1) Selection for tough-rachis grains. Within the gene pool of wild wheat and barley were variants whose rachis was tough enough so that it did not shatter on contact.

Normally these variants would have left few descendents, because of the inadequacy of their seed-dispersal mechanism. When man harvested with sickles or flails, however, he automatically selected for the tough-rachis grains because their heads stayed intact despite the rough treatment of the harvest. When seeds from the harvest were planted, the next generation of plants contained an abnormally high proportion of tough-rachis individuals, and each successive generation reinforced the trend.

2) The development of techniques for removing the seeds from their glumes. Sometime before 7000 B.C. man discovered that by roasting the grain he had collected he could render the glumes so dry and brittle that they could be crushed by abrasion; roasting, moreover, killed the wheat or barley germ so that it would not sprout, and the grain could be stored even through the winter rainy season. Many of the preceramic villages excavated throughout the Near East contain clay ovens appropriate for roasting grain in this manner, and nearly all seem to have stone grinding slabs of one kind or another on which the dry grain could be abraded out of its glume. Further grinding resulted in "groats," or coarse grits of grain which could be cooked up into a mush or gruel. (By and large, the tough-glumed primitive grains were unsuitable for bread-making.)

3) Actual genetic change in the grain species themselves, resulting in new strains. Because early cultivated grain was somewhat shielded by man from the natural selection pressures to which uncultivated grain was subjected, the chance that random mutants would survive was much greater. One of the first mutations that occurred, apparently, was a change from the standard adhering-glume kernel to a "naked" kernel which could be easily freed by threshing. According to Stubbe (1959), a single gene controls the difference between "hulled" and "naked" barley, and when a mutation took place at that locus, sometime before 7000 B.C., free-

threshing barley was born. A second genetic change was that which transformed standard wild barley (*Hordeum spontaneum*), which has only two fertile kernel rows, into mutant barley with six fertile rows (*Hordeum hexastichum*). Helbaek, who has actually produced the six-row mutant in his laboratory by subjecting wild two-row barley to x-rays (Helbaek 1960*b*), feels that ecological factors probably determined the early distribution of these two strains: two-row barley is adapted to the fairly late (April and May) rainfall of the cool Zagros Mountain uplands, while mutant six-row barley may be more successfully adapted to much drier spring weather and the irrigation farming of the Mesopotamian plain (Helbaek 1960*a*). Archaeological remains tend to support this. The two-row form seems to be the only one known so far from the highlands before 5000 B.C., while six-row barley is known from lowland Khuzistan by 6000 B.C.; the two-row strain does not seem to have caught on in the lowlands, possibly because it was poorly adapted to the climate there. Present data, in fact, suggest that although the cool uplands probably contributed the original ancestor (two-row hulled barley) it may have been the lowland ecology which stabilized the important "naked" and "six-row" strains (see Fig. 3).

Another important early genetic change was polyploidy, an actual increase in the chromosome number, which produced new strains of wheat. Wild emmer wheat (*Triticum dicoccoides*) is tetraploid—that is, it contains 4 × 7 chromosomes and has tough glumes enclosing the kernels. A native annual grass of well-watered mountains, it prefers the 400- to 750-millimeter rainfall zone, from Palestine and Syria to the Zagros Mountains of Iran and Iraq. By 6000 B.C., however, on the Anatolian plateau of central Turkey, a mutant had been produced which was free-threshing: this was hexaploid wheat (*Triticum aestivum*), with 6 × 7 chromosomes.[5] Such polyploid strains, together with irrigation, were instrumental in the spread of

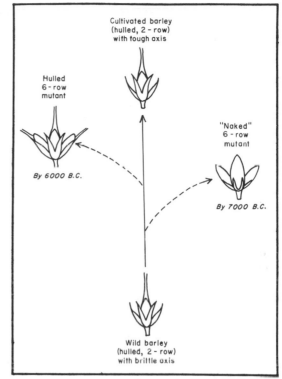

FIG. 3. *Simplified diagrams of barley spikelets, showing some of the changes which took place after domestication. Data courtesy of Helbaek (see text).*

free-threshing wheat throughout southwest Asia.

Mutations and changes in gene frequency also played a role in the establishment of races of domestic animals, and once again there were biological obstacles to be overcome by early herders. Some of the adaptive and nonadaptive changes which took place were as follows.

1) A change in the sex and age ratios within the captive population. If early herds of domesticated sheep or goats were small, as we assume they were, how did the animals avoid being eaten during the winter and survive until the spring lambing season? Work by Charles A. Reed (1960) and Dexter Perkins (1964) on archaeological bones from early villages in Kurdistan suggests that some kind of conservation may have been prac-

264

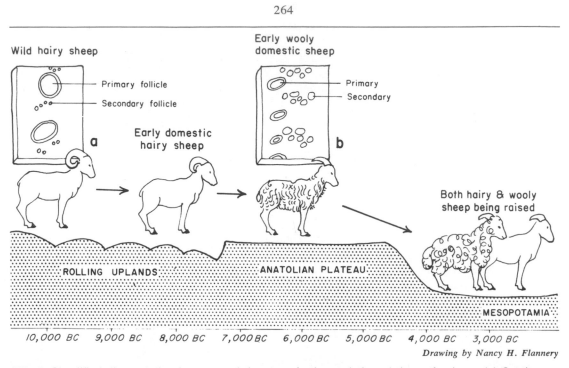

FIG. 4. *Simplified diagram showing some of the steps in the evolution of domestic sheep. (a) Section, as seen through a microscope, of skin of wild sheep, showing the arrangement of primary (hair) and secondary (wool) follicles; (b) section, similarly enlarged, of skin of domestic sheep, showing the changed relationship and the change in the size of follicles that accompanied the development of wool. [After Ryder (1958), see text]*

ticed. Perkins notes that the proportion of immature sheep relative to adult sheep at Zawi Chemi, Iraq, was far higher than that in any normal wild herd, an observation from which he infers domestication (see also Dyson 1953). Evidently the young animals were eaten, while the older breeding stock was saved. The practice was much the same at the village of Jarmo, where Reed noted a high proportion of butchered young males, as if the females were being held back for breeding. Such practices would have resulted in an abnormally high proportion of adult females in the herd, and consequently in milk surpluses in late winter and early spring. Although wild sheep and goats produce very little milk in comparison to today's domestic breeds, such seasonal surpluses may eventually have been exploited by early herders. Today, milk, yogurt, and cheese are part of the whole trading complex of southwest Asian pastoralists.

2) Changes leading to wool production. Wild sheep (*Ovis orientalis*) have a coat like a deer or gazelle, and are no woolier than the latter. Microscopic examination of their skin reveals two kinds of follicles: "primaries," or hair follicles which produce the visible coat, and "secondaries," which produce the hidden, wooly underfur. In the skin of wild *Ovis* the secondary follicles lie intermingled with the primaries in groups of three to five. After domestication, genetic changes moved the secondaries out to the side, away from the primaries, and greatly increased their numbers; while wild strains of sheep or goat may have a ratio of only two to four secondaries for each primary, the ratio may be as high as seven to one in fine Merino sheep. The wool of the domestic sheep grows from these dense clusters of secondary follicles (Ryder 1958). Wool may already have been spun as early as 6000 B.C. at Catal Hüyük in Anatolia (Mellaart 1964). Both

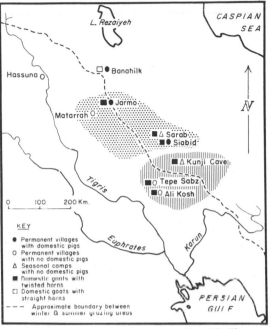

Drawing by Nancy H. Flannery

FIG. 5. *Map of Greater Mesopotamia, showing areas where transhumance is believed to have been of importance in prehistoric times. Ceramic objects from sites in the stippled area (Jarmo, Sarab, Matarrah) all have one set of traits; those from sites in the hachured area (Kunji, Ali Kosh, Tepe Sabz) all have another set. The rapid spread of the twisted-horn goat in both areas suggests that flocks may have been moved from one elevation to another seasonally; so does the almost complete absence of the domestic pig, an animal unsuitable for transhumant herding. In the summer grazing area (northeast of the dashed line), many sites appear to be seasonal shepherds' camps in caves or on valley floors. These camps seem to have stronger ties, from the standpoint of traits of ceramic objects, with sites in the adjacent winter grazing area (southwest of the dashed line) than with other sites in their own environmental zone (see text).*

"hairy" and "wooly" sheep were known by 3000 B.C. in Mesopotamia (Hilzheimer 1941), and the now-famous Dead Sea Scrolls, dating to the time of Christ, have been shown by Ryder (1958) to have been written on parchment made both from hairy and from wooly sheep (see Fig. 4).

3) Nonadaptive genetic changes, such as the twisted horns of domestic goats. One of the most interesting (if poorly understood)

changes which followed domestication was one affecting the horns of the goat (*Capra hircus*). The wild goat of the Near East has scimitar-shaped horns whose bony cores are quadrangular or diamond-shaped in cross section near the skull. Sites dating from 8500 to 7000 B.C. are known where goat domestication is inferred from the ratio of immature animals to adult animals, but no changes in the cross section of the horn during this period are noted. By 6500 B.C., from the Jordan Valley to the Zagros Mountains, there are scattered occurrences of goats whose horn cores show a flattening of the medial surface, and thus a triangular or almond-shaped cross section. By 6000 B.C. in the Mesopotamian area, from the Assyrian steppe to the oak-pistachio woodlands, a new type of horn core makes its appearance: the core is medially flattened in section, and it also shows signs of a corkscrew twist like that of the modern domestic goat in southwest Asia. The irregular geographic distribution of the trait suggests that it was strongest in the Iran-Iraq area, occurring only sporadically elsewhere before 4500 B.C., even at 3500 B.C. not all sites in the Palestinian area show goats of a uniformly "twisted horn" type (Reed 1960). Possibly its rapid spread in the Zagros was due to transhumant herding (see Fig. 5).

4) The problem of pig domestication. One of the questions most frequently asked is why the pig was domesticated at 6000 B.C. in some parts of the Near East, like the Zagros Mountain valleys (Reed 1961:32), but was apparently never domesticated in prehistoric time in other areas, such as the Khuzistan steppe (Hole, Flannery, and Neely 1965). The most common answer is that this was the result of religious or dietary laws; but in fact, the reasons may be ecological. According to Krader (1955:315), "the disappearance of the pig from Central Asia is not the clear-cut case of religious determination that might be supposed. The pig is not a species suitable to pastoral nomadism . . . it is nomadism with its mastery of the steppe ecology and movements of herds and herdsmen which is the decisive

factor in the disappearance of pigs from this part of the world." Figure 5 shows the sites where domestic pigs are known either to have been, or not to have been, present in the Mesopotamian area between 6000 and 5000 B.C. Since pigs seem to be incompatible with transhumant herding, the areas where they do *not* occur may be those where there was greatest reliance on seasonal movement of flocks.

Effects on Human Life and Cultural Ecology

In the past it has been customary to treat each of the Mesopotamian environmental zones as if it were a "cultural and natural area"—a region characterized by a certain flora and fauna and exploited by a certain group of inhabitants who knew it particularly well.[6] There are hints that such a situation obtained in Palestine, for there Perrot (1962: 162) has distinguished two archaeological traditions, one adapted to the moist Mediterranean side of the mountains, the other adapted to the arid eastern foothills.

In 1956 Fredrik Barth pointed out that the "cultural and natural area" concept did not fit northern Pakistan, and there are a considerable number of data to suggest that it does not fit the Mesopotamian area at 6000 B.C. either. Barth showed that a single valley system might be occupied by three distinct ethnic groups, each of which occupied only a portion of the total resources, leaving the rest open for other groups to exploit. The first group consists of sedentary agriculturalists who practice intensive irrigation agriculture on the river floodplain, growing two crops a year and never moving to a higher elevation. A second group raises one crop a year in this same floodplain area, but its members also migrate annually with their flocks up through five seasonal campsites to high mountain meadows. Still a third group is made up of pastoral nomads who are assimilated into the society of the intensive agriculturalists as a special "herder caste,"

contributing milk and meat in exchange for grain; they are permitted to use prime grazing land not needed by the sedentary farmers (Barth 1956).

At 6000 B.C. there are striking contrasts between archaeological sites in the oak-pistachio belt and the Assyrian steppe of the Greater Mesopotamian area which suggest Barth's model. Jarmo, at an elevation of 750 meters in the oak woodlands, was a village of permanent, mud-walled houses with courtyards and ovens; Tepe Sarab, at an elevation of 1260 meters, has no obvious houses, and only the kind of ashy refuse beds that might occur around a tent camp. The pottery objects at the two sites are nearly identical, but Jarmo has goats, sheep, and even domestic pigs, along with two strains of wheat and one of barley, whereas Tepe Sarab has only goats and sheep, and no grinding stones suggestive of local agriculture. The ages of the domestic goats show that Tepe Sarab was occupied in late winter or early spring. In this case we suspect that the camp at 1260 meters may have been occupied by seasonal herders who obtained their grain from more permanent farming villages at 750 meters (Braidwood and Howe 1962; Flannery 1962: 7–17; Reed 1963).

From the Assyrian steppe of Khuzistan, southwestern Iran, come further data of the same type. From 7000 to 6500 B.C. at the site of Ali Kosh, goat-grazing and tiny amounts of agriculture supplemented the collection of wild legumes: from 6500 to 6000 B.C. the growing of wheat and barley greatly increased at the expense of wild plants. At 6000 B.C. a striking expansion of sheep and goat grazing occurred, and amounts of wild wheat and wild barley lessened, while the pod-bearing perennial *Prosopis* came to the fore (Hole, Flannery, and Neely 1965) We doubt that this was a simple case of abandonment of agriculture; *Prosopis*, Helbaek reminds us, is intimately associated with herding peoples in southwest Asia, and the increase in domestic sheep and goats suggests that this was a time when, in conformity with Barth's ecological model, Ali Kosh became primarily a "herding village" coexisting a symbiotic framework with "farming villages" in adjacent areas.

Finally, we have the occurrences of typical Khuzistan pottery at a shepherds' camp in Kunji Cave, 1200 meters up, in the mountains of western Iran.[7] This part of Luristan seems to have stronger cultural ties with lowland Khuzistan than with other mountain areas in the same environmental zone, suggesting that at 6000 B.C. some valleys in Luristan were summer grazing land for herds that wintered in Khuzistan.

Summary and Speculation

The food-producing revolution in southwestern Asia is here viewed not as the brilliant invention of one group or the product of a single environmental zone, but as the result of a long process of changing ecological relationships between groups of men (living at varying altitudes and in different environmental settings) and the locally available plants and animals which they had been exploiting on a shifting, seasonal basis. In the course of making available to all groups the natural resources of every environmental zone, man had to remove from their natural contexts a number of hard-grained grasses and several species of ungulates. These species, as well as obsidian and native copper, were transported far from the biotopes or "niches" in which they had been at home. Shielded from natural selection by man, these small breeding populations underwent genetic change in the environment to which they had been transplanted, and favorable changes were emphasized by the practices of the early planter or herder.

Successful cultivation seems to have intensified exchanges of natural resources and cultivars between groups, and there are hints that the diversity of environments made village specialization in certain commodities the best means of adapting to the area. We have suggestive evidence that by 4000 B.C. the redistributive economy had produced regional temple-and-market towns which regulated the produce of a symbiotic network of agriculturists engaged in intensive irrigation, transhumant herders, and perhaps even traders who dealt in obsidian, copper, salt, asphalt, fish, and regional fruits (Hole, Flannery, and Neely 1965).

NOTES

1. The foregoing discussion is based in part on published studies of faunas from the sites of Shanidar Cave and Zawi Chemi (Perkins 1964), Zarzi Cave, and Palegawra Cave, all in Iraq (for a summary, see Braidwood and Howe 1960:169–70), and Bisitun Cave in Iran (see Coon 1951). It is based, also, on personal examination of unpublished faunal collections from Karim Shahir in Iraq (Braidwood and Howe 1960) and from the following Iranian sites: Qaleh Daoud Cave (see Hole 1962), Warwasi Rock Shelter (see Braidwood and Howe 1962:135) and Kunji Cave and Gar Arjeneh Rock Shelter (F. Hole and K. Flannery, unpublished data).

2. For a good summary of the differences in ecology between sheep and goat, see Perkins 1959. Perkins explains the skeletal differences, especially differences in metapodial length, which reflect the somewhat different habitats occupied by *Ovis* and *Capra*.

3. The plants were identified by Dr. Hans Helbaek of the Danish National Museum (see Hole, Flannery and Neely 1965:106).

4. This, and all subsequent discussion of the ecology of the early cereals, is based on personal communications from Hans Helbaek or on one of the following articles by Dr. Helbaek: 1960*a*, 1960*b*, 1963.

5. See note 4 above.

6. For the origins of the "cultural and natural area" hypothesis, see Kroeber 1939.

7. F. Hole (of Rice University) and I made a test excavation of Kunji Cave in 1963; the data have not been published.

Carrying Capacity and Dynamic Equilibrium in the Prehistoric Southwest

THIS ESSAY is one specific result of an examination of the implications of a general model of carrying capacity as a dynamic equilibrium system (Zubrow 1969). The model is used to account for archaeological data from the Hay Hollow Valley in eastern Arizona. Before considering the model, I wish to make my general assumption base explicit. First, I am assuming the validity of a neo-Malthusian approach. Malthus's major argument, that food limits population, which first appeared in the *Essay on Population*, has been encapsulated by an anonymous writer in the following verse.

> To get land's fruit in quantity,
> Takes jolts of labor ever more,
> Hence food will grow like one, two, three,
> While numbers grow like one, two, four.
> (Samuelson 1961:16)

Since its original publication in 1798, there have been many criticisms of the "Essay." First and most trivial, his ratios have been shown to be in error. Second, Malthus hypothesized that each advance in technology is absorbed by an increase in population

Reproduced by permission of the Society for American Archaeology from *American Antiquity*, vol. 36, no. 2, 1971, pp. 127–38. The bibliographical references have been placed in the general bibliography for this volume. This research was made possible by grants GS-1910 and GS-2381 of the National Science Foundation and assistance from the Field Museum of Natural History and the University of Arizona.

which prevents any increase in the standard of living. This was disproved by the Industrial Revolution. As an empirical generalization it was valid for most of the preindustrial world prior to 1760. However, as a general law, it fell due to the fallacious assumption that increases in production could never exceed increases in population.

The neo-Malthusians such as Boulding and Peacock feel that the general Malthusian model applies where the Industrial Revolution has not changed the potential for production by several quantum leaps. In these economies which are labor intensive, population is a major factor in determining the production function and the law of diminishing returns eventually limits production. Although Malthus's concept of a stable standard of living is rejected, the conclusion that population growth is a correlate of technological change is viable. Thus, in the neo-Malthusian model the ratios are replaced by population pressure in a series of organized, spatially differentiated ecosystems, each with its own level of consumption expectations based on food chains with internal and external ecological connections.

My second assumption is that it is possible to measure prehistoric populations and resources through indirect indices. Archaeological surveys have traditionally served two functions. First, they provide the archaeologist with an approximation of the unexcavated material remains. Second, they may be used to provide an estimate of population. It is a crude estimate, perhaps, of absolute population but it provides a better estimate of relative population size. The more intensively an area is surveyed and the more systematically it is sampled, the more refined is the estimate. An effective indirect index for monitoring the changes in prehistoric resource systems is pollen analysis which reflects vegetation changes.

With this background, one may turn to the model of carrying capacity as a dynamic equilibrium system. Carrying capacity is the maximum number of organisms or amounts of biomass which can maintain itself indefinitely in an area, in other words, a homeostatic equilibrium point. It is a homeostatic equilibrium in that there is a tendency toward the maintenance of a state of balance between opposite forces or processes which result in a diminishing net change or a stable constant. It is dynamic in that the point at which the state of balance exists may change over time and space.

What are the two opposing forces which determine the equilibrium? On the one hand, Liebig's extended law (Broughey 1968:2) states population size is determined by maxima and minima of specific resources. On the other hand, the "prime dynamic mover" appears to be reproduction. A population will tend to keep reproducing and growing in size until an ultimate limit is reached which is determined by the supply of nutrients and energy. When there is a change in the supply of nutrients and energy, a change in the carrying capacity results, and there is a consequence growth or decrease of the biomass until a new equilibrium is reached. Letter A of Fig. *1* denotes an equilibrium point which has been defined above as carrying capacity. If a change in the resource curves takes place from Resource 1 to Resource 2, there results a disequilibrium with resources being greater than population. One would expect the biomass or population to grow along the population curve until a new equilibrium point B is reached. Similarly, one may pre-

dict what would happen in the other cases— a decrease in the resource curve or an increase or decrease in the population curve.

Neo-Malthusian models such as the one just described have both advantages and disadvantages. The primary advantages are first, given the initial conditions one may predict the expected consequences, and second, one may quantify both the initial conditions and the expected results. The primary disadvantage of this type of neo-Malthusian model building is that contemporary demographic and ecological data do not lend themselves to testing the model. This is because the time span for which data exist is too short in relation to long term ecological processes. Secondarily, modern technological development with its concomitant diversity of resources, complex trade patterns, and ease of mobility, complicate the data to the point where it is necessary to use factor and discriminant analyses to remove the masking data patterns and variables.

Archaeology is thus in a unique position to evaluate this type of model. Its data span long time periods and some of the societies it considers have not developed the complex resource networks, trade systems, and technologies which distinguish modern industrial nation states. As presented initially the model is oversimplified. It does not take into account the spatial differentiation or temporal change in resource patterns. First, consider the implications of the spatial differentiation of resources holding the temporal changes in the resource base constant. One may imagine a complex heterogeneous resource pattern as exemplified by Fig. *2* where there are four distinct resources. If this complex pattern is divided into a set of homogeneous resource spaces (which I shall call for the rest of this essay resource zones), it will be easier to build the more generalized model. The simplified model presented in Fig. *1* accounts for one resource zone. In order to account for the heterogeneous pattern, one needs only to sum the models of the individual resource zones. This is exemplified in Fig. *2* where the

270

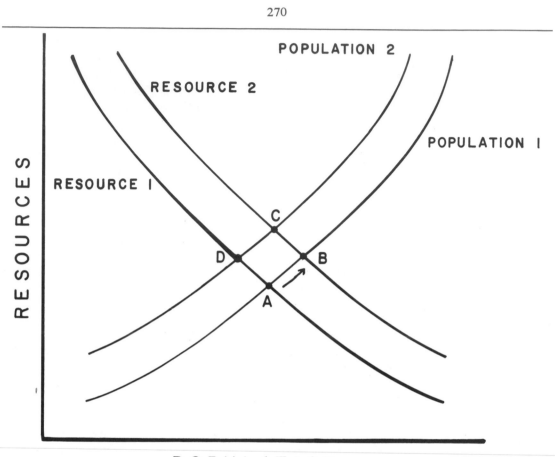

FIG. 1. *Carrying capacity as a dynamic equilibrium system. Note: Resource 1 and resource 2 refer to iso-resource curves (or resource levels) in which resources plus population equal an energy or biomass constant.*

Drawing by Patricia Mail

total carrying capacity for the heterogeneous area will be the sum of the carrying capacities of the individual resource zones. This is denoted on the figure by E being equal to A + B + C + D.

Now adding the temporal variable one may note that external conditions such as climate, may cause different resource curves to exist at different points in the chronology. Thus, over time there might be changes in the individual resource zone curves, as well as in the summation curves. These changes need not be uniform.

With this more or less general introduction to the model, one may turn to the specific problem. It has often been noted that the distribution of settlements follows a definite pattern through time which is partially dependent upon the spatial distribution of resources (Kroeber 1939; Haggett 1966). The hypothesis to be examined is that the development of populations in marginal resource zones is a function of optimal zone exploitation. In order to operationalize this hypothesis in terms of the model, one must set up a series of resource zones with consecutively diminishing resource curves as in Fig. *3*.

It is easy to define at this point what is meant by optimal and marginal resource zones. Optimal means the resource zone with the highest resource curve. All the other

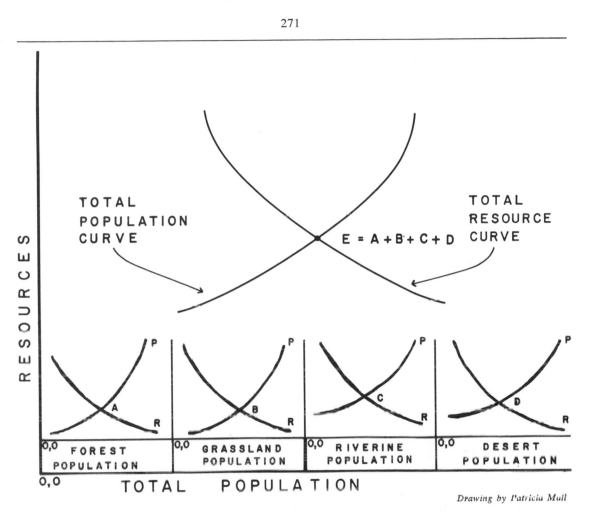

Drawing by Patricia Mull

FIG. 2. *Heterogeneous resource model. The summation of homogeneous resource zones.*

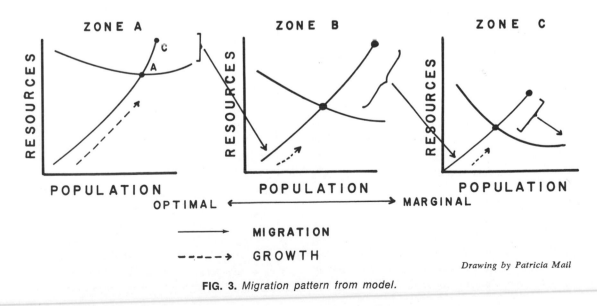

Drawing by Patricia Mail

FIG. 3. *Migration pattern from model.*

272

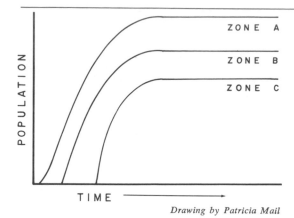

FIG. 4. *Population predictions by zones from heterogeneous model without change in resource curves.*

zones are marginal. The lower the resource curve the more marginal the resource zone. One may predict on the basis of the model what will happen as a population starts to grow in the optimal resource zone (Fig. *3*). If the population is less than the carrying capacity, it will increase until it reaches the carrying capacity. If the population overshoots the carrying capacity as a result of simple population growth or as a result of population growth combined with immigration then the population surplus (the distance C to A in Fig. *3*) has two choices— gradual extinction or out-migration of the surplus to the next zone which is more marginal. In the more marginal zone the process would repeat itself. But each time one moves from a zone to a more marginal zone it takes less population to reach carrying capacity. If there is no change in the resource curves over time one would expect the following sequence of events. First, a population filling up the optimal zone to carrying capacity, then a little later a second zone filling up to a smaller carrying capacity, and then a little later a third zone filling up to a smaller carrying capacity, etc. There are indications, however, discussed by Birdsell (1957), Stott (1969), and Isard (1960) that the out-migration process might begin shortly before carrying capacity is reached for popula-

tion pressure would be beginning to be felt. On the basis of our model, the predicted population curves by zone would look similar to Fig. *4*. However, one must remember that the resource curves have been held constant through time. If they should begin to drop, the resulting carrying capacity decrease would result in larger out-migration. This possibility is shown in Fig. *5*.

To what extent do the data support the first hypothesis? I have made two tests. The first uses the archaeological population indices from the Hay Hollow Valley in east central Arizona while the second simulates actual carrying capacity values. The results of both must be compared to the model's predictions.

Topographic zones were defined at the Hay Hollow Valley which show some ecological differentiation. Zone I is a mesa top with juniper-pinyon vegetation and basaltic soils. Zone II is the side of the mesa. Zone III is upper saltbush grassland. Zone IV is the upper highland terrace with juniper-pinyon vegetation. Zone V is the lower highland terrace and zone VII the lower grass bottomlands. Zone VI has no habitation sites and is thus excluded.

Survey data have been collected in three samples which when combined cover intensively an area of 18.4 square miles. There

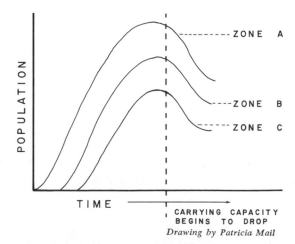

FIG. 5. *Population predictions by zones from heterogeneous model with change in resource curves.*

273

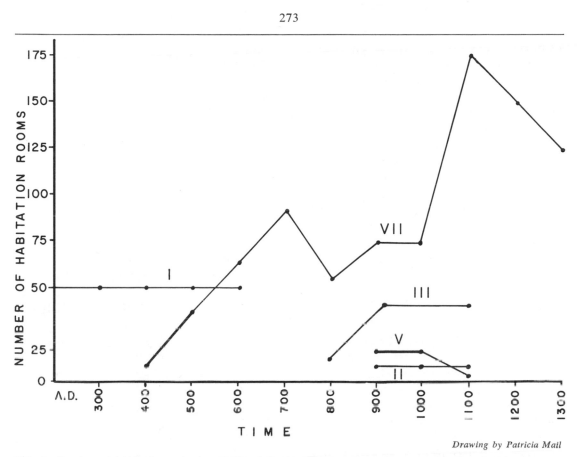

Drawing by Patricia Mail

FIG. 6. *Number of habitation rooms per zone based on 52 sites. The 100% sample (compiled by Schiffer; Zubrow).*

are two samples in which 25% of the area has been surveyed and one sample in which 100% of the land has been covered. The survey technique consisted of setting up grids and then having 5–10 people spaced 10 yards apart walking back and forth across a grid square searching for sites until the entire grid was covered. On the basis of these surveys, room and population estimates have been done on the basis of surface evidence and by regression analysis by Fred Plog and Michael Schiffer. There have been minor corrections of the data on the basis of my excavations of seven sites that had been previously surveyed. Paul S. Martin and David Gregory have developed a chronology of the sites based on tree-ring dated ceramics which has been partially cross checked with radiocarbon dates.

Solely on the basis of the density of the present flora and the proximity to water resources which effect agriculture, one would expect the resource curve of zone VII to be the highest. There is diminishing carrying capacity potential in the other zones. Fig. 6 shows the number of habitation rooms by zone in the 100% sample. The similarity of the shapes of the curves in Figs. 4, 5, and 6 is clear. If one uses the total number of sites as an index of population, then Fig. 7 clearly shows the greater similarity to 5 rather than 4. It should be noted that these results indicate a decrease in the resource curves after A.D. 1150. This decrease has been explained in an article by Schoenwetter and Dittert (1968) as a result of a change in effective moisture caused by a change in the seasonal rainfall pattern at approximately this date. Hevly (1970) explains this decrease in resources with multiple factors including 1) a change in rainfall pattern from summer to winter dominant or to a biseasonal pattern, and 2) a change in the temperature pattern from warm to cool.

It is clear, however, that the changing resource curves should be verified independently of the model and the population indices for the valley. In order to do this, a series of pollen analyses were undertaken by Hevly. The clearest indicator of climatic change, particularly of moisture and temperature, was the pinyon pollen. This correlated positively with changes of both agricultural and gathered economic pollens to a high degree. In order not to confuse cause with effect nor to take into account the cultural filter on the potential resource curves, I will use the changes in pinyon pollen as a relative index of the change in the resource curves. Given the above, the bar-graph section of Fig. 10 (the pinyon pollen curve) shows independently that there is a drop in the resource curves after A.D. 1150.

Actual qualification of the model for maximum carrying capacity values is shown in Table 1. The area of each ecological zone is calculated from aerial photographs and maps. The amounts of dry grams of biomass produced are taken from Odum's values for agriculture and arid areas, and it is assumed on the basis of the United Nations world sample that 2500 kilocalories per day are necessary and sufficient to maintain an average individual in the population. Consumption is 5% of total produced biomass. This is an arbitrary but reasonable estimate. Examining Table 1, one would expect the population size to decrease by zone in the following order: zone VII with the largest population, zone V, zone III, zone IV, zone II, and finally zone I with the smallest population.

Since these area figures of Table 1 include both land covered in the 100% and 25% samples, one must utilize Fig. 7 to test the validity of the simulated zone ordering. Turning to Fig. 7 then, one gets the following actual distribution of sites through time by zone: zones VII, II, V, III, IV, I. Only one zone is out of the expected sequence.

There are several possible reasons for this which will also point out some of the simplifying assumptions in this preliminary simulation. First, I have assumed that the sites are located in the same zone as they utilize. Second, I have assumed the geographic size of the zones remains constant over time. Third, I have not attempted to define multiple utilization of zones by the population of a site. These assumptions however are not insurmountable. For example, one should be able to use the actual location of each site in comparison to the zonal boundaries to determine a function which would predict multiple zonal use of resources for each site.

TABLE 1

Carrying capacity calculations

Zone:	VII	V	III	IV	II	I
Area: square miles	9.92	2.84	.92	1.43	2.15	1.17
Biomass: grams per square meter per day	2.0	1.0	.5	.4	.2	.3
Kilocalories per gram of biomass	4.0	4.0	4.0	4.0	4.0	4.0
Kilocalories	20×10^7	15×10^7	9×10^7	6×10^7	4×10^7	3×10^7
At 5% consumption rate the number of people at carrying capacity	4110	290	190	120	80	70

275

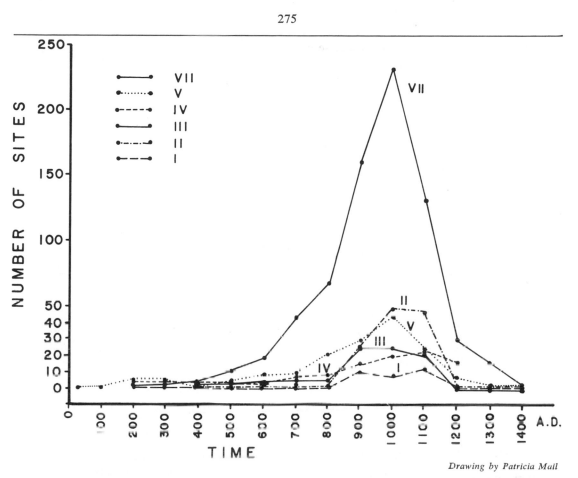

Drawing by Patricia Mail

FIG. 7. *Number of sites by time and zone based on the 100% and the two 25% samples.*

On the basis of the two tests it would appear that the data generally support the hypothesis that the development of populations in marginal resource zones is a function of optimal zone exploitation. The model not only allows one to operationalize the hypothesis but suggests the interaction of the underlying variables.

Human populations are not simply mechanistic. First, they do not grow exactly to the carrying capacity point and then have an intrinsic growth rate of zero. Instead, they will sometimes overshoot the carrying capacity point and with the resulting disequilibrium there will be an increase in the mortality rate and out-migration as previously shown. When this occurs there is a certain amount of leeway, for the standard of living acts as a buffer. Survival may result for a

population above carrying capacity at the expense of lowering the standard of living. However, if the intrinsic growth rate is still positive, the decrease in the standard of living is only a delaying action and eventually the Malthusian checks will catch up. Second, human populations do not grow continuously. Instead, the reality of generations results in a time lag. In other words, given a real population there will be particular age cohorts which will have a larger influence in population growth than others. This will result in unequal growth through time. These two factors, the buffering of the standard of living and the time lag make the more careful examination of the homeostatic mechanism and the conditions under which it functions necessary.

Utilizing our graphical model, the popula-

276

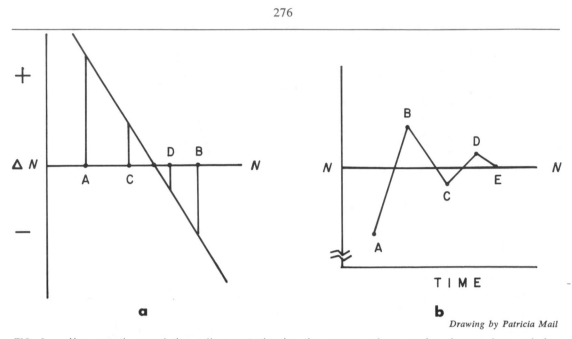

FIG. 8. *a. Homeostatic population adjustment showing the process of successive changes in population size (after MacArthur 1966:137). b. Homeostatic population adjustment showing the change in population size as a time plot (after MacArthur 1966:137).*

Drawing by Patricia Mail

tion's homeostatic adjustment would be presented as a decreasing oscillation on the population curve around the carrying capacity point. Alternatively, Robert MacArthur (MacArthur and Connell 1966) has shown the oscillation in terms of the size of the change of population. Thus, in Fig. *8a* a population of initial size A, will fluctuate through time to become sizes B, C, D, etc. Note B is placed so that the distance from A to B equals the perpendicular of the line segment above A. In this and the following figure, N is the size of the population and N is the change in the size of the population. This may be replotted across time as in Fig. *8b*. As MacArthur points out, if the population grew continuously there need not be a time lag nor an oscillation. His graphs do not show the buffering effect of the standard of living. If a lower standard of living is tolerable, the horizontal axis N (Fig. *8a*) is lowered, which results in a higher equilibrium point for N (Fig. *8b*) in the time curve plot. It should be noted that this may take place after the oscillation process has begun which would result in an asymetrical oscilla-

tion and is the essence of the population dynamics in Geertz's involution concept (Geertz 1968).

MacArthur notes that if the slope of the line of N/N is greater than 63, a threshold is reached so that the oscillations become more violent through time. They increase rather than decrease and instead of a homeostatic process one has a deviation amplifying process such as discussed by Magorah Maruyama (Maruyama 1968) in "The Second Cybernetics: Deviation Amplifying Mutual Causal Processes" (Fig. *9*). The graphical model of carrying capacity as a dynamic equilibrium system would suggest that population extinction such as seen in the Hay Hollow Valley about A.D. 1400 could result solely from a decrease in the resource curves to the point that no population could be supported. MacArthur's model provides in the deviation amplifying process an alternative explanation to resource depletion as a cause for extinction. Possibly both processes are involved. These mechanisms augment traditional explanations for the abandonment of the Southwest.

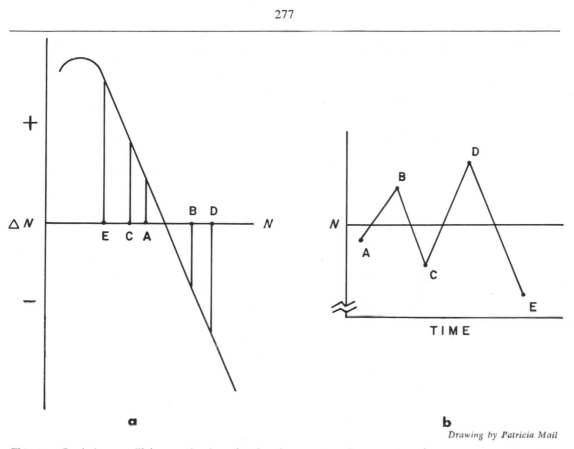

FIG. 9. a. Deviation amplifying mechanism showing the process of successive changes in population size (after MacArthur 1966:137). b. Deviation amplifying mechanism showing the change in population size as a time plot (after MacArthur 1966:138).

Up to this point we have been relating population size and zonal distribution to resources but we have not related settlement pattern variables such as population aggregation, spatial aggregation, or residential area to the resources. If the population is above the carrying capacity point or at carrying capacity when the resource curves begin to drop, and if access to resources is related to population size, then one would expect the smaller villages to be depopulated first. For example, let us imagine three villages, one with a population of 100, one with a population of 40, and one with a population of 20. If there is a 50% decrease in resources which causes a loss of population of 50%, the three villages would have populations of 50, 20, and 10. If there was another 50% decrease, the three villages would be 25, 10, and 5. The

smallest village would no longer have sufficient manpower to continue its functions as a village including its subsistence, religious, and political activities. Thus, the smallest population would migrate either to one of the other villages or out of the area. If the population migrated to another village there would be an average of 20 people per village; if they migrated out of the area, there would be an average of 17.5 people per site and if the smallest village somehow continued to exist there would be 13 people per site. The point to be noted here is that if small villages continue, the average number of people per village is smaller than if they do not. One might suggest that during periods of resource depletion there will be population aggregation. In other words, as resources decrease there will be fewer sites but relatively more

278

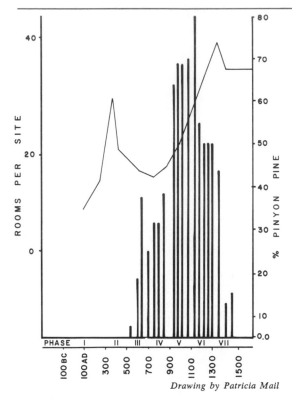

Drawing by Patricia Mail

FIG. 10. *Population aggregation and resource index in the Hay Hollow Valley. The population aggregation is measured by rooms per site as a line graph while the resource index is the percentage of pinyon pollen presented as a bar graph.*

people living in each site as the small villages become extinct. Utilizing the 100% survey data the results may be seen in Fig. *10*. The bar graphs are the pinyon pollen serving as an indirect index of resources as discussed previously. The line is the average number of rooms per site which is taken to be an index of population aggregation. During the major period of resource depletion, from A.D. 1150 on, the number of rooms per site remains quite high. This indicates that during this period there is population aggregation. This conclusion is justified since the smaller sites which would have lowered the average number of rooms per site are not having that effect.

At the same periods of time that we note population aggregation we would expect spatial aggregation. This is the result of the

increasing necessity for the population to utilize areas of optimal resource production during periods of resource depletion. If one examines the data in Fig. *11*, this relationship may be seen graphically. The bar graphs are the resource indices which are the same as in the previous graph. The line calculated by David Gregory is the measurement of the nearest neighbor statistic between sites. This is an index of the continuum between perfect spatial dispersion and aggregation. Perfect hexagonal dispersion is 2.15 and complete aggregation is 0.0. From the diagram it is clear that after A.D. 700 the spatial relationship between sites is one of aggregation whenever the pinyon pollen index is below 50%.

The third variable, residential area, should also decrease during periods of resource

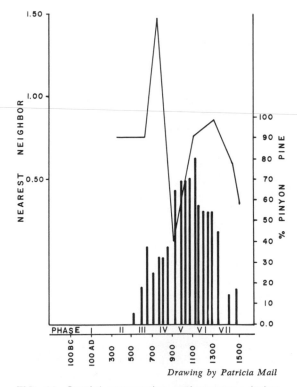

Drawing by Patricia Mail

FIG. 11. *Spatial aggregation and resource index in the Hay Hollow Valley. Spatial aggregation is measured by the nearest neighbor statistic calculated between sites and shown as a line graph. The resources index is the percentage of pinyon pollen represented by a bar graph.*

depletion. Whenever the population is above the resource curve, there are insufficient resources to meet the demand. As a result a set of resource priorities will need to be established. For example, under these conditions a village should allocate more of its labor force to subsistence tasks than to building of large residential structures. Thus, one would expect that residential area will decrease during resource depletion due to the priority of subsistence in the expenditure of resources. The data in Fig. *12* represents a sample of the 100% survey chosen by time, and ecological zone. The resource curve is the same as the two previous figures. There is a close correlation between residential area as measured by average room size and the resource index. The results show a clear decrease in residential area as resources decrease.

In conclusion, this essay has: 1) built a model of carrying capacity as a dynamic equilibrium system, 2) operationalized the model in order to test the hypothesis that the development of populations in marginal resource zones is a function of optimal zone exploitation, 3) presented data supporting the above hypothesis from the Hay Hollow Valley of Arizona, 4) presented MacArthur's homeostatic and deviation amplifying model as an alternative to diminishing resource curves to explain the extinction of the Hay Hollow population in A.D. 1450, and 5) examined the effects on settlement pattern of

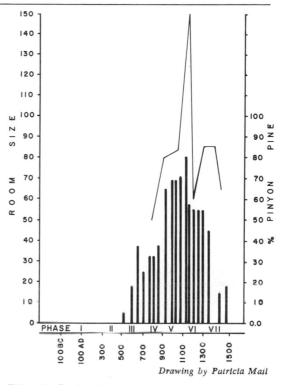

Drawing by Patricia Mail

FIG. 12. *Residential area and resource index in the Hay Hollow Valley. Residential area is measured by the average room size graphed as a line. The resource index is the percentage of pinyon pollen represented by a bar graph.*

disequilibriums caused by population excess. Specifically, it has considered how these disequilibriums, as defined by the model, effect the variables of population aggregation, spatial aggregation, and residential area.

Chapter **24** FRED T. PLOG and CHERYL K. GARRETT

Explaining Variability in Prehistoric Southwestern Water Control Systems

THE EXISTENCE of prehistoric water control systems in the southwestern United States has been documented for a very long time. Adolph Bandelier, for example, noted the occurrence of irrigation channels in the valley of the Little Colorado in the 1890s (1892: 388–89). Few of these early discussions went beyond noting the existence of such features and detailed information was and still is sparse. Water control techniques have been given primary attention in only a handful of reports.

This situation is rapidly changing as ecological studies and a materialist orientation become more important in the discipline. A wide variety of data on the interaction of prehistoric populations and their natural environments are being obtained. Agricultural practices, whether or not they involve water control technology, are an important aspect of this concern and more such investigations will probably be undertaken in the near future.

In the past, a critical problem in archaeology has been the general lack of overlap between research projects carried on by different investigators, even when those projects attacked the same problem. When a particular phenomenon has been investigated, the attributes on which the research focused have varied considerably from one investigator to another. Artifacts, features, and settlement patterns have an infinite number of attributes that we might wish to record,

and we select from these those which we perceive to be important. Differences in data collection sometimes reflect varying evaluations of priorities by investigators, while at other times they result from a failure to develop a precise problem focus. In the former instance, the variability is healthy and belongs in the discipline. In the latter it is not. Without a problem focus it is unlikely that we will collect those data or record those attributes that will lead to a solution of the problem at hand.

If we wish a coherent research picture — one that allows variability in priorities but insures comparability by maintaining a shared problem focus, then we should begin a discussion of those problems that we expect to solve with water control data and the relevant techniques for solving them. This essay is an attempt at such a discussion. It discusses some questions that have been critical for us in our research in the upper Little Colorado and some ways in which answers to these questions might be obtained.

We wish to clarify a number of assumptions that will underly our approach to explaining variability in water control systems. First, we see the question at hand as one that involves a primary focus on behavior rather than culture, at least in so far as the latter term is characteristically used by archaeologists in reference to norms, templates, and artifacts. We do not wish to oversimplify the distinction between culture and behavior. We recognize the widespread variability in the use of these terms in American anthropology today. Some anthropologists use *culture* to refer to ideational variables so as to make such variables primary and others to distinguish between what individuals think and what they do. Some regard behavior as the primary referent of the term *culture*. We simply wish to make clear our own inclination to focus on decisions and actions as they relate to information on the one hand and produced artifacts on the other. We use information as a referent for what is in one's head rather than the more restrictive concept of norm. The evidence of water control systems that the archaeologist finds results from the actions of populations behaving in their habitats. It does not result from the mindless application of a water control template held by a prehistoric population to the entire land mass it controlled.

Evidence already acquired shows no one-to-one correspondence exists between water control systems and culture areas. There is no unique Anasazi strategy or Mogollon strategy. Within the upper Little Colorado region, for example, one finds significant variability from valley to adjacent valley. The notion that a single ideal strategy should have existed for so diverse an area leads to an absurd picture of prehistoric Southwesterners trying to build the same water control system throughout a region with total insensitivity to, and total ignorance of, the relationships between water control systems and the habitats in which they were utilized.

Flannery has recently noted that we "no longer think of the pre-ceramic plant collectors as a ragged and scruffy band of nomads: instead they appear as a practiced and ingenious team of lay botanists who know how to wring the most out of a superficially bleak environment" (1968a:69). It seems equally appropriate to deal with southwestern agriculturalists as a skilled team of soil conservationists and agronomists.

Such a decision seems justified when one considers the comparative abilities of modern and prehistoric farmers in coping with southwestern environments. It is sometimes argued by modern farmers in the Upper Little Colorado that one is safer putting in an irrigation ditch by digging out a prehistoric one than by hiring an engineer. Moreover, when one compares modern and prehistoric settlement patterns in the area, it is clear that prehistoric agriculturalists never built their villages on prime agricultural land while modern settlements nearly always occur on the best arable land.

We will not be concerned with the source of the information that prehistoric farmers used in practicing their art. Since most water control techniques were practiced throughout the Southwest, this information seems to be widespread. No doubt the information spread by word of mouth, by observation, and by invention and reinvention. Diffusion and invention are topics which we leave to other investigators already working on such problems. Our analysis will operate in terms of two concepts—variety and selection. We have assumed that a variety of water control techniques were available to prehistoric populations. We wish to examine the selective pressures operating on this variety that would have led to the use of a particular technique in a particular area and different techniques in other areas.

In pursuing this goal, we must answer four questions: 1) what are the components of a water control system? 2) how do water control systems vary in time and space? 3) which natural and social environmental variables affect this temporal and spatial variability? and 4) what kinds of effects does a water control system have on its natural and social environment? While the last two questions are the focus of our interest and that of most other archaeologists, the first two must be answered as a first step toward attacking these larger issues.

The first question—what are the components of a water control system?—demands the creation of a typology of water control

282

strategies, that is, the technical components of which the system is composed. At present it seems worthwhile to distinguish three components or strategies: gridding, terracing, and irrigation. A grid is a single line of rocks, one rock high, that follows the contour of a slope and serves to slow water passing over it. Gridding means constructing a number of such rows in close proximity. It is similar to the modern practice of contour plowing, which reduces the loss of soil and water due to erosion but does not drastically modify the land surface. A terrace is constructed of rocks at least two tiers high with earth fill behind them. In contrast to gridding, terracing significantly modifies the contour of the land on which it is practiced. The nature of irrigation seems clear and requires no definition here. This typology is obviously incomplete but will serve as a basis for continuing the current discussion. As work with problems involving water control systems continues, we expect a far more precise and comprehensive terminology to be developed.

The second question focuses on the temporal and spatial dimensions of variability in water control systems. It is clear that such systems have been utilized for a great period of time in the Southwest, beginning as early as 300 B.C. and continuing to the present. However, the specific temporal variability in individual areas, which will be critical to understanding subsistence patterns, is unknown. Spatial variability appears to be of considerable magnitude. To repeat an earlier point, adjacent valleys that are accepted as having been occupied by members of the same culture (e.g., Mogollon) have highly variable water control systems. Thus, it does not appear that variability in water control systems follows accepted cultural boundaries but is quite clearly a behavioral response to local environmental variability.

Once we have adequately answered the first two questions, we can turn to a third question—which natural and social environmental variables affect the temporal and spatial patterning of the distribution of water

control systems? This critical question encompasses an extremely broad range of information and we may profitably break it down into somewhat more specific issues. Examples of essential topics are: What factors in the natural and social environment of a population lead to the decision to control water? What factors define an optimal water control system for an environment? What variables determine a population's ability to afford a system?

The decision to control water must be a response to problems in subsistence. Pressures on the food supply may come from the natural environment, in which case variables such as decadic and yearly rainfall and soil quality are critical. On the other hand, a variety of demographic variables such as population size and density might affect the security of a population's food base. We must understand variables like these if we are to explain why water control procedures are ever utilized.

A more comprehensive set of variables become critical when we confront the issue of the efficiency of different systems in different habitats. Variables previously mentioned —soil, decadic rainfall, and yearly rainfall— as well as the slope of the land and the type and distribution of surface water are most critical. We must learn to evaluate the probability that a particular strategy can be practiced under different combinations of these variables, the increase in productivity that will result from the practice, and the extent to which the practice will minimize the risk of subsisting in the environment.

An example of the effect of one of these variables, slope, on the availability or fitness of the three strategies can be seen in Fig. 1. The X axis represents slope, increasing from left to right, while the Y axis measures the potential productivity of the strategies. Thus, the graph shows the productivity of each strategy under varying slope conditions. The peaks of the curves occur at the particular slope on which the strategy will be maximally productive. Each strategy can be employed

283

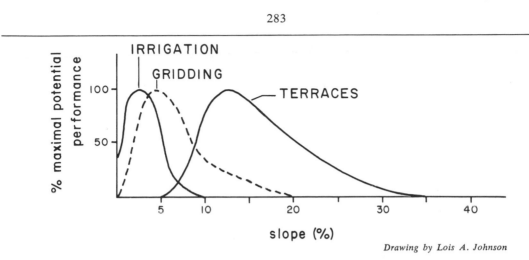

Drawing by Lois A. Johnson

FIG. 1. *Efficiency of water control strategies with varied slope.*

over a range of slope conditions, but at the cost of decreasing productivity. These curves are based on soil conservation and agricultural studies of the effectiveness of different strategies on different slopes (in Bennett 1939; Frevert et al 1955; Hughes and Henson 1957). In Figure 2, however, the curves are reproduced individually with plots of the relative frequencies of different slope measurements for different prehistoric cases. The data on the graph are from the Salt and Gila River Valleys (Turney 1929; Midvale 1965), the Upper Little Colorado, and Point of Pines (Woodbury 1961). In spite of the limited data, the frequencies roughly correlate with the predictions. This same kind of graph can be constructed for any variable to yield information on the fit between our expectations based on modern data and observed prehistoric cases.

Other factors in the natural and social environment of a population become crucial in attempting to determine that population's ability to afford a water control system. Both natural and human resources must be present. Natural resources vary for each strategy and include such items as rocks for grids and terrace walls, soil for filling terraces, and sufficiently nonporous soil or adobe for lining irrigation canals. The human resource required is energy. The energy necessary for building and maintaining each system varies

greatly—from simply lining up rocks for grids, to building and filling and maintaining terrace walls, to digging and cleaning irrigation channels and supervising the flow of water. Thus, the availability of resources necessary for the systems affects the final decision on the combination of strategies.

A final question concerns the effect of a water control system once it has been constructed on its natural and social environment. Some evidence of the effect of irrigation on its natural environment in the Southwest is already available. A comparison of old irrigation canals in the Salt River Valley (Midvale 1965) with current locations of heavy alkalai deposits (United States Department of Agriculture 1926) show a close correlation. Obviously, this irrigation system was affecting its natural environment in a major way. Examples of treatments of the effect of a water control system on its social environment are Wittfogel's *Oriental Despotism* (1957) and Adams's *Land Behind Baghdad* (1965) and *The Evolution of Urban Society* (1966). This kind of problem has not been studied in any detail in the Southwest.

The remainder of this essay is focused on our attempt to construct a model that defines the environment of a water control system and describes the decisions that lead to the construction of a particular system in a

284

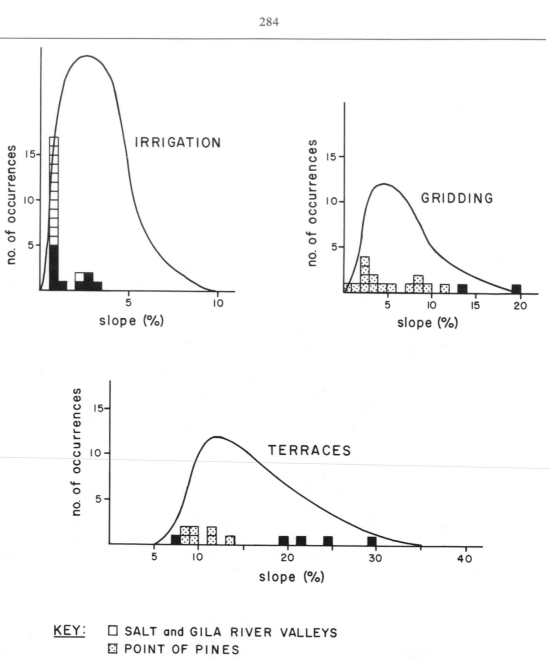

KEY: □ SALT and GILA RIVER VALLEYS
      ▨ POINT OF PINES
      ■ UPPER LITTLE COLORADO

Drawing by Lois A. Johnson

FIG. 2. *Actual distribution of water control strategies on various slopes.*

particular environment. The specific bit of information we attempt to derive from the model is an explanation of why different mixes of irrigation, terracing, and gridding are found in different loci. To reemphasize an earlier point, it is not our feeling that this variability is cultural; that is, it does not correspond to classically defined culture areas within the Southwest. The question on which this model centers, then, is: Why does the ratio of irrigation to terracing to gridding vary from one valley habitat to the next? We

285

attempt to answer the question by constructing a model that simulates the decisions that result in a particular irrigation, terracing, and gridding mix. If the simulation is successful, the expectations (predictions) derived from it on the basis of measuring relevant prehistoric variables for a particular habitat should correspond to the observed pattern of variability in the habitat. The decision-making process involves three steps: 1) decision to control water, 2) determination of the range of feasible optimal systems for controlling water in the habitat in question, and 3) determination of the system with optimal cost/benefit ratio for the habitat. Three main boxes in the model in Figure *3* represent the three decisions.

Why does a population decide to control water, to begin a farming strategy more complex than the maintenance of circumvillage dry farming plots? This decision is not one that occurs merely as a result of obtaining information on water control strategies. Some stimulus—such as change in the population's natural or social environment—to which water control is an appropriate response must be identified. This stimulus probably involves factors discussed in the article in this book by Ezra Zubrow on population and carrying capacity. Carrying capacity is itself dependent on other variables such as soil quality, decadic rainfall variability, and yearly rainfall variability.

An evaluation of the relationship between extant population and carrying capacity leads to an estimation of the food resource problem that a population faces. The existence of a food resource problem in conjunction with information on water control technique is likely to lead to the adoption of such techniques. We do not argue that water control is adopted when population exceeds carrying capacity. Rather, the probability of adopting a water control system is some direct function of the ratio between population and carrying capacity. When the ratio exceeds some tolerance level, a food resource problem is identified. As this variable approaches some tolerance level, the probability of adopting a water control system approaches one.

A need to control water having been determined, a second decision involves designing an appropriate system for the habitat in question. We treat this decision not as a question of norms or templates but as one that involves variability within a system and selective pressures from the system's environment acting on that variability. To repeat an oft-recited statement, systems adapt to variability, not to averages. Selection acts on behavioral variability, not on behavioral norms. This situation is not unique to the question at hand, nor even to anthropology. When one attempts to explain variability from an evolutionary perspective—whatever the discipline—two sets of data are required; 1) a set that represents the variability in the system for the trait in question and 2) a set that represents the selective pressures operative in the environment.

In approaching a problem of population ecology, Richard Levins (1968) has created a neat conceptual basis for approaching selectivity-variability problems. Variability within a system is represented by what Levis calls adaptive sets—sets that represent the fitness of alternative combinations of two or more strategies for some particular environmental variable. Selective pressures are represented by adaptive functions—lines that measure the actual distribution of the environmental variable in the habitat being studied.

Formally an adaptive set is created by plotting fitness values over the environmental variability of one strategy on the X axis and values for the other strategy over the same environmental variable on the Y axis. Figure *4* shows the adaptive set constructed by plotting the values from Figure *1* for irrigation (on the X axis) versus those for gridding (on the Y axis) on slopes on which both are possible. Optimally fit combinations of strategies lie along the side of the set that is farthest from the origin.

The adaptive function is a line; its shape

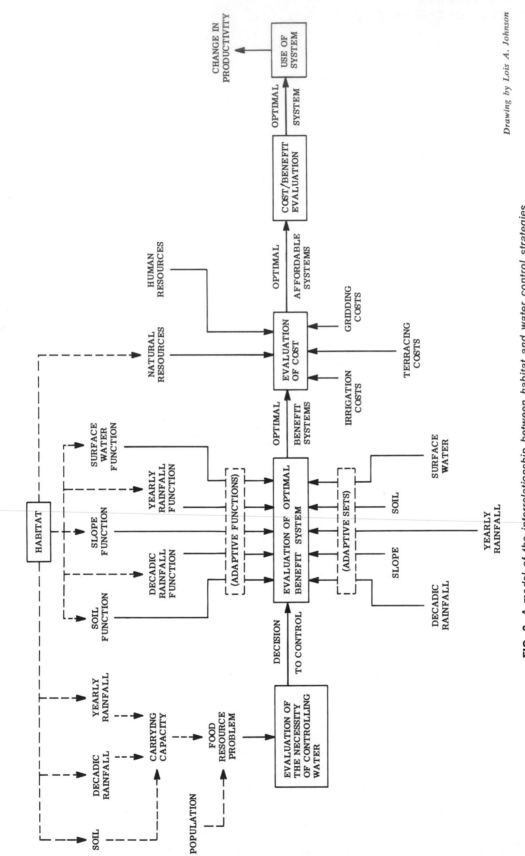

FIG. 3. A model of the interrelationship between habitat and water control strategies.

287

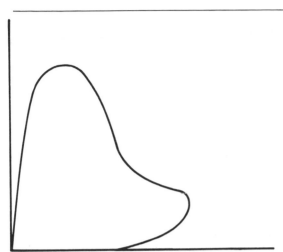

ADAPTIVE SET
Drawing by Lois A. Johnson

FIG. 4. *Adaptive set, such as might be constructed for griddings and terraces over varied slope.*

and slope vary with the actual distribution of values of environmental variables in the habitat being observed (see Figure 5). It measures, then, the actual distribution of, for example, areas of different slope in the environment. The point or points of contact

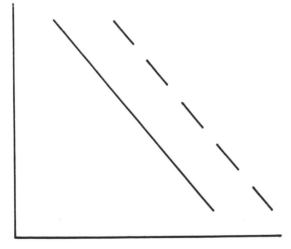

ADAPTIVE FUNCTION
Drawing by Lois A. Johnson

FIG. 5. *Adaptive function, such as might define the distribution of the slope variable in a particular environment.*

between the adaptive set and function (see Figure 6) represent the strategy or combination of strategies that would be most fit for a particular habitat. Adaptive set/adaptive function analyses can be made for each of the variables in the model: slope, soil, decadic rainfall variability, and surface water type. In this fashion, an optimal mix of irrigation, terracing, and gridding for the habitat can be determined.

One or a number of optimal strategies having been designed for a particular habitat, the next decision is an evaluation of the cost of the system in the habitat. This involves a determination of the alternative costs of the strategies and a consideration of whether the costs can be met with the human and natural resources at hand. Again, appropriate modern

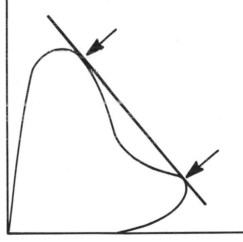

ADAPTIVE SET–ADAPTIVE FUNCTION
Drawing by Lois A. Johnson

FIG. 6. *The arrows indicate the points of contact between adaptive set and adaptive function, representing the most efficient combination of strategies for the environment.*

data are available. The cost ratio of the three strategies for a ten-year period in the modern case is approximately 1:2:40 for gridding to terracing to irrigation (based on data in Heady and Jensen 1954). Archaeological experiments with the time and resources involved in the construction of the strategies

288

can lead to a similar series of inequalities or ratios. After the cost of alternative systems has been estimated, those optimal benefit systems that cannot be afforded are deleted from further consideration and those that can be afforded are evaluated further.

The nature of the evaluation is a cost/benefit analysis. If more than one combination of strategies provides an optimal benefit for the habitat and if more than one is affordable, the system selected will be that one for which the lowest cost/benefit ratio (that is, the greatest benefit for the least cost) is obtained. This system is the one that will be put into operation. Once the system is in operation, it affects the food resource problem variable and leads to either further action or no further action in controlling water.

This model had focused exclusively on technological responses to food resource problems. There are clearly others that would warrant consideration in dealing with agricultural practices in general. Population control, aggregation, shifting the balance between hunting and gathering and agriculture, selecting natural environmental alternatives, or practicing a spatially diversified system such as the one Hack describes for the Hopi (1942) are all alternatives. Incorporating them all in a simple model is beyond our present capability.

In the long run, it is precisely such a model that will lead to the solution of the most interesting problems. It will do this by permitting a rigorous treatment of the differential impact of technologically generalized and technologically specialized agricultural strategies on the cultural system employing them. Might it be the case that the Hopi and Zuni survival of the Western Anasazi abandonment represents a selection for a simpler, more diversified system? Was the widespread process of population aggregation prior to the abandonment an attempt to meet the price of an increasingly expensive technology or to provide resources for more and more technology? It seems far more likely that we will be satisfied with explanations of events such as these that explain with established evolutionary propositions such as the Law of Evolutionary Potential (Sahlins and Service 1960) and Geertz's Involution (Geertz 1963) rather than invoking particularistic event-centered explanations such as drought or warfare.

Changes in the Adaptations of Southwestern Basketmakers: A Systems Perspective

RECENTLY A number of scientists in various disciplines have suggested that a "general systems theory" would be useful in integrating the knowledge of science as a whole so that each discipline may benefit from the insights and progress of others (Boulding 1956a). Advocates of this theory have asserted that generalizations may be made about the nature of reality no matter whether this reality is chemical, physical, biological, social or cultural. Furthermore, they have suggested that such generalizations may be couched in a special set of terms which would serve as a lingua franca, as it were, of the sciences. Consequently, general systems theory may be defined as a set of terms and concepts along with their definitions, principles, and hypothesized laws which concern systems on a number of different levels of complexity.

General systems theory seems to have gained its initial impetus from the fields of electronics – particularly computer technology – and communications. Certainly much of the terminology of the theory has been used in such fields for many years. Nevertheless, it has been individuals in the biological, behavioral, and social sciences who have been most active in popularizing the theory (cf. issues of the *General Systems Yearbook*). Anthropologists, however, have been somewhat reticent in expounding the theory compared to other social sciences (e.g. Buckley 1967, 1968) in spite of the fact that an anthropologist conceived of a culture as a living thermodynamic system at a comparatively early date (White 1959:33). Within the subdiscipline of archaeology, however, the theory has several explicit proponents (Binford 1962; Hole and Heizer 1969:44–46, 372–77; Clarke 1968:43–81). Of these archaeologists Hole and Heizer and Clarke have presented fairly detailed descriptions of the theory and, to a degree, have demonstrated how cultures may be viewed as systems. I propose here that the full import of the theory to archaeology, and generally anthropology, is yet to be fully realized, and it shall be my intent here to point out some of the added implications of the theory and to outline a model based on general systems theory for explaining changes in prehistoric Basketmaker adaptations in the American Southwest.

A system may be defined in a number of ways – even strictly within the framework of general systems theory (cf. Bertalanffy 1950: 143, Hall and Fagen 1956). For our purposes it will be necessary to emphasize in a definition the content of a system and the nature of the relationships between its parts. In the first place, any concrete system contains only matter and energy (White 1959: 33; Miller 1965:193). A third phenomenon, information, may also be present, but it is always carried by, or is manifested as, a form of either matter or energy and does not have an independent existence (Miller 1965:194–

95). All three, regardless of form, are at least logically observable and measurable as variables. Matter and energy exist in a system as a set of parts or components, that is, they exist as nonrandom localizations in space and time (Miller 1965:202). Components of concrete systems may be demonstrated to be systems themselves, but for our purposes we need not delve into this possibility here. Several different types of relationships between components may be defined and observed: there may simply be proximities between components in space and/or time; there may be determinancies between components which are manifested as covariances; or there may be passages of matter or energy from one component to another which often, if not always, account for deterministic relationships.

Systems may be nonliving or living. Nonliving systems may be static, in that matter and energy are in temporally constant states of organization; or they may be dynamic, in that matter and energy are in states of flux through the system. Living systems are always dynamic and are characterized, as are many nonliving systems, by homeostatic devices which serve to maintain steady-states within the system through the passage and interpretation of information. Thus the movement of matter and energy through dynamic systems is maintained as a set of equilibrium fluxes (Miller 1965:224). Movements of matter and energy through space and time are referred to as processes and they may be either simple transfers or have the additional characteristic of being converted from one form to another during the process.

Living systems are open systems in that matter and energy (often in the form of information) enter the system from its environment at relatively low states of entropy, are consumed in its maintenance, and then are expelled as waste into its environment at relatively high states of entropy. A living system is dependent upon relative constancy in the form and quantity of these inputs and outputs, and although environmental variations occur, the system maintains its internal steady-state by mitigating the effects of these variations through the use of various homeostatic devices. A living system is therefore adaptive in this ability to cope with variability in its environment.

While systems theorists have devoted considerable attention to the processes involved in the diversity of systems and their means of maintenance, comparatively little attention has been given to systemic change (cf. tabulations of systems theory literature by Young 1964). The minimal attention given to this provocative topic has been devoted to the growth of systems and to various aspects of disequilibrium (Young 1964:78–80, Boulding 1956b). The following statements, therefore, represent an attempt to develop some general definitions of certain kinds of systemic variability and change which will be relevant to future discussion.

Two types of systemic variability may be defined—qualitative and quantitative. Qualitative variability between two systems would involve differences in the structural arrangements and articulations or the functions of components. Qualitative differences between two qualitatively identical systems, or the same system at different points in time, would exist if there was either different sizes of components, different numbers of components of preexisting types, or different amounts of matter or energy processed by components. Observed as directional variability with some degree of continuity, quantitative variability has been called a cline if it is distributed through space, a trend if it is distributed through time, and cyclic if it deviates alternatively through either dimension. Growth has been defined by Boulding as quantitative increase through time (1956b), although some of his types of growth appear to verge on what is defined here as qualitative variability. Systemic change as defined here is not simply growth. Instead it consists of qualitative differences between systemic structures at different points in time, and of course some of the matter or energy would be passed on from the old to the new system. If this were not so, we would be dealing with such phenomena as replacement rather than change.

Certainly two of the most useful aspects of general systems theory, insofar as it concerns the explanation of systemic change, are the concepts of adaptation and steady-state. A living system is always attempting to maintain a status quo by adaptive responses to variability in its environment by seeking a set of equilibrium fluxes in the internal flows of matter and energy. In light of this, it stands to reason that changes in systems can only be brought about by changes in inputs and outputs which are extensive enough to disturb the equilibrium fluxes to points where homeostatic mechanisms no longer function adaptively in maintaining a steady-state. As a general rule we may conclude that if we are seeking explanations of systematic change we must look at the interfaces between the system and that portion of the environment to which it is articulated by inputs and outputs of matter and energy. When the system no longer can adapt to new variables, it has two choices: either change or become extinct.

In the process of adapting to new environmental variability, a system may readapt through quantitative variation or minor qualitative changes affecting only a few components. But if this new environmental variability is extreme or persistent enough, quantitative or minor qualitative variation may finally become inadequate, and overall structural or qualitative change must ensue if the system is to remain a system. Because of interdependence between components of a system, we would expect change to be abrupt and comprehensive. When one component is disrupted, many related components will be similarly affected, resulting in relatively complete disorganization. This would be followed immediately by a reorganization, and "transitional" states would be nonexistent. Consequently, systematic change would never be conceived as a "continuum."

General systems theory has its greatest relevance to anthropology (and archaeology as anthropology), as well as to any other discipline, through its role in deductive-nomological explanation (cf. Hempel and Oppenheim 1948; Hempel 1966:49–54 for a specific meaning of this form of explanation). It provides us with a set of principles and laws from which our hypothesized explanations of cultural differences and similarities may be deduced. In a discipline such as anthropology, which still fails, for the most part, to follow the strictures of logical deduction, the theory has particular utility in that it provides us with a basis for deducting hypothetical laws concerning the set of phenomena with which we deal—that is, we may deduce cultural laws. And from these, in turn, we may deduce our hypotheses to explain particular observed cultural "events." Through this deductive process we may eventually rid anthropology and specifically archaeology of a number of spurious, often implicit assumptions concerning the nature of culture and cultural process, several of which will be taken up later.

Two of the most important laws upon which general systems theory itself is based are the first and second laws of thermodynamics. The first law, in one of its many forms, states that matter and energy can be neither created nor destroyed; it can only be transferred from one locus to another or transformed from one state to another. From the perspective of general systems theory we may therefore say that a system can neither create nor destroy its matter-energy. Consequently, unless the system is growing or shrinking in size, the amounts of matter or energy contained within it are constant, and the total inputs will equal the outputs.

The second law of thermodynamics has even more relevance to general systems theory, for it justifies the existence of open systems which process matter and energy. The law states that matter and energy tend to disperse toward states of random distribution or entropy. Consequently systems exist in the face of, or in spite of, natural tendencies toward entropy, and if a system is to maintain itself in a steady-state, that is, if the components and their organization are to remain extant, there must be replenishing inputs of matter and energy to replace that which has degenerated to relatively high states of entropy. Likewise, there must be outputs of the entropy so that it does not accumulate within the system. Once inputs and outputs have stopped, such as when a living system dies, entropy begins to increase.

Another aspect of the second law of thermodynamics asserts that any conversion or transfer of matter-energy results in some energy being converted to other forms at higher states of entropy. In other words, conversion or transfer cannot take place without some energy "consumption." So the work that a system does in its maintenance results in energy loss as entropy, necessitating inputs of new matter-energy at low states of entropy for continued maintenance. A system could never hope to survive by only reusing that energy contained in it at some particular moment in time.

These are only a few of the major principles or laws of general systems theory, but they will suffice to allow us to deduce a series of assumptions concerning cultural systems. (See Miller 1965 for a number of other hypothetical laws of general systems theory.) In the first place, we must view a cultural system as consisting of matter, energy and information. From this perspective, our conceptualizations of real or veredicial systems —or particular portions of them—would deal with units of analysis which have observable and measurable analogs in matter, energy and information. This stricture would necessitate ridding anthorpology of a plethora of terms and concepts which presently have questionable or unspecified analogs in the components and processes of real cultural systems. Abstractions such as "norms," "rules," "ideas," "goals," or "influences" are among the more obvious which fall into this category.

Secondly, the components of cultural systems would be viewed as being organized into subsystems, with patterns of dependent relationships. Until recently, much of anthropology has rejected any such principle of determinism, being content to view culture as sets of independently varying traits. Driver and Kroeber made this most explicit in initiating a program for measuring the differences and similarities between cultures. They said, "We believe that culture traits are in the main if not in absolutely all cases independent" and that ". . . all traits can occur independently of each other" (1932:212–13). Such a perspective is still prevalent in archaeological procedures for measuring cultural variability by reference to differences in sets of artifact types (a critique of this perspective is found in Binford 1962). These assertions of the independence of cultural parts not only are incompatible with viewing a culture as an organization of interacting parts; they also reflect a rejection of the possibility that all cultural phenomena are potentially explainable since explanation, by definition, asserts a relationship between parts of a system.

Third, a cultural system would be considered a type of living system, and like all living systems it would be viewed as dynamic in the sense that matter and energy flow through it in its maintenance and its opposition to natural tendencies toward entropy. Moreover, like any living system, culture must adapt to variability in those features of its environment to which it is articulated by inputs and outputs of matter, energy, and information. Of course, such points of view are not new in anthropology. Leslie White had discussed culture as a living system some years ago (White 1959:35). For our purposes, however, it is necessary to expand his discussion to include a few more specifics.

Components of cultural systems consist of groups of humans, artifacts, and symbols, the latter existing as artifacts or as differential flows of matter and energy. All three are organized into structures commonly denoted respectively as social organization, technology, and ideology. Matter and energy flow through the cultural system as foods, fuels,

293

raw materials, and a variety of other energy forms, often in well-defined spatial patterns called logistical networks. Symbols and ideology, in serving their homeostatic functions, are also characterized by explicit patterns of movement called communications networks. Movement through both types of networks is made possible by technology.

Human cultural behavior exists as a set of activities which are the bases of social and demographic structures. The set of activities of a cultural system may be divided into two major categories: extractive activities and maintenance activities (Binford and Binford 1966a:268). Extractive activities are those which deal with the procurement of matter, energy, and information from the environment while maintenance activities are those which are concerned with replenishing, through internal conversions and transfers of matter, energy and information, those portions of the components which have reached critically high states of entropy. Other maintenance activities of an ideological sort would be devoted to preserving the structural relationships between components.

The artifacts of a technology may also be viewed as having characteristic behaviors with respect to their functions as components in cultural systems. Using the concepts offered by Philip Wagner (1960:92–94), they may be divided into two basic categories: tools and facilities. Modifying his definitions somewhat, tools are artifacts which concentrate energy in the process of doing work, that is, they facilitate energy transfers and conversions. On the other hand, facilities function to impede energy transfers and conversions by containing or maintaining it in some particular form, or they function to minimize its spatial dispersion during periods of transfer or conversion.

Cultural systemic change would by definition involve the replacement of one qualitative type of cultural system by another. Such a change could conceivably be observed as a gradual replacement and/or revision of structural relationships between components

—a change so gradual as to be observed as largely quantitative when looking at the differences over comparatively short periods of time. In contrast to this gradual accumulation of small qualitative differences, "true" systemic change would more likely be very abrupt. If a component or a set or organization of components in a cultural system were to change markedly in form and behavior, the rest of the system should also have to make comparatively major adjustments.

Since we are viewing cultural change as involving two qualitatively different living systems, an explanation of cultural change would necessarily have to assert that the determinants of change exist outside the cultural system. The change would simply be an adaptation to new environmental variability. This perspective is a major departure from what archaeologists normally have thought to be relevant considerations in explaining prehistoric cultural change—that is, the geographic origins of the new cultural content. Even if foreign "origins" could be documented, the question remains as to why such foreign "traits" became part of the new system. If we are really interested in explaining cultural change, we would be interested in the interfaces between the cultural systems and their environments—specifically the points where matter and energy enter or leave systems. Changes in inputs of foods or fuels, for instance, would necessitate adjustments not only in extractive activities or technology but also in the manner in which people are organized to carry out these activities and the ideological means by which this organization is maintained. It follows from this discussion that the explanation of the change from one cultural system to another must take the form of a cultural-ecological study in that we are concerned with the relationship between cultural systems and their environments.

As an example of abrupt, relatively comprehensive cultural systemic change, I shall consider the shift in the northern portion of the Southwestern United States from the cultural-temporal period called Early Basket-maker (Basketmaker II) to that designated as Late Basketmaker (Basketmaker III). I would argue that this change involved a major shift in the proportions of products extracted from the environment, a shift in the technical means used to extract and utilize these products, and finally a shift in the organization of social groups associated with these activities.

Those Southwestern archaeologists who have considered the shift from Early to Late Basketmaker generally recognize the following developments as heralding the beginning of Late Basketmaker (cf. Morris 1939:11–29; McGregor 1965:170–86, 206–17 for syntheses of this shift): 1) An increased dependence on farming, 2) the addition of fired pottery containers to the previously exclusive use of basketry containers, and 3) a shift from spear-thrower (atlatl) to bow-and-arrow hunting. These changes are generally believed to have occurred around A.D. 400, and in addition to the "pure" Basketmaker in the Durango District, we are now aware of similar developments in adjacent areas of the San Juan Basin—for example, the Navajo Reservoir District (Eddy 1966).

Traditional explanations of these changes have centered around two themes: the migration of people, or the transmission of traits or ideas from the Mogollon area of the central Southwest (Gladwin 1957:72; McGregor 1965:206, 209, 216; Eddy 1966:479), where the cultural developments which occurred in the San Juan Basin are known to have occurred earlier (Wheat 1955:205 ff). The argument supporting a migration of peoples from the Mogollon to the Basketmaker areas is based on similarities between the two areas of various traits such as the brown color of pottery, pithouse architecture, and maize farming. However, such similarities are certainly not reliable indicators of population movement, and even if Mogollon peoples had expanded into the San Juan Basin, taking their culture with them, we must ask what happened to the indigenous San Juan popu-

lation and their culture. To say that the culture of the indigenous population was influenced by the culture of the invaders alludes to the equally unsatisfactory explanation of these changes by reference to diffusion of these "traits," "ideas," or "influences" from the Mogollon area. Even if diffusion or influence did take place, we must still explain why knowledge of the behavior of foreign peoples was accepted, which, in essence, is our original explanatory question. In the end, citation of diffusion or migration is largely irrelevant to the explanation of cultural change.

Explanation, in fact, never lies in citing particular origins or historical background (Spaulding 1968). Rather, an explanation is an argument that a particular phenomenon, or set of phenomena, is manifest or behaves in a specified manner because of the existence of another independent phenomenon or set of phenomena, and that this covariation is an example of a general class of covariations stated in a covering law or set of laws (Hempel 1966:49–54; Fritz and Plog 1968). In this regard, a law or set of related laws may be considered a premise. If it is true, then the observed articulation between phenomena is also true, given that the conditions for subsumption under the law are met. Cultural change, therefore, can only be explained by citation of independent, determining variables which covary with the cultural variability and by subsumption of this covariation under a law or laws relevant to human behavior.

The explanation of the Early-to-Late Basketmaker cultural change which I propose here is predicated on the assertion that a culture is a living, adaptive system. Starting with this assumption, general systems theory serves as a guide to constructing hypotheses regarding this explanatory problem. In formulating such an hypothesis the theory forces us initially to consider differences in the various forms of matter and energy which entered and left the Early and Late Basketmaker systems, as well as differences in the manner in which this matter and energy flowed through the systems as equilibrium fluxes. Specifically, the explanation which I would like to consider treats regional population density as largely an independent variable. I argue that population density was increasing through the Early Basketmaker period throughout the San Juan Basin, and that this disequilibrium between population input and output in Early Basketmaker cultural systems eventually caused enough stress on other components to induce a change to the Late Basketmaker systems.

Population density in the American Southwest was probably in a state of disequilibrium from a time not too long after the end of the Pleistocene epoch, and this disequilibrium was probably ultimately initiated by the broad environmental changes of the transition from the Pleistocene to the post-Pleistocene climate. Man's adaptations of the post-Pleistocene Archaic stage no longer involved the degree of mobility of the preceding Lithic stage (Willey and Phillips 1958:111). Instead, movement was relatively more restricted, and as a result the old homeostatic mechanisms normally controlling population numbers among mobile hunter-gatherers (infanticide, etc.) no longer operated. The American Southwest was very likely an area which received excess population from other areas where adaptations were of a relatively sedentary type. Coastal California, for instance, may have been providing population to interior areas for at least the last six millenia before Christ. Early Basketmaker culture, in fact, may represent an essentially Archaic type of cultural system undergoing a noticeable amount of stress. A consideration of the reasons underlying population increase, however, are not really essential to the particular problem at hand, which is the relationship between increase in population density, whatever its origin, and the rest of the Early and Late Basketmaker systems. My somewhat speculative comments, based on Binford's considerations of post-Pleistocene adaptations in an Old World setting (1968c), illustrate the need for much more research concerning the dynamics of population increase, not only in the Southwest, but also in North America as a whole.

Before going any further into the relationship between population density and cultural systems, a sketch of the biotic environment in which the Basketmaker populations lived is necessary. In the American Southwest certain regions are characterized by a large variety of edible plants and animals occurring in relatively high densities. By and large these regions are pinyon-juniper-covered plateaus or mesas, at altitudes between 6,500 and 7,500 feet above sea level, which are dissected, often deeply, by canyons with relatively permanent stream-flows. The canyon slopes and floors provide a number of biotic forms quite different from those of the plateaus. Thus we have two different biotic communities which alternate with each other over considerable areas of land. The pinyon-juniper plateau biotic community provides such edibles as pinyon nuts and juniper berries, prickly-pear cactus, and yucca, while the canyon biotic community produces a variety of annuals such as composites, amaranth, and a number of grasses. Taking advantage of both biotic communities are a variety of such animals as deer and rabbit, and these animals are often in much higher densities than in situations where either of the biotic communities is continuous. This phenomenon of higher densities of these animals (and possibly some plants) in situations where two biotic communities meet has been called by ecologists the edge effect, and the zone of contact or transition between two biotic communities is known as an ecotone (Odum and Odum 1959:278).

Early Basketmaker populations were also probably maximizing on the existence of two adjacent biotic communities. Still centered largely around hunting and gathering of wild foods, Early Basketmaker subsistence would have been most successful in these ecotone situations, and where the ecotones between the pinyon-juniper and canyon biotic communities were most frequent, so would be human populations. It is even possible that Early Basketmaker populations were relatively sedentary in these ecotone situations because of the close proximity of quantities of different resources coming from each biotic community, and it is also possible that population was increasing in such situations of greater sedentariness. Regardless of how varied the sources of populations increase might have been, a saturation distribution would ultimately have been reached. That is, the carrying capacity of the land, in terms of type of subsistence of Early Basketmaker culture, would have been reached. In terms of the proposed explanation, it is argued that the Early Basketmaker settlements in such regions as the vicinity of Kayenta, Arizona; Durango, Colorado; and the Navajo Reservoir District (Kidder and Guernsey 1919; Guernsey and Kidder 1921; Nusbaum 1922; Morris and Burgh 1954; Eddy and Dickey 1961)—essentially the northern half of the San Juan Basin—represent saturation distributions.

Once all of the environmental niches in which Early Basketmaker culture could flourish had been filled, less favorable portions of the San Juan Basin—probably the somewhat dryer areas of the southern San Juan Basin—would have begun to receive excess population. When the shift to a new type of adaptation was finally the only recourse, this would likely have occurred first in these dryer, marginal areas.

This brings us to the crux of the explanatory model. It is argued that increase in population density resulted in a reorganization of the Early Basketmaker cultural systems and that these reorganized cultural systems, as a systemic type, are what we know as Late Basketmaker, or Basketmaker III. This new systemic type would include, among others, such local phases as the Sambrito phase of the Navajo Reservoir District (Eddy 1966: 478–84) and the earlier portion of the La Plata phase of the Mesa Verde District (Hayes 1964:88) and Durango district (Morris and Burgh 1954:73; Gladwin 1957:

53). It is proposed that this cultural change involved two different technical aspects: 1) the development of more efficient means of food production whereby a given amount of food, as measured by units like calories, could be extracted from smaller amounts of land per capita population, and 2) the development of technological means whereby food could be preserved over longer periods of time and then reconstituted with minimal nutritional loss. Both of these developments involve the increased use and proliferation of facilities, which may be divided into three types based on their functions in retarding matter and energy dispersion. The first type, the agricultural field, is related to production of matter and energy, or rather its extraction or capture from the environment. While fields are not popularly thought of as facilities created by man, it should be pointed out that they are maintained in weeded and tilled artificial conditions, and in such conditions they serve as repositories of the mineral and organic energy which cultigens consume. Where farming was practiced during Early Basketmaker times, it was evidently a relatively casual activity, and fields were probably often no more than gardens from which relatively small yields were obtained. During Late Basketmaker times, however, fields were probably much more extensive in acreage, were located on landforms from which more dependable yields could be obtained, and were tilled and weeded more consistently in order to extract higher yields. Thus, increased farming, particularly of maize, allowed much higher inputs of subsistence energy from much smaller amounts of land than that which would yield nutritionally equivalent amounts from wild products. Therefore, a larger population than one existing primarily on a hunting-gathering subsistence could have been supported in the pinyon-juniper dissected plateaus or in areas somewhat marginal to these regions. It should be emphasized, however, that as far as the model is concerned the population pressure favored this development of productive facilities, rather than vice versa. In other words, increasing population input into the Basketmaker environments is the independent variable while the developments of productive and economic facilities are the dependent variables.

Another type of facility, the underground bottle-shaped roasting oven, has been found in large numbers in some Late Basketmaker sites while they are rare in Early Basketmaker sites. There are several possibilities as to how this type of facility is related to other cultural components in minimizing food energy loss during storage and fuel energy loss during food preparation. In fact, these ovens may actually have entered into the energy flow networks of Late Basketmaker cultural systems in several different ways in increasing economy of energy expenditure. Generally, these facilities would have enhanced efficient energy conversion by containing the maize and heat energy in bounded units of space. More specifically, the roasting of those ears of maize not reaching maturity naturally would have enhanced its storage and nutritional qualities (Cushing 1920). Also, roasting green corn would have increased its nutritional value by exploding its starch grains (Ford 1968:2–3). After the roasted corn had been dried, it would have taken less heat energy to cook it into a palatable and nutritious form. In the winter, when firewood would have been more difficult to acquire, or in areas marginal to pinyon-juniper woodlands the use of ovens could have made quite a difference. Finally, the roasting of green corn would have killed any insect pests within the ears. The importance of these ovens, regardless of their specific position or positions in an energy flow network, is well demonstrated in the work at the Navajo Reservoir District. While some pit ovens were discovered associated with remains of the Early Basketmaker period (Los Pinos Phase), by far much larger numbers were found in sites or components of the Late Basketmaker period (Sambrito Phase) (Eddy 1966:214–40, 352).

A pottery container is another facility used in energy conversion, but in this regard the process is reconstitution rather than preservation. Pottery vessels are relatively quickly made and are certainly more versatile than baskets in culinary activities. They may be applied directly to the fire, thus eliminating the need for basket-boiling with heated rocks. With a larger portion of the diet consisting of maize, pottery cooking may have been necessary simply to minimize the time necessary to reconstitute maize. Pottery vessels also allow foods to be simmered for long periods of time without constant attention – a quality which not only would have been necessary to make maize not previously roasted nutritious but also would have been of great value during periods of peak daily activity in the fields. Thus, pottery would have entered into the Late Basketmaker energy flow systems as a component minimizing the expenditure of energy in food preparation by decreasing both fuel expenditure and human energy expenditure while maximizing the amount of food energy available in maize.

The initial use of fired pottery from the Navajo Reservoir sites of the Los Pinos and Sambrito Phases may date as early as A.D. 300, and Chapin Gray sherds were found associated with these types in deposits dating after about A.D. 450 (Eddy 1966:451, 454–55). Later, Late Basketmaker pottery occurs in greater quantities in sites all over the San Juan Basin, including such types as Lino Gray, Chapin Gray, and Obelish Gray (Colton 1955; Abel 1955).

The last type of facility to be considered is that for preservation or storage. Food storage by Early Basketmaker populations is well documented compared to what we know of pre-Basketmaker or Archaic adaptations, but beginning in Late Basketmaker times, there is a marked increase in storage space and a shift to different forms of storage facilities. Early Basketmaker population was apparently dense enough to necessitate gaining time utility of both wild and domestic seeds through their storage over the leanest season of the year. Nevertheless, enough wild plants were probably available during winter and early spring to avoid having to store large amounts. However, as population density increased toward Late Basketmaker times more seeds would have to be stored. Since wild seed-bearing plants were not increasing concomitantly, farming would have been increased, not only to compensate for diminishing amounts of harvestable wild seeds per capita population, but also to compensate for per capita decreases in wild foods used in winter and early spring. Therefore, we would expect Late Basketmaker storage facilities to have been considerably larger in volume per capita population, reflecting both increased dependence on farming and the expansion of the time utility of stored foods.

In Early Basketmaker times storage facilities were subterranean or semisubterranean cists in the floors of dry caves of the Kayenta District and adjacent portions of southern Utah or in and around houses in the Durango and Navajo Reservoir Districts (Kidder and Guernsey 1919; Guernsey and Kidder 1921; Nusbaum 1922; Morris and Burgh 1954; Eddy and Dickey 1961). While the number of cists at any one of these sites is often large, the refuse or burials found in most indicate that only a few were in use at any one time—probably two to four based on Morris and Burgh's site descriptions. This would represent approximately 30 to 60 cubic feet of storage space per household. By Late Basketmaker times the volume of storage space increased markedly. In the Navajo Reservoir District during the Sambrito Phase storage continued in underground cists, and the number per household apparently increased, if the 40-odd roasting-storage cists found at the Oven Site are any indication (Eddy 1966:214). At other Late Basketmaker sites dating toward A.D. 600–700 the increase in storage space is even more pronounced. Shabik'eshchee Village in the Chaco District contained a number of semisubterranean storage rooms about eight feet in diameter—much larger than Early Basketmaker cists (Roberts 1929). In other Late Basketmaker sites of the Durango, La Plata, Ackmen-Lowry, and other districts storage facilities took the form of above-ground, rectangular, contiguous rooms (Morris and Burgh 1954:85; Morris 1939; Martin 1939). Although it is difficult to determine the volume of storage space per capita of Late Basketmaker population due to sampling error during excavation and problems of establishing contemporaneity between houses and storage rooms, a guess that volumes per capita more than doubled compared to Early Basketmaker volumes is probably conservative. The shift to aboveground storage rooms would seem to have occurred when labor expended in building and maintaining increased numbers of storage facilities was less for the aboveground as opposed to the underground types and when site locations shifted to landforms with sandier bases.

Covarying with the changes in storage and conversion facilities is a shift from one type of hunting weapon to another—the atlatl and dart to the bow-and-arrow. This change is probably directly related to the restructuring of human activities from Early to Late Basketmaker times. Specifically, the increased variety and numbers of facilities in Late Basketmaker cultural systems implies concomitant increases in maintenance activities associated with tending fields and building and repairing storage and conversion facilities. Human energy input into such activities would have been much higher than previously, and this situation would have put stress on another process of the cultural system—this being the extraction of protein-rich food resources from the environment in order to supplement the protein-poor maize in maintaining health. While beans would certainly have been helpful in supplying this needed protein, meat would have supplied a higher quality protein if less time-consuming methods of hunting were practiced. The bow-and-arrow would have provided this efficiency by providing the advantages of ambush, by expanding the hunt to more thickly wooded lands, and perhaps by increasing the variety of smaller animals which could be effectively hunted. Reflected in the much smaller size of projectile points, all the above-cited archaeological work in the San Juan Basin indicates that the shift to the bow-and-arrow occurred relatively abruptly with the inception of the Late Basketmaker period.

To summarize, an attempt was made to develop a series of hypotheses having to do with the changes from Early to Late Basketmaker cultural systems in the proportions of the kinds of energy entering the systems and the manners by which this energy was processed. The model of change was based on what we already know about Early and Late Basketmaker facilities as well as some predictions about poorly documented aspects of our knowledge of Basketmaker facilities. It was argued that the archaeological record reflects changes in the energy flow networks involving processes of energy storage and conversion. While storage and conversion facilities were present in the Early Basketmaker cultural systems, it was proposed that these were inefficient with respect to the larger amounts of maize required for per capita subsistence of Late Basketmaker populations. These efficiencies are measured primarily in terms of the amount of human energy and fuel expended to produce a given unit of food. In addition to the replacement of Early Basketmaker facilities by larger and/or more efficient Late Basketmaker forms, roasting ovens may have been an entirely new type of facility added to the system serving to enhance the energy conservation capabilities of the other storage and conversion facilities.

The stress forcing the development of the larger and more complex Late Basketmaker facility system was argued to have been the increases in population input into the San Juan Basin which ultimately resulted in decreases in the inputs of wild foods from the environments of the basin. In spite of the new efficiencies obtained in the development of the Late Basketmaker facilities system,

the total amount of energy expended by Late Basketmaker populations in obtaining a per capita subsistence was undoubtedly much higher than before. In other words, the more facilities that must be involved in supporting a human population, the greater is the per capita energy expenditure. Late Basketmaker populations had to pay the consequence of living in denser numbers in roughly the same environment as their predecessors by expending more energy in their sustenance. Incidentally, this relationship between population density and the amount of energy expended in the operation of cultural systems may be conceived as a cultural law covering the model of Early-to-Late Basketmaker evolutionary development. More specifically, this law states that with an increase in population density we would expect a concomitant increase in the amount of energy processed through facilities. The similarity between this law and White's law of evolution is not fortuitous (White 1959:56). Such a change will occur when the environmental carrying capacity with respect to a given facilities system is finally reached.

Little was mentioned regarding changes in human activities and social organization because of the complexities of obtaining reflections of these in the published archaeological record. Besides the previously mentioned likelihood that many more extractive and maintenance activities would have been involved in building and maintaining facilities in Late Basketmaker times, we would also expect that human energy output was minimized by combining the labors of several families in communal activities. The increase in size of Late Basketmaker communities beyond those of Early Basketmakers may be used as a reflection of this change in activity structure. Early Basketmaker sites probably contained no more than two or three houses occupied contemporaneously (in spite of the designation of such sites as "villages") while Late Basketmaker communities were considerably larger, particularly toward A.D. 600–700. Thus, not only did the facilities system change, but also the population very likely was articulated to them in a different manner than before. That these social changes were coupled with a wide variety of technical changes, all occurring within a comparatively short span of time, lends considerable support to the assertion that the changes from Early to Late Basketmaker was truly an overall systemic change. Formal similarities between Early and Late Basketmaker facilities certainly exist, but this only reflects the principle that in formulating a new cultural system as much of the old system will be included as possible. What is really relevant to identifying cultural systemic change is the manner in which cultural components (technical and social components in the present context) are articulated with each other by energy flow networks.

To adequately test the previously mentioned hypotheses having to do with the relationships between population density, environment, facilities, and social organization in terms of the energy flow networks which joined all of these components, much effort would have to be devoted to development of test implications. This would be far beyond the scope of an essay which is intended to demonstrate how systems theory may be deductively applied to an archaeological problem of explanation. So I will direct my attention to only a few hypotheses having to do with the relationship between population density and the geographic distributions of resources. In terms of economy of effort devoted to testing the model, this would be a good point to begin.

First, we would expect that if population was increasing from the Archaic, through Early Basketmaker, and into Late Basketmaker times, there would be increasing numbers of contemporaneous house units through this period of time, controlling for increase in household size and community size. Systematic surveys of whole districts would provide the necessary data, however, the number of published surveys is still scant and many of the earlier surveys are subject to the possibility of gross sampling error.

Nevertheless, the available data do indicate that the numbers of sites increased markedly during Late Basketmaker times. This is apparent in the remarks of Morris and Burgh (1954:73) and Gladwin (1957:53) concerning Late Basketmaker sites in the Durango District, and it is also evident in Morris's work in the La Plata District and Herold's summaries of site distribution of Mesa Verde and adjacent regions (1961). But the postulated increase is not so obvious in the Navajo Reservoir District. This anomaly may be accounted for by the fact that Late Basketmaker sites, as opposed to Early Basketmaker sites, are invariably covered by later occupational debris and were revealed only by excavation (Eddy 1966:478). In fact, superimposition of Late Basketmaker sites by later occupational debris is probably a widespread phenomenon. Similar cases are evident in Morris's work in the La Plata district (1939) and in Morris and Burgh's comments concerning distributions of Late Basketmaker and Pueblo I sites in the Durango District (Morris and Burgh 1954:86). It is significant, therefore, that in spite of the obscurity of Late Basketmaker site distributions the number is still much greater than that of Early Basketmaker sites.

Through knowledge of site distributions and the distributions of flora and fauna exploited by Early Basketmakers, which was previously postulated to be in situations where well-watered canyons are flanked by pinyon-juniper woodland, we should be able to discover whether or not population pressures did exist at the end of the Early Basketmaker period. If the population was at an extent where all resources in a region were fully exploited—that is, where all biotic resources were being consumed at, near, or just beyond their reproductive capacity, we would have a saturation distribution of population. In identifying a saturation distribution, we would need to know the amount of land area in various biotic communities necessary for a given population number. This, of course, would have to be determined from other sources of information, such as human dietary requirements of present-day or historic populations living in saturation distributions.

Going on to the ecological relationships of Late Basketmaker sites, we would expect that their distribution would be correlated with the distribution of farmable land. Here landform and soil characteristics would be important, and although we know comparatively little about the optimal landform and soil conditions for growing aboriginal varieties of maize with particular forms of farming technology, alluvial fans or bottomlands of sandy loam, containing some ground water throughout the summer, would certainly be a close estimation. Such land would be found in the canyon bottoms of the comparatively well-watered pinyon-juniper plateau country of the San Juan Basin—in other words, in the localities occupied by Early Basketmaker populations. But such land optimal for farming comprises a very small and scattered percentage of the land surface, so as population density increased we would expect Late Basketmaker sites to be located in marginal areas where the growing season was still long enough for maize and where larger tracts of land are available for farming. These lands are probably floodplains which are watered by runoff and sheet floods more than they are by rainfall, groundwater, or springs. In the San Juan Basin such locations are at lower altitudes, downstream from the centers of Early Basketmaker site distributions. Nevertheless, we would expect at least some of the variability in site locations to be determined by densities of such fauna as deer and by locations of firewood. A hint of a shift in the distributions between Early and Late Basketmaker times is evident in Herold's analysis (1961:65–69). This analysis, based on all known data up to that time, indicates a general shift to southerly portions of the San Juan Basin during Late Basketmaker times —that is, a shift to lower, broader portions of drainages where farmable land is more abundant. In addition, Morris and Burgh and Gladwin imply that Late Basketmaker sites are located farther south and downstream in

the Animas Valley than Early Basketmaker sites (Morris and Burgh 1954:85; Gladwin 1957:53), and Morris reports sites in environmentally analogous portions of the La Plata District. An exception to this marked trend is the high density of Late Basketmaker sites on Mesa Verde (Herold 1961:67), but this anomaly may be a result of the comparatively unique environmental characteristics of this district. By and large, then, the data do support the contention that Late Basketmaker population density shifted to portions of the San Juan Basin where larger albeit less than optimal tracts of arable land are located.

In conclusion, I have attempted to demonstrate through the course of this essay that if we begin with a set of assumptions about the nature of living systems derived from general theory, we would expect cultural systems, as a type of living system, to have certain characteristics dealing with inputs and outputs of matter and energy and with flows of energy through the system which account for dependent relationships between parts of the cultural system. To put it another way, general systems theory forces us to look at aspects of a cultural system's technology, social organization, and ideology as components through which measurable quantities of matter and energy pass in specific patterns of flow. Moreover, general systems theory forces us to assume that a cultural system will remain in steady-state until such a time that changes of significant magnitude take place in the cultural system's inputs and/or outputs. As an example of cultural systemic change, a model of the changes in Basketmaker agricultural facilities systems was developed based on known archaeological data. It was argued that changes in facilities reflect changes in how foods, fuels, and human energy were processed or converted from one form to another. From the perspective that facilities are those aspects of technology which impede or control the flow of energy, the change to a Late Basketmaker facilities system represented new means of economizing foods, fuels, and human work.

302

NOTE

This essay is a revision of an earlier paper entitled "General Systems Theory and its Application to a Problem of Archaeological Explanation: Basketmaker Settlement in the Northern Southwest," presented in the symposium "Archaeological Theory and Method—1968" at the Pecos Conference, El Paso, Texas, August 1968. I wish to express my gratitude to Lewis R. Binford for introducing me to General Systems Theory and its pertinence to anthropological problems of explanation.

The Hopewell Interaction Sphere in Riverine–Western Great Lakes Culture History

"HOPEWELL" or "Hopewellian" has become a household term in eastern North American archaeology over the years, yet it has been used in so many contexts and in so many ways that its meaning is blurred. A brief glance at the literature finds Hopewellian referring alternately to a culture type, a culture phase, a temporal horizon, and a form of burial complex or cult, to list only the more common usages. As the tempo of archaeology in this country increases, so does interest in the prehistoric expressions to which the name "Hopewell" is applied. In turn, this forces us to reconsider the nature of the commonality of these expressions and to seek an understanding of the cultural processes responsible for this commonality.

At the outset, anyone who reviews the archaeological expressions labelled Hopewell is faced with a number of regionally distinct cultural systems, whether he looks at the structure of burial, community patterning, or regional demography. These regional expressions exhibit in common a number of artifact styles and exotic raw materials. The most important of the latter are copper, marine shells, mica, and obsidian, with a host of natural products such as tortoise shell, shark and alligator teeth, meteoric iron, etc., of

Reprinted from Illinois State Museum Scientific Papers, vol. 12, 1964, *Hopewellian Studies,* edited by Joseph R. Caldwell and Robert L. Hall, pp. 85–106. By permission of the author and the Illinois State Museum

minor significance. Finished goods occurring in many, though not all, regions include bicymbal copper earspools; "pulley-type" earspools of pottery, copper breastplates, panpipes, and celts, chipped obsidian artifacts; marine shell containers and beads; cut mica sheets, sometimes taking geometric or representational forms; worked bear canine teeth; plain and effigy platform pipes; human figurines of pottery; and a special class of pottery vessels described as Hopewell series in Ohio and Illinois. These items were obtained through participation in a logistics network for which the term *Hopewell Interaction Sphere* is used here.[1]

Detailed formal comparison of Hopewell artifacts in various regions would show, I believe, that primarily raw materials and stylistic concepts, not finished goods, were moving through the network. In addition, certain general conformities in burial practices (with which these artifacts are most often associated) suggest that the interaction also involved dissemination of ideological rationalizations for use of these goods. It is clear from the evidence that considerable local reinterpretation of diagnostic Hopewell artifact forms and ideological concepts (as reflected chiefly in the structure of burial) occurred. The increasing body of radiocarbon dates available suggest 100 B.C. as an approximate beginning for the Interaction Sphere, and A.D. 300 to 350 for its attenuation.

It tends to be overlooked that, while final

304

disposition of Hopewell items was usually in the graves of selected dead, this neither makes these specifically mortuary goods nor indicates that the various local expressions were part of any pan-regional burial complex or cult. There is ample evidence, particularly from recently excavated habitation sites in the Illinois River Valley and in the Scioto drainage of southern Ohio, that typical Hopewell finished goods and raw materials were kept and utilized in the community where they were frequently lost. In short, the artifacts and materials circulated within the Hopewell Interaction Sphere were not mortuary items per se. It is better to conceive of them as status-specific objects which functioned in various ritual and social contexts within community life. Eventually all or a portion were removed from this milieu and deposited as personal belongings or contributed goods with the dead, reaffirming the status of the deceased.

Evidence for a "Hopewellian mortuary complex" on a pan-regional basis does not exist. Certainly this is not what is implied in the interaction sphere concept. The Hopewell Interaction Sphere simply refers to relations of a still undetermined nature, though involving idea and goods exchange, between groups scattered over a broad area of eastern North America. Though a distinct burial pattern is associated with Hopewell objects in the Riverine–Western Great Lakes Area, one need only look at the form and content of Mound City, Turner, Seip, and other Ohio earthworks and compare them with the "Hopewell" burial sites in Illinois to realize that societies on quite different levels of complexity participated in the interaction sphere, albeit differentially. The structure of burial varies markedly between these divergent cultural systems.

Therefore, for purposes of the present discussion the term "Hopewell" is used to describe the prehistoric logistics network within which quantities of raw materials circulated, together with an array of stylistic and probably ideological concepts that underwent local modification.

What the mechanisms of interaction were between local groups and between far-distant ones remains to be demonstrated, as do the specific functional contexts within which these items were used in each participating society. And, of course, the degree and form of participation has yet to be explicated for the various local manifestations.

It is clear that by Early Woodland times (ca. 800 B.C.) a number of regional traditions are definable for the eastern Woodlands (Caldwell 1958). These are, in fact, macro-style zones based largely on ceramic decorations and vessel form. More importantly, they are correlated with differences in ecological adaptation; such diversity is an important continuation of the increasing adaptive specificity Caldwell regards as the primary theme of Archaic and Woodland culture history. Abruptly, Hopewell forms appear in restricted locales in all of these traditions.

Explanations for differences in participation in the Hopewell Interaction Sphere between these traditions and between localities within each tradition have yet to be made. Eventually these will be phrased in terms of the processes responsible for the continuities and change between the various still-to-be-defined cultural systems represented in both the participating and nonparticipating localities. Specific historical explanations have been offered which attempt to fix the origin of Hopewell styles in a given locality or region. Such explanations, even if archaeologically substantiated, do not in fact explain Hopewell development anywhere. They describe the results of cultural process without elucidating the process itself.

To solve the problem of whether the raptorial bird motif, characteristic of the Marksville ceramic series in the lower Mississippi, was created in the north and moved south, or vice versa, does not tell what cultural changes in both regions (and perhaps others as well) were prerequisite to and responsible for the widespread interaction reflected in this style sharing.

Binford (1964b) has called for the "regional approach" in designing archaeological research programs. This is characterized as "the detailed and systematic study of regions that can be expected to have supported cultural systems. . . . The isolation and definition of the *content, structure,* and *range* of a cultural system together with its ecological relationships is viewed as a research objective."

Research programs designed to achieve these objectives are necessary if we are to explain the sudden appearance of Hopewell styles within certain locales and their extensive distribution throughout eastern North America. Excavation programs might well focus initially on regions where Hopewell manifestations are documented. In each it will be important to elucidate changes in the cultural system, both in its articulation with the physical environment and with other cultural systems impinging on it. It might be suggested, for example, that the rapid spread and marked uniformity of Hopewell styles within the middle and lower Illinois Valley attests to the expansion of a dominant mode of adaptation at the expense of less efficient ones. It remains then to demonstrate of what this new adaptation consisted.

Within this frame of reference this essay deals with two problems:

1) The attempt to define each of two regional traditions or macro-style zones encompassed within the Riverine–Western Great Lakes area in which extensive Hopewell activity is documented (see Fig. *1*).

2) To present evidence for local diversity within these traditions with respect to participation in the Hopewell Interaction Sphere. This is measured in terms of typical Hopewell artifact distributions. In turn, these are correlated with quantitative variation in site and artifact data employed as indices of population density and with the differential distribution of Hopewell-related mortuary activity. An hypothesis is advanced to explain the contrasts and similarities between localities; this in turn suggests processes responsible for the form and distribution of the interaction sphere.

Two of the seven regional traditions outlined by Caldwell are of concern here – the Havana and Crab Orchard. Without attempting a definitive distributional study, artifact styles diagnostic of the Havana tradition extend from northeastern Oklahoma and western Missouri eastward to include the Illinois River system and all of the State of Illinois south to the Big Muddy–Crab Orchard drainage near the Ohio River. On the Mississippi, Havana manifestations are known from as far south as the mouth of the Kaskaskia River, as far north as the Red Cedar River in Wisconsin and the southern edge of the Anoka Sand Plain just north of Minneapolis. Eastward it encompasses the middle Wabash Valley and, on the basis of recent excavations by the University of Michigan, appears to extend into the Saginaw basin (James B. Griffin, personal communication). Significantly, the boundaries of the Havana tradition are coextensive with those of the eastern Prairie (Brown 1965).

To date, the Havana tradition is best documented in terms of continuities in ceramics, and to a lesser extent in chipped stone, established on Illinois Valley materials. Most diagnostic is the Havana pottery series. According to the recent projectile point typology developed by Howard Winters, the corner-notched Snyders point is typical while the Dickson broad-bladed type of the Belknap type-cluster is also important. The latter falls within the range of "Gary" points described in the literature. Lacking adequate distribution studies, we can speculate that Havana is characterized by high frequencies of small, rectangular flint hoes, lamellar flake blades, end-scrapers made on lamellar flakes, and to a lesser extent, disc-shaped scrapers made from a lamellar flake core. Celts are the dominant woodworking tool with perhaps a survival of the three-quarter grooved axe. Diagnostic Havana burial practices cannot be described since mortuary evidence except for the Hopewellian phase is unknown.

The Crab Orchard tradition includes an area across southern Illinois on a line from the lower Wabash to the Fountain Bluff

306

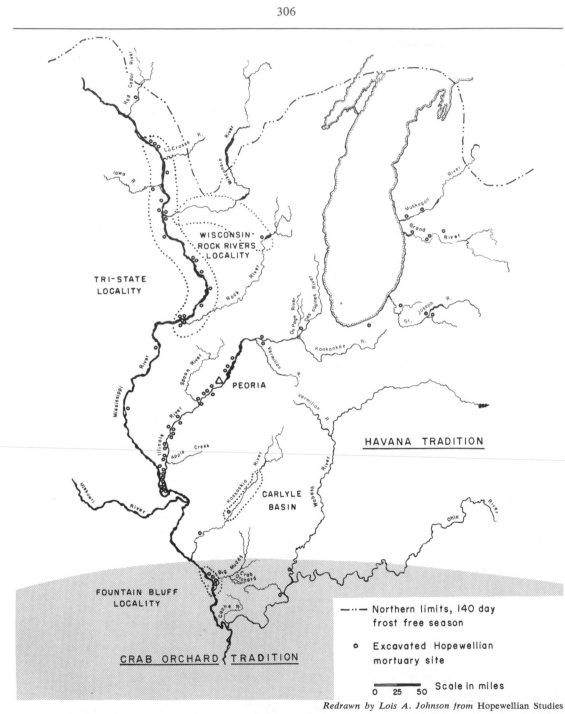

FIG. 1. *Documented Hopewellian burial components within the Havana and Crab Orchard traditions.*

locality on the Mississippi (see Fig. *1*). Crab Orchard is distinguished primarily by its cordmarked and fabric-impressed, grog (i.e. crushed sherd) tempered pottery. Winters's (n.d.) recent survey disclosed that during the Middle Woodland period this fabric-impressed ware occurs alone in the lower Cache River Valley whereas it, together with cordmarked surfaces, constitutes a pottery assemblage in the upper reaches of that valley. The northern cordmarked tradition, which obtains its fullest expression in Havana, is earliest exemplified in southern Illinois by Sugar Hill Cordmarked centering in the nearby Big Muddy–Crab Orchard drainage. Evidence from the upper Cache testifies to the early fusion of the northward spreading fabric-impressed ceramic, diagnostic of Caldwell's Middle Eastern tradition (1958:23), with this local cordmarked pottery.

In short, the upper Cache River Valley is a shatter zone in which northern and southern traditions overlap. Here, and in the adjacent Big Muddy, cordmarking carries over and together with fabric-impressing is characteristic of the Crab Orchard tradition. Other diagnostic Crab Orchard styles include the Tamms Expanding-Stem type-cluster in Winters's forthcoming projectile point classification. Petaloid celts occur in relatively high frequencies. Grooved axes are absent. Finally, and importantly, the northern limits of the Carb Orchard style zone are coterminous with those of the Oak-Hickory Forest.

Over the past 35 years the Riverine–Western Great Lakes area has been the scene of intensive archaeological activity. In consequence, enough data have accumulated to allow the tentative definition of several geographically restricted localities. On the basis of commonality in artifact styles, general uniformity in numbers and types of sites, and degree of mortuary activity, these can be treated for purposes of discussion as units persisting throughout the duration of the Havana and Crab Orchard traditions.

These include the Illinois River Valley, the Tri-State and Fountain Bluff localities on the Mississippi, the Carlyle Reservoir in the Kaskaskia Valley, the middle and lower Wabash, the Wisconsin-Rock rivers locality, the Big Muddy–Crab Orchard drainage, and the Cache River Valley. Current and projected work in the Spoon, Du Page, La Crosse and lower Rock River valleys will soon allow us to delimit additional localities.

Prerequisite to assessing similarities and contrasts in cultural development from one locality to another is establishment of an adequate chronology. Within the Havana tradition we must depend at present on the pottery sequence established on Illinois Valley materials. This can be broken down into two major phases, with an episode of rapid and extensive change forming a juncture between them. In absolute terms, this sequence conforms to the Middle Woodland period which dates from about 400 B.C. to A.D. 350. A comparable breakdown is not available for lithic and other artifact classes. Therefore, ceramics alone must serve to assess a) the history of style change within each of the aforementioned Havana (and to some extent, Crab Orchard) localities, and b) the degree of interaction between localities during each phase.

Unpublished data from the writer's recent stratitests at the Snyders and Apple Creek sites, along with materials from the 1961 Illinois State Museum excavations at the Pond site, are combined with earlier studies by Baker, Griffin, Morgan et al. (1941), Griffin (1952a), Fowler (1955), and Powell (1957) in constructing the following sequence.

Unfortunately, little is known of the ceramics of the preceding Black Sands [2] and Morton complexes (Griffin 1952a:98–101), but the Early Havana phase (ca. 400 B.C. to 100 B.C.) is highlighted by changes in vessel morphology and by the advent of stamping treatments among the decorative attributes. Included are crescent, ovoid, and straight dentate stamped varieties. Until excavation of the single component Pond site in the middle Illinois Valley, this early phase was poorly understood. Pond yielded ceramics of the Havana series only. The dominant surface treatment is smoothed-over cordmarked (i.e. cord impressions almost totally obliterated), with other cordmarking rare. The predominant Havana decorative attributes are crescent and ovoid stamping, with straight dentate stamping of secondary importance. The carry-over of earlier Morton concepts is reflected in the emphasis on lower rim band decoration and continuation of the herringbone pattern. Use of rim nodes occurs infrequently in early Havana.

The succeeding, or "Hopewellian," phase

of the Havana tradition in the Illinois Valley marks a significant change in the pottery assemblage. Introduction of the fully developed Hopewell pottery series occurs. Local or foreign antecedents for this ceramic have yet to be confirmed. Within the Havana series crescent and ovoid stamping diminish while straight dentate-stamped rims and zoned bodies, together with cordmarked surfaces, predominate. Rim nodes assume importance at this time.

It was originally thought that following the Hopewellian phase of the Havana tradition there was a sufficient stylistic carry-over to warrant definitions of a "Late Havana" phase. Indeed, in the Weaver ceramic series cord-wrapped-stick and plain-stamped rims represent carry-overs of Havana decorative attributes. In the Apple Creek series of the White Hall phase (ca. A.D. 350–A.D. 650) in the lower Illinois Valley cordmarked or cord-wrapped-stick stamped upper rims separated from a smooth-surfaced neck by a row of hemiconical punctates are typical. While the decorative devices are not always the same, the relationships of decorative elements on the exterior of the Apple Creek vessels duplicate that of the earlier Hopewell series.

The fact that Weaver and Apple Creek pottery includes a few Havana and Hopewell series decorative or morphological attributes does not warrant considering these as local variants of a third or "Late" Havana phase. Such terminology only obscures a significant episode of rapid and extensive stylistic change. While changes do occur in the Havana series from the Early Havana to the Hopewellian phases, these changes are limited and the term Havana series is still legitimately applied to the pottery of both phases. But the diagnostic pottery series of the following cultural phase are sufficiently different that they cannot be classified as a later variant within the Havana series.

In sum, the Hopewellian phase of the Havana tradition, at least from the Illinois Valley evidence, terminates with an episode of extensive change in ceramics and other artifact classes, including those diagnostic of both the Hopewell Interaction Sphere and the Havana tradition as well. For this region at least, this marks the end of the interaction sphere and the Havana tradition. While these impressions appear to fit the evidence, the degree of carry-over in artifact styles and burial forms of the Hopewellian phase into the various succeeding phases classified as Late Woodland remains to be demonstrated through quantitative studies.

It is probable that when more extensive work has been done, the long Hopewellian phase (ca. 100 B.C. to A.D. 350) may be divisible into two or more phases on the basis of documented stylistic changes. To date, however, no one has demonstrated style change within what is defined herein as the Hopewellian phase in the Illinois Valley or any other locality within the Havana tradition. Speculation on this question is common archaeological parlor conversation, and there have been attempts through pottery seriation (Fowler 1955) to show change. However sampling vagaries alone call into question the results of these attempts at using the seriation technique.

To date, detailed distributional studies of the two-phase Havana ceramic complex within the Riverine–Western Great Lakes area remain to be undertaken, but available evidence confirms a markedly localized and variable pattern of occurrence. Marked shifts in distribution between the Early Havana and Hopewellian phases are also indicated.

Seventy-three mortuary components excavated in the Riverine–Western Great Lakes area have yielded artifacts typical of the Hopewell Interaction Sphere. In the broadest sense these sites display a structural similarity, i.e. linear arrangements of small earth mounds covering high-status burials placed in central log crypts. They, too, have an irregular geographical distribution (Fig. 1). It is noteworthy that localities manifesting the strongest expression of Hopewellian phase ceramics as described for the Illinois Valley are those in which the Hopewell Interaction Sphere was most active as reflected in its diagnostic raw materials, artifact forms and burial modes.

The phase-by-phase shift in distribution of Havana ceramic types, when correlated with the initial appearance of Hopewell goods and related mortuary activity, is significant. Involvement of the Tri-State and Fountain Bluff localities and the Illinois, Kaskaskia, and Wabash valleys in a vigorous interaction during the Hopewellian phase, documented in the sharing of ceramic and mortuary forms, follows an early phase in which distribution of pottery types is much more restricted. No evidence for a common mortuary pattern exists for the early Havana phase. There are hints that in the succeeding early phases of the Late Woodland period a localization of burial practices parallels a breakdown of the widespread sharing of Havana and Hopewell pottery styles; the latter involves the appearance of a number of cordmarked wares, each with a strong local expression (e.g. Weaver, Apple Creek, Leland, Canteen or Jersey Bluff, Snyders Bluff, Raymond, Lewis, etc.).

The picture thus created is one of rapid and extensive change in ceramics marking the advent of the Hopewellian phase in the Illinois Valley, associated with development of an interaction sphere involving groups in a limited number of the Havana and Crab Orchard localities recognized here. Contemporary with this is the emergence of a broadly similar burial pattern whose most extensive expression is found in these same localities. By contrast, this series of events is unknown for the Wisconsin-Rock and the Big Muddy–Crab Orchard, Spoon, and Cache river localities. Evidence for their participation in the interaction is restricted largely to adoption of a few Havana and Hopewell series decorative devices (e.g. straight dentate and cord-wrapped-stick stamping; cross-hatch rim incising), with incorporation of these into a local ceramic complex. Again, Hopewell artifacts and associated burial forms in the Riverine–Western Great Lakes area are not documented for these localities.

Accompanying these changes there occurs in the Hopewellian phase of the Havana and Crab Orchard traditions a significant rise in number and size of habitation sites. Midden deposits become deeper and artifact densities higher. These and additional factors point to a large-scale population expansion during Hopewellian times, at least in the lower and middle Illinois Valley from which our best evidence comes. It can be speculated that investigation would disclose a similar phenomenon for all localities participating in the vigorous interaction and sharing a common Hopewell burial mode at this time.

To explain this parallel and generally synchronous emergence of a) ceramic styles, b) a logistics network, c) mortuary practices, and suggestively, d) a marked population expansion as well, it is important to assess their distribution in a number of ecological contexts. Fowler (1957) has proposed the idea of an independent development of horticulture in the central Mississippi basin on a late Archaic horizon. He noted the affinity of certain local plant species to soils disturbed by human habitation and asked whether these might not be linked to the beginning of a simple cultivation, one requiring no special technological preparedness, a minimum investment of labor, and little alteration of overall subsistence patterns. Finally, and importantly, this beginning horticulture was restricted to a highly localized ecological situation.

What model of changing subsistence-settlement patterns and social organization best accounts for the advent of cultivation in the context suggested by Fowler? Earliest plant manipulation leading to horticulture may well have occurred in an adaptive milieu featuring a collecting adjustment noteworthy for its high level productivity and subsistence security in a context of marked residential stability. Extending this picture, subsistence activities are seen as strongly oriented to exploitation of natural plant resources (though hunting may still have been important).

In eastern North America this adaptive milieu is approximated during late Archaic times in the valley–riverine area centering about the confluence of the Ohio, Missouri, Illinois, and Mississippi rivers. Here there is abundant evidence for a shift to an aquatic adaptation with a heavy reliance on shellfish. Deep midden deposits, quantities of storage-refuse pits, and high artifact densities reflect the efficient, diversified collecting adjustment to which Caldwell (1958) has given the name "Primary Forest Efficiency." Both seasonal reoccupation of the same site from year to year and a shift to natural plant foods are indicated (Caldwell 1958:12 ff). The high level of residential stability implied is prerequisite to the development of a "dump heap" situation in which the commensalism, likely so important to earliest plant manipulation, was possible.

It is further suggested that in this context the reorientation of labor responsibilities, from one emphasizing a division between procurement and preparation to one differentiating male-female subsistence roles along lines of major food resources, may have provided for the first time a social milieu in which experimental manipulation of commensal plants could have occurred.[3]

While Braidwood and Reed (1957:21) feel that an efficient, highly productive collecting pattern like that described by Caldwell for the Eastern Woodlands may have mitigated against the development of horticulture, the present hypothesis contends that it provided for the first time in this area a milieu in which this shift could occur. During the preceding middle Archaic a hunting-oriented subsistence pattern can be postulated emphasizing a division of labor along lines of procurement and preparation, i.e. men procured the animal, women prepared it. Such a division of labor, with its ritual enunciation in a variety of contexts, may well have constituted an effective barrier to plant manipulation. Not until the late Archaic, with its greater emphasis on plant resources and greater permanence of settlement, can we postulate a shift in division of work responsibilities with women acting importantly for the first time in a procurement role.

The crucial element is not local vs. tropical origins for horticulture in eastern North America, but the adaptive milieu within which this important shift in food-getting practices would be expected, whatever the origin of the plant forms themselves. The subsistence-settlement system, with functionally related aspects of social organization (e.g. division of labor), important for the development of an hypothetical eastern agricultural complex based on commensal plants might be expected to duplicate that necessary for the effective adoption and utilization of introduced cultigens.

It is argued here that a complex of factors set the stage for plant manipulation in certain riverine situations. The most important factors were: a) increased subsistence security and residential stability prerequisite to establishment of a "dump heap" situation; b) an increasing reliance on natural plant foods; c) a shift in division of labor which brought women into food procurement on a large scale for the first time.

If for the moment we accept this hypothesis for the inception of cultivation in the valley-riverine area, it becomes important to point up certain ecological correlates of the localized Hopewell distribution, since they provide the foundation for a second hypothesis in terms of which the Hopewell development can be understood.

First, the northern limits of Hopewell distribution correspond closely with those of the 140-day frostless season (Fig. 1).

Second, localities manifesting the Hopewell complex are largely restricted to the major river valleys. Within the Havana and Crab Orchard traditions this has a two-fold application:

a) A sharp drop-off in number of Hopewellian components in the Illinois River Valley north of Peoria, a point at which the flood plain narrows markedly from the 4 to 5 miles characteristic of the Valley in its middle and lower reaches.

b) Lack of evidence for the Hopewellian phase ceramic assemblage in the smaller

311

valleys tributary to the Illinois, Mississippi, and Wabash. Known Hopewell burial components are restricted in large part to the aforementioned valleys with their broad alluvial bottoms. It should be noted, in this connection, that recent surveys of the Spoon, Cache, Rock, and Wisconsin rivers, together with earlier work in the Big Muddy–Crab Orchard drainage, indicate this absence is not merely the result of a failure to explore these lesser waterways. Maxwell (1951) has called our attention to such a picture of differential development in southern Illinois. Here, he noted the contrast between the extensive Hopewell mortuary activity in the Fountain Bluff–Mississippi Valley area and its complete absence in contemporary Crab Orchard expressions immediately to the east. Ecologically, the latter area constitutes the heavily dissected hill country and narrow stream valleys of the Big Muddy–Crab Orchard drainage.

Finally, within the lower Illinois Valley, Hopewell burial components are restricted to the main stream course. They are not found along the numerous minor streams leading into the Illinois. Habitation sites attributed to the builders of these mounds have a like distribution, whereas both burial and occupation sites of pre- and post-Hopewell expressions are well represented along these minor streams. Even more significant, Hopewellian phase living sites have a distribution in the main valley that suggests their placement was governed in part by dominant subsistence interests.

In summary, the evidence shows that localities manifesting Hopewellian forms can be correlated with a series of ecological zones ranging in increasing specificity from the entire region lying south of the 140-day frost line, to the flood plains of the major river valleys, to (in the case of habitation sites) the immediate environs of shallow backwaters and stream banks in and immediately proximal to the alluvium.

It can be postulated that this distribution reflects a correlation between these cultural events and the importance of a simple, mudflat horticulture, an hypothesis that sees a low-level, technologically simple cultivation as an important feature conditioning the degree to which Woodland expressions in different locales underwent a shift to a higher level of complexity exemplified in the Hopewell mortuary expression.

Caldwell proposed that, following establishment of a Primary Forest Efficiency in the Eastern Woodlands, regional florescences are recognizable closely tied to intensive exploitation of natural food resources in various particularly favorable ecological niches. He discounted, however, the role of cultivation in explaining these developments. We hypothesize that in large degree the same features which made certain localities favorable to the development of Primary Forest Efficiency provided a context for cultural events leading to an early plant manipulation. It was in the lush river valleys that density and diversity of natural food resources were greatest; here might be expected the emergence of a collecting adaptation strongly oriented to plant foods and characterized by the high level of subsistence security and residential stability regarded as important preconditions to an incipient horticulture.

We agree with Caldwell, therefore, that perhaps productive differential can be ascribed an important place in explaining the regionalization noted in post-Archaic times, but it is held that development of a simple horticulture only served to increase differing economic potentialities already present as a result of distributional variation in natural food resources.

Substantive evidence for an early horticulture, or at least intense local plant utilization, is beginning to appear in increasing quantities. To a large extent this reflects a greater awareness on the part of excavators to the importance of plant remains in archaeological sites. Some time ago Jones (1936) identified marsh elder (*Iva* sp.) and lamb's-quarter (*Chenopodium* sp.) in human feces recovered from the Newt Kash Hollow rockshelter in Kentucky; grass in which the coprolites occurred has been radiocarbon dated at 640 B.C. ± 300 (M–31). The associated cultural materials are Adena. Gilmore (1931) found seeds of these and other eastern plants associated with Ozark Bluff-Dweller remains in Arkansas and Missouri. Regardless of whether the seeds represent cultigens, as Gilmore contended, it is clear the inhabitants of these shelters were collecting and storing them in some quantity.

Blake (1939:84–85) examined the *Iva* seeds from these Kentucky and Ozark rockshelters and from them defined a new variety —*Iva ciliata* Willd., var. *macrocarpa* Blake. He states: "It seems more likely that the rockshelter form represents a large-fruited strain developed by selection than that it is a distinct species or the normal wild ancestral form of the modern plant." Black (1963) has recently reviewed the archaeological status of marsh elder and notes that the achenes of the prehistoric seeds from the sites used by Blake to define a cultivated variety are "up to 3 or 4 times longer than those of any wild variety." Yarnell (1963:548) states that in discussions with Raymond C. Jackson, a botanist who has recently completed a detailed analysis of the genus *Iva,* he "seems to be of the opinion that . . . large seed size is likely to be the result of artificial selection (that is, primitive plant breeding), at least in marsh elder (*Iva*) and sunflower." Furthermore, Black reminds us that the cultivated *Iva* (reclassified by Jackson as *Iva annua,* var. *macrocarpa*) occurs in archaeological sites largely in association with the sunflower, a native North American cultigen. It is pointed out that var. *macrocarpa* has been identified from a site (Newt Kash Hollow) that lies outside the range of modern varieties of *Iva annua,* and that its occurrence (thus far) is restricted to archaeological contexts.

This discussion becomes particularly relevant to the problem of Hopewell development with the recovery of marsh elder seeds at the Stilwell site. These have been tentatively identified by both Black and Yarnell as var. *macrocarpa.* Stilwell is a White Hall phase

site in the lower Illinois Valley. It would appear that marsh elder cultivation was going on in that region by at least the 4th or 5th century A.D.

Similar studies to those already undertaken with *Iva* have not been carried out for the genera *Chenopodium* and *Amaranthus,* other likely cultigens in the proposed eastern agricultural complex. Sauer (1950), in a well-documented study, presents evidence for the widespread cultivation of amaranths in modern-day and early historic times, suggesting this reflects their ancient domestication and once great economic importance. The extensive use of these seeds by gathering peoples is well known. Jones (1953:91) points out that amaranths "are almost ideal plants for seed gathering. . . . They produce a prodigious number of seeds concentrated in compact terminal position and at a convenient height. The seeds fall readily at maturity. There is hardly a plant which would yield a greater amount of food in a short time." Sauer (1950) presents rather convincing evidence that the yield of grain amaranths per unit of land may be greater than that of corn.

In addition to the occurrence of amaranths and chenopods in association with the cultivated variety of *Iva* in the Kentucky and Ozark sites, each Havana site in the lower Illinois Valley in which this writer has utilized the flotation method for extracting plant remains from pit and hearth matrices has yielded carbonized seeds of these and other genera. Dr. Hugh C. Cutler of the Missouri Botanical Garden has identified chenopods associated with the Hopewellian component at the Snyders site (Struever 1962) and seeds of the same genus at Stilwell where the aforementioned marsh elder was recovered. Yarnell has recently found small marsh elder and other seeds in the initial phases of analyzing plant remains from the Apple Creek site. At Newbridge, a White Hall site just two miles from Apple Creek, large masses of carbonized seeds were taken from several pits during our 1962 field season.

The evidence begins to make it appear that

Iva, Amaranthus, and *Chenopodium* seeds have not been recognized for their importance in Havana subsistence because of difficulties in recovering them from archaeological contexts. At the Apple Creek site we inaugurated production-scale flotation extraction of plant remains from pit fills associated with Hopewellian and White Hall phase occupations. Large quantities of plant remains were found which had already escaped detection in the standard screening process. Indeed, the subsistence activities of the Apple Creek inhabitants look at present quite different than had we not used the flotation process. The difference lies in large part within the realm of plant foods, with flotation bringing to light an array of carbonized remains that reflects a strong dependence on nuts and seeds.

In sum, archaeological evidence does exist for the early utilization, and in the case of *Iva,* for the early cultivation of economically useful commensal plants. Recent work in Havana living sites in the lower Illinois Valley, a region of particularly extensive Hopewell development, discloses the importance of certain among these in the local subsistence. How many of these species were cultivated and to what extent remains to be ascertained.

The mud flats bordering sloughs and streams in the alluvium provide a functional equivalent to Anderson's (1952) "dump heap" situation. *Chenopodium, Amaranthus,* and *Iva* establish themselves only when some external factor has intervened to obliterate the potential competitors and open up a patch of raw soil. These genera do not belong to a stable plant association. Their niche is a habitat disrupted either by man or by natural agencies. They colonize natural scars in the mantle of vegetation. Such disturbed places were created by the annual spring floods which by cutting and filling constantly opened new areas. The most extensive of such scars would be the flats of shallow backwaters covering large sectors of the flood plain. It is difficult to imagine another situation in which a disturbed habitat is created

with a regularity and geographic extent comparable to that of the broad alluvial bottomlands. It is here one might expect the early manipulation of commensal plants to have played an important role prehistorically in the development of higher levels of economic productivity.

One concomitant of man's dispersal of the chenopod, amaranth, and marsh elder populations into artificial habitats might have been, as Sauer (1952) indicates, the development of new strains especially adapted to new conditions. Hybridization and selective modification in varying habitats might have given rise to highly productive varieties.

Assuming this hypothesis has some basis in fact, it then becomes useful in understanding the development and parallel distribution of the Hopewell Interaction Sphere and associated burial modes, and the diagnostic Hopewellian ceramic complex within the Havana and Crab Orchard traditions.

It is postulated that an important shift in subsistence restricted to the broad river valleys was responsible for a cultural disequilibrium and subsequent population expansion. Data for the latter are available from the lower Illinois Valley alone, but it is inferred that additional work would disclose a like situation for the Tri-State, Fountain Bluff, Wabash Valley, and other localities. Budding off of daughter communities (at the expense of less complex groups) followed the major streams to which the new adjustment was restricted. Hopewell burial practices followed a similar distributional pattern since as a concomitant of increased cultural complexity their emergence, it is held, was closely linked to the shift in subsistence and the resulting changes in population and internal organization.

Disruption of established territoriality and breakdown of the strong local orientation characteristic of a late Archaic collecting adjustment may account in part for the high degree of stylistic commonality in ceramics and burial forms observed here for certain of the Havana and Crab Orchard localities. Perhaps the rapid extension of a more com-

314

plex culture type at the expense of simpler ones is reflected in the breakdown of local style orientations, representative of a stable situation, and replacement of them by a broad style zone indicating some form of group identity. The logistics network necessary to maintenance of a common ceremonial-mortuary institution, once established in various localities, may have been one basis for this. Again, these localities all lie within major river valleys, supporting the inference that a new, ecologically restricted subsistence base is an important condition for understanding these events.

The Wisconsin–Rock rivers locality exemplifies a different developmental picture. Here an adaptation something like Caldwell's Primary Forest Efficiency may well have persisted throughout Middle Woodland times. This is expressed in a strong localism in ceramics, i.e. considerable stylistic variability between pottery assemblages from presumably contemporaneous manifestations on the lower Wisconsin River and in the Lake Koshkonong and "Driftless" areas of southern Wisconsin (Joan E. Freeman and Robert J. Salzer, personal communications; Wittry 1959). Correlatively, the infrequent occurrence of sherds representative of the Hopewell series indicates this locality was marginal to the previously described interaction sphere. A few decorative devices, locally reinterpreted, alone attest to historical ties with the other localities. Besides stylistic differences, data from recent surveys pertinent to distribution, number, and size of habitation sites suggest nothing comparable to the marked population expansion recognized in the lower Illinois Valley (Freeman, personal communication). In turn, Hopewell mortuary sites are almost unknown for this locality.

A similar situation is becoming apparent for the Des Plaines–Du Page rivers locality of northeastern Illinois. Ten years of survey have disclosed, in addition to the complete absence of Hopewell series sherds, many small habitation sites yielding cordmarked pottery of the Havana series but with asso-

ciated decorative types largely missing (David J. Wenner, personal communication). At the only excavated site from which a large sample has been recovered, the major decorative treatment is rim punctuation. The stylus application resembles that of an important Havana type in the upper Illinois Valley (Steuben Punctated), but the executed design is entirely a local reinterpretation. Again, as in the Wisconsin-Rock rivers locality, sites here are exceedingly small and the artifactual material sparse.

The local diversity in culture history within the Havana and Crab Orchard traditions during the Middle Woodland period is dramatized by the strong expression of Havana and Hopewell pottery types, together with interaction sphere artifacts and associated burial modes, in the Mississippi Valley immediately west of the Wisconsin–Rock rivers locality (McKern 1931; Logan 1958). The evidence testifies that while groups here participated in an active logistics network and maintained a distinctive burial complex, others along the nearby Wisconsin, La Crosse, Rock, DuPage, and Des Plaines shared little in these activities. This is related, we hypothesize, to events stemming from a shift in subsistence pattern in one locality and not the other, a circumstance linked to differing ecological conditions.

The preceding discussion has taken as its first objective the attempt to define two broad regional style zones (i.e. traditions) situated within the Riverine–Western Great Lakes area during the Middle Woodland period, one coextensive with the eastern Prairie, the other with the northern fringes of the Oak-Hickory Forest. A comparison of archaeological data from a number of localities within these traditions discloses that certain among them participated in an episode of rapid and extensive culture change with the advent of what is defined as the Hopewellian phase.

Innovations in material culture include a host of imported raw materials and finished items, none of which appear to have had their primary function in subsistence technology, and most of which accrued to selected persons who occupied status positions in what in some instances appear to be internally ranked societies. These are diagnostic artifacts of the Hopewell Interaction Sphere. The Hopewellian phase in the Havana and Crab Orchard traditions (in addition to several other traditions recognized within eastern North America) is characterized by the sharing of these distinctive artifact styles between a number of widely scattered, geographically restricted localities.

It is thought that population expansion and internal reorganization were important corollaries of the documented innovations in material culture; especially significant were shifts to higher levels of cultural complexity as expressed within the social subsystem in mortuary activity. A comparison of the Ohio, Illinois, and Michigan Hopewellian mortuary sites is sufficient to indicate that several culture types on different levels of complexity were involved.

The aforementioned increase in cultural complexity associated with the Hopewellian phenomena is perhaps best reflected in the inclusion of local manifestations scattered from the Florida Gulf Coast to the Muskegon Valley of Michigan, from western New York State to Kansas City, Missouri, in a network of interaction. These events bypassed broad geographical areas in which contemporary groups do not appear to have undergone marked change. Except for their absorption and reinterpretation of a few decorative attributes characteristic of the Hopewell pottery series, these areas appear not to have participated in the interaction sphere (though in fact this may only indicate that they occupied a different role within the interaction). Unfortunately, until recently archaeological research has largely ignored problems of culture history in these areas for the more glamorous prospects of the Hopewellian centers.

The repeated use of the word *interaction* in these pages highlights a major problem for future research: the elucidation of the specific cultural mechanisms through which intercourse between the various Hopewellian groups was carried out. The general word *interaction* as used in the preceding discussion attempts only to indicate that some form (or forms) of communication, intercourse, or articulation existed prehistorically to enable far-distant groups to share an assemblage of imported raw materials, artifact styles, and precepts governing the interment of certain dead.

Finally, evidence has been presented to show that this increase in cultural complexity within the Riverine–Western Great Lakes area was encompassed within a series of ecological zones. From this, together with newly recovered archaeological plant remains, stems the hypothesis that the localized shifts to higher levels of complexity may be tied to the adoption of a technologically simple horticulture in specific locales.

NOTES

1. This essay was originally presented as a paper at the annual meeting of the American Anthropological Association, Philadelphia, November 18, 1961; revised and submitted for publication May 6, 1963.

2. The 1962–63 excavations of Gregory Perino (Thomas Gilcrease Foundation) and the author at the Peisker Site in the lower Illinois Valley have produced detailed evidence of Black Sands ceramic and lithic styles.

3. The writer owes to Prof. Lewis R. Binford the initial statement of this hypothesis.

Archaeology as Anthropology: A Case Study

RECENTLY, certain archaeologists have expressed concern over the few contributions that archaeology has made to the general field of anthropology (Taylor 1948; Willey and Phillips 1958; Binford 1962). A combination of advances in methodology and the adoption of cultural models which focus on cultural processes has resulted in contributions that go beyond mere taxonomy and inventories of stylistic traits. Many aspects of extinct cultural systems (for example, social organization) are not directly reflected in material objects and are therefore difficult for the prehistorian to interpret. This essay [1] indicates one way in which archaeology can elucidate some of the features of social life.

Selected data obtained during the excavation of one prehistoric community in eastern Arizona were used to answer questions concerning aspects of its social system. The purposes of this study were: 1) to augment the cultural history of the upper Little Colorado area and to provide a clearer understanding of the role of the region in the prehistoric Southwest, 2) to demonstrate the value of combining systematic sampling procedures with traditional as well as new methods of data processing (for example, computer processing), and 3) to make specific contributions to the growing body of anthropological knowledge and theory (for example, to dem-

Reprinted from *Science,* vol. 144, 19 June 1964, pp. 1454–55. By permission of the author and the American Association for the Advancement of Science. Copyright 1964 by the American Association for the Advancement of Science.

onstrate the presence of localized matrilineages in the Southwest by A.D. 1200).

In this report I describe the analysis of one community, the Carter Ranch Site, located in eastern Arizona and occupied approximately from A.D. 1100 to 1250. This area today is semiarid with most of its precipitation occurring during the summer months as torrential storms. Palynological studies, which permit inferences concerning the past climate, indicate that there have been no great climatic changes in the past 3500 years. There is evidence that a minor shift in the rainfall pattern, from one of roughly equal winter-summer precipitation to the present pattern,[2] took place by about A.D. 1000. It was after this shift became pronounced that the Carter Ranch Pueblo was occupied.

By A.D. 1000, the area was covered by a network of small villages (pueblos) consisting of one or two multiroom buildings. By 1250, most of the region was abandoned; very large Pueblo villages were located on two permanent streams in the area. The area was totally abandoned by 1500.

The Carter Ranch Site consisted of 39 dwelling rooms built as a main block with two wings surrounding a plaza which contained two kivas (underground ceremonial structures). A detached Great Kiva (a large ceremonial building built partly aboveground) was situated about 10 meters northwest of the room block. The site was located in a valley containing about 60 sites roughly contemporary with it.

During the course of the occupation of the

Carter Ranch Site, ecological pressures became more acute as the shift in rainfall became more pronounced. The cultivation of corn probably became difficult and mutual economic assistance in the form of cooperation between villages would seem to have been advantageous under conditions of such economic stress. The appearance of Great Kivas suggests the development of multicommunity patterns of solidarity with a religious mechanism to "cement the tics." In the area's settlement system, the Carter Ranch Site functioned as a ceremonial center and united a number of communities into one sociopolitical sphere.

A series of analyses were undertaken to determine the social system of the community itself. One was a detailed design element analysis of the ceramics from the site. The smallest elements of design, which were defined from more than 6000 sherds, were considered important because they might not have been "in focus" to the potter who might therefore have selected them in an unconscious manner. If there were a system of localized matrilineal descent groups in the village, then ceramic manufacture and decoration would be learned and passed down within the lineage frame, it being assumed that the potters were female as they are today among the western Pueblos. Nonrandom preference for design attributes would reflect this social pattern.[3]

The distribution of 175 design elements was plotted for the site and was found to be nonrandom, certain designs being associated with distinct blocks of rooms. This suggested the presence of localized matrilineal groups. To test this phenomenon further, the frequencies of the design elements were subjected to a multiple regression analysis on the I.B.M. 7094 computer. This analysis showed that there were three groupings of rooms and kivas on the basis of similarities and differences of occurrence of elements of design on the pottery from the floors. Each group of rooms was associated with a kiva. There were two main groups, one each in the southern

and northern parts of the village. A small cluster of rooms in the northeastern portion of the village with an associated kiva was similar to the main block of rooms localized in the southern part of the Pueblo. I interpret this as a group which segmented from the lineage in the southern part and began a separate localized lineage in the northeastern portion of the community.

The various kinds of pottery excavated during 1961 were subjected to a regression analysis.[4] Nonrandom groups of ceramics appeared to be correlated with certain rooms, suggesting that specific tasks were carried out in particular types of rooms. Rooms of several different types were repeated in each room block. This probably reflects household units housing an extended family or lineage segment. Nonceramic artifacts obtained during the 1961 and 1962 excavations, and ceramic types from the 1962 season were subjected to a multiple regression analysis on the I.B.M. 7094. The pottery types were associated with particular types of rooms, exactly as in the previous analysis. Other artifacts were much less confined in distribution. Each dwelling was used for several functions, with an activity or set of related activities prevalent in each room. This is precisely the pattern of room utilization in the modern western Pueblo household.

One group of ceramics was associated with ceremonial units, such as kivas, indicating that a set of stylistically distinct vessels were associated with ritual activities. Vessels of these types were also associated with the burials, suggesting graveside ritual.

A cemetery of three separate areas was excavated in the midden east of the site. In the northern midden were interments that were oriented east-west, whereas the southern midden had burials oriented north-south. An analysis of design elements on the ceramics in the graves indicated that the burials in the northern section of the midden were associated with the localized descent group in the northern part of the village, and that the southern burial area was associated with the descent group localized in the southern portion of the site. The burials in the center of the midden were mixed, both in terms of their orientation and the occurrence of design elements. Almost all of the ornaments and unusual items that probably reflect differences in status, included as grave goods from the entire sample of burials, were from this central area. Likewise, the burials in the central portion of the midden had twice as many vessels per burial as the burials in other areas of the midden. This central cluster of burials probably represents individuals of relatively high status from all localized social groups in the community, buried in a separate section of the cemetery. The importance of the site as a ceremonial focal point suggests that high status would have been earned by individuals through participation in ritual activities rather than acquired through inheritance.

The regression analyses of artifacts reflect a rigid division of labor at the site. For example, weaving implements were found with a male burial indicating that weaving was a male activity, and these items were strongly correlated with artifacts used in ritual activities associated with the kivas. This suggests that weaving was a masculine task and was carried out in the kiva, just as it is today in the western Pueblos. The distribution of tools associated with female activities was quite different from that of items associated with male activities. Most tasks were evidently performed by groups organized according to sex.

These analyses permit comparisons to be made between the modern western Pueblos and one portion of their prehistoric background. The presence of localized matrilineages and lineage segments at the Carter Ranch Site demonstrates continuity for this western Pueblo trait for more than 700 years. A similar pattern for the household as the basic local unit can now be documented. Other stable processes are now demonstrable. These include the basic form of the rigid division of labor and particular activities associated with each of the sexes.

Significant differences can be shown as

well. One of the most striking is the change in intercommunity integration and a related change in the intracommunity pattern itself. Communities made up of from one to three localized matrilineages (probably corresponding to single clans as well) were united through the mechanism of centralized ritual. Strong mechanisms for multicommunity integration are not present among the modern western Pueblos.

Related to these changes was a change in the nature of the organization of the community itself. Villages up to A.D. 1300 probably were more commonly composed of single localized lineages. The economic advantages accruing to larger aggregates of people in the face of environmental pressures resulted in the establishment of communities of more than a single lineage after 1300. Strong localized lineages are not conducive to a strong village integration when a village consists of several lineages. I would expect the development of integrative ties that crosscut social groups to develop within the village under these circumstances. These would be such things as the development of societies with strong ritual functions, the breakdown of the association of kiva with clan, and the assumption by the kivas of more villagewide significance (for example, by association with societies). Crosscutting integrative mechanisms such as these would promote community solidarity at the expense of the disruptive lineage strength, and this is the pattern today among the western Pueblos.

These examples serve to document my case for the potential use of this approach in investigations of prehistoric communities. The method and theory incorporated in this study can be used to advantage in testing hypotheses of reconstruction, as well as for providing background to aid in understanding the development of certain sociological phenomena.

NOTES

1. This study is a result of a series of investigations in eastern Arizona conducted by the Chi-

cago Natural History Museum (now Field Museum of Natural History), directed by Paul S. Martin, chief curator, Department of Anthropology. The full report of the work (Longacre 1963) contains details of the evidence and methodology which supported the conclusions reported. Martin (1962) made a preliminary report of the results.

2. Palynological studies by Schoenwetter and Hevly under the direction of P. S. Martin, University of Arizona, have yielded data concerning past climatological conditions in eastern Arizona: P. S. Martin, J. B. Rinaldo, W. A. Longacre, C. Cronin, L. G. Freeman, and J. Schoenwetter (1962); P. S. Martin, J. B. Rinaldo, W. A. Longacre, L. G.

Freeman, J. A. Brown, R. H. Hevly, and M. E. Cooley (1964).

3. The first demonstration of a correlation between changes in social organization or residence and the distribution of design attributes used in ceramic manufacture, or both, was made by J. D. F. Deetz (1960), by utilizing data from the historic period in the Plains. The usefulness of this distribution of design elements as a tool for sociological interpretation in prehistory was first realized by C. Cronin (1962).

4. This was undertaken, with the aid of Univac, by L. G. Freeman and J. A. Brown, University of Chicago (1964).

A Prehistoric Community in Eastern Arizona

THERE HAVE been, in recent years, a number of promising contributions related to the elucidation of prehistoric sociocultural systems. Most of these are concerned with settlement patterns, ceremonial structures, mortuary practices, social status, and craft specialization (Sears 1961). Several other contributions are also notable (Longacre 1963, 1964; Freeman and Brown 1964; Deetz 1960, 1965).

There is a growing feeling, represented especially by the above kinds of study, that there is much to be gained by attempting to describe (and perhaps explain) complete or whole sociocultural systems—much as it is done by ethnologists. How complete these descriptions can be is a matter of justifiable concern, but it is evident that at least some headway is being made in this direction.

This article [1] presents an outline of a case study which may be of value to those interested in the so-called systems or structural approach to the interpretation of archaeological data. It should provide some fodder usable in evaluating this kind of concern; and, at the very least, it is an example of certain ways in which prehistoric material can be interpreted. The explicit purposes of the study were twofold: a) to describe as much of the internal structure and social organization of a prehistoric society as was possible to discover, and b) to attempt to develop a hypothesis

Reprinted from the *Southwestern Journal of Anthropology*, vol. 22, no. 1, 1966, pp. 9–30. By permission of the author and publisher.

pertinent to explaining adaptive changes in this organization.

The focus of the analysis was on Broken K Pueblo, located eleven miles east of Snowflake, Arizona (excavated by the Chicago Natural History Museum [now Field Museum of Natural History], with National Science Foundation support). This archaeological site is a rectangular, ninety-five room,[2] single-storied, surface masonry pueblo, dating from about A.D. 1150 to 1280 (see plan, Fig. *1*). The largest and latest site in the Hay Hollow Valley, it is located in a savanna-woodland vegetation zone. The climate is semiarid today, and the landscape has been heavily dissected by the prevailing pattern of torrential summer thundershowers.

Theory and Method

The basic theoretical model employed is simply that human behavior is patterned or structured. To put it in its simplest form, people do certain things in certain places within their communities, and they leave behind them many of the structured remains of these activities (e.g., artifacts). It may be useful to state this as a formal postulate since it is fundamental to succeeding interpretations.

The spatial distributions of cultural materials are patterned or structured (nonrandom), and will be so within an archaeological site.

A) These patterns reflect the loci of patterned behavior that existed in prehistoric times.

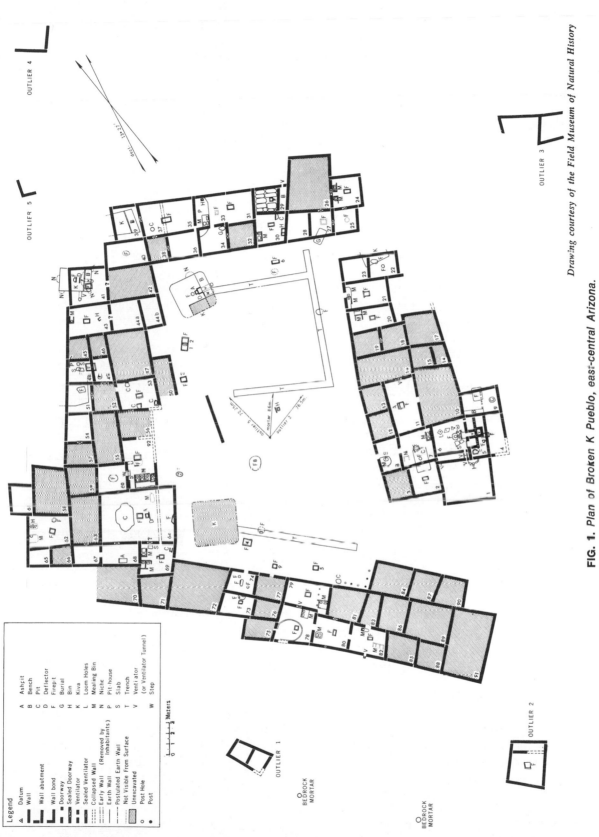

FIG. 1. Plan of Broken K Pueblo, east-central Arizona.

Drawing courtesy of the Field Museum of Natural History

Legend

△	Datum
	Wall
	Wall abutment
	Wall bond
	Doorway
	Sealed Doorway
	Ventilator
	Sealed Ventilator
	Collapsed Wall
	Early Wall (Removed by Inhabitants)
	Earth Wall
	Postulated Earth Wall
	Not Visible From Surface
	Unexcavated
o	Post Hole
•	Post

A	Ashpit
B	Bench
C	Pit
D	Deflector
F	Firepit
G	Burial
H	Bin
K	Kiva
L	Loom Holes
M	Mealing Bin
N	Niche
P	Pit-house
S	Slab
T	Trench
V	Ventilator (or Ventilator Tunnel)
W	Step

0 1 2 3
Meters

OUTLIER 1

OUTLIER 2

OUTLIER 3

OUTLIER 4

OUTLIER 5

BEDROCK MORTAR

BEDROCK MORTAR

322

B) The kind of behavior represented in these loci depends on the nature or behavioral meaning of the item or set of items, the distribution of which is being studied.

C) These behavioral meanings can be determined with the aid of specific ethnographic evidence or general worldwide comparative evidence. There is a great variety of such "meanings" with which items (or stylistic elements) can be associated: 1) Some items or stylistic elements have functional meanings (i.e., they are associated with certain economic, sociological, or religious activities). 2) Some of these functional classes of items may reflect the composition of *social segments* (e.g., specific classes of items may be used by men, women, hunters, priests, etc.). 3) Within any given class of items there may be stylistic differences associated with the various social segments (e.g., men, women, hunters, priests, households, lineages, clans, etc.).

As has been suggested by others (Eggan 1952:37; Binford 1962, 1964*b*, 1965; Rootenberg 1964; and others), it should be possible to isolate some of these patterns archaeologically. The problem with respect to Broken K Pueblo was to find as many clusters or patterns in the data as possible, and then attempt to interpret them as reflecting parts of a village activity structure and social organization.

The site was too large to permit complete excavation, considering the time and resources available. Largely for this reason, a system of simple random sampling was employed. Nearly all of the existing walls at the site were discovered and mapped prior to excavation. Forty-six rooms were then excavated in the initial sample. The sample was not considered an end in itself, however; eight additional rooms were excavated, as the necessity for doing so became apparent. All the excavated rooms, both surface and subterranean, are shown in Fig. *1* as unshaded rooms, which, including outliers, total 54.

Naturally deposited stratigraphic levels were excavated as separate units; and those levels containing cultural materials were screened, in an effort to ensure comparability of samples. Materials found in direct association with floors were kept separate from those in "fill" levels. All possibly relevant materials were saved, and charcoal and fossil pollen samples were taken from most rooms.

A large portion of the data from the site was quantified and manipulated statistically. Three multivariate analyses (factor analyses) were performed on the I.B.M. 7094 computer at the University of Chicago.[3] These analyses permitted the development of non-random clusters of pottery-types and ceramic design elements; and the clusters or factors were used in various distribution studies.

The Temporal Variable

In order profitably to study a community structure, prehistoric or otherwise, it is necessary that the structure be defined at a specific point or points in time. The reason it must be studied synchronically is that it may tend to change through time and gradually develop into a different structure. While it is reasonable to compare structures which have existed at different points in time, it would not be very meaningful to consider them all as a single structure.

Since Broken K was not constructed at a specific point in time, it was important that it not be assumed (initially) to represent a synchronic structure. Various lines of evidence, primarily architectural and stratigraphic, were employed in this intrasite dating effort;[4] and it was discovered that, in general, the southern portion of the site was somewhat earlier than the northern portion. This does not imply, however, that the southern portion had been abandoned prior to the northern occupation. There were many rooms in the southern portion that did not contain refuse deposits, and there was much more evidence of remodeling in that area than in the northern portion of the site. It therefore seems likely that people were living in that portion until the end of the occupation of the site. This suggests that we can consider the entire

A Prehistoric Community
James N. Hill

site as a roughly contemporaneous unit, at least near the end of the occupation. But contemporaneity cannot at present be unequivocally demonstrated, however, and the reader should be aware of this fact in considering some of the subsequent interpretations. This problem clearly illustrates the importance of accurate intra-site dating when problems such as those dealt with in this essay are considered.

Room Types and Functions

Archaeologists have long recognized that there are differences in types of rooms found in prehistoric pueblo sites. Ordinarily, a large room containing a firepit and mealing bin is called a living room or habitation room; a small room without such features is called a storage room. A ceremonial room is often recognized as being a subterranean structure (or surface structure) with a roof-entrance, a

firepit, a ventilator, some wall niches, and a bench or platform along one or more of the walls—among other distinctive attributes.

This kind of classification is probably adequate with respect to ceremonial rooms, since these rooms often contain many attributes similar to those in present-day Hopi and Zuni ceremonial rooms. It may not be very adequate, however, for isolating habitation and storage rooms. The differences between these room types are not always obvious, and a classification of them on the basis of one or two attributes may not always be reliable.

Twelve different attributes were used in isolating these room types at Broken K. One of the attributes was floor area. I noticed that some of the rooms were much larger than others. Simple statistical manipulations showed that there were in fact two different modes of room size. Approximately half of the nonceremonial rooms were small, ranging

TABLE 1

Distribution of artifact types

Artifact type	Mean no. per habit. room	Mean no. per storage room	Mean no. per kiva	Total	Dominant room types	
Projectile points	.92	.08	.50	21	H	K
Arrowshaft tools	.88	.11	.00	25	H	
Antler flakers	.08	.08	.25	5		K
Saws	.28	.04	.00	8	H	
Graver-burins	.20	.20	.00	10	H S	
Flake knives	1.70	.23	.00	48	H	
Bifacial knives	.20	.07	.00	7	H	
Utilized flakes	2.40	1.00	2.00	96	H S	K
Blades	.16	.16	.00	8	H S	
Cores	.92	.23	1.50 *	35	H	K
Scrapers	3.00	.84	3.00 *	108	H	K
Choppers	2.60	.44	4.70 *	96	H	K
Axes	.32	.00	.00	8	H	
Mauls	.28	.11	.00	10	H	
Hammerstones	3.70	.69	2.00 *	118	H	K
Metates	1.10	.15	.25	32	H	
Manos	6.60	1.00	.25	192	H	
Worked slabs	.88	.15	.75	29	H	K
Worked sherds	1.50	.15	.25	42	H	
Bone awls	1.60	.27	.25	48	H	
Bone rings and ring material	1.00	.11	.25	30	H	
"Ornamental items"	.96	.19	.50	31	H	K

* All from a single kiva (kiva beneath Room 41)

TABLE 2

Distribution of nonartifact materials

Item	Mean no. per habit. room	Mean no. per storage room	Mean no. per kiva
Firepits	1.0	0.0	1.0
Mealing bins	1.0	0.0	0.0
Ventilators	0.5	0.0	1.0
Lithic waste	98.0	30.0	37.0
Animal bone	120.0	26.0	29.0
Seeds	9.3	4.2	2.5
Pollen grains (economic)	22.0	51.0	17.0

in size from 2.5 to 6.5 square meters in floor area; while other rooms ranged in size from 6.6 to 16.0 square meters.[5]

By means of a series of Chi-square tests of association, it was found that the small class of rooms generally contained few internal structural features (no slab-lined features) and very few artifacts; but they did contain large amounts of the pollen of "economic" plants.[6] The large rooms, on the other hand, were significantly associated with firepits, mealing bins, ventilators, artifacts (including potsherds), lithic waste, animal bone, and seeds; but they contained very little economic pollen. The distributions of the major classes of artifacts, in terms of statistical means, is given in Table 1. Other pertinent distributions appear in Table 2.

The factor analysis of pottery types was particularly interesting in that it indicated that each type of room was dominated by a different constellation or cluster of pottery types. Of the thirteen types analyzed, five of them were dominant in habitation rooms; two of them were dominant in storage rooms; and two were largely peculiar to ceremonial rooms. The four remaining types were common to both habitation and ceremonial rooms (cf. Table 3).

The primary goal of this room-type analysis was not the establishment of the types themselves; rather, it was a first step in arriving at some of the functional characteristics of the rooms. Many of the functions of these room-types, and the centrally located plaza as well, were determined by examining the differential spatial clustering of both artifact and non-artifact materials, as outlined above. The functional meanings of these materials were derived from direct ethnographic evidence or worldwide comparative evidence in most cases. Some of the probable functions of the room types are listed in Table 4. In addition to these functions, it seems possible that the habitation rooms also served as centers for the manufacture of pottery, the manufacture of ground and pecked stone implements, and the manufacture of ornamental items. These suggestions are somewhat doubtful, however. In the case of pottery manufacture, for example, the ethnographic evidence suggests occurrence outside of the rooms rather than within them.

In any event, nearly all of the functions given in Table 4 are found to have been carried out in analogous types of rooms among the recent Hopi and Zuni Indians. Thus, this pattern of room usage seems to have changed very little among the western Pueblos during the last 700 years.

TABLE 3

Distribution of pottery types
(Indicates room-types in which pottery-types are dominant, as determined by factor analysis)

Pottery type	Habit.	Storage	Kiva
Brown plain corrugated, smudged interior	X		
Brown indented corrugated, smudged interior	X		
McDonald indented corrugated	X		
Tularosa black-on-white	X		
Snowflake black-on-white, Hay Hollow variety	X		
Brown indented corrugated	X		X
Patterned corrugated	X		X
Snowflake black-on-white, Snowflake variety	X		X
Pinto polychrome	X		X
Brown plain corrugated			X
St. Johns black-on-red			X
McDonald corrugated		X	
St. Johns polychrome		X	

325

TABLE 4
Functions of the room types

Habitation	Storage	Kiva
Food preparation	Storage of plant foods	Ceremonies
Eating		Weaving
Water storage and use	Storage of non-plant items	Manufacture of hunting tools
Manufacture of hunting tools	"Work"	

It is significant that, were it not for the pollen data recovered from nearly all of the rooms at the site, it would have been impossible to state with any certainty that the so-called storage rooms actually did serve in a storage capacity. They generally contained so much more *Zea* and *Cucurbita* pollen than did the other rooms that their storage function can hardly be denied (Chi-square, significant at .001 level). The tentative demonstration that pollen data can be used in isolating functionally specific areas within a site may represent a methodological advancement. It may, in the future, be possible to isolate functionally different sites by this method. Seasonally occupied sites might be particularly susceptible to differentiation in this manner.

William A. Longacre claims to have demonstrated the existence of two, and possibly three, "localized matrilineages" at a somewhat earlier site in the Hay Hollow Valley (Carter Ranch Site, Longacre 1963, 1964, 1970). His demonstration was based on the occurrence of a nonrandom distribution of ceramic design elements at the site. He was able to show that the north and south halves of the site were different in terms of their constellations or clusters of design elements; and since modes of design style are transmitted from mother to daughter within the localized matrilineal framework among the present-day western Pueblos, he was able to interpret the localized clusters of design elements at Carter Ranch Site as representing the loci of extinct matrilineages. Although there is some

question concerning his demonstration of lineality, it is likely that his major conclusions are correct.

The factor analyses of ceramic design elements and pottery types, as well as other data from Broken K, have led to somewhat similar conclusions. At this site, however, there seem to have been five such localized units; and I have chosen to call them "uxorilocal residence units" instead of "localized matrilineages." [7] These units can be grouped into two larger, more inclusive residence units. The locations of the units may be seen in Figure 2. Their existence, although tentative, was demonstrated as follows:

1) Nonrandom distributions of ceramic

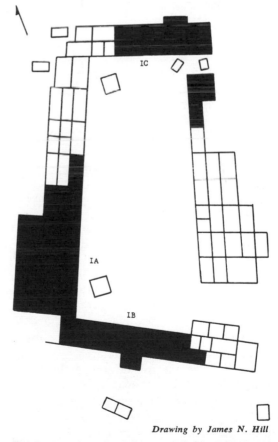

Drawing by James N. Hill

FIG. 2. *Approximate locations of the inclusive residence units of Broken K Pueblo. Shaded areas indicate Residence Unit no. I and its subunits; the unshaded areas represent Residence Unit no. II and its subunits.*

326

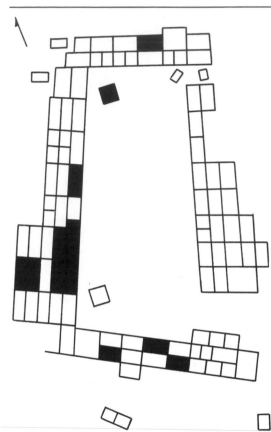

Drawing by James N. Hill

FIG. 3. *Distribution of Factor 1, analysis of pottery types found on floors. The shaded area, indicating the distribution of Factor 1, delineates the general locus of Residence Unit no. I.*

design elements, pottery types, firepit types, storage pits, "chopper" types, and animal bone indicated discrete localizations within the pueblo (which could not be explained in terms of functionally specific areas). An example of these distributions is presented in Figure 3. The distributions of all of the above categories are given in Table 5.

2) Through the use of ethnographic evidence, it was found that these items and stylistic elements were probably associated with female activities (except perhaps choppers and animal bone, for which there is no clear evidence). No items clearly associated with male activities were found to cluster in localized areas of the pueblo.

3) All of the female-associated items

(above) were found to have been usable in the day-to-day maintenance of a residence unit.

4) Each unit was found to have had temporal continuity—at least sixty-five years. (This seems conservative, for the entire length of occupation was *ca.* 130 years; both the north and south halves of the site were thus probably occupied for at least 65 years each.)

It seems likely that this evidence is sufficient for the establishment of uxorilocal residence units, especially when it is considered in the light of the fact that such units are characteristic of the modern Pueblos. Of all residence systems known, only uxorilocal and

TABLE 5

Distribution of stylistic categories used in isolating the loci of residence units

Stylistic category	Residence units				
	IA	*IB*	*IC*	*IIA*	*IIB*
Firepits, type IV	X	X	X	X	
Factor 2, pottery types, floors	X	X	X		
Factor 1, pottery types, floors	X	X	X		
Factor 12, ceramic design, floors	X	X	X		
Factor 2, ceramic design, floors	X	X	X		
Storage pits, 7–15 present	X	X	X		
Factor 13, ceramic design, floors	X	X			
Firepits, type I	X	X			
Flake choppers, floors	X	X			
Factor 5, ceramic design, floors	X				
Factor 4, ceramic design, fills	X				
Prairie dog bone, floors	X				
Factor 9, ceramic design, fills	X		X		
Factor 6, ceramic design, floors		X			
Factor 3, pottery types, floors				X	X
Factor 4, pottery types, floors				X	X
Factor 1, ceramic design, fills				X	X
Factor 2, ceramic design, fills				X	X
Firepits, type III				X	X
Factor 3, ceramic design, floors				X	
Factor 9, ceramic design, floors				X	
Mountain sheep bone, floors				X	
Gopher bone, floors				X	
Firepits, type V			X	X	
Factor 4, ceramic design, floors					X
Factor 3, ceramic design, fills					X
Firepits, type II					X
Storage pits, none present					X

TABLE 6

Residence patterns and their hypothetical distribution correlates

Residence pattern	Definition	Distribution of female stylistic items	Distribution of male stylistic items
Uxorilocal	Husband and wife live in vicinity of wife's maternal relatives	Nonrandom	Random
Matrilocal	Husband and wife live in vicinity of wife's mother	Nonrandom	Random
Matrilocal, with resident male head	Same, but a mother's brother and his family reside within the group	Nonrandom	Random
Virilocal	Husband and wife live in vicinity of husband's relatives—patrilineal or matrilineal	Random	Nonrandom
Patrilocal	Husband and wife live in vicinity of husband's father	Random	Nonrandom
Avunculocal	Husband and wife live in vicinity of husband's maternal uncle	Random	Nonrandom
Neolocal	Husband and wife live separate from either mate's relatives	Random	Random
Bilocal	Husband and wife live either in vicinity of husband's or wife's relatives	Random	Random
Duolocal	Husband and wife live separately, with own relatives	Nonrandom	Nonrandom

duolocal[8] systems should be reflected by highly nonrandom distributions of female-associated items or stylistic elements; and in the latter case, one would expect male-associated items to distribute in a nonrandom manner also (cf. Table 6).

We must assume here, of course, that the entire site was occupied synchronously; as I have already indicated, this cannot be demonstrated with certainty—not, at least, until techniques for intrasite dating are vastly improved. Still, on the basis of the slim evidence presented previously, the assumption of contemporaneity seems reasonably likely. If this was not the case, there is no reason to conclude that the exposition to this point is invalid; even when the early and late halves of the site are considered separately, the nonrandom distributions of female-associated items still emerge. We would simply have indications of fewer residence units existing at a given point in time.

The two large residence units at Broken K (I-A,B,C and II-A,B, Fig. 2) can perhaps be considered as representing residence groups (rather than simple aggregations of women) because there is some evidence that they were integrated internally. This is suggested by the fact that the subunits within each large unit were much more similar to one another with regard to the above mentioned stylistic elements than any one of them was to the other large unit. This sharing of stylistic elements suggests that there was less social distance within each large unit than there was between large units; and it may also be an indirect measure of economic cooperation—but the latter inference is clearly stretching a point. It is also possible, however, that each large unit controlled or used its own kiva. This is suggested because, in general, each ceremonial room had stylistic affinities with only one of the two large units. That ceramic design style can by itself indicate shared control or use of kivas is not completely certain, of course; if such were found to be the case among present-day Pueblo groups, the above inference would be much stronger. As it stands, the possibility is simply a suggestion susceptible to further testing.

To carry this analysis a step further, it is possible that these residence units were "corporate" groups.[9] This is suggested, provided that one can accept the above evidence of style sharing and common participation in kivas. It also seems possible, however, that non-movable property was inherited within each group (i.e., rooms). Most rooms were apparently inhabited for at least sixty-five years, or roughly three generations, by the same group; and this suggests that they were inherited.

Thus it is likely that Broken K Pueblo contained two major uxorilocal residence units (possibly "groups"), each with at least two subunits—and corporateness might be postulated. It is not possible to infer the existence of matrilineal descent, nor would such an inference be desirable, considering the present state of social anthropological understanding of descent rules. Furthermore, we clearly cannot excavate social rules or norms of any sort.

A comparison of the localization of residence units at this site with the two residence units inferred for Carter Ranch Site is illuminating. In terms of number of rooms, the units at Carter Ranch Site were the same size as the subunits of the two major units at Broken K (*ca.* twenty rooms per unit); and they may have been equivalent in terms of social organization. This suggests the possibility that Carter Ranch Site as a whole was equivalent to only one of the major units at Broken K. It may be that as villages increased in size through time, there was an increasing number of large units per village.

The modern Hopi and Zuni also have a hierarchy of social organizational units—line-ages, clans, and so forth. It may be that the largest units at Broken K (I and II) were roughly equivalent to clans (or phratries), while the subunits were equivalent to lineages (or clans); but this cannot, of course, be demonstrated. It may, in the future, be possible to compare prehistoric pueblos with one another with respect to equivalent social units. Eventually it may be feasible to compare other kinds of sites in a similar manner.

Adaptive Responses

A number of sociological changes were evidently occuring between A.D. 1050 and 1300 in the Southwest, changes which may have been promoted by an environmental shift. Although this is merely a hypothesis, there is some rather good evidence for such a shift. It is documented by the nearly simultaneous occurrence of the following events: 1) a shift from a relative abundance of arboreal pollen to a relative abundance of nonarboreal pollen (Schoenwetter 1962; Hevly 1964), 2) a shift from a relative abundance of large sized *Pinus* pollen grains (probably *P. ponderosa*) to a relative abundance of small sized grains (probably *P. edulis*) (Schoenwetter 1962; Hevly 1964), 3) a shift in the widths of tree-rings, from wide to narrow (probably reflecting a shortage of "effective" soil moisture) (Douglass 1929; Schoenwetter and Eddy 1964; Hevly 1964), and 4) a widespread cycle of erosion (Bryan 1925; Hack 1942; Schoenwetter and Eddy 1964). There are a number of reasons for thinking that these events may have been related to one another and that they reflect prehistoric conditions inimical to agriculture.

There seem to have been responses to an environmental shift throughout the Southwest. Of major importance was a general decrease in population which was in full force by about A.D. 1250. At about the same time, many villages were abandoned, and people appear to have aggregated into fewer but larger villages along major drainageways. At the same time, it is possible that there was an increase in the

329

scope of intervillage integration, as indicated by the fact that "Great Kivas" [10] became more common between *ca.* A.D. 1000 and 1200. These kivas may have been associated with intervillage ritual institutions. There is also a suggestion of a broadened scope of intravillage integration, as evidenced by the fact that the ratio of ceremonial rooms to other types of rooms became continuously smaller through time (Steward 1937).

The same trends are noted in the vicinity of Broken K and Carter Ranch Site. Furthermore, in comparing the two sites themselves, it was found that there is a small amount of evidence suggesting a trend toward a broadened scope of intravillage integration. Broken K, the later of the two sites, seems to have reached a more advanced stage in this respect, and the evidence is as follows:

1) At Carter Ranch Site, both small residence units apparently owned or controlled their own kivas; while at Broken K, kivas were shared by the small units (subunits) within each *major* residence unit. (This inference is less than sure, however, since we do not really know that shared design-elements in kivas represent shared ownership or control.)

2) The residence units were less strictly localized at Broken K than at Carter Ranch Site, suggesting that internal social division may have been less formal or less important.

3) The architecture and room features at Broken K were much more homogeneous stylistically than was the case at Carter Ranch Site. (This suggests an increased scope of style sharing and communication.)

This evidence cannot be considered conclusive for inferring an increased scope of intravillage integration. One reason for this is that it is difficult to infer aspects of social integration from living arrangements and style distributions alone. There are certainly other hypotheses which could be presented.

The hypothesis offered here is supported to some extent by the fact that the degree of residence localization among present-day Hopi and Zuni Indians seems to be indicative of the degree of intravillage integration in these pueblos. Since the residence units at Broken K appear to have been more localized than are modern western Pueblo residence units, it may be that they were also less integrated (cf. Kroeber 1917:90–200; Parsons 1925:112; Titiev 1944; Eggan 1950; and others).

In addition to the hypothesized increasing scope of integration and aggregation, however, there is direct evidence that the people of Broken K were responding to an environmental shift. The idea that agriculture was becoming difficult is supported by the fact that there was a significant replacement of domesticates (corn and squash) with wild food crops through time; the quantities of fossil pollen grains representing known domesticates decrease, both within Broken K itself, and between Carter Ranch Site and Broken K.[11] The numbers of charred corn cobs and squash seeds show the same trend.[12] At the same time, the pollen and seeds of "wild" plants increased through time.

An increase in the frequencies of food-grinding implements through time may reflect the fact that more such tools were needed to process the increased amount and variety of wild plants being collected. Furthermore, there was a 20 percent increase in storage space between the early and late portions of the site, suggesting a possible need to store increased quantities of seed for planting in the event of crop failure. We know that among the modern Hopi, the recent assurance of a stable food supply has led to a decrease in the amount of food stored for long periods of time (Whiting 1939:11).

There is also evidence that hunting may have become difficult at Broken K. The hunting of deer, mountain sheep, and jackrabbits was replaced through time by the hunting of cottontail;[13] and the relative proportion of hunting tools to other kinds of artifacts declined at the same time.

There are, of course, other possible explanations for these responses besides the idea that they were prompted by a shift in the physical environment. The possibilities of flood, fire, inner cultural tendency, internal dissension, and disease have all been suggested at one time or another; and most archaeologists consider them unlikely. The possibility that enemy attack was involved cannot be lightly dismissed; but the fact that people were aggregating along drainageways, and in generally nondefensive locations, suggests that warfare is a somewhat unlikely explanation. There is very little evidence for it in the Southwest at this time period.

It may be, of course, that the trend toward aggregation, and the possible trend toward an increasing scope of integration, were prompted by changes in the physical environment wrought by man himself rather than by strictly natural causes. It is also possible that some of the responses discussed here were not at all related to an environmental shift and a decreasing productivity of agriculture and hunting. Further, one might reasonably suggest that under the environmental conditions hypothesized, the inhabitants of the area would disperse rather than aggregate and integrate. Still, once these people were committed to a stable, sedentary agricultural economy, it seems likely that they might have attempted to maintain it in the face of conditions that would probably promote dispersal among less sedentary peoples. The impression is given, in the ethnographic literature, that the Hopi and Zuni would find it difficult or impossible to revert to a strictly hunting and gathering existence.

After Broken K was abandoned, the inferred process of aggregation and integration appear to have continued—both in east-central Arizona and throughout major portions of the Southwest. By 1540, there were only a few remaining large pueblos—at Hopi, Zuni, and along the Rio Grande. An examination of the ethnographic evidence indicates that the Hopi and Zuni have a much wider scope of intravillage integrative mechanisms than are apparent at either Carter Ranch Site or Broken K (cf. Kroeber 1917:183; Parsons 1925:112; Bunzel 1932:476; Eggan 1950:

116). It is particularly notable that today there is very little descent-group localization, and ceremonial society members are recruited from the entire village.

Hopi and Zuni economic integration is extremely important on a villagewide scale (cf. Forde 1931; Beaglehole 1937; Goldman 1937). It is doubtful that individual families or lineages could exist as independent units. It seems at least possible that, beginning about A.D. 1050, an environmental shift made subsistence so difficult for Pueblo adaptive systems that previously separate family or lineage groups were forced to aggregate for mutual support (to maintain an agricultural existence). This aggregation, in turn, may have led to the development of broadened integrative mechanisms which served to bind larger groups together.

Conclusions

This short essay has presented an example of some of the kinds of inferences which may be made concerning the internal structure and social organization of a prehistoric Pueblo site.[14] It has also examined some of the evidence related to an ultimate explanation of changes in site structure through time. Even though the results are tentative, it is hoped that they are suggestive of some of the kinds of problems and inferences with which archaeologists might reasonably deal. This is not to say that the kinds of concerns discussed here should be the primary concerns in archaeology—far from it. I merely suggest that this line of research will not be detrimental, and it should be useful to pursue it further, especially since the techniques for doing so are developing rapidly.

The specific hypotheses developed here do not provide any answers, and they would not be acceptable to many archaeologists as explanations. They are not intended as explanations but, rather, as testable hypotheses. Future research will alter their usefulness, no doubt.

If it is indeed possible to define the outlines

331

of prehistoric activity structures and residence units in the Pueblo Southwest, it may also be possible to do it elsewhere. Having defined these outlines, it should be possible to learn something about the processes of change.

One of the crucial concerns for those who are interested in this approach would seem to lie in the further development of research designs and techniques that can be used in recovering and analyzing data that will be useful in making more complete descriptions of prehistoric sociocultural systems and more complete explanations of their change in time and space.

NOTES

1. A paper similar to this essay was presented by William A. Longacre and the author at the Sixty-fourth Annual Meeting of the American Anthropological Association, Denver, Colorado (Symposium on Prehistoric Social Organization). The primary archaeological data used in this study were provided by fieldwork carried out by the Chicago Natural History Museum (now Field Museum of Natural History) in east-central Arizona during the summers of 1962–63. The excavations were directed by Dr. Paul S. Martin, chief curator of anthropology.

2. The room-count is complicated by the fact that the initial wall-trenching (to discover all of the rooms in the pueblo prior to sampling) failed to locate all of the rooms accurately. Rooms 31 and 33 should be considered a single room, as should rooms 35 and 37 (cf. Fig. 1). Room 44 had to be divided into rooms 44a and 44b. Room 92 is located in the west wing; it is numerically out of place because it was not discovered until the simple random sample had already been chosen, thus "freezing" the room numbers. There are five outliers not included in the room-count, but only two of them (to the south of the pueblo) are clearly rooms. The outliers were not included in the initial population sampled and thus were not numbered; but all of them were excavated. There may be one or two undiscovered rooms in the northeast portion of the east wing. The "kiva" in the southwest corner of the plaza was excavated (contrary to map designation); it was either not a kiva, or it was unfinished, since there were no kiva features in this rectangular pit. It had been excavated by the prehistoric inhabitants, partially into the sandstone bedrock.

3. For a discussion of factor analysis, see Fruchter 1954.

4. Pollen data were also found useful in intrasite dating. A pollen chronology for the area (Schoenwetter 1962; Hevly 1964) indicated a gradual temporal shift in the relative proportions of pollen types, characterized primarily by decreasing percentages of arboreal pollen (especially *Pinus*) and increasing percentages of nonarboreal pollen during this time period (*ca.* A.D. 1000–1300). Most of the rooms at the site which, on the basis of other evidence, had been considered "early" contained 20 to 40 percent *Pinus* pollen; while "late" rooms generally contained less than 20 percent. The "late" rooms contained significantly more nonarboreal pollen (especially Compositae, Chenopodiaceae, Amaranthaceae, an Gramineae). It might not be valid to claim that pollen data can be used widely in intrasite dating, but further experimentation seems called for.

5. Seven rooms exceeded 16.0 sq. m. in floor area; one was as large as 33.5 square meters. The distribution did not suggest a definite third mode, however.

6. Economic plants are defined as those for which there is evidence of their introduction into the site by man rather than by natural agencies. In the present case, they include *Zea, Cucurbita, Cleome, Opuntia,* and several others.

7. Uxorilocal residence is defined as a residence situation in which husband and wife live in the vicinity of the wife's maternal relatives.

8. Duolocal residence is defined as a residence situation in which husband and wife live separately, each with his own relatives.

9. A "corpoate" group is defined here as a group of related people who cooperate economically and transmit nonmovable property within the group.

10. "Great Kivas" are defined as large ceremonial structures, generally exceeding thirty feet in diameter or length and containing somewhat more elaborate features than do other kivas (cf. Wormington 1959:86; Vivian and Reiter 1960:83–96). A clear definition of Great Kivas has not yet been given, however.

11. Early rooms at Broken K contained between 6 and 85 grains of "economic" pollen while the late rooms generally contained 0 to 5 grains (Chi-square, .05 level).

12. Out of 53 charred corn cobs found at the site, 46 of them were in early rooms. Of 70 squash seeds, 49 of them were found in early rooms.

13. Tested by Chi-square (.01 level).

14. It has not been possible to include all of the necessary supporting data for this study in the text. A more detailed version of this study is published as "Broken K Pueblo: Prehistoric Social Organization in the American Southwest" (*Anthropological Papers of the University of Arizona,* no. 18, Tucson). Further relevant data are published in "Chapters in

332

the Prehistory of Eastern Arizona, 3" (Paul S. Martin, William A. Longacre, and James N. Hill), *Fieldiana: Anthropology,* vol. 57. Raw counts of artifact and sherd types are in *Archives of Archaeology,* no. 27 (Society for American Archaeology and the University of Wisconsin Press). Field notes and collections are at the Field Museum of Natural History. Publications on special aspects of this study are as follows: Hill 1968; Hill and Hevly 1968; and Longacre 1966.

The Olmec Were-Jaguar Motif in the Light of Ethnographic Reality

IN VIEW of the strides Olmec archaeology has made since the early 1940s and the increasingly more sophisticated definition of the formal qualities and distribution of the Olmec style, it is regrettable that there has not been a more searching analysis of the content and meaning of the extraordinary art of this earliest of American civilizations. Few attempts have been made to interpret Olmec iconography in depth; instead, its treatment has been more descriptive than analytical. One can hardly blame the Mesoamericanist for his caution. As Michael Coe (1965*b*: 751) has observed, we have neither the benefit of definite knowledge nor of inscriptions, readable or otherwise, which might help in discovering the mythical basis of Olmec iconography. It is the purpose of this paper, however, to demonstrate that we are not altogether without resources. Of these the most important is ethnographic analogy, long recognized by archaeologists as a valuable tool for interpretation but largely neglected until now in the analysis of pre-Columbian art, at least that of Mesoamerica.[1] Compounding the problem is the limbo to which most art historians and anthropologists have consigned the study of pre-Columbian art.

Reprinted by permission of the author and publisher from Elizabeth P. Benson, editor, *Dumbarton Oaks Conference on the Olmec, October 28th and 29th, 1967* (Washington, D.C.: Dumbarton Oaks Research Library and Collection, Trustees for Harvard University, 1968), pp. 143–74.

As a result it finds a congenial niche in neither discipline.

Attempts have been made at interpretation of at least some of the more pervasive elements of Olmec art. Miguel Covarrubias (1957:50–83) drew numerous analogies between characteristic features of Olmec art and the meaning these, or their derivatives, assumed in later Mesoamerican civilizations. Largely on this basis it is frequently suggested that the jaguar may have been a rain deity in Olmec times or at least that the pervasive feline motif was connected with rain and fertility. Covarrubias, who saw the Olmec as a kind of "mother culture" which directly or indirectly gave rise to all the subsequent major civilizations, was inclined to regard all of the jaguar deities and the feline aspects of different gods in the later Mesoamerican civilizations as Olmec-derived, describing them as "an interesting unfolding of an ancient concept, the 'Olmec' jaguar deity, into various personalities that acquire individual characters during a millennium-long, varied adoption by different peoples" (1957:59). This is a provocative idea but it is not necessary to invoke a unilineal stylistic evolutionism to account for the feline element or even the were-jaguar motif which may be found in all Mesoamerican religious art, though certainly nowhere as predominant or pervasive as among the Olmec.

Matthew Stirling (1955:19, Pl. 25) has offered a hypothetical basis for some elements of Olmec iconography by relating a remark-able Olmec stone sculpture realistically de-picting a jaguar in the act of copulation with a human female, discovered by him at Potrero Nuevo, to a possible origin myth in which the feline played an ancestral role. Com-menting on Stirling's hypothesis, Coe (1965b: 751–52) agrees that it is reasonable to con-clude

that this union resulted in a race of infants combining the features of the jaguar and man in varying degrees. These are usually shown as somewhat infantile throughout life, with the puffy features of small, fat babies, snarling mouths, fangs, and perhaps even claws. The heads are cleft at the top. . . . They are always quite sexless, with the obesity of eunuchs.[2]

All writers agree that Olmec iconography centers on a "jaguar cult," with the were-jaguar and its corollary, the peculiar combi-nation of infantile and feline features (the "jaguar-babyface" motif), as the hallmarks of the Olmec style. Coe (1965b) lists among the main attributes of the adult were-jaguar the V-shaped cleft at the top of the head, the snarling mouth with jaguar fangs (sometimes absent), the flame-like element for brows, and infrequently a small, pointed beard. He observes that these are among the most com-mon iconographic motifs in Olmec figurines, effigy axes, jade plaques, masks, and monu-ments. It might be added that plants some-times sprout from the cleft. There are also representations of other creatures, including dragon-serpents, raptorial birds, and flying were-jaguars with large bat-like wings. Two such winged jade jaguars, found in Guana-caste Province, Costa Rica, are in the Brook-lyn Museum (Coe 1965b: Fig. 16).

The so-called jaguar cult among the Olmec is variously interpreted, but many of these explanations suffer from ethnographic bias in tending to ascribe to a culture of another time those attitudes and concepts which seem most "natural" to us and which are therefore un-critically assumed to possess universal validity. We often read that the Olmec must have chosen the jaguar as their principal deity be-cause it was the most powerful and most

feared animal in their tropical environment. But this is not how people choose their gods, and indeed it is by no means borne out by the ethnographic data on the jaguar's role in con-temporary or recent Indian societies. True, the jaguar is often greatly feared for its power (natural and supernatural) and wherever it occurs it plays a very special role in the Indian *Weltanschauung*. The supernatural jaguar may be master of the air, of his own species, of all animals and all food plants; he may be bringer of rain, devourer of the planets, foster parent and antagonist of the mythical twins, guardian of sacred places and of gods, and (almost universally) avatar of living and deceased shamans. But he is rarely elevated to the status of deity in the true sense of the term, much less the principal deity, even in cultures where we can speak of a pervasive jaguar cult. Occasionally, certain gods or the spirits of the dead are given some jaguar characteristics (e.g., prominent ca-nines), but this is not the same thing as the deification of the jaguar.

Heinz Walter (1956:94–96) discovered only four instances of a real jaguar deity in the ethnographic literature. Even here analysis of the data revealed that in three cases the jaguar deity was in reality only an institu-tionalized version of the well-known "master of the species" concept which is characteristic of hunting cultures but can still be found in the world view of many tropical forest culti-vators. The master of the species is a super-natural being, but not a god. Of the four tribes three are Bolivian, the Arawakan Mojo, the Tacana Araóna, and the Panoan Pacaguára; the fourth is the Shipáya, a Tupían-speaking group living between the Xingú and Tocatíns Rivers in northeastern Brazil. The Araóna, whose territory adjoins Arawakan-speaking groups to the west and north, appear to be strongly influenced by Andean religion; sig-nificantly, their jaguar god has the Quechua name *Baba Tsutsu*. Among the Mojo a super-natural jaguar was venerated in a temple hut, attended by a special shaman, called *cama-coy*. These shamans were recruited from men who had survived a jaguar attack in the forest and were therefore thought to be favored by the feline deity. If a hunter succeeded in killing a jaguar he had to remain in the temple for several days while the jaguar shaman made sacrifices (especially *chicha*) in his behalf. The supernatural jaguar revealed to the shaman the dead animal's secret name which the hunter then assumed.

There is no reason to doubt Walter's assessment of this jaguar god as an original master of the species who became institutionalized and deified with a temple-priest cult under the influence of Andean high cultures. For example, the deified jaguar is asked to lead the hunter to his prey; if the hunter is attacked by a jaguar and survives, it is a sign of the benevolent attitude of the god as master of the jaguars, and if he succeeds in killing a jaguar, the god, as master of the species, must be propitiated. Also, the shaman asks the deity to prevent attacks on the settlement by jaguars which prowl in the forest. The skull and paws of a slain jaguar are preserved as hunting cultures ritually preserved skulls, horns, and bones of animals to assure their resurrection (Zerries 1954:165–68; Eliade 1964:63, 159). Finally, it hardly accords with the idea of a deity that the jaguar shaman can engage the supernatural jaguar in combat and force his will upon him in order to protect his community. From these battles the shaman frequently emerges exhausted, with his clothing torn and his face and body covered with blood. Similar bloody encounters between shamans and animal spirits, demons, and the souls of sorcerers occur in other cultures.

Only *Kumupári,* the creator-culture hero and war-and-cannibalism god of the Shipáya, is a real deity in jaguar form (Nimuendajú 1948). However, he too is a special case, because he was a formerly anthropomorphic creator who only assumed jaguar form when he became angry with mankind.

One fact emerges with great clarity from the ethnographic evidence: the jaguar does not derive any unique mythic quality from its animal characteristics. On the contrary, dangers or benefits ascribed to the jaguar spring not from its nature as a dangerous predator but from its inherent supernatural attributes. The jaguar is in fact a man. The world view of the hunter is rooted in the qualitative equivalence of man and all wild animals. They differ only in outer form, and in ancient times even this differentiation did not exist. The jaguar, however, is equivalent only to one category of men who alone possess supernatural powers: the shamans. Moreover, shamans and jaguars are not merely equivalent, but each is at the same time the other.

To return to Olmec art, it seems significant that the jaguar in purely zoomorphic form is rare. Only later is he represented simply as the animal; even then his bearing and associated iconographic elements underline supernatural rather than natural qualities. In Olmec art the jaguar is almost everywhere the were-jaguar, i.e., the feline anthropomorph or the anthropomorphic feline. This man-jaguar motif ranges on a conceptual and representational continuum, from predominant zoomorphism on one end, to nearly complete anthropomorphism on the other. An example of the first extreme is the Dumbarton Oaks statuette (Fig. *1,* right); it has the head, body, feet, and tail of a jaguar but its legs, arms, and clenched hands are clearly human. At the other end of the continuum are the companion piece at Dumbarton Oaks (Fig. *1,* left) and the remarkably similar statuette from the Constance McCormick Fearing Collection (Fig. *3*). Both are completely human except for the unmistakable facial characteristics of a jaguar. A head fragment (Fig. *2*) in storage at the Museo Nacional de Antropología in Mexico City presumably belongs in the same category, although the body of this piece is missing.

Within the range of were-jaguar imagery are the portable and monumental two- and three-dimensional sculptures which are almost entirely anthropomorphic except for the "jaguar mouth." These may appear haughty, stern, or full of brooding power; sometimes the expression is lively, suggesting speech or debate (e.g., the famous figurine-and-celt cache from La Venta). Where the face has a pronounced grimace one wonders whether

336

FIG. 1. *Were-jaguars of serpentine in the Dumbarton Oaks Collection. Height: left, 7¾ in.; right 3⅛ in. Provenience: Tabasco.*

the artist meant to represent the fierce snarl of the jaguar, as is often suggested, or a feeling of intense inner torment or ecstasy. This may also be true of figurines where the grimace is accompanied by a strangely contorted body posture, as in the miniature "dancing were-jaguars," reminiscent of the Olmecoid *danzantes* at Monte Albán (Covarrubias 1946:Pl. 8; Coe 1965b:Fig.*11*). The most completely human although generally sexless were-jaguar types are the hollow ceramic "jaguar-babyface" figurines characteristic of Tlatilco and Las Bocas.

Of particular significance is Coe's observation that human beings

without noticeably jaguar or baby-like characteristics do occur on the monuments and in the

climax region, but seldom on the portable art and hardly anywhere outside the area. It is of course not beyond probability that the Olmec artist tended to look at everybody as having a little bit of jaguar-baby in him, but it would be safer to consider as portraits only those depictions without such an aspect. The individuality of some of these human portraits is so strong that they must represent historical personages. Most of these are bearded, like the famous "Uncle Sam" figure on Stela 3, La Venta, and like this, they often have hooked noses. (Coe 1965b:755)

Occasionally the two distinct types, those with and without were-jaguar characteristics, are juxtaposed, as on La Venta Stela 3, where there are several were-jaguars above the two principal personages. The seated figure in Chalcatzingo Petroglyph 1, though carved in characteristic Olmec style, also seems to lack were-jaguar features, as does the bearded reclining figure in Petroglyph 2. A were-jaguar face appears, however, as a mask or an apparition, at the back of his head, and three other standing figures in the same petroglyph unequivocally represent were-jaguars (Coe

FIG. 2. *Head fragment of a were-jaguar. Collections of the Museo Nacional de Antropología, Mexico. Height of head: just over 3 in. Found in Huimanguillo, Tabasco.*

The Olmec Were-Jaguar Motif
Peter T. Furst

Photograph by Peter T. Furst

FIG. 3. Serpentine were-jaguar from the Constance McCormick Fearing Collection, Santa Barbara, California. Height: 4¼ in. Reported provenience: Tabasco.

1965a:Fig. 10; 1965b:Fig. 3). Much has been made of this apparent ethnic differentiation in Olmec art. Soustelle (1966:35) raises the question "whether these two distinct ethnic types correspond to one or more migrations or invasions." Covarrubias (1957:58) also mentioned this but rightly warned that it is

of course dangerous to attempt to identify a people by physical characteristics shown in their art; there is no such thing as a uniform ethnic type, and it is well known that peoples seldom portray their characteristic type; they rather incline to portray that which results from the aesthetic ideals of their elites.

Nonetheless, the fact remains that the Olmec perceived and depicted two distinct types (three, if we add the colossal heads). I agree with Coe that only those sculptures which lack jaguar features should be con-

sidered true portraiture. It follows that those with were-jaguar features, however attenuated, represent conceptual and symbolic, rather than ethnic, reality. The question is why the Olmec artist should have experienced certain individuals in his culture as "jaguars," and what he meant to convey when he translated this emotional experience into two- and three-dimensional form. The South American shaman-jaguar transformation complex seems to me to hold the key to the interpretation of much, if not all, Olmec were-jaguar imagery, for the Olmec were-jaguar has its analogy in a large number of contemporary Indian cultures of diverse linguistic affiliation throughout the northern half of South America as well as Central America; there is at least strong inferential, if not direct, evidence that the same jaguar shaman concept formerly extended to Mesoamerica as well.

Two of the illustrated figurines (Fig. 1, left; Fig. 3) and the head fragment (Fig. 2) are a good departure point for this discussion because they share certain peculiar characteristics which are not readily apparent in most other Olmec were-jaguars but which seem to be of great significance for the shaman-jaguar transformation hypothesis.

At first glance the larger Bliss figurine and the Fearing statuette share so many stylistic and iconographic characteristics that they might well have been made by the same artist. Even the raw material—a very dark-green serpentine—is the same. However, closer examination reveals sufficient differences in the treatment of detail, such as hands and feet, to suggest that the two pieces probably came from different artists working in the same tradition and expressing the same underlying concept. It is of course possible that one master conceived and carved both pieces but left minor details to be completed by apprentice artists. In any case, there seems little doubt that the two Bliss pieces came from the same master's hand. Indeed, they are said to have been found together in Tabasco (Lothrop 1957:234). The precise provenience of the Fearing figure is unknown but it also is said to have been discovered in Tabasco. The museum catalogue gives the provenience of the Mexico City head fragment as Huimanguillo, Tabasco, located approximately fifty miles southeast of La Venta on the left bank of the Grijalva River. Whether these sculptures were originally carved in Tabasco is, of course, another matter. The Mexico City head is of a different stone, but in style and iconography it strongly resembles the heads of the Fearing and Bliss pieces. In all three, as also in the standing jaguar, the eyes were inlaid with small pyrites. These are still in place in the two Bliss statuettes but are missing in the Fearing piece and the Mexico City head. As is frequently true of portable Olmec art, there are traces of cinnabar embedded in various orifices, carved depressions, and minute imperfections in the polished surface of the stone.

All these pieces bear witness to the extraordinary gift of Olmec sculptors for handling material and tools with the delicacy and precision of the jeweler, yet imbuing their creations with monumentality and tremendous plastic force. Coe (1965b:749) puts it very well when he says of Olmec art: "no matter how small the object, it always looks much larger than it really is."

Upon superficial examination, the Fearing and Bliss figures and the Mexico City head seem to be wearing jaguar masks. The Bliss statuette was so interpreted by Lothrop (1957:234) who thought it represented a woman. Leaving aside for the moment the absence of overt male sexual characteristics which, along with certain fine-line engraved markings on the front of the body, misled Lothrop into assuming the figure to be female, the details of the head make it clear that the artist did not intend to portray a masked being, but rather conceived the jaguar features as an integral element of the personage portrayed. All three figures have a clearly defined dividing line differentiating the jaguar features of the face from the rest of the head. However, what the carver has done is to leave the back of the head raised, rather than the

front, and this part, together with the ears, is unquestionably human rather than feline. This curious phenomenon gives one the distinct feeling not of a mask (which would stand out, however slightly, from the front of the head) but rather of the human skin carved or peeled away to reveal the jaguar beneath. The fact that the same imagery is repeated precisely in all three pieces indicates that we are dealing not with a stylistic aberration but with a well-defined mode of representing a phenomenon which the Olmec believed to be real and which the artist (perhaps himself a religious specialist) had experienced emotionally.

The sculptures are highly naturalistic representations of the human figure, marvelously rendered with faithful attention to the interplay of muscles and body posture to convey the feeling of great inner tension and potential power. At the same time the jaguar face is convulsed into a tortured grimace. But this conveys far more the feeling of some emotional stress almost beyond bearing—indeed, the ecstatic experience par excellence—than the ferocity of a snarling feline. If these figures are what I think they are, then this problem resolves itself, since the ecstatic experience, the breakthrough in plane, so to speak, is characteristic of all shamanism, and the ecstatic experience of jaguar transformation, with or without the use of narcotics, is a characteristic of shamanism throughout tropical South America.

Some comments should be made here about Stirling's intriguing interpretation of Monument 3 from Potrero Nuevo in relation to the feline element in Olmec art. Indeed it might illustrate what the Olmec believed about their origin, although mythical matings between animals and humans are a frequent theme in the traditions of peoples who do not regard a particular animal as their ancestor, but who do conceive of absolute qualitative equivalence and interchangeability of outer form between man and beast, deriving from a complete lack of differentiation in the mythical "first times."

On the other hand, there are traditions in

The Olmec Were-Jaguar Motif
Peter T. Furst

tropical South America in which jaguars play an ancestral, generative role as original fathers or mothers; in fact, several peoples regard themselves, or are regarded by their neighbors, as Jaguar-Men or People of the Jaguar. According to Gerardo Reichel-Dolmatoff (1950–51:266), the Chibchan Kogi of Colombia "are the People of the Jaguar, their land is the Land of the Jaguar, their ancestors are the Jaguar People." In the Kogi creation myth cycle, ancestral jaguars, or jaguar-people, play the central role. A long series of jaguar people was born of the Universal Mother even before the birth of the first human people, and there are numerous stories of *Habia Nabia,* the Jaguar Mother; *Kashindukúa,* the Jaguar Father with attributes of the Great Shaman; *Duginávi,* the Jaguar Brother; *Námaku,* the Jaguar Chief, and others (Reichel-Dolmatoff 1950–51:265–66). It is important to note here that the jaguar people were anthropomorphic and zoomorphic at the same time and that they could transform themselves at will into one or the other form. Of the mythical ancestors, it is said that they were jaguars in human form and that when night came they changed into jaguars because of the knowledge possessed by *Kashindukúa.* Jaguars are responsible for all the food plants of the Kogi (a concept they share with the Tacana of Bolivia and other tribes) and in the cosmology jaguars will be instrumental in the end of the world. It should be stressed, however, that in the Kogi world view jaguars represent less a danger than the essential vital force. It goes without saying that jaguar ancestry and shaman-jaguar transformation are by no means mutually exclusive.

On a different conceptual level, the Apapocúva-Guaraní of Brazil regard their neighbors, the Caingang, as jaguars in a very real sense, not because their ancestors were jaguars but rather because they have the souls of jaguars (Nimuendajú 1914:305–6). This belief is founded in the Apapocúva concept of the dualistic human soul, called *ayvucué* and *acyiguá,* respectively. These represent the two sides of human nature: all that is good, quiet, and well-behaved is in the *ayvucué,* and all that is intemperate and violent in the *acyiguá.* For example, appetite for mild vegetable foods has its origin in the *ayvucué,* whereas desire for meat comes from the *acyiguá.* Since the latter represents the animal component of the dual soul, the properties of the animals which contributed to its formation determine the temperament of the person concerned. The worst thing that can happen is for a man to have the *acyiguá* of a dangerous beast of prey, such as the jaguar, because the *acyiguá* of such an animal always has dominance over the *ayvucué.* For this reason, according to Kurt Nimuendajú, the Caingang are not comparable to or symbolic of jaguars, but are by nature jaguars, appearing in human form. It is not just that the Apapocúva regard the Caingang as jaguar people, the latter also characterize themselves as jaguars in the literal sense (Nimuendajú 1914:371). In preparation for fighting they paint themselves with black spots or stripes and their war cries sound like the cry of the jaguar. According to Nimuendajú, the identity is taken so literally that occasionally there is a kind of "psychological disorientation" by which a *minanti,* or "dreamer" of jaguars, turns into a *mi-vé,* or "seer" of jaguars. The *mi-vé* believes himself to be the intended lover of the daughter of the master of the jaguars, separates himself from all his relatives and friends and prowls the forest alone until he enters a trance in which a supernatural jaguar appears and shows him the way to the jaguar people or the jaguar woman.

This is reminiscent of shamanic initiation with implicit or explicit ritual death and rebirth through a supernatural jaguar (or a Great Shaman in jaguar form), reported for some other South American peoples. For example, among the Arawakan Ipurina of the Juruá-Purús region of Amazonas: "The young man who is to become a shaman is sent into the forest; there he remains until a great jaguar appears to him; through him he is certified and he returns to his village as an initiated shaman" (Kunike 1915:20). Seclusion deep in the forest with strict abstentions to achieve the proper initiatory vision is reported also by Paul Ehrenreich (1891) for other Arawakan tribes, among them the Paresi of the Mato Grosso, although he mentions the jaguar initiation specifically only for the Ipurina.

A very detailed story of shamanic initiation by the Great Jaguar Shaman was recorded among the Bolivian Tacana by Karin Hissink and Albert Hahn (1961:401–2). The tradition concerns a twelve-year-old boy who walked into the forest to collect the fruits of the *sayal* palm. While he climbed about in the crown of the tree, *Iba Bana,* the giant-winged jaguar who is also a great *yanacona* (shaman), sat down by the tree to wait for the boy. The boy stepped on *Iba Bana*'s back and *Iba Bana* flew off with him into another world. When the boy failed to return home his mother consulted a *yanacona,* who, by means of coca, divined the boy's fate and told her not to worry: " 'Your son is alive. He is not on this earth. *Iba Bana* has taken him away to his world. He will come back after one year. He will return at the same time that *Iba Bana* took him away. . . .' So the mother knew that her son was to become a *yanacona.*" When the son reappeared on the day the *yanacona* had prophesied, he walked in silence into the cult house where he collapsed before the altar as though dead. The *yanaconas* rubbed him with narcotic powder to bring him back to life but it was not until after sundown that he finally stirred. Again the *yanaconas* rubbed him with narcotic powder. Then they carried him home and laid him in his hammock. When the boy finally awoke he told his parents not to cry, because he was alive and the *edutsi* (deified spirit beings or gods) did not want them to weep. Thus, ends the narrative, "the parents and the people knew that he had become a *yanacona.*"

Of the Sanemá, a Venezuelan Yanoáma group, Johannes Wilbert (1963:222) reports that the future *héwiawan* (literally "Bat-Person") goes alone into the forest where he encounters *Omáokóhe,* a giant supernatural bipedal jaguar who is Master of all the Felines and who strips him of his human flesh — without, however, injuring any of his bones. The initiate asks the Great Jaguar to replace his flesh and *Omáokóhe* covers his skeleton with the flesh of a supernatural bat. Zerries (1964: 238) points to the close linguistic relationship between this Great Jaguar *Omáokóhe* and the Yanoáma culture hero and creator deity *Omáo,* one of the celestial twins whose mother was eaten by a Great Jaguar. Her uterus containing the unborn twins was rescued by Frog Woman who became the twins' foster mother. The twins later cause the Great Jaguar's death and *Omáo* creates the first people out of trees. He leaves the earth when his twin brother attempts the seduction of his wife (Wilbert 1963). To what extent *Omáokóhe,* as the initiatory Great Jaguar of the *héwiawan* and possible hypostasis of *Omáo,* can be identified with the Great Jaguar who is the antagonist of the celestial twins *Omáo* and *Soáo,* is difficult to determine, though the data are certainly suggestive (Zerries 1964:238).[3]

Whereas the jaguar-twin motif complex may have only peripheral significance in the present context, the feline as the initiatory being of the shaman is of the greatest significance. If one concept cutting across geographic, linguistic, and cultural boundaries among South American Indians can be singled out, it is that of the qualitative identity between jaguars and shamans and accordingly their interchangeability of form. Alone among men, shamans are capable of transforming themselves into jaguars whose inherent qualities they share; the reverse side of the coin is that jaguars — at least those appearing under unusual circumstances or those attacking human beings — are not animals, but transformed shamans or sorcerers, or the soul bearers of deceased shamans who assist their living disciples as tutors and spirit helpers (Karsten 1964). Even where a real temple cult has developed around a jaguar deity (or deified Master of the Jaguar Species), as among the aforementioned Mojo of Bolivia, the concept of shaman-jaguar transformation exists. Those who escape unharmed from a jaguar in the forest are considered to be favored by the feline deity and are initiated into a guild of jaguar shamans who carry out all the rituals connected with jaguars and who are able to call and propitiate their spirits. According to Zerries (1961:19–20), they are also reported to have the capability of transforming themselves into jaguars.

One of the earliest accounts of shaman-jaguar transformation in South America is that of Pater Martin Dobrizhoffer (1822), a German priest who served among the Abipon, a Guaicurú-speaking tribe of Paraguay, in the mid-1700s. In a chapter, "Of the Conjurers, or rather the jugglers and cheats of the Abipones," he writes that all his Indians believe in the power of conjurers

to inflict disease and death, to cure all disorders, to make known distant and future events; to cause rain, hail, and tempest; to call up the shades of the dead and consult them concerning hidden matters; *to put on the form of a tiger,*[4] to handle every kind of serpent without danger, etc., which powers, they imagine, are not obtained by art, but imparted to certain persons by their grandfather, the devil. (Dobrizhoffer 1822:67)

Subsequently he describes his vain attempts to convince the Indians that there was no such thing as the transformation of a shaman into a jaguar:

At another time, when these bugbears imagine anyone inimical or injurious to them, they will threaten to change themselves into a tiger, and tear everyone of their hordesmen to pieces. No sooner do they begin to imitate the roaring of a tiger, than all the neighbors fly away in every direction. From a distance, however, they hear the feigned sounds. "Alas! his whole body is beginning to be covered with tiger spots!" cry they. "Look, his nails are growing," the fear-struck women exclaim, although they cannot see the rogue who is concealed within his tent, but that distracted fear presents things to their eyes which have no real existence. It was scarce possible to persuade them out of their absurd terrors: "You daily kill tigers in the plain," said I, "without dread, why then should you weakly fear a false imaginary tiger in the town?"

"You fathers do not understand these matters," they replied with a smile. "We never fear, but kill tigers in the plain, because we can see them. Artificial tigers we do fear, because they can neither be seen nor killed by us." (77–78)

Compare this to the account of a Tacana informant recorded by Hissink and Hahn (1961:398) during the 1952–54 Frobenius Expedition to Bolivia:

A *yanacona* (shaman) tried several times to tempt me to learn how to become a jaguar. As such I would have power over other people. The *yanacona* took me into the forest and I had to take up a certain spot. When I heard twigs breaking next to me and looked in that direction the *yanacona* stood there beside me in the form of a jaguar. I was frightened and wanted to flee. Then the *yanacona* again stood in front of me in his previous form and laughed at me. After this experience I was no longer tempted to learn the art of transformation.

In certain areas and language groups the conceptual equation of shaman and jaguar goes so far that a single linguistic term is used for both. This is true especially in the north west Amazon basin (eastern and southeastern Colombia and northwest Brazil). According to Theodor Koch-Grünberg (1909–10, Vol. 2:155), all of the Betoi speaking tribes use the same basic word for shaman and jaguar. A good example is the Detuana group of Betoi languages (Hanke 1964:40–59). The common term for shaman here is *dzaika,* that for jaguar *dzaja.* The same linguistic identity of shaman and jaguar is to be found among the Tucanoan-speakers of the same general area (Bödiger 1965). Indeed, the Tucanoan term is a very close cognate to that used by the Betoi-speakers and, as we shall see, also by the Witoto, whose language is classified as independent by Čestmír Loukotka (1968).

Approximately thirty tribes belong to the Tucanoan language family. These are separated by the Witoto and some Carib-speaking tribes into a western and an eastern group, with little, if any, cultural contact between them. All, however, share the concept of shaman-jaguar transformation and most, if not all, use the same or a closely related term for

342

both. According to Ute Bödiger's recent survey of the Tucanoan world view, the common name for either shaman or jaguar among the Siona is *yái,* and among the Corrugaje, *dyái* (Bödiger 1965:42–44; 150–53). Both belong to the western group. Arsenio, a shaman of the Siona, was called *yaiguaje,* "one of the jaguar people," or "jaguar man." The same terminology was reported earlier by Plácido de Calella (1940–41). The Witoto, whose culture in many respects seems intermediate between that of Paleo-Intian hunters and Neo-Indian tropical forest cultivators, call their shaman *ikodyai* (Preuss 1921:22). Bödiger points out that this term consists of two Tucanoan words, *dyái,* jaguar, and *iko,* soul.

The close relationship between shaman and jaguar which exists among the western Tucanoans, including the Siona, Corrugaje, Koto, Pioje, Macaguaje, and Tama, can be demonstrated for the eastern Tucanoans also. Here, identical terms for jaguar and shaman are to be found among the Tuyuka, Uasona, Uaiana, Ömöa, and Buagana (*yéi* or *yái*); the Tucano (*yaí*); the Uanana and Uaikana (*yáiro* and *yáido,* respectively); and the Cubeo (*yauwi* or *yaví*).

Because of the scarcity of published ethnographic data for the Tucanoan-speakers, especially in the area of religion, it is difficult to say whether all jaguar spirits or all spirits with jaguar characteristics can be seen as the souls of former shamans, even though this seems to apply at least to the western Tucanoan-speakers and even though all Tucanoan tribes believe in shaman-jaguar transformation, to which transmigration of the soul of the dead shaman into the jaguar is usually the corollary. Among the Macaguaje, a western tribe, the jaguar is definitely not only the living shaman's avatar but also the shaman's teacher and spirit helper. According to Bödiger, this is presumably so because shamans receive their knowledge from deceased shamans and the jaguar embodies such a soul. Significant is the fact that the Siona call their shaman not only *yai* or *yaiguaje,* jaguar or jaguar man,

but also *uattí,* meaning spirit, because he is equated with the *uattí* spirits which he controls and with whom he makes contact in trances induced by the narcotic *yagé.* However, the *uattí* spirits themselves are embodied in jaguars, so that there seems little doubt that the *uattí* are the souls of dead shamans acting as the helpers and teachers of the *yaiguaje* (Bödiger 1965:44). Since shamans are themselves jaguars, no shaman is ever attacked by a jaguar. Calella (1940–41:737–50) says of the *yaiguaje* of the Siona that when they "encounter a jaguar in the forest, they call out, My name is *yái!* Then the jaguar does not harm them."

Thanks to a recent monograph by Irving Goldman (1963), the data for the shaman-jaguar equation among the Cubeo are somewhat more complete than for most other Tucanoan-speakers. The Cubeo have a concept of supernatural power which they call *parié.* There are two kinds of shamans, one called the *pariékokü,* or man of power, and the other *yaví,* or jaguar (Goldman 1963: 262–67). Every *yaví* is a *pariékokü,* but not every *pariékokü* is a *yaví.* Rather, according to Goldman, "the *yaví* is the supreme shaman, the one who can take the form of a jaguar, who consorts with jaguars, who maintains the jaguar as a dog . . ." (262).

Goldman's informants (none of whom was a *yaví* because no *yaví* was willing to discuss his work with him) were not entirely agreed whether all jaguars or only some were *yavís:*

Some informants said flatly that every jaguar was a *yaví* or the dog of a *yaví,* or a jaguar into which a *yaví's* soul had entered. When a *yaví* dies, his ghost spirit (*dekókü*) becomes a jaguar. According to this view, the jaguar is feared because he is not an animal but a fiercely predatory man. Other informants explained that there are both ordinary jaguars and jaguars who are *yavís.* Both views agreed on the point that the fierceness of the jaguar is of human origin. Those who believed in ordinary jaguars said those were the kind that might run from a man. (1963:263)

Koch-Grünberg (1909–10, Vol. 2:155) says of the same tribe that their shamans also turn into jaguars when they get old simply by donning jaguar skins. Much the same is true of the Carib Taulipang, whose shamans

> are completely convinced that they are able to transform themselves into jaguars by putting on the *kaikuse-zamatále* ("the jaguar's dress"). In so doing they reverse their entire body, so that the stomach is turned upward. The back descends to become the stomach. Hands and feet become rounded and armed with claws, like the paws of the jaguar, and are turned backward. (Koch-Grünberg 1916–28, Vol. 3:200)

In his magical incantations for curing, the Taulipang shaman merges his own personality with that of the supernatural jaguars who live under the earth or in the water. They assist him as his spirit helpers and he becomes— indeed he already is one of them. In one such chant transcribed by Koch Grünberg (1917–28, Vol. 3:225–26) the shaman speaks of the illnesses sent by the various animals of the forest or the savannah to "weaken the flesh." He too is threatened by them, but by using pepper plants in a magical way he succeeds in frightening away the illnesses of animal origin and so becomes immune to them. When the people are struck by such a disease, he chants,

> [they] must call upon me, for I am the black jaguar. . . . I drive away the illness. They have to call on me. I am the tapir-jaguar. I too am here. . . . It is me they have to invoke if they wish to frighten it (the illness) away. I am the puma-jaguar. I too am here. . . . I extract the illness from their backs. It is me they have to call. I am the multi-colored jaguar I too am here.

The ethnographic literature leaves no doubt that most—if not all—Carib-speaking tribes in northern Brazil, Venezuela, and the Guianas shared these concepts of shaman-jaguar equivalence and metamorphosis. For example, while Koch-Grünberg was staying with the Yecuana (Makiritare), a jaguar came within a few feet of the house and remained there for some time, growling and snarling, before he finally turned tail and disappeared into the forest. When the ethnographer mentioned the incident to one of the Indians he was told:

> "That was no jaguar, that was a shaman trying to get his bench." I said, "Then why didn't he let me know? I would have put the bench outside for him." Hanging inside the house is a large stool, carved of heavy wood in the form of a jaguar, of the kind required by shamans for their nocturnal cures. (Koch-Grünberg 1917–28, Vol. 1:291)

While visiting another Yecuana group, the Majongkong, during a raging grippe epidemic, he was permitted to witness a lengthy curing ceremony during which the shamans, painted with stripes and red spots and seated on their jaguar benches, chanted and howled like jaguars all night and much of the following day. When he rose around noon to find something to eat he was warned by the young men not to enter the forest because it was full of prowling jaguars who had been summoned by the cries of "their human colleagues, the shamans" (Koch-Grünberg 1916–28, Vol. 1: 234). Here, as elsewhere, narcotic trances play an important role in spiritual transformation.

Some beliefs of the Tacana-speakers of northern Bolivia regarding shaman-jaguar transformation have been mentioned. Central to Tacana cosmology is the concept of a great flying jaguar who is a transformed human being, who functions as master of all animal species and of many natural phenomena, and who is a powerful shaman. The mythological material available for the Tacana has been greatly enriched by recent studies of Hissink and Hahn (1961).

There seems no doubt that Tacana religion and ritual are influenced by Andean concepts; one might add that these and other tribes of the Bolivian highlands and adjoining tropical lowlands seem to share with the pre-Hispanic Andean high cultures certain basic motifs. A hypothesis of ancient cotradition finds support in the extraordinary degree of correspondence noted by Hissink and Hahn (1961:539–53) between their mythic data and Andean art motifs, including the flying were-jaguar, the

344

double-headed serpent with sawtooth back as sky symbol, masters or guardians of animals and plants with feline characteristics, anthropomorphized objects such as tools and weapons, etc. The common Tacana term for shaman, *yanacona,* stems from the Quechua, although in Inca as well as Spanish colonial times its meaning was very different (Friederici 1947:662). *Caquiahuaca,* the principal deity of the Tacana, who is identified with a sacred mountain and mountain chain, is likewise of Andean origin. Nevertheless, the Tacana world view is basically similar to that of the South American tropical forest cultivators, with an underlying, and still very strong, component of typical hunting ideology. The latter is evident in such concepts as those of masters, mothers, or guardians of various animal and plant species; qualitative equivalence and interchangeability of form between animals and men, derived from an original state when animals, men, and plant life were as yet undifferentiated; propitiation of slain animals, etc. Another notion which clearly derives from hunting ideology is that a hunter who kills more animals of a certain species than he and his family can consume may be punished with illness and even death by the guardian of that species (Hissink 1964:202–4). The same idea extends to guardians of plant life. The *yanacona's* task is to divine the origin of such illnesses and to determine the proper propitiatory acts to effect a cure.

The flying jaguar represents a significant motif complex in Tacana cosmology and myth. Flying jaguar beings are variously known as *iba bana* (*iba* = jaguar, *bana* = tree) and *ebaquie iba* (*ebaquie* = up high or above, *iba* = jaguar) (Hissink and Hahn 1961:328–33). The airborne jaguar is dualistic; he functions as antagonist and as benefactor, as a danger to man and the universe as a whole, and as master or guardian of the air, earth, water, and all animal and plant species; as bringer of the seasons, wind, and rain; as guardian or emissary of the deities (*edutsi*) and especially of *Caquiahuaca Edutsi*; as earth bearer or supporter of the earth bearers;

as regulator of darkness and light (by alternately raising and lowering the earth or the earth bearers); and as the initiatory being of shamans. When a flying jaguar threatens the community, the *yanaconas* can put him in a temporary trance by blowing narcotic tobacco snuff at him; they then drive him away. Under certain conditions he may even be killed by magical means. The flying jaguars themselves are believed to be powerful *yanaconas*; originally they were human beings who were transformed at their own request or as punishment for some transgression by the old Earth Mother and female creator deity, *Eaua Quinahi.*

Still other supernatural jaguar beings, likewise regarded as great *yanaconas*, and *Marúri*, the Master of the Jaguar Species, who is at one and the same time the *iba bana* of the Earth Mother, *Eaua Quinahi,* and *Marúri aba*, the *iba bana* of the creator god, *Caquiahuaca*.

Marúri aba, also characterized only by the name *iba bana,* is the first guardian who has to be overcome on the journey to *Caquiahuaca* [presumably by the shaman]. . . . *Marúri aba* is not only guardian and watchman of *Caquiahuaca.* He is also dispatched by the latter as his messenger. In that case he grows wings and appears as a flying jaguar. (Hissink and Hahn 1961:331–32)

The Tacana distinguish several classes of *yanacona*, the two most prestigious being the *tata hanána*, who functions as priest in a regular temple cult as well as shaman, and the *mau*, who is the typical shaman without priestly overtones. The *tata hanána* is directly responsible to the *edutsi*, or deified beings, especially *Caquiahuaca Edutsi* and *Eaua Quinahi,* the Earth Mother, to whom he travels in his narcotic trances. The *mau* answers to the supernatural master of shamans, called *Mau Isháua.* Both are believed able to transform themselves into jaguars (the *mau* also has the jaguar as his principal spirit helper); restore themselves and others to a complete state and new life after initiatory dismemberment (ritual death and rebirth); travel to other worlds; enter trances and establish contact with the spirits by coca-chewing, tobacco-smoking, and the use of other hallucinogenic substances; predict the future; diagnose and cure illnesses; recover strayed or kidnapped souls; drive away the *ebaquie iba* by means of narcotic tobacco powder; and cause their enemies to fall ill or die (Hissink and Hahn 1961:390–401). The difference between the *tata hanána* and the *mau* seems to correspond to that between the *héwiawan* and the *sablí* of the Venezuelan Sanemá (Wilbert 1963). Another type of *yanacona* is the *ayahuasca* shaman, who relates to a supernatural master of the hallucinogenic *Banisteria* vine to reach the trance state essential to Tacana shamanizing (Hissink 1964:202).

The direct method of changing form at will and without any special preparation has been mentioned in the account of the *yanacona* who alternately appeared to his disciple as a man and as a jaguar. Another method is to "think" one's *enidu*, or shadow soul, into leaving one's body, climb a tree, and jump down headfirst. The *enidu* reaches the ground in the form of a giant jaguar with numerous lives and a heart formed of the hairs of different forest animals. Jaguar transformation can also be achieved by tumbling or somersaulting. Informants varied in their opinions on the vulnerability of such a transformed jaguar, some insisting that there was no way of killing one, others that thirteen arrows are necessary, still others that the same featherless arrow without a point (*puma*) which can be used magically on a flying jaguar is effective also for the were-jaguar. Should a were-jaguar be killed by magical means, he returns to human shape and is buried as a human; if the were-jaguar is a transformed shadow soul, his injury or death is duplicated in the *enidu's* owner (Hissink and Hahn 1961:397–98).[5]

Ecstatic intoxication and sexual abstention need still to be considered in relation to shamanism, to shaman-jaguar equivalence and transformation in South America, and by extension, to certain motifs in Olmec art. Psycho-active intoxicants, at least in the form of

some narcotic snuff powder, most probably akin to the *Piptadenia* and *Virola* snuff, have been known and used in South America for more than three millennia.[6] The earliest paraphernalia for snuffing now known are a whale-bone snuff tablet and a snuffing tube discovered by Junius B. Bird near Huaca Prieta, Chicama Valley, Peru, and dated by him ca. 1200 B.C. (Wassén 1967:257). These, and the many effigy snuffing implements of more recent date discovered in archaeological sites in Chile, Argentina, Peru, Uruguay, and the Amazon basin provide a remarkable thread of continuity, both in form and iconography, which leads from the prehistoric lowland tropical forest cultures to the Andean civilizations and from them directly into the historic period and the contemporary ethnographic scene (Wassén 1964, 1965, 1967). The archaeological evidence and related ethnographic data have important bearing on the shaman-jaguar complex as well as on the phenomenon of shamanic flight or celestial ascent.

S. Henry Wassén (1965; 1967:233–89) and Zerries (1965:185–94) have recently demonstrated that the well-known "alter ego" carvings from the lower Amazon depicting a jaguar behind and above a man are in fact paraphernalia connected with the preparation, storage, and use of the powerful psychotomimetic *Piptadenia* snuff. Zerries (1965: Figs, 5, 7, and 8) illustrates three wooden jaguar-supported *Piptadenia* mortars from the confluence of the Trombetas and the Amazon; two are double-headed, the heads facing in opposite directions. One cannot but wonder whether the famous carved stone mortar in the shape of a jaguar from Chavín de Huantár in the collection of the University of Pennsylvania Museum (Dockstader 1967:Pl. 90) might not also have been used for the preparation of *Piptadenia* snuff or some other narcotic. This may apply also to the elaborately carved Central American jaguar metates or grinding tablets (Dockstader 1967: Pls. 150, 152, 192), especially in view of the fact that ceramic snuffing tubes with small

346

bowls have been found in archaeological sites in Costa Rica (Stone 1958:16; Wassén and Holmstedt 1963:23; Wassén 1965:24–26, and Fig. 2).[7] The juxtaposition or combination of jaguars and birds on snuffing paraphernalia is closely bound to the widespread concept of birds as tobacco spirits or patrons of ecstatic intoxication, and as the avatars or spirit helpers of the shaman in his celestial flight, which he experiences in a state of ecstasy induced with psychotropic substances (Wassén 1965:24–29). Wassén (1967:277–83) derives the motif of the feline as such on ethnographic snuffing paraphernalia in lowland South America and archaeological counterparts from Chile, Peru, Argentina, and Uruguay directly from the concept of the shaman as jaguar (see Wassén 1967: Figs. 8, 16, 18, 22, 30; Dockstader 1967:Pl. 183). The combination of jaguar (shaman) and bird in relation to intoxicants with psychotomimetic effects may perhaps explain the origin of the Tacan feathered and winged were-jaguars (*iba bana* and *ebaquie iba*) who are regarded as great *yanaconas*.

In Olmec art we also find the bird-jaguar motif, e.g., the winged were-jaguars from Guanacaste, Costa Rica, the incised jade "spoon" from Guerrero, and the incised La Venta jade earplugs illustrated by Coe (1965b:754, Figs. *29–31*). The "spoon" has a were-jaguar face in profile inside the bowl and a bird on the handle, facing in the opposite direction. The American Museum of Natural History also owns a jade "spoon" with a carved bird head at one end. The clearest Olmec depiction of a raptorial bird, perhaps an eagle, with a "kan cross" in the eye, appears on an obsidian core from La Venta; more or less anthropomorphized birds or "were-birds" with raptorial characteristics are found on several other objects from La Venta and elsewhere (Coe 1965b:753). There are also the jade pendant from the Dumbarton Oaks Collection in the shape of a human head with a duck bill (Lothrop 1957:Pl. 1), and the famous duck-billed anthropomorphic Tuxtla Statuette which, though no longer

purely Olmec, is at least derived from the Olmec style.

I have long thought that the Olmec jade "spoons" might be stylized birds, but until I saw the ilustrations by Wassén (1967) of stylized bird-shaped stone carvings with cavities, found in the shell middens at Santa Catarina, Brazil, and read his discussion of their likely use as receptacles for *paricá* snuff powder, the possibility of the jade spoons as receptacles for psychotomimetic snuff had not occurred to me. This is speculative since we do not know whether the Olmec shamans used snuff or other narcotics; however, in view of the great antiquity of snuffing and the widespread use of psychotropic plants in South and Central America, as well as in Mexico, it would be surprising if they did not. At the time of the Conquest, *piciétl*, a bright green psychotomimetic powder made of the dried and pounded leaves of the *Nicotiana rustica* L. was used for ritual cleansing in curing and as an ecstatic intoxicant; in some areas of Mexico it is still used in native religious ritual and curing (Wasson 1966:330). According to Fray Bernardino de Sahagún (1950–63, Book 11:146) *piciétl* "intoxicates one, makes one dizzy, possesses one." The powder can be inhaled directly through the nose; formerly it was also mixed with lime and made into a wad for chewing, much as coca and lime are chewed in the Andes. The subject of snuffing in Mexico has hardly been broached, although there is some literature on other hallucinogens (see, for example, Safford 1920; Furst and Myerhoff 1966; Hoffman 1966: 349–57; Miller 1966:317–28; Wasson 1966: 329–57). No Olmec objects securely identifiable as snuffing tubes are known. However, many collections of Olmec jade include longitudinally drilled tubes which could have served as snuffers, even though such objects are generally described as beads. Also, as in South America, Olmec snuffing tubes might have been made of wood or bird bone.

In South America the ethnographic data we have on ecstatic intoxication in relation to shamanic transformation (especially Koch-

Grünberg) make it clear that the narcotic substances taken by the shaman do not *cause* him to assume jaguar form but rather allow the jaguar already within to reveal himself—as, in the analogous Jekyll-and-Hyde story, the brew which Jekyll drinks does not change him into something alien to himself but only into his other self. Nor is the shaman in the power of the intoxicant; it is he who controls it, and through it, the spirits of nature—so long as the proper ritual requirements are fulfilled. Related specifically to jaguar metamorphosis, the psychotomimetic intoxicant might be seen as a mechanism enabling the shaman to intensify his emotions to the point of experiencing completely his other self.

This is the case with shamans of the Carib tribes of the Orinoco-Ventuari whom Koch-Grünberg visited extensively. On ritual occasions, all the adult men consumed quantities of *kahí*, a powerful narcotic beverage made from vines belonging to the genus *Banisteriopsis*, but only shamans became jaguars during ecstatic intoxication. One Yecuana showed Koch-Grünberg the vine and told him that within it was contained "the shaman, the jaguar" (Koch-Grünberg 1917–28, Vol. 1: 323). In highly charged curing ceremonies (e.g., during a grippe epidemic) the shamans, seated on jaguar-effigy stools, achieved ecstasy and became jaguars while consuming great amounts of the *Banisteria* beverage; as jaguars, they called on their spirit helpers and wrestled with the disease demons. However, there were evidently circumstances when the jaguar inherent in the shaman might inadvertently come out without any special effort and when metamorphosis into a jaguar was actually quite inappropriate to the occasion. To quote Koch-Grünberg (1917–28, Vol. 3: 201) again:

Akúli [a Carib shaman informant] told me that in the course of a big dancing ceremony held in the dance house on the Roraima he himself had changed into a jaguar, and this before the very eyes of the people, who fled and barricaded the house. He had climbed up one of the house posts and fallen down. When the people had told him about it the following day he had been most embarrassed.

Metamorphosis through a psychoactive substance, in this case tobacco, is implicit also in a Warao tradition in which a man teaches his brother the secret of transforming himself into a jaguar by the intensive smoking of a magic cigar. As jaguars they raid a burial place and dig up the dead. An Indian comes along and fatally wounds the brother, who thereupon changes back into a man and dies. The other brother, in the form of a jaguar, avenges his death by killing the Indian (Wilbert 1970). One is reminded here of the Tacana tradition that a were-jaguar can be successfully opposed only by magical means (arrow, tobacco powder)—prerogatives of the shaman—and that if a transformed jaguar is fatally wounded he changes back into a man. There also comes to mind the precautionary question of the Sanemá (Yanoáma) hunter when he meets any jaguar in the forest: "Are you a jaguar or are you a shaman?" If the jaguar replies that he is a shaman the hunter prudently retreats, for to challenge or threaten a transformed shaman would assure fatal consequences (Johannes Wilbert, personal communication).

Sexual abstention before, during, and after all ritual acts and during initiatory training, is a well-documented shamanic phenomenon which may shed light on the real meaning of the peculiar characteristic of sexlessness in Olmec were-jaguar figurines. Sexual abstinence applies especially to all activities connected with the various psychotomimetic plant substances used by the shaman to achieve contact with the other world.

The Tucanoans, for example, believe that the power which the shaman exercises over nature and the spirits which rule over the plant and animal species, is concentrated in his power over the narcotic *Banisteria* beverage (here called *yagé*), and that this unique power would be gravely endangered by sexual activity during its preparation and its use by the shaman (Bödiger 1965:45–48). Among the Siona, *yagé* is prepared in a special place by a novice shaman. The training of the novice has two major phases, the first designed to cleanse the body through various narcotic plant and bark extracts, to initiate him into the knowledge only shamans have of the forest, and to impress him with his duties to the community, at whose service he will place himself without reservation following his initiation. This phase is already accompanied by food and sexual taboos. The second and most important phase is that of initiating him into the use of *yagé*, which brings about the trances during which he will establish contact with the other world. During this time the taboo against all sexual relations is vital, for, as he is told by the shaman: "If you do not strictly avoid women, the *yagé* will not give you its visions" (Bödiger 1965: 47–48). The *yagé* jealously insists on complete sexual abstention and if this condition is not observed, the shaman might die when he uses it. Noting that the Guardian of *Yagé* is conceived as female, Bödiger (1965:49) cites an analogous situation among the Cuna of Panama and Colombia whose shamans must abstain from sexual intercourse while searching for medicinal plants, because the female plant spirits are extremely jealous.[8]

The novice shaman of the Jívaro likewise has to abstain from sexual intercourse during his training (Karsten 1955:172). No married couple can live in the same house with him and even his food must be prepared by an unmarried man or a virgin. Should he violate these taboos the consequences would be fatal, for the mystical poison which he has absorbed into his body would not only fail to "ripen" but, on the contrary, cause his death.

Perhaps the most arduous initiatory experience was that of the Carib shaman, who had to observe the strictest sexual abstention in the face of erotic excitation by pubescent girls who each night painted his entire body with red paint and even danced with him (Andrés 1938:336). These girls made twelve ceramic bowls which, decorated with a spiral stairway symbolizing the ladder to the sky, were designed to transport the novice to the other world with the help of Grandfather King Vulture, the most important of the spirit helpers. According to Koch-Grünberg (1917–28, Vol. 3:335–37), the Carib shaman's training lasted for three years and more, during which the novice not only abstained from sex but was permitted to eat so little that he was reduced to a virtual skeleton (reduction to skeleton = initiatory death).

Food taboos and length of initiatory training vary but the sexual taboo is evidently universal during all ritual acts for the rest of the shaman's life. Two examples from contemporary Mexico are of interest, one from the Huichols of the Sierra Madre Occidental in Jalisco and Nayarit, with whom I have worked since 1965, and the other from the highland Maya area. During his training, which includes a minimum of five pilgrimages from West Mexico to the sacred peyote country in San Luis Potosí, in the north-central high desert, the Huichol *mara'akáme* (shaman-priest) must observe long periods of strict sexual abstention and numerous food taboos. Sexual abstinence is a strict requirement immediately before, during, and immediately after all ceremonial activities, especially for the duration of the peyote pilgrimage, which may last between forty and forty-five days. Maud Oakes (1951:57–58) reports much the same thing for Todos Santos Cuchumatán, a Mam-speaking community in the Department of Huehuetenango, Guatemala, where she had the following conversation with the sister of the *Chimán Nam* (shaman-priest) Macário:

"When he was young, Macário's wife ran away with another man. She ran away because she wanted a man for a husband, not a *Chimán Nam*."

"What do you mean?" I asked.

"The *Chimán Nam* can never touch a woman during *costumbre*[9] time and five to twenty days before. Now Macário performs much *costumbre* throughout the year, though not much during the rainy season. Because of all this his wife ran away and he never took another woman."

349

We should perhaps reexamine the asexual phenomenon in Olmec art in the light of these strong sexual taboos which seem to be almost universally associated with shamanic initiation, ecstatic transport, and other shamanic ritual, as well as with priesthood in general, rather than interpreting it as the portrayal of a pathological condition or priestly emasculation (Dávalos Hurtado 1951). There is frequently a strong sexual element in shamanism which expresses itself in different ways in different geographical and cultural contexts: change of sex, sexual relations between shamans and tutelary spirits or celestial instead of human wives, transmutation of sexual energy, etc.; all imply abstention from a normal sexual life for the shaman (Eliade 1964:71–74, 79–81, 257–58). Dávalos Hurtado (1951:133–41) may have come close to the truth in interpreting the Olmecoid "danzantes" of Monte Albán as priests engaged in an ecstatic ritual dance, but I suggest that the flower-like designs or scrolls which replace their sexual organs, as well as the absence of sexual organs on were-jaguar figurines, be considered as metaphorical rather than literal, symbolizing ritual celibacy rather than recording sexual atrophy or castration.

Except for the Huichols and perhaps remnants of the Lacandon Maya in Chiapas, nowhere in modern Mesoamerica has aboriginal belief and ritual survived to nearly the extent that it has in tropical South America. While jaguar symbolism in pre-Columbian art can often be clearly identified with priestly status,[10] there is also persuasive documentary and linguistic evidence for shaman-jaguar equivalence in comparatively recent times. As George Foster convincingly demonstrated, the component parts of the Mesoamerican phenomenon of nagualism are in fact

merely local manifestations of native American beliefs. . . . In many parts of North and South America the native peoples believed that certain individuals possessed the power to transform themselves into animals in which form they did mischief. Ancient Mexico and Guatemala shared this belief. (1944:87)

There are two closely related aspects to nagualism. On one hand, the nagual is the sorcerer who changes into an animal. But in some areas, notably Oaxaca, Veracruz, Chiapas, and Guatemala, nagualism also pertains to the belief that a person has an animal alter ego, or companion animal.[11] According to Foster (1944:92–93), the bond between man and his animal is so close

that there is practical spiritual identity; it is but a step to assume that the human can take at will the animal form. The idea that when either companion animal or human is injured and dies the other suffers a like fate is the most striking characteristic of this aspect of the phenomenon. Modern and early accounts cite the innumerable cases in which an animal is shot and at the precise moment someone in a nearby village drops dead, his body showing the same wounds as the animal.

This is much like the beliefs about were-jaguars and other alter ego animals in South America and elsewhere. The term nagual comes from the Aztec stem *naual*, which through affixation of the article *tli* becomes *naualli*; compounds from the stem denote something hidden or disguised (Foster 1944: 85, 88–89). Georg Friederici (1926:69) explains *nagual-nauali* as

the bewitched one, the enchanted one, one disguised as werewolf, the sorcerer in animal form; the animal spirit which stands in the closest relationship with a human from birth on and in a sense is one with him. . . . The personal spirit, the alter ego of the individual. Through its aid the adept can practice sorcery etc., and especially acquire the power of "shape-shifting," that is, transforming himself at will into some animal.

Sahagún (1950–63, Book 10:31) differentiates between *qualli naualli* (good sorcerers) and *tlaueliloc naualli* (bad sorcerers):

The sorcerer [is] a wise man, a counselor, a person of trust—serious, respected, revered, dignified, unreviled, not subject to insults. The good sorcerer [is] a caretaker, a man of discretion, a guardian. Astute, he is keen, careful, helpful; he never harms anyone. The bad sorcerer [is] a doer [of evil], an enchanter. He bewitches women; he deranges, deludes people; he casts spells over them; he charms them; he enchants them; he causes them to be possessed. He deceives people; he confounds them.

There is another reference which hints strongly at jaguar transformation by "sorcerers" (*naualli*) or "conjurers" (*nonotzaleque*). In his discussion of the so-called *ocelutl*, by which he evidently means not the ocelot but the jaguar, Sahagún (1950–63, Book 11:3) describes the use of the skin as follows:

The conjurers went about carrying its hide—the hide of its forehead and of its chest, and its tail, its nose, and its claws, and its heart, and its fangs, and its snout. It is said that they went about their tasks with them—that with them they did daring deeds, that because of them they were feared; that with them they were daring. Truly they went about restored. The names of these are conjurers, guardians of tradition, debasers of people.

As in South America, the shaman can transform himself simply by donning a jaguar skin. A possible Olmec analogy is the ceramic were-jaguar figurine dressed in a jaguar skin from Atlihuayan, Morelos (Covarrubias 1957:61).

Jaguars ("lions" or "tigers") and birds are mentioned in early accounts as the animal metamorphosis of the *naualli*. In Nicaragua, *nawa*, a local form of the Aztec *naua*, is used by the Sumu Indians specifically for jaguar. This is

an identification understandable when it is realized that this animal is perhaps the most common and ancient disguise of the transforming witch. These Indians believe in witches who change themselves into owls and other forms, but they are not called naguals. (Foster 1944:100)

There remains some linguistic evidence for an ancient equation between shaman-priest and jaguar in the Maya area in the so-called Books of Chilam Balam, the sacred writings of the Maya of northern Yucatán. *Chilam* means priest, shaman, or interpreter of the gods, while *balam* means jaguar. Chilam Balam may be translated as Priest-Jaguar or

Jaguar Priest. However, *balam* can also mean priest (Roys 1967:111, footnote 3) or "sorcerer" (Recinos 1950:94, footnote 1). Of the four original ancestors of the Quiché Maya, three were named Balam. This identification of the priestly ancestors with the jaguar is explained by Recinos as follows: "It must be noted that *balam* also has the meaning of sorcerer, and that the ancient Quiché, who believed in sorcery and incantations, saw their first fathers as sorcerers and wizards."

Such beliefs are a common theme in origin myths in North and South America and in the Old World as well: the first ancestors are human and animal at the same time, without qualitative or formal differences between them. Eventually the bond is broken and animal and man assume their permanent shape, with the exception of the shamans who alone are capable of reestablishing mystical solidarity, because they can transform themselves at will into their animal alter egos or their animal tutelary spirits. To quote Mircea Eliade (1964:94): "Each time a shaman succeeds in the animal mode of being, he in a manner re-establishes the situation that existed *in illo tempore*, in mythical times, when the divorce between man and the animal world had not yet occurred."

The phenomenon of Mesoamerican nagualism, as an agglutination of two apparently different concepts, that of animal transformation and that of the companion animal or animal alter ego, has its almost identical counterpart among the Buryat of Siberia, an area where shamanism was preserved, until recently, in its classic forms. Here the shaman's tutelary animal spirit, called *khubilghan* (from *khubilkhu*, "to change oneself," "to take another form"),

not only enables the shaman to transform himself; it is in a manner his "double," his alter ego. This alter ego is one of the shaman's "souls," the "soul in animal form," or, more precisely, the "life soul." Shamans challenge one another in animal form, and if his alter ego is killed in the fight, the shaman very soon dies himself. (Eliade 1964:94–95)

Nagualism can apparently be understood as a local manifestation of shamanism in general, even though in Mexican syncretic folk beliefs the transforming shaman has become the "sorcerer" who does mischief in his animal form.

The above evidence does not negate the possibility of deification of the jaguar or of certain gods appearing in jaguar form, especially where deities developed out of deified ancestors or their animal counterparts or alter egos. Among the contemporary Tzotzils the companion animals of the elders and shamans are the largest members of the cat family, with a great jaguar as the alter ego of the most important elder of the community (Holland 1964:304). The companion animals

of the elders and curers are lineage gods which occupy the highest levels of the sacred mountain. . . . The companion animal of the *principal of principales,* a giant jaguar, has the most imposing position from which he consults directly with the ancestor gods in matters concerning the rule of his inferiors.

The contemporary beliefs of the Tzotzil in a society of companion animals centered around sacred mountains

may have had prehistoric Maya counterparts centered around lineage pyramids in ancient Maya archaeological sites. Ancient Maya ancestor worship may have functioned as a supernatural system of social control, as it still does among the Tzotzil and Tzeltal. (Holland 1964:306)

In discussing the role of ethnographic analogy in the interpretation of archaeological materials, Raymond Thompson (1958:5) observed that

the archaeologist who formulates an indicated conclusion is suggesting that there is a correlation between a certain set of archaeological material percepta and a particular range of sociocultural behavior. He must test this conclusion by demonstrating that an artifact-behavior correlation similar to the suggested one is a common occurrence in ethnographic reality.

Furthermore, Thompson said, in order to support the proposed correlation, it must be dem-

onstrated that it derives from a pattern of repeated occurrences in a large number of cultures. This condition I believe has been fulfilled for the suggested correlation between the Olmec were-jaguar motif, and, by extension, at least some of its analogies in post-Olmec times, and the widespread, indeed almost universal, shaman-jaguar identity in contemporary or recent Indian cultures. If the analysis has any validity, the were-jaguar figurine ceases to be naturalistic portraiture, depicting an ethnic type, an aesthetic ideal, or a pathological condition—or a combination of all three. Rather, the feline characteristics become a kind of badge of office, the manifestation of the supernatural jaguar qualities inherent in priest or shaman, his spiritual bond and identity with the jaguar, and his capacity, unique among men, of crossing the boundary between animals and humankind by achieving total spiritual transformation. From this it is but a small step to deified lineage ancestors, creator gods, or gods controlling the natural phenomena, as Great Shamans—and hence their depiction in ceremonial art with jaguar characteristics.

The "scientific world view" to which we are all captive makes it difficult to reach meaningfully into the metaphysical, esoteric areas of the past—or, for that matter, the present—but at least we can be certain that in pre-Hispanic art, as in the art of other non-Western peoples, things are rarely what they appear to be at first glance. The question is how to achieve that second look and make it yield meaningful results. It seems obvious that the most valuable and perhaps the only tool at our disposal in this respect is ethnographic analogy, which, as Kwang-Chih Chang (1967:229) properly observes, "is the principal theoretical apparatus by which an archaeologist benefits from ethnological knowledge." It is probably also the only theoretical apparatus by which we may eventually achieve classifications in pre-Columbian art which agree reasonably closely with the cognitive systems of its creators, rather than only with our own.

352

NOTES

1. Some European scholars have made use of analogies between ethnographic reality and archaeological materials in Central and South America. An especially useful contribution is that of O. Zerries (1962) on the "alter ego" concept and the role of the harpy eagle among South American Indians, which he relates to the numerous Central American gold representations of this bird. Hissink and Hahn (1961) drew attention to the extraordinary degree of correspondence betwen mythic motifs of the contemporary Tacana of Bolivia and the iconography of pre-Hispanic art, including Chavín, Paracas, Nazca, Moche, and Tiahuanaco. Another valuable study is that on the significance of the frog in South and Central America by S. H. Wassén (1934a:613–58; 1934b:319–70). The same author has also clarified the cultural-historical problem of narcotic intoxication by snuffing in relating the archaeological evidence to ethnographic reality in this area and the West Indies (Wassén 1965, 1967; Wassén and Holmstedt 1963).

2. The apparent physical deformities associated with the feline-infant motif, such as obesity, puffed eyelids, cleft, drawn mouth exposing toothless gums, and absence of sexual characteristics, have given rise to various hypotheses. Of these the least attractive and most tenuous is that they might represent some kind of interaction of observed glandular disturbances and genetic or chromosomal defects with the Olmec aesthetic ideal (Covarrubias 1957:58).

Certainly some physical deformities and even certain symptoms of disease were occasionally depicted in pre-Columbian art. Whatever the reasons why certain formal conventions arose and became institutionalized in funerary or ritual art, especially in West Mexico, it is doubtful that they were inspired exclusively or even largely by disease.

3. The relationship of the jaguar to the celestial twins is extremely complex and to do it justice would take us to far afield from the central theme of this paper. Suffice it to say that the motif is widely distributed and often involves the jaguar as both antagonist and benefactor of the twins. Zerries (1964:241–44) cites numerous versions in which the mother of the twins is killed by the Jaguar People or a Great Jaguar, whereupon the pair is rescued and raised by a foster mother. She, in turn, combines the attributes of Frog Woman and Mother of the Jaguars or is transformed from frog to feline. She is later slain by the twins in revenge for their real mother's death, but this is really a creative act in that from her bones or ashes grow the first cultivated plants. Valuable studies of the celestial twin motif complex in South America are those of Ehrenreich 1905; Gusinde 1930; Métraux 1928, 1932;

and Kuhne 1955. Also useful in Zerries's (1934:237–44) discussion because it centers on the distribution of the basic myth and its various elements among Carib- and Arawak-speakers and the marginal or hunting-and-gathering tribes, such as the various Yanoáma groups and the Warao in Venezuela, northern Brazil, and the Guianas.

4. Italics mine.

5. Koch-Grünberg writes (1917–28, vol. 3:201) of a Taulipang shaman-chief who was greatly feared as an evil sorcerer. He appeared in the form of a jaguar to one of Koch-Grünberg's informants, who succeeded in wounding the jaguar with an arrow. The sorcerer was said to have fallen ill at the same moment.

6. The two most widely used psychoactive preparations are a drink whose main ingredient is an extract from one species of the genus *Banisteriopsis,* and a powerful snuff powder whose main constituent is usually the crushed seed of the *Piptadenia* tree. These snuffs are variously known as *parica, yopo, cohobo, villca,* etc. *Datura* and tobacco are also widely used, and in several regions snuff powders and narcotic infusions are prepared with several varieties of psychotropic plants mixed together. See Cooper (1949:525–58), S. H. Wassén and B. Holmstedt (1963), and Wassén (1964, 1965, 1967).

7. Since this was written, small pipe-like effigy bowls as well as undecorated bowls equipped with longitudinally perforated stems or tubes have been found in association with beautifully fashioned naturalistic figurines and typical Olmec pottery in a new pre-Classic site at Xochipala, Guerrero, in western Mexico. The undecorated bowls especially resemble later ceramic snuffing instruments from Central America, but the construction of all these Xochipala artifacts strongly suggests an important snuffing complex in Olmec times, ca. 1200 to 900 B.C., at least in Guerrero. Two hollow tomb figurines from Colima depicting males (one of them horned) snuffing from gourd snuffers held to the nose, as well as small Colima redware snuffing pipes, are also known to me. The kind of snuff used in West Mexico is of course unknown. Possibly it was tobacco; however, it should be noted that several species of the genus *Anadenanthera* (formerly *Piptadenia*), including especially *A. flava* and *A. constricta,* are found in West Mexico. Their possible narcotic properties are not known at this time. It might also be of more than passing interest that the major hallucinogenic alkaloid of some *Anadenanthera* species, bufotenine, is also present, as its name implies, in toads of the common genus *Bufo* found all over Central and South America (Daly and Myers 1967:970, Table 1). Frogs or toads are a pervasive archaeological motif and in mythology are frequently identified with jaguar transformation (Zerries 1964:242–44).

353

8. Perhaps this is the reason why the hallucinogenic *Ipomoea* seeds are called "seeds of the Virgin" or "La Señorita" in Oaxaca, and why they must be ground by a virgin (B. P. Reko 1934; Wasson 1966). It must also be virgins who gather and grind the divinatory mushrooms in the Valley of Juxtlahuaca in the Mixteca, and the leaves of the *Salvia divinorum* in Ayautla and San José Tenango in the Sierra Mazateca (Wasson 1966:346).

9. Literally "custom," used to mean prayer, ceremony, ritual, etc., of the traditional, non-European kind.

10. For example, Roys (1967:198) notes that the jaguar appears frequently "in the older Maya art, indeed it goes back to some of the earliest monuments; but before the appearance of an intrusive Nahua culture in Yucatan this animal is always connected with the priesthood. Only in the Toltec temples do we begin to find it a symbol of the warrior class." One cannot help wondering whether the plumed and often anthropomorphic jaguars in the Teotihuacán murals, especially the conch-blowing jaguar procession below the Palacio del Quetzalpapálotl, are not metaphorical representations of priests, especially since, at least in Aztec times, the blowing of conches, even war conches, was the exclusive prerogative of the priesthood (Sahagún 1950–63, Book 2).

11. See also Holland (1961, 1964). Holland's work provides a useful example of the value of ethnographic analogy for the interpretation of some aspects of Maya civilization.

PART 7

Archaeological Strategy for the Study of Complex Agriculturalists

Introduction

If the invention of domestication has always been recognized as the proper domain for archaeology, then so has its corollary, the rise of cities. The phenomenon of civilization and its principal characteristic, urbanism, are understood to be founded on agriculture. And this usually means a type of agriculture made possible by complex technology. Here resides, for example, the irrigation hypothesis. This is the proposition made by Wittfogel that irrigation under some circumstances leads to a social organization characterized by elites and pyramidally arranged power. Since the first cities are all founded on agriculture supported by complex irrigation practices, it is reasoned, and not lightly, that agriculture, irrigation, autocracy, and cities are linked factors.

Aside from the complex technology that comes into existence with certain kinds of agriculture, are economic and social forms and radically new forms of religious organization (Bellah 1970:9–15). There are in this section some of the significant efforts in American archaeology to cope with aspects of urbanism and its allied traits. Certainly the theoretical foundation for the study of urbanism had been laid by Gordon Childe and Julian Steward. These men had pointed out the issues within the problem-domain of the rise of cities and each had contributed his share of competence and publicity to a series of provocative solutions. What we see now, however, acknowledges and builds upon Childe and Steward as a base and goes on as well.

Whether or not Robert Adams would feel comfortable being called a new archaeologist is an open question. That he is mentor, initiator, and guide for numbers of them is not such a debatable issue, however. Adams began in the middle 1950s to address the problem of the rise of cities. He took the remarkable step of making a general comparative statement about the factors behind the rise of cities and their early transformations as seen in the archaeological record. The article reprinted here is one of his earliest statements and cites evidence from ancient Mesopotamia and pre-Columbian Mesoamerica. This model of presentation undoubtedly enjoyed inspiration from Julian Steward. But to have an ethnologist, even one trained in archaeology, discuss the uniform qualities in civilization and to have an archaeologist do the same thing are not parallel. Steward could stand safe in a comparative field. Adams faced the particularists in their own house. (See Adams 1966 for the most up-to-date and comprehensive statement on this subject.)

Even now one would suppose that a decade and a half had changed the intellectual climate in archaeology sufficiently to permit and even encourage such trial efforts. But that is distinctly not the case. While one can not observe active discouragement of generalization, one does not catch many archaeologists prepared to go beyond the study of the ecological adjustment of a given culture to the more general phenomenon of which he may have examined a specific instance. It is only slowly becoming part of our world view that such an attempt is within the range of acceptable or anticipated alternatives for archaeologists. An inability to transcend the particulars of a culture seems to characterize all living generations of archaeologists. One of the potential exceptions to this flaw in archaeology rests in some recent archaeological efforts. The two articles in an earlier section of this volume by Binford and Flannery on domestication present hypotheses that are removed or removable from the spatial limitations of one site or region. These are, of course, conscious efforts at responsible generalization. Zubrow's article in the section on horticulture aims at a demographic model applicable to more than the American Southwest. Rathje's and Morris's pieces in this section do the same although more indirectly. Given the rarity of the phenomenon of the invention of domestication and the rise of cities, a comparative stance may be required. Regardless of the cause, however, these domains are partly responsible, as well as are their chief scholars, for the acceptability of generalizing research in archaeology.

The difference between the research effort of the 1950s and the 1970s is well characterized by Adams. "I feel the payoffs are likely to be greater at present for relatively systematic analyses of diachronic changes in individual examples of major institutional structures. Naturally, the themes for such analyses ought to be those that will support future comparative treatment, for the point is precisely that we still have an adequate base of *organized, relevant* knowledge about each individual area to support generalizations about comparative processes at other than an intuitive level" (personal communication).

An attempt to provide such organized and relevant knowledge is one of the unifying features of this section. As Adams's own work demonstrates, it is with the advent and effects of urbanism that archaeological research holds some of its richest potential and rewards.

The original articles by Morris and Rathje in this section are both examples of recognized problems in the domain of urbanism addressed by archaeologists who possess a generalizing world view; who act on the assumption that economics are fundamental, that culture is an efficient set of subsystems, that change is explained by cultural variables and not by climatic ones; and who see their work as contributing, however modestly, to more than Inca ethnohistory or Maya archaeology. Although neither author would disparage either field, the orientation of both demands conscious awareness of the source of his explanatory ideas as well as his effect on them.

Rathje's article may be the first substantive breath of fresh air in Maya studies since Morley attempted to synthesize Maya history and J. Eric Thompson transformed his daydreams into successful social science. And Morris's article fingers a type of urbanism created as a function of empire building.

It may be analytically incorrect to classify early colonial New England under complex agriculturalists. But the point is only of academic interest. The research performed in New England on the gravestones of God's elect in the New World is among the most interesting in the field right now. The work of Deetz and Dethlefsen on colonial artifacts, especially gravestones, illustrates the growing use to which historical archaeology is put and an increase of interest in ideology on the part of archaeologists. It may also represent the dawn of the notion that archaeology is doing more than going from the range of living ideas to the pattern of dead artifacts. It may well be that an important part of the subdiscipline's future will be spent going from living artifacts to the systems, including the system of ideas, that produced them. This would involve us in a science of material culture which would not exclude the past but would include the present. Our aim would not only be the reconstruction of subsystems of culture from material remains but would include how artifacts function in aiding other subsystems to work. The distinction is between asking what an artifact, living or dead, is used for and asking what it does to you when you use it.

Artifacts function at all levels of culture: economic, social, and religious. How, for example, does the unique settlement plan of nineteenth-century Mormon farming towns in the Great Basin reinforce and reflect the social and religious systems carried on within them? Streets divide property and ease transportation. That may be their economic function. But they also divide land up equally or unequally and arrange number, position, and distance of neighbors and in such a way that spatial divisions facilitate the social organization. The settlement plan may provide a three-dimensional representation of the heavenly sphere, thus reifying ideological abstractions. These, as Binford pointed out, are levels of functional variability. But what are the physical properties of a settlement plan street layout that allow it to function at all levels as it does? How does it manipulate space, for example? This is an area in which there are few answers and fewer researchers.

This section and its articles are not offered as a guide to the future in American archaeology. It represents only the best of the present. It offers no more than some competent experiments and some ideas for future experimentation.

Chapter **30** ROBERT M. ADAMS

Some Hypotheses on the Development of Early Civilizations

GROSS PARALLELS in patterns of development of early civilizations have long invited closer inspection. Attempts to formulate these processes of growth into a single general statement of cause and effect have been out of fashion in anthropology for many years now, but interest has remained high in the general problem of comparison. Leaving aside studies concerned particularly with progressive changes in styles or technologies, the greatest promise seems to attach currently to studies focused on the growing network of formal, supra-kin institutions which characterized each of the early civilizations for which archaeological or historic documentation exists.

The approach taken here has much in common with that of V. Gordon Childe (1942, 1952), and certainly leans heavily on the rich store of archaeological insight he has made available for the Old World. Childe is only tangentially concerned with the minutiae of historical process, however. He sees the achievement of civilization as the resolution of a series of contradictions between population growth, environmental limitations, and the like on one hand, and the kind and degree of means and organization of production on the other, but has never prepared a systematic account of the step-by-step resolution of these contradictions. Usually the functional inter-

relationships of his stages and the presumed agencies of change are either given highly generalized and rationalistic explanations or are assumed and not inquired into. In this respect, Julian Steward's functional interpretations of eras and sequences in his study of "Culture Causality and Law" (1949) furnish the more useful model, although his formulations to date remain on the whole programmatic rather than specific. Perhaps most directly, this essay utilizes Gordon R. Willey's conception of developmental trends as tools for comparative study (Willey 1950). Concerned with the direction of change over time of particular recurrent institutions in variable sociocultural settings, this approach makes possible an appreciation of many significant cross-cultural regularities and differences even where the limitations of archaeological evidence preclude a full understanding of these institutions in their wider functional contexts.

What is attempted here is not a review of the whole range of material dealt with by Willey, Steward, or Childe, but rather a more intensive and tentatively explanatory—if still preliminary and necessarily brief—examination solely of the transition to full urban life. Partly, it is hoped to shed additional light on the apparent interplay of forces leading to this momentous change. Partly, it may be useful simply as a series of reflections on the processes Steward and Willey have outlined from a point of view, unlike their own, that has been shaped primarily by Old World data.

Reprinted from *American Antiquity,* vol. 21, no. 3, 1956, pp. 227–32. By permission of the author and the Society for American Archaeology.

Finally, it also stems in part from the desire to see a comparative method restored to common use in archaeology as an important mode of analysis.

Ideally, a comparison of developmental trends in civilization should embrace every society which developed an essentially independent configuration of the attributes of civilized life, whether or not it received a number of its component traits by diffusion from some other area. In practice, however, a narrower approach is dictated by present limitations in our data. Thus, the backgrounds for civilization in China and the Indus Valley remain practically unknown, while knowledge of the formative stages of civilization in Egypt is derived almost entirely from graves and hence contains crucial areas of uncertainty on domestic life and settlement pattern. By contrast at least, we are much better off in Mesoamerica, Peru, and Mesopotamia, so that it seems useful to limit a comparative discussion to these regions. Even in this latter group, of course, the gross outlines of development are not yet clear and unambiguous, and it is cheerfully expected that the hypotheses on social process put forward here will need substantial revision in the light of further work.

Our story begins in each region with an established network of agricultural communities, perhaps centering their socioreligious life around small shrines like those known for Coastal Chavín in Peru and the Early Ubaid of Mesopotamia. Such excavations as have been conducted in private houses of the time suggest little inter-community specialization beyond that normally to be expected based on age and sex differences, although a distinction between towns or regional seats and smaller, less differentiated hamlets perhaps already was coming into being (for example, Tlatilco and Zacatenco in the Valley of Mexico, if the radiocarbon evidence that these sites are roughly contemporary can be trusted).

My point is that the formal integration of these communities into areal groupings seems in each case first to have been achieved on a significant scale by individuals whose authority devolved from their positions as religious spokesmen. Thus, one recalls that the earliest monumental architecture consists of unambiguous temples only, save possibly in Mesoamerica where Armillas (1951a:23) has argued that temple mounds were briefly preceded by funerary mounds for which an important role in the day-to-day religious life cannot yet be established. Moreover, in spite of regional differences in emphasis (compare Willey 1950:235) the archaeological provenance makes it likely that subsequent elaborations of craftsmanship, whether luxury ceramics, ritual objects, or architectural embellishments, were provided mainly for the temples and their spokesmen rather than for the satisfaction of private and secular tastes, and the variations of style which are characteristic of this "Early Classic" era seem to be polarized in local traditions ranging around the more important of the emerging temple centers. In fact, to judge from the placing and content of tombs and representational art, individual status differences were largely derived from, or at least closely connected with, leadership in the temples. Finally, the initially open and undefended aspect of these communities together with the rarity of military equipment and pictorial representations of martial activities is perhaps more consistent with the assumption of temple dominance than with a well-developed secular authority and strong status differences. Peru is somewhat precocious in this respect, for Willey (1953:358) traces the construction of defensive redoubts and presumably intervalley raiding back to the White-on-red horizon, not long after the earliest monumental ceremonial structures.

This early temple dominance is perhaps most understandable where irrigation or other systems of intensive cultivation requiring the planned efforts of sizeable groups were necessary and practical, as in southern Mesopotamia and some of the coastal Peruvian valleys, for one could argue that their construction and maintenance increasingly required a kind of authoritative leadership not well developed in villages engaged independently in subsistence agriculture. But, as is shown in lowland Mesoamerica, increasing population and growing diversity in intra- and intercommunity tasks could lead to the rise of the same institutions even where irrigation was an apparently negligible factor.

For a time, it seems probable that the religious elite played an increasingly important role in the administration of group activities as communities grew larger and more complex. Archaeological evidence for these growing administrative functions perhaps can be seen in the general replacement of structures apparently intended exclusively for sacred use by structures which, while retaining an important sacred component, are modified for use as dwellings for the elite or as administrative centers (compare Thompson 1954: 93). The change in emphasis from temple to "palace" in the A-V complex at Uaxactun (Smith 1950, Figs. 2–5), the frequent substitution by late Mochica times in North Coast Peru of pyramid-dwelling-construction-"palace" complexes for the isolated pyramid mounds characteristic of earlier periods (Willey 1953:354–56), and the increasing importance of storehouses and other ancillary buildings within temple precincts during the Protoliterate and Early Dynastic periods in Mesopotamia (compare, for example, the Tell Uqair Painted Temple [Lloyd and Safar 1943] with later temples from the Diyala region [Delougaz 1940; Delougaz and Lloyd 1942]) furnish convenient examples.

But the growth processes we are concerned with here did not end with the institutionalization of temple authority. It is our second hypothesis that forces inherent in temple control, some of them only coming into being in societies already integrated by temple leadership, gradually weakened the foundations on which temple supremacy rested. The increasing heterogeneity of society, for example, although largely a product at first of elaborations of the temple establishments, must have decreased the effectiveness of purely religious sanctions in the administration of community affairs. Warfare, previously confined mainly to raids, increased in scale and importance. Partly this may have been the result of an increasingly precarious balance of population with agricultural resources, as Steward (1949:23) suggests, but it should be remembered also that the increasing wealth in the temples offered vastly greater inducements to military activity than had existed previously. Thus in a sense, an era of temple dominance—however "classic" its religious or artistic expression—may be viewed as a transitional period necessary for the emergence of social groups and concepts profoundly at variance with those reflected in the traditional homogeneity and group solidarity of folk-village life.

Under the influence of all these forces the effective integration of communities in each of the areas required an increasingly authoritarian, militaristic, and centralized character that was also fundamentally in opposition to the traditional activities of the temple. The priestly hierarchies met this crisis with varying success, but only survived as corporate entities still responsible for an important share of the secular affairs of the groups under their charge where they were able to adopt the same autocratic outlook as their rising secular competitors. Architectural manifestations of this shift in outlook perhaps may be seen in the circumvallation of temple compounds in Early Dynastic Mesopotamia (Delougaz 1940) and in the enclosure of North Coast Peruvian pyramid mounds within fortified redoubts (Willey 1953:358). An increasingly warlike aspect to the clergy can be documented more graphically in the Late Classic of the lowland Maya area with numerous reliefs and the Bonampak murals (Armillas 1951b).

While this trend was underway, individuals also began to emerge, either from the ranks of temple personnel or independently, who sought to provide political and especially military leadership with less regard for the old priestly prerogatives or for the propitiation of deities the temples served. Here one thinks of the "barbarians" active in the Toltec forces (Armillas 1951*a*:29), of the rise of kings alongside temple hierarchies in Early Dynastic Mesopotamia (Falkenstein 1954:795 and following), and of the somewhat more fluid distinction between nobility and clergy among the Inca (Kirchoff 1949). To some extent, the competition for control that seems to have ensued may consciously have been directed toward the expansion of royal wealth and authority at the expense of the temples. We have the complaint of a Mesopotamian reformer, for example, that the oxen of the god (read temple) were being appropriated illegally to plow the fields of the ruling lord (Barton 1929:79). The suppression of a priestly attempt to seize control under the Inca in Peru is reported to have resulted in changes in governmental structure which also may have been thus openly motivated (Kirchoff 1949:308). But consciousness is not a necessary assumption for the argument, and it seems certain that some kind of religious authority was invoked by every contending party. In Mesoamerica, for example, it has been suggested (Armillas 1951*a*:29) that the legendary struggle for power between two gods, Quetzalcoatl and Tezcatlipoca, may reflect a civil war between established supporters of the former and rising groups bent on military expansion. Perhaps more generally characteristic of the secular rulers was a tendency to expand the areas in which they might act on their own authority without acknowledgment of divine jurisdiction. A successful Early Dynastic ruler in southern Mesopotamia, for example, stressed repeatedly the support he had received from his city's chief deity, and sought to justify this support by proclaiming himself the "man who carries out the word (of the god)" (Barton 1929:35), while his Akkadian successors generally invoked the names of their deities only to curse those who might later attempt to deface their monuments (Barton 1929:121).

The point is that the steps which needed to be taken by any leadership, whether priest, war leader, or king, would seem to have un-dermined or at least circumscribed the capacity of religious leaders *qua* religious leaders effectively to control many of their communities' most important activities. Thus, the need for a specialized defensive force probably was felt by the temples more strongly than any other institutional body—note that a burning temple served as the Aztec symbol for a conquered town, while the looting of its temples must have been almost invariably associated also with the capture of a Sumerian city (Barton 1929:58, 89)—yet the appointment of permanent warriors served quickly to enhance the authority of the secular figures who commanded them and weakened further the internal position of the temples. It is not surprising that Early Dynastic and Akkadian rulers in Mesopotamia frequently began to acquire large estates worked by armed followers responsible only to them (Falkenstein 1954:800), that an Aztec tradition records the granting of captured lands and their occupants to leading warriors in fief from the king (Valliant 1944:97), or that the ruling Inca rewarded the nobility in his victorious armies with land (Bram 1941:73) and llamas by the hundreds (Kirchoff 1949:299). All of these measures contributed to undermining the political authority of the temples, both directly and by providing incentives for successful conquest which could only increase the frequency of military crises and thus weaken temple leadership further.

Similarly, an extension of the market first may have been encouraged by the temples as a way of solidifying their control and strengthening the integrative ties in the communities under their charge. In all three areas, craft products previously reserved for sacred use were finally made available to the populace at large. For example, there was a breakdown in the long-established separation between ceremonial-mortuary and domestic pottery traditions in Tiahuanaco, Peru, with mold-making technics applicable to mass production being applied to the latter for the first time (Ford and Willey 1949:68). In lowland Mesoamerica we find effigy censers, apparently manufactured by craftsmen in a tightly integrated tradition, not only in the ceremonial precincts of Mayapan but also in household shrines (Smith and Ruppert 1953). In Early Dynastic Mesopotamia, one can point to an extension in the use of cylinder seals from almost exclusively sacred precincts to even some of the more modest private houses and graves. But in the long run, the growth of the market acted to make both craftsmen and consumers less dependent on the temples and created an independently powerful group of private traders. This in turn widened popular demands for luxury products, and metal for tools and weapons, which could only be obtained by the very kind of increasing emphasis on aggrandizement that strengthened warrior castes at the expense of temple leadership.

Although these trends proceeded at different rates in each nuclear area or subarea (compare Willey 1950:239–40), the end result tended uniformly to be the overshadowing of authority based specifically in the temples by the authority of dynasts ruling nascent territorial states and bending every effort toward military and political expansion.

Whatever names we give the units of time into which the sequence of events thus briefly described is divided up, it is clear, first, that these historical processes are continuous, so that any set of units is in a very real sense artificial, and second, that the exact combination and sequence of trends is highly variable not only as we compare Mesopotamia with Mesoamerica and Peru, but also between cultural or ecological subareas of these larger entities. If the purpose of time divisions is to facilitate comparison, it would seem to follow that rigorous chronological distinctions between successive eras are both highly dubious and not likely to occur as significant parallels in different historical traditions. What will occur, if there is any substance to the hypotheses offered here, are significant parallels in the most characteristic expressions that successive eras assume, what Steward calls their "culminations." Thus, the origins of militar-

ism may differ widely, ranging, to take their time dimension alone, from Late Formative in Peru to Late Florescent or Classic in southern Mesopotamia and parts of Mesoamerica; but an era in which this has become the dominant trend always follows an era of temple dominance in the sequences of early civilizations and exhibits many striking regularities as we move from one area to another. Our remaining task, then, is to outline a series of culminations behind which might lie the interplay of conflicting and mutually reinforcing trends already suggested.

The Formative Era is not of primary interest here. It is characterized by subsistence farming, village settlements, perhaps a few small shrines, and the general absence of craft specialization and class distinctions in the archaeological record. This definition differs from that of most New World culture historians only in that the era is explicitly considered to have ended when the changed needs of communities transformed earlier part-time cult specialists into a theocratic class serving as a kind of organizing authority. On present evidence, this may have occurred after Eridu IX in southern Mesopotamia and Gawra XIV in Assyria; after Providencia and perhaps Tlatilco in highland Mesoamerica and near the end of Chicanel in the Petén; after the Chavín horizon in at least the Virú Valley of Peru, but before the construction of Chavín de Huántar in the highlands. But we would stress again the futility, for comparative purposes at least, of defining eras with more concern for their precise chronological limits than for their characteristic content.

A Florescent or Classic Era is posited next, here as elsewhere, embracing the growth of temple centers and culminating in the dominance of priestly hierarchies. Perhaps its most important criteria may be found in largely coterminous religious and political institutions, equipped with a newly formalized religious symbolism; in small groups of craft specialists producing mainly for the temples; in the general absence of status distinctions beyond those found in the temple establishments; in the presence of warfare but not yet of a full-time soldiery.

Finally, a Militaristic or Dynastic Era corresponds roughly to the attainment of a way of life which may be called urban whatever the size of its settlements. Politically, it comes to be characterized by a new kind of secular-territorial government, although the older religious elites continued their sacred functions alongside the new administrators. A considerable portion of the energies of these states were directed toward expansion, and warfare was a common and accepted instrument of policy. Systems of developed class distinctions, including slavery, were at the basis of society, and productive facilities, principally land, tended gradually to pass into large-scale private ownership. Mass-produced craft products were made available by greatly increased numbers of artisans to large sections of society through a market. In southern Mesopotamia, the beginning of the Early Dynastic period coincides pretty well with the attainment of this level, as may the occupation of Tula in Central Mexico. Perhaps the shift from ceremonial centers to differentiated "urban elite" and "lay" centers, which Schaedel (1951:234) believes began in North Coast Peru at about the time of the Tiahuanaco horizon, also corresponds to this transition; however, the social complexity implied by some Mochica pottery may suggest an earlier beginning for parts of the area.

Such a general outline as this obviously can never be reconciled completely with the specific historical sequences to which it has been applied. At present it is still largely speculative, supported by the weak and ambiguous lines of evidence that have been alluded to only because they seem frequently to converge to form a pattern. Moreover, it is at best a schematization, concerned only with the rough shaping of major integrative institutions under the pressure of social forces which apparently paralleled each other in every area where civilization came into being. The institutions produced by these forces, of course, were everywhere different, for they were not the outcome of a smoothly inevitable course of societal growth but of opposing trends developing simultaneously and at different rates. Moreover, they were certainly also affected by local differences in technology, sources of subsistence, physical and biological environment, and a host of nonmaterial factors. But in their main outlines these institutions were nonetheless frequently very similar, and the advantage of this, or any, provisional scheme is that, with its aid, local points of variance can quickly be exposed for inspection. Sometimes it may be shown that the individual sequence has been wrongly interpreted due to a failure to consider the generalized processes believed to have been at work from a comparative study of the data. At other times the particular sequence will be substantiated and, strengthened by this renewed scrutiny, will demand revision of the general scheme itself or at least of explanations offered for other areas in light of the variation thus documented. Systematically in this fashion, it should be possible to increase both understanding of developments within each early civilization and capacity to generalize about historical processes involved in the appearance of all of them.

NOTE

This essay is a slightly modified version of a paper entitled "Institutional Patterns and the Development of Civilization," which was read at the annual meeting of the Society for American Archaeology in Bloomington, Indiana, on May 5, 1955. Some of the problems dealt with here are also touched on in a symposium on irrigation civilizations (Steward et al. 1955) that appeared too late to be utilized.

Praise the Gods and Pass the Metates:
A Hypothesis of the Development of Lowland
Rainforest Civilizations in Mesoamerica

WHY DID lowland rainforest civilization evolve in its ecological setting? This is a question that has been considered by many— Sanders, Tolstoy, Ford, M. Coe, W. Coe, Willey, Ekholm, Millon, Bernal, and Fried. This essay [1] will develop a hypothesis to explain the evolution of two Mesoamerican lowland rainforest civilizations—the Olmec and the Maya, the earliest and the largest respectively. [2]

The environmental configuration of the pertinent rainforests must be considered to explain the growth of the cultures that thrived in them (Fig. 1). Expansive rainforest environments have been characterized as lacking the potential to stimulate sociopolitical development because: 1) the rainforest environment is redundant in terms of access to resources, 2) transportation of goods is difficult, and 3) slash-and-burn agriculture is the most practical subsistence technique. As a result of these problems there is said to have been little effort invested toward trade and redistribution (M. Coe 1961a:68; Sanders 1964:233); nucleated centers were rarely maintained and a scattered slight settlement was typical (Sanders 1964:229, 237; Meggers 1954:807; Webb 1964:304, 386, 436, 439; M. Coe 1961a:67–68, 76, 84); and there were no obvious changes in the subsistence system through time which would have required community efforts and caused

the growth of ceremonialism (Webb 1964: 386; Palerm and Wolf 1957).

"In summary, there were few integrative factors operating in (lowland rainforests) toward the formation of large socio-political groupings and many disruptive ones. . . . The ecological system lacks any characteristics that one can link with the integration of a large society" (Sanders 1964:236). Therefore, it has always puzzled many Mesoamerican archaeologists that the first civilization of Mesoamerica, the Olmec, and one of the most complex, the Maya, developed within the rainforest environment. Accepting the preceding characterization of the environment, a review of past models is useful in outlining the problem of the rise of rainforest civilizations. [3]

1. Past Hypotheses

In 1954, Meggers's cross-cultural survey of tropical forest areas concluded that: "(1) advanced cultural traits did not diffuse into (the tropical forest) from adjacent regions of higher culture in spite of frequent 'opportunity'; and (2) more advanced cultures that attempted to colonize the tropical forest were unable to preserve their more advanced culture in so doing" (1954:809). Based on these conclusions Meggers hypothesized that lowland Maya civilization could not have evolved within the Peten rainforest,

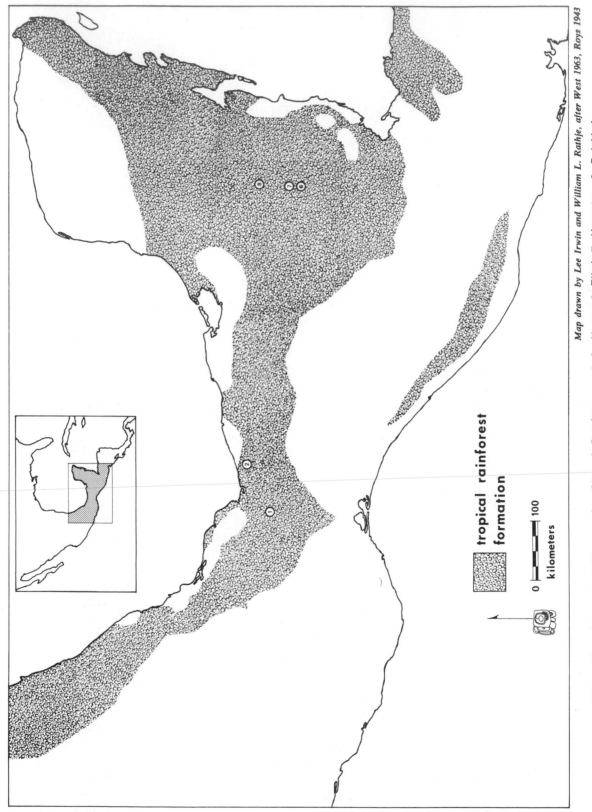

FIG. 1. The rainforests of Mesoamerica. Sites: 1, San Lorenzo; 2, La Venta; 6, Tikal; 7, Uaxactun; 8, Balakbal.

Map drawn by Lee Irwin and William L. Rathje, after West 1963, Roys 1943

that it must have been introduced full-blown into the lowlands, and that its history must have been one of continual decline (1954: 817). Yet, by Meggers's own admission, for 400 years the Maya culture not only held its own, it actually advanced, before rolling over on its back in a 600-year denouement (1954: 819). This contradiction of expectations and the recent emphasis by Sanders and Price (1968:142–45, 169) on the role of outside stimuli on the development of the Maya raise an important question. Sanders has asserted that there would have been little functional advantage to sustain a well-integrated civilization in a rainforest environment (1964:236; Sanders and Price 1968:169). Since acceptance usually occurs only where a diffusing complex is useful, what was the function of complex sociopolitical organization in the Maya lowlands? Meggers and Sanders and Price provide no answer.

Willey has suggested that "ceremonial centers arose in response to population increase and out of the desire to maintain and symbolize kinship and religious unity" (1966a: 98). According to this hypothesis, parent villages thus became seats of religious and political authority (1966a.98). Population growth and village budding do not always develop nucleating ceremonial centers, especially in the Mesoamerican rainforest environment. In this lowland tropical forest, population growth does not create population concentration. Because of their subsistence base, swidden agriculture, individual households are forced to remain dispersed. In addition, the production of similar goods by every household undercuts the value of kinship connections between households which have split off from one another. Thus, without some other stimuli, population growth and the symbolizing of kinship and ideological unity among scattered slash-and-burn agriculturalists certainly did not require the degree of elaboration evident in two of the world's most flamboyant civilizations, the Olmec and the Maya.

Before his recent excavations at the major Olmec site of San Lorenzo (Site 6, Fig. *1*), Michael Coe made some suggestions about the development of rainforest civilizations. "It is a simple step from the segmented society exercising communal rights to the person who directs the society and remains above it. . . . Each respective area was organized directly into the support by tribute or corvee labor of a royal and/or religious cult as represented by the growth of non-urban ceremonial centers" (1961a:68). Is the origin of civilization through "the compulsion of tribute and corvee labor" (1961a:85) a simple step? Webb has cogently argued that in tropical forest areas "thinly scattered population . . . can easily decamp if coerced" (1964:304; cf. Carneiro 1968:134–35, 142). What function did the cult provide which would be reciprocated in terms of generous contributions of labor and libations?

Webb answers that ". . . the worship of the dieties of the Theocratic stage would be one factor which could provide the concentration of population and of work needed to bring in the Classic stage among the Maya . . . despite the fact that this meant a settlement pattern that worked against the easiest use of the environment" (1964:420). "There would be no need—of a basic economic sort —for a theocratic leadership and all its works . . . —except the 'ideological' one of bonding the cult and the organization necessary to that end" (1964:422; Morley and Brainerd 1956:45, 57). That the cult exists to glorify itself is an ineffectual hypothesis. There are many areas in Mesoamerica which were more compatible to forming compact settlements and organizing corvee labor, where theocratic dieties didn't seem to warrant many temples, much less a complex cult.

Recently there has been a rash of new hypotheses to explain the early rise of rainforest civilization. The most popular involves the amazing productivity of natural river levee lands in the Olmec area (and does not apply to the Maya development) (Fig. *4*). These narrow strips of land produce 3.15 metric tons of corn per hectare, compared to loma

368

(nonlevee) lands which yield 2.25 metric tons per hectare (M. Coe 1968a:107; 1969: 11, 14–15). Loma lands can be planted twice a year, levee lands only once (1969:14–15). "The Gulf Coast florescence can be explained on the basis of the high productivity of swidden agriculture in this region" (Sanders and Price 1968:134). "The possession of the (natural levee lands) provides the (modern) local political and economic leaders with much of their power. We think that they must have given a similar power base to the Olmec leaders of 1000 B.C." (M. Coe 1968a:107). As to the actual character of Olmec civilization, M. Coe concludes that it is possible that "some pre-San Lorenzo chief decided that he wanted monuments carved in basalt to glorify himself and his distinguished ancestors" (1968a:126–27; 1968b:65). The production of such monuments required leaders who "held the tributary populace in a firm grip, forcing from them incredible expenditures of labor" (1968a:86). Although "potent sanctions" are evoked to explain the organization of labor (M. Coe 1961a:89; 1968a:86; Webb 1964:304), these sanctions have not been enumerated.

The Olmec natural levees are certainly crucial to the development of a base of power, but are incomplete, in themselves, as an explanation for the rise of Olmec civilization. The power of differential access to "strategic" goods and resources has been cited as stimulating redistribution activities and sociopolitical complexity (Sahlins 1958:1963; Flannery and M. Coe 1968:281–82; Fried 1967: 52, 186–235). However, it was Michael Coe himself who originally pointed out that in areas producing the same commodities, distribution systems would serve no important integrative function (1961a:81). Loma land production in the area of San Lorenzo (Site 1, Fig. 4) is more than sufficient to feed the families of nonlevee land farmers (M. Coe 1969:14). In fact, the present controllers of the levee land obtained that land by using the procedes from loma land production (1969: 15). What economic resource, much less sanction, could the levee land controllers hold

over the loma farmers? If everyone has a surplus of corn, corn is a poor wage or inducement to work. Without a means to invest excess corn toward integrative ends, all a levee owner can gain is weight (cf. Carneiro 1958, 1968). Therefore, as Coe concludes: "subsistence and technology are a precondition, but not a necessary cause of the rise of civilization" (1968a:126; 1968b:65; cf. Binford 1968c). "While the possession of the river levee lands had something to do with the crystallization of Olmec culture and all its paraphernalia, we need new models to explain why and how this happened" (M. Coe 1969: 20). The function of the sociopolitical integration of lowland rainforest civilization is still the crucial question.

2. Background to the Hypothesis

To reconstruct the function of complex sociopolitical development in the Mesoamerican rainforests an understanding of the conjunction of environment and technology is crucial. Every household[4] needs basic resources to efficiently exploit a given niche. Basic resources are those for which evidence is present (archaeological, ethnohistoric, and/ or ethnographic) in every household participating in a specific subsistence configuration —in this case the maize agricultural complex.[5]

Three basic resources necessary for successful maize agriculture in rainforest environments are igneous or hard stone for grinding tools, obsidian for razor-sharp cutting tools, and salt (See 5. Basic Resources for Tropical Lowland Agriculture).[6] These commodities do not occur naturally in the rainforests of Mesoamerica and were considered crucial enough to be imported everywhere in the lowlands in quantity and over vast distances.

Most areas of highland Mesoamerica were not far from one or more sources of these commodities. Teotihuacan, for example, is situated in a valley which furnished all three. In the lowlands these resources are few and far between. Because of this highland/lowland dichotomy of resource distributions,

369

there is also a highland/lowland dichotomy in the way in which these goods are mined, worked, collected, and redistributed. Wolf (1967; see also Chapman 1957:115) has isolated two systems of goods distribution functioning in Mesoamerica today: 1) a "solar" market system involving regular interaction of individual household units (Nash 1967); 2) an extramarket commercial network composed of itinerant merchants, merchant groups, and "stores."

In the highlands the two function "side by side" (Wolf 1967:313). Where different resource zones are usually closely spaced, a network of local markets provides for distribution of essential goods ("economic symbiosis" — Fig. 2; also see Sanders 1968). In this system "the unit of production, consumption, and market interaction is the household" (Tax and Hinshaw 1969:84; McBryde 1945: 82; Nadar 1969:347; Nash 1967:97; Wolf 1967:301–10). "Given the fact that households, not firms, are the economic organization around which the economy is built, the limits of planning, continuity, scale, and technological complexity in economic life become readily apparent" (Nash 1967:97).

In the lowlands, where many basic resources are not within local reach, the extramarket commercial network functions nearly alone. The highland household's market function of procuring, working, and marketing certain strategic goods is replaced in the lowlands by suprahousehold organizations (Wolf 1967; Fig. 3). Local market interaction networks are virtually nonexistent. Buying and selling is done through hacienda supplystores, local shops, stores and emporiums in cities, and traveling merchants, all depending heavily on freight transport provided by post-Conquest means: mules, trucks, motor boats, airplanes.[7] Ultimately, as Redfield phrased it, today the city and its complex organization make the trade by bringing large quantities of goods within the reach of small store owners and itinerant merchants (Redfield 1941:156; Wolf 1967:311).

The importance of the store and its extension, the itinerant merchant, are clear in Quintana Roo. Through commerce with outside suprahousehold units the natives obtain salt, knives, machetes, "indispensible" matches, metal corn mills, pepper, pots, pans, plates, cups, dishes, and spoons of metal and enamel, whiskey, rifles, gunpowder, soap, needles, axes, shirts, hats, gold jewelry, and colored beads (Villa Rojas 1945:26, 45, 53, 55, 65). According to the data provided by Villa Rojas, a merchant was somewhere in the area of the nine villages he studied for all but about three days a month (1945:42).

In sum, today there is a difference in the way highland and lowland populations procure and distribute essential goods: the highlands depend mainly upon interacting household units; the lowlands depend upon suprahousehold organizations interacting with households. This highland-household/lowland-suprahousehold dichotomy seems to have been equally valid before the Conquest (Thompson 1964).[8] For example, comparing pre- and post-Conquest highland and lowland Maya merchants in Guatemala, Thompson concludes: "Accounts, unfortunately not detailed, have survived of the merchant class among the Chontal and Yucatec Maya, but there are no such descriptions for the highlands. That may be accidental, but it is more probable that it is because long-distance travel, perhaps into hostile territory, calls for larger and more organized bodies than does land travel over shorter routes" (1964:22).

Lowland long-distance trade was "not simply an extension of the face to face exchanges common in the market place" (Chapman 1957:115; Thompson 1964:22). Large accumulations of resources were necessary to maximize effort in distant resource areas. Bearers[9] had to be obtained, fed, and led. Complex organization was needed to provide for security and leadership. Routes had to be carefully planned and expeditions precisely timed. Organization at the opposite end of the line, usually in the form of resident representatives and factorics, was crucial. Even with detailed planning and established trading factories "commerce was a continual adventure" (Soustelle 1961:61). "Sometimes mer-

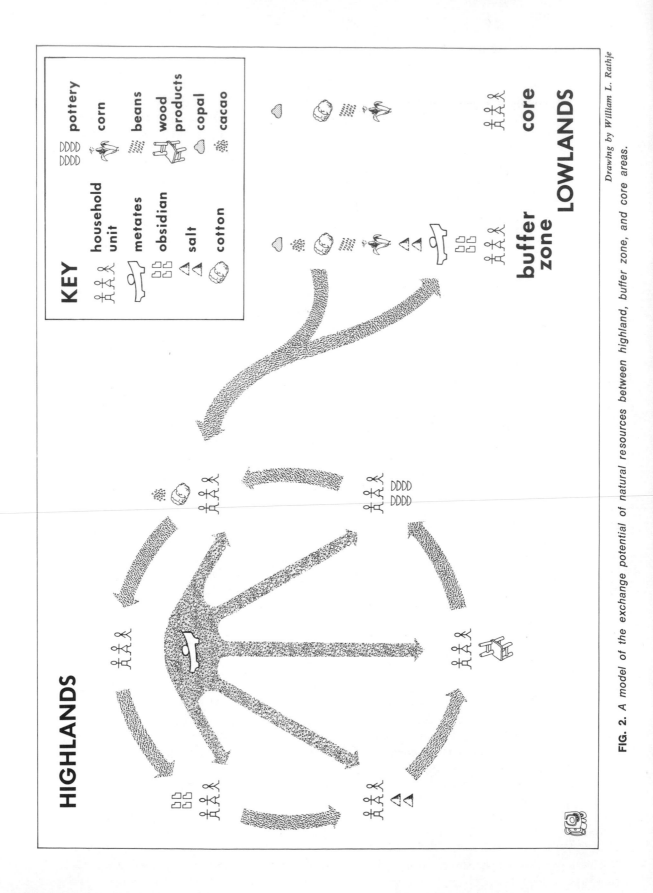

FIG. 2. *A model of the exchange potential of natural resources between highland, buffer zone, and core areas.*

Drawing by William L. Rathje

chants were abused or killed in another state in quarrels over debt or other disagreements" (Roys 1965:671). Even more dangerous than foreign cities were the treks to and from them (Chapman 1957:122, 124–25; Thompson 1964:22). In sixteenth-century Honduras, one chronicler commented that "salt was difficult to obtain because the merchants who carried it were often killed on the road" (Roys 1943:120). Thus, the problem of policing trade routes had to be continually faced (Chapman 1957:122, 124–25). Because of these factors the prerequisites of long-distance trade were concentration of resources and complex organization far above that which a single household could muster.[10]

Slash-and-burn agriculture necessitated a dispersed settlement pattern that made the distribution of highland resources to individual lowland households difficult. Before the Conquest and the mule, the upper limit a cargador could carry was 100 lbs., or two metates and six manos. The utter impossibility of door-to-door selling of highland resources from highland bases into an area stretching several thousand square miles should be apparent. "Trade as an extension of the lowland environment required an elaborate system of redistribution" (Leone 1968: 128). "If there ever was a trend to village isolation, this was contradicted from earliest times by the necessity to co-operate with immediate neighbors," (1968:127) to obtain basic resources not available in the redundant rainforest environment.

Evenly distributed bases where goods could be concentrated as a source of supply for households would be selected for in rainforest environments. The lowland ceremonial center provided the suprahousehold concentration of capital, organizational potential, integration of scattered population, as well as bases of distribution and supply necessary for pre-Conquest lowland trade; the ceremonial center was the minimal unit of autonomous economics (Leone 1968:127–28).

The need within every household for basic resources therefore created a bridge between

ecology and sociopolitical organization (Sahlins 1958, 1963; Fried 1967). Such organization functioned to insure procurement and distribution of needed resources. Households are quite capable of autonomous direction of their own production; however they are not always capable of independently obtaining the basic commodities needed to maintain their subsistence level. Thus individual households must often give up some of their autonomy to organizations for centralized procurement and redistribution (Sahlins 1963:300; 1958:3; Fried 1967:191).

Independently, a lowland household would have a difficult time obtaining the items necessary for its economic success. For trade in basic resources to reach every household consistently, goods and authority, extracted at the expense of every household, had to be concentrated into a very few hands. This situation selected for lowland developments in sociopolitical interaction and organization. The advantages of a consistent supply of basic resources provided a way to invest capital and administrative ability in a fashion that brought political, economic, and social integration and control. Those people who could key into long-distance trade successfully would have restricted access to basic resources that could increase the efficiency of every household unit. Such individuals would become integrative nuclei to scattered household populations.[11]

The pre-Columbian merchant, especially in the lowlands,[12] was a part of the ruling elite.[13] There are references from the lowlands of actual rulers (Roys 1965:677) or members of ruling families who were merchants (Tozzer 1941:39; Roys 1943:107).

Trade and the managerial activities connected with it in the lowlands provide an equally good avenue to social, political, and economic power today.[14] The San Lorenzo area (Site 1, Fig. *1*) provides an excellent example. Most harvested crops are more than sufficient to feed the grower's family. The farmer "uses what is left over to sell for cash so that the other things in life which he has

372

come to need—transistor radios, wristwatches, canned goods—can be bought" (M. Coe 1969:140). Michael Coe found that one group of brothers "occupied all important political posts in [the modern town of San Lorenzo] Tenochtitlan" (1969:15). He refers several times to the acquisition of levee lands as crucial to their rise (1968a:107; 1968b:65; 1969:15). However, little power comes from having surplus corn unless it is invested. The Tenochtitlan brothers "became storekeepers, loaning out money on huge rates of interest against future crops whose ultimate price disposition they controlled through their deals with buyers and middlemen" (1969:15). Wolf's survey article outlines much the same pattern: "control and credit by the wealthy has resulted in a monopolization of production equipment and distributive outlets that underwrites a social and economic dominance easily translatable into political terms" (1967:308). Obviously, in pre-Conquest Mesoamerica, the exact means may not have been the same, but the lowland patterns of resource distribution provide a road to political, economic, and social power for those who could control long-distance trade.

Thus, environmental redundance, transportation difficulties, and dispersed settlement patterns, far from being disruptive in the face of missing basic resources, turn Sanders's (1964:236) statement around—there were many integrative factors operating in large, populated, expanses of rainforest toward the formation of well-integrated sociopolitical groupings. However, both the Olmec and Maya civilizations collapsed and were never replaced. Obviously, there are other influences to be weighed.

Lowland environments have usually been studied as single units; however, sectors within lowland rainforest plains also deserve attention. Large lowland expanses can be divided into two parts: 1) the inner core or central area (Figs. 4, 7) landlocked and separated from resource areas by 2) the outer buffer zone which borders the highlands or important transportation systems (navigable river

complexes, the ocean, mountain passes, etc.) and surrounds the inner core. This division is between areas near to, and areas removed from, highland resources; however, there are no major differential distributions of resources in the lowlands which create or correspond to this division. Thus, although the core area is more remote from strategic resources, it can only offer the same environmental resources as the closer buffer zone in exchange.

The difference between highland and lowland internal trade is crucial to an understanding of the difference between buffer zone and core area development. The highland market system provides a network through which scarce resources can easily move (Fig. 2). In the highlands there are many raw materials that are restricted in natural distribution. Because of the clustering of differing ecological niches, these resources lie within the collection, manufacture, and redistribution capabilities of individual household units. A metate maker can exchange his product for salt, obsidian tools, ceramics, and wood products, as well as lowland resources from buffer zone areas. Through this interaction metates are distributed to areas with salt, obsidian, clay, and wood resources, and into lowland buffer zones. Metates can theoretically pass through as many hands as there are differentially distributed resources. In the highlands the permutations of redistribution are virtually inexhaustible.

In the lowlands exchange is limited by ecological redundance (Fig. 2).[15] Both the buffer zone and the lowland core are part of the same biome and therefore contain the same resources. The buffer zone can exchange its resources in bordering highland regions for basic resources. Since the only scarce commodities the buffer zone requires are located in the highlands, there is little economic motivation for the buffer zone to act as a middle man between highland resource areas and the lowland core. The lowland core must therefore compete with buffer-zone areas for highland resources. That is not an easy task. The buffer zone is closer to highland resource zones and the central core has no natural resources desired in the highlands which are not available in the buffer zone. The ecology and geographic position of the core area select for the development of a complex organization capable of maximizing resources to compete with the buffer zone for highland commodities. This includes the ability to mount large trading expeditions, maintain open trade routes, support factories, schedule efforts to deal with numerous resource areas, and manufacture commodities desired in both resource and buffer zones.

If complex organization is necessary to obtain resources, then community ceremonial interaction and luxury paraphernalia are equally necessary to maintain stratification and organization (cf. Flannery 1968b:100; Fried 1967:32; Rappaport 1968:105–9; Binford 1962; Sabloff and Tourtellot 1969). The environment and geographic position of the core also select for the elaboration of ideology, services, and products that reinforce community integration. Such capabilities and commodities are the only scarce exchangeable resources the core area can tap to obtain basic resources directly from the highlands and indirectly through buffer zone intermediaries. Core exports will therefore be the by-products of community stratification: socio-technic and ideotechnic products and the rational for their manipulation—a specific ceremonial configuration producing access to the supernatural by means of temples, altars, ritual and astronomical knowledge, ceremonial paraphernalia, and other items of status reinforcement (Fig. 3).[16]

Additional repercussions of the core's environment also affect development patterns. There is a limit on sociopolitical development in lowland rainforests (Meggers 1954; M. Coe 1961a; Sanders 1964; Sanders and Price 1968). The only scarce resources that lowland core areas have to market for strategic resources are the products of superior sociopolitical organization. Therefore, when the sociopolitical development of buffer zone and/or resource areas reaches the level allowed by the core area's rainforest environment, the best the core area can do is compete for basic commodities on an equal organizational base. Because of spatial advantages, buffer and highland zones will obviously control strategic resources and the core area will find it hard to sustain complex organization without reinforcing returns in proportion to that organization. In addition, if the competition for resources includes increased dependence upon military superiority, the core will be unable to reach a new level of organization that can protect its trade routes and markets from usurpation by state-level competitors. (Webb 1964; Fry 1970; Erasmus 1968). Under such conditions, the core area organization would wither as population was drawn off into thriving buffer zone and resource areas. It also follows from this argument that the core area cannot even develop to potential limits if, at the time of settlement, buffer zone and resource areas have already reached the sociopolitical capacity of the lowland rainforest.

Accepting the preceding conceptions of environment, subsistence base, technology, and basic resources, I hypothesize that complex sociopolitical organization in the lowland rainforests of Mesoamerica developed originally in response to the demand for consistent procurement and distribution of nonlocal basic resources useful to every household. To test the hypothesis three predictions can be projected and compared with available archaeological data:

Prediction 1.

The earliest evidence of complex sociopolitical organization will occur in resource-deficient core areas. No sites of equal complexity will be found in the surrounding buffer zone. If complex organization first appears and develops in the buffer zone, such organization will not spread into the central core.

Prediction 2.

Core area influence will spread to areas vital to the procurement of basic resources—into the buffer zone, along trade routes, into resource areas. This influence will take the form of wholesale importation of techniques

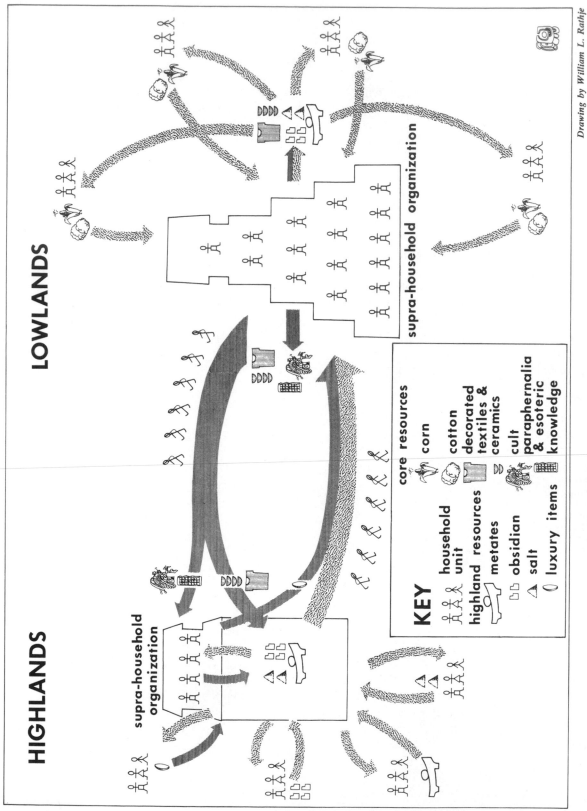

HIGHLANDS

LOWLANDS

supra-household
organization

supra-household organization

KEY

household
unit

highland resources

metates

obsidian

salt

luxury items

core resources

corn

cotton

decorated
textiles &
ceramics

cult
paraphernalia
& esoteric
knowledge

Drawing by William L. Rathje

FIG. 3. *A model of the exchange functions of the core's cult organization.*

and commodities utilized to sustain complex sociopolitical organization – cult ideology, cult technology, and manufactured cult paraphernalia from the core area.

Prediction 3.

Once buffer zone and resource areas attain complex organization (with the help of core exports), core area manufactured goods and cult will be displaced by local buffer zone and resource area equivalents. When the core area reaches its maximum development, and buffer zone and resource areas reach a similar or higher level of complexity, the core's complex organization will collapse.

The two largest lowland rainforest zones in Mesoamerica (Fig. *1*) will serve as test areas for the preceding predictions – the Veracruz-Tabasco plain (Fig. *4*) and the center of the Yucatan Peninsula (Fig. *7*).

3. Tests

Prediction 1.

The earliest evidence of complex organization will occur in resource-deficient core areas. No sites of equal complexity will be found in the surrounding buffer zone. If complex sociopolitical organization first appears in the buffer zone, it will not spread to the central area.

Test 1-A: The Olmec. Neither obsidian nor hard stone suitable for metates is available in the Veracruz-Tabasco rainforest plain (Fig. *4*; Roys 1965:677; Webb 1964:442; M. Coe 1968a:89; Covarrubias 1946:104; Bernal 1969:68). Obsidian is found in distant highland locations (Heizer et al. 1956; M. Coe and Cobean 1970); hard stone can be obtained in the mountains (especially the Tuxtla Mountains, Fig. *4*, No. 5) that largely surround the plain. The only salt source on the Gulf Coast plain is a small salt pan located fifteen miles east of Espiritu Santu (Fig. *4*; Scholes and Warren 1965:784).

Conquest and post-Conquest settlement patterns provide a crude index of the exchange value of natural resources and the ease of obtaining nonlocal strategic supplies. The most populous areas were the lower Coatzacoalcos River region, below San Lorenzo (Site 1, Fig. *4*), and the base of the Tuxtla Mountains [17] (Scholes and Warren 1965:719; Covarrubias 1946:70; Bernal 1969:23–24). The fertility of the soils around the Tuxtlas has been extensively praised (Covarrubias 1946:27; M. Coe personal communication). The Veracruz-Tabasco central core (Fig. *4*), the area of least resource exchange potential, is defined on the basis of distance from basic resources, low population density at the time of the Conquest, and lack of post-Conquest and modern development (Covarrubias 1946:27, 39; Bernal 1969:23).

The importance of the major river systems (the Coatzacoalcos and Tonala) is derived not so much from their potential as transportation routes but from their natural levees and resultant corn production capabilities. Those who controlled levee lands were able to invest produce in support of complex organizations that obtained and distributed basic resources over vast distances. Such organizations integrated a dispersed population and produced the Olmec civilization.

San Lorenzo (Site 1, Figs. *4, 5*), on the Coatzacoalcos River, is the earliest known Olmec Cult center (M. Coe, Diehl, and Stuiver 1967; M. Coe 1968a, 1968b; Tolstoy 1969; Bernal 1969). Even the possibly pre-Olmec phases show massive projects necessitating large-scale sociopolitical interaction (M. Coe 1968a:79; 1968b). Basalt metates and obsidian cutting tools are present in the earliest levels excavated (M. Coe and Cobean 1970; M. Coe personal communication). San Lorenzo is positioned where the coastal plain core area coincides with river levee lands (Fig. *4*). San Lorenzo is also equidistant from surrounding highland resource zones. La Venta (Site 2, Figs. *4, 5*), a second early site (Berger, Graham, and Heizer 1967; Heizer 1968), is not located near San Lorenzo, but on the Tonala River in the heart of another section of the core area. The Olmec Cult developments at the sites in the Tuxtlas re-

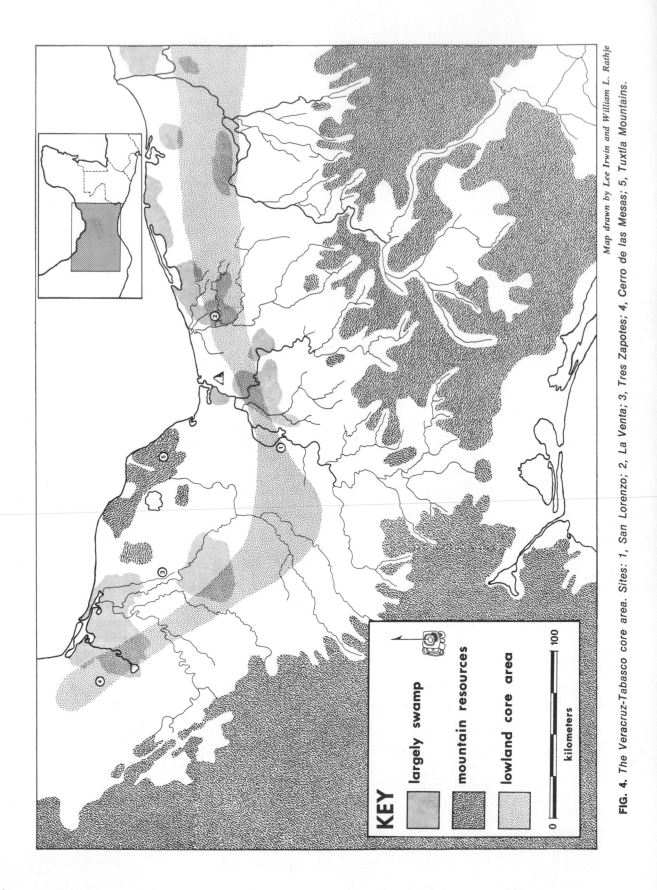

FIG. 4. *The Veracruz-Tabasco core area. Sites: 1, San Lorenzo; 2, La Venta; 3, Tres Zapotes; 4, Cerro de las Mesas; 5, Tuxtla Mountains.*

Map drawn by Lee Irwin and William L. Rathje

KEY

largely swamp

mountain resources

lowland core area

0   100

kilometers

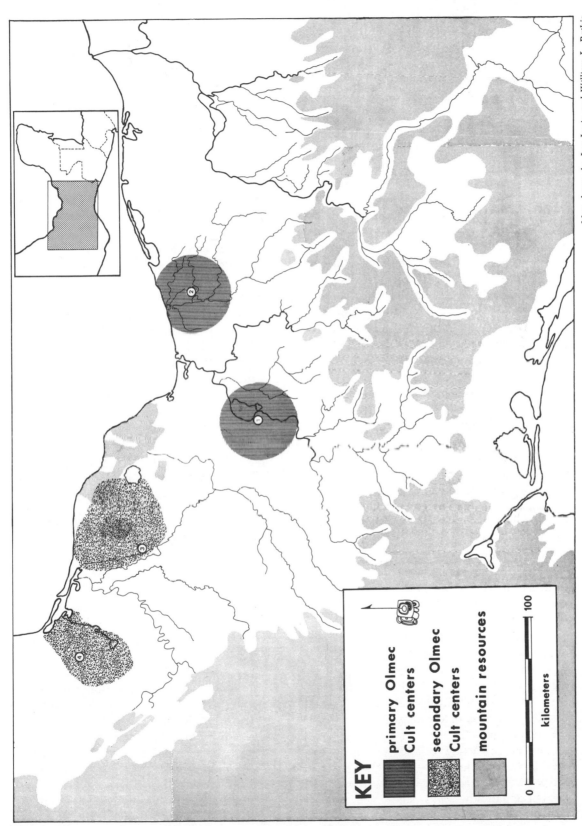

FIG. 5. *Principal lowland Olmec Cult centers. Sites: 1, San Lorenzo; 2, La Venta; 3, Tres Zapotes; 4, Cerro de las Mesas.*

378

gion that have been excavated are not as early as Cult remains at either San Lorenzo or La Venta (Weiant 1943; Drucker 1943a, 1943b; M. Coe 1965c). The rise of complex organization in the Valley of Mexico (Tolstoy and Paradis 1970; Tolstoy 1969) and Oaxaca (Flannery 1968b; Flannery et al. 1967) also postdate the inception of the Olmec Cult in the Gulf Coast core area. Thus, the Olmec civilization arose in the Veracruz-Tabasco core area before similar developments occurred in either buffer or highland resource zones. Prediction 1 seems to be confirmed.

Test 1-B: The Maya.—This test offers an opportunity to compare predictions.[18] According to R. E. W. Adams's interpretation of Sanders and Price (1968): "They point out the agricultural advantages of alluviated flood plains versus the interfluves of swidden agriculture. They argue that chiefdoms with their higher density populations and economic advantages would develop first in these ecological niches" (1969:21). Economic symbiosis (Sanders 1964, 1968) would also spur development in areas of adjacent highland and lowland environments, or perhaps in areas where numerous lowland microenvironments cluster, as near the coast. In sum, the first Maya Cult developments should occur, if stimulated greatly by economic symbiosis and population growth, in the buffer zone.

Adams argues that this prediction is confirmed: "it is noteworthy that the known early settlements of the Southern lowlands are located along rivers (Barton Ramie, Site 26, Fig. *8*; Altar de Sacrificios, Site 11, Fig. *8*; and Seibal, Site 29, Fig. *8*)" (Adams 1969: 21). Sanders and Price (1968) are not predicting the location of settlements however early; they are predicting the location of the first development of complex chiefdoms and the Maya Cult—for which I do not feel Xe or any other early Preclassic settlements in the buffer zone qualify. As Adams reported, Xe pottery at Altar is "widely spread over the site but apparently not associated with mound building" (1964:372).

Most of the buffer zone did not develop complex organization until the Late Classic— skipping any major Preclassic or Early Classic development (Piedras Negras, Site 13, Fig. *8*—W. Coe 1959:143–44; Palenque—Rands and Rands 1957:147; Seibal, Site 29, Fig. *8* —Willey, A. L. Smith, Sabloff, and Tourtellot personal communications). Altar de Sacrificios however, showed substantial Preclassic and Early Classic development (Willey and A. L. Smith personal communications). It matured after the sites in the northeast Peten and will be considered in detail in Test 2-B. Some buffer-zone areas never did develop much complexity, especially the coast and the cacao-producing areas of Belize (Belize Valley, No. 26, Fig. *8*—Willey et al. 1965; Ricketson 1929; San Jose, Site 25, Fig. *8*—Thompson 1939). Altun Ha is a case in point (Pendergast 1969a, 1969b, 1969c). The site was the product of a somewhat varied environment and exportable marine resources. Although overflowing with jade and other luxuries, Altun Ha does not show the large-scale sociopolitical integration apparent at the mammoth sites of the northeast Peten.

The culture history of the Belize Valley is especially interesting. This area seems well suited for the development of complex sociopolitical integration: limited land of alluvial productivity (cf. Carneiro 1968; Webb 1964; M. Coe 1968a, 1968b); zones of differing production capabilities (alluvial plain, nonalluvial lands, riverine and coastal resources, cf. Sanders 1964, 1968); good means of communication and transportation (the Belize River cf. Sanders 1964, 1968); and fairly dense population (Sanders 1964, 1968; Carneiro 1968; Webb 1964; Fried 1967).[19] What was the result? No major ceremonial centers have been found in the Belize Valley. In fact, the only major centers, in terms of size, found in the whole of Belize are in the west, on the edge of the northeast Peten— an area lacking many of the developmental prerequisites found in the Belize Valley. The recorded Belize Valley post-Conquest pattern of political fragmentation—"each village appears to have been independent" (D. E.

Thompson 1967:31, 33)—seems to have been much the same as hundreds of years earlier.

If the lowland Maya civilization did not originate in the buffer zone, did it first coalesce in the core as I predict? The core area of least resource exchange potential must be defined. Because of the ethnohistoric record, it is possible to plot the population distributions for post-Conquest southern Yucatan. The only area that can be confirmed by available data as largely uninhabited (relative to other reported regions) is the center of the northeast Peten (Fig. 6; J. E. S. Thompson 1951: 390; 1967:29; Scholes and Roys 1968:463–64; Cortes 1908:2:269; Means 1917:124–29; Sanders 1962:110). This pattern of thin post-Classic population in the northeast Peten is also supported archaeologically (Bullard 1960, 1970). The area is still largely uninhabited today (Maler 1910:150; Lundell 1937:4; Bullard 1960:357). The northeast Peten is one of the areas most remote from salt, obsidian, and igneous resources (Fig. 7). Obviously, it is not an area with any special exportable environmental resource not found abundantly in the rest of the Maya lowlands (Sanders and Price 1968:169). Sanders sums it up best:

During the period from the 6th to the 10th century the Maya lowland area was one of the most densely populated parts of Mesoamerica, and the demographic center was precisely in that part of the area which since that period has been extremely thinly settled. (1962:110)

I define the northeast Peten as the Maya lowland core (Fig. 7), the area hardest to reach, with the least potential for exchange—the one area that was too much trouble to settle and supply with basic resources in the sixteenth century.

Most Mayanists today believe that the Maya Cult, in a recognizable constellation, crystallized first within the lowland core area —the northeast Peten (Willey 1966a:117; Longyear 1952:69; Morley and Brainerd 1956:49; Thompson 1965:335; W. Coe 1965; Sanders 1962:114; 1964:208). The two largest Maya sites, Mirador (Site 28, Fig. 7–I. Graham 1967) and Tikal (Site 6, Fig. 7), are within this core area. One confirmation of the priority of core developments is furnished by dated stelae. The earliest inscriptions recorded by Morley (1937–38) occur within the core area (Sites 6, 7, 8, 9, Fig. 7). Another early stela (late cycle eight) was discovered in 1970 by Ian Graham (personal communication) at El Zapote (Site 35, Fig. 7). These data confirm the priority of Maya Cult developments in the lowland core and Prediction 1.

Prediction 2.

Core area influence will spread to areas vital to the procurement of basic resources— into the buffer zone, along trade routes and into resource areas. This influence will take the form of wholesale importation of techniques and commodities utilized to sustain complex sociopolitical organization—cult ideology, cult technology, and manufactured cult paraphernalia from the core area.

Test 2-A: The Olmec.—The extensive spread of the Olmec Cult has been a matter of record for years. The distribution of Olmec sociotechnic and ideotechnic complexes—Olmec figurines, votive axes, decorated ceramics, motifs, and style—has been well documented in Guerrero, Morelos, Puebla, the Valley of Mexico, the Isthmian and Guatemalan Pacific Coast, etc. (M. Coe 1968a: 91–103, map p. 102; 1965a; 1965b; Bernal 1969:123–85, Fig. *15*; Grove 1968, 1970; Tolstoy 1969; Tolstoy and Paradis 1970; Flannery 1968b; Williams, Heizer, and Graham 1965; Heizer 1968; Lowe 1970).

Recent explanations of this phenomenon conclude that the only model that "fits neatly into the patterning of site distribution is the trade route theory" (Grove 1968:182; M. Coe 1965a:123; 1968a:91–103; Tolstoy and Paradis 1970; Lowe 1970; Bernal 1969). San Lorenzo materials studied by Michael Coe and Cobean (1970) have demonstrated that the earliest obsidian came from sources in

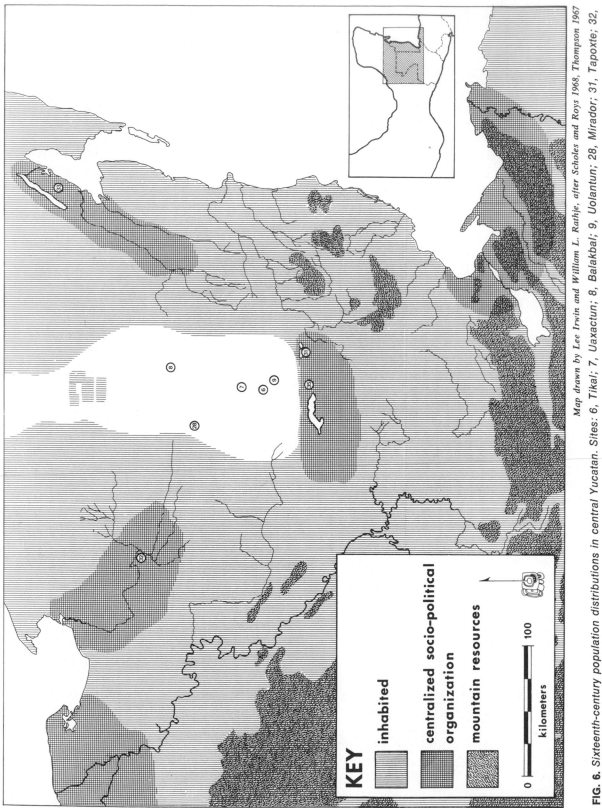

FIG. 6. *Sixteenth-century population distributions in central Yucatan. Sites: 6, Tikal; 7, Uaxactun; 8, Balakbal; 9, Uolantun; 28, Mirador; 31, Tapoxte; 32, Itzamkanac; 33, Chetumal; 35, El Zapote.*

Map drawn by Lee Irwin and William L. Rathje, after Scholes and Roys 1968, Thompson 1967

KEY

inhabited

centralized socio-political organization

mountain resources

kilometers

0   100

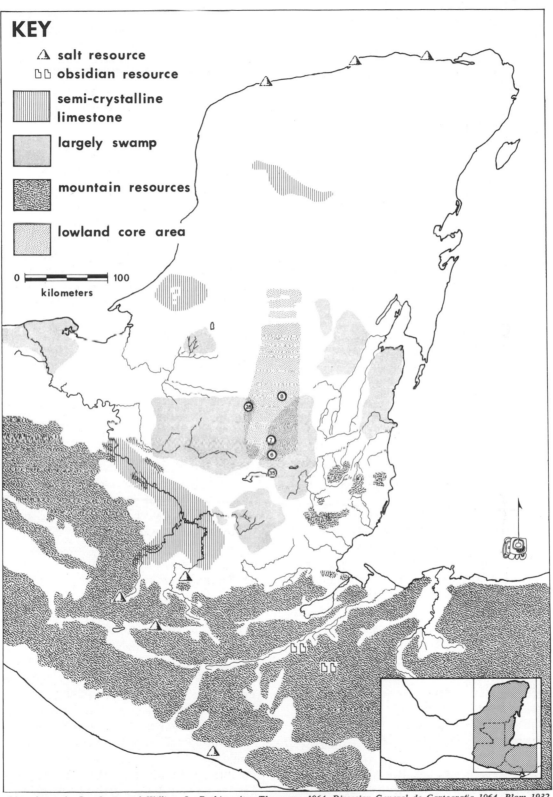

KEY

△ salt resource
◨◨ obsidian resource
▦ semi-crystalline limestone
▨ largely swamp
▧ mountain resources
▨ lowland core area

0 ─────── 100
kilometers

Map drawn by Lee Irwin and William L. Rathje, after Thompson 1964, Direccion General de Cartografia 1964, Blom 1932, Graham 1967, Hendges 1902

FIG. 7. *The central Yucatan core area and surrounding resource zones. Sites: 6, Tikal; 7, Uaxactun; 8, Balakbal; 28, Mirador; 35, El Zapote.*

382

Puebla (Guadelupe Victoria) and Guatemala (El Chayal). Obsidian procurement also provides an explanation for the intense Olmec influence evident in the Valley of Mexico (M. Coe and Cobean 1970; Tolstoy and Paradis 1970). The search for exotic materials to be used to maintain stratification and community integration—jade for earplugs, figurines, votive axes, necklaces; magnetite for mirrors; serpentine for votive offerings—explains the Olmec Cult presence in such places as Guerrero and Oaxaca (M. Coe 1965a:123; 1968a: 91–103; Flannery 1968; Grove 1968; Lowe 1970; and others). In sum, Prediction 2 seems to be confirmed; Olmec influence in the recoverable form of Cult paraphernalia diffused in a manner consistent with the procurement of basic and exotic resources.

Test 2-B: The Maya. — There have been several good studies of resource distribution and trade in the Maya area.[20] The spread of the Maya Cult, however, has not been analysed from a trade/resource point of view. The brief survey below (Fig. 8) follows the diffusion of the stela cult as recorded by Morley (1937–38) and Graham (1967; and personal communication).

After the original appearance of the stela cult at Tikal (Site 6, Fig. 8), Uaxactun (Site 7, Fig. 8), Balakbal (Site 8, Fig. 8), Uolantun (Site 9, Fig. 8), and El Zapote (Site 35, Fig. 8), in the northeast Peten, it spread into the buffer zone. Three early cycle 9 stela were erected at Tres Islas, located south of Seibal (Site 29, Fig. 8) on the Rio Pasion route of access to the Guatemalan highlands (I. Graham personal communication). No mounds have been found at Tres Islas and the monuments may have served as trade route markers, somewhat equivalent to such highland Olmec phenomena as the rock carvings at Chalcatzingo (M. Coe 1968a:91–92; Grove 1968).

The Usumacinta and Pasion drainage was a major trade route in the sixteenth century (Roys 1943:59, 106; Scholes and Roys 1968:30; Thompson 1964:19, 44). During the Maya Classic this drainage produced

Peidras Negras (Site 13, Fig. 8), Yaxchilan (Site 12, Fig. 8), and Altar de Sacrificios (Site 11, Fig. 8) as significant stela-cult members. Altar de Sacrificios is a buffer zone site which stands in a special relationship to the Guatemalan highlands. Its unique river junction location "is quite distinct from an ordinary riverbank location" (Willey and A. L. Smith 1969:47). The only two salt sources near the lowlands are located up the Chixoy River from Altar (Fig. 7; Thompson 1964: 20–22, 36; Hendges 1902). The area above the salt pans has many sources of hard stone. During the Early Classic strong influences from the Peten spread throughout the highlands (Rands and R. E. Smith 1965:144). Most interesting is the fact that later, when much of the highlands became isolated from lowland core area influence, the salt-producing Chixoy area did not. "Not only did this zone remain within the Peten diffusion sphere, but burials continued to be well stocked and in the Chama district one of the great polychrome styles of Mesoamerica emerged (Rands and R. E. Smith 1965:131). Much of the Peten influence must have passed through strategically located Altar de Sacrificios into important highland resource areas. Altar's position was, therefore, crucial to the procurement needs of the core, and it is not surprising that it is the only major site on the Usumacinta-Pasion with a significant Early Classic occupation.

Another important buffer zone cult center developed at Copan (Site 10, Fig. 8), geographically in the highland resource zone near obsidian sources and on a Post-Classic trade route (M. Coe and Cobean 1970; Longyear 1952:71; Thompson 1964:13). The culture history of this site is especially interesting in terms of the hypothesis and prediction. During the Copan Archaic a minimal population of farmers and gatherers had only sporadic contact with the outside. In the Early Classic the Maya Cult arrived. Trade with outside regions increased dramatically, including the "wholesale importation" of ceremonial paraphernalia and pottery from the

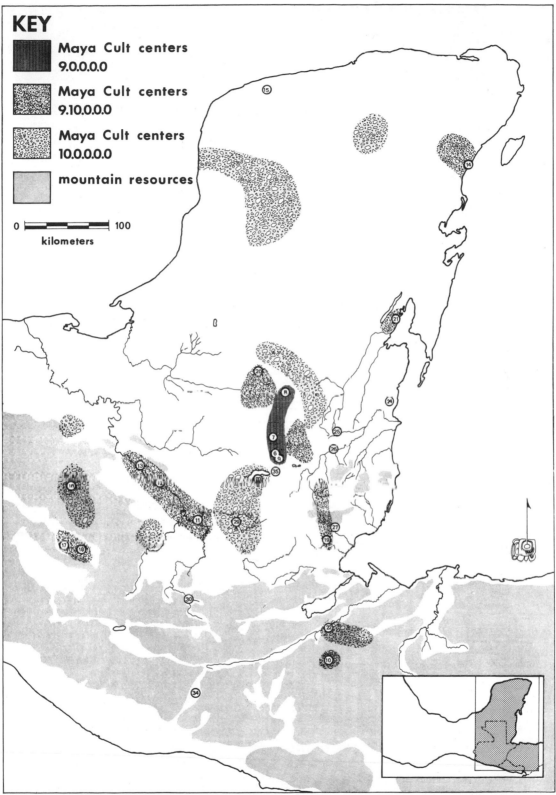

FIG. 8. *The spread of the Maya Cult as represented by the spread of the stela cult. Sites: 6, Tikal; 7, Uaxactun; 8, Balakbal; 9, Uolantun; 10, Copan; 11, Altar de Sacrificios; 12, Yaxchilan; 13, Piedras Negras; 14, Tulum; 15, Dzibilchaltun; 16, Tonina; 17, Comitan; 18, Chinkultic; 19, Pusilha; 20, Calakmul; 21, Ichpaatun; 22, Quirigua; 23, Tayasal; 24, Altun Ha; 25, San Jose; 26, Barton Ramie; 27, Lubaantun; 29, Seibal; 30, Chama Valley; 34, Kaminaljuyu; 35, El Zapote.*

northeast Peten (Longyear 1952:32, 68, 70).

Tulum (Site 14, Fig. 8) was a stela cult member located across from Cozumel, long a stopping point in the salt trade between northern Yucatan, Belize, and Honduras (Thompson 1964:16). Also of note is the seemingly one-way trade between the Peten and Dzibilchaltun (Site 15, Fig. 8), where "literally thousands of Peten trade pieces pepper the Early Period deposits" (Andrews 1965:305). Perhaps these two pieces form part of the early development of a Peten–northern Yucatan salt trade. The Maya Cult center at Tulum, most probably, served the Peten centers as a buffer zone procurement base.

Cult sites appeared in Chiapas at Comitan (Site 17, Fig. 8), Chinkultic (Site 18, Fig. 8), and Tonina (Site 16, Fig. 8). Tonina is near Ocosingo, a major modern source of metates "made of volcanic stone found along the San Martin River" (Villa Rojas 1969a: 206). These sites are situated near passes that potentially connect the Usumacinta drainage and the Maya lowlands with Central Mexico, the Isthmus, the Central Depression of Chiapas and the salt wells at Ixtapa and Zinacantan. Later additions to the fold of the cult include Pusilha (Site 19, Fig. 8) and Ichpaatun (Site 21, Fig. 8), in the area of major cacao production (Thompson 1964: 49), and Quirigua (Site 22, Fig. 8), located on the Montagua River just below the obsidian source near Zacapa (Roys 1943:116; Thompson 1964:30). In general, the Maya stela cult expansion followed the paths of resource procurement. While this occurred, the Maya Cult also spread north – probably as its ability to support new markets for basic resources and ceremonial goods increased.

Obviously from its complexity, the spread of the Maya Cult required that sites in the buffer zone import specialists trained at centers in the northeast Peten core area. Sociotechnic and ideotechnic Cult products were subject to wholesale importation by buffer zone sites. The following are typical assessments of the distribution of core area ceramics during the Cult's early development:

Beginning with the Protoclassic and continuing into the Early Classic Period in the Southern Subregion, is a trend toward the massive production and extensive distribution of Peten Gloss Ware monochrome and polychrome types. (R. E. Smith and Gifford 1965:533)

Decorated and monochrome black gloss ware types from the environs of the Peten ceremonial centers reached Barton Ramie in abundance or were imitated by craftsmen who must either have been schooled in the Peten or instructed by persons directly emanating from Peten sources. (Willey et al. 1965:350)

Types and modes are duplicated throughout the southern lowlands with little tolerance for local divergence in decorated pottery. (Willey, Culbert, and Adams 1967:310)

The ideology and technology of temple architecture, glyphic writing, astronomical knowledge, stela erection, carved eccentrics and jades, diffused similarily. Morley and Brainerd conclude: "The area of Classic Maya culture constituted nearly 100,000 square miles, a major segment of Mesoamerica. . . . Over this region there is evidence of a rapid spread of calendric innovations and an identity of religious symbolism as well as a series of concurrent changes in pottery. . . . This remarkably wide-spread homogeneity occurred in an area notable nowadays for its nearly impassible terrain" (1956:46).

Prediction 3.

Once buffer zone and resource areas develop complex sociopolitical organization, the core area manufactured goods and cult will begin to be replaced by local buffer zone and resource area equivalents. When the core area reaches its maximum development, and buffer zone and resource areas reach a similar or higher level of complexity, the core's complex organization will collapse.

Test 3-A: The Olmec. – There is little question that in its later days the Olmec civilization, in order to obtain basic and exotic commodities, dealt and competed with rising state organizations in Oaxaca and the Valley of Mexico (Sanders and Price 1968; Flannery 1968b; Flannary et al. 1967; Tolstoy 1969;

Tolstoy and Paradis 1970). The most recent interpretations indicate that early Olmec/highland contacts included massive importation of Olmec Cult paraphernalia, but that as time progressed, local products replaced these items: "Analysis of the burial ceramics in comparison to assemblages from other Middle Preclassic sites suggests that Tlatilco and other sites of its type are not one-period sites, but exhibit at least two phases, the earliest phase related to highland Olmec, the later to a localization of styles" (Grove 1970:183; Bernal 1969:160–67; Valley of Mexico—Tolstoy and Paradis 1970; Oaxaca—Flannery et al. 1967; Flannery 1968*b*; Morelos and Western Puebla—Grove 1968, 1970). It is also of note that after the abandonment of San Lorenzo and La Venta, buffer zone sites, like Tres Zapotes (Site 3, Fig. *4*), in major cacao production zones continued to be occupied (M. Coe 1965*c*; Bernal 1969:106–17). Upon the fall of Olmec civilization, control of the pan-Mesoamerican trade network established by the Olmec passed to the state-level urban civilizations of Monte Alban and Teotihuacan (Conrad 1970).

Test 3-B: The Maya.—During the Early Classic in the Maya lowlands, many centers "resorted to almost wholesale importation" of ceremonial objects from the central core of the Maya Cult (Longyear 1952:72). However, in the Late Classic site after site in the buffer zone replaced core imports or copies with local products. This was especially true of pottery:

The monotonous homogeneity of Tzakol is replaced by a trend toward local diversity, with a number of local varieties and styles in painted decoration. (Willey, Culbert, and Gifford 1967:310)

As the Late Classic period develops, this leads with cumulative swiftness to ever-widening separation between pottery of one subregion and that of another. In addition, important ceramic differences are also manifest between geographical units within the Southern Subregion. (R. E. Smith and Gifford 1965:533)

Some well-known examples of this trend are Copador ware from Copan (Longyear 1952),

Chama polychrome from the Chixoy River Valley (Site 30, Fig. *8*) (Rands and R. E. Smith 1965) and Chixoy, Pasion, and Boca pottery from Altar de Sacrificios (Adams 1962). The Early Classic/Late Classic transition in the Belize River Valley is especially relevant. The Maya Cult faded from the Barton Ramie area as another buffer zone or resource area became important in external Belize Valley trade relations:

The flow of pottery influences from the Peten to the east was all but terminated. (Willey et al. 1965:360)

To an appreciable extent Barton Ramie potters suddenly dropped the use of clays and calcite tempering materials previously employed in favor of volcanic ash (which does not occur locally). (Willey et al. 1965:371, 373)

Local variation, similar to that in ceramics, occurred in Late Classic stela carving, architecture, and craft production.

In the Late Classic there are also hints of monopolization of resources by buffer zone sites. W. Coe noted that "the production of eccentric obsidians was dependent on the supply of exhausted cores" (1959:144). "For some reason or other, Uaxactun's (core) production of eccentric objects seems to have ceased at a time when Piedras Negras (buffer zone) artisans were making them in increasing quantities" (1959:145).[21] The amount of jade discovered in Late Classic deposits at the buffer zone site of Altun Ha makes even the quantities found at Tikal pale (Pendergast 1969*a*, 1969*b*). In addition, some terminal Late Classic substela caches at Seibal include rough unworked jade boulders (Tourtellot personal communication), which perhaps earlier would have found their way to artisans in the northeast Peten.

During the Late Classic, external events greatly impinged upon the Maya highlands and lowlands. The chaotic dispersions of state-level groups from Central Mexico placed tremendous pressure on the Maya trading network (Jimenez Moreno 1966*b*; Miles 1965; de Borhegyi 1965; Webb 1964; Fry 1970; Erasmus 1968). The signs of militarism increased (Sabloff and Willey 1967), as did the Mexican domination of source areas and trade networks aimed at directing basic resources to regions that could pay for them with valuable natural resources: jade, cacao, salt, etc. (Miles 1965; de Borhegyi 1965; Webb 1964; Jimenez Moreno 1966b; Erasmus 1968). As a result of inability of the Maya Cult to challenge these incursions with an effective military or an exportable environmental resource, at the end of the Late Classic the northeast Peten core area was largely depopulated.

4. Summary

As a sedentary agricultural life became a workable means of existence, it spread into the Gulf coast and Guatemalan lowlands between 1500 and 1000 B.C. The demand for certain basic resources spread with the agricultural economy: salt for dietary requirements, obsidian cutting tools, and igneous stone grinding implements—the sources for which are located primarily outside these lowland areas. In order to obtain these resources exchange networks were established.

As lowland settlements developed further and further from resource areas, trade relations became extended and more effort had to be made to sustain the reliability of supply. Since neither lowland environment nor technology could increase the dependibility of supply, the rudiments of human interaction became crucial in guaranteeing the distribution of needed commodities. The efforts of a complex sociopolitical system investing accumulated resources and human energy into organizing and leading trading expeditions, maintaining relations with resource areas, and producing exchangeable commodities were necessary to satisfy lowland resource demands. This situation provided a selective advantage for the development of a social organization and religious system and their array of paraphernalia, capable of integrating large groups of scattered slash-and-burn agriculturalists. Cult centers evolved as foci of community economic and ceremonial interaction.

The proliferation and refinement of paraphernalia, technology, and ideology occurred for another reason—such commodities were highly exportable. By using them, both the Olmec and the Maya established a pan-Mesoamerican trade network. This network procured exotic materials as well as basic resources. Basic resources supported the agricultural subsistence level and provided distributors with effective means for influencing the actions of individual households. In the case of the Olmec, jade and magnetite were made into ornaments that sustained stratification. Also, huge basalt heads and massive offerings of serpentine emphasized the authority of the leaders of community effort and represented control of resource areas. Such expressions of efficiency were rewarded by more and more people investing in an obviously successful system.

Thus the disadvantages of dispersed settlement, great distance from resources, poor transportation, and central location in an area whose redundance mitigated against local exchange all worked at integrating communities and selecting for highly organized sociopolitical systems. Every household needs many resources to efficiently exploit any given environment. In the rainforest an unusually large number of these valuable resources are not locally available. Since every household would benefit directly from procurement and distribution of basic resources, the returns on investment supporting an organization with that function would be incredibly high. Complex organization in the Mesoamerican rainforests developed in response to the need for consistent procurement and distribution of nonlocal basic resources useful to every household. When complex organization no longer successfully fulfilled its function, it collapsed.

To maximize their resources both the Olmec and the Maya were forced to export their only competitive advantage—the means of sustaining complex organization. The Olmec found their most ravenous markets in areas with the potential to develop far above the rainforest maximum. As the Gulf coast and Maya lowland core areas exported their techniques of integration, their respective competitors—both mercantile and military—became more vigorous and successful. Buffer zone and highland sociopolitical systems, in order to obtain returns to match their investments, usurped and reoriented the trade networks which the procurement organizations in the lowland core area depended upon. The complex organizations of the core areas soon found that their ability to collect and distribute resources no longer matched their size and investments. The means of coercion and symbols of power became increasingly difficult to acquire. The subsistence level of the populace of the core area began to falter. The complex organizations in the lowland rainforest core no longer fulfilled their function and disintegrated. The ability to sustain complex socio-political organization developed early in areas lacking basic resources. Inevitably the centers of complex sociopolitical development shifted from these areas to areas possessing natural resources.

5. Basic Resources for Tropical Lowland Agriculture

Metates.

As W. Coe observed "surely one must ultimately turn to mundane metates and manos to answer the essential questions" (1959:36). "The one utensil found in every household throughout Yucatan, the region of the Usumacinta, and every other part of Mexico as well, is the stone metate for grinding corn" (Tozzer 1907:19; McBryde 1945: 47,60–61; Roys 1943:106). Many houses, in fact, have more than one set of grinding stones (Roys 1943:319; Laughlin 1969*b*: 303; McBryde 1945:47; Haviland 1963: 474). The demand for metates is not great at any one time, but it is consistent. In a study of 37 small towns in highland Chiapas, Pozas found that one out of seven specialized in

manufacturing metates (1959:104). During two months of observation in 1936, McBryde noted a daily influx of 16 metates and 48 manos to the market at Quezaltenango, a town of over 20,000 inhabitants. Surely a sustaining area the size of Tikal—the latest population estimate is 49,000 (Haviland 1969)—made somewhat similar demands.

Metates are usually made of volcanic rock, andesite, basalt, quartzite, etc.[22] Because of the restriction of most of these materials to the highlands, there has always been a brisk flow of metates to the lowlands (McBryde 1945:72; Covarrubias 1946:278, 291; Nader 1969:341; Harvey and Kelly 1969:655, 665); but just how essential were highland metates to Veracruz-Tabasco and southern Yucatan?

The Veracruz Tabasco plain lacks useful stone resources almost entirely (Fig. *4*; Roys 1965:677; Webb 1964:442; M. Coe 1968*a*: 89; Covarrubias 1946:104; Bernal 1969:68). Thus, if corn were to be ground on a mano and metate, they had to be imported. Because of their size and weight, cargadors traveling short distances usually carry "2 metates and 6 manos at a time, a load of about 100 lbs." (McBryde 1945:73). In the highlands, where the interacting units are households, metates are peddled "a few at a time because of the great weight" (1945:61). Distribution distance from production centers is limited. Nahuala metates, accepting McBryde's map (1945:72, map 18), rarely occur over 40 miles from their source of manufacture. Thus, both La Venta (Site 2, Fig. *4*—80 kilometers from stone) and San Lorenzo (Site 1, Fig. *4*—50 kilometers from stone) lay at the center of scattered populations, but at the outer limits of highland-style trade in metates.

Metates of imported basalt occur in the earliest levels at San Lorenzo (M. Coe 1968*a*:82; personal communication) and La Venta (Drucker 1952:145). Today, manos and metates of Oaxaca basalt are still imported into the lowland Veracruz-Tabasco plain (Covarrubias 1946:43, 278; Nader 1969:314). It is a moot point whether or not the Olmec could have survived without metates of imported stone. They found them critical enough to efficiency to invest considerable effort in their procurement and distribution—long before they began importing huge stone heads.

Hard stone metates are just as necessary in southern Yucatan as in the Veracruz-Tabasco plain, but there is a more complex distribution of possible resources in the Maya homeland. The whole of Yucatan is a huge chunk of limestone. Limestone metates have an interesting distribution. Subcrystalline limestone metates are rarely found since natural limestone is too soft to be efficient. Limestone metates occur in quantity only in areas close to major sources of semicrystalline limestone—sources such as on the upper Usumacinta River and near the Sierra de Yucatan (Fig. 7; Roys 1943:106; Tozzer 1907:3–4; Shattuck et al. 1933:14). Limestone metates have been excavated in abundance in northern Yucatan, near the Sierra source, at Mayapan, Chichen Itza, etc. At present, numbers of limestone metates in southern Yucatan have come from only two sites: Piedras Negras (Site 13, Fig. 8), sixteen metates (W. Coe 1959:34); Calakmul (Site 20, Fig. 8), twelve metates (Stromsvik 1937:123). Piedras Negras is in a resource area on the Usumacinta. There is reason to believe that the metates found at Calakmul were imported from northern Yucatan (Stromsvik 1937). Twenty-seven of the twenty-eight metates are surface finds. Stromsvik's analysis of Calakmul grinders concludes that because they are in ceremonial rather than domestic contents "this rude type of grinder may date from a terminal period of cultural degeneracy when the religious structures had fallen into disuse" (1937: 126).

The only metate found at Piedras Negras in a good excavated provenience was basalt (W. Coe 1959:Fig. 38, 39). On the Usumacinta at Seibal (Site 29) and Altar de Sacrificios (Site 11), even though semicrystalline limestone was available, most of the metates are made of nonlocal metamorphic conglomerates. Such materials occur naturally in the Altos Chuchumatanes of the Guatemalan highlands. Organized importation is implied since the meandering rivers of the area are too slow for such stone to have been brought downstream from the Highlands to the Central Lowlands naturally (Pohl personal communication).

In areas where both igneous and limestone sources were readily available, metates were carved almost exclusively from the volcanic stone. The metates from San Jose (Site 25, Fig. 8), Barton Ramie (Site 26, Fig. 8), and Altun Ha (Site 24, Fig. 8), located near the Maya Mountains of Belize (Fig. 7), are mainly granite. In addition, about one third of the metates from Altun Ha are scoria, imported from the Guatemalan highlands (Pendergast personal communication). The structural fill of Lubantuun (Site 27, Fig. 8) contained amazingly large quantities of "tripod metates of lava" (Thompson 1964:15; Kidder 1947:35). At Copan (Site 10, Fig. 8), in a highland biome, "by far the greater proportion of metates are simple, legless fragments of volcanic stone" (Longyear 1952:105).

In areas where major deposits of semicrystalline limestone and igneous rock were lacking, specifically in the northeast Peten, domestic metates were made of imported stone. The metates excavated at Uaxactun (Site 7, Fig. 8) were a mixed bag. Several large metates were found in ceremonial center Group A: 4 granite, 4 vesicular lava, 4 hard limestone. The majority "date from a time when Group A had ceased to be a 'ceremonial precinct' " (Kidder 1947:34). The excavation of Group E also produced surface finds of grinding stones "usually of granite or conglomerate, more rarely of hard limestone" (Ricketson and Ricketson 1937:193). Over two thousand metates have been recorded at Tikal (Site 6, Fig. 8). Only 15 percent were limestone; 85 percent were made of imported stone (Culbert 1970). The Tikal housemound project has produced data from Late

Classic housemounds at the periphery of the ceremonial precinct. Forty-five of the forty-eight reported domestic metates were made of imported materials: thirty-four quartzite, six granite, five travertine, two limestone, and one flint (Haviland 1963:450–51). It may be suggested that this is a biased sample, that housemounds closely associated with ceremonial precincts would have had access to trade and that the presence of nonlocal metates represented access to luxuries. Again, Tikal data provide a rebuttal, although based on a small sample. Robert Fry, in his excavations for the sustaining area survey, discovered no limestone metates of any type. Instead, he found that metates were made of igneous materials as far from the site center as 3.5 kilometers and as early as the Preclassic (Fry 1969:86; personal communication).

For the northeast Peten, and especially Tikal, the nearest source of granite, quartzite, and other igneous materials is the Maya Mountains of Belize (Thompson 1963:15; Haviland 1963:450). The distance from Tikal to this stone source is at least 90 kilometers. Whether or not the Tikal population could have survived without imported metates is, as in the Olmec case, a moot point. The data indicate that the northeast Peten imported massive quantities of igneous stone metates from distant sources as early as the Preclassic.

Obsidian.

The Olmec homeland offers little difficulty in defining obsidian or some other cutting stone as a necessity that had to be imported. If things were to be butchered, built, cut, carved, chopped, skinned, sawed, sliced, shaved, and pealed, importation of special-purpose stone to make knives, scrapers, drills, punches, choppers, and axes was mandatory since appropriate stone resources do not occur locally.[23] Obsidian is found in quantity in the lowest levels at San Lorenzo (M. Coe and Cobean 1970) and La Venta (Drucker 1952:145). The two sources of the earliest obsidian found at San Lorenzo are approximately 300 kilometers (Guadelupe Victoria, Puebla) and 500 kilometers (El Chayal, Guatemala) from the site (M. Coe and Cobean 1970).

The Peten presents a more complex situation. It, like the rest of Yucatan, is one big flint mine. Therefore, what is the place of obsidian in the tool complex? Sanders calls it a "luxury" (1964:21–27). Other Meso-americanists disagree. "Obsidian must have been a necessity for only this substance could produce the razor-sharp edge which was evidently desired" (Haviland 1963:427, 437, 438). Flake-blades were put to "frequent utilitarian use" (W. Coe 1959:14, 144) and were "essential to everyday life" (Thompson 1965.333).

Flake-blades of obsidian are incredibly abundant everywhere in the lowlands but especially in housemounds (Gann 1918:50; Willey et al. 1965: 441–45; Wauchope 1934; Haviland 1963:435–38; Fry 1969; Tourtellot personal communication). One argument for the efficiency produced by importing obsidian is its distribution in the lowlands and highlands. From Tikal housemounds the ratio of obsidian to flint tools is about 1:3 (Haviland 1963:435–38). In buffer zone Barton Ramie housemounds the ratio is 1:2 (Willey et al. 1965:441–45). In Seibal housemounds, near major trade routes, the ratio is 1.3:1 (Tourtellot personal communication). In the highlands obsidian flake-blades are frequently the only tools found in quantity (Woodbury 1965:170). In fact, at Copan, lying near sources of obsidian, the inhabitants ignored flint and used obsidian almost exclusively (Longyear 1952:13).

Thus, housemound excavation data from the Maya lowlands indicate that: 1) there are no areas where flint served alone in the production of cutting tools; 2) obsidian was utilized everywhere, in some places exclusively; and 3) the amount of obsidian in the tool complex is a direct function of the distance from obsidian sources. Thus obsidian seems to have been needed, at least, to supplement flint tool complexes and was imported everywhere in quantity.

Salt.

Another basic resource of importance is salt. Sanders also seems to consider mineral salt a "luxury" (1964:234). Some authorities disagree. Salt is "as essential as water, and for precisely the same reason. . . . The chemical requirements of the human body demand that the salt concentration in the blood be kept constant" (Bloch 1963:89). The importance of salt "as an article of diet among agricultural peoples who eat comparatively little meat can scarcely be exaggerated" (Roys 1943:53; Pozas 1959:89; Redfield 1941:44; Villa Rojas 1945:26, 45, 65; Thompson 1964:20; Blom 1932:535; Mendizabal 1929). Bloch concludes that in areas depending primarily on a vegetarian diet "a human being needs a minimum of 2 to 5 grams of additional salt per day in mineral form" (Bloch 1963:89).

The salt consumption of natives recorded ethnographically is much greater than 5 grams. For example, a family of 6 living in highland Chamula, Chiapas, is likely to purchase and consume 1.6 liters of salt every twenty days (based on data from over 30 families—Pozas 1959:90). Salt has an incredible variety of important uses. It is an ingredient in such basic foods as atole, pozole, and kol. Vegetables, including black beans, squash, chaya, and chayote, are cooked in salt water. Salt is often mixed with chili. It is always present at mealtimes and liberally applied. Fish and meat are preserved with salt; this use is especially important in the humid lowlands. Salt also functions in curing, exorcism and ritual, including an important role in ceremonies of change in political and religious office.

Salt was one of the most important items of trade in pre-Columbian Mexico (McBryde 1945:46, 60, 72). As Thompson noted, after the Conquest "traffic in feathers and gold ceased, but salt was an essential" (1964:20). Another index of its worth was reported by Roys: "salt was difficult to obtain because the merchants who carried it were often killed on the road" (1943:20). The commercial prosperity of northern Yucatan was due largely to its monopoly of the salt business of the Atlantic seaboard and the constant demand from inland Yucatan groups (Roys 1943:53).

The two areas of interest discussed in this essay provided markets for Yucatecan salt. At the time of the Conquest, Yucatecans supplied almost all of the salt consumed in the Veracruz-Tabasco coastal plain (Roys 1943:53, 105; Thompson 1965:353). The only source of local salt in the plain is the small one east of Espiritu Santu (Scholes and Warren 1965:784). Southern Yucatan is completely without a local salt supply. Salt for the Cehach (Cehache) area in the northwest Peten was shipped down the coast to Laguna de Terminos and up the Candelaria River (No. 32, Fig. 6). From its rapids and portages the salt was lugged overland to the north Peten (Roys 1943:52; Scholes and Roys 1968:59). Salt was transported from the north by sea to the Belize, New, Hondo, etc. River valleys and to Chetumel. Salt for the Usumacinta and Mopan drainages was obtained from beds on the lower Chixoy River (No. 30, Figs. 7, 8), in the lower altitutes of the Guatemalan highlands (Thompson 1964:20–22, 36).

The ashes of burned boten leaves are slightly saline and in an emergency can be substituted for salt (Gann 1918:22). Thompson concludes from direct observation that this technique "is hardly a source for a large population" (1965:333). It does not even seem to be an adequate source for a small population. At the time of the Conquest, the Cehach area, which had an estimated population density of only two persons per square mile, was actively trading for mineral salt (J. E. S. Thompson 1967:29).

Perhaps the best way to drive home the concept of this essay is to demonstrate the potential that salt has for organizing people. By the time of the Conquest, trade routes were well established, and thriving buffer-zone merchant communities were supplying parts of the interior of southern Yucatan with basic resources. One group they were supplying was the Acala,[24] located somewhere on the upper Usumacinta. The two largest Acala towns, Cagbalam and Culhuacan, consisted of 300 and 140 houses respectively. J. E. S. Thompson concluded on the basis of climactic data that "clearly there was no centralized government" interrelating villages (1967: 30). However, when Tovilla passed through the region in 1630, the salt trade had been disrupted and the organization that had controlled the salt source had been displaced. Tovilla reported that while he was in the area the Acala sent an expedition of "140 men to extract salt" from the beds in the Chixoy Valley (1960, Bk. 2, Chs 8, 9; Thompson 1964:22). Whether this group came from an individual town or from the Acala area as a whole, it represents large-scale community interaction in response to the need for basic resources.

The preceding data support the proposition that certain tools and condiments not occurring naturally in the rainforests of Mesoamerica were considered crucial enough through time to be imported everywhere in the lowlands in quantity and over vast distances—i.e., that hard stone for metates, obsidian for flake-blades, and salt are resources crucial to successful agricultural subsistence in lowland Mesoamerica. These data are not meant to imply that people could not survive in lowland rainforests without importing vast quantities of basic resources. The point to be made is, rather, if 1) the inhabitants of the lowlands were aware of the existence of desirable but distant resources, 2) the possession of basic resources conferred specific economic advantages upon their possessors, and 3) the distances to basic resources were not totally prohibitive, then those people who could key into long-distance trade successfully would have had restricted access to basic resources that could increase the efficiency of every household

unit. Thus, resource controllers could have become integrative nuclei to scattered household populations.

NOTES

1. Special thanks to Gordon R. Willey who made this essay possible; to Michael Coe and Robert Fry for unusually generous assistance; to C. C. Lamberg-Karolovsky for detailed constructive criticisms and encouragement; and to Kent Day, William Fitzhugh, James Humphries, John Ladd, Mark Leone, Renato Rosaldo, Jeremy Sabloff, Edward Sisson, and Gair Tourtellot for willing ears and considered opinions.

2. Civilization as defined by Sanders (1964:236–37; 1968:106); stratified vs. ranked as defined by Fried (1967:52, 115, 186–225).

3. Models for both Olmec and Maya development will be considered together because I feel they deal with the same phenomena.

4. Household is defined as the minimal production/consumption unit, i.e., nuclear family, extended family, etc.

5. Under the term *resources* are included the commodities made from them, i.e. resources: igneous stone; commodity: metates. For a similar definition and methodological use of *basic resources* see Fried 1967:52, 186–87, 191; Leone 1968:43, 126–28.

6. It should be noted that as stratification develops, nonutilitarian commodities become essential to the maintenance of sociopolitical integration (Fried 1967:32; Flannery 1968*b*:100; Rappaport 1968:105–9; Binford 1962; Sabloff and Tourtellot 1969).

7. Wolf 1967; Villa Rojas 1969*b*:263; Covarrubias 1946; and personal communications from M. Coe, Willey, and Sisson.

8. See also Chapman 1957:131, 133, 138, 143; Scholes and Roys 1968; Roys 1943:51.

9. Chapman states that the basic load per bearer in long-distance trade was 50 lbs. (1957:137); however, sources from the highlands today claim the average load per cargador carried on short treks weighs 100 lbs. (McBryde 1945:73).

10. Concentration of resources—Tax and Hinshaw 1969:86; Wolf 1967:308–12; Soustelle 1961: 61, 86; Scholes and Warren 1965:785; Roys 1943: 50–51; Roys 1965:662, 670; Chapman 1957:123, 128. Complex organization—Nash 1967:97; Wolf 1967:310; Redfield 1941:156; Covarrubias 1946:39, 149, 155, 283; Thompson 1964:22; Soustelle 1961: 59, 61; Roys 1943:50–51, 120; Roys 1965:671; Webb 1964:426; M. Coe 1968*a*:45; Fig. *3*.

11. Fried defines stratification as "a system by which adult members of a society enjoy differential

rights of access to basic resources" (1967:52; cf. Sahlins 1958, 1960, and 1963).

12. Chapman notes that the "Yucatan trader was apparently much more closely identified with his political rulers than was the Aztec trader" (1957:132).

13. Soustelle 1961:60–61, 64, 65; Scholes and Warren 1965:785; Roys 1943:107; Roys 1965:662, 670, 677; M. Coe 1961a:58, 85; Carrasco 1961:485, 489; Calnek 1962:41–43; Webb 1964:426; J. E. S. Thompson 1967:35; Tozzer 1941:39; Fry 1970.

14. Palerm 1967:27; Bunzel 1952:90; Wolf 1967: 306–8, 313–14; Fried 1967:108, 191.

15. The recent understanding of the diversity of the resources of the lowlands is largely the product of M. Coe's work at San Lorenzo (1968a, 1969). In terms of the Maya lowlands both Tozzer (1907: 49) and Duby and Blom (1969:282) recorded that the Lacandon traded among themselves. The following important resources in the Peten are a few representatives of those differentially distributed: mahogany, botan palm, allspice, ramon, cacao, vanilla, zapote, Spanish cedar, cahune, cotton, building stone, ocote pitch pine (Willey and A. L. Smith 1969:41, 42, 43, 47; Roys 1943:7; Thompson 1964:33; M. Coe 1961a:80, 81). Put together at one point this means that a site like Altar de Sacrificios had to import woods "serviceable for construction," thatch, "suitable building stone," and cotton (Willey and A. L. Smith 1969:41–43, 47).

The point is obviously not whether there is differential distribution of resources, but the degree of this distribution. In comparison to the highlands, the differential distribution of products of the Peten is minimal and resource areas are usually extremely large, i.e. the habitat of mahogany (Willey and A. L. Smith 1969:41; Roys 1943:7).

16. Polychrome pottery, decorated textiles, ornaments, and other products of craft specialization.

17. At the Conquest, these areas were major producers and exporters of cacao (M. Coe personal communication).

18. This comparison in no way disclaims the importance of economic symbiosis and population growth in stimulating sociopolitical development, especially in the highlands; it merely tries to demonstrate that additional factors have affected lowland cultural development.

19. For estimates of Belize Valley population see Willey et al. 1965; Webb 1964:398; Sanders 1964:209; Haviland 1963; etc.

20. Blom 1932; J. E. S. Thompson 1929, 1964, and 1967; Chapman 1957; Mendez 1959.

21. Testing for obsidian reuse (Michels 1969) would be valuable in determining consistency of obsidian supply.

22. Tozzer 1907:19; Haviland 1963:450–51; Pendergast personal communication; Longyear 1952:106; Laughlin 1969a:162; de Borhegyi 1965: 10; M. Coe 1968a:67, 82; Drucker 1952:145; Fry personal communication; Nader 1969:341; McBryde 1945:47, 61; Covarrubias 1946:278, 291; Thompson 1964:15; Blom 1932:536; Ricketson and Ricketson 1937:193.

23. M. Coe 1968a:89; Roys 1943:50, 54; Roys 1965:677; Drucker 1952:145; Bernal 1969:28.

24. In 1964 (p. 22) J. E. S. Thompson identifies the salt recipients as Lacandon. However, in 1967 (p. 3) he states that Tovilla called them Lacandon, but that they "were almost certainly Acala."

Chapter 32 CRAIG MORRIS

State Settlements in Tawantinsuyu: A Strategy of Compulsory Urbanism

MOST OF the archaeological research on early cities has focused on cases we assume to have developed gradually and spontaneously. The concern has been primarily with *in situ* growth and differentiation in settlements and in explaining how such changes came about in terms of social, ecological, and ideological variables largely indigenous to the vicinity or region where the development occurred. The availability of important natural resources and a propitious position for trade or exchange are factors which have frequently been looked for in studying the growth of an urban center.

There are circumstances, however, in which large, internally differentiated settlements can arise in response to other stimuli, such as centralized state planning and directed population movement. We are familiar with modern cases, like Canberra or Brasilia, and Oppenheim (1957:36) speaks of "forced urbanism" in the Assyrian empire. In these cases the nature and growth of substantial settlements are understandable only in reference to a larger system and to politically based direction coming from far away.

It is becoming increasingly clear that a form of compulsory settlement was a common and extremely important feature of Andean political and economic organization during the Inca period. While many of these state installations were relatively small, several contained well over 1,000 buildings, and most were built quite rapidly during the latter half of the fifteenth century and the first three decades of the sixteenth. The hand of the state is clearly evident in the character of the centers, as well as in their founding and rapid growth.

The nature of these settlements can in part be derived from materials in the European ethnohistorical sources, and an understanding of the sociopolitical and economic contexts into which they fit largely depends on these sources. But I would argue that only archaeological data can provide the crucial tests of ideas found in the chronicles and in the work of their modern commentators and analysts.

The archaeological study of state settlements in Tawantinsuyu, the name given by the Inca to the territory they ruled, has not yet been very systematic or extensive. Rowe's pioneering work in Cuzco (Rowe 1944: 1967) and Menzel's (1959) important studies of the south coast have provided essential bench marks, but most of the archaeological work lies ahead. Even for the few instances of state installations discussed below, the evidence is still very fragmentary. However, it seems worthwhile to bring some of the results together, not only to present some preliminary conclusions, but to help provide a foundation on which more systematic work can build in the future.[1]

The Inca settlements which will be discussed are located in the Peruvian central highlands near the modern towns of Huánuco and Cerro de Pasco. They are but a part of a vast system of settlements totalling at least 170 (Poma [1615] 1936:1084–93) which the Inca built along the road networks in the territory they controlled. One road network followed the coast, and the other ran through the highlands from Quito to Cuzcó and on through Argentina into Chile. In 1964 and 1965 we visited Taparaku, Huánuco Pampa, (Huánuco Viejo), Tunsukancha and Pumpu, the remains of four settlements on the Cuzco-Quito road.[2] Two of the sites, Taparaku and Tunsukancha, are small, having only about 100 to 300 structures. Pumpu and Huánuco Pampa are at least four times that size. The contrast in size has long been recognized (Cieza [1550] 1959:68–69) and reflects a contrast in function. The small installations are usually referred to as *tampu*, the famous Inca way-stations, while the larger centers have been called "administrative centers," indicating their much broader range of activities. The *tampu* were separated by the approximate distance of a day's travel, with an administrative center occurring occasionally (usually every four to six days) instead of a *tampu*. All four of the ruins visited are located on high plateaus, or *puna*, since the road kept to the heights; at 3,736 meters the city of Huánuco Pampa is easily the lowest of the four.

Huánuco Pampa and Pumpu clearly fit into most archaeological definitions of urban centers. They are large; they have zones which furnished impressive buildings and large amounts of space for activities which were in some sense ceremonial; the residential architecture suggests marked social and economic stratification. Even the small *tampu* sites have what were apparently high status residential compounds, although they may have been used only occasionally (Morris 1966). But in Huánuco Pampa, and to a lesser extent Pumpu, this elite residential zone is large. Essentially it is a palace sector with associated administrative and ceremonial buildings covering more than half a square kilometer. All of the centers thus show the hallmarks of a complex, stratified society, but it is the administrative centers which so suggest an urban settlement form. They have the large, dense populations which are differentiated in terms of socioeconomic status and occupational specialization and are the most typical feature of cities, whether ancient or modern.

In addition to these more typical urban characteristics, there are other qualities of the settlements along the Inca road which are unusual, and which imply a rather special kind of urban center—both in terms of their internal structure and in terms of their relationships to the regions in which they are set. It is these unusual features which have led to terms like compulsory and imposed urbanism to contrast with the more organic kinds of cities.

Perhaps the most notable of these atypical characteristics is not manifested so much by the archaeological record of the state settlements themselves. It emerges instead from the comparison of the settlements along the Inca roads with the villages and towns of the ethnic groups local to the region, like the Yacha and the Chupaychu, described by Iñigo Ortiz de Zúñiga (1955–61, 1967). What we see is a profound difference between the imperial and the local sites in the stylistic attributes of both architecture and ceramics. This contrast suggests both the intrusiveness of the centers along the road and an interaction pattern between them and the local towns and villages which is very different from the relatively easy and casual flow of people, goods and ideas between city and village which we frequently visualize.

The pottery of the four sites along the Inca road showed clear Cuzco stylistic derivation. The similarity to the capital is such that it can only be ascribed to deliberate imitation, not mere influence. For example, local versions of most of the major vessel forms illustrated by Rowe (1944:48) for the Late Inca period in Cuzco are found in these sites. The villages, on the other hand, adhere to their pre-Inca ceramic traditions with only slight changes during the period of the construction

State Settlements in Tawantinsuyu
Craig Morris

and use of the state centers (D. E. Thompson 1967, 1968, 1969; Morris 1967).

The striking formal differences between the local ceramics and those associated with the state installations are paralleled by a clearly defined distribution pattern. The occurrence of local pottery in the state centers we studied was limited to five or six sherds out of many thousand. The distribution of the ceramics usually associated with the state centers was largely restricted to those centers. Large quantities of such state ceramics were found only in the village site which documents showed to have been the residence of the most important local *kuraq*, or leader (Ortiz [1562] 1967:55–59). This tends to suggest that such ceramics were essentially restricted to state settlements and certain significant points of political contact in the region.

The contrasts in the formal characteristics of the archaeological materials and their well defined distribution patterns, thus allow us to isolate archaeologically a state settlement system on the one hand and the villages of the local ethnic groups on the other. We can only interpret the road and the sites it joins as a system of settlements in some way foreign to the region in which they occur. Indeed, we might postulate that the state settlements were peopled by basically different groups, were it not that we know from documents (Ortiz [1562] 1955–61, 1967) that many of the people who inhabited them came not from Cuzco, but from the local villages whose archaeological remains are so different.

A second characteristic of these settlements which is unusual, and also indicative of their planned nature, is the suddenness of their appearance on the archaeological horizon. Stratigraphic tests in Huánuco Pampa and Tunsukancha and extensive surface collections from all four sites revealed no pre-Inca occupation. We know from historical sources that the region in question was not consolidated until after Thupa Inca took command of the army, which Rowe (1945:271–77) dates at about 1463. If this is correct, the construction we can now see was accomplished

in a period of no more than seventy years immediately preceding the Spanish Conquest in 1532. For a settlement to attain a size of well over a thousand structures in such a short period of time is unusual for the ancient world; for a whole series of them to be founded and grow at once over a wide area is even more unusual.

A third indication of the special character of the settlements is a preoccupation with storage. The enormous quantities of goods accumulated in storehouses have struck European observers since the Spanish first traveled the Inca roads. In 1965 and 1966 I conducted an archaeological study of parts of the Inca storage system, with the majority of the effort focused on these provincial settlements, particularly Tunsukancha and Huánuco Pampa. The hypotheses which guided that research drew on the ideas of Polanyi (1957) and Murra (1956, 1962a), holding that one of the functions of the large administrative centers was the redistribution of a wide variety of goods throughout an ecologically and culturally diverse hinterland. The postulate was that the storage complex served largely as the center of such a redistributive network, and therefore that the settlements in which they were located functioned as redistributive centers of exchange analogous to the market centers found in other contexts.

It is clear that the question requires extensive quantitative information, only part of which was supplied by the archaeology of my study. I was convinced, however, that while the redistribution of certain goods is not to be doubted, the primary function of the storehouses at centers like Huánuco Pampa (where 38,000 cubic meters of space was provided in 497 storehouses) and Pumpu was to supply the needs of the settlements themselves. There is little or no evidence of food production adjacent to the centers, and in any case they are not located in very productive zones. The source of their food, dozens of village communities, some quite far away, is clear from the written records (Ortiz [1562] 1967). Most of the storage seems to have been devoted to comestibles of varieties not substantially different from those available in most villages, accumulated to protect the settlements from famine or other disruptions in production or delivery. The extent to which provincial state settlements were also centers of redistributive exchange, important in the economy of the region as a whole, remains to be measured accurately, but at this point redistribution to the villages would not seem to rank near the top of the list of important functions they served.

A fourth factor to be considered, is that the architecture and planning of the settlements is marked by what seems to be a high proportion of buildings suited for temporary housing. There are also facilities which would more likely be used by individuals than families. The long rectangular structures surrounding the plazas in the hearts of the sites are examples of this apparent emphasis, as are the 43 neatly aligned buildings in what Harth-Terré (1964:13) refers to as the *cuartel* or barracks at Huánuco Pampa. We cannot talk definitively about architectural functions and permanent as opposed to temporary housing, because the documents now available do not provide direct evidence and pertinent archaeological associations must await extensive excavations. However, the implications of these aspects of settlement planning are that they assigned priorities to certain kinds of activities which were not primarily residential in the usual sense. The emphasis was instead on transient and perhaps *corvée* and military housing. Not only do these types of housing seem to have provided a physical core around which the settlements were planned, but in some cases they probably occupied as much or more space than residences characterized by a family-style dwelling unit.

Two final factors which call attention to a certain artificiality of the settlements along the Inca road are 1) the rapidity of their depopulation following the decapitation of the Inca state and 2) the apparent lack of important cemeteries associated with the ruins. Both of these factors tend to suggest that the population which inhabited the settlements had important external ties and perhaps regarded home as elsewhere. We know from historical sources (Varallanos 1959:125–42) that the Spanish attempt to maintain an important settlement at Huánuco Pampa was abortive. Furthermore, there is almost no definitive archaeological evidence of occupation during colonial times at any of the sites mentioned.

It would be premature to regard the present lack of evidence for burying grounds as conclusive. The settlements were not long established, and thus cemeteries would not have been extensive; also our search was not exhaustive and additional work may reveal burials. But at least there were no clearly defined burial areas of large size, which would certainly have been discovered by treasure hunters if not by us, nor were there any architectural remains which suggest the large above-the-ground burial chambers common in parts of the Andes.

There are two avenues of approach in searching for explanations of the characteristics of the Inca settlements summarized above. One of these is to try to place them in the context of the Inca institutions in which they developed and functioned. We need to look for their essential contributions to the wider political and economic system and how they interacted with other institutions which conditioned their form and determined some of their particular characteristics. The other avenue is to look more broadly still, to see if any general framework of the development of settlement forms and socioeconomic institutions is helpful.

Probably the most useful formulation of the development of urban phenomena is that of Adams (1956, 1966). It holds the origin of systems of centralized authority in society to have been first based in institutions which were primarily religious. But as a result of internal and external forces which he outlines, these institutions were transformed, resulting in structures of authority which were basically secular and militaristic. It is the latter part of his schema, dealing with what he calls the Militaristic or Dynastic era, which we are interested in here. Although a process of secularization may well have been continuing during the Inca period, the basic change with which Adams is dealing had clearly occurred much earlier in Andean prehistory, as Schaedel (1951) and others have demonstrated. In any case, it is the character of the result more than the major process which is of primary concern here.

The effects an increasingly secular and militaristic kind of organization has on the settlements associated with the centers of political control are also outlined by Adams (1960: 165–66). We see them very clearly in some of the less extraordinary characteristics of the sites mentioned above. There are the possible barracks areas, the presence of royal residences or lodges, however small, in all the centers, the enlargement of some of these palaces into lavish administrative and elite residential complexes. If the identifications I have made are correct, the storage destined for secular state use at Huánuco Pampu was many times that allotted to the deities (Morris 1967). Polo ([1571] 1916:59) also tells us the state's storehouses were larger than those of the Sun.

I stress this not simply as a way of explaining that military and palace-administrative activities were a central theme of the Inca road and the installations it connected. Cieza pointed that out in the sixteenth century. The point is to emphasize the importance and potential of a well established and militaristic central authority with substantial control over large amounts of power and economic goods. In the state settlements more than 550 kilometers from the capital at Cuzco one sees the external dimensions of such an authority structure as it has greatly expanded. In examining and evaluating the role of such settlements it is necessary to come to grips with questions of why they were essential to an expanding primitive state on the one hand, and how they were possible within the context of such a state on the other.

Perhaps the most crucial element in the dynamic of an expanding state is the kind of relationships it has with the people it seeks to incorporate and the way it initiates those relationships. In the case of the Inca it is how the local *ayllu* community and sometimes larger ethnic and economic units were enclosed within the state framework, as Murra (1964, 1968) has pointed out. This was accomplished by a series of mechanisms, not yet fully understood, which grew out of traditional principles of reciprocity (Murra 1956, 1958, 1962b, 1964, 1967).[3] It is some of these mechanisms which appear to explain many of the peculiar characteristics of the provincial state settlements and will be mentioned below.

From the standpoint of the state, it was the necessity for mobilizing the resources which sustained the elite and staffed and fed the armies of expansion which was the most important aspect of this relationship. It was also important that the proper resources be at the right place at the right time, particularly during periods of military operations. This latter requirement was quite an order for a territory spanning more than 2,500 kilometers of the world's harshest terrain with a technology of transportation and communication which was almost neolithic.

In working out responses to these needs in varied and frequently difficult or marginal situations, Inca administrative procedures in the provinces took shape. An administrative bureaucracy was required for mediating between the state and local communities. Local ethnic leaders and bureaucratic structures were used where possible. When they were absent, or when there were quarrels or conflicts between existing groups, new structures had to be created. Also required was a well-planned system of logistics and communications; without it, sustained conquest over long distances would have been difficult and even the beginnings of real consolidation would have been impossible.

In spite of contrasts in size and some other features, the four Inca sites dealt with here were part of a coherent whole, a network of roads and settlements which extended much of the length of Tawantinsuyu and which were vital parts of a mechanism which tied the state, however loosely, to the rather diverse peoples of its provinces. First, they and the other settlements of the network provided the nodes of the elaborate communication and logistic system which enabled the movement of armies, workers, officials, goods and information over long distances with remarkable efficiency and reliability considering the technological level of the Inca. The smaller *tampu* installations, like Taparaku and Tunsukancha, provided the minimal links in this network. Second, the settlements provided for the centralization of a series of administrative, ceremonial and economic operations which were essential in terms of securing the political, military and economic base on which the state was supported. The administrative centers, like Huánuco Pampa and Pumpu, with their palace-administrative-ceremonial zones and their large storage facilities were crucial here.

Whether other activities, like craft production, were important aspects of some of these settlements has yet to be determined. Several of the crafts, particularly cloth, were important parts of the state's reciprocal obligations, and therefore essential elements in the whole system whereby labor was mobilized for the state's support (Murra 1962b). The centralization of craft production in centers such as Huánuco Pampa and Pumpu would have provided greater efficiency and more direct state control in the production of critical goods. At this point there are only hints that craft production was an important activity in these settlements, but if it is confirmed, their importance and interest will be expanded further. Future archaeology should be able to solve problems such as this with relative ease.

The functions served by these state settlements are thus not surprising, given the expanse of Tawantinsuyu. They are what we would expect from a rapidly expanding state which took seriously the eventual consolidation of large areas, many of which might be called underdeveloped. What is perhaps un-

usual is the extent to which the Inca could undertake such a program of compulsory settlement. While the eclipse of Inca power by the Spanish prevented any real test of the full realization or longevity of the Inca system, its attempts at territorial incorporation and control were in many respects the most ambitious of any of the world's early "conquest" states. We cannot pretend at this point to fully understand this apparent precosity in political achievements, but we can understand part of the institutional basis through which state centers were built and populated. It is through a working out of some of these institutions that many of the singular characteristics of the settlements are explained.

Taking first the seeming importance of temporary and nonfamily dwelling units, it is clear that much of this can be explained simply on the basis of one of the settlement system's major functions. A fairly substantial number of transients had to be cared for. And it is reasonable that garrisons may have been stationed in larger centers like Huánuco Pampa. But aside from these activities, it is highly likely that a substantial portion of the population which was not directly involved in the military, or transient in the strictest sense of the word, was also not composed of permanent residents.

The state was supported almost entirely by labor, not tribute in kind. This fact had far reaching importance in other aspects of state organization and in the nature of its cities. Labor was converted into the goods and services necessary for state operation. The primary source of labor was the *mit'a* labor tax which was levied upon heads of households in rotation. It was a form of labor service which might be exacted to cultivate state fields near the taxpayer's own village; or it might involve military service, work on construction projects such as roads, bridges, irrigation and terracing, or other service which meant leaving home for varying periods of time. The *mit'a*, theoretically at least, was a purely temporary form of service which did not separate people from their village communities for long duration, much less permanently (Murra 1964, 1968; Rowe 1946: 265–69).

Part of the personnel which maintained and populated the state provincial settlements was almost certainly composed of *mit'a* laborers. Cieza (1959:109) tells us that over 30,000 people "served" Huánuco Pampa, which is very different from saying that 30,-000 people inhabited the center on a permanent basis. Ortiz ([1562] 1955–61: testimony of Juan Chuchuyauri, February 5, 1562) lists the community of Paucar as a source of those who served the *tampu* of Tunsukancha, a day and a half's walk away. A high proportion of *mit'a* inhabitants would explain the rapid post-Inca depopulation and the difficulty in locating a cemetery. Thus we have ethnohistorical, historical, and archaeological information all suggesting a population which in part consisted of rotating *mit'a* taxpayers. This probably not only meant a turnover in individual residents, but fluctuation in numbers as well, since it is doubtful that activities in the settlements along the roads were entirely free of influence from the agricultural and ceremonial calendar.

Cobo (1956·2:114) also says "a great number of people of service sent by the neighboring towns for their *mit'a*" were to be found in at least the larger state centers. But he lists others: *mitmaqkuna,* the "colonists" which the Inca transplanted in whole community units; *aqllakuna,* the women frequently portrayed as "virgins" associated with the Sun temples, but also weavers for the state (Murra 1956:304); and the chief delegate of the Inca or royal governor. Certainly there was at least a core of relatively permanent residents in these settlements. The problems of sorting out the relative importance of the various categories of state servants in the population as a whole can perhaps be partially solved archaeologically by studies of the nature of the domestic units and socioeconomic statuses related to the various kinds of housing in the centers' several habitation areas.

As was seen above, much of the distinctiveness between the centers along the roads and the villages indigenous to the area is the result of state planning and construction. But does that alone account for the exclusive occurrence of materials in the "state style" in these centers? Why was there not more mixing? There are at least two sets of principles which further account for the stark contrasts noted in the archaeology.

One of these had to do with the reciprocities on which the state depended for its labor revenues. The state's side of the reciprocity was to provide for those working for it (Murra 1956:168). Since it is probable that nearly all of the productive activities in these centers were directly related to the state, it would have assumed nearly total responsibility to provide housing, pottery and all else that was needed. The pervasive nature of the state stamp on everything down to the crudest cooking pot would tend to affirm that the state lived up to its obligations with almost unbelievable rigidity. This appears to be the soundest explanation for the lack of evidence we had expected to find of the various ethnic groups who served the centers (Murra 1962a; Morris and Thompson 1970). And the great storage effort further underscores the reality of the state's obligations, as well as suggesting the marginality of the areas in which they frequently had to be discharged.

The second set of rules and implications involved are those which regulated travel. Both the use of state roads and entrance into many of the settlements along them was controlled, if not actually restricted (Santillan [1563–64] 1927:88; Rowe 1946:271). While casual interchange between local communities for barter and other purposes was undoubtedly common, such was not likely the case between local communities and the *tampu* and administrative centers. Contact with the centers was mainly channeled along other lines, like the provision of labor and military service and the delivery of the state's goods.

I have tried to set forth above a tentative view of the nature of a segment of the vast system of *tampu* and administrative centers located along the Inca roads in the provinces of Tawantinsuyu. It is very difficult to answer many of the important questions regarding the general significance of these kinds of centers to the development of Andean civilization as a whole. To what extent are the four examples in the Peruvian central highlands typical of all the stops along the royal Inca roads? When did this form of state-imposed installations arise in the Andes; was it an Inca innovation? The literature, however, does hold several suggestions. It tends to indicate that such compulsory settlements were widespread, but that state centers were not exclusively of this type. It also indicates that settlements having at least many of the same characteristics as those outlined here may antedate the Inca by several hundred years.

It is expected that most of the Inca installations which were part of the system of roads had the same major functions as those described above. But this does not mean that they were all built and maintained or operated in the same way, or that all of the activities within them followed a single pattern —or the double pattern of *tampu* and administrative centers. The points developed above must not be applied too broadly. There were local variations, probably extensive ones, and when more research is done these will emerge more clearly. There are, however, two comments which can be made on the basis of what is now known. While the centers were planned and their construction partially supervised by state architects, the details of the architecture and even some rather major aspects of planning varied considerably even in the four settlements discussed above—witness the difference between Huánuco Pampa and Pumpu (Thompson 1969).

The other point deals with the manner in which the centers were established and populated. It seems likely that the observations Menzel (1959:140) has made for the south coast holds more generally: "the Incas took advantage of existing centralization . . . building their administrative centers at the focus of native authority. . . . In valleys in

which there was no centralized authority already the Incas imposed their own, constructing an administrative center at some convenient point to serve as the focus of Inca control." The important considerations were an appropriate position along the road and the jobs that had to be done in forming relationships with local populations. If these could be satisfied by partially taking over existing facilities or by grafting the necessary Incaic facilities onto an already existing population center, then it was done. The resident population presumably would have furnished most of the personnel needs for state activities. In this case a new series of activities was merely added onto an organic settlement. Due to the long history of urbanism and population concentration on the coast, these alternatives to compulsory settlements were probably much more common there than in the highlands where the Inca showed a distinct preference for keeping their road network to the high *puna* areas where the permanent population was generally sparse. In these more isolated zones where a centralized organization was not well developed one had to be imposed, the resources to support it mobilized, and the facilities to house it built. The result is the seemingly urban, yet quasi-artificial, administrative centers which complement the *tampu* along the highland road.

The question of the origins of this type of settlement in the Andes is one which has yet to be studied. However, if the arguments of Rowe (1963), Menzel (1968:91–93), Lumbreras (1969:155, 170) and others are correct, the spread of the styles which mark the Middle Horizon indicates the expansion of a highly centralized state society involving military conquest. It would not be surprising to find that some of the settlements of that period, particularly its earlier phases, showed the intrusive and compulsory character of those in Tawantinsuyu about 500 years later. The large centers identified with the Huari expansion are even less well known than those of the Inca. But Rowe has pointed out the prevalence of formal storage complexes at several important Middle Horizon sites, and I would concur that the existence of these "complexes provides evidence that the expansion of Huari was not a matter of peaceful penetration or raiding. It represents the formation of an imperial state with a well organized administration" (Rowe 1963:14).

The significance of compulsory urbanism as a strategy of expansion cannot become clear until the settlements it produced are themselves better understood. We can, however, grasp some of its most important features. In its earliest cases at least, it would appear to be a product of a particular kind of society: one controlled by a powerful and partially militaristic centralized governmental institution. It thus cannot emerge until such institutions have developed, and is a new form of settlement that may arise with them. The main functions it serves are political control in hinterland areas and the mobilization and channeling of goods and services to support the ruling elite and state operations. The locations and size of compulsory settlements seem primarily to depend on the extent to which existing patterns of authority and settlement can be used to accomplish vital state tasks. Therefore they tend to be particularly large and numerous in areas characterized by certain conditions of ecological and sociopolitical marginality.

One of the most interesting problems related to such settlements would be the changes they would undergo if they were utilized over extremely long periods of time. Here again we have mainly questions without answers. But it appears probable that if in some cases they became centers of craft production or exchange, their dependence for survival on the state which founded them would decrease, and their difference from other, spontaneous settlements would come to lie mainly in their origins. It may be then that this form of settlement is intrinsically ephemeral—lasting only as long as the state needs or can maintain it, or else ultimately acquiring a basically different and independent character. The important point, however, continues to be the connection between these compulsory settlements and the expansion of the state. They seem to show that certain minimal elements of urbanism, both as a mode of organization and a form of settlement, are so basic to the growth and maintenance of imperialistic state society, that in areas where they are not extant they must be created.

NOTES

1. This essay draws on material collected by the "study of Inca provincial life," 1963–66, sponsored by the Institute of Andean Research and financed by the National Science Foundation (GS 42). I wish to acknowledge the contributions of all who collaborated with that project, they go well beyond what can be covered by bibliographic citations. To Dr. John V. Murra, the project's director, go special acknowledgements—including those for comments and criticisms of this paper.

2. The reader interested in further information or greater detail on the work in these sites is referred particularly to D. E. Thompson (1967, 1968, and 1969), Morris (1966) and Morris and Thompson (1970).

3. These local groups varied greatly in size as well as level of complexity. Terms such as "ethnic" and "peasant" alone do not adequately characterize them. Murra's (1967) study of the Chupaychu should be consulted for greater detail. His articles on the Lupaca (Murra 1964, 1968) are also pertinent, although concerned with a different area.

Death's Head, Cherub, Urn and Willow

ENTER ALMOST any cemetery in eastern Massachusetts that was in use during the seventeenth and eighteenth centuries. Inspect the stones and the designs carved at their tops, and you will discover that three motifs are present. These motifs have distinctive periods of popularity, each replacing the other in a sequence that is repeated time and time again in all cemeteries between Worcester and the Atlantic, and from New Hampshire to Cape Cod.

The earliest of the three is a winged death's head, with blank eyes and a grinning visage. Earlier versions are quite ornate, but as time passes, they become less elaborate. Sometime during the eighteenth century—the time varies according to location—the grim death's head designs are replaced, more or less quickly, by winged cherubs. This design also goes through a gradual simplification of form with time. By the late 1700s or early 1800s, again depending on where you are observing, the cherubs are replaced by stones decorated with a willow tree overhanging a pedestaled urn. If the cemetery you are visiting is in a rural area, the chances are quite good that you will also find other designs, which may even completely replace one or more of the three primary designs at certain periods. If you were to search cemeteries in the same area, you would find that these other designs have a much more local distribution. In and around Boston, however, only the three primary designs would be present.

If you were to prepare a graph showing how the designs change in popularity through time, the finished product might look something like three battleships viewed from above, the lower one with the bow showing, the center one in full view, and the third visible only in the stern. This shape, frequently called a "battleship-shaped" curve, is thought by archaeologists to typify the popularity career of any cultural trait across time. Prepared from controlled data taken from the Stoneham cemetery, north of Boston, where the style sequence is typical of the area around this eighteenth-century urban center of eastern Massachusetts, the graph below shows such a curve.

It is appropriate here to interrupt and pose the question: why would an archaeologist study gravestones from a historic period?

Whether archaeology can be considered a science in the strict sense of the word is much debated. One of the hallmarks of scientific method is the use of controls in experimentation that enable the investigator to calibrate his results. Since archaeology deals largely with the unrecorded past, the problem of rigorous control is a difficult one. Much of modern archaeological method and theory has been developed in contexts that lack the necessary controls for precise checking of accuracy and predictive value. For this reason, any set of archaeological data in which such controls are available is potentially of great importance to the development and testing of

Reprinted by permission of the authors and the publisher from *Natural History,* vol. 76, no. 3, 1967, pp. 29–37.

explanatory models, which can then be used in uncontrolled contexts.

For a number of reasons, colonial New England grave markers may be unique in providing the archaeologist with a laboratory situation in which to measure cultural change in time and space and relate such measurements to the main body of archaeological method. All archaeological data—artifacts, structures, sites—can be said to possess three inherent dimensions. A clay pot, for example, has a location in space. Its date of manufacture and use is fixed in time, and it has certain physical attributes of form. In a sense, much of archaeological method is concerned with the nature and causes of variation along these dimensions, as shown by excavated remains of past cultures.

The spatial aspect of gravestones is constant. We know from historical sources that nearly all of the stones in New England cemeteries of this period were produced locally, probably no more than fifteen or twenty miles away; an insignificant number of them came from long distances. This pattern is so reliable that it is possible to detect those few stones in every cemetery that were made at a more remote town. Once placed over the dead, the stones were unlikely to have been moved, except perhaps within the cemetery limits.

Needless to say, the dimension of time is neatly and tightly controlled. Every stone bears the date of death of the individual whose grave it marks, and most stones were erected shortly after death. Like the spatial regularity, this temporal precision makes it possible to single out most of the stones that were erected at some later date.

Control over the formal dimension of gravestone data derives from our knowledge of the carvers, who, in many instances, are known by name and period of production, and who, even if anonymous, can be identified by their product with the help of spatial and temporal control. Thus, in most cases stones of similar type can be seen to be the product of a single person, and they reflect his ideas regarding their proper form.

Furthermore, it is known that the carvers of the stones were not full-time specialists, but rather workers at other trades who made stones for the immediate population as they were needed. We are dealing, then, with folk products, as is often the case in prehistoric archaeology.

Other cultural dimensions can also be controlled in the gravestone data with equal pre-

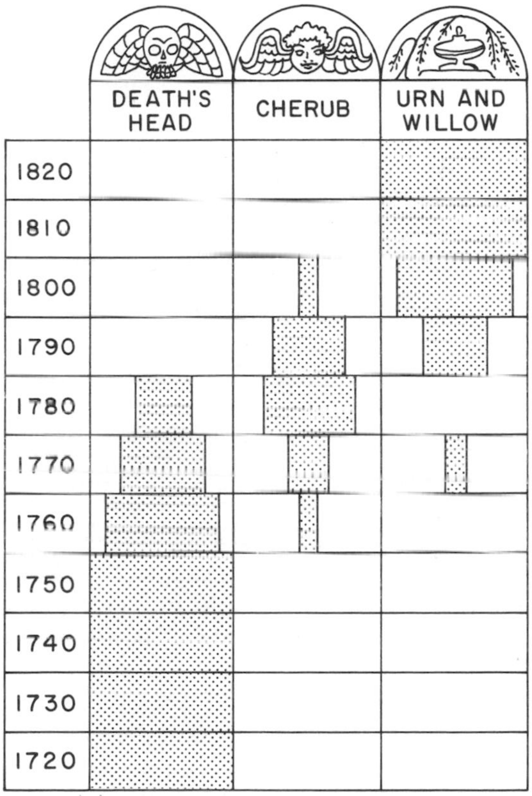

Redrawn by Lois A. Johnson from Natural History

FIG. 1. *Stylistic sequence from a cemetery in Stoneham, Massachusetts.*

cision, and with the addition of these, the full power of these artifacts as controls becomes apparent: probate research often tells the price of individual stones; status indication occurs frequently on the stones, as well as the age of each individual. Since death is related to religion, formal variations in the written material can be analyzed to see how they reflect religious variations. Epitaphs provide

404

a unique literary and psychological dimension. Spatial distributions can be measured against political divisions. In short, the full historical background of the seventeenth, eighteenth, and nineteenth centuries permits both primary and secondary control of the material, and with the resulting precision, explanations become quite reliable.

With such controls available to the archaeologist, the pattern of change in colonial gravestone design and style can be used with great effect to sharpen our understanding of cultural process in general.

To return to the battleship-shaped curves in this essay, what does this mean in terms of culture change? Why should death's heads be popular at all, and what cultural factors were responsible for their disappearance and the subsequent rise of the cherub design? The most obvious answer is found in the ecclesiastical history of New England. The period of decline of death's heads coincides with the decline of orthodox Puritanism. In the late seventeenth century, Puritanism was universal in the area, and so were death's head gravestones. The early part of the eighteenth century saw the beginnings of change in orthodoxy, culminating in the great awakenings of the mid-century. In his recent, excellent book on the symbolism of New England gravestones, *Graven Images,* Allan Ludwig points out that the "iconophobic" Puritans found the carving of gravestones a compromise. While the use of cherubs might have verged on heresy, since they are heavenly beings whose portrayal might lead to idolatry, the use of a more mortal and neutral symbol—a death's head—would have served as a graphic reminder of death and resurrection.

Given the more liberal views concerning symbolism and personal involvement preached by Jonathan Edwards and others later in the eighteenth century, the idolatrous and heretical aspects of cherubs would have been more fitting to express the sentiment of the period.

It is at this point that available literary controls become valuable. Each stone begins by describing the state of the deceased: "Here lies" or "Here lies buried" being typical early examples. Slowly these are replaced by "Here lies [buried] the body [corruptible, what was mortal] of." This slightly, but significantly, different statement might well reflect a more explicit tendency to stress that only a part of the deceased remains, while the soul, the incorruptible or immortal portion, has gone to its eternal reward. Cherubs reflect a stress on resurrection, while death's heads emphasize the mortality of man. The epitaphs that appear on the bottoms of many stones also add credence to this explanation of change in form over time. Early epitaphs, with death's head designs, stress either decay and life's brevity:

> My Youthful mates both small and great
> Come here and you may see
> An awful sight, which is a type of which
>   you soon must be

or a Calvinistic emphasis on hard work and exemplary behavior on the part of the predestined:

> He was a useful man in his generation, a
> lover of learning, a faithful servant of Harvard College above forty years.

On the other hand, epitaphs with cherub stones tend to stress resurrection and later heavenly reward:

> Here cease thy tears, suppress thy fruitless
>   mourn
> his soul—the immortal part—has upward
>   flown
> On wings he soars his rapid way
> To yon bright regions of eternal day.

The final change seen in gravestone style is the radical shift to the urn and willow design. It is usually accompanied by a change in stone shape; while earlier stones have a round-shouldered outline, the later stones have square shoulders. "Here lies the body of" is replaced by "In memory of," or "Sacred to the memory of," quite different from all earlier forms. The earlier stones are markers, designating the location of the deceased or at least a portion of him. In contrast, "In memory of" is simply a memorial statement, and stones of this later type could logically be erected elsewhere and still make sense. In fact, many of the late urn and willow stones are cenotaphs, erected to commemorate those actually buried elsewhere, as far away as Africa, Batavia, and in one case—in the Kingston, Massachusetts, cemetery—"drowned at sea, lat. 39 degrees N., long. 70 degrees W." The cultural changes that accompany the shift to urn and willow designs are seen in the rise of less emotional, more intellectual religions, such as Unitarianism and Methodism. Epitaphs change with design and in the early nineteenth century tend more to sentiment combined with eulogy.

This sequence of change did not occur in a vacuum, unrelated to any cultural change elsewhere; indeed, the sequence of three major types also takes place in England, the cultural parent of the Massachusetts colony, but about a half century earlier. Thus cherubs have become modal by the beginning of the Georgian period (1715), and urns and willows make their appearance, as a part of the neoclassical tradition, in the 1760s. In fact, the entire urn and willow pattern is a part of the larger Greek Revival, which might explain the squared shoulders on the stones—a severer classical outline.

Thus far we have been discussing formal change through time, and some of the fundamental causes. We have seen that New England is changing in harmony with England, with an expectable time interval separating the sequences. But we have not identified the relationship of all of this to archaeological method.

The battleship-shaped curve assumption is basic to many considerations of culture process in general and to such dating methods as seriation. Seriation is a method whereby archaeological sites are arranged in relative chronological order based on the popularity of the different types of artifacts found in them. The approach assumes that any cultural item, be it a style of pottery or a way of making an arrowhead, has a particular popularity period, and as it grows and wanes in popularity, its prevalence as time passes can be represented graphically by a single peaked curve. Small beginnings grow to a high frequency of occurrence, followed in turn by a gradual disappearance. If such an assumption is true, it follows that a series of sites can be arranged so that all artifact types within them form single peaked curves of popularity over time. Such an arrangement is chronological, and tells the archaeologist how his sites relate to one another in time.

By plotting style sequences in this manner in a number of cemeteries, we find that the assumption, not previously measured with such a degree of precision, is a sound one: styles do form single peaked popularity curves through time. By adding the control of the spatial to the form-time pattern explained above, we gain a number of understandings regarding diffusion—the spread of ideas through time and space and how this, in turn, affects internal change in style. In looking now at the three dimensions we will see that all of the secondary cultural controls become even more important.

The style sequence of death's head, cherub, and urn and willow design is to be found in almost every cemetery in eastern Massachusetts. However, when we inspect the time at which each change takes place, and the degree of overlap between styles from cemetery to cemetery, it becomes apparent that this sequence was occurring at a widely varying rate from place to place. The earliest occurrence of cherubs is in the Boston-Cambridge area, where they begin to appear as early as the end of the seventeenth century. Occasional early cherubs might be found in more distant rural cemeteries, but in every case we find them to have been carved in the Boston area and to be rare imports from there. The farther we move away from the Boston center, the later locally manufactured cherubs make their appearance in numbers. The rate at which the cherub style spread outward has even been approximately measured, and shown to be about a mile per year. It is not common in archaeology to make such precise measurements of diffusion rate – the usual measurements are cruder, such as hundreds of miles in millenniums.

We can view Boston and, more significantly, nearby Cambridge as the focus of emphasis of Puritan religion with its accompanying values, and inquire what factors might contribute to the initial appearance of cherubs and the change in religious values in this central area. We have noted that the change had already been accomplished in England by the early eighteenth century, so that when the first cherubs begin to appear in numbers in Cambridge, they were already the standard modal style in England. While cherubs occur in Boston, they never make a major impression, and as many death's heads as cherubs are replaced by the urn and willow influx.

On the other hand, in Cambridge cherubs make an early start and attain a respectable frequency by the late eighteenth century. Although they never attain a full 100 percent level there, as they do in most rural areas, they do at least enjoy a simple majority. When the cherub stones in Cambridge are inspected more closely, we find that roughly 70 percent of them mark the graves of high status individuals: college presidents, graduates of Harvard, governors and their families, high church officials, and in one case, even a "Gentleman from London." From what we know of innovation in culture, it is often the more cosmopolitan, urban stratum of society that brings in new ideas, to be followed later by the folk stratum. If this is true, then the differences between Boston and Cambridge indicate a more liberal element within the population of Cambridge, reflected in the greater frequency of cherub stones there. This is probably the case, with the influence of the Harvard intellectual community being reflected in the cemetery. It would appear that even in the early eighteenth century, the university was a place for innovation and liberal thinking. Cambridge intellectuals were more likely to be responsive to English styles, feel-

ings, and tastes, and this could well be what we are seeing in the high number of cherub stones marking high-status graves.

Introduced into Cambridge and Boston by a distinct social class, the cherub design slowly begins its diffusion into the surrounding countryside. Carvers in towns farther removed from Cambridge and Boston – as far as fourteen miles west in Concord – begin to change their gravestone styles away from the popular death's head as early as the 1730s, but fifty miles to the south, in Plymouth, styles do not change until the fifties and sixties and then in a somewhat different cultural context. We find, however, that the farther the cemetery is from Boston, and the later the cherubs begin to be locally manufactured, the more rapidly they reach a high level of popularity. The pattern is one of a long period of coexistence between cherubs and death's heads in the Boston center, and an increasingly more rapid eclipsing of death's heads by cherubs in direct proportion to distance, with a much shorter period of overlap. One explanation is that in towns farther removed from the diffusion center, enforcement of Puritan ethics and values would lessen, and resistance to change would not be so strong. Furthermore, revivalism and the modification of orthodox Puritanism was widespread from the late thirties through the sixties in rural New England, although this movement never penetrated Boston. Such activity certainly must have conditioned the rural populace for a change to new designs.

We have, then, a picture of the introduction of a change in the highly specific aspect of mortuary art, an aspect reflecting much of the culture producing it. We see the subsequent spread of this idea, through space and time, as a function of social class and religious values. Now we are in a position to examine internal change in form through time, while maintaining relatively tight control on the spatial dimension.

One significant result of the use of gravestone data with its accompanying controls is the insight it provides in matters of stylistic

FIG. 2. *Some gravestone locations and movements of carvers.*

evolution. The product of a single carver can be studied over a long period of time, and the change in his patterns considered as they reflect both ongoing culture change and his particular manner of handling design elements. The spatial axis extending outward from Boston shows not only systematic change in major style replacement rates but also a striking pattern of difference in style change. We find that in many cases, the farther removed we become from Boston, the more rapid and radical is change within a given single design. This has been observed in at least five separate cases, involving a number of the styles of more local distribution; we can inspect one

of these cases closely, and attempt to determine some of the processes and causes of stylistic evolution.

The design in question is found in Plymouth County, centering on the town of Plympton. Its development spans a period of some seventy years, and the changes effected from beginning to end are truly profound. Death's heads occur in rural Plymouth County, as they do elsewhere in the late seventeenth century. However, in the opening decade of the eighteenth century the carver(s) in Plympton made certain basic changes in the general death's head motif. The first step in this modification involved the reduction of the lower

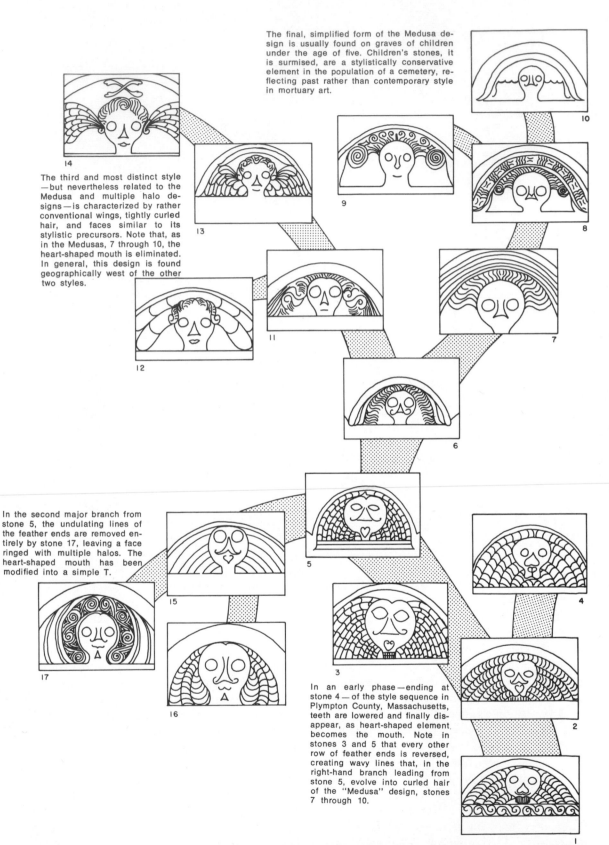

The final, simplified form of the Medusa design is usually found on graves of children under the age of five. Children's stones, it is surmised, are a stylistically conservative element in the population of a cemetery, reflecting past rather than contemporary style in mortuary art.

The third and most distinct style —but nevertheless related to the Medusa and multiple halo designs —is characterized by rather conventional wings, tightly curled hair, and faces similar to its stylistic precursors. Note that, as in the Medusas, 7 through 10, the heart-shaped mouth is eliminated. In general, this design is found geographically west of the other two styles.

In the second major branch from stone 5, the undulating lines of the feather ends are removed entirely by stone 17, leaving a face ringed with multiple halos. The heart-shaped mouth has been modified into a simple T.

In an early phase—ending at stone 4—of the style sequence in Plympton County, Massachusetts, teeth are lowered and finally disappear, as heart-shaped element becomes the mouth. Note in stones 3 and 5 that every other row of feather ends is reversed, creating wavy lines that, in the right-hand branch leading from stone 5, evolve into curled hair of the "Medusa" design, stones 7 through 10.

Redrawn with slight modifications by Lois A. Johnson from photographs in Natural History

FIG. 3. *Evolution of styles in a Plympton cemetery.*

portion of the face, and the addition of a heart-shaped element between nose and teeth. The resulting pattern was one with a heartlike mouth, with the teeth shrunken to a simple band along the bottom. The teeth soon disappear entirely, leaving the heart as the sole mouth element. This change is rapidly followed by a curious change in the feathering of the wings.

While early examples show all feather ends as regular scallops crossing the lines separating individual feathers, shortly after the first changes in the face were made, every other row of feather ends had their direction of curvature reversed. The resulting design produces the effect of undulating lines radiating from the head, almost suggesting hair, at right angles to curved lines that still mark the feather separation. These two changes, in face and wing form, occupy a period of 35 years from 1710 through 1745. During the later forties this development, which has so far been a single sequence, splits into two branches, each the result of further modification of wings. In the first case, the arcs marking feather separations are omitted, leaving only the undulating radial lines. Rapid change then takes place, and soon we are confronted with a face surmounted by wavy and, later, quite curly hair. The heart mouth has been omitted. We have dubbed this style "Medusa." In the second case, the separating lines are retained, and the undulating lines removed; the result in this case is a face with multiple halos. At times, space between these halos is filled with spiral elements, giving the appearance of hair, or the halos are omitted entirely. The heart-shaped mouth is retained in this case and modified into a T-shaped element.

Both of these styles enjoy great popularity in the fifties and sixties, and have slightly different spatial distributions, suggesting that they might be the work of two carvers, both modifying the earlier heart-mouthed design in different ways. Yet a third related design also appears in the forties, this time with tightly curled hair, conventional wings, and a face similar to the other two. Although this third design seems to be a more direct derivative of the earlier death's head motif, it is clearly inspired in part by the Medusa and multiple halo designs. This tight-haired style has a markedly different spatial distribution, occurring to the west of the other two, but overlapping them in a part of its range. Of the three, only the Medusa lasts into the seventies, and in doing so presents us with something of an enigma. The final form, clearly evolved from the earlier types, is quite simple. It has a specific association with small children, and has never been found marking the grave of an adult, and rarely of a child over age five.

The carver of the fully developed Medusa was probably Ebenezer Soule of Plympton; a definitive sample of his style is found in the Plympton cemetery. Normal Medusas, except for the late, simple ones marking children's graves, disappear abruptly in the late sixties. In 1769, and lasting until the eighties, stones identical to Soule's Medusas, including the simple, late ones, appear in granite around Hinsdale, New Hampshire. Fortunately, a local history has identified the carver of some of these stones as "Ebenezer Soule, late of Plympton." This alone is of great interest, but if Soule did move to Hinsdale in 1769, who carved the later children's stones in Plymouth County? As yet, no answer is known.

This development raises two interesting considerations. First, we see that a style, the Medusa, which had been used for the general populace, ends its existence restricted to small children. This pattern has been observed elsewhere, with children's burials being marked by designs that were somewhat more popular earlier in time. In other words, children are a stylistically conservative element in the population of a cemetery. While no clear answer can be given to this problem, it may well be that small children, not having developed a strong, personal impact on the society, would not be thought of in quite the same way as adults, and would have their graves marked with more conservative, less explicitly descriptive stones.

The second problem raised by the Medusas is their reappearance in Hinsdale. If, as archaeologists, we were confronted with the degree of style similarity seen between Hinsdale and Plympton in mortuary art, might we not infer a much greater influence than a single individual arriving in the community? After all, mortuary art would be about the only distinctively variable element in material culture over eighteenth-century New England, and such a close parallel could well be said to represent a migration from Plympton to Hinsdale. One man moved.

Placing this striking case of stylistic evolution in the broader context of culture change and style change in eastern Massachusetts, we find that it is paralleled by other internal modifications of death's head designs in other remote rural areas. The closer we move toward Boston, the less change takes place within the death's head design, and in Boston proper, death's heads from 1810 are not that different from those from 1710. Yet 1710 death's heads in Plympton and elsewhere had changed so radically by 1750 that it is doubtful that we could supply the derivation of one from the other in the absence of such an excellently dated set of intermediate forms. This difference in rate of change can be explained by referring back to the long, parallel courses of development of both death's head and cherub in the diffusion area's Boston center. However, culture change in the area of religion, marked by a shift of emphasis from mortality to immortality, probably generated a desire for less realistic and less grim designs on stones. Given this basic change in religious attitudes, what were the alternatives facing carvers in Boston as opposed to the Ebenezer Soules of rural New England? In Boston it was simply a matter of carving more cherub stones and fewer death's head stones; neither had to be altered to suit the new tastes. The choice between cherub and death's head in Boston has been seen as ultimately a social one, and if there was a folk culture component within Boston, there was nothing but folk culture in the more democratic, less-stratified

rural areas. With no one to introduce cherubs and to call for them with regularity in the country, carvers set to work modifying the only thing they had—the death's head. The more remote the community, the later the local cherubs appear, diffusing from Boston, and the more likely the tendency to rework the common folk symbol of skull and wings. Thus we get Medusas and haloed T-mouthed faces populating the cemeteries of Plymouth County until cherubs finally appear. Even then, the waning popularity of the death's head in this area might be more the result of Soule's exit than their unsatisfactory appearance compared to the new cherubs.

Only a few applications of gravestone design analysis have been detailed here. A three-year program is presently under way, through which we hope to pursue numerous other aspects of this fascinating study. There is a large and important demographic dimension to these data; since precise date of death is given, as well as age at death, patterns of mortality and life expectance through time and space can be detailed. The results of this work, in turn, will add a biological dimension of style to the cultural one described above. Studies of diffusion rate, and its relationship to dating by seriation will be continued. Relationships between political units—counties, townships, and colonies—and style spheres will be investigated to determine how such units affect the distribution of a carver's products. Finally, a happy byproduct will be the preservation on film of over 25,000 gravestones, a vital consideration in view of the slow but steady deterioration these informative artifacts are undergoing.

Aside from the value of this work to archaeology and anthropology in general, one final comment must be made. Compared to the usual field work experienced by the archaeologist, with all of its dust and heavy shoveling under a hot sun, this type of archaeology certainly is most attractive. All of the artifacts are on top of the ground, the sites are close to civilization, and almost all cemeteries have lovely, shady trees.

Bibliography/Index

Bibliography

Abel, Leland J.
1955 Pottery types of the Southwest. Ceramic Series, no. 3. Flagstaff: Museum of Northern Arizona.

Aberle, David F.
1960 The influence of linguistics on early culture and personality theory. *In* Essays in the science of culture: in honor of Leslie A. White. Gertrude Dole and Robert Carneiro, eds. New York: Thomas Y. Crowell.

Aberle, Kathleen Gough
1967 Anthropology and imperialism. Paper presented at the 1967 Southwestern Anthropological Association meetings. Reissued by the Radical Education Project, Ann Arbor.

Adams, Richard E. W.
1964 The ceramic sequence at Altar de Sacrificios and its implications. International Congress of Americanists, Mexico, D.F., 1962. Actas y Memorias 35(3):371–78.
1969 Maya archaeology 1958–1968, a review. Latin American Research Review 4(2):3–45.

Adams, Robert M.
1956 Some hypotheses on the development of early civilizations. American Antiquity 21:227–32.
1960a The evolutionary process in early civilizations. *In* The evolution of man: mind, culture, and society, Sol Tax, ed. Chicago: University of Chicago Press.
1960b The origin of cities. Scientific American 203(3):153–68.
1962 Agriculture and urban life in early southwestern Iran. Science 136:109–22.
1965 Land behind Baghdad: a history of settlement on the Diyala Plains. Chicago: University of Chicago Press.

1966 The evolution of urban society. Chicago: Aldine Publishing Company.
1968 Archeological research strategies: past and present. Science 160:1187–92.

Alcock, L.
1951 A technique for surface collecting. Antiquity 25:75–98.

Alexander, H. L., Jr.
1963 The Levi Site: a Paleo-Indian campsite in central Texas. American Antiquity 28:510–28.

Allee, W. C., et al.
1949 Principles of animal ecology. Philadelphia: W. B. Saunders.

Anderson, Edgar
1952 Plants, man, and life. Boston: Little, Brown.

Andrés, Friedrich
1938 Die Himmelsreise der caraibischen Medizinmänner, Zeitschrift für Ethnologie 70:331–42.

Andrews, E. W.
1965 Archaeology and prehistory in the northern Maya lowlands: an introduction. *In* Handbook of Middle American Indians, vol. 2: Archaeology of southern Mesoamerica, Gordon R. Willey, ed. Austin: University of Texas Press.

Antevs, Ernst
1962 Late quaternary climates in Arizona. American Antiquity 28:193–98.

Arkin, H., and Colton, Raymond
1957 Tables for statisticians. New York: Barnes and Noble, Inc.

Armillas, Pedro
1951a Tecnologia, formaciones socio-económicas y religion en Mesoamerica. *In* The civilizations of ancient America, Sol Tax, ed. Twenty-ninth International Congress of Americanists, Selected

Papers, vol. 1. Chicago: University of Chicago Press.

1951*b* Mesoamerican fortifications. Antiquity 25(98):77–86.

Ascher, R.
1959 A prehistoric population estimate using midden analysis and two population models. Southwestern Journal of Anthropology 15:168–78.

Ascher, R., and M.
1965 Recognizing the emergence of man. Science 147:243–50.

Baker, Frank C., et al.
1941 Contributions to the archaeology of the Illinois River Valley. Transactions of the American Philosophical Society, Vol. 32(1).

Bandelier, Adolph
1892 Final report of investigations among the Indians of the southwestern United States carried on mainly in the years from 1880 to 1885, Part 2. Papers of the Archaeological Institute of America, American Series, 4. Cambridge, Mass.: J. Wilson.

Barber, Bernard
1961 Resistance by scientists to scientific discovery. Science 134:596–602.

Barka, Norman F.
1965 Historic sites archaeology at Portland Point, New Brunswick, Canada 1631–c.1850 A.D. Ph.D. dissertation, Harvard University.

Barron, Frank
1969 Creative person and creative process. New York: Holt, Rinehart and Winston.

Barth, Fredrik
1956 Ecologic relationships of ethnic groups in Swat, North Pakistan. American Anthropologist 58:1079–89.

Bartholomew, George A. Jr., and Birdsell, J. B.
1953 Ecology and the protohominids. American Anthropologist 55:481–98.

Barton, George A.
1929 The royal inscriptions of Sumer and Akkad. New Haven: Yale University Press.

Bayard, Donn T.
1969 Science, theory, and reality in the "new archaeology." American Antiquity 34: 376–84.

Beaglehole, Ernest
1937 Notes on Hopi economic life. Yale University Publications in Anthropology, no. 15. New Haven: Yale University Press.

Beals, Ralph L., and Hoijer, Harry
1953 An introduction to anthropology. New York: Macmillan Co.

Bellah, Robert N.
1970 Beyond belief: essays on religion in a post-traditional world. New York: Harper & Row.

Benedict, Francis G.
1936 The physiology of the elephant. Washington, D.C., Carnegie Institution of Washington, Publication 474.

Benfer, Robert A.
1967 A design for the study of archeological characteristics. American Anthropologist 69:719–30.

Bennett, Hugh Hammond
1939 Soil conservation. New York: McGraw-Hill Book Company.

Bennett, John W.
1943 Recent developments in the functional interpretation of archaeological data. American Antiquity 9:208–19.

Bennett, Wendell C., ed.
1948 A reappraisal of Peruvian archaeology. Menasha, Society for American Archaeology, Memoir no. 4.

Bennyhoff, J. A.
1952 The Viru Valley sequence: a critical review. American Antiquity 17:231–49.

Berger, R.; Graham, J. A.; and Heizer, R. F.
1967 A reconstruction of the age of the La Venta Site. Berkeley, Contributions of the University of California Archaeological Research Facility, no. 3.

Bernal, Ignacio
1969 The Olmec world. Berkeley: University of California Press.

Bertalanffy, Ludwig von
1950 An outline of general systems theory. British Journal of the Philosophy of Science 1:134–65.

Binford, Lewis R.
1962 Archaeology as anthropology. American Antiquity 28:217–25.
1963 "Red ocher" caches from the Michigan area: a possible case of cultural drift. Southwestern Journal of Anthropology 19:89–108.
1964a Archaeological and ethnohistorical investigation of cultural diversity and progressive development among aboriginal cultures of coastal Virginia and North Carolina. Ph.D. dissertation, University of Michigan.
1964b A consideration of archaeological research design. American Antiquity 29:425–41.
1965 Archaeological systematics and the study of culture process. American Antiquity 31:203–10.
1967 Smudge pits and hide smoking: the use of analogy in archaeological reasoning. American Antiquity 32:1–12.
1968a Archeological perspectives. *In* New perspectives in archeology, Sally R. and Lewis R. Binford, eds. Chicago: Aldine Publishing Company.
1968b An ethnohistory of the Nottoway, McHerrin and Weanock Indians of southeastern Virginia. Ethnohistory 14(3–4):103–218.
1968c Post-Pleistocene adaptations. *In* New perspectives in archeology, Sally R. and Lewis R. Binford, eds. Chicago: Aldine Publishing Company.
1968d Some comments on historical versus processual archaeology. Southwestern Journal of Anthropology 24:267–75.
1968e Methodological considerations of the archeological use of ethnographic data. *In* Man the hunter, R. B. Lee and I. DeVore, eds. Chicago: Aldine Publishing Company.

Binford, Lewis R. and Sally R.
1966a The predatory revolution: a consideration of the evidence for a new subsistence level. American Anthropologist 68:508–12.
1966b A preliminary analysis of functional variability in the Mousterian of the Levallois Facies. In Recent studies in paleoanthropology, J. D. Clark and F. C. Howell, eds. American Anthropologist 68(2:2):238–95.

Binford, Sally R. and Lewis R., eds.
1968 New perspectives in archeology. Chicago: Aldine Publishing Company.

Birdsell, Joseph B.
1953 Some environmental and cultural factors influencing the structuring of Australian aboriginal populations. American Naturalist 87(Supplement):171–207.
1957 Some population problems involving Pleistocene man. Cold Spring Harbor Symposia on Quantitative Biology 22:47–69.
1958 On population structure in generalized hunting and collecting populations. Evolution 12:189–205.
1968 Some predictions for the Pleistocene based upon equilibrium systems among recent hunters. *In* Man the hunter, Richard B. Lee and Irven DeVore, eds. Chicago: Aldine Publishing Company.

Black, M. J.
1963 The distribution and archaeological significance of the marsh elder *Iva annua* L. Ann Arbor, Papers of the Michigan Academy of Science, Arts and Letters 48:541–47.

Blake, S. F.
1939 A new variety of *Iva ciliata* from Indian Rock Shelters in the south-central United States. Rhodora 41:81–86.

Bloch, M.
1931 Les caractères originaux de l'histoire rurale francaise. Oslo.

Bloch, M. R.
1963 The social influence of salt. Scientific American 209(1):88–96.

Blom, Frans
1932 Commerce, trade and monetary units of the Maya. Middle American Research Series, Publication no. 4. New Orleans: Tulane University.

Boas, Franz, ed.
1938 General anthropology. New York: D. C. Heath.

Bödiger, Ute
1965 Die religion der Tukan. Kölner ethnologische Mitteilungen 3. Cologne.

416

de Borhegyi, S. F.
1965 Archaeological synthesis of the Guatemalan highlands. *In* Handbook of Middle American Indians, vol. 2: Archaeology of southern Mesoamerica, Gordon R. Willey, ed. Austin: University of Texas Press.

Boring, Edwin G.
1961 The beginning and growth of measurement in psychology. Isis 52(168): 238–57.

Bose, Saradindu
1964 Economy of the Onge of Little Andaman. Man in India 44:298–310.

Boughey, Arthur S.
1968 Ecology of populations. London: Macmillan & Co.

Boulding, Kenneth
1956a General systems theory—the skeleton of science. General Systems 1:11–17.
1956b Toward a general theory of growth. General Systems 1:66–75.

Braidwood, Robert J.
1951a Prehistoric men. 2d ed. Popular Series, Anthropology no. 37. Chicago: Chicago Natural History Museum.
1951b From cave to village in prehistoric Iraq. Bulletin of the American Schools of Oriental Research 124:12–18.
1952a From cave to village. Scientific American 187(4):62–66.
1952b The Near East and the foundations for civilization. Condon Lectures. Eugène: University of Oregon Press.
1959 Archaeology and the evolutionary theory. *In* Evolution and anthropology: a centennial appraisal, Betty J. Meggers, ed. Washington, D.C.: Anthropological Society of Washington.
1960a The agricultural revolution. Scientific American 203(4):130–41.
1960b Levels in prehistory: a model for the consideration of the evidence. *In* Evolution after Darwin, Vol. 2: The evolution of man, Sol Tax, ed. Chicago: University of Chicago Press.
1963 Prehistoric men. 6th ed. Popular Series, Anthropology no. 37. Chicago: Chicago Natural History Museum.

Braidwood, Robert J. and Linda
1950 Jarmo: a village of early farmers in Iraq. Antiquity 24:189–95.

Braidwood, Robert J., and Howe, Bruce
1960 Prehistoric investigations in Iraqi Kurdistan. Oriental Institute Studies in Ancient Oriental Civilization, no. 31. Chicago: University of Chicago Press.
1962 Southwestern Asia beyond the lands of the Mediterranean littoral. *In* Courses toward urban life, R. J. Braidwood and G. R. Willey, eds. Chicago: Aldine Publishing Company.

Braidwood, Robert J., and Reed, Charles A.
1957 The achievement and early consequences of food production. Cold Spring Harbor Symposia on Quantitative Biology 22:19–31.

Braidwood, Robert J., and Willey, Gordon
1962 Conclusions and afterthoughts. *In* Courses toward urban life, R. J. Braidwood and G. R. Willey, eds. Chicago: Aldine Publishing Company.

Braidwood, Robert J., and Willey, Gordon R., eds.
1962 Courses toward urban life. Chicago: Aldine Publishing Company.

Braithwaite, R. B.
1960 Scientific explanation. New York: Harper and Row.

Bram, Joseph
1941 An analysis of Inca militarism. Monographs of the American Ethnological Society, no. 4. New York: J. J. Augustin.

Breuil, H.
1921 Observations suivantes: M. Cartilhac, La question de l'hiatus entre le Paléolithique et le Néolithique. L'Anthropologie 31:349–55.
1946 The discovery of the antiquity of man. Journal of the Royal Anthropological Institute of Great Britain and Ireland 75:21–31.

Brew, John Otis
1946 Archaeology of Alkali Ridge, southeastern Utah, with a review of the prehistory of the Mesa Verde Division of the San Juan and some observations on archaeological systematics. Papers

of the Peabody Museum of American Archaeology and Ethnology, vol. 21. Cambridge: Harvard University.

Broholm, H. C., and Hald, M.
1935 Danske Bronzealders Dragter. Nordiske Fortidsminder 2(5/6). Copenhagen.

Brothwell, D., and Higgs, E., eds.
1963 Science in archaeology. London: Thames and Hudson.

Brown, John Allen
1888 On some small highly specialized forms of stone implements found in Asia, North Africa, and Europe. Journal of the Royal Anthropological Institute of Great Britain and Ireland 18:134–39.
1892 On the continuity of the Palaeolithic and Neolithic periods. Journal of the Royal Anthropological Institute of Great Britain and Ireland 22:66–98.

Brown, James Allison
1965 The prairie peninsula: an interaction area in the eastern United States. Ph.D. dissertation, microfilm, University of Chicago Library.

Brown, J. A., and Freeman, J. L. G.
1964 A UNIVAC analysis of sherd frequencies from the Carter Ranch Pueblo, eastern Arizona; with comments by Paul S. Martin. American Antiquity 30:162–67.

Bryan, Kirk
1925 Date of channel trenching (arroyo cutting) in the arid Southwest. Science 62:338–44.
1965 Paleoamerican prehistory. Pocatello, Occasional Papers of the Idaho State University Museum, no. 16.

Buckley, Walter
1967 Sociology and modern systems theory. Englewood Cliffs: Prentice-Hall.

Buckley, Walter, ed.
1968 Modern systems research for the behavioral scientist. Chicago: Aldine Publishing Company.

Buettner-Janusch, John
1957 Boas and Mason: particularism versus generalization. American Anthropologist 59:318–24.

Bullard, William R., Jr.
1960 Maya settlement pattern in the northeastern Petén, Guatemala. American Antiquity 25:355–72.
1970 The status of postclassic archaeology in Petén, Guatemala. Paper presented at the Society for American Archaeology meeting, May 1970, Mexico City.

Bunzel, Ruth
1932 Introduction to Zuni ceremonialism. *In* Forty-seventh Annual Report of the Bureau of American Ethnology. Washington, D.C.
1952 Chichicastenango: a Guatemalan village. Monographs of the American Ethnological Society, no. 22. New York: J. J. Augustin.

Burkitt, M. C.
1925 The Transition between Palaeolithic and Neolithic times, i.e. the Mesolithic period. Proceedings of the Prehistory Society of East Anglia 5:16–33.

Buttler, W., and Haberey, W., eds.
1936 Die bandkeramische Ansiedlung bei Köln-Lindenthal. Leipzig.

Caldwell, Joseph R.
1958 Trend and tradition in the prehistory of the eastern United States. Menasha, Memoirs of the American Anthropological Association, no. 88.
1962 Interaction spheres in prehistory. Paper presented at the Annual Meeting of the American Association for the Advancement of Science, Philadelphia.

Calella, Plácido de
1940–41 Apuntes sobre los Indios Sionas del Putumayo. Anthropos 35/36:737–50.

Callen, Eric O.
1965 Food habits of some pre-Columbian Mexican Indians. Economic Botany 19:335–43.

Calnek, Edward E.
1962 Highland Chiapas before the Spanish conquest. Ph.D. dissertation, University of Chicago.

Camden, William
1695 Britannia. London.

deCandolle, Alphonse L. P. P.
1959 Origin of cultivated plants. Reprint of the 2d ed., 1886. New York: Hafner.

Carneiro, Robert L.

1957 Subsistence and social structure: an ecological study of the Kuikuru Indians. Ph.D. dissertation, University of Michigan, mimeographed.

1958 Agriculture and the beginning of civilization. Berlin, Ethnographisch-Archäologische Forschungen, no. 4.

1968 Slash-and-burn cultivation among the Kuikuru and its implications for cultural development in the Amazon Basin. *In* Man in adaptation: The Cultural Present, Y. Cohen, ed. Chicago: Aldine Publishing Company.

Carrasco, Pedro

1961 The civil-religious hierarchy in Mesoamerican communities: pre-Spanish background and colonial development. American Anthropologist 63: 483–97.

Carrington, Richard

1958 Elephants: a short history of their natural history, evolution and influence on mankind. London: Chatto & Windus.

Carr-Saunders, Alexander M.

1922 The population problem: a study in human evolution. Oxford: Clarendon Press.

Chamber's Technical Dictionary

1962 C. F. Tweney and L. E. Hughes, eds., 3d rev. ed. New York: Macmillan Co.

Chang, Kwang-chih

1967a Rethinking archaeology. New York: Random House.

1967b Major aspects of the interrelationship of archaeology and ethnology. Current Anthropology 8:227–34.

1968 Toward a science of prehistoric society. *In* Settlement archaeology, K. Chang, ed. Palo Alto: National Press Books.

Chapman, Anne C.

1957 Port of trade Enclaves in Aztec and Maya civilization. *In* Trade and market in the early empires, Karl Polanyi, Conrad M. Arensberg and Harry W. Pearson, eds. Glencoe: Free Press.

Childe, V. Gordon

1925 The dawn of European civilization. New York: Alfred A. Knopf.

1929 The Danube in prehistory. London: Oxford University Press.

1931 The forest cultures of northern Europe: a study in evolution and diffusion. Journal of the Royal Anthropological Institute of Great Britain and Ireland 61:325–48.

1937 Adaptation to the postglacial forest on the north Eurasiatic plain. *In* Early man, G. G. McCurdy, ed. Philadelphia: J. B. Lippincott.

1942 What happened in history. Harmondsworth: Penguin Books.

1944a Archaeological ages as technological stages. Journal of the Royal Anthropological Institute of Great Britain and Ireland 74:1–19.

1944b Progress and archaeology. London: Watts.

1951a Man makes himself. New York: New American Library.

1951b Social evolution. New York: Henry Schuman.

1952 New light on the most ancient East. 4th ed. London: Routledge and Kegan Paul.

1956 The new Stone Age. *In* Man, culture, and society, Harry L. Shapiro, ed. New York: Oxford University Press.

Cieza de León, Pedro

[1550] 1959 The Incas of Pedro de Cieza de León, translated by Harriet de Onis and edited by Victor W. von Hagen. Norman: University of Oklahoma Press.

Clark, J. Desmond

1951 Bushman hunters of the Barotse forests. Northern Rhodesia Journal 1(3):56–65.

1962 Africa south of the Sahara. *In* Courses toward urban life, R. J. Braidwood and G. R. Willey, eds. Chicago: Aldine Publishing Company.

Clark, John Grahame Douglas

1932 The Mesolithic age in Britain. Cambridge: The University Press.

1936 The Mesolithic settlement of northern Europe: a study of the food-gathering peoples of northern Europe during the early post-glacial period. London: Cambridge University Press.

1945*a* Farmers and forests in Neolithic Europe. Antiquity 19:57–71.

1945*b* Man and nature in prehistory, with special reference to Neolithic settlement in northern Europe. Institute of Archaeology, Occasional Paper no. 6: 20–28. London: University of London.

1947*a* Forest clearance and prehistoric farming. Economic History Review 17:45–51.

1947*b* Sheep and swine in the husbandry of prehistoric Europe. Antiquity 21:122–36.

1948*a* Fowling in prehistoric Europe. Antiquity 22:116–30.

1948*b* The development of fishing in prehistoric Europe. Antiquaries Journal 28: 45–85.

1952*a* Archeological theories and interpretation: old world. *In* Anthropology today, A. L. Kroeber, ed. Chicago: University of Chicago Press.

1952*b* Prehistoric Europe: the economic basis. London: Methuen.

1952*c* Die mittlere Steinzeit. *In* Historia Mundi, Fritz Kern, ed. Vol. 1, pp. 318–45. Munich.

1954 Excavations at Star Carr; an early Mesolithic site at Seamer near Scarborough, Yorkshire, England. London: Cambridge University Press (reprinted 1971).

1963 A survey of the Mesolithic phase in the prehistory of Europe and southwest Asia. Atti de 6 Congresso Internazionale delle Scienze Preisstoriche e Protostoriche 1:97–111. Rome: Collegio Romano.

1969 World prehistory: a new outline. 2d ed. Cambridge: Cambridge University Press.

1971 Star Carr: a case study in bioarchaeology. Reading, Mass.: Addison-Wesley.

Clarke, David L.
1968 Analytical archaeology. London: Methuen.

Cleland, Charles E., and Fitting, James
1968 The crisis of identity: theory in historic sites archaeology. Papers of the Conference on Historic Sites Archaeology, 1967, Stanley South, ed. 2(2):124–38.

Cobo, Bernabé
[1653] 1956 Historia del Nuevo Mundo. Biblioteca de Autores Españoles, vols. 91–92. Madrid.

Cochran, William G.
1963 Sampling techniques. New York: John Wiley.

Coe, Michael D.
1961*a* Social typology and the tropical forest civilizations. Comparative Studies in Society and History 4:65–85.

1961*b* La Victoria: an early site on the Pacific coast of Guatemala. Papers of the Peabody Museum of Archaeology and Ethnology, Vol. 53. Cambridge: Harvard University.

1962 Mexico. New York: Frederick A. Praeger.

1965*a* The jaguar's children: pre-classic central Mexico. New York: Museum of Primitive Art.

1965*b* The Olmec style and its distributions. *In* Handbook of Middle American Indians, vol. 3: Archaeology of Southern Mesoamerica, Gordon R. Willey, ed. Austin: University of Texas Press.

1965*c* Archaeological synthesis of southern Veracruz and Tabasco. *In* Handbook of Middle American Indians, vol. 3: Archaeology of Southern Mesoamerica, Gordon R. Willey, ed. Austin: University of Texas Press.

1968*a* America's first civilization. New York: American Heritage Publishing Co.

1968*b* San Lorenzo and the Olmec civilization. *In* Dunbarton Oaks Conference on the Olmec, Elizabeth P. Benson, ed. Washington, D.C., Dunbarton Oaks Research Library and Collection.

1969 Photogrammetry and the ecology of Olmec civilization. Paper presented at the Working Conference on Aerial Photography and Anthropology, Cambridge, Mass.

Coe, Michael D., and Cobean, Robert
1970 Obsidian trading at San Lorenzo, Tenochtitlan. Paper presented at the Society for American Archaeology meeting, Mexico City.

Coe, Michael D., and Flannery, Kent V.
1964 Microenvironments and Mesoamerican prehistory. Science 143:650–54.

1967   Early cultures and human ecology in south coastal Guatemala. Smithsonian Contributions to Anthropology, vol. 3. Washington, D.C.: Smithsonian Press.

Coe, Michael D.; Diehl, R. A.; and Stuiver, M.
1967   Olmec civilization, Veracruz, Mexico: dating of the San Lorenzo phase. Science 155:1399–1401.

Coe, William R.
1959   Piedras Negras archaeology: artifacts, caches, and burials. Museum Monographs. University Museum. Philadelphia: University of Pennsylvania.
1965   Tikal, Guatemala, and the emergent Maya Civilization. Science 147:1401–19.

Cole, Fay-Cooper
1951   Kincaid, a prehistoric Illinois metropolis. Chicago: University of Chicago Press.

Colton, Harold S.
1955   Pottery types of the Southwest. Ceramic Series, no. 3. Flagstaff: Museum of Northern Arizona.

Conrad, G. W.
1970   Toward a systematic view of Mesoamerican prehistory: inter-site sociopolitical organization. Ph.D. dissertation, Harvard University.

Cook, S. F., and Heizer, R. F.
1951   The physical analysis of nine Indian mounds of the lower Sacramento Valley. Berkeley, University of California Publications in American Archaeology and Ethnology 40:281–312.
1962   Chemical analysis of the Hotchkiss Site (CCo–138). University of California Archaeological Survey, Reports no. 57(1):1–24.
1965   The quantitative approach to the relation between population and settlement size. University of California Archaeological Survey, Reports no. 64.

Cook, S. F., and Treganza, A. E.
1947   The quantitative investigation of aboriginal sites: comparative physical and chemical analysis of two California Indian mounds. American Antiquity 13:135–41.
1950   The quantitative investigation of Indian mounds. Berkeley, University of California Publications in American Archaeology and Ethnology 40:223–62.

Coon, Carleton S.
1951   Cave explorations in Iran, 1949. Museum Monographs. University Museum. Philadelphia: University of Pennsylvania.

Cooper, John M.
1949   Stimulants and narcotics. *In* Handbook of South American Indians. Washington, D.C., Bulletin of the Bureau of American Ethnology, no. 143(5).

Cortes, Hernando
1908   Letters: the five letters of relation to the emperor Charles V, Francis A. MacNutt, trans. and ed. 2 vols. New York: G. P. Putnam.

Coutil, L.
1912   Tardenoisien, Capsien, Getulien, Ibero-Maurusien Intergetulo-Néolithique, Tellien Loubirien, Geneyenien. Congrès International d'Anthropologie et d'Archéologie Préhistorique, 14th Session 1:301–36. Geneva.

Covarrubias, Miguel
1946   Mexico South; the isthmus of Tehuantepec. New York: Alfred A. Knopf.
1957   Indian art of Mexico and Central America. New York: Alfred A. Knopf.

Cowgill, George L.
1964   The selection of samples from large sherd collections. American Antiquity 29:467–73.
1968   Archaeological applications of factor, cluster and proximity analysis. American Antiquity 33:367–75.

Crabtree, D., and Butler, B. R.
1964   Notes on experiments in flint knapping, 1: heat treatment of silica minerals. Tebiwa 7:1–6. Pocatello: Idaho State University Museum.

Cressey, George B.
1960   Crossroads: land and life in southwest Asia. Philadelphia: J. B. Lippincott.

Cronin, Constance
1962   An analysis of pottery design elements indicating possible relationships between three decorated types. *In* Chapters in the prehistory of eastern Arizona 1, by Paul S. Martin and

others. Fieldiana: Anthropology, vol. 53. Chicago: Chicago Natural History Museum.

Culbert, T. P.
1970 Socio-cultural integration and the classic Maya. Paper presented at the Society for American Archaeology meetings, Mexico City.

Cumont, M.
1907 Quelques mots au sujet de Tardenoisien et de la transition du Paléolithique au Néolithique. Sociéte Royale Belge d'Anthropologie et de Préhistoire, Bulletin 26:ccv–ccviii.

Cushing, Frank Hamilton
1894 Primitive copper working: an experimental study. American Anthropologist 7:93–117.
1920 Zuni breadstuff. Indian Notes and Monographs, vol. 8. New York, Museum of the American Indian, Heye Foundation.

Daly, John W., and Myers, Charles W.
1967 Toxicity of Panamanian poison frogs (*Dendrobates*): some biological and chemical aspects. Science 156:970–73.

Damas, David
1968 The diversity of Eskimo societies. *In* Man the hunter, R. B. Lee and I. DeVore, eds. Chicago: Aldine Publishing Company.

Daniel, Glyn E.
1943 The three ages; an essay on archaeological method. Cambridge: Cambridge University Press.
1950 A hundred years of archaeology. London: Duckworth.
1962 The idea of prehistory. Baltimore: Penguin Books.
1967 The origins and growth of archaeology. Harmondsworth: Pelican Books.

Darwin, Charles R.
1875 The variation of animals and plants under domestication, vol. 1, 2d ed. London: Murray and Sons.

Dávalos Hurtado, Eusebio
1951 Una interpretación de los Danzantes de Monte Albán. *In* Homenaje al Doctor Alfonso Caso. Mexico: Instituto Nacional de Antropología e Historia.

Davis, D. R.
1966 Recent plant invasions in the arid and semi-arid Southwest of the United States. Annals of the Association of American Geographers 56:408–23.

Dawkins, William Boyd
1894 On the relation of the Palaeolithic to the Neolithic period. Journal of the Royal Anthropological Institute of Great Britain and Ireland 23:242–54.

Deetz, James D. F.
1960 An archaeological approach to kinship change in eighteenth century Arikara culture. Ph.D. dissertation, Harvard University.
1965 The dynamics of stylistic change in Arikara ceramics. Illinois Studies in Anthropology, no. 4. Urbana: University of Illinois Press.
1967 Invitation to archaeology. Garden City: Natural History Press.
1968a The inference of residence and descent rules from archeological data. *In* New perspectives in archeology, Sally R. and Lewis R. Binford, eds. Chicago: Aldine Publishing Company.
1968b Late man in North America: archeology of European Americans. *In* Anthropological archeology in the Americas, Betty J. Meggers, ed. Washington, D.C.: Anthropological Society of Washington.

Deevey, Edward S., Jr.
1960 The human population. Scientific American 203(1):194–204.

Delougaz, Pinhas
1940 The temple oval at Khafājah. Oriental Institute Publications, vol. 53. Chicago: University of Chicago Press.

Delougaz, Pinhas, and Lloyd, Seton
1942 Pre-Sargonid temples in the Diyala region. Oriental Institute Publications, vol. 58. Chicago: University of Chicago Press.

Deming, William Edwards
1950 Some theory of sampling. New York: John Wiley.

Dethlefsen, Edwin, and Deetz, James
1966 Deaths heads, cherubs and willow trees: experimental archaeology in colonial

cemeteries. American Antiquity 31: 502–10.

Digby, Adrian
1949 Technique and the time factor in relation to economic organization. Man 49:16–18.
1962 Time the catalyst: or why we should study the material culture of primitive peoples. Advancement of Science 19(80):349–57.

DiPeso, C. C.
1953 Clovis fluted points from southeastern Arizona. American Antiquity 19:82–85.

Direccion General de Cartografia
1964 Atlas Preliminar de Guatemala. Segunda Edition.

Dittert, Alfred E. Jr.; Hester, James J.; and Eddy, Frank W.
1961 An archaeological survey of the Navajo reservoir district, northwestern New Mexico. Santa Fe, Monographs of the School of American Research and Museum of New Mexico, no. 23.

Dixon, Keith A.
1966 Obsidian dates from Temesco, Valley of Mexico. American Antiquity 31:640–43.

Dobrizhoffer, Martin
1822 An Account of the Abipones, an equestrian people of Paraguay. 3 vols. London.

Dockstader, Frederick J.
1967 Indian art of South America. Greenwich, Conn.: New York Graphic Society.

Dollar, Clyde D.
1968 Some thoughts on theory and method in historical archaeology. Papers of the Conference on Historic Sites Archaeology, 1967, Stanley South, ed. 2(2): 3–34.

Douglass, A. E.
1929 The secret of the Southwest solved by talkative tree-rings. National Geographic Magazine 56:736–70.

Driver, Harold E., and Kroeber, A. L.
1932 Quantitative expressions of cultural relationships. *In* University of California Publications in American Archaeology and Ethnology, vol. 31. Berkeley.

Drucker, Philip
1943a Ceramic stratigraphy at Cerro de las Mesas, Veracruz, Mexico. Washington, D.C., Bulletin of the Bureau of American Ethnology, no. 141.
1943b Ceramic sequences at Tres Zapotes, Veracruz, Mexico. Washington, D.C., Bulletin of the Bureau of American Ethnology, no. 140.
1952 La Venta, Tabasco: a study of Olmec ceramics and art. Washington, D.C., Bulletin of the Bureau of American Ethnology, no. 153.

Duby, G., and Blom, F.
1969 The Lacandon. *In* Handbook of Middle American Indians, vol. 7: Ethnology, Evon. Z. Vogt, ed. Austin: University of Texas Press.

Duggan-Cronin, Alfred M.
1942 The Bushman tribes of southern Africa. Kimberley: Alexander McGregor Memorial Museum.

Dumond, D. E.
1965 Population growth and cultural change. Southwestern Journal of Anthropology 21:302–24.

Duncan, O. T.; Cuzzort, Ray; and Duncan, Beverly
1961 Statistical geography. Glencoe: Free Press.

Durkheim, Emile
1897–98 Morphologie sociale. L'année sociologique 2:520–21.

Dyson, R. H., Jr.
1953 Archaeology and the domestication of animals in the Old World. American Anthropologist 55:661–73.

Eddy, Frank W.
1966 Prehistory in the Navajo reservoir district, northwestern New Mexico. 2 vols. Santa Fe, Museum of New Mexico Papers in Anthropology, no. 15.

Eddy, Frank W., and Dickey, Beth L.
1961 Excavations of Los Pinos phase sites in the Navajo reservoir district. Santa Fe, Museum of New Mexico Papers in Anthropology, no. 4.

Edgington, Eugene S.
1969 Statistical inference: the distribution-

free approach. New York: McGraw-Hill Book Company.

Eggan, Fred
1950 Social organization of the western Pueblos. Chicago: University of Chicago Press.
1952 The ethnological cultures and their archaeological backgrounds. *In* Archaeology of eastern United States, James B. Griffin, ed. Chicago: University of Chicago Press.

Ehrenreich, Paul M.
1891 Beiträge zur Völkerkunde Brasiliens. Veröffentlichungen aus dem Königlichen Berlin, Museum für Völkerkunde 2:1–80.
1905 Die Mythen und Legenden der südamerikanischen Urvölker und ihre Beziehungen zu denen Nordamerikas und der Alten Welt. Berlin.

Eliade, Mircea
1964 Shamanism: archaic techniques of ecstasy. Bollingen Series, no. 86. New York: Pantheon Books.

Emerson, E. F.
1932 The tension zone between the grama grass and pinon juniper association in northeastern New Mexico. Ecology 13:347–58.

Erasmus, Charles J.
1968 Thoughts on upward collapse: an essay on explanations in anthropology. Southwestern Journal of Anthropology 24:170–94.

Faegri, K.
1943 Studies on the Pleistocene of western Norway, 3: Bømlo. Naturvitensk r. Nr. 8. Bergens Mus. Årbok.

Falkenstein, A.
1954 La Cité-Temple Sumérienne. Journal of World History 1:784–814.

Figgins, J. D.
1931 An additional discovery of a "Folsom" artifact and fossil remains. Denver, Proceedings of the Colorado Museum of Natural History 10(4):23–24.
1933 A further contribution to the antiquity of man in America. Denver, Proceedings of the Colorado Museum of Natural History, vol. 12(2).

Findley, J. S.
1964 Paleoecological reconstruction: vertebrate limitations. *In* The reconstruction of past environments. J. J. Hester and James Schoenwetter, eds. Taos, Fort Burgwin Research Center, Publication no. 3.

Firbas, F.
1949 Spät- und nacheiszeitliche Waldgeschichte der Alpen. Jena.

Fish, Carl Russell
1910 The relation of archaeology and history. Wisconsin Archaeologist 9(4):93–100.

Flannery, Kent V.
1962 Early village farming in southwestern Asia. *In* Proceedings of the 1961 annual spring meeting of the American Ethnological Society, V. E. Garfield, ed. Seattle: University of Washington Press.
1966 The postglacial "readaptation" as viewed from Mesoamerica. American Antiquity 31:800–805.
1967 Review of "An introduction to American archaeology, vol. 1: North and Middle America," by Gordon R. Willey. Scientific American 217(2):119–22.
1968a Archeological systems theory and early Mesoamerica. *In* Anthropological archeology in the Americas, Betty J. Meggers, ed. Washington, D.C.: Anthropological Society of Washington.
1968b The Olmec and the Valley of Oaxaca: a model for inter-regional interaction in formative times. *In* Dumbarton Oaks Conference on the Olmec, Elizabeth P. Benson, ed. Washington, D.C., Dumbarton Oaks Research Library and Collection.
1969 Origins and ecological effects of early domestication in Iran and the Near East. *In* The domestication and exploitation of plants and animals, P. J. Ucko and G. W. Dimbleby, eds. Chicago: Aldine Publishing Company.
n.d. Vertebrate fauna and hunting patterns. *In* Prehistory of the Tehuacán Valley, vol. 1: environment and resources. Andover, Mass.: R. S. Peabody Foundation. (Published 1968)

Flannery, Kent V., and Coe, Michael D.
1968 Social and economic systems in formative

Mesoamerica. *In* New perspectives in archeology, Sally R. and Lewis R. Binford, eds. Chicago: Aldine Publishing Company.

Flannery, Kent V., et al.
1967 Farming systems and political growth in ancient Oaxaca, Mexico. Science 158:445–54.

Foley, Vincent P.
1968 Some thoughts on theory and method in historical archaeology: a critique. Papers of the Conference on Historic Sites Archaeology, 1967, Stanley South, ed. 2(2):142–57.

Fontana, Bernard L.
1965 On the meaning of historic sites archaeology. American Antiquity 31:61–65.
1968 Bottles, buckets, and horseshoes: the unrespectable in American archaeology. Keystone Folklore Quarterly 1968 (Fall):171–84.

Fontana, Bernard L., et al.
1962 Johnny Ward's Ranch: a study in historic archaeology. Kiva 28(1–2):1–115.

Ford, James A.
1951 Greenhouse: a Troyville-Coles Creek period site in Avoyelles Parish, Louisiana. New York, Anthropological Papers of the American Museum of Natural History 44(1).
1952 Measurements of some prehistoric design developments in the southeastern States. New York, Anthropological Papers of the American Museum of Natural History 44:313–84.
1954 The type concept revisited. American Anthropologist 56:42–57.
1969 A comparison of formative cultures in the Americas: diffusion or the psychic unity of man. Smithsonian Contributions to Anthropology, vol. 11. Washington, D.C.: Smithsonian Institution Press.

Ford, James A., and Willey, Gordon R.
1949 Surface survey of the Virú Valley, Peru. New York, Anthropological Papers of the American Museum of Natural History 43(1).

Ford, Richard I.
1968 Jemez Cave and its place in an early horticultural settlement pattern. Paper presented at the Thirty-third Annual Meeting of the Society for American Archaeology, Santa Fe.

Forde, C. Daryll
1931 Hopi agriculture and land ownership. Journal of the Royal Anthropological Institute of Great Britain and Ireland 61:357–405.
1949 Habitat, economy and society: a geographical introduction to ethnology. London: Methuen.

Foster, George M.
1944 Nagualism in Mexico and Guatemala. Acta Americana 2:85–103.
1960 Culture and conquest. Viking Fund Publications in Anthropology, no. 27. Chicago: Wenner-Gren Foundation.

Fowler, Melvin L.
1955 Ware groupings and decorations of Woodland ceramics in Illinois. American Antiquity 20:213–25.
1957 The origin of plant cultivation in the central Mississippi Valley: a hypothesis. Unpublished paper presented at the annual meeting of the American Anthropological Association.

Fox, Cyril F.
1923 Archaeology of the Cambridge region. London: Macmillan & Co.

Freedman, L. G., Jr., and Brown, James A.
1964 Statistical analysis of Carter Ranch pottery. *In* Chapters in the prehistory of eastern Arizona, 2, by Paul S. Martin et al. Fieldiana: Anthropology 55. Chicago: Chicago Natural History Museum.

Frevert, Richard K., et al.
1955 Soil and water conservation engineering. New York: John Wiley.

Fried, Morton H.
1960 On the evolution of social stratification and the state. *In* Culture in history: essays in honor of Paul Radin, Stanley Diamond, ed. New York: Columbia University Press.
1967 The evolution of political society: an essay in political anthropology. New York: Random House.

Friederici, Georg C.
1926 Hilfswörterbuch für den Amerikanisten; Lehnwörter aus Indianer-Sprachen und

Erklärungen altertümlicher Ausdrücke, Deutsch-Spanisch-Englisch. Halle (Salle).

1947 Amerikanistisches Wörterbuch. Abhandlungen aus dem Gebiet der Auslandskunde, vol. 53. Hamburg.

Fritz, John M.
1968 Archaeological epistemology—two views. M.A. thesis. Department of Anthropology, University of Chicago.

Fritz, John M., and Plog, Fred T.
1968 The Nature of archaeological explanation. Paper presented at the Thirty-third Annual Meeting of the Society for American Archaeology, Santa Fe.
1970 The nature of archaeological reasoning. American Antiquity 35(4):405–12.

Fruchter, Benjamin
1954 Introduction to factor analysis. Princeton: D. Van Nostrand Company.

Fry, R.
1969 Ceramics and settlement in the periphery of Tikal, Guatemala. Ph.D. dissertation, University of Arizona.
1970 Mesoamerican trading systems and the Maya collapse. Paper presented at the Society for American Archaeology meetings, Mexico City.

Furst, Peter T.
1965a Radiocarbon dates from a tomb in Mexico. Science 147:612–13.
1965b West Mexican tomb sculpture as evidence for Shamanism in prehispanic Mesoamerica. Antropológica 15:29–60.

Furst, Peter T., and Myerhoff, Barbara G.
1966 Myth as history: the jimson weed cycle of the Huichols of Mexico. Antropológica 17:3–39.

Gabel, W. Crieghton
1958a The Mesolithic continuum in western Europe. American Anthropologist 60:658–67.
1958b European secondary Neolithic cultures. Journal of the Royal Anthropological Institute of Great Britain and Ireland 88:97–107.
1960 Seminar on economic types in pre-urban cultures of temperate woodland, arid, and tropical areas. Current Anthropology 1:437–38.

Galloway, R. W.
1970 The full glacial climate in the southwestern United States. Annals of the Association of American Geographers 60:245–57.

Gann, Thomas W. F.
1918 The Maya Indians of southern Yucatán and northern British Honduras. Washington, D.C., Bulletin of the Bureau of American Ethnology, no. 64.

Garretson, Martin S.
1938 The American bison: the story of its extermination as a wild species and its restoration under federal protection. New York: New York Zoological Society.

Garrod, D. A. E.
1932 A new Mesolithic industry: the Natufian of Palestine. Journal of the Royal Anthropological Institute of Great Britain and Ireland 62:257–69.

Garrod, D. A. E., and Bate, D. M. A.
1937 The Stone Age of Mount Carmel, Excavations at the Wady el-Mughara, vol. 1. Oxford: Clarendon Press.

Gearing, Fred
1958 The structural poses of 18th century Cherokee villages. American Anthropologist 60:1148–57.
1962 Priests and warriors. Menasha, Memoirs of the American Anthropological Association, no. 93.

Geertz, Clifford
1963 Agricultural involution: the process of ecological change in Indonesia. Berkeley: University of California Press.
1964 Ideology as a cultural system. *In* Ideology and discontent, David Apter, ed. New York: Free Press.
1966 Religion as a cultural system. *In* Anthropological approaches to the study of religion, Michael Banton, ed. Association of Social Anthropologists Monograph no. 3. New York: Frederick A. Praeger.

Gifford, E. W.
1916 Composition of California shellmounds. Berkeley, University of California Publications in American Archaeology and Ethnology 12:1–29.

Gifford, James C.
1960 The type-variety method of ceramic classification as an indicator of cultural phenomena. American Antiquity 25:341–47.

Gimbutas, Marija
1956 The prehistory of eastern Europe. *In* American School of Prehistoric Research, Harvard University, Bulletin no. 20. Cambridge.
1963 European prehistory: Neolithic to the Iron Age. *In* Biennial review of anthropology 1963, Bernard J. Siegel, ed. Stanford: Stanford University Press.

Girod, P.
1906 Les Stations de l'Âge du Renne dans les vallées de la Vézère et de la Corrège. Paris.

Gjessing, G.
1944 Circumpolar Stone Age. Acta Arctica Fasc. II:40–46. Copenhagen.

Gladwin, Harold S.
1957 A history of the ancient Southwest. Portland, Me.: Bond Wheelwright Co.

Gladwin, Winifred and H. S.
1928 A method for designation of ruins in the Southwest. Globe, Arizona, Gila Pueblo, Medallion Paper 1.

Glob, P. V.
1951 Ard og Plov i Norden Oldtid. Jysk Arkaeologisk Selsk. Skr., Bd. 1. Aarhus.

Goldman, Irving
1937 The Zuni Indians of New Mexico. *In* Cooperation and competition among primitive peoples, Margaret Mead, ed. New York: McGraw-Hill Book Company.
1963 The Cubeo; Indians of the northwest Amazon. Illinois Studies in Anthropology, no. 2. Urbana: University of Illinois Press.

Goodenough, Ward H.
1963 Cooperation in change. New York: Russell Sage Foundation.

Goodman, L. A., and Kruskal, W. H.
1954 Measures of association for cross classifications. Journal of the American Statistical Association 49:732–63.

Graham, Ian
1967 Archaeological explorations in El Peten, Guatemala. Middle American Research Institute, Publication no. 33. New Orleans: Tulane University.

Greengo, R.
1951 Molluscan species in California shell middens. University of California Archaeological Survey, Report no. 13.

Greenwood, R. S.
1961 Quantitative analysis of shells from a site in Goleta, California. American Antiquity 26:416–20.

Griffin, James B.
1952a Some early and Middle Woodland pottery types in Illinois. *In* Hopewellian communities in Illinois, Thorne Deuel, ed. Illinois State Museum, Scientific Papers 5:93–129.
1952b Culture periods in eastern United States archaeology. *In* Archaeology of eastern United States, James B. Griffin, ed. Chicago: University of Chicago Press.
1960a Climatic change: a contributory cause of the growth and decline of northern Hopewellian culture. Wisconsin Archaeologist 41:21–33.
1960b Some prehistoric connections between Siberia and America. Science 131: 801–12.
1961 Comments on Edmonson: Neolithic diffusion rates. Current Anthropology 2:92–93.

Grove, David C.
1968 The pre-classic Olmec in central Mexico: site distribution and inferences. *In* Dunbarton Oaks Conference on the Olmec, Elizabeth P. Benson, ed. Washington, D.C., Dunbarton Oaks Research Library and Collection.
1970 The San Pablo pantheon mound: a middle preclassic site in Morelos, Mexico. American Antiquity 35:62–73.

Guernsey, Samuel J., and Kidder, Alfred V.
1921 Basket-Maker caves of northeastern Arizona. Papers of the Peabody Museum of American Archaeology and Ethnology, vol. 8(2). Cambridge: Harvard University.

Gusinde, Martin
1930 Das Brüderpaar in der Südamerikanischen Mythologie. *In* 23d International
Congress of Americanists. New York.

Haag, William G.
1959 The status of evolutionary theory in
American history. *In* Evolution and
anthropology, a centennial appraisal,
Betty J. Meggers, ed. Washington,
D.C.: Anthropological Society of
Washington.

Hack, John T.
1942 The changing physical environment of
the Hopi Indians of Arizona. Papers
of the Peabody Museum of American
Archaeology and Ethnology, vol.
35(1). Cambridge: Harvard University.

Hafsten, V.
1961 Pleistocene development of vegetation
and climate in the southern high plains
as Evidenced by Pollen Analysis. *In*
The Paleoecology of the Llano Estacado, Fred Wendorf, ed. Santa Fe,
Fort Burgwin Research Center, Publication no. 1.

Haggett, Peter
1965 Locational analysis in human geography.
London: Edward Arnold.

Hainline, Jane
1965 Culture and biological adaptation.
American Anthropologist 67:1174–97.

Halbwachs, Maurice
1960 Population and society: introduction to
social morphology. Glencoe: Free
Press.

Hall, A. D., and Fagen, R. E.
1956 Definition of system. General Systems
1:18–28.

Hammel, E. A.
1968 Anthropological explanations: style in
discourse. Southwestern Journal of
Anthropology 24:155–69.

Hanke, Wanda
1964 Verlöschende Urzeit im Inneren Brasiliens. Voelkerkundliche Forschungen in
Südamerika, vol. 11. Braunschweig.

Hanson, Norwood Russell
1958 Patterns of discovery. Cambridge: Cambridge University Press.

Harrington, J. C.
1952 Historic sites archaeology in the United
States. *In* Archaeology of the eastern
United States, James B. Griffin, ed.
Chicago: University of Chicago Press.
1955 Archaeology as an auxiliary science in
American History. American Anthro-
pologist 57:1121–30.

Harrington, M. R.
1933 Gypsum Cave, Nevada. Los Angeles,
Southwest Museum Papers, no. 8.

Harris, Marvin
1968 The rise of anthropological theory. New
York: Thomas Y. Crowell.

Harth-Terré, Emilio
1964 El Pueblo de Huánuco Viejo. Arquitecto
Peruano 320/21:1–20.

Harvey, H. H., and Kelly, I.
1969 The Totonac. *In* Handbook of middle
American Indians, vol. 7: ethnology,
Evon Z. Vogt, ed. Austin: University
of Texas Press.

Hatt, G.
1937 Landbrug i Danmarks Oldtid. Copenhagen.

Hatt, Robert T.
1959 The mammals of Iraq. Museum of
Zoology, Miscellaneous Publications,
no. 106. Ann Arbor: University of
Michigan.

Haury, Emil W.
1936 The Mogollon culture of southwestern
New Mexico. Globe, Arizona, Gila
Pueblo, Medallion Paper 20.
1953 Artifacts with mammoth remains, Naco,
Arizona, 1: discovery of the Naco
Mammoth and the associated projectile points. American Antiquity 19:1–
14.
1962 The greater American Southwest. *In*
Courses toward urban life, Robert J.
Braidwood and Gordon R. Willey,
eds. Chicago: Aldine Publishing Company.

Haury, Emil W.; Sayles, E. B.; and Wasley,
William W.
1959 The Lehner Mammoth Site, southeastern Arizona. American Antiquity 25:
2–30.

Haviland, William A.
1963 Excavation of small structures in the

428

northeast quadrant of Tikal, Guatemala. Ph.D. dissertation, University of Pennsylvania.

Hawkes, Christopher
1954 Archaeological theory and method. American Anthropologist 56:155–68.

Hayes, Alden C.
1964 The archaeological survey of Wetherill Mesa, Mesa Verde National Park—Colorado. Archaeological Research Series, no. 7–A. Washington, D.C.: National Park Service.

Haynes, C. Vance
1964 Fluted projectile points; their age and dispersion. Science 145:1408–13.
1967a Carbon–14 dates and early man in the New World. *In* Pleistocene Extinctions: the search for a cause, P. S. Martin and H. E. Wright, eds. New Haven: Yale University Press.
1967b Quaternary geology of the Tule Springs area, Clark County, Nevada. Anthropological Papers, no. 13(1). Carson City: Nevada State Museum.

Haynes, C. Vance, and Agogino, G. A.
1965 Prehistoric springs and geochronology of the Clovis Site, New Mexico. American Antiquity 31:812–21.

Hays, William L.
1965 Statistics for psychologists. New York: Holt, Rinehart and Winston.

Heady, Earl O., and Jensen, Harald
1954 Farm management economics. Englewood Cliffs: Prentice-Hall.

Heer, O.
1866 Die Pflanzen der Pfahlbauten. vi. Pfahlbautenbericht. Mitteilungen d. Antiqu.-Ces. in Zurich 15:310–17.

Heizer, Robert F.
1942 Archaeological evidence of Sebastian Rodriguez Cermeno's California visit in 1595. California Historical Society Quarterly 20:5–22.
1960 Physical analysis of habitation residues. *In* The application of quantitative models in archaeology, Robert F. Heizer and Sherburne F. Cook, eds. Viking Fund Publications in Anthropology, No. 28. Chicago: Quadrangle Books.
1968 New Observations on La Venta. *In* Dumbarton Oaks Conference on the Olmec, Elizabeth P. Benson, ed. Washington, D.C.: Dumbarton Oaks Research Library and Collection.

Heizer, Robert F., and Williams, Howel
1965 Notes on Mesoamerican obsidians and their significance in archaeological studies. *In* Sources of stones used in prehistoric Mesoamerican sites. Berkeley, University of California, Archaeological Research Facility, Contributions 1:94–103.

Helbaek, H.
1950 Tollund Mandens Sidste Maaltid. Aabøger 311–28.
1952 Early crops in southern England. Proceedings of the Prehistoric Society 18:194–233.
1960a Paleo-ethnobotany of the Near East and Europe. *In* Prehistoric investigations in Iraqi Kurdistan, R. J. Braidwood, B. Howe, et al. Studies in Ancient Oriental Civilization, no. 31. Chicago: University of Chicago Press.
1960b Ecological effects of irrigation in ancient Mesopotamia. Iraq 22:186–96.
1963 Paleo-ethnobotany. *In* Science in archaeology, D. Brothwell and E. Higgs, eds. London: Thames and Hudson.

Helm, June
1968 The nature of Dogrib socioterritorial groups. *In* Man the hunter, R. B. Lee and I. DeVore, eds. Chicago: Aldine Publishing Company.

Hemmings, E. Thomas
1970 Early man in the San Pedro Valley, Arizona. Ph.D. dissertation, University of Arizona.

Hempel, Carl G.
1966 Philosophy of natural science. Englewood Cliffs: Prentice-Hall.

Hempel, Carl G., and Oppenheim, Paul
1948 Studies in the logic of explanation. Philosophy of Science 15:135–75.

Hendges, M.
1902 Guatemala map. Bureau of the American Republics.

Herold, Joyce
1961 Prehistoric settlement and physical environment in the Mesa Verde area. Anthropological Papers, Department

of Anthropology, no. 53. Salt Lake City: University of Utah.

Herskovits, Melville J.
1948 Man and his works. New York: Alfred A. Knopf.

Herve, Georges
1899 Populations Mesolithiques et Néolithiques de l'Espagne et du Portugal. Revue Mensuelle de L'Ecole d'Anthropologie de Paris 9:265–80.

Hevly, Richard Holmes
1964 Pollen analysis of Quaternary archaeological and lacustrine sediments from the Colorado plateau. Ph.D. dissertation, University of Arizona.

Hill, James N.
1965 Broken K: a prehistoric society in eastern Arizona. Ph.D. dissertation, University of Chicago.
1966 A prehistoric community in eastern Arizona. Southwestern Journal of Anthropology 22:9–30.
1968 Broken K pueblo: patterns of form and function. *In* New perspectives in archeology, Sally R. and Lewis R. Binford, eds. Chicago: Aldine Publishing Company.
1970 Broken K pueblo: prehistoric social organization in the American Southwest. Anthropological Papers of the University of Arizona, no. 18. Tucson: University of Arizona Press.

Hill, James N., and Hevly, Richard H.
1968 Pollen at Broken K pueblo: some new interpretations. American Antiquity 33:200–210.

Hilzheimer, M.
1941 Animal remains from Tel Asmar. Oriental Institute Studies in Ancient Oriental Civilization, no. 20. Chicago: University of Chicago Press.

Hissink, Karin
1964 Krankheit und Medizinmann bei Tacana-Indianern. *In* Festschrift für Ad. E. Jensen. Munich.

Hissink, Karin, and Hahn, Albert
1961 Die Tacana; Ergebnisse der Frobenius-Expedition nach Bolivien 1952 bis 1954, vol. 1: Erzählungsgut. Stuttgart.

Hofman, Albert
1966 The active principles of the seeds of the Rivea Crymbosa (L.) Hall F. (Ololiuhqui, Badoh) and *Ipomoea Tricolor* Cav. (Badoh Negro). *In* Summa Antropológica en homenaje a Roberto J. Weitlaner. Mexico City: Instituto Nacional de Antropología e Historia.

Hole, Frank
1962 Archeological survey and excavation in Iran, 1961. Science 137:524–26.
1966 Investigating the origins of Mesopotamian civilization. Science 153:605–11.

Hole, Frank, and Helzer, Robert F.
1969 An introduction to prehistoric archeology. 2d ed. New York: Holt, Rinehart and Winston.

Hole, Frank; Flannery, Kent V.; and Neely, J.
1965 Early agriculture and animal husbandry in Deh Luran, Iran. Current Anthropology 6:105–6.

Holland, William R.
1961 Relaciones entre la Religión Tzotzil Contemporánea y la Maya Antigua. Mexico City, Anales del Instituto Nacional de Antropología e Historia 13:113–31.
1964 Contemporary Tzotzil cosmological concepts as a basis for interpreting prehistoric Maya civilization. American Antiquity 29:301–6.

Holmes, William H.
1901 Aboriginal copper mines of Isle Royale, Lake Superior. American Anthropologist 3:684–96.

Hough, Walter
1915 The Hopi Indians. Cedar Rapids: Torch Press.

Howard, Edgar B.
1935 Evidence of early man in North America. Museum Journal 24(2–3). University Museum. Philadelphia: University of Pennsylvania.

Hughes, Harold D., and Henson, Edwin R.
1957 Crop production. New York: Macmillan Co.

Hume, Ivor Noël
1969 Historical archaeology. New York: Alfred A. Knopf.

Huntingford, G. W. B.
1955 The economic life of the Dorobo. Anthropos 50:605–84.

Hyrenius, Hannes
1959 Population growth and replacement. *In*

430

The study of population: an inventory and appraisal, P. M. Hauser and Otis Duncan, eds. Chicago: University of Chicago Press.

Irwin-Williams, Cynthia
1967 Picosa: the elementary southwestern culture. American Antiquity 32:441–57.

Isard, Walter
1960 Methods of regional analysis: an introduction to regional science. New York: John Wiley.

Iversen, J.
1941 Landnam i Danmarks Stenalder. Dansk Geologisk Unders. ii R. nr. 66. Copenhagen.

Jackson, C. F., and Knaebel, J. B.
1934 Sampling and estimation of ore deposits. Washington, D.C., Bulletin of the U.S. Bureau of Mines, no. 365.

Jennings, Jesse D.
1968 Prehistory of North America. New York: McGraw-Hill.

Jennings, Jesse D., and Norbeck, Edward
1955 Great Basin prehistory: a review. American Antiquity 21:1–11.

Jessen, K., and Helbaek, H.
1944 Cereals in Great Britain and Ireland in prehistoric and early historic times. Det Kong. Danske Vidensk. Sels. Biol. Skr., vol. 3(2) Copenhagen.

Jiménez-Moreno, Wilberto
1966a El Hallazgo de los Restos del Padre Kino. Mexico City, Instituto Nacional de Antropología e Historia, Buletín, no. 25:17–21.

1966b Mesoamerica before the Toltecs. *In* Ancient Oaxaca, John Paddock, ed. Stanford: Stanford University Press.

Jones, Volney H.
1936 The vegetal remains of the Newt Kash Hollow Shelter. University of Kentucky Reports in Anthropology and Archaeology 3(4):147–67.

1953 Review of the Grain Amaranths: a survey of their history and classification, by J. D. Sauer. American Antiquity 19:90–92.

Kaplan, David
1960 The law of cultural dominance. *In* Evolution and culture, Marshall D. Sahlins and Elman R. Service, eds. Ann Arbor: University of Michigan Press.

Kaplan, Lawrence
1965 Archaeology and domestication in American *Phaseolus* (Beans). Economic Botany 19:358–68.

Karsten, Rafael
1955 Zur Psychologie des indianischen Medizinmannes. Zeitschrift für Ethnologie 80:170–77.

1964 Studies in the religion of the South American Indians east of the Andes, Arne Runeberg and Michael Webster, eds. Societas Scientarium Fennica, Commentationes humanarum litterarum 29(1). Helsinki.

Kenyon, Kathleen M.
1959 Some observations on the beginnings of settlement in the Near East. Journal of the Royal Anthropological Institute of Great Britain and Ireland 89:35–43.

Kidder, Alfred V.
1947 The artifacts of Uaxactun, Guatemala. Washington, D.C., Carnegie Institution of Washington Publication 576.

Kidder, Alfred V., and Thompson, J. E.
1938 The correlation of Maya and Christian chronologies. *In* Cooperation in research. Washington, D.C., Carnegie Institution of Washington, Publication 501.

Kirchoff, Paul
1949 The social and political organization of the Andean peoples. *In* Handbook of South American Indians, Julian Steward, ed. Bulletin of the Bureau of American Ethnology, no. 143(5). Washington, D.C.: Government Printing Office.

Kluckhohn, Clyde
1935 A Note on the sources of the drawings in the Del Rio volume on Palenque. Maya Research 2:287–90.

1939 The place of theory in anthropological studies. Philosophy of Science 6:328–44.

1940 The conceptual structure in Middle American Studies. *In* The Maya and Their Neighbors, C. L. Hay, R. L.

Linton, et al., eds. New York: Appleton-Century.

Koch-Grünberg, Theodor
1901–10 Zwei Jahre unter den Indianern. Reisen in Nordwest-Brasilien 1903/1905. 2 vols. Berlin.
1917–28 Vom Roroima zum Orinoco. Ergebnisse einer Reise in Nordbrasilien und Venezuela in den Jahren 1911–1913. 5 vols. Berlin-Stuttgart.

Kozlowski, Leon
1926 L'Époque Mésolithique en Pologne. L'Anthropologie 36:47–74.

Krader, Lawrence
1955 Ecology of central Asian pastoralism. Southwestern Journal of Anthropology 11:301–26.

Kroeber, Alfred L.
1916 Zuni potsherds. New York, Anthropological Papers of the American Museum of Natural History 18:1–37.
1935 History and science in anthropology. American Anthropologist 37:539–69.
1939 Cultural and natural areas of native North America. Berkeley, University of California Publications in American Archaeology and Ethnology, vol. 38.
1948 Anthropology. New York: Harcourt, Brace.
1952 The nature of culture. Chicago: University of Chicago Press.
1953 Introduction. *In* Anthropology today, A. L. Kroeber, ed. Chicago: University of Chicago Press.

Kroeber, Alfred L., and Kluckhohn, Clyde
1952 Culture: a critical review of concepts and definitions. Papers of the Peabody Museum of American Archaeology and Ethnology, vol. 47(1). Cambridge: Harvard University.

Krumbein, W. C.
1965 Sampling in paleontology. *In* Handbook of paleontological techniques, Bernhard Kummel and David Raup, eds. San Francisco: W. H. Freeman.

Kuhn, Thomas S.
1962 The structure of scientific revolutions. Chicago: University of Chicago Press.
1970 The structure of scientific revolutions. 2d enl. ed. International Encyclopedia of Unified Science 2:2. Chicago: University of Chicago Press.

Kuhne, Heinz
1955 Der Jaguar im Zwillingsmythus der Chiriguano und dessen Beziehung zu anderen Stämmen der Neuen Welt. Archiv für Völkerkunde 10:16–135.

Kunike, Hugo
1915 Jaguar und Mond in der Mythologie des andinen Hochlandes. Leipzig.

Kushner, Gilbert
1970 A consideration of some processual designs for archaeology as anthropology. American Antiquity 35:125–32.

Larrabee, Edward M.
1965 Historic sites archaeology in relation to other archaeology. Paper presented at the Society for American Archaeology meeting.

Lathrap, Donald W.
1968 The hunting economics of the tropical forest zone of South America: an attempt at historical perspective. *In* Man the hunter, Richard B. Lee and Irven DeVore, eds. Chicago: Aldine Publishing Company.

Laughlin, R. M.
1969a The Tzotzil. *In* Handbook of Middle American Indians, vol. 7: ethnology, Evon Z. Vogt, ed. Austin: University of Texas Press.
1969b The Huastec. *In* Handbook of Middle American Indians, vol. 7: ethnology, Evon Z. Vogt, ed. Austin: University of Texas Press.

Laughlin, William S.
1968 Hunting: an integrating biobehavior system and its evolutionary importance. *In* Man the hunter, R. B. Lee and I. DeVore, eds. Chicago: Aldine Publishing Company.

Lazarsfeld, Paul F., and Rosenberg, Morris, eds.
1955 The language of social research. Glencoe: Free Press.

Lee, Richard B.
1965 Subsistence ecology of !Kung Bushman. Ph.D. dissertation, University of California, Berkeley.
1968 What hunters do for a living, or how to make out on scarce resources. *In* Man the hunter, R. B. Lee and I. DeVore,

eds. Chicago: Aldine Publishing Company.

Lees, G. M., and Falcon, N. L.
1952   The geographical history of the Mesopotamian plains. Geographical Journal 118:24–39.

Leone, Mark
1968   Economic autonomy and social distance: archaeological evidence. Ph.D. dissertation, University of Arizona.

Leopold, Aldo Starker
1959   Wildlife of Mexico: the game birds and mammals. Berkeley: University of California Press.

Levins, Richard
1968   Evolution in changing environments: some theoretical explorations. Princeton: Princeton University Press.

Linton, Ralph
1936   The study of man. New York: Appleton-Century.
1945   Present world conditions in cultural perspective. *In* The science of man in world crisis, Ralph Linton, ed. New York: Columbia University Press.

Lloyd, S., and Safar, F.
1943   Tell Uqair. Journal of Near Eastern Studies 2:131–58.

de Loe, Baron A.
1908   Contribution à l'étude des temps intermédiares entre le Paléolithique et le Néolithique. XII Congrès International d'Anthropologie et d'Archéologie préhistorique, Monaco, 1907. 1:422–23.

Logan, Wilfred D.
1958   Analysis of Woodland complexes in northeastern Iowa. Ph.D. dissertation, University of Michigan.

Longacre, William A.
1963   Archaeology as anthropology: a case study. Ph.D. dissertation, Department of Anthropology, University of Chicago.
1964   Archeology as anthropology: a case study. Science 144:1454–55.
1966   Changing patterns of social integration: a prehistoric example from the American Southwest. American Anthropologist 68:94–102.
1968   Some aspects of prehistoric society in east-central Arizona. *In* New perspectives in archeology, Sally R. and Lewis R. Binford, eds. Chicago: Aldine Publishing Company.
1970   Archaeology as anthropology: a case study. Anthropological Papers of the University of Arizona, no. 17. Tucson: University of Arizona Press.

Longyear, J. M., III
1952   Copan ceramics: a study of southeastern Maya pottery. Washington, D.C., Carnegie Institution of Washington, Publication 597.

Lothrop, Samuel K.; Foshag, W. F.; and Mahler, Joy
1957   Pre-Columbian art: Robert Woods Bliss collection. New York: Phaidon Publications.

Loukotka, Čestmír
1968   Classification of South American Indian languages. Johannes Wilbert, ed. Los Angeles: University of California, Latin American Center.

Lowe, Gareth W.
1959   Archaeological exploration of the upper Grijalva River, Chiapas, Mexico. Papers of the New World Archaeological Foundation, no. 2 (Pub. no. 3). Provo, Utah: Brigham Young University.
1970   A provincial Olmec occupation sequence at San Isidro in the middle Grijalva basin. Paper presented at the Society for American Archaeology meeting, Mexico City.

Lowie, Robert
1946   Evolution in cultural anthropology: a reply to Leslie White. American Anthropologist 48:223–33.

Lumbreras, Luis Guillermo
1969   De Los Pueblos, Las Culturas y Las Artes del Antiguo Perú. Lima: Monclos-Campodonico.

Lundelius, E. L.
1964   The use of vertebrates in paleoecological reconstruction. *In* The reconstruction of past environments, J. J. Hester and James Schoenwetter, eds. Taos, Fort Burgwin Research Center, Publication no. 3.

Lundell, C. L.
1937   The vegetation of Peten. Washington,

D.C., Carnegie Institution of Washington, Publication 478.

MacArthur, Robert H., and Connell, J. H.
1966 Biology of populations. New York: John Wiley.

McBryde, F. W.
1945 Cultural and historical geography of southwest Guatemala. Institute of Social Anthropology, Publication no. 4. Washington, D.C.: Smithsonian Institution.

McCarthy, Frederick D.
1957 Habitat, economy, and equipment of the Australian Aborigines. Australian Journal of Science 19:88–97.

McCarthy, Frederick D., and McArthur, Margaret
1960 The food quest and the time factor in Aboriginal economic life. Records of the American-Australian Scientific Expedition to Arnhemland 2:145–94. Parkville, Australia: University of Melbourne Press.

McCary, Ben C.
1951 A workshop site of early man in Dinwiddie County, Virginia. American Antiquity 17:9–17.

MacCurdy, George Grant
1924 Human origins: a manual of prehistory. 2 vols. New York: D. Appleton.

McGregor, John C.
1965 Southwestern archaeology. 2d ed. Urbana: University of Illinois Press.

McKern, W. C.
1931 A Wisconsin variant of the Hopewell culture. Bulletin of the Milwaukee Public Museum 10(2).
1935 Certain culture classification problems in Middle Western archaeology. In The Indianapolis Archaeological Conference, issued by the Commitee on State Archaeological Surveys. National Research Council, Circular no. 17.
1939 The Midwestern taxonomic method as an aid to archaeological culture study. American Antiquity 4:301–13.

MacNeish, Richard S.
1954 An early archaeological site near Pánuco, Vera Cruz. In Transactions of the American Philosophical Society, vol. 44. Philadelphia.

1961 First annual report of the Tehuacán archaeological-botanical project. Andover, Mass.: R. S. Peabody Foundation for Archaeology, Report no. 1.
1962 Second annual report of the Tehuacán archaeological-botanical project. Andover, Mass.: R. S. Peabody Foundation for Archaeology, Report no. 2.
1964a Ancient Mesoamerican civilization. Science 143:531–37.
1964b The food-gathering and incipient agriculture stage of prehistoric Middle America. In Handbook of Middle American Indians, vol. 1: natural environment and early cultures, Robert C. West, ed. Austin: University of Texas Press.

Maler, Teobert
1910 Explorations in the department of Peten, Guatemala and adjacent region: Motul de San José; Peten-Itza: reports of explorations for the museum. Memoirs of the Peabody Museum of American Archaeology and Ethnology, vol. 4(3). Cambridge: Harvard University.

Mangelsdorf, Paul C., and Smith, C. E., Jr.
1949 New archaeological evidence on evolution in maize. Botanical Museum Leaflets, vol. 13(8). Cambridge: Harvard University.

Mangelsdorf, Paul C.; MacNeish, Richard S.; and Galinat, Walton
1964 Domestication of corn. Science 143:538–45.

Manninen, I.
1932 Die finnisch-ugrischen Völker. Leipzig.

Martin, Paul S. (Arizona)
1963a Early man in Arizona: the pollen evidence. American Antiquity 29:67–73.
1963b The geochronology of pluvial Lake Cochise, southern Arizona, 2, pollen analysis of a 42 meter core. Ecology 44:436–44.
1963c The last 10,000 years: a fossil pollen record of the American Southwest. Tucson: University of Arizona Press.

Martin, Paul S. (Arizona); Schoenwetter, James; and Arms, B. C.
1961 Southwestern palynology and prehistory: the last 10,000 years. Geochronology

434

Laboratories. Tucson: University of Arizona.

Martin, Paul S. (Chicago)
1939 Modified Basket Maker sites; Ackman-Lowry area, southwestern Colorado, 1938. Anthropological Series 23(3). Chicago: Field Museum of Natural History.
1954 Comments on Southwestern archaeology, its history and theory by Walter W. Taylor. American Anthropologist 56: 570–72.
1962 Archeological investigations in east central Arizona. Science 138:826–27.
1971 The revolution in archaeology. American Antiquity 36:1–8.

Martin, Paul S. (Chicago), and Rinaldo, John B.
1950 Turkey Foot Ridge Site; a Mogollon village, Pine Lawn Valley, western New Mexico. Fieldiana: Anthropology vol. 38(2). Chicago: Chicago Natural History Museum.

Martin, Paul S. (Chicago); Quimby, George I.; and Collier, Donald
1947 Indians before Columbus. Chicago: University of Chicago Press.

Martin, Paul S. (Chicago); Rinaldo, John B.; and Antevs, Ernst
1949 Cochise and Mogollon Sites, Pine Lawn Valley, western New Mexico. Fieldiana: Anthropology vol. 38(1). Chicago: Chicago Natural History Museum.

Martin, Paul S. (Chicago), et al.
1962 Chapters in the prehistory of eastern Arizona, 1. Fieldiana: Anthropology vol. 53. Chicago: Chicago Natural History Museum.
1964 Chapters in the prehistory of eastern Arizona. 2. Fieldiana: Anthropology vol. 55. Chicago: Chicago Natural History Museum.

Maruyama, Magoroh
1963 The second cybernetics: deviation-amplifying mutual causal processes. American Scientist 51:164–79.

Mason, J. Alden
1938 Observations on the present status and problems of Middle American archaeology. American Antiquity 3:206–23, 300–317.

Mason, Ronald J.
1962 The Paleo-Indian tradition in eastern North America. Current Anthropology 3:227–78.

Mathiassen, T.
1942 Dyrholmen, En Stenalderboplads paa Djursland. Copenhagen.

Maxwell, Moreau S.
1951 Woodland cultures of Southern Illinois: archaeological excavations in the Carbondale area. Museum Publications in Anthropology, Bulletin no. 7. Beloit, Wisc.: Beloit College.

Means, Philip Ainsworth
1917 History of the Spanish conquest of Yucatan and the Itzas. Papers of the Peabody Museum of American Archaeology and Ethnology, vol. 7. Cambridge: Harvard University.

Meggers, Betty J.
1954 Environmental limitation on the development of culture. American Anthropologist 56:801–24.

Mehringer, P. J.
1967 The environment of extinction of the late Pleistocene megafauna in the arid southwestern United States. *In* Pleistocene extinctions, P. S. Martin and H. E. Wright, eds. New Haven: Yale University Press.

Mehringer, P. J., and Haynes, C. V.
1965 Pollen evidence for the environment of early man and extinct mammals at the Lehner Mammoth Site, southeastern Arizona. American Antiquity 31:17–23.

Meighan, C. W., et al.
1958 Ecological interpretation in archaeology: Part 1. American Antiquity 24:1–23.

Mellaart, James
1961 Excavations at Hačilar: 4th Report. Anatolian Studies 11:39–75.
1963 Excavations at Čatal-Hüyük 1962: 2d Preliminary Report. Anatolian Studies 13:43–103.
1964 A Neolithic city in Turkey. Scientific American 210(4):94–104.

Mendez, A. C.
1959 El Comercio de los Mayas Antiguos. Acta Anthropologica 2(1).

de Mendizábal, Miguel O.
1929 Influencia de la Sal en la Distribución Geográfica de los Grupos Indígenas de Mexico. *In* Obras completas, vol. II. Mexico, D. F.

Menghin, Oswald
1925 Die mesolithische Kulturentwicklung in Europa. Deutsches Archäologisches Institut, Röm.-Germ., Komsn. Bericht., 17:154.

Menzel, Dorothy
1959 The Inca occupation of the south coast of Peru. Southwestern Journal of Anthropology 15:125–42.
1968 New data on the Huari Empire in Middle Horizon Epoch 2A. Ñawpa Pacha 6:47–114.

Métraux, Alfred
1928 La religion des Tupinamba et ses rapports avec celle des autres tribus Tupi-Guarani. Bibliothèque de l'école des hautes études, sciences et religieuses, vol. 45. Paris.
1932 Mitos y cuentos de los indios Chiriguanos. Revista del Museo de la Plata 33:119–84.

Michels, Joseph W.
1969 Testing stratigraphy and artifact reuse through obsidian hydration dating. American Antiquity 34:15–22.

Midvale, Frank
1965 Prehistoric irrigation of the Casa Grande Ruins Area. Kiva 30:82–86.

Miles, S. W.
1965 Summary of preconquest ethnology of the Guatemala-Chiapas highlands and Pacific slopes. *In* Handbook of Middle American Indians, vol. 2: Archaeology of southern Mesoamerica, Gordon R. Willey, ed. Austin: University of Texas Press.

Miller, James G.
1965 Living systems: basic concepts, structure and process; cross-level hypotheses. Behavioral Science 10:193–237, 337–411.

Miller, Walter S.
1966 El Tonalamatl Mixe y Los Hongos Sagrados. In Summa Antropológica en homenaje a Roberto J. Weitlaner.

Mexico, D.F., Instituto Nacional de Antropología e Historia.

Mindeleff, Victor
1891 A Study of Pueblo architecture: Tusayan and Cibola. *In* Annual Report of the Bureau of Ethnology, no. 8. Washington, D.C.

Moone, J. R.
1958 An environmental appraisal of the desert culture concept. M. A. thesis, University of Colorado.

de Morgan, Jacques Jean Marie
1924 Prehistoric man: a general outline of prehistory. New York: Alfred A. Knopf.

Morley, Sylvanus G.
1937–38 The inscriptions of Peten. 5 vols. Washington, D.C., Carnegie Institution of Washington, Publication 437.

Morley, Sylvanus G., and Brainerd, George W.
1956 The ancient Maya. 3d rev. ed. Stanford: Stanford University Press.

Morris, Craig
1966 El Tampu Real de Tunsucancha. *In* Cuadernos de Investigación, no. 1 (Antropología):95–107. Huánuco: Universidad Nacional Hermilio Valdizán.
1967 Storage in Tawantisuyu. Ph.D. dissertation, University of Chicago.

Morris, Craig, and Thompson, Donald E.
1970 Huánuco Viejo: an Inca administrative center. American Antiquity 35:344–62.

Morris, Earl H.
1939 Archaeological studies in the La Plata district, southwestern Colorado and northwestern New Mexico. Washington, D.C., Carnegie Institution of Washington, Publication 519.

Morris, Earl H., and Burgh, Robert F.
1954 Basketmaker 2 sites near Durango, Colorado. Washington, D.C., Carnegie Institution of Washington, Publication 604.

de Mortillet, Adrien
1896 Les petits silex taillés, à contours géométriques trouvés en Europe, Asie et Afrique. Revue de l'Ecole d'Anthropologie 6:376–405.

de Mortillet, Gabriel
1885   Le Préhistorique antiquité de l'Homme. 2d ed. Paris: C. Reinwald.

Munson, Patrick J.
1969   Comments on Binford's "Smudge pits and hide smoking: the use of analogy in archaeological reasoning." American Antiquity 34:83–84.

Murdock, George Peter
1949   Social structure. New York: Macmillan Co.

Murra, John V.
1956   The economic organization of the Inca state. Ph.D. dissertation, University of Chicago.
1958   On Inca political structure. *In* Systems of political control and bureaucracy in human societies, Verne F. Ray, ed. Proceedings of the 1958 Annual Spring Meeting of the American Ethnological Society. Seattle: University of Washington Press.
1962*a* An archaeological "restudy" of an Andean ethnohistorical account. American Antiquity 28:1–4.
1962*b* Cloth and its functions in the Inca state. American Anthropologist 64:710–28.
1964   Una Apreciación Etnológica de la Visita. *In* Visita Hecha a la Provincia de Chucuito . . . en el año 1567, Garci Diez de San Miguel, ed. Documentos Regionales para la Etnología y Etnohistoria Andinas, no. 1. Lima: Casa de la Cultura del Perú.
1967   La Visita de los Chupachu como Fuente Etnológica. *In* Visita de la Provincia de León de Huánuco, vol. 1, Iñigo Oritz de Zúñiga, et al. Documentos para la Historia y Etnología de Huánuco y la Selva Central. Huánuco.
1968   An Aymará kingdom in 1567. Ethnohistory 15:115–51.

Nader, L.
1969   The Zapotec of Oaxaca. *In* Handbook of Middle American Indians, vol. 7: ethnology, Evon Z. Vogt, ed. Austin: University of Texas Press.

Nagel, Ernest
1961   The structure of science. New York: Harcourt, Brace, and World.

Nash, Manning
1967   Indian economics. *In* Handbook of Middle American Indians, vol. 6: social anthropology, Manning Nash, ed. Austin: University of Texas Press.

Neely, James A.
1967   Organización Hidráulica y Sistemas de Irrigación Prehistóricos en el Valle de Oaxaca. Mexico City, Instituto Nacional de Antropología e Historia, Boletín no. 27:15–17.

Nesbitt, Paul H.
1938   Starkweather ruin. Logan Museum Publications in Anthropology, Bulletin no. 6. Beloit, Wisc.: Beloit College.

Nielsen, Harry A.
1967   Methods of natural science: an introduction. Englewood Cliffs: Prentice-Hall.

Nilsson, Sven
1838–43 Skandinaviska Nordens Urinvånare. Lund.

Nimuendajú, Curt
1914   Die Sagen von der Erschaffung und Vernichtung der Welt als Grundlagen der Religion der Apapocúva-Guaraní. Zeitschrift für Ethnologie 46:284–403.
1948   Tribes of the lower and middle Xingú River. *In* Handbook of South American Indians. Washington, D.C., Bulletin of the Bureau of American Ethnology 143(3).

Northrop, F. S. C.
1947   The logic of the sciences and the humanities. New York: Macmillan Co.

Nusbaum, Jesse L.
1922   A Basketmaker cave in Kane County, Utah. Miscellaneous Paper 29. New York, Museum of the American Indian, Heye Foundation.

Oakes, Maud
1951   The two crosses of Todos Santos: survivals of Mayan religious ritual. Bollingen Series, no. 27. New York: Pantheon Books.

Obermaier, Hugo
1925   Fossil man in Spain. New Haven: Yale University Press.

Odum, Eugene P., and Odum, H. T.
1959   Fundamentals of ecology. 2d ed. Philadelphia: W. B. Saunders.

437

Oldfield, F., and Schoenwetter, James
1964 Late Quaternary environment and early man on the southern high plains. Antiquity 38:226–29.

Oppenheim, A. L.
1957 A bird's-eye view of Mesopotamian economic history. *In* Trade and market in the early empires, Karl Polanyi, Conrad M. Arensberg, and Harry W. Pearson, eds. Glencoe: Free Press.

Ortiz de Zúñiga, Iñigo
[1562] 1955–61 Visita fecha por mandado de Su Magestad . . . Revista del Archivo Nacional del Perú, Lima.
[1562] 1967 Visita de la Provincia de León de Huánuco en 1562. Documentos para la Historia y Etnología de Huánuco y la Salva Central, vol. 1. Huánuco: Universidad Nacional Hermilio Valdizán.

Osborn, Henry Fairfield
1919 Men of the old Stone Age, their environment, life and art. 3d ed. New York: Charles Scribner's.

Osgood, Cornelius
1951 Culture: its empirical and non-empirical character. Southwestern Journal of Anthropology 7:202–14.

Owens, J. G.
1892 Natal ceremonies of the Hopi Indians. A Journal of American Ethnology and Archaeology 2:163–75.

Palerm, Angel
1967 Agricultural systems and food patterns. *In* Handbook of Middle American Indians, vol. 6: social anthropology, Manning Nash, ed. Austin: University of Texas Press.

Palerm, Angel, and Wolf, E. R.
1957 Ecological potential and cultural development in Mesoamerica. *In* Studies in human ecology. Washington, D.C., Pan American Union, Social Science Monographs, no. 3.

Parry, John H.
1961 The establishment of the European hegemony, 1415–1715. New York: Harper & Row.

Parsons, E. C.
1925 A Pueblo Indian journal 1920–1921.

Menasha, Memoirs of the American Anthropological Association, no. 32.

Parten, Mildred
1950 Surveys, polls and samples: practical procedures. New York: Harper and Brothers.

Pendergast, David M.
1969a An inscribed jade plaque from Altun Ha. Archaeology 22:85–91.
1969b Altun Ha, British Honduras (Belize). The sun god's tomb. Toronto, Royal Ontario Museum, Division of Art and Archaeology, Occasional Paper, no. 19.
1969c Altun Ha: a guidebook to the ancient Maya ruins. Belize.

Pennington, Campbell W.
1963 The Tarahumar of Mexico. Salt Lake City: University of Utah Press.

Perkins, D., Jr.
1959 The post-cranial skeleton of the caprinae: comparative anatomy and changes under domestication. Ph.D. dissertation, Harvard University.
1964 Prehistoric fauna from Shanidar, Iraq. Science 144:1565–66.

Perrot, Jean
1960 Excavations at 'Eynan (Ain Mallaha); Preliminary Report on the 1959 Season. Israel Exploration Journal 10: 14–22.
1962 Palestine-Syria-Cilicia. *In* Courses toward urban life, R. J. Braidwood and G. R. Willey, eds. Chicago: Aldine Publishing Company.

Peters, E.
1930 Die altsteinzeitliche Kulturstätte Petersfels. Augsburg.

Peters, E., and Toepfer, V.
1932 Der Abschluss der Grabungen am Petersfels bei Engen im badischen Hagau. Prähistorische Zeitschrift 23: 155–99.

Phillips, Philip
1955 American archaeology and general anthropological theory. Southwestern Journal of Anthropology 11:246–50.

Phillips, Philip; Ford, James A.; and Griffin, James B.
1951 Archaeological survey in the lower Mississippi Alluvial Valley, 1940–1947.

438

Papers of the Peabody Museum of American Archaeology and Ethnology, vol. 25. Cambridge: Harvard University.

Piette, Ed.
1895a Études d'ethnographie préhistorique. L'Anthropologie 6:276–92.
1895b Hiatus et lacune vestiges de la période de transition dans la grotte du Mas-d'Azil. Bulletin de la Société d'Anthropologie de Paris 6(4th series): 235–67.

Piggott, Stuart
1951 William Camden and the Britannia. Proceedings of the British Academy 1951: 199–217.

Pilling, Arnold R.
1967 Beginnings. Historical Archaeology 1:1–22. Society for Historical Archaeology.

Piña Chán, Román
1958 Tlatilco. Mexico, D. F., Instituto Nacional de Antropología e Historia, Serie Investigaciones, no. 1.

Piña Chán, Román, and Covarrubias, Luis
1964 El Pueblo del Jaguar. Museo Nacional de Antropología, Mexico.

Pittioni, Richard
1962 Southern Middle Europe and southeastern' Europe. *In* Courses toward urban life, R. J. Braidwood and G. R. Willey, eds. Chicago: Aldine Publishing Company.

Pitt-Rivers, A. Lane-Fox
1906 The evolution of culture and other essays, J. L. Myres, ed. Oxford: Clarendon Press.

Plog, Fred T.
1968 Archaeological survey—a new perspective. M.A. thesis, Department of Anthropology, University of Chicago.
1969 An approach to the study of prehistoric change. Ph.D. dissertation, Department of Anthropology, University of Chicago.

Polanyi, Karl
1957 The economy as instituted process. *In* Trade and market in the early empires, Karl Polanyi, Conrad M. Arensberg and Harry W. Pearson, eds. Glencoe: Free Press.

Polo de Ondegardo, Juan
[1571] 1916 Relación de los fundamentos acerca del notable daño que resulta de no guardar a los Indios sus Fueros . . . Lima, Colección de Libros y Documentos Referentes a la Historia del Perú, Serie I, vol. 3.

Poma de Ayala, Guaman
[1615] 1936 Nueva Coronica y Buen Gobierno. Paris, Travaux de l'Institute d'Ethnologie, no. 23.

Pound, R., and Clements, F.
1900 The photogeography of Nebraska. Published by the Botanical Seminar. Lincoln: University of Nebraska.

Powell, B. Bruce
1957 Hopewellian pottery of the lower Illinois Valley: The Snyders Site ceramics. Papers of the Michigan Academy of Science, Arts and Letters 42:219–24.

Pozas, R.
1959 Chamula: Un Pueblo Indio de los Altos de Chiapas. Memorias del Instituto Nacional Indigenista, vol. 8. Mexico, D.F.

Preuss, Konrad T.
1921 Religion und Mythologie der Uitoto. Textaufnahmen und Beobachtungen bei einem Indianerstamm in Kolumbien, Südamerika, vol. 1. Gottingen.

Quimby, George I.
1962 A year with a Chippewa family, 1763–1764. Ethnohistory 9:217–39.

Rands, Robert L. and B. C.
1957 The ceramic position of Palenque, Chiapas. American Antiquity 23(2:1): 140–50.

Rands, Robert L., and Smith, R. E.
1965 Pottery of the Guatemalan highlands. *In* Handbook of Middle American Indians, vol. 2: archaeology of southern Mesoamerica, Gordon R. Willey, ed. Austin: University of Texas Press.

Rappaport, Roy A.
1967 Ritual regulation of environmental relations among a New Guinea people. Ethnology 6:17–30.
1968 Pigs for the ancestors: ritual in the ecology of a New Guinea people. New Haven: Yale University Press.

Ray, C. N., and Bryan, Kirk
1938 Folsomoid point found in alluvium beside a mammoth's bones. Science 88: 257–58.

Recinos, Adrián
1950 Popol Vuh: the sacred book of the ancient Quiché Maya. Norman: University of Oklahoma Press.

Redfield, Robert
1941 The folk culture of Yucatan. Chicago: University of Chicago Press.
1947 The folk society. American Journal of Sociology 52:293–308.

Reed, Charles A.
1960 A review of the archaeological evidence on animal domestication in the prehistoric Near East. *In* Prehistoric investigations in Iraqi Kurdistan, R. J. Braidwood, B. Howe, et al. Oriental Institute Studies in Ancient Oriental Civilization, no. 31. Chicago: University of Chicago Press.
1961 Osteological evidences for prehistoric domestication in southwestern Asia. Zeitschrift für Tierzüchtung und Zuchtungsbiologie 76.31–38.
1963 Osteo-archaeology. *In* Science in archaeology, D. Brothwell and E. Higgs, eds. London: Thames and Hudson.

Reichel-Dolmatoff, Gerardo
1950–51 Los Kogi. Revista del Instituto Etnológisco Nacional, vol. 4. Bogotá.

Reko, Blas P.
1934 Das mexikanische Rauschgift Ololiuqui. El México Antiguo 3(3–4):1–7. Sociedad Alemana de Mexicanistas, Mexico, D.F.

Ricketson, Oliver G., Jr.
1929 Excavations at Baking Pot, British Honduras. Washington, D.C., Carnegie Institution of Washington, Publication 403.

Ricketson, Oliver G., Jr., and Edith B.
1937 Uaxactun, Guatemala, Group E—1926–1931. Washington, D.C., Carnegie Institution of Washington, Publication 477.

Ritchie, William A.
1955 Recent discoveries suggesting an early Woodland burial cult in the Northeast. Albany, New York State Museum and Science Service, Circular no. 40.

Roberts, Frank H. H., Jr.
1929 Shabik'eshchee Village, A late Basketmaker site in the Chaco Canyon, New Mexico. Bulletin of the Bureau of American Ethnology, no. 92. Washington, D.C.: Government Printing Office.
1935 A Folsom complex. Preliminary report on investigations at the Lindenmeier Site in northern Colorado. Washington, D.C., Smithsonian Instituion, Miscellaneous Collections, no. 94.
1936 Additional information on the Folsom complex. Washington, D.C., Smithsonian Institution, Miscellaneous Collections, no. 95.

Rootenberg, S.
1964 Archaeological field sampling. American Antiquity 30:181–88.

Roth, H. Ling
1887 On the origin of agriculture. Journal of the Royal Anthropological Institute of Great Britain and Ireland 16:102–36.

Rouse, Irving
1939 Prehistory in Haiti: a study in method. New Haven: Yale University Publications in Anthropology, no. 21.
1955 On the correlation of phases of culture. American Anthropologist 57:713–22.
1960 The classification of artifacts in archaeology. American Antiquity 25:313–23.
1968 Prehistory, typology, and the study of society. *In* Settlement archaeology, K. Chang, ed. Palo Alto: National Press Books.

Rowe, John H.
1944 An introduction to the archaeology of Cuzco. Papers of the Peabody Museum of American Archaeology and Ethnology, vol. 27(2). Cambridge: Harvard University.
1945 Absolute chronology in the Andean area. American Antiquity 10:265–84.
1946 Inca culture at the time of the Spanish conquest. *In* Handbook of South American Indians. Bulletin of the Bureau of American Ethnology, no.

143(2). Washington, D.C.: Government Printing Office.

1963 Urban settlements in ancient Peru. Ñawpa Pacha 1:1–27.

1967 What kind of settlement was Inca Cuzco? Ñawpa Pacha 5:59–76.

Roys, Ralph L.
1943 The Indian background of colonial Yucatan. Washington, D.C., Carnegie Institution of Washington, Publication 548.

1965 Lowland Maya native society at Spanish contact. *In* Handbook of Middle American Indians, vol. 3: archaeology of southern Mesoamerica, Gordon R. Willey, ed. Austin: University of Texas Press.

Roys, Ralph L., ed. and trans.
1967 The book of Chilam Balam of Chumayel. Norman: University of Oklahoma Press.

Rudner, Richard S.
1966 Philosophy of social science. Englewood Cliffs: Prentice-Hall.

Russell, Carl P.
1967 Firearms, traps, & tools of the mountain men. New York: Alfred A. Knopf.

Russell, L. S.
1962 Mammalian migrations in the Pleistocene. *In* Problems of the Pleistocene epoch and Arctic area 2(2):48–55. Montreal: McGill University Museum Publications.

Rust, A., ed.
1937 Das Altsteinzeitliche Rentierjägerlager Meiendorf. Neumünster.

1943 Die alt- und mittelsteinzeitlichen Funde von Stellmoor. Neumünster.

Ryder, M. L.
1958 Follicle arrangement in skin from wild sheep, primitive domestic sheep and in parchment. Nature 182:781–83.

Sabloff, Jeremy A., and Willey, Gordon R.
1967 The collapse of Maya civilization in the southern lowlands: a consideration of history and process. Southwestern Journal of Anthropology 23:311–36.

Sabloff, Jeremy A., and Tourtellot, Gair
1969 Exchange systems and the ancient Maya. Paper presented at the American Anthropological Association meetings, New Orleans.

Sackett, James R.
1966 Quantitative analysis of Upper Paleolithic stone tools. *In* Recent studies in paleoanthropology, J. Desmond Clark and F. Clark Howell, eds. American Anthropologist 68(2:2):356–94.

1968 Method and theory of Upper Paleolithic archeology in Southwestern France. *In* New perspectives in archeology, Sally R. Binford and Lewis R. Binford, eds. Chicago: Aldine Publishing Company.

Safford, William E.
1922 Daturas of the Old World and New: An account of their narcotic properties and their use in oracular and initiatory ceremonies. *In* Smithsonian Institution, Annual Report for 1920. Washington, D.C.

Sahagun, Fray Bernardino de
1950–63 Florentine codex, general history of the things of New Spain, Arthur J. O. Anderson and Charles E. Dibble, eds. and trans. Monographs of the School of American Research, no. 14. School of American Research, Santa Fe; University of Utah Press, Salt Lake City.

Sahlins, Marshall D.
1958 Social stratification in Polynesia. Seattle: University of Washington Press.

1960 Political power and the economy in primitive society. *In* Essays in the science of culture: in honor of Leslie A. White, Gertrude E. Dole and Robert L. Carneiro, eds. New York: Thomas Y. Crowell.

1961 The segmentary lineage: an organization of predatory expansion. American Anthropologist 63:322–45.

1963 Poor man, rich man, big man, chief: political types in Melanesia and Polynesia. Comparative Studies in Society and History 5:285–303.

1968 Notes on the original affluent society. *In* Man the hunter, Richard B. Lee and Irven DeVore, eds. Chicago: Aldine Publishing Company.

Sahlins, Marshall D., and Service, Elman R., eds.

1960 Evolution and culture. Ann Arbor: University of Michigan Press.

Samuelson, Paul A.
1961 Economics: an introductory analysis. New York: McGraw-Hill Book Company.

Sanders, William T.
1961 Ceramic stratigraphy at Santa Cruz, Chiapas, Mexico. Papers of the New World Archaeological Foundation, no. 13. Provo, Utah.
1962 Cultural ecology of the Maya lowlands, part 1. Estudios de Cultura Maya 2: 79–121.
1964 Cultural ecology of the Maya lowlands, Part 2. Estudios de Cultura Maya, 4.
1965 The cultural ecology of the Teotihuacan Valley. Department of Sociology and Anthropology, Pennsylvania State University, multilithed.
1968 Hydraulic agriculture, economic symbiosis and the evolution of the state in central Mexico. *In* Anthropological archeology in the Americas, Betty J. Meggers, ed. Washington, D.C.: Anthropological Society of Washington.

Sanders, William T., and Price, B. J.
1968 Mesoamerica: the evolution of a civilization. New York: Random House.

Santillán, Hernando de
[1563–64] 1927 Relación del Origen, Decedencia, Politica y Gobierno de los Incas. Lima, Colección de Libros y Documentos Referentes a la Historia del Perú, Serie 2, vol. 9.

Sauer, Jonathan D.
1950 The grain amaranths: a survey of their history and classification. Missouri Botanical Garden, Annals 37:561–632.
1952 A geography of pokeweed. Missouri Botanical Garden, Annals 39:113–25.

Sayles, E. B.
1945 The San Simon branch, excavations at Cave Creek and in the San Simon Valley, 1: material culture. Globe, Arizona, Gila Pueblo, Medallion Paper 34.

Sayles, E. B., and Antevs, Ernst
1941 Cochise culture. Globe, Arizona, Gila Pueblo, Medallion Papers 29.

Schaedel, Richard P.
1951 Major ceremonial and population centers in northern Peru. *In* The civilizations of ancient America, Sol Tax, ed. Twenty-ninth International Congress of Americanists, Selected Papers, vol. 1. Chicago: University of Chicago Press.

Schoenwetter, James
1962 The pollen analysis of eighteen archaeological sites in Arizona and New Mexico. *In* Chapters in the prehistory of eastern Arizona, 1, by Paul S. Martin, et al. Fieldiana: Anthropology, vol. 53. Chicago: Chicago Natural History Museum.

Schoenwetter, James, and Dittert, A. E., Jr.
1968 An ecological interpretation of Anasazi settlement patterns. *In* Anthropological archeology in the Americas, Betty J. Meggers, ed. Washington, D.C.: Anthropological Society of Washington.

Schoenwetter, James, and Eddy, Frank W.
1964 Alluvial and palynological reconstruction of environments, Navajo Reservoir District. Santa Fe, Museum of New Mexico Papers in Anthropology, no. 13.

Scholes, France V., and Roys, R. L.
1968 The Maya Chontal Indians of Acalan-Tixchel: a contribution to the history and ethnography of the Yucatan Peninsula. 2d ed. Norman: University of Oklahoma Press.

Scholes, France V., and Warren, D.
1965 The Olmec region at Spanish conquest. *In* Handbook of Middle American Indians, vol. 3: archaeology of southern Mesoamerica, Gordon R. Willey, ed. Austin: University of Texas Press.

Schott, C.
1935 Urlandschaft und Rodung. Vergleichende Betrachtungen aus Europa und Kanada. Zeitschrift d. Ges. f. Erdkunde zu Berlin 81–102.

Schuyler, Robert L.
1969 Historic sites archaeology and its relevancy to the question of professional and amateur archaeology. Newsletter of the Archaeological Survey Associa-

tion of Southern California 16(1): 1–2.

1971 The history of American archaeology: an examination of procedure. American Antiquity 36:383–409.

Schwabedissen, Herman
1962 Northern continental Europe. *In* Courses toward urban life, R. J. Braidwood and G. R. Willey, eds. Chicago: Aldine Publishing Company.

Sears, William H.
1960 Ceramic systems and Eastern Archaeology. American Antiquity 25:324–29.
1961 The study of social and religious systems in North American archaeology. Current Anthropology 2:223–46.

Sellards, E. H.
1952 Early man in America. Austin: University of Texas Press.

Semenov, S. A.
1964 Prehistoric technology. New York: Barnes and Noble.

Service, Elman R.
1962 Primitive social organization. New York: Random House.

Setzler, Frank M.
1943 Archaeological explorations in the United States, 1930–1942. Acta Americana 1:206–20.

Shantz, H. L., and Zon, R.
1924 Atlas of American agriculture and natural vegetation. Washington, D.C.: U.S. Department of Agriculture.

Shapere, Dudley
1965 Philosophical problems of natural science. New York: Macmillan Co.

Shattuck, G. C., ed.
1933 The peninsula of Yucatan; medical, biological, meteorological and sociological studies. Washington, D.C., Carnegie Institution of Washington, Publication 431.

Shetelig, Haakon, and Falk, H. Jalmar
1937 Scandinavian archaeology. London: Oxford University Press.

Simpson, George Gaylord
1949 The meaning of evolution. New Haven: Yale University Press.

Slonim, M. J.
1960 Sampling in a nutshell. New York: Simon and Schuster.

Smith, A. L.
1950 Uaxactun, Guatemala: excavations of 1931–1937. Washington, D.C., Carnegie Institution of Washington, Publication 588.

Smith, A. L., and Ruppert, Karl
1953 Excavations in house mounds at Mayapan, 2. Washington, D.C., Carnegie Institution of Washington, Department of Archaeology, Current Reports 10:180–206.

Smith, C. Earle, Jr.
1965a Agriculture, Tehuacán Valley. Fieldiana: Botany 31(3):55–100. Chicago: Chicago Natural History Museum.
1965b Flora, Tehuacán Valley. Fieldiana: Botany 31(4):107–43. Chicago: Chicago Natural History Museum.
1967 Plant remains from the Tehuacán project. *In* Prehistory of the Tehuacán Valley, vol. 1: environment and resources, Douglas S. Byers, ed. Published for the R. S. Peabody Foundation, Phillips Academy, Andover, Mass., by the University of Texas Press, Austin.

Smith, Robert E., and Gifford, James C.
1965 Pottery of the Maya lowlands. *In* Handbook of Middle American Indians, vol. 2: archaeology of southern Mesoamerica, Gordon R. Willey, ed. Austin: University of Texas Press.

Smith, Watson
1962 Schools, pots, and potters. American Anthropologist 64:1165–78.

Soday, F. J.
1954 The Quad Site: A Paleo-Indian village in northern Alabama. Tennessee Archaeologist 10:1–20.

Solecki, Ralph S.
1963 Prehistory in Shanidar Valley, northern Iraq. Science 139:179–93.

Sollas, William J.
1924 Ancient hunters and their modern representatives. 3d ed. New York: Macmillan Co.

de Sonneville-Bordes, Denise
1960 Le Paléolithique supérieur en Périgord, 2 vols. Bordeaux: Imprimerie Delmas.
1963a Upper Paleolithic cultures in western Europe. Science 142:347–55.

1963*b* Le Paléolithique supérieur en Suisse. L'Anthropologie 67:205–68.

Soustelle, Jacques
1961 The daily life of the Aztecs on the eve of the Spanish conquest. London: George Weidenfeld & Nicolson.
1967 Arts of ancient Mexico. New York: Viking Press.

Spaulding, Albert C.
1946 Northeastern archaeology and general trends in the northern forest zone. *In* Man in northeastern North America, Frederick Johnson, ed. Papers of the Robert S. Peabody Foundation for Archaeology, vol. 3. Andover, Mass.: Phillips Academy.
1957 Review of method and theory in American archaeology, by Gordon R. Willey and Philip Phillips. American Antiquity 23:85–87.
1960*a* The dimensions of archaeology. *In* Essays in the science of culture: in honor of Leslie A. White, Gertrude E. Dole and Robert L. Carneiro, eds. New York: Thomas Y. Crowell.
1960*b* Statistical description and comparison of artifact assemblages. *In* The application of quantitative methods in archaeology, Robert F. Heizer and Sherburne F. Cook, eds. Viking Fund Publications in Anthropology, no. 28. Chicago: Quadrangle Books.
1968 Explanation in archeology. *In* New perspectives in archeology, Sally R. and Lewis R. Binford, eds. Chicago: Aldine Publishing Company.

Spencer, Robert F., and Jennings, Jesse D.
1965 The native Americans. New York: Harper and Row.

Spier, Leslie
1917 An outline for a chronology of Zuni Ruins. New York, Anthropological Papers of the American Museum of Natural History 18:209–331.

Stanton, W.
1965 The scientific approach to the study of man in America. Journal of World History 8:768–88.

Steiger, T. L.
1930 The structure of prairie vegetation. Ecology 11:170–217.

Stevens, Stanley Smith, ed.
1951 Handbook of experimental psychology. New York: Wiley.

Steward, Julian Haynes
1936 The economic and social basis of primitive bands. *In* Essays in anthropology presented to A. L. Kroeber, R. Lowie, ed. Berkeley: University of California Press.
1937 Ecological aspects of southwestern society. Anthropos 32:87–104.
1948 A functional-developmental classification of American high cultures. In A reappraisal of Peruvian archaeology, W. C. Bennett, ed. Society for American Archaeology, Memoir no. 4: 103–4.
1949 Cultural causality and law: a trial formulation of the development of early civilization. American Anthropologist 51:1–27.
1955 Theory of culture change. Urbana: University of Illinois Press.
1960 Evolutionary principles and social types. *In* The evolution of man: mind, culture and society, Sol Tax, ed. Chicago: University of Chicago Press.

Steward, Julian H., ed.
1955 Irrigation civilizations: a comparative study. Washington, D.C., Pan American Union, Social Science Monographs, no. 1.

Steward, Julian H., and Setzler, Frank M.
1938 Function and configuration in archaeology. American Antiquity 4:4–10.

Steward, Julian H., and Faron, Louis C.
1959 Native peoples of South America. New York: McGraw-Hill Book Company.

Stirling, Matthew W.
1955 Stone monuments of the Río Chiquito, Veracruz, Mexico. Bulletin of the Bureau of American Ethnology, no. 157 (Anthropological Papers, no. 43). Washington, D.C.: Government Printing Office.

Stocking, George
1968 Race, culture and evolution. New York: Free Press.

Stone, Doris Z.
1958 Introduction to the archaeology of Costa Rica. San José, Costa Rica: Museo Nacional.

Stott, D. H.

1969 Cultural and natural checks on population growth. *In* Environment and cultural behavior, Andrew P. Vayda, ed. Garden City: Natural History Press.

Stracey, P. D.

1963 Elephant gold. London: Weidenfeld and Nicolson.

Stromsvik, G.

1937 Notes on the metates from Calakmul, Campeche, and from the Mercado, Chichen Itza, Yucatan. Contributions to American Archaeology, vol. 3(1). Washington, D.C., Carnegie Institution of Washington, Publication 456.

Strong, William D.

1936 Anthropological theory and archaeological fact. *In* Essays in anthropology presented to A. L. Kroeber, R. H. Lowie, ed. Berkeley: University of California Press.

1948 Cultural epochs and refuse stratigraphy in Peruvian archaeology. *In* a reappraisal of Peruvian archaeology, Wendell C. Bennett, ed. Society for American Archaeology, Memoir no. 4.

Struever, Stuart

1962 Implications of vegetal remains from an Illinois Hopewell site. American Antiquity 27:584–87.

Stubbe, H.

1959 Considerations on the genetical and evolutionary aspects of some mutants of hordeum, glycine, lycopersicon and antirrhinum. Cold Spring Harbor Symposia on Quantitative Biology 24:31–40.

Swartz, B. K., Jr.

1967 A logical sequence of archaeological objectives. American Antiquity 32:487–97.

Tallgren, A. M.

1937 The method of prehistoric archaeology. Antiquity 11(42):152–61.

Taylor, Walter W.

1948 A study of archeology. Menasha, Memoirs of the American Anthropological Association, no. 69.

1952 Review of excavations in Big Hawk Valley, Wupatki National Monument, Arizona by Watson Smith. American Antiquity 18:399.

1968 Foreword. *In* A study of archaeology. Carbondale: Southern Illinois University Press.

1969 Review of "New perspectives in archeology," Sally R. and Lewis R. Binford, eds. Science 165:382–84.

Tax, S., and Hinshaw, R.

1969 The Maya and the Midwestern Highlands. *In* Handbook of Middle American Indians, vol. 7: ethnology, Evon Z. Vogt, ed. Austin: University of Texas Press.

Thompson, Donald E.

1967 Investigaciones Arqueológicas en las Aldeas Chupachu de Ichu y Auquimarca. *In* Visita de la Provincia de León de Huánuco en 1562, Iñigo Ortiz de Zúñiga, et al. Documentos para la Historia y Etnología de Huánuco y la Selva Central, vol. 1. Huánuco: Universidad Nacional Hermilio Valdizán.

1968 An archeological evaluation of ethnohistoric evidence on Inca culture. *In* Anthropological archeology in the Americas, Betty J. Meggers, ed. Washington, D.C.: Anthropological Society of Washington.

1969 Incaic installation at Huánuco and Pumpu. *In* El Proceso de Urbanización en America desde sus Orígenes Hasta Nuestros Días, Jorge Hardoy and Richard Schaedel, eds. Actas y Memorias del XXXVII Congreso Internacional de Americanistas. Buenos Aires.

Thompson, J. Eric S.

1929 Comunicaciones y Comercio de los Antiguso Mayas. Soc. de Geog. e Hist. de Guatemala. Anal. 6.

1939 Excavations at San Jose, British Honduras. Washington, D.C., Carnegie Institution of Washington, Publication 506.

1951 The Itza of Tayasal, Peten. *In* Homenaje al Dr. Alfonso Caso. Mexico, D.F.: Instituto Nacional de Antropología e Historia.

1954 The rise and fall of Maya civilization. Norman: University of Oklahoma Press.

1964 Trade relations between the Maya high-lands and lowlands. Estudios de Cultura Maya 4:13–49.

1965 Archaeological synthesis of the southern Maya lowlands. *In* Handbook of Middle American Indians, vol. 3: archaeology of southern Mesoamerica, Gordon R. Willey, ed. Austin: University of Texas Press.

1967 The Maya central area at the Spanish conquest and later: a problem in demography. Proceedings of the Royal Anthropological Institute of Great Britain and Ireland 1967:23–37.

Thompson, Raymond H.
1958*a* Preface. *In* Migrations in New World culture history, Raymond H. Thompson, ed. University of Arizona, Social Science Bulletin, no. 27.

1958*b* Modern Yucatecan Maya pottery making. Salt Lake City, Memoirs of the Society for American Archaeology, no. 15.

Thomsen, C. J.
1936 Ledetraad til Nordisk Oldkyndighed. Copenhagen.

Thomson, Donald F.
1939 The seasonal factor in human culture illustrated from the life of a contemporary nomadic group. Proceedings of the Prehistoric Society 1939:209–21.

Thorvildsen, K.
1950 Moseliget fra Tollund. Aarbøger for nordisk Oldkyndighed og Historie, 302–9. Copenhagen.

Thurstone, Louis Leon
1959 The measurement of values. Chicago: University of Chicago Press.

Titiev, Mischa
1944 Old Oraibi: a study of the Hopi Indians of Third Mesa. Papers of the Peabody Museum of American Archaeology and Ethnology, vol. 22(1). Cambridge: Harvard University.

Tolstoy, Paul
1958 Surface survey of the Northern Valley of Mexico: the Classic and Post-Classic Periods. Philadelphia, Transactions of the American Philosophical Society 48(5).

1969 Review of Mesoamerica: the evolution of a civilization, by W. T. Sanders and B. J. Price. American Anthropologist 71:554–58.

Tolstoy, Paul, and Paradis, L. I.
1970 Early and middle Preclassic culture in the Basin of Mexico. Science 167:344–51.

Tönnies, Ferdinand
1957 Community and society. Charles P. Loomis, trans. and ed. East Lansing: Michigan State University Press.

Tovilla, M. A.
1960 Relacion Historica Dyscreptiva de las Provincias de la Verapaz y de la del Manche de le Reyno de Guatemala, F. V. Scholes and E. B. Adams, eds. Guatemala.

Tozzer, Alfred Marston
1907 A comparative study of the Mayas and the Lacandones. Report of the Fellow in American Archaeology 1902–1905, Archaeological Institute of America. New York: Macmillan Co.

1934 Maya research. Maya Research 1:3–19.

1937*a* Prehistory in Middle America. Hispanic American Historical Review 17:151–59.

1937*b* Review of various publications by G. C. Vaillant. American Anthropologist 39:338–40.

1941 Landa's 'Relacion de las Cosas de Yucatan.' Papers of the Peabody Museum of American Archaeology and Ethnology, vol. 18. Cambridge: Harvard University.

Treganza, A. E., and Cook, S. F.
1948 The quantitative investigation of aboriginal sites: complete excavation with physical and archaeological analysis of a single mound. American Antiquity 13:287–97.

Troels-Smith, Hørgen
1953 Ertebølle Culture-Farmer Culture, Results of the Past Ten Years' Excavations in Aamosen Bog, West Zealand. Aarbøger for nordisk Oldkyndighed og Historie, 1–62. Copenhagen.

Turnbull, Colin
1968 The importance of flux in two hunting societies. *In* Man the hunter, R. B.

Lee and I. DeVore, eds. Chicago: Aldine Publishing Company.

Turney, Omar S.
1929 Prehistoric irrigation in Arizona. Phoenix: Arizona State Historian.

Taylor, E. B.
1881 Anthropology. London: Henry Holt.

Ucko, Peter, and Dimbleby, G. W.
1969 The domestication and exploitation of plants and animals. Chicago: Aldine Publishing Company.

United States Department of Agriculture
1926 Soil survey of the Salt River Valley area, Arizona. Washington, D.C.: U.S.D.A.

University of London
1953 The archaeology of Palestine. London, Institute of Archaeology, Occasional Paper no. 10: pp. 10–12.

Vaillant, George C.
1930 Excavations at Zacatenco. New York, Anthropological Papers of the American Museum of Natural History 32(1).

1931 Excavations at Ticoman. New York, Anthropological Papers of the American Museum of Natural History 32(2).

1935a Early cultures of the Valley of Mexico: results of the stratigraphical project of the American Museum of Natural History in the Valley of Mexico, 1928–1933. New York, Anthropological Papers of the American Museum of Natural History 35(3).

1935b Excavations at El Arbolillo. New York, Anthropological Papers of the American Museum of Natural History 35(2).

1944 Aztecs of Mexico. Garden City: Doubleday.

Van Zeist, W., and Wright, H. E., Jr.
1963 Preliminary pollen studies at Lake Zeribar, Zagros Mountains, southwestern Iran. Science 140:65–67.

Varallanos, Jose
1959 Historia de Huánuco. Buenos Aires: Imprenta Lopez.

Vavilov, N. I.
1951 The origin, variation, immunity and breeding of cultivated plants. Chronica Botanica 13(⅙).

Vayda, Andrew P.
1964 Anthropologists and ecological problems. *In* Man, culture, and animals, Anthony Leeds and Andrew P. Vayda, eds. Washington, D.C., American Association for the Advancement of Science Publication no. 78.

Vescelius, G. S.
1960 Archaeological sampling: a problem in statistical inference. *In* Essays in the science of culture: in honor of Leslie A. White, Gertrude E. Dole and Robert L. Carneiro, eds. New York: Thomas Y. Crowell.

Vestal, Paul A.
1952 Ethnobotany of the Ramah Navaho. Papers of the Peabody Museum of American Archaeology and Ethnology, vol. 40(4). Cambridge: Harvard University.

Vielle, Edmond
1890 Pointes de fleches typiques de Fère-en-Tardenois (Aisne). Bulletin de Société Anthropologique de Paris 1(6th series):959–64.

Villa Rojas, Alfonso
1945 The Maya of east central Quintana Roo. Washington, D.C., Carnegie Institution of Washington, Publication 559.

1969a The Tzoltel. *In* Handbook of Middle American Indians, vol. 7: ethnology, Evon Z. Vogt, ed. Austin: University of Texas Press.

1969b The Maya lowlands: The Chontal, Chol, and Kekchi. *In* Handbook of Middle American Indians, vol. 7: ethnology, Evon Z. Vogt, ed. Austin: University of Texas Press.

Vivian, Gordon, and Reiter, Paul
1960 The great kivas of Chaco Canyon. Monographs of the School of American Research and the Museum of New Mexico, no. 22. Santa Fe: Museum of New Mexico Press.

Vogt, E.
1937 Geflechte und Gewebe der Steinzeit. Basel.

Wagner, Philip L.
1960 The human use of the earth. Glencoe: Free Press.

Walter, Heinz
1956 Der Jaguar in der Vorstellungswelt der südamerikanischen Naturvölker. Ph.D. dissertation, University of Hamburg.

Waring, Antonio J., and Holder, Preston
1945 A prehistoric ceremonial complex in the southeastern United States. American Anthropologist 47:1–34.

Warnica, J. N.
1966 New discoveries at the Clovis Site. American Antiquity 31(3):345–57.

Wassén, S. Henry
1934a The frog in Indian mythology and imaginative world. Anthropos 29:613–58.
1934b The frog-motive among the South American Indians. Anthropos 29:319–70.
1964 Some general viewpoints in the study of native drugs especially from the West Indies and South America. Ethnos 29(½):97–120.
1965 The use of some specific kinds of South American snuff and related paraphernalia. Ethnologiska Studier no. 28. Etnografiska Museet, Göteborg.
1967 Anthropological survey of the use of South American snuffs. In Ethnopharmacologic search for psychoactive drugs, symposium proceedings, Public Health Service Publication no. 1645. Washington, D.C.

Wassén, S. Henry and Holmstedt, Bo
1963 The use of paricá, an ethnological and pharmacological review. Ethnos 28(1):5–45.

Wasson, R. Gordon
1966 Ololiuhqui and the other hallucinogens in Mexico. In Summa Antropológica en homenaje a Roberto J. Weitlaner. Mexico, D.F.: Instituto Nacional de Antropología e Historia.

Watanabe, Hitoshi
1964 The Ainu: a study of ecology and the system of social solidarity between man and nature in relation to group structure. Journal of the Faculty of Science, University of Tokyo, Section 5 (Anthropology), vol. 2(6).
1968 Subsistence and ecology of northern food gatherers with special reference to the Ainu. In Man the hunter, R. B. Lee and I. DeVore, eds. Chicago: Aldine Publishing Company.

Waterbolk, H. T.
1962 The Lower Rhine Basin. In Courses toward urban life, R. J. Braidwood and G. R. Willey, eds. Chicago: Aldine Publishing Company.

Watson, Don
1940 Cliff palace: the story of an ancient city. Ann Arbor: Edwards Brothers.

Wauchope, Robert
1934 House mounds of Uaxactun, Guatemala. Contributions to American Archaeology, vol. 7:109–60. Washington, D.C., Carnegie Institution of Washington, Publication 436.

Webb, Malcolm C.
1964 The Post-Classic decline of the Peten Maya: an interpretation in the light of a general theory of state society. 3 vols. Ph.D. dissertation, University of Michigan.

Wedel, Waldo R
1963 The High Plains and their utilization by the Indian. American Antiquity 29:1–16.

Weiant, C. W.
1943 An introduction to the ceramics of Tres Zapotes, Veracruz, Mexico. Bulletin of the Bureau of American Ethnology, no. 139. Washington, D.C.: Government Printing Office.

Wendorf, Fred
1961 Paleoecology of the Llano Estacado. Santa Fe, Fort Burgwin Research Center, Publication no. 1.

Wendorf, Fred, and Hester, J. J.
1962 Early man's utilization of the Great Plains environment. American Antiquity 28:159–71.

West, Robert C.
1963 The natural regions of Mesoamerica. In Handbook of Middle American Indians, vol. 1: natural environment and early cultures, Robert C. West, ed. Austin: University of Texas Press.

Whallon, Robert
1966 The Owasco Period: a reanalysis. Ph.D. dissertation, University of Chicago.

Wheat, Joe Ben
1955   Mogollon culture prior to A.D. 1000. Menasha, Memoirs of the American Anthropological Association, no. 82.

White, Leslie A.
1949   Science of culture. New York: Farrar, Strauss.
1954   Review of "Culture: a critical review of concepts and definition," by A. L. Kroeber and Clyde Kluckhohn. American Anthropologist 56:461–68.
1959   The evolution of culture. New York: McGraw-Hill Book Company.

Whitehead, Alfred North, and Russell, Bertrand
1925 & 1927 Principia mathematica. 2d ed. 3 vols. Cambridge: Cambridge University Press.

Whitehill, Walter Muir
1968   Historic sites archaeology in the study of early American history. *In* The reinterpretation of early American history, Ray Allen Billington, ed. New York: W. W. Norton.

Whiting, Alfred F.
1939   Ethnobotany of the Hopi. Flagstaff, Museum of Northern Arizona, Bulletin no. 15.

Wilbert, Johannes
1963   Indios de la Región Orinoco-Ventuari. Caracas, Fundación La Salle de Ciencias Naturales, Monografía no. 8.
1970   Folk literature of the Warao Indians, vol. 1: narrative material and motif content. Los Angeles: University of California, Latin American Center.

Willey, Gordon R.
1948   Functional analysis of "Horizontal styles" in Peruvian archaeology. *In* A reappraisal of Peruvian archaeology, W. C. Bennett, ed. Society for American Archaeology, Memoir no. 4.
1950   Growth trends in New World cultures. *In* For the dean: essays in anthropology in honor of Byron Cummings, E. K. Reed and D. S. King, eds. Santa Fe: Southwestern Monuments Association.
1953   Prehistoric settlement patterns in the Virú Valley, Perú. Bulletin of the Bureau of American Ethnology, no. 155. Washington, D.C.: Government Printing Office.

1966a   An introduction to American archaeology, vol. 1: North and Middle America. Englewood Cliffs: Prentice-Hall.
1966b   New World archaeology in 1965. Proceedings of the American Philosophical Society 110(2):140–45.
1968   One hundred years of American archaeology. *In* One hundred years of anthropology, John O. Brew, ed. Cambridge: Harvard University Press.

Willey, Gordon R., and Phillips, Philip
1958   Method and theory in American archaeology. Chicago: University of Chicago Press.

Willey, Gordon R., Ekholm, G. F.; and Millon, R. F.
1964   The patterns of farming life and civilization. *In* Handbook of Middle American Indians, vol. 1: natural environment and early cultures, Robert C. West, ed. Austin: University of Texas Press.

Willey, Gordon R.; Culbert, T. P.; and Adams, R. E. W., eds.
1967   Maya lowlands ceramics: a report from the 1965 Guatemala City conference. American Antiquity 32:289–315.

Willey, Gordon R., and Smith, A. L.
1969   The ruins of Altar of Sacrificios, Department of Peten, Guatemala; an introduction. Papers of the Peabody Museum of American Archaeology and Ethnology, vol. 62(1). Cambridge: Harvard University.

Willey, Gordon R., et al.
1965   Prehistoric Maya settlements in the Belize Valley. Papers of the Peabody Museum of American Archaeology and Ethnology, vol. 54. Cambridge: Harvard University.

Williams, Howel; Heizer, Robert F.; and Graham, John
1965   Sources of rocks used in Olmec monuments. *In* Sources of stones used in prehistoric Mesoamerican sites. Archaeological Research Facility, Contributions 1:1–39. Berkeley: University of California.

Williams-Hunt, P. D. R.
1949   A technique for anthropology from the air in Malaya. Singapore, Bulletin of

the Raffles Museum, Series B, no. 4:44–68.

Wilmsen, Edwin N.
1968   Functional analysis of flaked stone tools. American Antiquity 33:156–61.

Wilson, Thomas
1893   Minute stone implements from India. *In* Report of the U.S. National Museum, 1892. Washington, D.C.: Government Printing Office.

Winship, George Parker
1896   The Coronado Expedition, 1540–1542. *In* Annual Report of the Bureau of Ethnology, no. 14. Washington, D.C.

Winters, Howard D.
n.d.   The southern Illinois frontier—10,000 B.C. to A.D. 1500 Manuscript.

Wissler, Clark
1942   The American Indian and the American philosophical society. Proceedings of the American Philosophical Society 86:189–204.

Wittfogel, Karl A.
1956   Hydraulic civilization. *In* International symposium on man's role in changing the face of the earth, W. L. Thomas, ed. Chicago: University of Chicago Press.
1957   Oriental despotism. New Haven: Yale University Press.

Witthoft, John
1952   A Paleo-Indian Site in eastern Pennsylvania. Proceedings of the American Philosophical Society 96:464–95.

Wittry, Warren L.
1951   A preliminary study of the Old Copper Complex. Wisconsin Archeologist 32(1):1–18.
1959   Archaeological studies of four Wisconsin rockshelters. Wisconsin Archaeologist 40(4):137–267.

Wittry, Warren L., and Ritzenthaler, Robert E.
1956   The Old Copper Complex: an archaic manifestation in Wisconsin. American Antiquity 21:244–54.

Wolf, Eric R.
1967   Levels of communal relations. *In* Handbook of Middle American Indians, vol. 6: social anthropology, Manning Nash, ed. Austin: University of Texas Press.

Woodburn, James
1968   Background material on the Hadza of Tanzania. *In* Man the hunter, Richard B. Lee and Irven DeVore, eds. Chicago: Aldine Publishing Company.

Woodbury, Richard B.
1954   Review of "A study of archeology" by W. W. Taylor. American Antiquity 19:292–96.
1961   Prehistoric agriculture at Point of Pines, Arizona. Salt Lake City, Memoirs of the Society for American Archaeology, no. 17.
1965   Artifacts of the Guatemalan highlands. *In* Handbook of Middle American Indians, vol. 2: archaeology of southern Mesoamerica, Gordon R. Willey, ed. Austin: University of Texas Press.

Woodward, Arthur
1932   The value of Indian trade goods in the study of archaeology. Pennsylvania Archaeologist 3(1):8, 9, 16–19.
1937   The study of historic archaeology in North America. Boletin Bibliografico de Antropologia Americana 1:101–3.

Wormington, H. M.
1957   Ancient man in North America. 4th ed. Popular Series, no. 4. Denver: Denver Museum of Natural History.
1959   Prehistoric Indians of the Southwest. 3rd ed. Popular Series, no. 7. Denver: Denver Museum of Natural History.

Wynne-Edwards, V. C.
1962   Animal dispersion in relation to social behavior. Edinburgh: Oliver and Boyd.
1964   Population control in animals. Scientific American 211(2):68–74.

Yarnell, Richard A.
1963   Comments on Struever's discussion of an "Eastern agricultural complex." American Antiquity 28:547–48.

Yengoyan, Aram A.
1960   Preliminary notes on a model of the initial populating of the Philippines. Anthropology Tomorrow 6(3):42–48.

Young, O. R.
1964   A survey of general systems theory. General Systems 9:61–80.

Young, T. Cuyler, and Smith, P. E. L.
1966   Research in the prehistory of central western Iran. Science 153:386–91.

Zerries, Otto

1954 Wild- und Buschgeister in Südamerika. Wiesbaden, Studien zur Kulturkunde, vol. 11.

1961 Die Religionen der Naturvölker Südamerikas und Westindiens. Religionen der Menschheit 7:269–384.

1962 Die Vorstellung vom Zweiten Ich und die Rolle der Harpyre in der Kultur der Naturvölker Südamerikas. Anthropos 57:889–914.

1964 Waika. Die kulturgeschichtliche Stellung der Waikaindianer des oberen Orinoco im Rahmen der Völkerkunde Südamerikas. Munich.

1965 Drie unbekannte Holzschnittarbeiten aus Brasilianisch-Guayana im Museum für Völkerkunde zu Mannheim. Tribus 14:185–93.

Index

Accidental deviation. *See* Sampling

Activity loci, 168, 169, 170, 173, 177, 207

Adaptation: limited by environment, 94; role of culture, 94, 127; adaptive context, 96–87; adaptive area, 132; and scheduling, 228; and technology, 229; as a local problem, 244–45. *See also* Adaptive sets; Cultural ecology; Evolution

Adaptive sets, 285–86

Adena: copper tools, 100

African elephant, 211, 215. *See also* Hunting; Mammoths

Aggregation. *See* Social organization

Agricultural revolution: as an economic revolution, 241; origins of, 267

Agriculture: in American Southwest, 57; in temperate Europe, 67; origins of, 68, 241, 243, 244, 248, 251, 258, 260, 262, 311; subsistence base, 70; effect on social organization, 74, 231; in Mesoamerica, 222, 223; sedentary, 223; and population, 231, 246; and water control systems, 231, 280, 282; and seasonality, 232; and adaptation, 244, 245; selective situations favoring, 252; in Mississippi basin, 309; and adaptive milieu in North America, 310, and ecological niches, 313; plant characteristics, 313; productivity, 330; Gulf Coast florescence, 368. *See also* Domestication; Food production; Irrigation

Analogy: ethnographic, 105–6; in archaeological interpretations, 105–6, 110, 114; limitations of, 114; between nature and behavior, 114. *See also* Scientific method

Anasazi: ties to Snowflake, 13; influence on Mogollon, 53. *See also* Mogollon; Southwest, American

Andean political organization, 393. *See also* Inca

Animal husbandry: no trace in archaeological record, 68; as an adaptation, 245; and origins of agriculture, 255. *See also* Domestication

Anthropology: relation to archaeology, xi–xiii, 12, 16, 19, 21, 24, 28, 85, 93–101, 102, 108, 153; development as a discipline 14, 26, 81, 82; use of hypotheses, 38; goals of, 79, 123; research on social structure, 96; and cultural evolution, 101; as a social science, 123. *See also* Scientific method

Antiquarianism: in the genesis of archaeology, 62; in Mesoamerican studies, 79

Aquatic resources: and population density, 100; dependence on in post-Pleistocene era, 251; and food production, 252–53

Archaeological record: vestigial nature of, 63; as an indicator of sociocultural phenomena, 135, 195; an instrument in archaeological research, 137; defined, 137; and food supply, 230. *See also* Method; Scientific method

Archaeologist: professional myopia, 62, 78; similarity to ethnologist, 78; as technician, 141, 176

Archaic: increased sedentism in, 251; population growth, 251

Arguments of relevance: in archaeological theory, 133, 141; and archaeological data, 140, 141; characteristics of, 140, 147, 148, 149; absence of, 143; function of, 143, 147; development of, 146; validity of, 147; determination of content, 147; application of, 148, 152

Arikara: example of attribute analysis, 113

Art: colonial mortuary art, 115; problems in the study of, 333. *See also* Olmec art

Artifact: and human behavior, 84, 113; evolutionary ranking of, 85; and cultural systems, 89–90, 94–95; treated as traits, 93, 195; distribution of, 94, 158, 186; technomic, 95, 97, 99; sociotechnic, 95, 96, 97, 131; ideotechnic, 96, 97; typology, 113, 116, method of seriation, 116; defined, 164; dimensions of, 164; imply events, 164; diagnostic traits, 195; described in formal terms, 198; in Paleo-Indian collections, 212. *See also* Assemblages; Typology

Assemblages: and social system, 95, 113; relation to behavior, 113; major types, 130; variation in, 130, 207; and data gathering, 209

Attributes: typology, 113; in site classification, 171; identification procedures, 196

Bands. *See* Hunter-gatherers: Macrobands; Social organization

Basketmaker: shift to later Phase, 294, 296; population, 295, 299, 300, 301; carrying capacity, 296; agriculture, 296, 301; proliferation of facilities, 296; pottery, 297; food storage, 297–98; hunting, 298; activity structure, 299

Behavior: defined by process school, 103; opposed to culture, 281

Belize Valley, 378

Bilateral descent. *See* Kinship

Biotic species: relation of fluctuations to human population, 206

451

454

460